Visual QuickStart Guide

LiveMotion 1.0

for Windows and Macintosh

Elaine Weinmann
Peter Lourekas

Peachpit Press

For Alicia

Visual QuickStart Guide
LiveMotion for Windows and Macintosh
Elaine Weinmann and Peter Lourekas

Peachpit Press
1249 Eighth Street
Berkeley, CA 94710
510/524-2178
800/283-9444
510/524-2221 (fax)

Find us on the World Wide Web at: www.peachpit.com

Visual QuickStart Guide is a trademark of Peachpit Press, a division of Addison Wesley Longman

Cover design: The Visual Group
Interior design: Elaine Weinmann
Production: Elaine Weinmann and Peter Lourekas
Illustrations: Elaine Weinmann, Peter Lourekas, and Newfangled Graphics

Colophon
This book was created with QuarkXPress 4.1 on a Macintosh G3 and a Macintosh G4. The primary fonts used were ITC New Baskerville, Myriad, and CaflischScript from Adobe Systems Inc.

ISBN 0-201-70473-0

9 8 7 6 5 4 3 2 1

Printed and bound in the United States of America

How we pulled this off

No man or woman is an island. Don't get us wrong—we're definitely insane enough to attempt to do everything by our sweet lonesome. But this time we didn't, thank goodness. Here's a list of the people who were essential in getting this darling newborn baby off the ground.

Nancy Aldrich-Ruenzel, hard-working Publisher of Peachpit Press; *Marjorie Baer,* Executive Editor, for gathering info and giving us support; *Victor Gavenda,* brilliant, meticulous, and witty Technical Editor; *Cary Norsworthy,* our fabuloso Editor, who's always on top of things and is a delight to work with; *Gary-Paul Prince,* Publicist; *Keasley Jones,* Associate Publisher; *Lisa Brazieal,* Production Coordinator, and the rest of the wonderful staff at Peachpit. They're not just unfailingly helpful—they're interesting people, too.

Debbie D'Andrea, Marcus Chang, Michael Ninness, Joe Bowden, Chris Prosser, Ken Rice, and technical support at *Adobe Systems, Inc.*

Mies Hora at *Ultimate Symbol,* for sending us the beautiful and tremendously useful Nature Icons CD. Some of the illustrations in this book were created using these images. They're at www.ultimatesymbol.com.

Frith Breitzer, freelance writer, for writing the section on export.

Jane Taylor Starwood, proofreader and copy editor.

Emily Glossbrenner, indexer.

Dan Yee at *Newfangled Graphics,* for producing many of the illustrations.

And *Cherry,* for her stellar vocabulary, terrific sense of humor, sweet, joyous disposition, love, and untiring (and we mean un-tir-ing) patience.

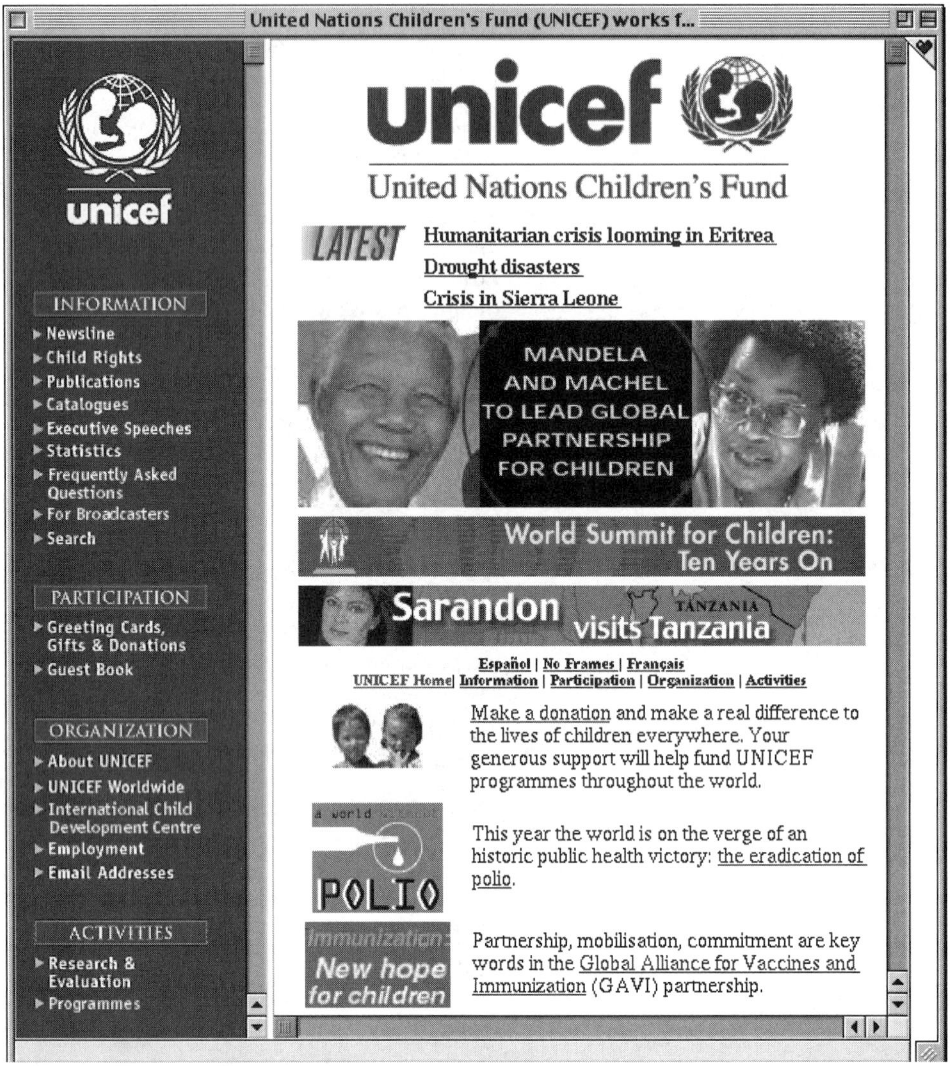

***www.unicef.org**, a well-designed site.*

Contents

3 Create Objects

4 Work with Objects

7 Text

8 Acquire Images

9 Edit Objects

Warmup 1

Are you a real greenhorn?

If you're an arch beginner and you don't yet know your way around a Macintosh machine, check out Robin Williams' *The Little Mac Book* (it really was little once upon a time!). Windows users, check out *The Little Windows 98 Book* by Alan Simpson. Both books are available from our favorite publisher, Peachpit Press. Or try *Macs for Dummies*, by David Pogue (IDG Books Worldwide).

1 ➤ This button consists of two objects: a ***text object*** *on top of a geometric* ***button object****. A* ***texture*** *was applied to top layer of the button.*

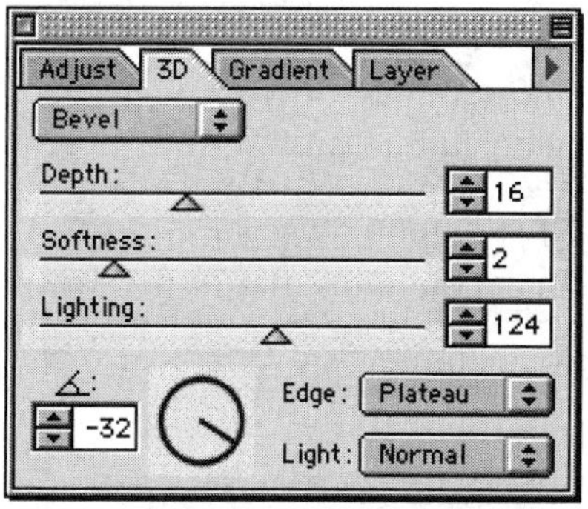

2 ➤ The ***3D*** *palette is used to apply a* ***Bevel*** *effect to the button's top layer.*

What the heck is LiveMotion, anyway?

YOU BOUGHT THIS BOOK because you're a devoted sycophant and you buy everything we write. Oh, your Web Design 101 professor forced you to buy it. Well, in any case, you're not exactly sure what the darn program does.

Here's the short answer, plain and simple. LiveMotion (the successor to ImageStyler) is used to construct flat or 3D buttons and other navigation devices, decorative elements, backgrounds, animations, and rollovers for Web pages. All without touching a single line of HTML code. Once your artwork is finished, you'll optimize it and then export it to a Web-page layout application (e.g., Adobe GoLive or Macromedia Dreamweaver).

So grab a nice hot cup (or cool glass) of something, put your feet up, and take a few minutes to read this let's-get-acquainted chapter. First, skim our broad overview of LiveMotion. Second, read our comprehensive introduction to LiveMotion's 21 palettes (aptly titled "Palettes galore"). And third, if you're new to Web design, read the glossary so you can start talking and thinking in "Webspeak."

Three types of objects

In LiveMotion, you will be creating three basic types of objects:

Geometric ➤ Ellipses, rectangles, and other regular or irregular shapes that are created with LiveMotion's drawing tools, (e.g., Rounded Rectangle tool, Ellipse, Pen tool).

Text ➤ Objects that are created with LiveMotion's Type tool ("text object" and "type object" mean the same thing).

(Continued on the next page)

Image ➤ Scanned images, images from bitmap editing programs (e.g., Photoshop), EPS text graphics from illustration programs, and objects created in LiveMotion using any of the Combine commands.

How the job gets done

A design is built by creating and arranging various objects into a **composition** inside the **composition window** (what is known as the "document window" in other applications).

Using menu or palette commands, any type of object can be **repositioned**; **transformed** (scaled, rotated, or skewed); **restacked**, **aligned**, or **distributed** relative to the other objects in the composition; **grouped**; **combined**; assigned an **opacity**, **color, gradient,** or **texture;** assigned a **3D, distort**, or **Photoshop filter** effect; or given a different **contour**. Changes made to an object are not permanent and can be **adjusted** or **undone** at **any** time.

And as in other **vector** applications, in LiveMotion you can adjust an object's properties over and over without diminishing its quality. (It may degrade slightly when it's optimized for the Web—oh, well—but let's not get into that now.)

Furthermore, up to 99 **object layers** can be assigned to each individual object. Layers work differently in LiveMotion than in Photoshop and Illustrator. Each subset of layers belongs to that object and that object alone—not to the overall composition. An object's layers match the outer shape of the object itself, not the rectangular "live canvas area" (e.g., the layers in a hexagonal object will have that hexagonal shape).

Each layer can be assigned its own individually editable attributes. These include **width, location, softness, color (solid or gradient), texture, 3D,** and **opacity**. For example, let's say you've created a button and you want to adjust the softness or opacity of the button's shadow without changing any other objects in the composition. Simply work on the button's shadow layer.

Text in LiveMotion functions like any other object. It can be scaled, rotated, or skewed,

Vector-schmector

In a **vector** application, shapes are constructed using mathematical coordinates. This makes them elastic and stretchable as well as precise at any resolution. Images in a raster (bitmap) application (e.g., Photoshop), on the other hand, are composed of a grid of tiny pixels. Since each pixel can be a different color, raster programs are well suited for creating photographic or painterly images and applying soft, graduated tones.

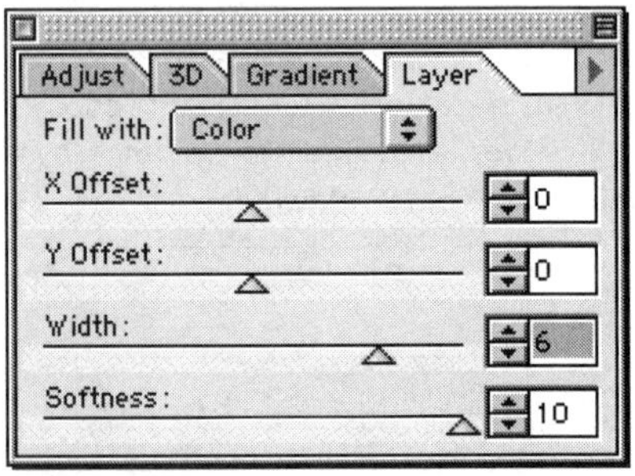

*1 ➤ The **Layer** palette is used to widen and soften the button's second layer to create a **shadow**.*

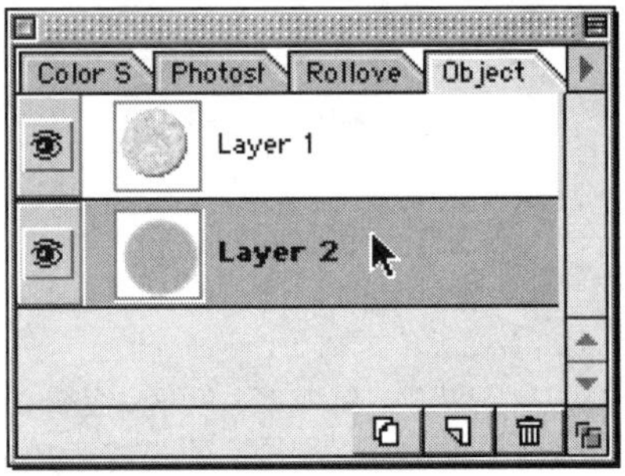

*2 ➤ As you can see from the thumbnails on the **Object Layers** palette, layers always match an object's shape.*

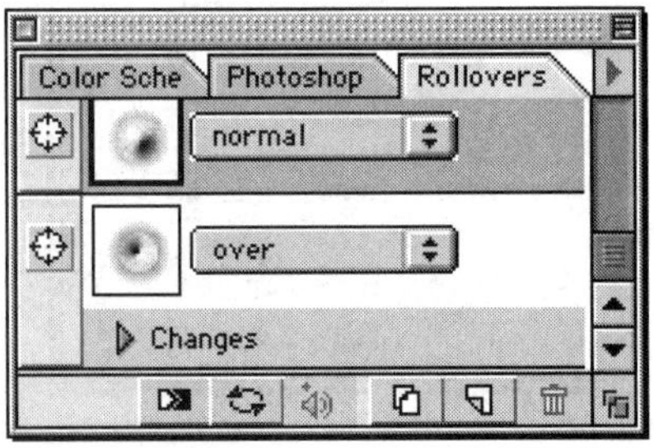

*3 ➤ The **Rollovers** palette is used to add states to an object (**Over, Down,** and **Out**).*

What really matters

When you're designing a Web site, always remember that your goal is to grab your viewer's attention—and keep their attention. A well-designed site is **easy to read, easy to use,** and **quick to download**. If it's also unique, entertaining, or even exciting to look at, so much the better. The purpose of a Web site, as with any medium, is to **communicate** information. Robin Williams' and John Tollett's *The Non-Designer's Web Book* (Peachpit Press) has a wealth of tips and suggestions for designing Web sites. Robin is a great communicator herself.

*1 ➤ This is the button's **Normal** state, when the pointer is not rolled over it or clicking on it.*

*2 ➤ This is the button's **Over** state, when the pointer is rolled over it. Different **Bevel** (3D palette) settings were used for the button's Normal and Over rollover states.*

and textures, styles, and 3D effects can be applied to it. Imagine the possibilities. Imagine all the hideous possibilities.

What else

Not only can you create cute little buttons in LiveMotion, but you can also create **flat** or **textured backgrounds** for Web pages. And you can apply the same texture to individual objects to give your design unity.

The features for creating **animations** and **rollovers** in LiveMotion are generating a lot of fanfare. Rollovers, remote rollovers, simple animations, and animations with rollovers make for lively and entertaining Web pages.

Streamlining production

You may be familiar with styles or style sheets in a word processing or layout application. Well, LiveMotion **styles** work the same way, except they're used to apply sets of object attributes (e.g., color, texture, opacity) instead of typographic or text formatting attributes (e.g., font, point size). Styles are saved and applied via the Styles palette.

Another method for streamlining production is to use **aliases**. When you modify an object that has alias objects linked to it, the aliases update too. If you create some great shapes, you can save them in the **Library** palette and use them again in any composition. You can even save an object with an animation to the Library palette or the Styles palette.

Moving on

You're finished creating the components of your Web page in LiveMotion, but your masterpiece isn't finished. At this point you can use the LiveMotion **Web** palette to attach a **URL** address to any object to serve as a link to other pages or sites. And then you'll perform the most critical task: You'll **optimize** individual objects or the whole composition for online viewing using the **Export** palette. Once that's accomplished, you're ready to take your LiveMotion files into a Web-page layout application (e.g., Adobe GoLive or Macromedia Dreamweaver). ▲

Palettes galore

Using the palettes

As you can see from the number of pages we've devoted to LiveMotion's **21 palettes** in this chapter alone, palettes are how things get done in this program. These pages serve as an introduction to the palettes, as well as a useful reference guide later on.

To **open** a palette, choose Window menu > Show [palette name]. The palette will appear at the front of its palette group. Palettes that are open when you quit/exit LiveMotion will appear in the same location when the program is re-launched.

To save screen space, the palettes are joined into default groupings, but you can compose your own **groups**. To display an open palette at the front of its group, click its tab.

To **shuffle** (rearrange) a palette within its existing palette group, drag the palette tab within the palette window.

To **separate** a palette from its group, drag its tab (palette name) away from the group (Figs. 1–2). To **add** a palette to any group, drag the tab over the group. Use the resize box (lower right corner) to **lengthen** or shorten a palette.

To neaten up your screen, you can **align** your palettes together, edge to edge, as shown in Figure 2.

➤ MacOS: Press Tab to **hide/show** all currently open palettes, including the Toolbox. Press Shift-Tab to hide/show all open palettes except the Toolbox.

Default palette groups

Toolbox

Web, Transform, Properties

Distort, Opacity, Color

Adjust, 3D, Gradient, Layer

Color Scheme, Photoshop Filters, Rollovers, Object Layers

Sounds, Library, Textures, Styles

Timeline

Choose Window menu > **Reset To Defaults** to restore the palettes to their factory-default settings as well as their factory-default locations on screen. The **Export** palette doesn't open when you choose the reset command.

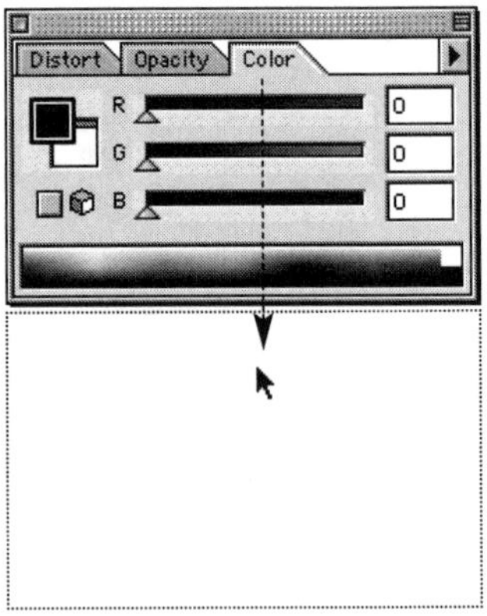

1➤ The Color palette is dragged out of its group.

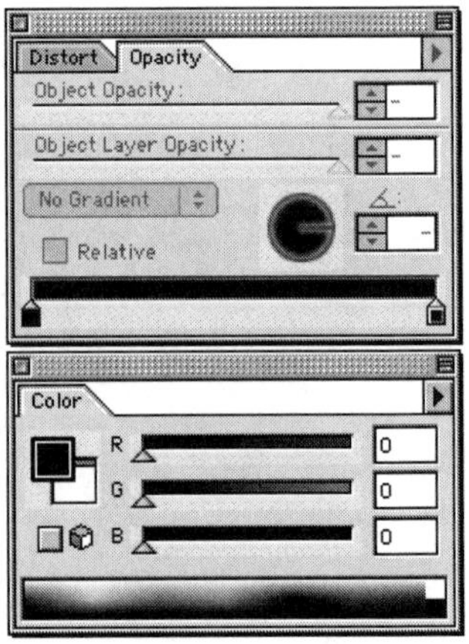

2➤ Now the Color palette is by itself.

You're gonna love this

To access **ANY** tool temporarily without actually switching to that tool, **press** and **hold** on the tool's shortcut key (letter). Try this—it's a real innovation!

The Toolbox

The Toolbox palette contains 18 tools for item creation and editing. If the Toolbox is hidden, choose View menu > Show Tools to redisplay it.

Choose a visible tool by clicking on it. To access a tool quickly, use its letter shortcut (see the boldface letters in the figure below). *Note:* When you use a tool shortcut, make sure the pointer is in the composition window, not in a palette field.

➤ If you forget a tool shortcut, rest the pointer on the tool without clicking—the tool name and shortcut (tool tip) will appear on screen.

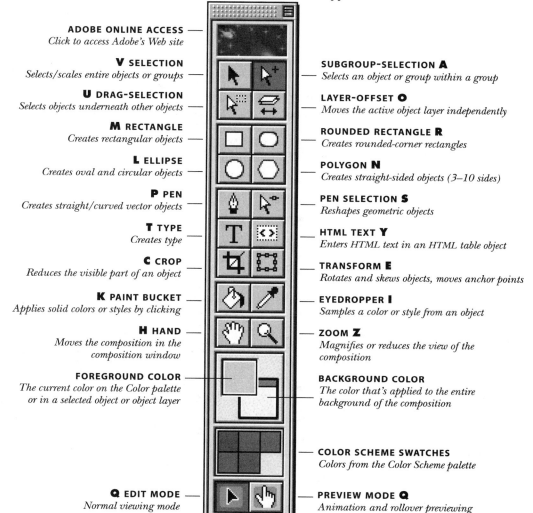

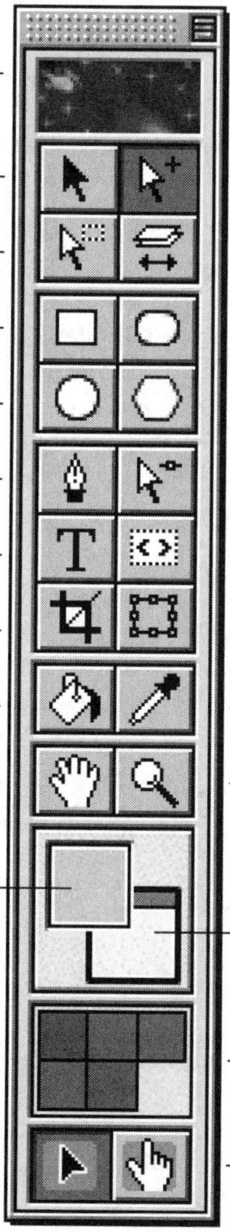

Properties palette

The Properties palette features change depending on what kind of object is selected (not what kind of tool is selected).

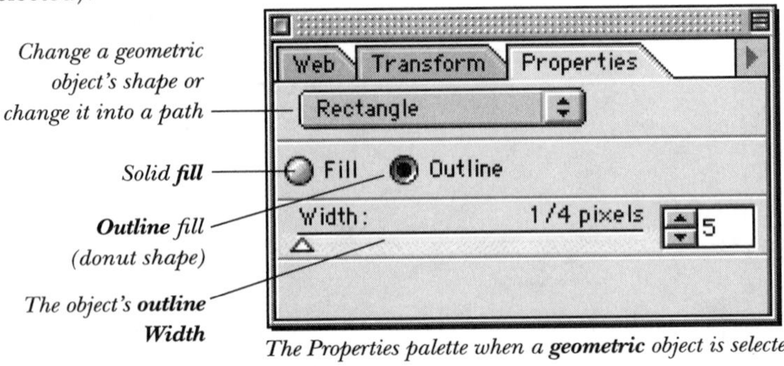

*The Properties palette when a **geometric** object is selected.*

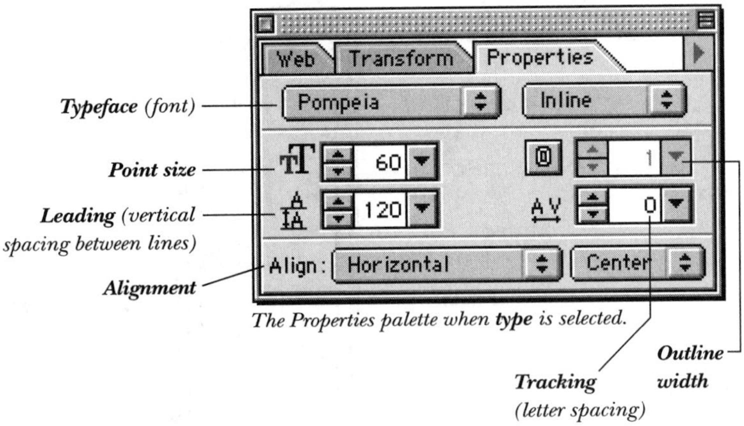

*The Properties palette when **type** is selected.*

Transform palette

Using the Transform palette, any LiveMotion object—whether it's a text, geometric, or image object—can be precisely repositioned, scaled, rotated, skewed horizontally, or skewed vertically.

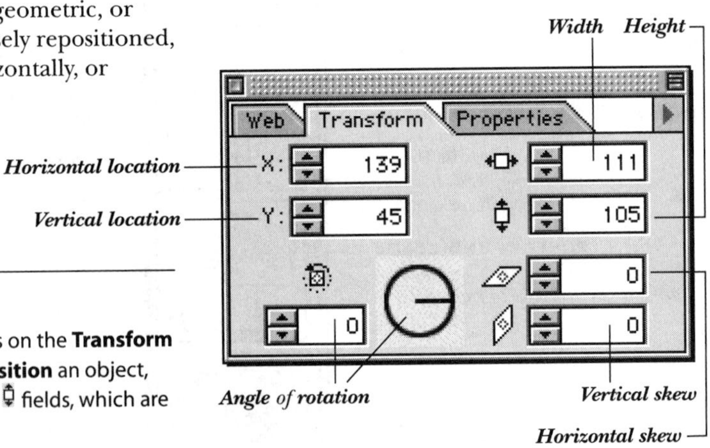

Don't get confused!

Don't confuse the **X** and **Y** fields on the **Transform** palette, which are used to **reposition** an object, with the **width** and **height** fields, which are used to **scale** an object.

Web palette

The Web palette is used to assign URL links for rollover states. It's also used to assign which HTML headline tags are to be replaced during batch HTML replacement. The palette has two panels. If the bottom panel is hidden, choose Detail View from the palette menu to display it.

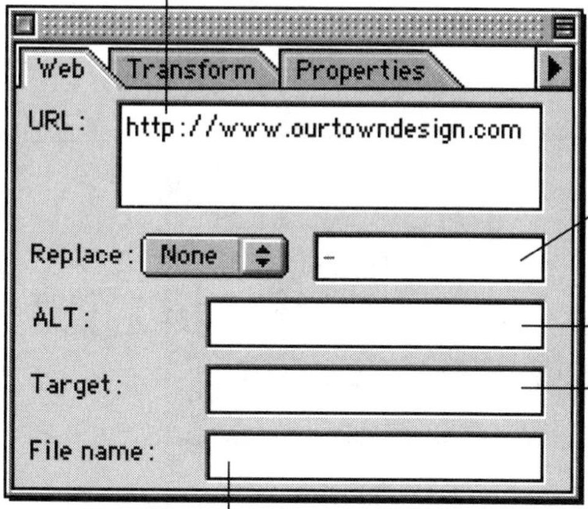

Color palette

The Color palette features a Foreground color square and a Background color square. The Foreground color is used to apply color to the currently active layer of the currently selected object or objects. The Background color fills the background of the entire composition.

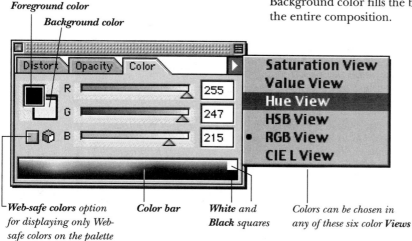

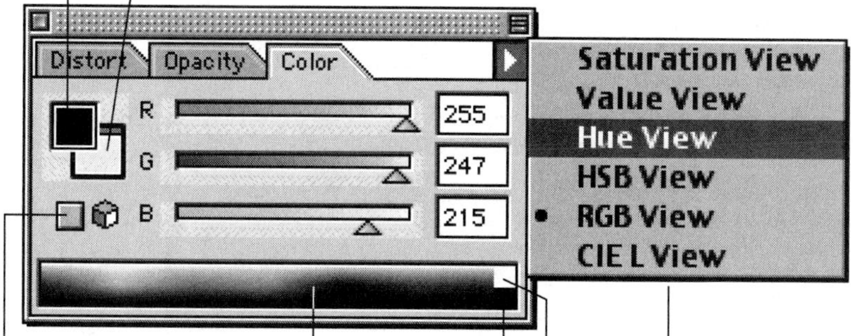

Opacity palette

The Opacity palette is used to assign an opacity setting to an entire object or to individual object layers, or to assign graduated opacity values to object layers via an opacity gradient.

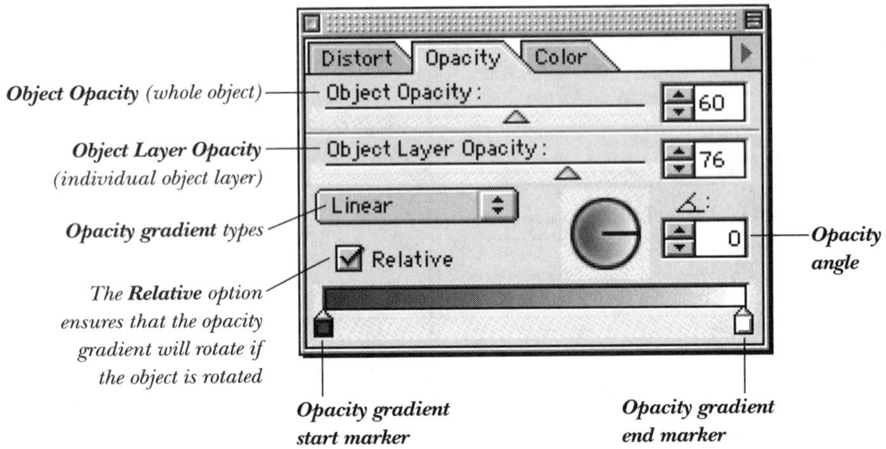

Distort palette

The Distort palette is used to apply special effects to a texture, an image, a gradient, or a non-solid background. The Distort effects include: Displace, Lens, Twirl, Spherize, Quantize, and Radial Quantize (the latter two create mosaic effects). The Distort palette options vary depending on which effect is currently chosen.

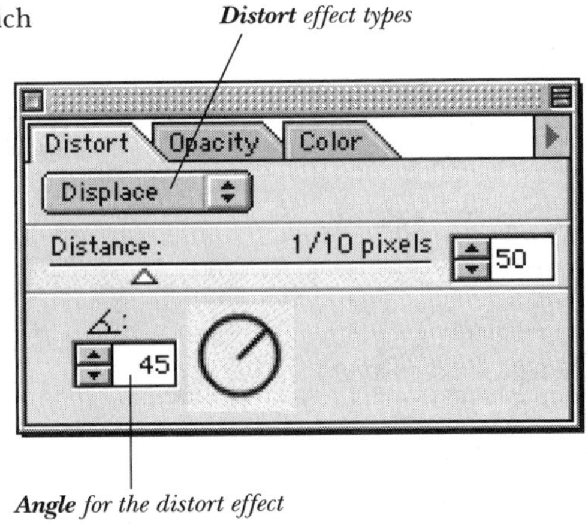

Layer palette

The Layer palette is used to change the attributes of the currently selected object layer: whether it is filled with a color, an image, the background color, or a texture; its position relative to the object's other layers; its width (whether it's wider or narrower than the other layers); and the softness of its edge.

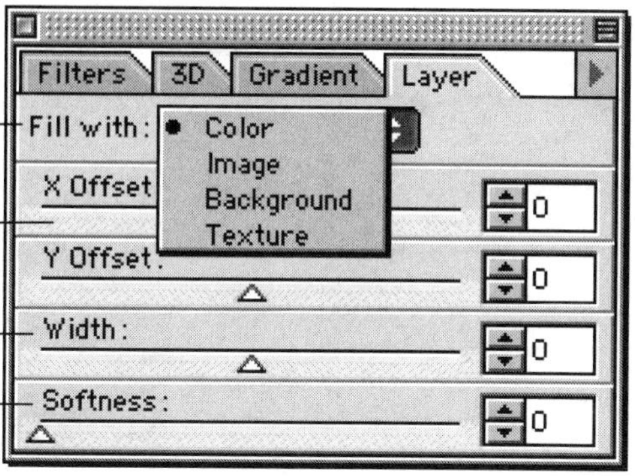

Gradient palette

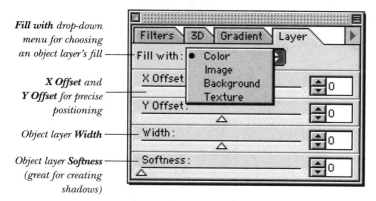

The Gradient palette applies a two-color blend to the entire active layer. You can choose from four gradient types: Linear, Burst, Double Burst, and Radial. You can also adjust the angle of the gradient and adjust where the gradient colors start and end within the object.

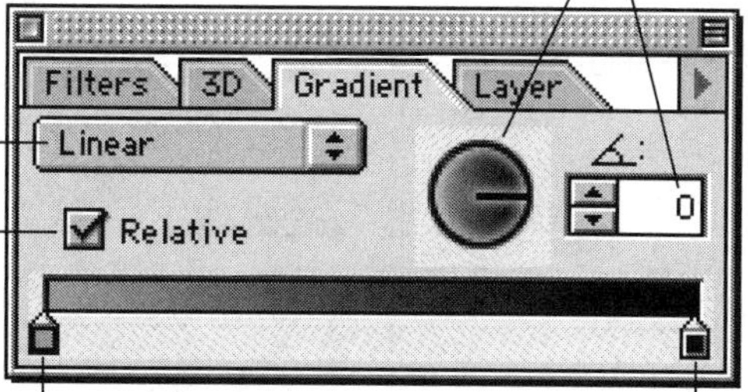

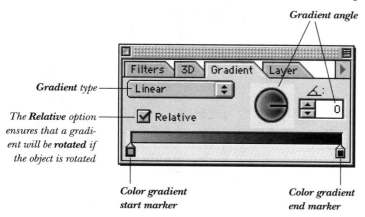

3D palette

The 3D palette applies Depth, Softness, and Lighting attributes to an object to make it look three-dimensional. You can choose from four preset 3D effects (Cutout, Emboss, Bevel, and Ripple) and you can adjust individual settings for each effect.

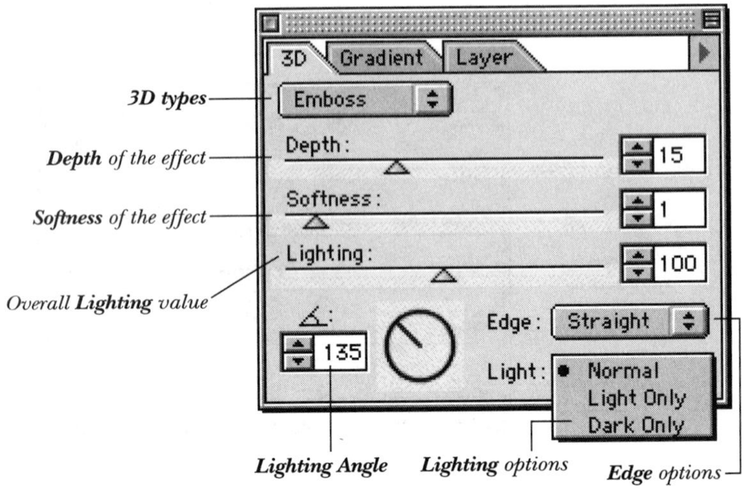

Adjust palette

The Adjust palette is used to perform brightness, contrast, and saturation adjustments; to apply a tint to or posterize a texture, gradient, or image (not a solid color); or to invert colors. The palette can be used on a solid color, an image, or a texture on an object layer or on the background of a composition.

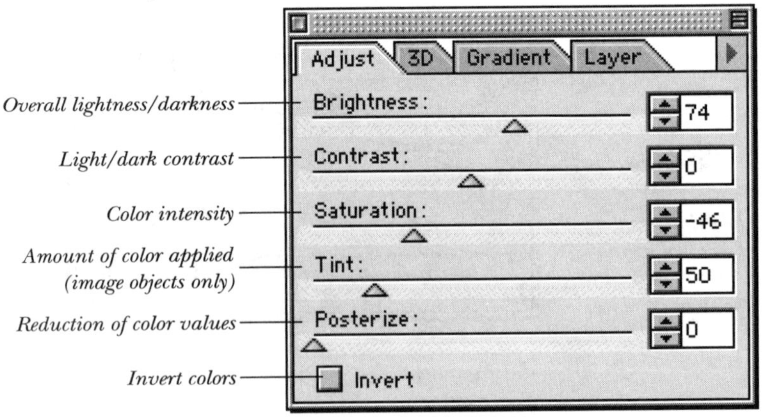

Object Layers palette

Each individual object in LiveMotion can contain up to 99 layers that match its shape, and each layer can be edited separately. The Object Layers palette is used to add/delete, select, hide/show, restack, and duplicate layers for individual objects.

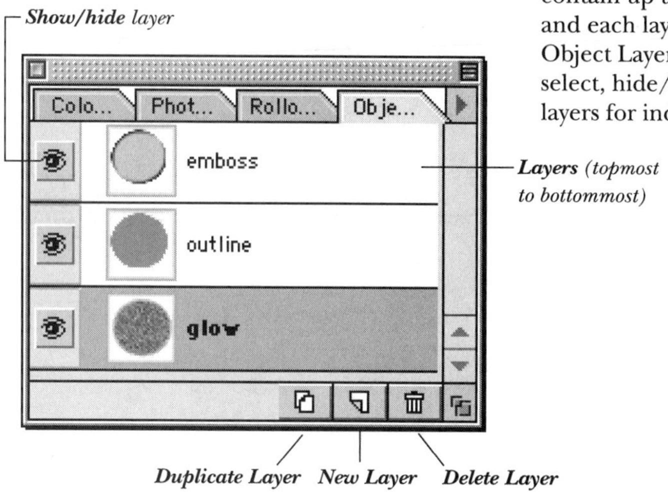

Rollovers palette

Rollovers are screen events that occur when the mouse moves over or clicks on an object in a browser. They are the life of a Web page. Every object has a Normal state (no action). To create a rollover, you will add a (mouse) Over and/or (mouse) Down state. You can also add a (mouse) Out state.

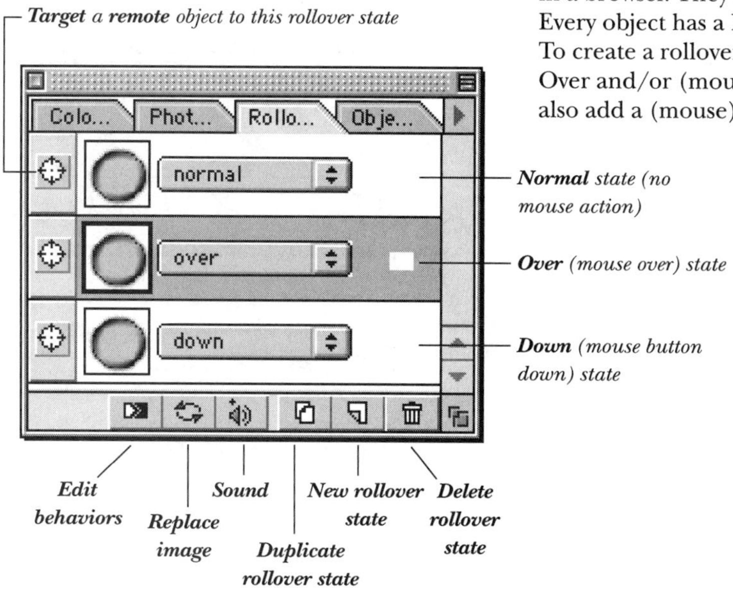

Photoshop Filters palette

Photoshop filters can be applied to image (bitmap) objects via the Filters submenu under the Object menu. The Photoshop Filters palette stores separate lists of the filters that have been applied to each object, so the palette list will change depending on which object is currently selected. (If more than one object is selected, the palette will only list the filters that are applied to the topmost of the selected objects.)

A filter effect can be turned off (or back on) by clicking the eye icon for that filter. To adjust the settings for a filter effect, no matter when it was applied, double-click the filter name on the palette and change the settings in the filter dialog box that opens.

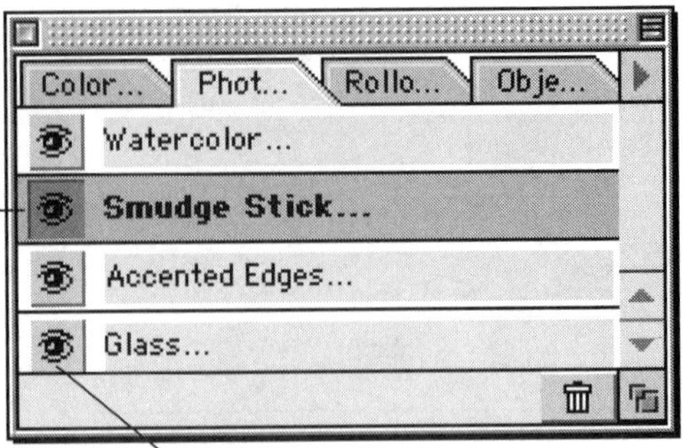

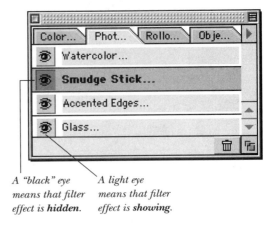

*A "black" eye means that filter effect is **hidden**.*

*A light eye means that filter effect is **showing**.*

Color Scheme palette

The Color Scheme palette simplifies color selection and application by creating arrangements of swatches that work well together. It's like an electronic interior decorator, except instead of compiling an assortment of swatches or paint chips, the Color Scheme palette chooses a harmonious assortment of Web-safe colors. The entire scheme can be shifted along the color wheel or hues can be clustered in groups via the color wheel relationship buttons. The current Color Scheme swatches are also displayed on, and can be chosen from, the bottom of the Toolbox.

Color Scheme swatches

*Circle used to move the whole scheme along the **color wheel***

*Menu for choosing the **Honey Comb** or **Triangles** swatch display mode*

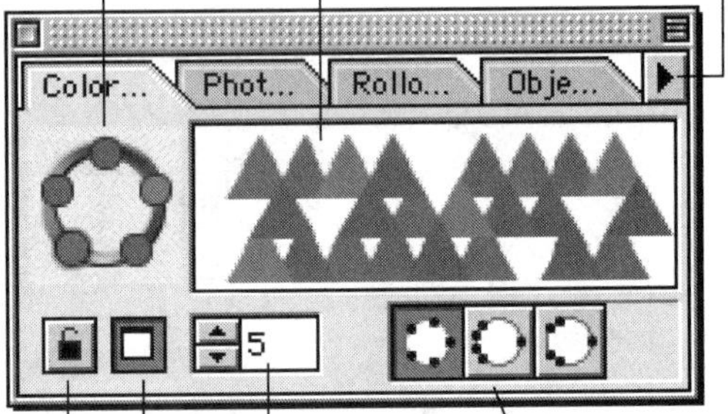

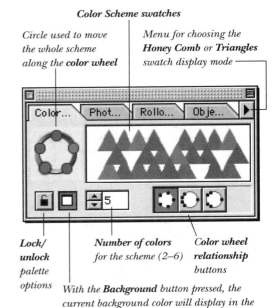

***Lock/ unlock** palette options*

***Number of colors** for the scheme (2–6)*

***Color wheel relationship** buttons*

*With the **Background** button pressed, the current background color will display in the background of the palette swatch window*

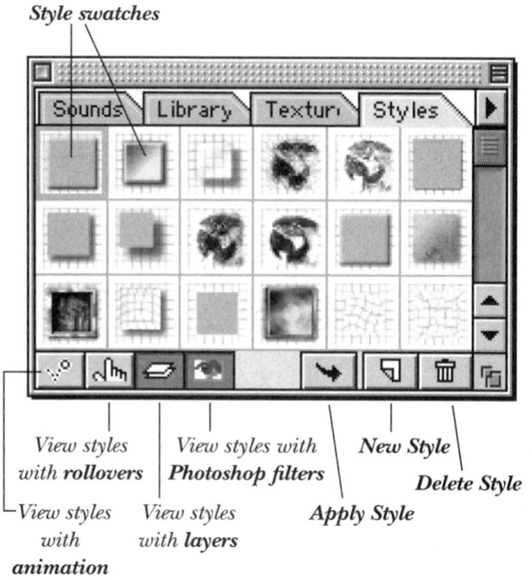

Styles palette

In LiveMotion, a style is a set of object layer attributes, such as Color, Adjust, 3D, Opacity, Distort, Gradient, Photoshop Filters, Textures, and Layer palette settings. A style can contain multiple layers and animation instructions. The same style can be assigned to any number of objects in a composition. Styles speed up production and help to ensure consistency from object to object (e.g., from button to button). You can use the preset styles that come with LiveMotion or you can create your own styles, and you can edit either kind. *Note:* Unlike a style in a word processing program, if you edit a style in LiveMotion, the objects to which it was already applied won't update.

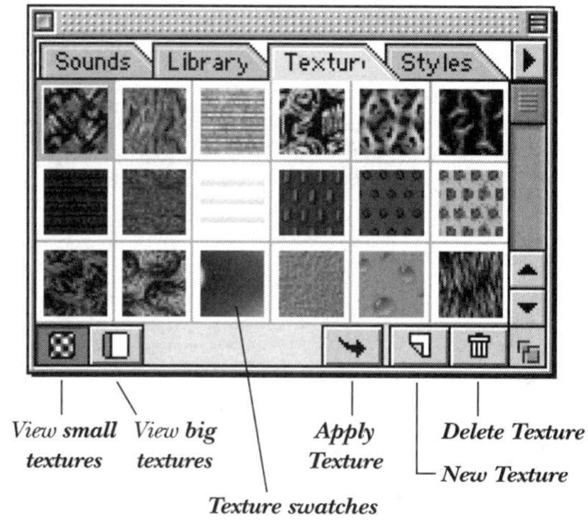

Textures palette

A texture is actually an image that's placed, pasted, or applied to an object layer or to the background of a composition. If the dimensions of the texture file are smaller than the background or object into which it is placed, it will repeat in a tile formation. You can use a preset texture or you can use any LiveMotion file (or exported LiveMotion file) as a tile to create your own textures.

Three ways to view

For the Library, Styles, or Textures palette, you can choose a view option from the palette menu: **Swatches** View (thumbnails without names), **Preview** View (names and one large thumbnail), or **Name** View (names with small thumbnails) .

Library palette

The Library palette is used for storing and retrieving LiveMotion, vector, or image objects. You can use any of the default objects or you can create and save your own objects in the library.

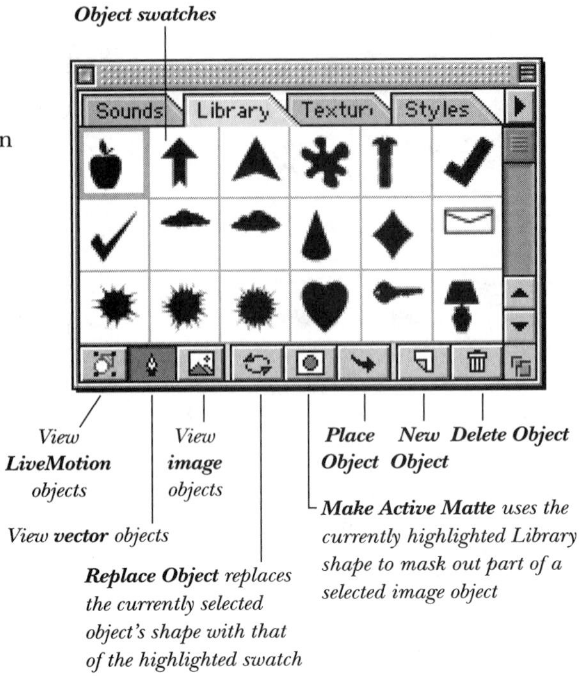

Sounds palette

Sounds add another dimension to animations and rollovers. The Sounds palette is used for storing, previewing, and applying sounds.

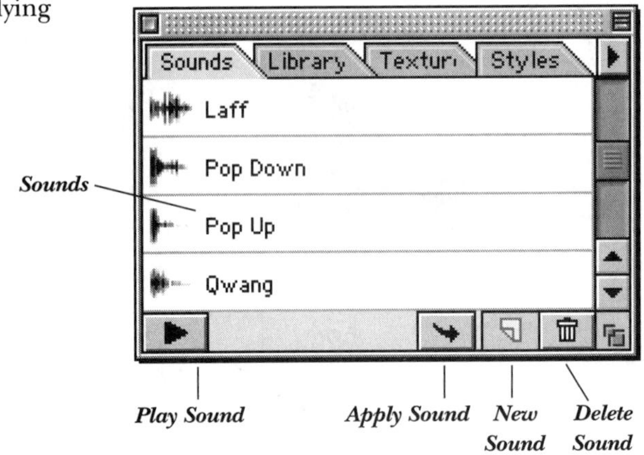

Export palette

The Export palette is used to optimize a LiveMotion object or composition for online viewing. First you'll choose a file format: Photoshop, JPEG, GIF, PNG-Indexed, PNG-Truecolor, or SWF. Then you will compare download size versus quality settings until you achieve an acceptable balance between the two. The options on the Export palette change depending on which export file format you choose.

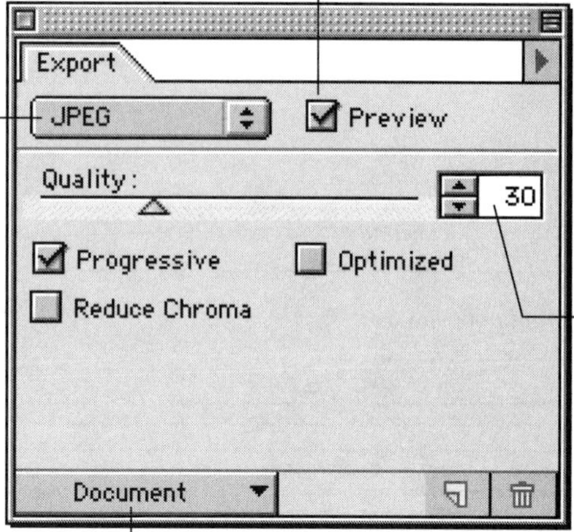

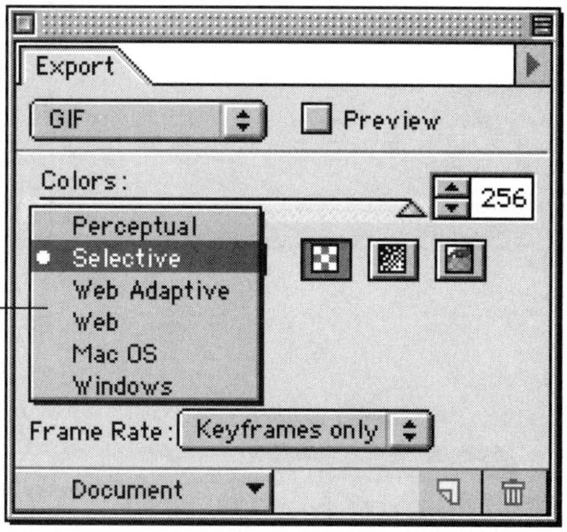

*The **color palette** to be used for optimization*

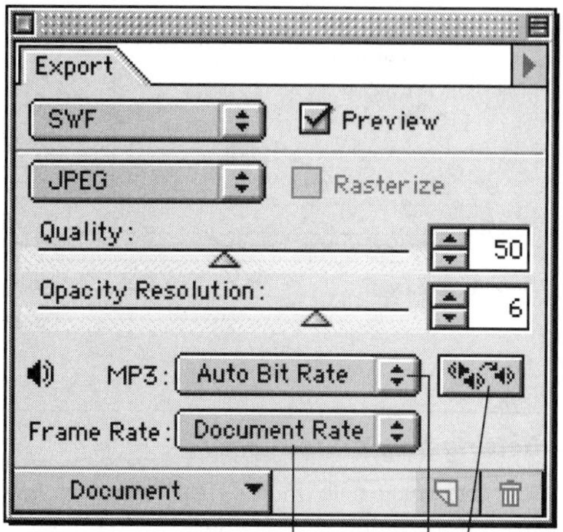

***Animation** setting* ***Sound** settings*

Timeline

Animation is motion. The Timeline editor is used to map object changes to specific points in time. Those changes can include making an object move across the screen, making it fade in or out, changing its color or opacity, transforming it, or even replacing it. This palette is used so heavily, there's even a shortcut for opening it: Command-T/Ctrl-T.

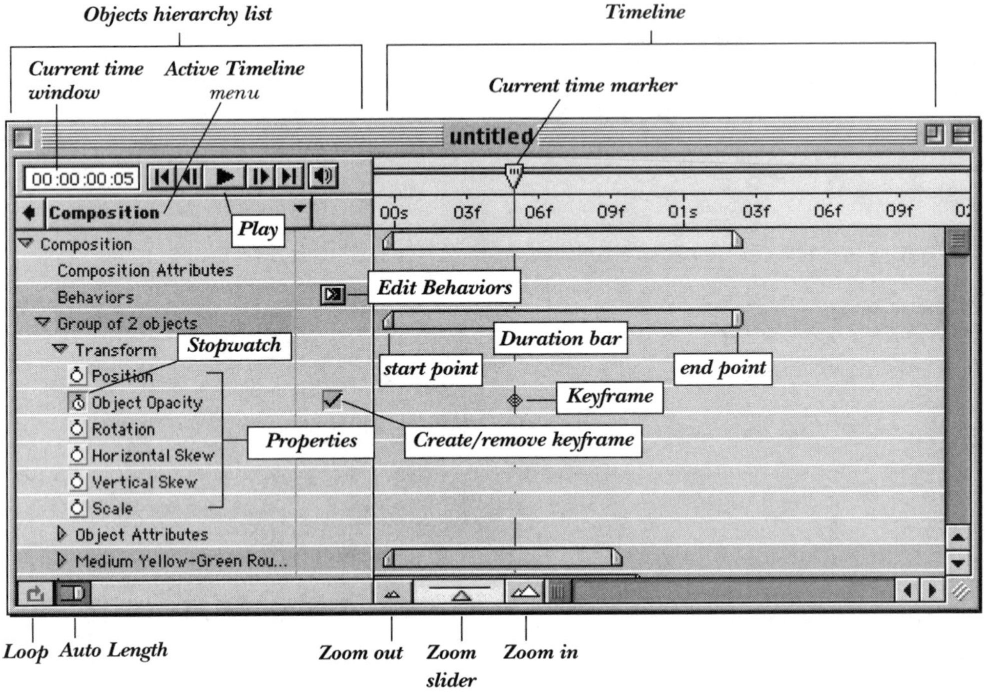

Getting help online

To access online help, choose Help menu > **LiveMotion Help**. When the Help window opens, you can navigate through topics via the Contents or the Index.

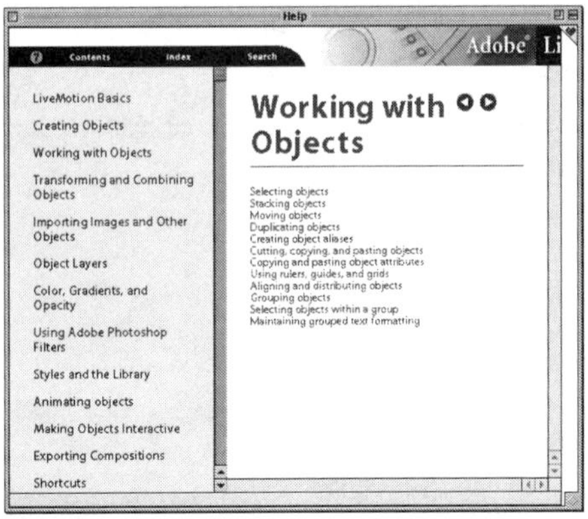

Webspeak demystified

HOLY MACKEREL. *What started out as a mini-glossary turned into a glossary-glossary. There are so many new words, many of them acronyms or slang, in this ever-changing field. Webspeak is a whole new language, and every Web designer needs to learn how to speak it. Skim the glossary now, then go back to it later on when you have a wider frame of reference. Pay particular attention to the individual definitions of (and differences between) the file formats: GIF, JPEG, PNG, and SWF. Terms that we use frequently in this book, especially in the Export chapter, are marked here with this symbol: ➤.*

alt label
Alternate label. A text label for a graphic link. Alt labels display as a Web page loads, and can be used as an alternate method for linking by Web viewers whose image display is turned off.

anti-aliasing ➤
The addition of pixels along the edges of objects or color areas to make them appear smoother (less jaggy) on screen. Anti-aliasing slightly increases a file's size. We recommend that you use it for most kinds of graphics, but not for small type.

bandwith
The speed at which data can be transmitted over the Internet. Bandwith is usually measured in bits per second (bps), thousands of bits per second (Kbps), or millions of bits per second (Mbps). A phone line, analog modem, for example, can transmit 56K bits per second. A cable modem can transmit at about 300 Kbps.

banner
A commercial advertisement on the Web. Banners usually occupy only a portion of a Web page, and are usually animated GIFs.

bitmap ➤
An image that's composed of pixels in a grid configuration (also called a "raster" image). Photoshop and other image-editing programs produce bitmap images. The Web is a bitmap arena.

bookmark/favorite
A browser feature that lets you save a link to a Web page so you can easily return to it later. In Netscape Communicator, it's called a bookmark; in Internet Explorer, it's called a favorite.

bot
Short for robot; also called a "spider." A bot is a software robot that scans the Web for addresses (URLs) to include in search engine databases.

browser ➤
An application (e.g., Netscape Navigator, Netscape Communicator, Internet Explorer) that enables a user to access, navigate through, and download from the World Wide Web.

client
A client is a computer station that requests a service of another computer system (usually a server on a network).

color depth
The number of bits used to represent the color of each pixel in an animation or a still image. A 1-bit image has only black and white pixels; a 8-bit image can contain up to 256 colors; a 24-bit image can contain up to 16.7 million colors.

color model
The method by which colors are defined. Computer monitors use red, green, and blue (RGB) light to produce a spectrum of color. This is called "additive" color. Documents are printed, on the other hand, using tiny dots of cyan, magenta, yellow, and black (CMYK) inks, or using individual mixed spot colors (e.g., Pantone). This is called "subtractive" color.

Regardless of which View you choose for the Color palette in LiveMotion—Saturation, Value, Hue, HSB, RGB, or CIEL—the colors will always be displayed as RGB.

compression ◄
The reduction of a file's storage size in order to speed up its download time over the Internet. Compression has no effect on the dimensions of an image.

CSS
Cascading Style Sheets. Sets of rules applied to HTML documents that control the location, fonts, point size, colors, and other attributes of HTML text and graphics. The style sheet, browser, and server ascertain what type of monitor, connection, and system the visitor is using and then the style sheet cascades down through its list to find the one that's most appropriate for that visitor. This enables every visitor to see a site at its best. A class is a group of HTML elements chosen by a Web designer to which the same layout attributes are applied via a cascading style sheet.

CLUT
Color Look-Up Table. A system for storing the values of all colors in graphic image. CLUTs are used by image-editing programs to convert images between color models and by the browsers to display images.

DHTML
Dynamic Hypertext Markup Language. A version of HTML that is used to describe text, graphics, animation, actions, layers, HTML, JavaScript, and cascading style sheets.

dithering ◄
The pseudo-blending of pixel colors to simulate missing colors. Dithering can cause an image to look grainy. It's used when a file's color depth is reduced for faster downloading.

download ◄
Transmit data from a server to a user's hard disk.

firewall
An Internet security system that's designed to prevent unwanted intruders from accessing sensitive data on a network.

frames
The division of a Web page into sections. A different HTML page can be loaded into each frame. Frames are used, for example, to create a column of buttons or a navigation bar that will remain visible as a viewer flips through various pages on a site.

frame rate
The rate at which an animation plays in frames per second. The higher the frame rate, the smoother the playback, and the larger the file size.

FTP
File Transfer Protocol. A method by which files are transmitted to, and downloaded from, an Internet server.

GIF, GIF89a ◄
Graphics Interchange File format. A widely used lossless, color bitmap file format used for compressing and saving graphics for display over the Internet. GIF is an 8-bit format, capable of saving up to 256 colors. GIF is generally better suited for sharp-edged graphics that contain flat color areas than for continuous-tone imagery.

The GIF89a format (unlike JPEG) is used for displaying multiple images in sequence (called "multiblocks") in order to create an animation effect. GIF89a also supports interlacing and single-color transparency. Files called "animated GIFs" or "transparent GIFs" are in GIF89a format.

hash table
A sequential list of hyperlinks (e.g., a list of page number links that a visitor can choose from).

host
A powerful Web server with a fast, permanent connection to the Internet. Host servers store Web sites for customers.

hotspot
A location in a graphic or image map, which when clicked on, links the viewer to another page or site.

HTML ◄
Hypertext Markup Language. The coding language that uses structural and style tags to create hypertext documents on the Web.

All Web pages must be written to fit into the structure of HTML, whether the tags are assigned to page elements by the Web designer or it's done invisibly behind the scenes, as in LiveMotion.

http
Hypertext Transfer Protocol. The method by which HTML files are transmitted over the Internet.

hyperlink
(*see* Link)

hypertext
Underlined text that a visitor clicks on to get to other Web pages.

image map ➤
An image on a Web site that contains more than one link. Each hotspot a visitor clicks in an image map activates a different link. To find out whether a graphic is an image map, move the mouse over it. If the hand icon appears there or the address changes in the status bar at the bottom of the browser window, it means the mouse is currently over an image map.

inline graphic
A graphic that's incorporated into an HTML file. Non-inline graphics have to be downloaded separately.

Intranet
A private, internal-use-only Web site that can only be accessed by members. To prevent entry by nonmembers, Intranet sites use an electronic security system known as a "firewall."

interlacing ➤
The gradual downloading of an image with successively increasing clarity and resolution until the final, highest resolution image renders on screen. The first, and lowest resolution image, is called the "low-source image." The GIF89a, PNG, and Progressive JPEG (not the standard JPEG) file formats support interlacing.

ISP
Internet Service Provider. A service that provides Internet access to its members (e.g., America Online, CompuServe, Earthlink).

JavaScript
A scripting language developed by Netscape that enables designers to add animation, rollovers, and sound effects to Web pages. JavaScripts are embedded into HTML files.

JPEG ➤
Joint Photographic Experts Group. A graphics file format used for saving bitmap images at varying degrees of compression. JPEG compression is lossy, meaning it causes image degradation, but the loss isn't necessarily noticeable or objectionable. JPEG is capable of saving millions of colors, but it doesn't support transparency, so you can't drop the background out from a JPEG image. Unlike GIF, JPEG can only be animated using JavaScript. JPEG is best suited for continuous-tone images.

An offshoot of JPEG, Progressive JPEG, uses interlacing to download images and has an even better compression scheme. Progressive JPEG isn't yet supported by all Web browsers.

keyframe
A frame in an animation that marks a key property of an object (e.g., its topmost position or its lowest opacity) at a specific moment in time. The insertion of additional frames between keyframes is called "tweening." Tweening is done automatically by the application. The number of frames inserted depends on the file's current frames-per-second rate.

LAN
Local Area Network. A computer network that's restricted to one specific geographic location.

link ➤
Short for hyperlink. A word or icon on a Web page that a viewer clicks to get to another page in the same site (an internal link) or to another site (an external link).

A link can be an underlined or boldface word, a picture, a word in another color, a 3D button, a rollover, or simply a word standing by itself. (Tip: Make it obvious.) Any kind of graphic link—still image or animation—is called hypermedia. When the pointer is over a link on a Web page, the link address displays at the bottom of the browser window. (*See also* navigation)

listserv
The transmission via e-mail of news or newsletters over the Internet only to subscribers.

loop
The continuous playback of an animation. An animation can be programmed to play once, a specific number of times, or forever.

lossy
A compression scheme (e.g., JPEG) that causes data loss from an image. A lossless compression scheme doesn't cause data loss (e.g., GIF). Data loss as a result of compression isn't always objectionable. It depends on the type of image being compressed and how much it's compressed.

MIME
Multipurpose Internet Mail Extensions. A method for attaching non-text files (e.g., photos, graphics, tables) to e-mail messages for transmission over the Internet.

navigation ➤
A navigation bar on a Web page typically lists various subjects or categories. Each category is a link that a visitor can click to access another part of the same site or another site. Each site has its own overall organizational scheme, or navigation system, the purpose of which is to help visitors access the information they need as quickly and easily as possible.

net
Short for Internet.

OpenType
A new type file format developed jointly by Adobe and Microsoft that allows fonts to be embedded into Web pages. When OpenType is used, visitors always see the Web page in the designer's font of choice—not in a substitute font.

optimize ➤
When a file is optimized, it is saved in one of the file formats used for online images (e.g., GIF, JPEG, PNG, or SWF), and compression, dithering, transparency, and other settings are chosen for it. The purpose for optimizing a file is to speed up the time it takes to download on the Web.

page
A Web page (HTML file). All Web pages contain text; many Web pages also contain graphics; and some Web pages also contain animations and/or rollovers.

PDF
Portable Document Format. A format developed by Adobe Systems, Inc. that compresses a file while preserving its formatting so it can be transferred from one computer to another. A PDF file can be viewed on screen or printed.

PNG ➤
Portable Network Graphics (pronounced "ping"). A lossless file format that's used for compressing and saving images on the Web. PNG supports 256-level (8-bit) transparency and only JavaScript animation, and has its own gamma correction mechanism. PNG can save up to 16.7 million colors, and it has a superior interlacing feature (the initial low-res image that you see as a PNG downloads is crisper than the initial image you see as a GIF downloads). PNG still isn't supported by all the browsers.

ppi
Pixels per inch. The unit of measurement used to measure image resolution (the amount of pixel data that is stored per inch). 72 ppi is a sufficient resolution for saving graphics for the Web.

QuickTime
The Apple Computer system software that compresses and displays desktop videos, animations, sounds, and still images.

QuickTime is used on both the MacOS and Windows platforms.

rollover ➤
An area on a Web page that triggers a screen event when the user moves the mouse over it or clicks on it. The screen event can be a change in color or opacity or it can be the appearance of an image, text, or an animation. A rollover can even include sound. When a rollover triggers a screen event at another location on a Web page, it's called a "remote" or "secondary" rollover. Every rollover has a Normal state (no action), and one or all of these states: Over (mouse over), Down (mouse down), or Out (mouse up).

search engine
A Web site that serves as a portal to help users locate Web pages. After a user enters a keyword, phrase, or URL (Web address) in an entry field, the search engine displays a list of sites bearing that string of words (with links to those sites). Popular search engine sites include: excite.com; hotbot.com; infoseek.com; yahoo.com; miningco.com, and altavisa.com.

Search engines are also used within individual Web sites to help visitors locate keywords within the site (e.g., go to Amazon.com or Barnesandnoble.com and type "Weinmann" in the Search field. A listing of our current and out-of-print books will appear). Some sites (e.g. Yahoo) also have directories in which Web sites are organized into categories.

server
A powerful computer that has a permanent connection to the Internet and serves as a storing house for Web sites. Also called a "host."

Shockwave
A Macromedia software component that compresses and exports Director movies for playback on the Web. The newest versions of Shockwave support streaming of movie elements.

slice
Slicing is the division of an image into sections, with each section fitting into one cell of an HTML table. Each slice can be optimized independently and can contain its own links, animations, and rollover effects.

source image
A graphic that displays on a Web page via a browser.

splash screen
The opening page that appears when a user first gets to a Web site. (Also the opening screen when an application launches.)

streaming
A method of transferring text, sounds, graphics, animation, and QuickTime video over the Web so it's processed by the visitor's system in a continuous stream—it starts displaying before the whole file is finished downloading.

SVG ➤
Scalable Vector Graphics. A new file format developed specifically for the Web. Vector graphics exported as SVG stay as vectors in the browsers—they don't have to be rasterized. In addition, the SVG format supports fills, gradients, blends, animation, and interactivity in both vector and raster graphics. It allows for searchable text. It allows visitors to zoom in on details on a Web page. And it produces smaller file sizes with faster download times. What more could anyone ask for?

SWF ➤
SWF is a Flash-based vector format that is used to export compositions containing animations. SWF files can be read by most browsers with the Flash plug-in. It is suitable for animations with solid-color areas and sharp-edged objects. It saves only solid-color backgrounds. For multi-layer objects, which cannot be saved as vectors, the SWF format will reference or embed a raster file (JPEG or PNG-Indexed).

tables
A method for organizing text and graphics into separate cells on a Web page.

tile
A bitmap graphic that's used in a repeating formation as a background for a Web page.

transparency ≺
A object's opacity. An object with 0% opacity is completely see-through. The GIF, PNG, SWF, and SVG file formats support transparency; JPEG does not.

tweening
The addition of frames in between keyframes in an animation.

upload
Transmit files from one computer to another over the Internet. In order to get a home page onto the Internet, the HTML files for the pages must be uploaded to the server chosen to host the Web site.

URL
Uniform Resource Locator. The address assigned to a particular page on the Internet.

vector
A method for describing and storing objects using mathematical coordinates. FreeHand and Illustrator are vector applications. A vector graphic can be converted into a bitmap graphic by a process known as rasterization.

web-safe ≺
The 216 colors that the Unix, Windows, MacOS, and other platforms have in common. When the Web-safe color box is checked on the LiveMotion Color palette, only Web-safe colors will be displayed on the palette.

World Wide Web ≺
The part of the Internet on which HTML pages are displayed and that uses HTTP to display them. World Wide Web pages can be viewed on any computer with a browser and access to the Internet.

E-mail/chat room shorthand

BFN
Bye for now

BG
Big grin

BTW
By the way

DIKU
Do I know you?

emoticon
just kidding ;-)

I'm sad :-(

[tilt your head to the left]

FWIW
For what it's worth

FYI
For your information

G
Grin

GMTA
Great minds think alike

IAC
In any case

IANAL
I am not a lawyer (but)

ILU
I love you

IMHO
In my humble opinion

IMNSHO
In my not so humble opinion

IOW
In other words

LLTA
Lots and lots of thunderous applause

LOL
Laughing out loud

OIC
Oh, I see

ROFL
Rolling on the floor laughing

THX
Thanks

TIA
Thanks in advance

TPTB
The powers that be

Rev Up 2

Creating and opening compositions

To launch LiveMotion (MacOS):

Open the LiveMotion folder on the hard drive, then double-click the LiveMotion application icon.

or

Double-click an alias of the application icon.

or

Click the LiveMotion application icon on the Launcher (Fig. 1).

or

Double-click a LiveMotion file icon (Fig. 2).

To launch LiveMotion (Windows):

Click the Start button on the Taskbar, choose Programs, choose Adobe, choose LiveMotion, then click Adobe LiveMotion (Fig. 3).

or

Double-click a LiveMotion file icon.

or

Open the LiveMotion folder in My Computer/Applications, then double-click the LiveMotion icon (Fig. 4).

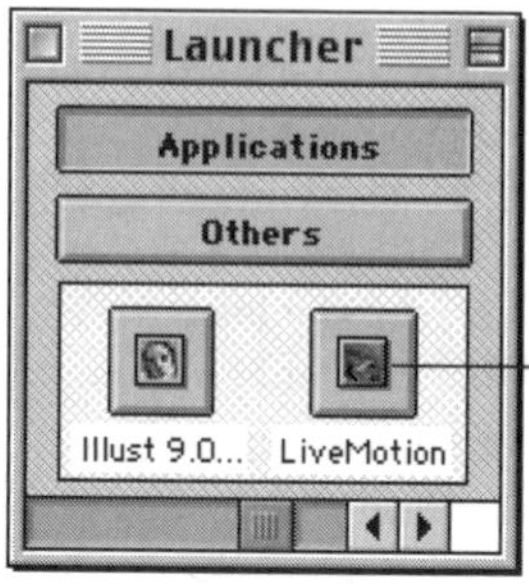

*1 ➤ Click the **LiveMotion application** icon on the **Launcher**.*

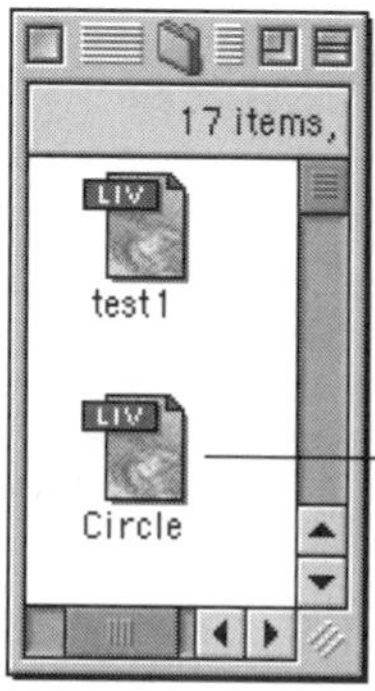

*2 ➤ Double-click a **LiveMotion file** icon (MacOS).*

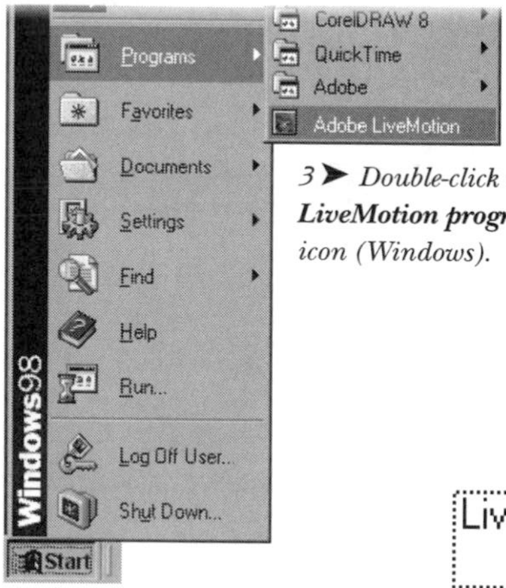

*3 ➤ Double-click the **LiveMotion program** icon (Windows).*

*4 ➤ Or double-click the **LiveMotion application** icon (Windows).*

The original dimensions of a LiveMotion composition are chosen when the composition is created, but they can be changed at any time. The current composition size is also the maximum size of any object you can import or export.

To create a new composition or resize an existing composition:

1. Choose File menu > New (Command-N/ Ctrl-N).
   or
   Open an existing document, then choose Edit menu > Composition Settings (Command-Shift-N/Ctrl-Shift-N).
2. Modify the Width and/or Height pixel values (Fig. 1).
3. If you're going to create an animation, make the frame rate 12 or 15. (An animation frame rate that's faster than 15 will require a very fast Internet connection to display properly.)
4. For now, choose Export: Entire Composition or AutoLayout (you can change this setting when you're ready to export the file), and check the Make HTML box.
5. Click OK (Return/Enter). If you're creating a new file, a new, untitled composition window will now open (Fig. 2). You can name it when you save it.

➤ The width and height values aren't linked. Changing the height has no effect on the width, and vice versa.

How big?

The final size of the Web page may be specified in LiveMotion or later on in a Web-page editing program (e.g., Macromedia Dreamweaver or Adobe GoLive). The larger the dimensions of the composition, the more pixels it will contain and the longer the page will take to download on the Web.

For most purposes, you should design for the pixel dimensions of the most common monitor size and resolution a viewer might use. At the present time, those dimensions are **800** pixels wide by **600** pixels high. If you want to subtract space for the browser menu bar at the top, make the Height **550** pixels.

Web viewers are usually willing to scroll vertically, but they're going to resist scrolling horizontally—it's **annoying**. Keep that in mind when you specify dimensions. Some designers refuse to cater to small monitors and design only for the large monitors (20-inch). 1,024 x 1,024 pixels is the maximum size composition you can create in LiveMotion.

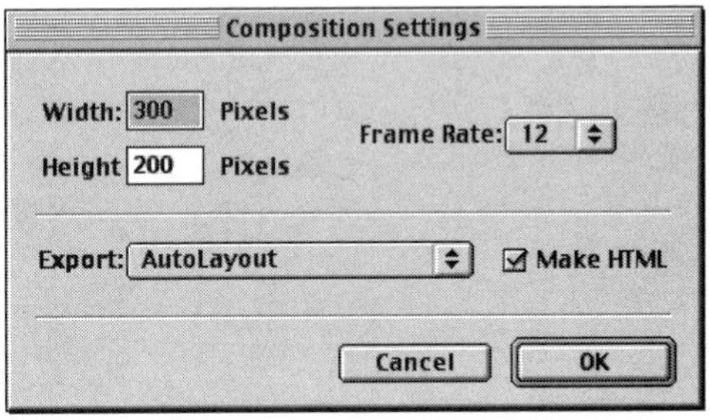

1➤ Choose or change an image's ***pixel dimensions*** *in the* ***Composition Settings*** *dialog box.*

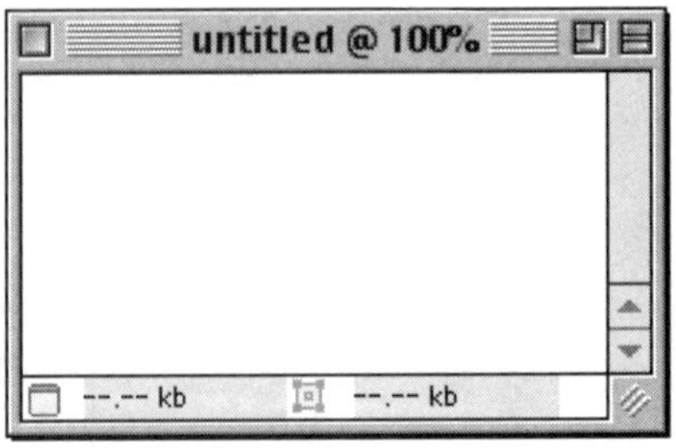

2➤ A new, untitled composition window.

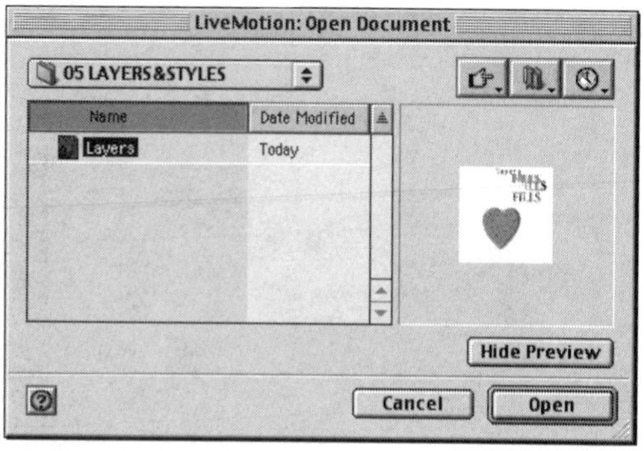

*1 ➤ Use the **Open Document** dialog box to open existing LiveMotion files.*

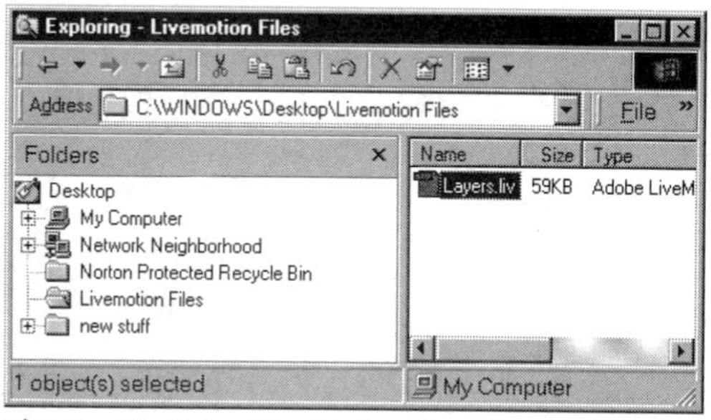

*2 ➤ Double-click a LiveMotion file in **Windows Explorer**.*

The Open Document dialog box is used to open LiveMotion files (the file extension is ".liv"). To import images or illustrations from other applications into LiveMotion, use the Place command (see page 102).

To open an existing LiveMotion file from within LiveMotion:

1. Choose File menu > Open (Command-O/Ctrl-O).
2. MacOS: If you see a Show Preview button (the preview is currently hidden), click it to display a thumbnail of the file (Fig. 1).
4. Locate and highlight a file name, then click Open (Return/Enter).
   or
   Double-click a file name.

To open a LiveMotion file from the Macintosh Finder/Windows Explorer:

Double-click a LiveMotion file icon (Fig. 2). LiveMotion will launch if it hasn't already been launched.

Navigating

As you're working in LiveMotion, you'll need to switch periodically between a zoomed-in view to work on small details and a zoomed-out view to survey the overall composition. There are a few methods for doing this. The current zoom level is indicated on the title bar of the composition window.

To change the view size:

Choose View menu > Actual Size (100%) (Command-Option-0 (zero)/Ctrl-Alt-0).

or

Zoom in using the Command-+ (plus)/Ctrl-+ shortcut (100%–800% in 100% increments).

or

Zoom out using the Command- - (minus)/Ctrl- - shortcut.

or

Choose the Zoom tool (Z), then click in the composition window to zoom in or Option-click/Alt-click in the composition window to zoom out (Fig. 1).

or

Choose the Zoom tool (Z), then drag in the composition window to zoom in on that chosen area (Fig. 2).

or

Choose Zoom in or Zoom out from the View menu (100%–800%).

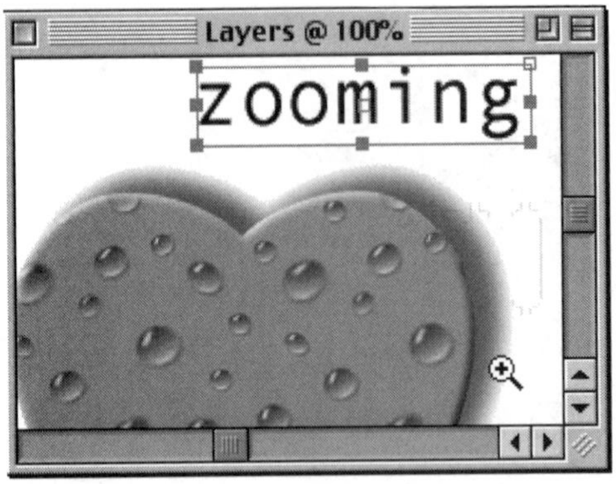

*1 ➤ Zooming in with the **Zoom** tool.*

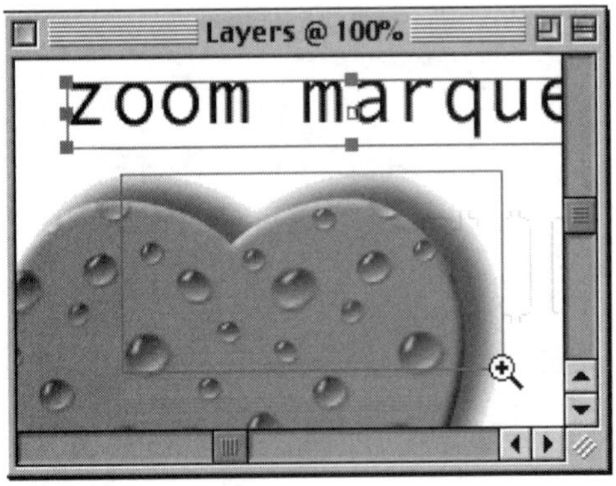

*2 ➤ Dragging a marquee with the **Zoom** tool to enlarge that chosen area.*

To work with multiple open compositions:

To **arrange** multiple windows, choose Window menu > Stack, Tile. MacOS: You can also choose Tile Vertical. Windows: You can also choose Cascade for a stairstep configuration.

To **switch between** open files, choose from the list of currently open documents on the Window menu.

To move a composition in its window:

1. Choose the Hand tool (H) or hold down Spacebar.
2. Drag in the composition window (Fig. 3).

*3 ➤ Moving the composition in the window using the **Hand** tool.*

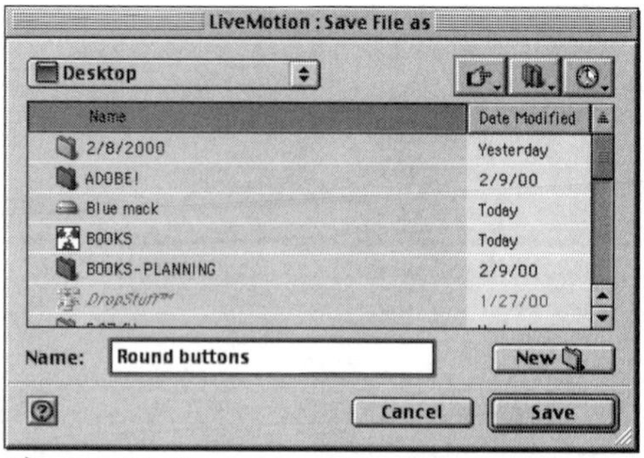

1 ➤ ***MacOS: Name** a new file and choose a **location** in which to save it in the **Save File as** dialog box.*

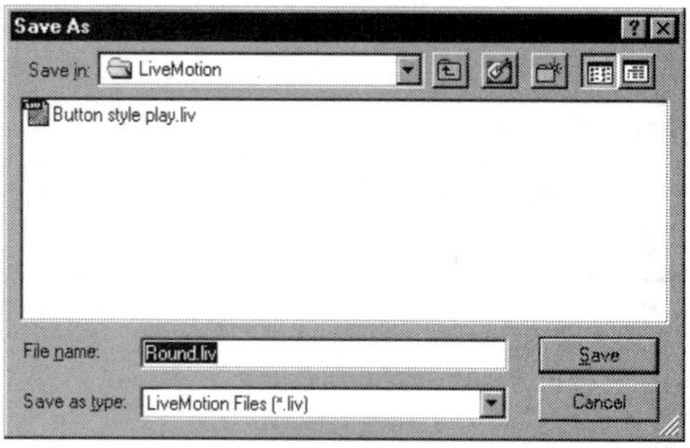

2 ➤ ***Windows: Name** a new file and choose a location in which to save it in the **Save As** dialog box.*

Saving

Both the Save and Save As commands save a file in the LiveMotion format. A LiveMotion file can be closed, reopened, and edited. When the layout is finished, you can export an optimized version of it to a Web-page layout program.

To save a new file in LiveMotion format:

1. Choose File menu > Save (Command-S/ Ctrl-S).
2. Enter a name in the Name field (MacOS)/ File Name field (Win) (Figs. 1–2).
3. MacOS: Highlight a folder in which to save the file, then click Open. Or to create a new folder, choose a location in which to save the folder, click New, type a name for the folder, then click Create.

   Windows: Navigate to the folder in which you want to save the file using the "Save in" pop-up menu.
4. Click Save (Return/Enter). The file name will appear on the composition window title bar.

➤ MacOS and Windows LiveMotion files are compatible. If you're going to share your files cross-platform, just be sure to use the .liv extension when saving files on the MacOS. MacOS: If the Append File Extension Preference is set to Always (instead of Never) in Edit menu > Preferences when you save a file for the first time, the file extension will be appended to the file name automatically. In Windows, the .liv extension is automatically added to every LiveMotion file.

Once a file has been saved, subsequently choosing the Save command won't open the Save dialog box—you'll just be saving over the existing file. Save frequently! Don't say we didn't warn you.

To save an existing file:

Choose File menu > Save (Command-S/ Ctrl-S) (Fig. 1).

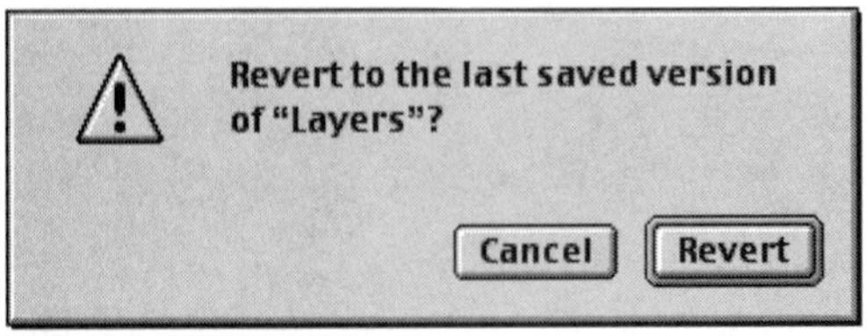

*1➤ The **Revert** command is a drastic measure, but it's there when you need it.*

Use Save As to save a version of the current file under a different name.

To save a file under a different name:

1. With an edited file open, choose File menu > Save As (Command-Shift-S/ Ctrl-Shift-S).
2. Enter a different file name in the Name/Filename field (Figs. 2–3).
3. Choose a location in which to save the file.
4. Click Save (Return/Enter). The original file will close automatically and a new file window will appear with the name you entered in the Save As dialog box on its title bar.

➤ Windows bug: If the file name you enter in the Save As dialog box contains a space, only the first word will be used. In other words, don't bother entering more than a one-word name.

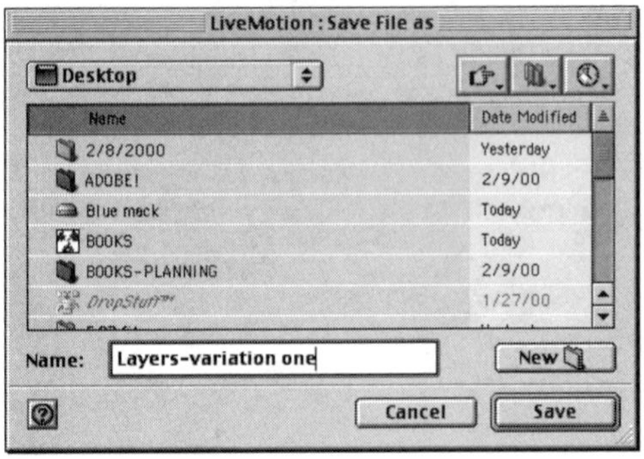

*2➤ The **Save As** command is useful if you want to spawn variations from the same composition (**MacOS**).*

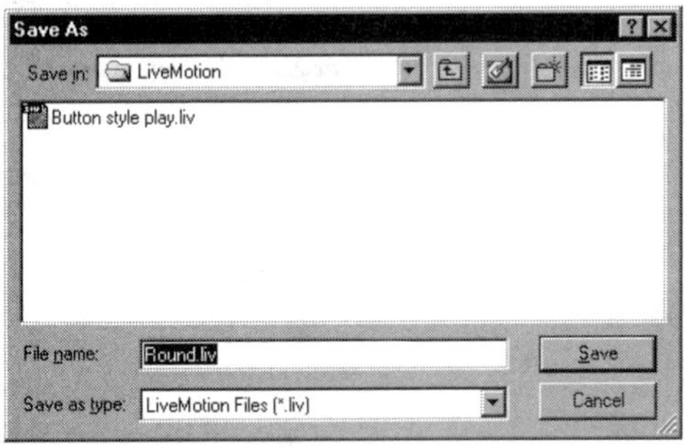

*3➤ This is the **Save As** dialog box in **Windows**.*

Context menus (Windows only)

Context-sensitive menus are on-screen menus that pop up when the time is right—and, of course, when you **Right-click** in the composition window. Context menus save you the trouble of having to mouse to the menu bar or to a palette.

There aren't a whole lot of context-menu choices in LiveMotion—at least not yet. Furthermore, not all of the commands that appear on a context menu may be applicable to or available for the objects that are currently selected. The menu offerings will change depending on which tool is selected and whether any objects are selected in your composition. We include choosing commands from context menus as an option in some of the instructions in this book.

Undoing

The Revert command restores the currently open composition to its last-saved version.

To revert to the last saved version:

1. Choose File menu > Revert (F12).
2. Click Revert. This cannot be undone!

You may resort to the Revert command occasionally, but it's a pretty drastic step. What you'll avail yourself of more frequently is the Undo command, which undoes most operations. Now that you know the Undo submenu is there, mistakes won't be cause for widespread panic.

To undo:

To Undo the last operation: Command-Z/ Ctrl-Z.

or

Choose from a list of the most recent operations on the Edit menu > Undo submenu.

➤ To Redo the last undo: Command-R/ Ctrl-R.

Ending a work session

To close a file:

MacOS: Click the close box in the upper left corner of the composition window.

Windows: Click the close box in the upper right corner of the composition window.
or
MacOS or Windows: Choose File menu > Close (Command-W/Ctrl-W).

If you try to close a composition that was modified since it was last saved, a warning prompt will appear (Fig. 1). You can close the file without saving (click Don't Save), save the file (click Save), or cancel the close operation altogether (click Cancel).

To quit/exit LiveMotion:

MacOS: Choose File menu > Quit (Command-Q).

Windows: Choose File menu > Exit (Ctrl-Q).

All open LiveMotion files will close. If changes were made to any open files since they were last saved, a warning prompt will appear. You can save the file(s) or quit/exit without saving the changes.

Accessing Adobe online

From the Adobe LiveMotion home page on the Web, you can obtain registration info, tips, software upgrades, and other goodies. If you have a technical question, e-mail Adobe at techdocs@adobe.com.

Note: We apologize for spelling out the obvious, but in order to access Adobe Online, your computer must have an Internet connection. To access Adobe Online using America Online as your Internet provider, you must sign on to AOL first.

1. In LiveMotion, click the spaceship image at the top of the Toolbox.
2. To update the Adobe Online screen, click Update, then click OK. The Adobe site will update your online screen.
3. Click a topic on the Adobe Online screen to launch your browser and connect to the Adobe home page on the Web. Once you reach the Adobe Web site, you can click on other topics to learn more about LiveMotion or about other Adobe products or services.

➤ While you're at it, study the site. Do you like the design? Did you get where you needed go to quickly?

➤ The Internet address for the Adobe home page is: http://www.adobe.com.

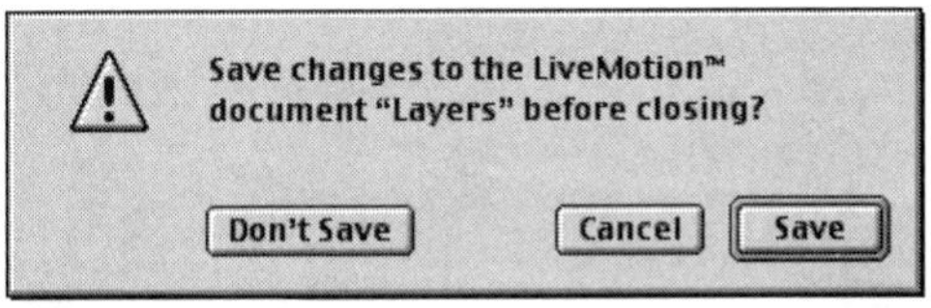

1➤ *This alert dialog box will appear if you attempt to* ***close*** *a composition that was* ***modified*** *since it was last* ***saved.***

Opening palettes

For the instructions in this practice exercise, you'll need to use several palettes. If the palette you need isn't already showing, choose the palette name from the **Window** menu. If the palette is visible on screen but hidden behind other palettes in its group, click the palette tab (name) at the top of the palette group to bring it to the front.

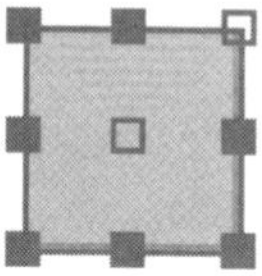

*1 ➤ A **square** is created.*

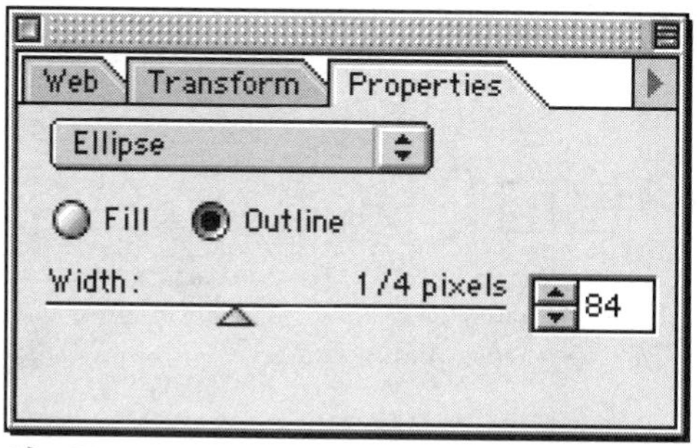

*2 ➤ The **Properties** palette is used for **changing** a geometric object's shape or converting it into an editable path; for changing an object's outline **Width;** and for switching between the **Fill** and **Outline** styles.*

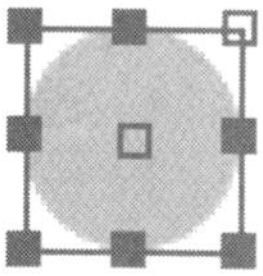

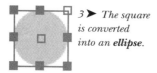

*3 ➤ The square is converted into an **ellipse**.*

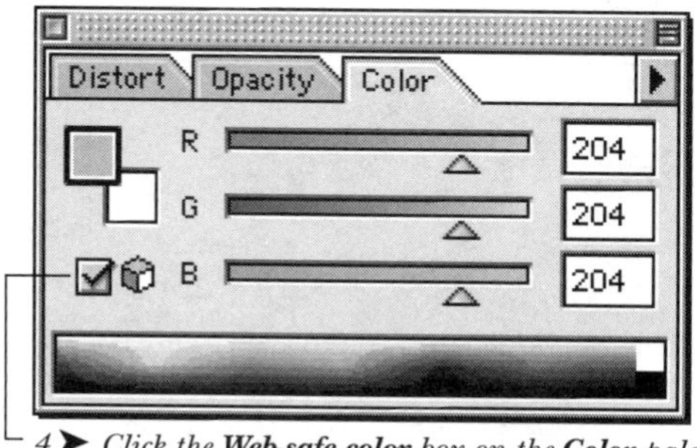

*4 ➤ Click the **Web-safe color** box on the **Color** palette.*

Dry run: create a button

LiveMotion is a vector application that remembers the original properties of any drawn or imported shape. So not only can any palette option be applied at any time to any object, these options can also be removed or changed at any time. Attributes are editable and reversible.

Just to give you a taste of what LiveMotion has to offer, we're offering an exercise to guide you through some of the steps you could follow to create a button. Note our use of the word "could," not "will." When you're working on your own, you'll make up your own steps and concoct your own designs.

DRAW THE BUTTON SHAPE

1. Choose the Rectangle tool (M).
2. Shift-drag in the composition window to create a square (Fig. 1). Leave the object selected (its selection border with selection handles will be visible).
3. Choose the Selection tool (V).
4. Show the Properties palette (Window menu > Properties). The palette will show options for the rectangle (or any geometric shape created with a drawing tool—Rectangle, Rounded Rectangle, Ellipse, Polygon, or Path) (Fig. 2). Changes made using this palette will affect the whole object and all its layers.

   See what happens to the object when you click the Fill button, then the Outline button. For this exercise, choose Fill.

   To change the object's shape, choose Ellipse from the pop-up menu (Fig. 3).
5. Show the Color palette.
6. From the Color palette drop-down menu (click the triangle at the palette's upper right), choose RGB View.
7. Check the "Web-safe color" box next to the little cube icon (Fig. 4) to turn that option on.

(Continued on the next page)

8. Click a light color on the color ramp at the bottom of the palette.
9. Save your document, and continue with the instructions below.

ADD AN EMBOSS EFFECT

1. Show the 3D palette.
2. Choose Emboss from the topmost pop-up menu, then choose these settings: Depth 8; Softness 2; Lighting 50; Angle 135; Edge: Straight; and Light: Normal (Figs. 1–2).

ADD A DROP SHADOW

1. Show the Object Layers palette (Window menu > Object Layers). *Note:* Don't confuse the Object Layers palette with the Layer palette.
2. Click the New Layer button at the bottom of the Object Layers palette (Fig. 3). A new layer will be created with the same shape.
3. Double-click the new layer name, rename it "Shadow," then click OK.
4. *Optional:* With the new layer still selected, choose a color for the shadow from the Color palette.
5. Show the Layer palette.

(Continued on the next page)

A whole new layer concept

In LiveMotion, you won't find layers that fit the rectangular "live canvas" area. Instead, you'll find **object layers** that belong to each individual object that you create. If an object is shaped like an arrow, for example, any layers that are assigned to that object will have that arrow shape.

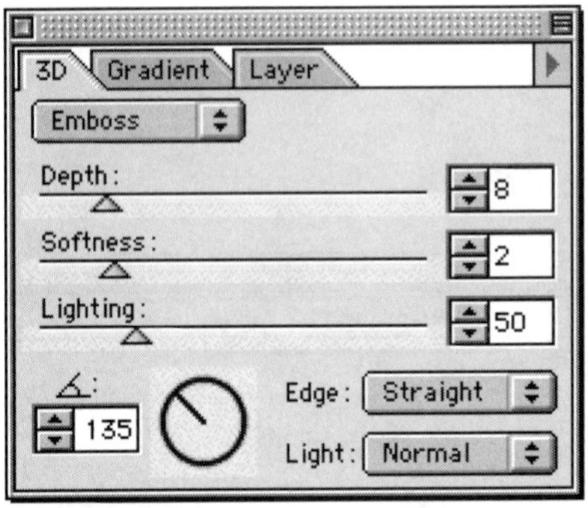

1 ➤ You can choose from four different effects on the 3D palette: ***Cutout, Emboss, Bevel,*** *and* ***Ripple.***

2 ➤ The ***Emboss*** *effect.*

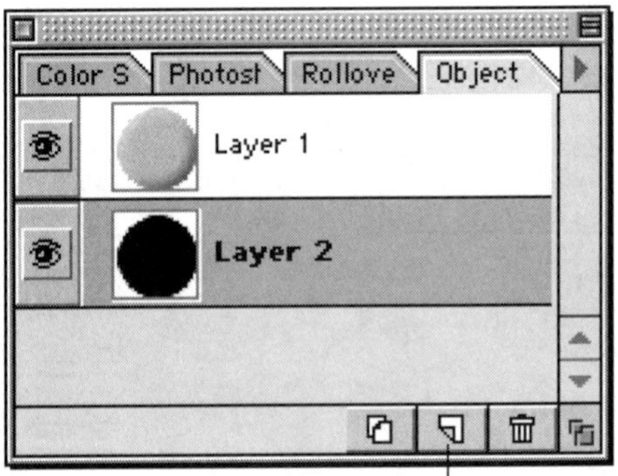

3 ➤ Click the ***New Layer*** *button.*

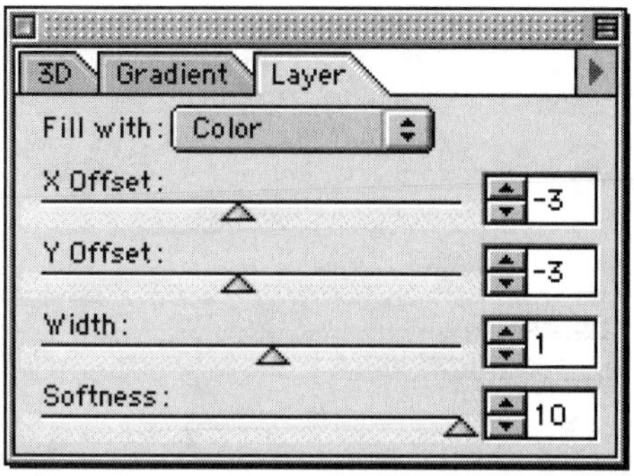

*1 ➤ The **Layer** palette is used to apply **position, width,** and **softness** values to the current layer.*

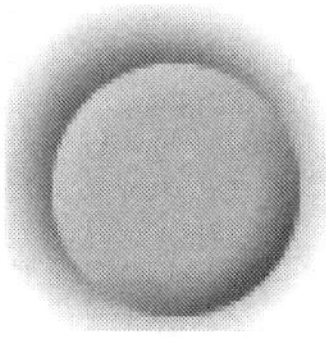

*2 ➤ The shadow layer is **nudged, widened,** and **softened**. Now the button looks even more three-dimensional.*

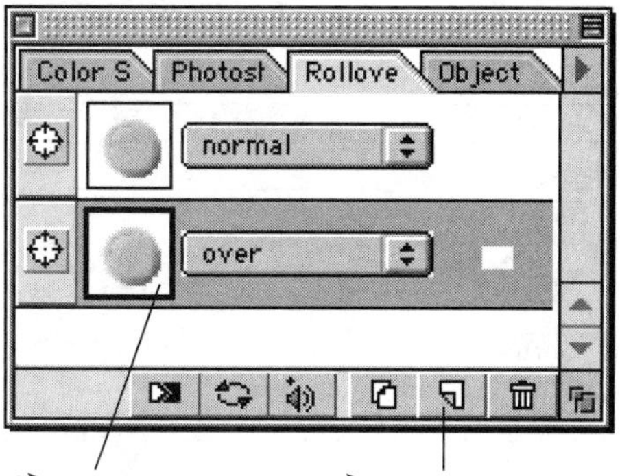

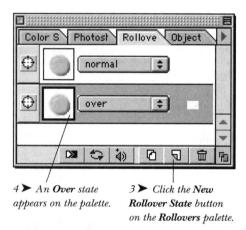

*4 ➤ An **Over** state appears on the palette.*

*3 ➤ Click the **New Rollover State** button on the **Rollovers** palette.*

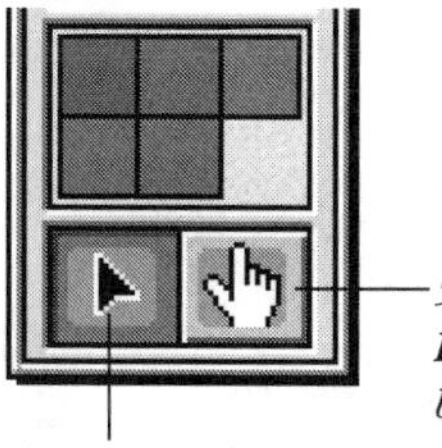

*5 ➤ Click the **Preview mode** button at the bottom of the **Toolbox**.*

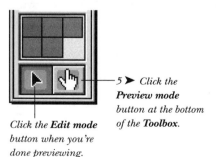

*Click the **Edit mode** button when you're done previewing.*

6. Make the X Offset -3, the Y Offset -3, the Width 1, and the Softness 10 (Figs. 1–2). Save your file.

➤ You can also offset a selected layer by dragging it with the Layer Offset tool (O) instead of using the Offset sliders on the Layer palette. New X Offset and Y Offset readings will display on the Layer palette. Don't try to do this by dragging an object's selection handles, though—you will resize all the object's layers instead of just one layer.

CREATE A ROLLOVER

A rollover is a change that happens to an object on a Web page when the mouse is moved over it or clicks on it.

1. Make sure the button is still selected (the selection handles should be visible). If it's not, choose the Selection tool (V), then click on the button. And select Layer 1 on the Object Layers palette.
2. Show the Rollovers palette (Window menu > Rollovers).
3. Click the New Rollover State button at the bottom of the Rollovers palette (Figs. 3–4).
4. With the new rollover state still selected (the Over state), choose a different color from the Color palette.
5. Click the Preview mode button at the bottom of the Toolbox (the pointing hand) (Fig. 5).

(Continued on the next page)

6. Move the mouse over the button, then away from the button, then over the button, and so on (Fig. 1). You've created a rollover! Click back on the Edit mode button at the bottom of the Toolbox when you're done previewing the rollover.
7. You wanna do more? Click the New Rollover State button on the Rollovers palette again. A Down state will appear on the palette (Fig. 2).
8. Show the 3D palette, then choose Ripple from the pop-up menu on the palette. Also adjust the Depth and/or Lighting, if desired (Fig. 3).
9. Click the Preview mode button at the bottom of the Toolbox again, then move the mouse over the button, click on the button, then move the mouse away from the button, then over the button (Fig. 4). Show off your rollover to your boss or a loved one. They'll think you're a genius.

   We don't expect you to remember any of these steps. Just file them away in the back of your mind—they'll serve as a frame of reference as you go through the book.

*1➤ When the mouse is moved over the button in **Preview mode** (the **Over** state is active), the button's second color displays.*

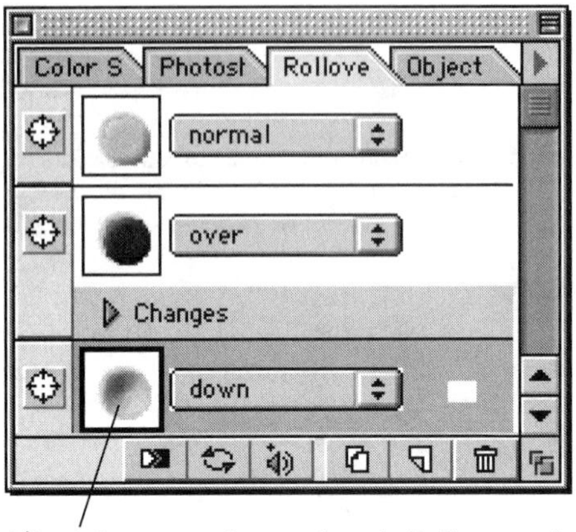

*2➤ A **Down** state is created on the **Rollovers** palette.*

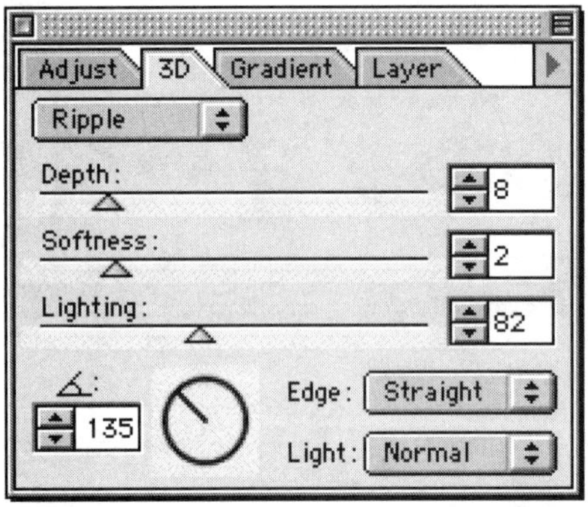

*3➤ The **3D: Ripple** effect is applied to the **Down** state.*

*4➤ When this button is clicked (the **Down** state) in **Preview mode**, the Ripple effect appears.*

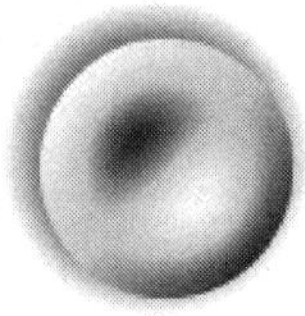

Create Objects 3

Fill or outline?

Double-clicking the Rectangle, Rounded Rectangle, Ellipse, or Polygon tool causes the **Properties** palette to display. You can choose whether an object will have a Fill or an Outline property before or after it's drawn (read about these properties on page 86).

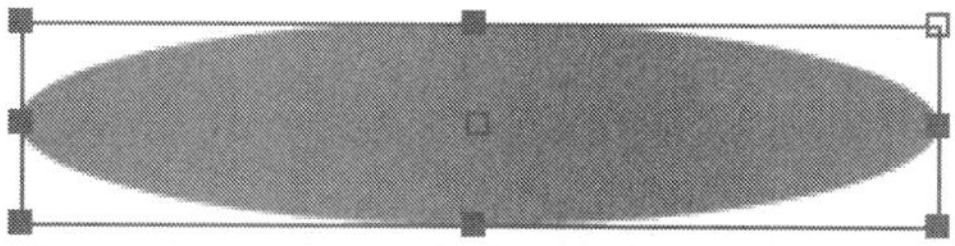

1 ➤ The completed ellipse is selected automatically and filled with the current ***Foregound*** *color.*

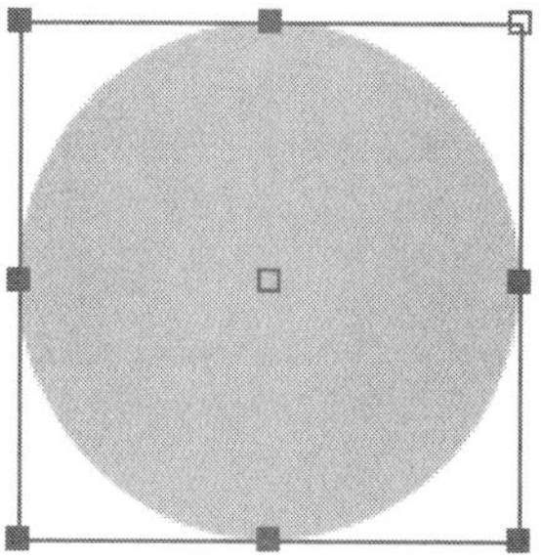

2 ➤ An ellipse drawn with ***Shift*** *held down.*

Drawing geometric objects

AS WE MENTIONED in Chapter 1, three different types of objects can be created in LiveMotion: geometric, text, and image. In the first part of this chapter we'll teach you how to create simple geometric shapes using LiveMotion's Rectangle, Rounded Rectangle, Ellipse, and Polygon tools, as well as more irregular shapes using the Pen tool. In the latter part of the chapter you'll learn how to use the Library palette to store and retrieve shapes.

When you use any of the geometric drawing tools, your newly formed object will be filled automatically with the current Foreground color (more about color in Chapter 8).

To create a rectangle or an ellipse:

1. Choose the Rectangle tool (M) ☐, the Rounded Rectangle tool (R) ▢, or the Ellipse tool (L) ○.
2. Press and drag diagonally in the composition window. The shape will preview as you drag. When you release the mouse, the object will be selected (Fig. 1).

   To create a square or a circle, hold down Shift while dragging (Fig. 2).

➤ To change the amount of curvature on a rounded rectangle, see page 43.

➤ If the Toolbar Behavior: Auto-Revert to Arrow Tool box is checked in Edit menu > Preferences (Command-K/Ctrl-K), after you use the Rectangle, Rounded Rectangle, Ellipse, or Polygon tool, the Selection tool will be chosen automatically. If you turn this option off, the tool won't change.

In LiveMotion, you can create a three- to ten-sided polygon.

To create a polygon:

1. Double-click the Polygon tool (N).
2. Choose the number of sides for the polygon using the Sides slider or field on the Properties palette.
3. Drag diagonally in the composition window. The shape will preview as you drag. When you release the mouse, the object will be selected (Fig. 1).

   To create a symmetrical polygon in which all the sides are of equal length, hold down Shift while dragging (Fig. 2).

➤ You can also use the Sides slider or field to change the number of sides on a polygon after it's drawn. The current Sides value will remain in effect until you change it.

*1➤ A **polygon** drawn **without** holding down Shift.*

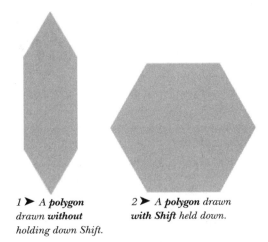

*2➤ A **polygon** drawn **with Shift** held down.*

You can't really draw a line in LiveMotion. What you can do is draw a long and very narrow rectangle.

To draw a line:

1. Choose the Rectangle tool (M).
2. Draw vertically or horizontally to create a long, skinny rectangle (Fig. 3).
3. *Optional:* To make a vertical line skinnier, change the width value on the Transform palette; to make it longer or shorter, change the height value (Figs. 4–7). To make a horizontal line skinnier, change the height value; to make it longer or shorter, change the width value. One pixel is the minimum.

➤ You can use the Styles palette or any other method to embellish the line.

*3➤ A **skinny rectangle** is drawn.*

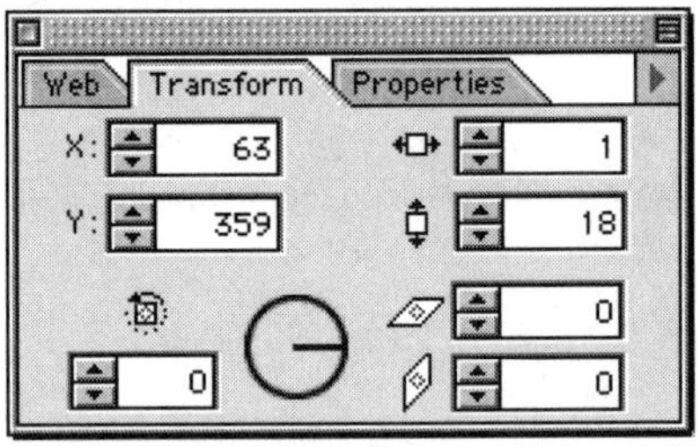

*4➤ Its **width** is changed to **1 pixel**.*

*5➤ Now the rectangle looks like a **line**.*

6➤ An alias is made from the line. The lines are used to divide text links. (You'll learn about aliasing in the next chapter.)

7➤ This line (rectangle) was drawn horizontally and then stylized to make it look glowy.

Think pixels!

Unless you're 21 years old and in college (we're so much older than that it's **not funny**), you may have had a little experience measuring things in picas and points—if not by hand using a Schaedler ruler then at least in an electronic page layout program. Stick the Schaedler in a keepsake box next to your Beatles cards and start thinking and measuring things in pixels. Remember, you're creating objects that will never ever leave the on-screen environment.

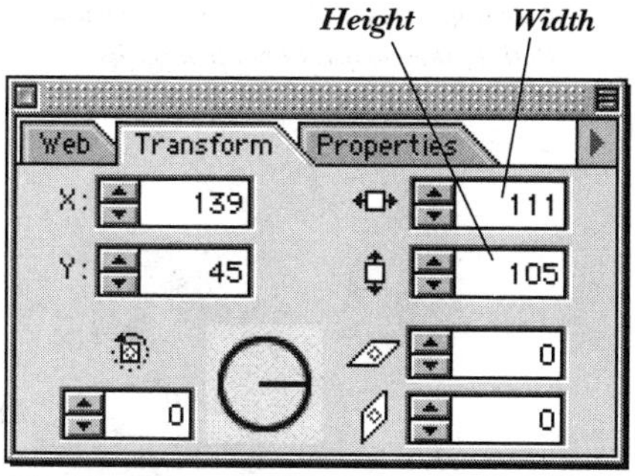

1 ➤ Transform palette.

You can't create a geometric object from scratch using precise dimensions, but you can use the Transform palette to adjust the width and/or height of any existing object.

To create a rectangle, ellipse, or polygon of precise dimensions:

1. Create a rectangle, rounded rectangle, ellipse, or polygon, and leave the object selected. If it's not selected, press "V" to choose the Selection tool, then click on the object. You can be sloppy about the original object's size, since you're about to change it.
2. Show the Transform palette (Window menu > Transform) (Windows users: F9).
3. Change the pixel values in the width and/or height field (pressing Tab to move from one field to the next), or click the arrows (Fig. 1). *Note:* Don't confuse the width and height fields with the X and Y fields, which are used to change an object's location.
4. Press Return/Enter to exit the palette.

➤ To create a perfect square or other symmetrical object, copy the value in the width field, then paste it into the height field, or vice versa.

➤ You can change the dimensions of more than one object at a time.

The pre-fab shape-drawing tools (Rectangle, Ellipse, etc.) are all well and good—if that's the shape you happen to need. But what if you want to create a button that's shaped like a bird or a flower or an amoeba? For that you'll need to learn how to use the Pen tool. Not at all surprisingly, it works just like the Pen tool in Adobe Illustrator.

The Pen creates curved and straight segments (Fig. 1). The segments are joined by points.

- Points that join two curved segments have direction lines (antennae) that move in tandem. Direction lines are used for reshaping curves.
- Points that join a curved segment and a straight segment have one direction line.
- Points that join two straight segments have no direction lines.

To draw an object with the Pen tool:

1. Choose the Pen tool (P).
2. Click in the composition window to create a starting point.
3. Move the pointer, then click again to create a straight segment or drag a short distance to create a curved segment. Continue to click or drag to complete the shape (Fig. 2).
4. To close the shape, move the pointer back over the starting point (a tiny circle will appear next to the Pen pointer) and click on it (Figs. 3–4).
   or
   To end the shape but leave it open, choose a different tool (Fig. 1).
5. To reshape the object, follow the instructions on page 44.

➤ To convert the last-created point from a corner point to a smooth point, Option-drag/Alt-drag it. Option-click/Alt-click to convert a point from smooth to corner.

➤ The shape will automatically be assigned the current Foreground color. That color will appear as a Fill or as an Outline, depending on which of those options is currently chosen for the object on the Properties palette.

On the button

You're by no means stuck with making round buttons. Make them in the shape of type, a bar, a candy bar—whatever suits your fancy. It's not like you'd be violating a centuries-old tradition.

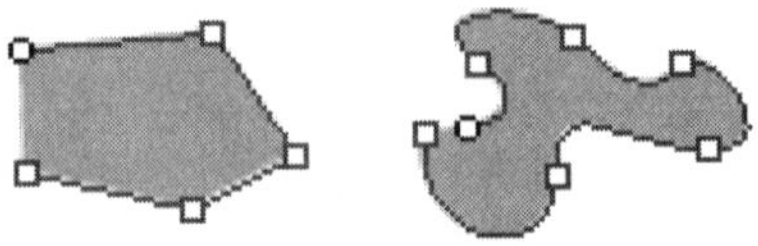

*1 ➤ Two objects drawn with the **Pen** tool: A **straight-sided** object and a **curved** object. Both of these objects are **open** paths.*

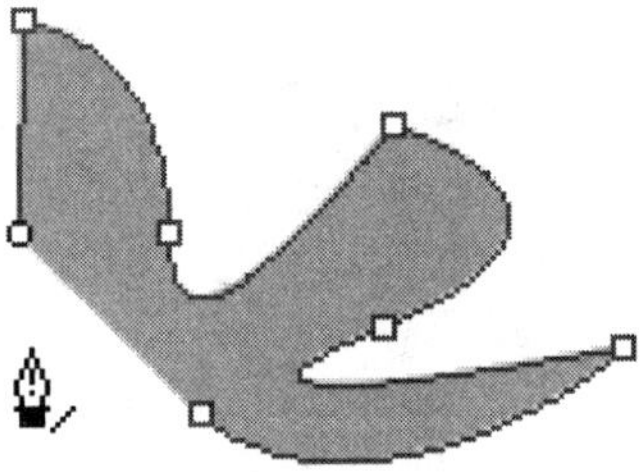

*2 ➤ Drawing a **path**.*

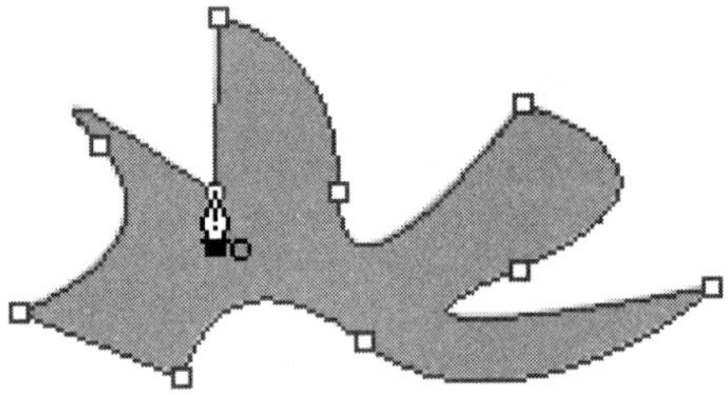

*3 ➤ **Closing** the path.*

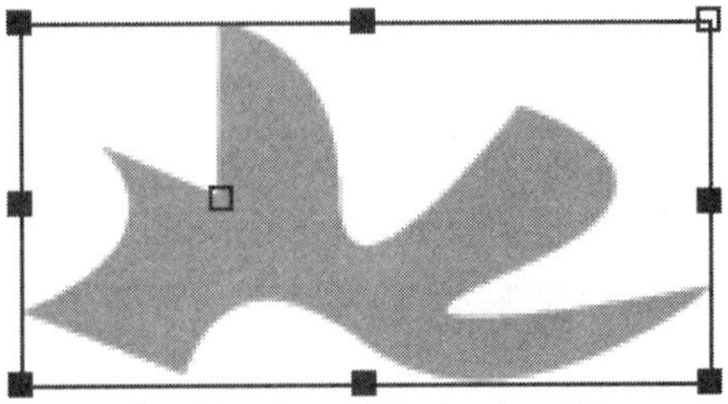

4 ➤ After the path is closed and then selected using the Selection tool.

Tutorial

If you feel like a klutz when you use the Pen tool, remember, you can always draw a geometric shape using the Rectangle, Ellipse, Rounded Rectangle, or Polygon tool instead and then reshape it (see page 44).

You can also use Object menu > Combine > Unite to join multiple shapes into one larger shape (see page 118). The objects will automatically be converted into a path, and the object's points will be available for reshaping.

*1➤ Draw an ellipse using the **Ellipse** tool.*

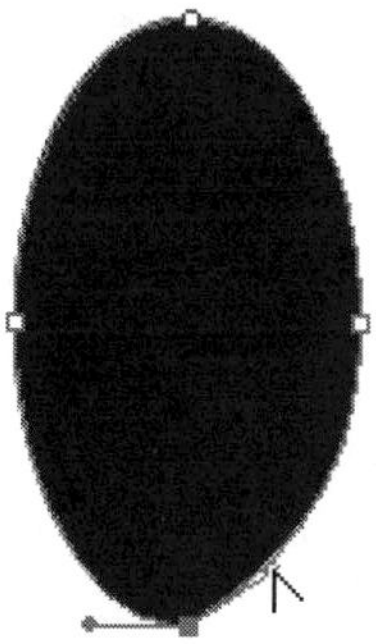

*2➤ Choose the **Pen-selection** tool, click on the path, then click on the bottommost point. **Option-drag/Alt-drag** each of the direction lines from that point upward.*

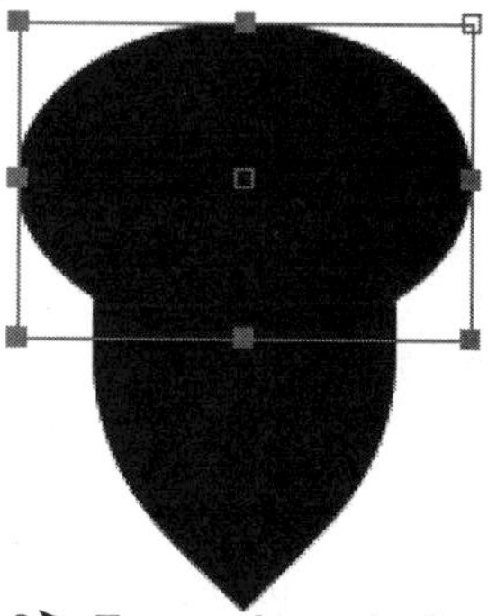

*3➤ To create the cap for the acorn, draw another **ellipse** and place it on top of the existing one.*

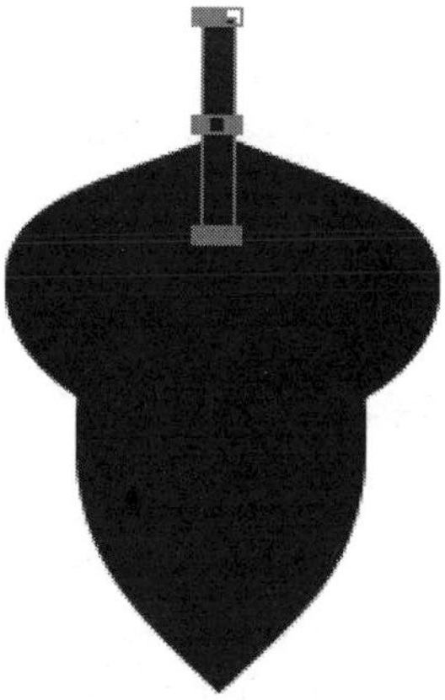

*4➤ To create the stem, draw a narrow rectangle using the **Rectangle** tool.*

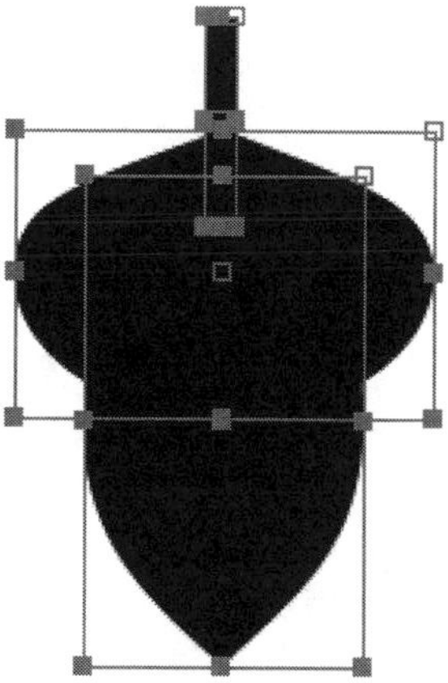

*5➤ Marquee the three objects with the **Selection** tool.*

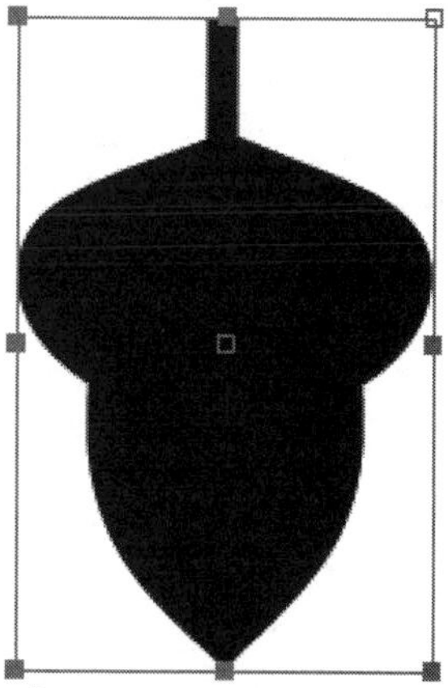

*6➤ Choose **Object** menu > **Combine** > **Unite**. The three objects are united into one.*

Selecting and deleting

You can't edit any object in any way, shape, or form unless it's selected. We cover selection methods more in depth in the next chapter, but here's a quick introduction.

To select an object or objects:

METHOD 1

1. Choose the Selection tool (V).
2. Click on the object's fill or outline (an object can't have both) (Figs. 1–3). Shift-click to select multiple objects.

METHOD 2

1. Choose the Selection tool (V) or the Drag-selection tool (U).
2. Drag a marquee **completely** around the object or objects you want to select (Figs. 4–5). A selection border will now surround all the objects that fell within the marquee.

   Note: Only objects that fall entirely within the marquee you drag will become selected. This is different from the way selection marquees work in other applications that you may be accustomed to.

To deselect objects:

METHOD 1

1. Choose the Selection tool (V) or the Drag-selection tool (U).
2. Click in a blank area of the composition window.

METHOD 2

Choose Edit menu > Deselect All (Command-Shift-A/Ctrl-Shift-A).

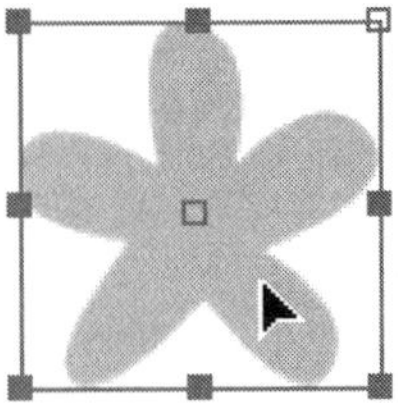

*1 ➤ If the object has a **Fill** property, you can click anywhere inside it to select it.*

*2 ➤ If the object has an **Outline** property, click on the outline to select it (or marquee the whole object).*

*3 ➤ Clicking here **won't work**.*

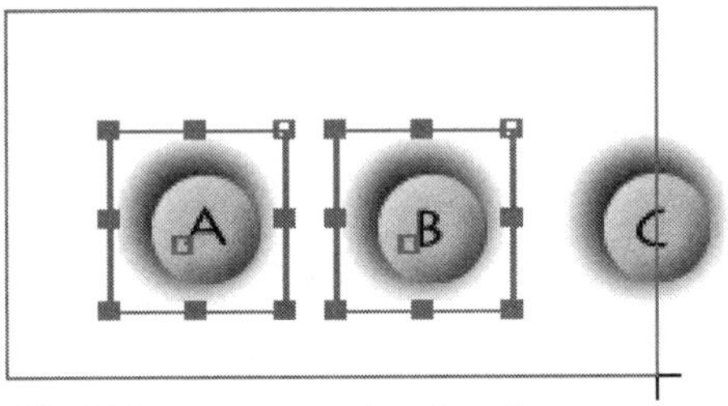

4 ➤ If the mouse were to be released now, only the first two buttons would become selected.

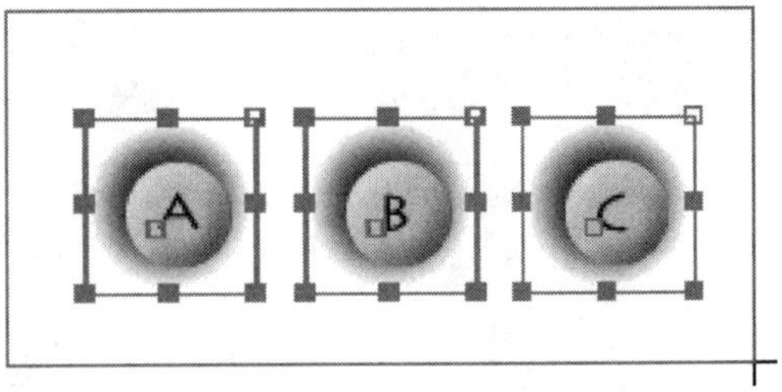

*5 ➤ The three buttons are **completely surrounded** by the marquee, and all three become selected.*

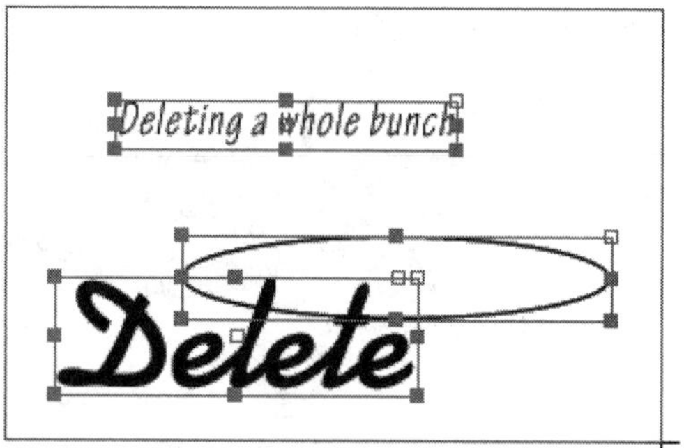

1 ➤ When you select objects, make sure your selection marquee ***completely*** *surrounds all the objects you want to delete.*

Here's how to get rid of any useless junk that's lying around.

To delete one object:

1. Choose the Selection tool (V), then click on the object you want to delete.
2. Press Delete/Backspace.
   or
   Choose Edit menu > Clear or Cut. The Cut command will place the objects on the Clipboard.

To delete several objects:

1. Select the objects you want to delete using the Selection tool (V), the Drag-selection tool (U), or the Subgroup-selection tool (A) (Fig. 1).
2. Press Delete/Backspace.
   or
   Choose Edit menu > Clear.
   or
   Edit menu > Cut. The Cut command will place the objects on the Clipboard.

Reshaping

Here's an advantage of working with a vector program: You can take any geometric object (drawn with a drawing tool in LiveMotion) and instantly change it into another standard geometric shape or into a path (e.g., you can change an ellipse into a rectangle). Or you can take a path and change it into a standard geometric object. Any previously applied effects and layer attributes are preserved.

In addition to the shape pop-up menu, other options may also be available on the Properties palette, depending on what type of shape is currently selected. For a polygon, for example, you can switch between the Fill and Outline options, adjust the Outline width, or add or remove sides.

To change an object's geometric properties:

1. Select a geometric object (Fig. 1).
2. Show the Properties palette (Window menu > Properties).
3. Choose **Rectangle, Rounded Rectangle, Ellipse, Polygon**, or **Path** from the pop-up menu (Figs. 2–3). If you turn an object into a path, its direction lines and points will then become available for reshaping.
4. Click the **Fill** or **Outline** button (Fig. 4). This is an either/or situation—an object can't have an outline and a fill simultaneously. (Read more about Fills and Outlines on page 86.)
5. Move any of the available sliders at the bottom of the palette.

   Change the **Width**, if the Outline option is currently selected.

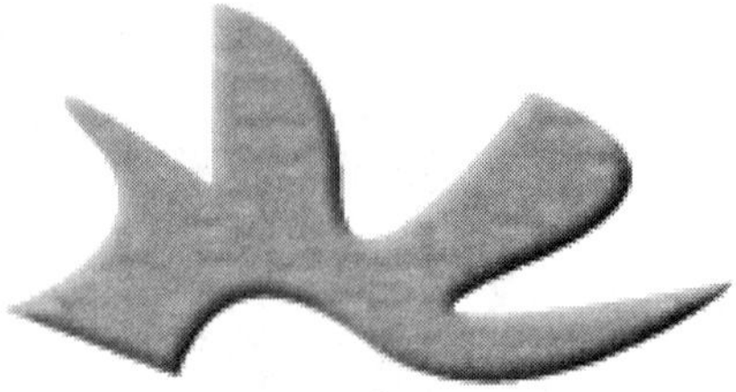

*1 ➤ A **Path** object.*

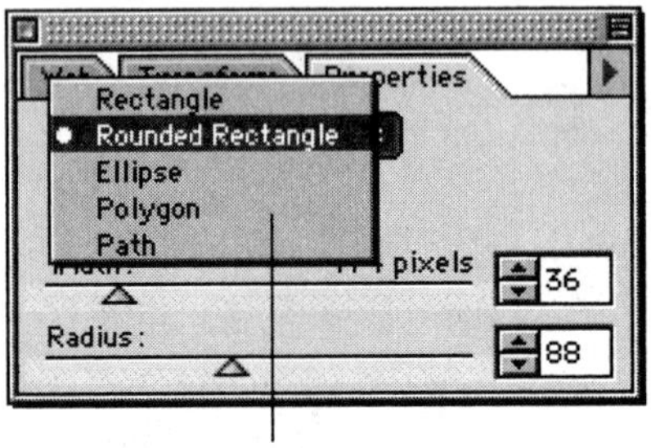

*2 ➤ A different shape is chosen from the pop-up menu on the **Properties** palette.*

*3 ➤ The Path is turned into a **rounded rectangle**. Previously applied lighting, color, and other attributes are **preserved**.*

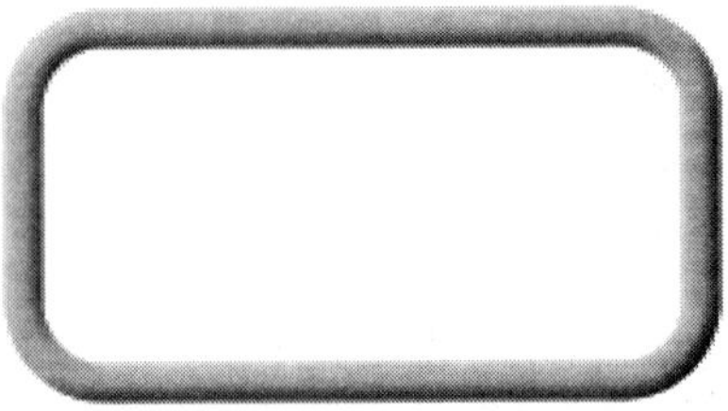

*4 ➤ The **Outline** button is clicked.*

We kid you not

If you turn an irregular path into a standard geometric object (an ellipse, a rectangle, or a polygon) using the pop-up menu on the Properties palette, and then turn it back into a path, it will revert to its **original irregular shape**! (Fig. 4)

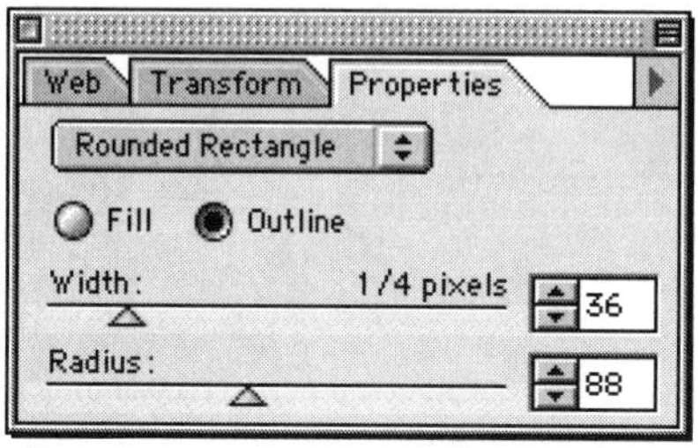

1 ➤ *The **Radius** slider is moved to the right.*

2 ➤ *The corners are now more rounded.*

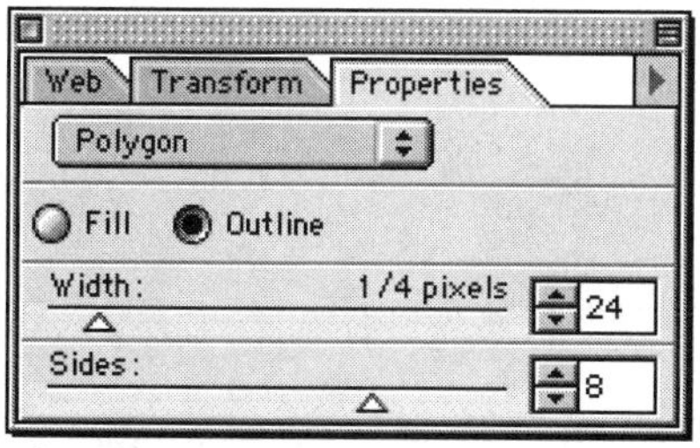

3 ➤ *The **Properties** palette when a **Polygon** is selected.*

For a rounded rectangle, you can move the **Radius** slider or click the up or down Radius arrow to make the corners more or less rounded (Figs. 1–2). The higher the Radius value, the more curved the corners. (This value is the maximum radius that a circle could have and still fit inside the corner of the rectangle.) The Radius can't be greater than half the length of the smaller sides of a rectangle. In fact, choosing a higher radius than that value will have no effect. A Radius of zero will turn the object into a square-cornered rectangle.

For a polygon, move the **Sides** slider or click a Sides arrow to add or delete sides from the shape (3–10) (Fig 3).

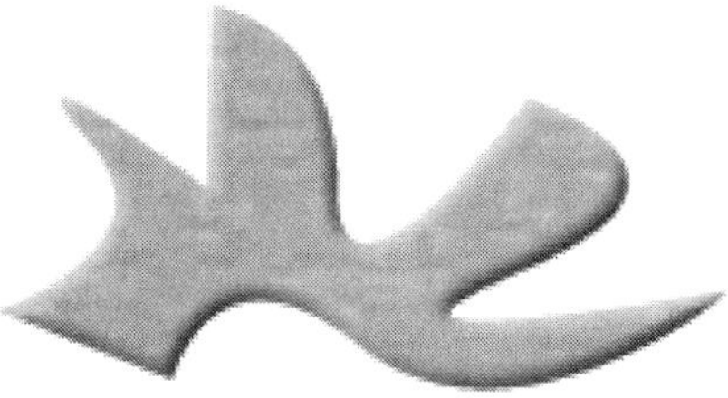

4 ➤ *If you turn a path into a standard geometric object via the Properties palette and then choose Path from the same pop-up menu, you'll get back to your original, irregular path.*

It's only that Rare Pen Tool Genius who can draw a new shape perfectly without having to reshape or adjust it afterwards. The rest of us mortals end up having to fiddle with a shape until it looks right. You can also reshape an object that was drawn with the Rectangle, Rounded Rectangle, Ellipse, or Polygon tool.

To reshape a geometric object:

1. Choose the Pen-selection tool (S).
2. Click on the object you want to reshape. The object's points should now be visible—not its selection border.
3. To **move** a **point** or a **segment**, position the pointer right on the point or segment (not on a direction line), then, when the white arrow pointer displays, drag the point or segment (Figs. 1–2).
   or
   To **reshape** a **curve**, click on a point to select it, then pull or rotate one or both of its direction lines (Fig. 3).
   or
   To **add** a point, move the pointer over a segment, then Command-click/Ctrl-click (the Pen pointer will have a plus sign) (Figs. 4–5). (You can also add a point with the Pen tool—but don't hold down Command-Ctrl.)

(Continued on the next page)

Why stop here

You're not limited to the techniques we discuss on this page for reshaping. You can also reshape an object by dragging a corner handle of the object's **selection border** (except the upper right handle) with the Selection tool. Or you can use any of the **transformation** techniques we discuss in Chapter 9.

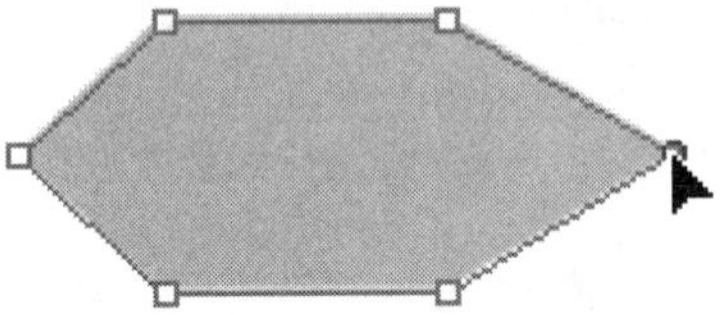

*1➤ If you move a **point**, that point and its **adjacent segments** will move along with it.*

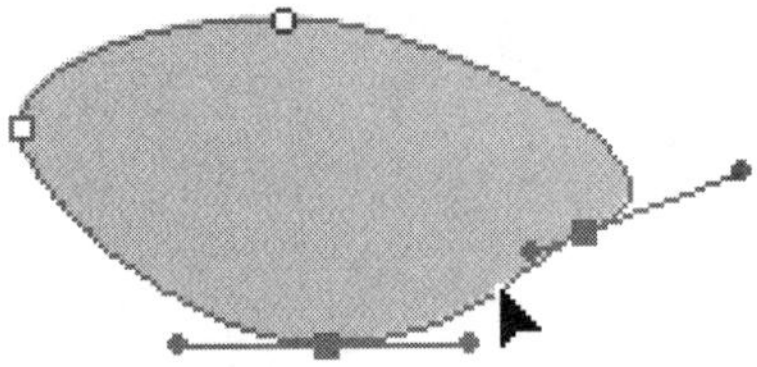

*2➤ If you move a **segment**, that segment, the two points that connect it, and the segment adjacent to each point will move along with it.*

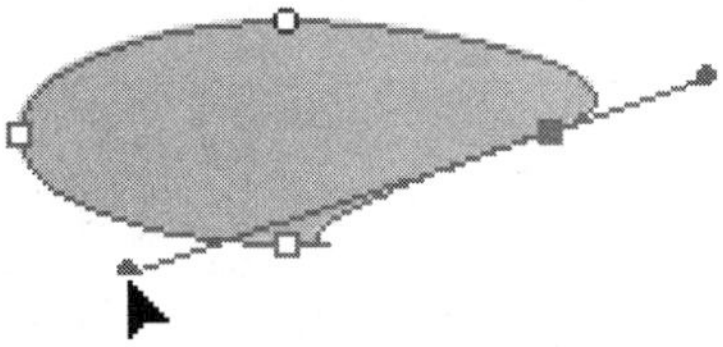

*3➤ You can also reshape a curve by moving a **direction line**.*

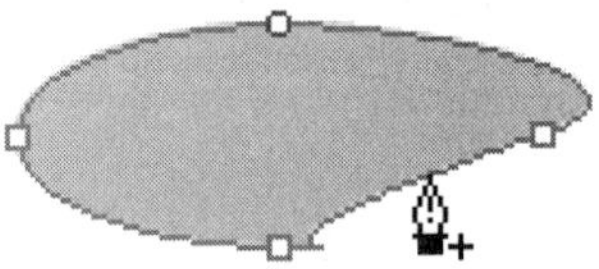

*4➤ To **add** a **point**, click on a **segment**.*

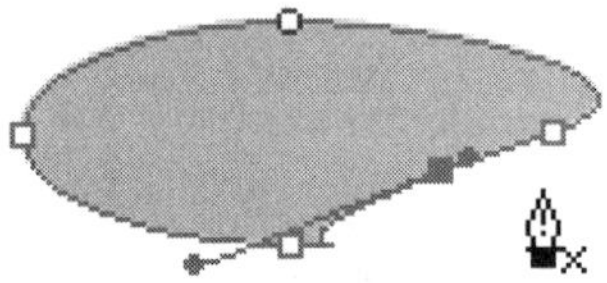

5➤ A point is added.

Power reshaping

Access the Pen-selection tool temporarily when another tool is chosen	**S**
Convert a point	**S** and **Option/Alt** click or drag
Add or delete a point	**S** and **Command/Ctrl** click

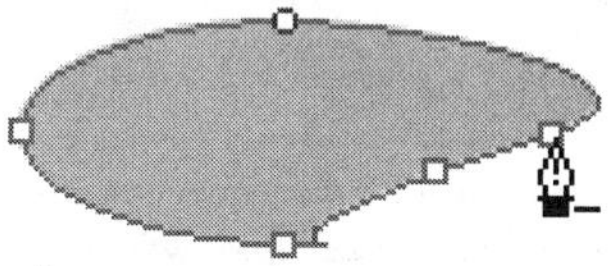

*1 ➤ To **delete a point**, click on it.*

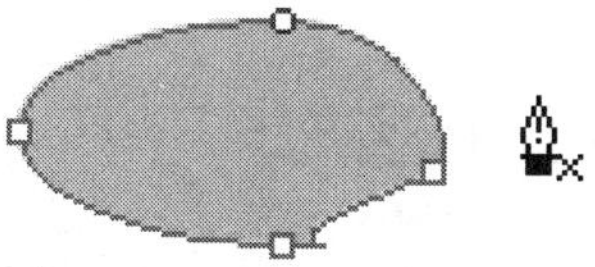

2 ➤ The point is deleted.

*A **smooth** point was converted into a **corner** point.*

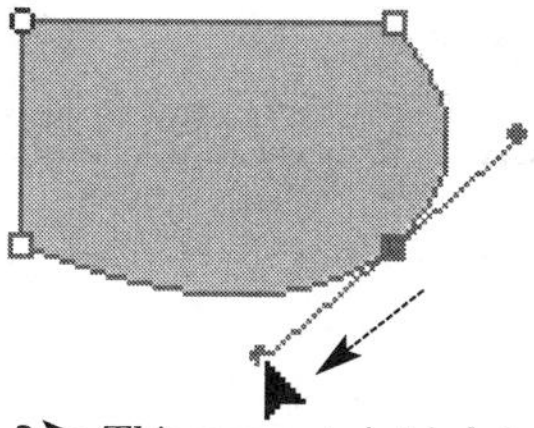

*3 ➤ This **corner** point is being converted into a **smooth** point.*

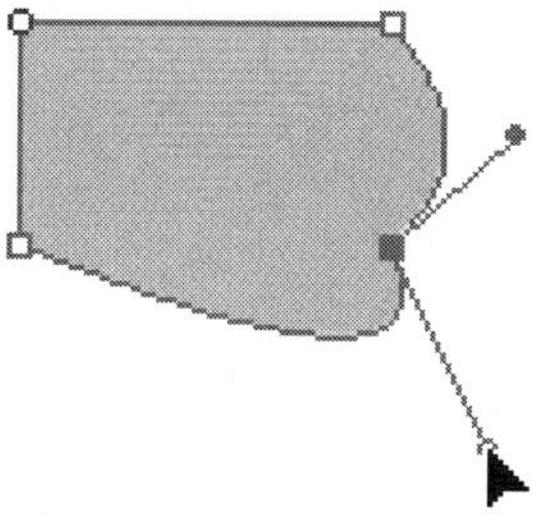

*4 ➤ Direction lines that move in tandem are being converted into direction lines that move **independently**.*

or

To **delete** a point, move the pointer right over the point, then Command-click/Ctrl-click it (the Pen pointer will have a minus sign) (Figs. 1–2). (You can also do this with the Pen tool—don't hold down Command-Ctrl.)

or

To convert a **corner** point into a **smooth** point, Option-drag/Alt-drag the point (Fig. 3). If the shape gets twisted, rotate the direction line back to untwist it.

or

To convert a **smooth** point into a **corner** point, Option-click/Alt-click the point.

or

To convert a point with direction lines that form a straight line into a point with direction lines that move **independently** of each other, Option-click/Alt-click the direction point at the end of either direction line, then rotate the direction line (Fig. 4).

➤ To convert a selected rectangle, rounded rectangle, ellipse, or polygon into a path by another method, choose Path from the pop-up menu on the Properties palette.

➤ We said this only two pages ago, but it bears repeating: If you turn an irregular path into a standard geometric object (an ellipse, a rectangle, or a polygon) using the pop-up menu on the Properties palette, and then turn it back into a path either by choosing Path from the same pop-up menu or by clicking on it with the Pen-selection tool, it will revert to its original irregular shape.

Shapes and the Library palette

What are shapes?

Each of the three basic object types (geometric, text, and image) are built from the same elements (Figs. 1–2):

- An overall **shape** (contour)
- A **layer** or layers
- **Removable effects** that are applied to individual layers

Earlier in this chapter you learned how to create geometric objects: rectangles, rounded rectangles, ellipses, polygons, and irregularly shaped paths. Now we focus on storing and retrieving vector and bitmap shapes (contours) from the Library palette.

Shapes can be used in many ways:

- A shape can be placed from the Library palette onto the composition as a **new object**
- A shape from the Library palette can be used to replace a selected object's **contour** without changing its other attributes
- The shape's contour can become the active **matte** for an image object (see page 122)
- A shape can be **imported** from another application (e.g., Adobe Illustrator, Adobe Photoshop, or Macromedia FreeHand), saved on the Library palette, and used as an image object in LiveMotion.

*1 ➤ This button has is a circle **shape**; it has three **layers**; and various **effects** are applied to its layers.*

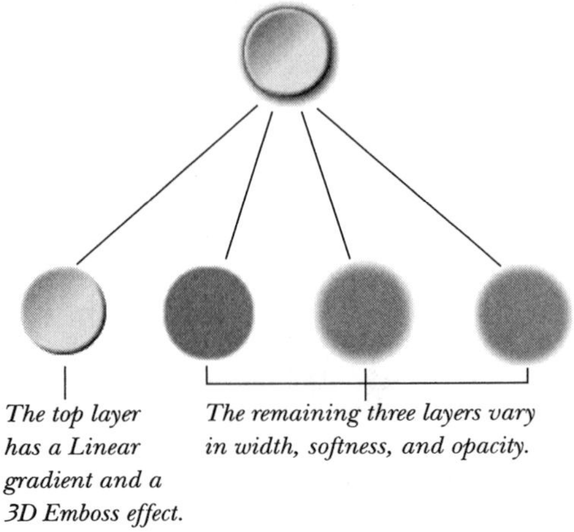
The top layer has a Linear gradient and a 3D Emboss effect.
The remaining three layers vary in width, softness, and opacity.

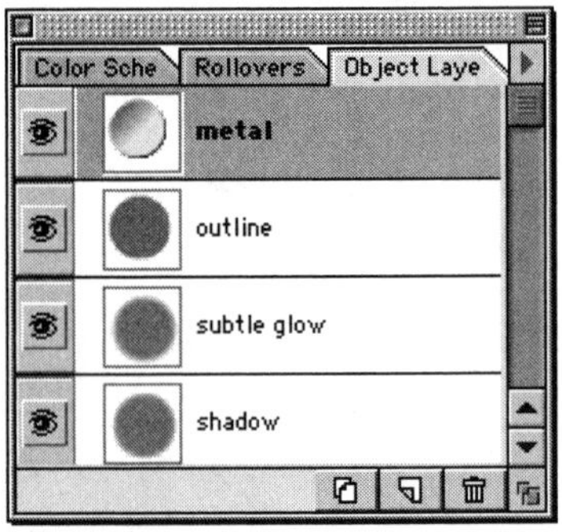

*2 ➤ This is what the **Layers** palette looks like for the button object shown in the previous figure.*

Using the views

If you already know the names of the shapes you want to work with, use Name View. If you're shopping around, use Swatches View to find a swatch you might want to place, click on the swatch, then choose Preview View to preview it before you place it.

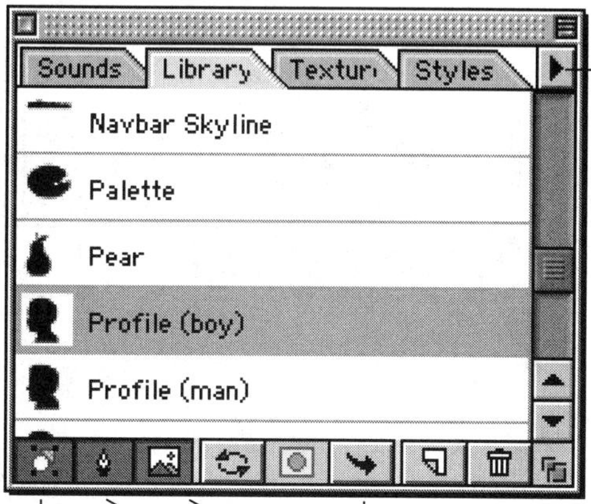

*1 ➤ The Library palette in **Name** view. A name is selected for placing into a composition.*

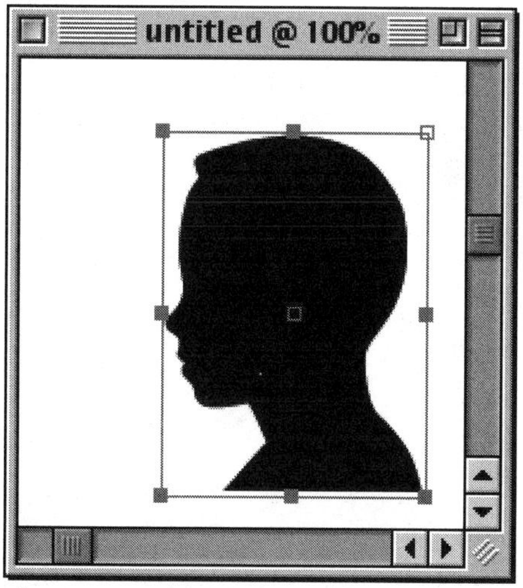

*2 ➤ A **shape** is **placed** into the composition window.*

Let's get acquainted with the Library palette.

To choose Library palette display options:

Show the Library palette (Window menu > Library), then choose a view from the palette command menu (Fig. 1):

Swatches View to display the shapes as swatch thumbnails without names.

Preview View to display the shapes by name, with a large thumbnail swatch for the selected shape.

Name View to display the shapes alphabetically by name with small thumbnail swatches.

To block the display of certain categories of images on the palette, deselect the **LiveMotion** objects, **Vector** objects, or **Image** objects box at the bottom of the palette.

➤ In any view, if you click anywhere on the palette and start typing a swatch name, the swatch with the closest-matching name will become highlighted.

Follow these instructions to add a Library shape to a composition as a new object. It will be placed with all the attributes it was stored with (e.g., color, texture, opacity, style, contour, object type).

To place a Library shape into a composition:

1. Show the Library palette (Window menu > Library).
2. Drag a swatch thumbnail or name into the composition window. The newly placed object will be selected.
   or
   Click on a swatch thumbnail or a swatch name, then click the Place Object button at the bottom of the palette (Fig. 1). If you place a shape this way, it will appear in the center of the composition itself—not the center of the composition window. If you don't see the shape, choose View menu > Actual Size view or use the Hand tool to move the shape into view.

➤ You can also drag a file icon from the Desktop into a LiveMotion composition.

If you use the Library palette's Replace Object button instead of the Place Object button, the contour of the selected object in the composition will be replaced by the shape you highlight on the palette, but the object will keep all its original attributes (e.g., color, style, size, transformation). The new shape will be squeezed, stretched, or possibly even cropped, to fit within the selected object's selection border.

Note: If you replace an image object with a shape, the object will be filled automatically with the current Foreground color and the image will disappear.

To replace the shape of an existing object with a Library shape:

METHOD 1

1. Choose the Selection tool (V) or the Drag-selection tool (U), then select the object whose contour you want to replace with that of a shape (Fig. 1).
2. Click on a swatch thumbnail or a shape name on the Library palette (Fig. 2), then click the Replace Object button at the bottom of the palette (Return/Enter) (Figs. 3–4).
   or
   Double-click a swatch thumbnail or name.

METHOD 2

Drag a swatch or shape name from the Library palette over the object (the object doesn't have to be selected). Release the mouse when the object's selection border appears.

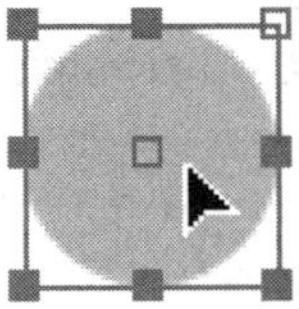

1 ➤ The original object.

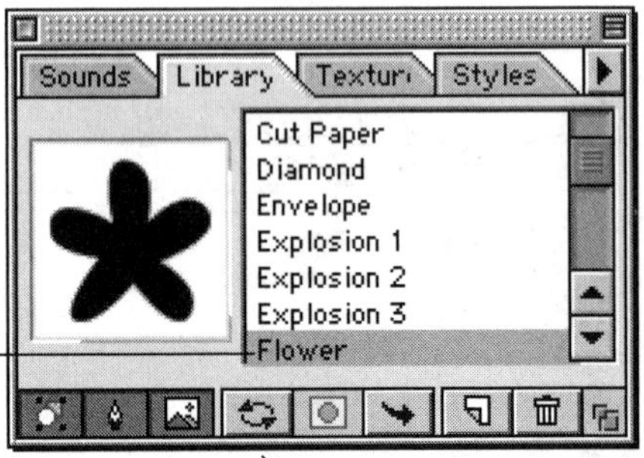

2 ➤ Click a shape on the Library palette.

*3 ➤ Then click the **Replace Object** button.*

*4 ➤ The object's **shape** changes, but **not** its **color**.*

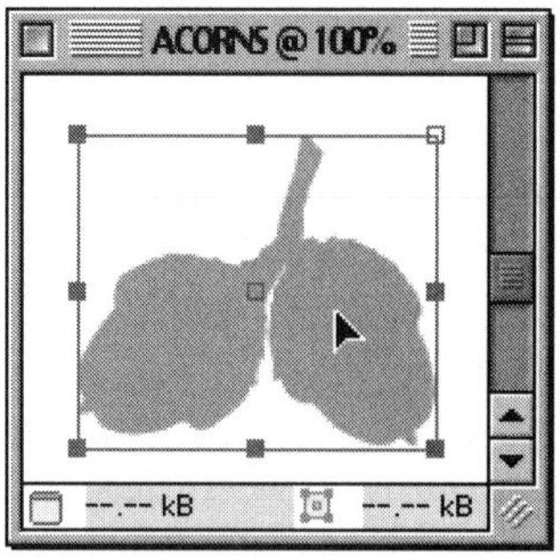

1 ➤ ***Drag** the object you want to save from the composition window...*

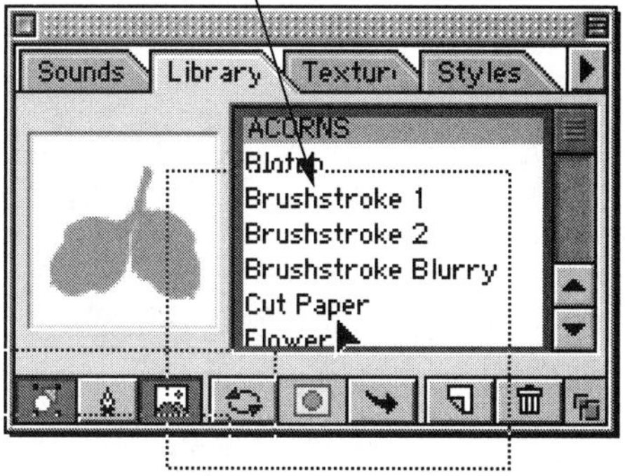

2 ➤ *...into the **Library** palette.*

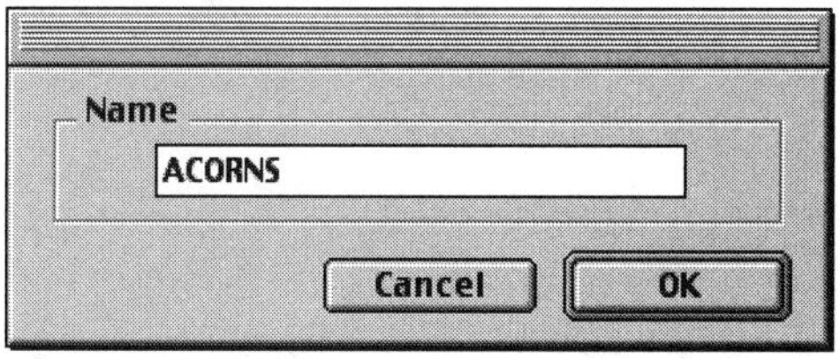

3 ➤ ***Name** the object.*

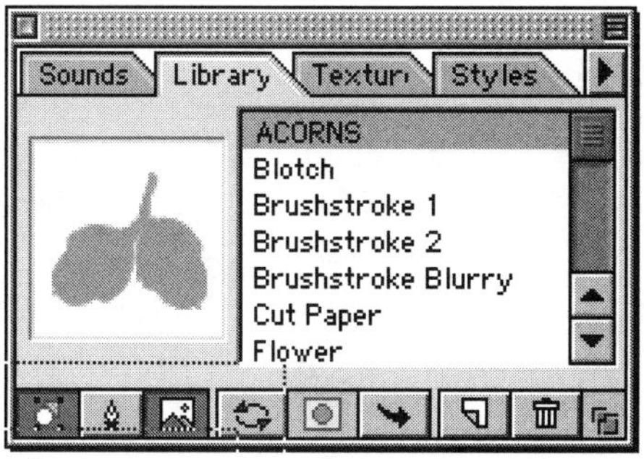

4 ➤ *The object appears on the **Library** palette.*

When an object is saved as a shape on the Library palette, the color, texture, opacity, style, Photoshop filter effect, contour, object type, rollover states, animations, and transformation attributes that are applied to its layers are saved along with it. All kinds of objects can be saved to the Library: geometric, text, and image. Once it's saved in the Library, a shape can be used in any LiveMotion composition. Skim through the following four methods before you decide which one to use.

To save an object as a shape:

METHOD 1

1. Choose the Selection tool (V) or the Drag-selection tool (U).
2. Drag the object you want to save as a shape from the composition window into the Library palette (Figs. 1–2).

   Note: In the first-release version of LiveMotion 1.0, you cannot drag a shape into the Library palette if the palette overlaps the composition window. Move the palette away from the composition window before you drag a shape into it.
3. Type a name for the shape (Fig. 3), then click OK (Return/Enter) (Fig. 4).

METHOD 2

1. Click the New Object button at the bottom of the Library palette.
2. Locate the file that contains the shape you want to add to the Library palette, then click Open.
3. Type a name for the shape, then click OK (Return/Enter). If you use a name that's already being used on the palette for an object of the same type, an alert box will display asking whether you want to replace the existing shape.

(Methods 3 and 4 are on the following page.)

METHOD 3

1. On the MacOS Desktop or in Windows Explorer, make sure the file has the desired name and is in a format that LiveMotion can import. In Windows, make sure the file has the correct extension.
2. Drag the file icon into the Library folder inside the LiveMotion folder. In order for the new shape to appear on the Library palette, you must quit/exit and then relaunch LiveMotion.

METHOD 4

1. Make sure the file is in a format that LiveMotion can import. In Windows, make sure the file has the correct extension.
2. Make sure LiveMotion is the active application and the Library palette is showing. Reshape the LiveMotion composition window, if necessary, so you can see both the file icon and the Library palette at the same time.
3. Drag the file icon from the Desktop into the LiveMotion Library palette.
4. Type a name for the shape, then click OK (Return/Enter).

➤ If you save a shape that has been rotated, it will be saved in the library in its original, un-rotated state.

Note: When a shape is deleted from the Library palette, it is also deleted from your hard drive.

To delete a shape from the Library palette:

1. On the Library palette, click on the shape that you want to remove.
2. Click the palette Delete Object (trash) button.
3. MacOS: Click Delete (Return). Windows: Click Yes (Enter).

Work with Objects 4

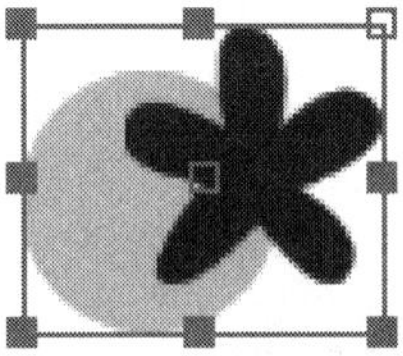

*1 ➤ A selected object or objects will have a blue, rectangular **selection border** with eight handles. Note: If View menu > **Active Export Preview** is on, the selection border will be **red**.*

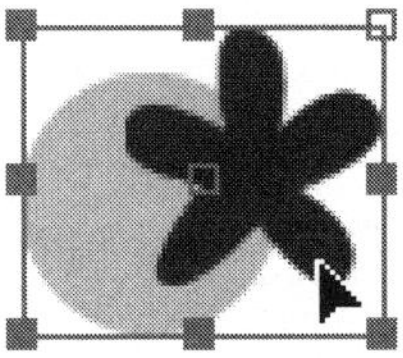

*2 ➤ The **Selection** tool selects objects or whole groups by **clicking**.*

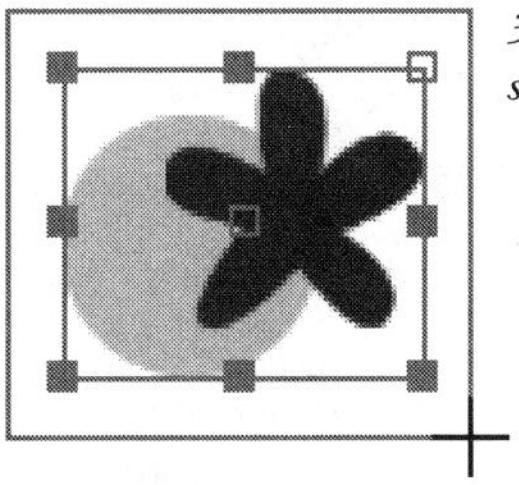

*3 ➤ The **Drag-selection** tool selects objects by **dragging**.*

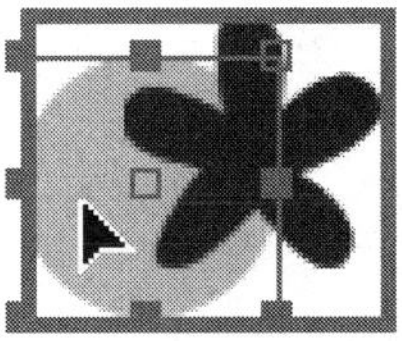

*4 ➤ The **Subgroup-selection** tool selects objects or nested groups within **groups**.*

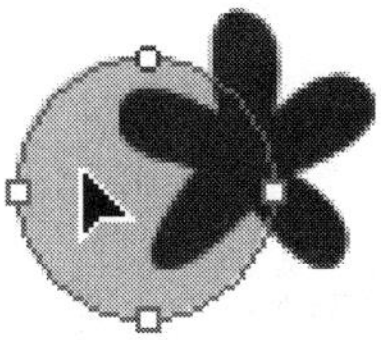

*5 ➤ The **Pen-selection** tool makes path **segments** and **points** visible.*

Selecting

The selection tools

WE THINK OF SELECTING objects as a form of non-verbal communication between the user and the application. Before you can modify any element in a composition, you have to send a signal to LiveMotion that tells the application which object you want to work on. LiveMotion does wondrous and remarkable things, but it can't mindread.

The signaling process is accomplished by clicking on or marqueeing an object with a selection tool. Once an object is selected, the next step is to choose which of that object's layers you want to change (Fig. 1). Layer selection is discussed in Chapter 6, but let's learn the basic selection methods first.

There are four selection tools:

- ➤ The **Selection** tool (V) selects whole objects (Fig. 2).
- ➤ The **Drag-selection** tool (U) selects by dragging a marquee—not by clicking (Fig. 3). It's handy for grabbing hold of objects that are hiding behind other objects.
- ➤ The **Subgroup-selection** tool (A) selects subgroups or objects that are nested inside larger groups (Fig. 4). Grouping is discussed on pages 58–59.
- ➤ The **Pen-selection tool** tool (S) is used to make an object's points and direction lines visible for reshaping (Fig. 5).

The selection tools are also used for reshaping, moving, and resizing objects.

When an object is selected, its selection border becomes visible. The selection border is used for scaling and rotating.

To select an object or objects:

METHOD 1

1. Choose the Selection tool (V) or the Subgroup-selection tool (A).
2. Click on the object. Shift-click to select multiple objects. *Note:* If it's a geometric object and it has a Fill (Properties palette), click anywhere inside the object (Fig. 1). If it's a geometric object with an Outline, click on its outline.

➤ If you click on a blank area of an object with the Selection tool, you'll select the next closest object behind it, if there is one.

METHOD 2

1. Choose the Selection tool (V), the Drag-selection tool (U), or the Subgroup-selection tool (A).
2. Drag a marquee **completely** around the object or objects you want to select (Figs. 2–3).

When you select an object with the Pen-selection tool, all of its points and segments become visible for moving or reshaping.

To make an object's points and direction lines visible:

1. Choose the Pen-selection tool.
2. Click on the object (Fig. 4). The object's points should now be visible—not its selection border (Fig. 5). To reshape an object, see pages 42–45.

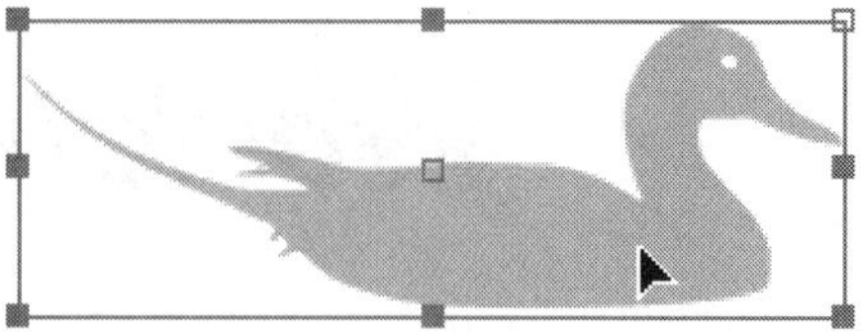

1➤ To select an object, ***click*** *on its* ***fill*** *(or its outline).*

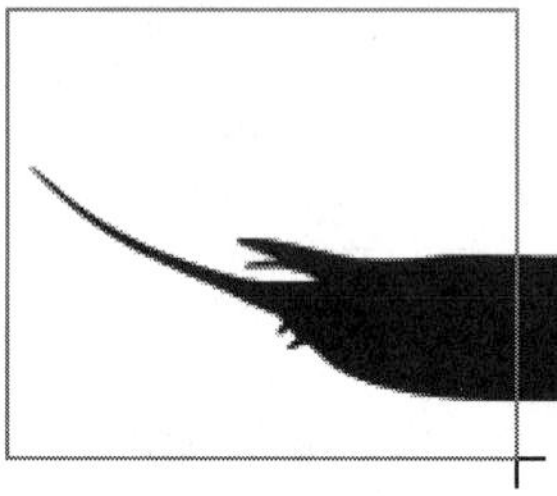

2➤ Trying to select by ***marqueeing****. If the mouse were released at this point, the object would not become selected.*

3➤ Selecting by ***marqueeing****. The marquee* ***surrounds*** *the object completely, so it becomes selected.*

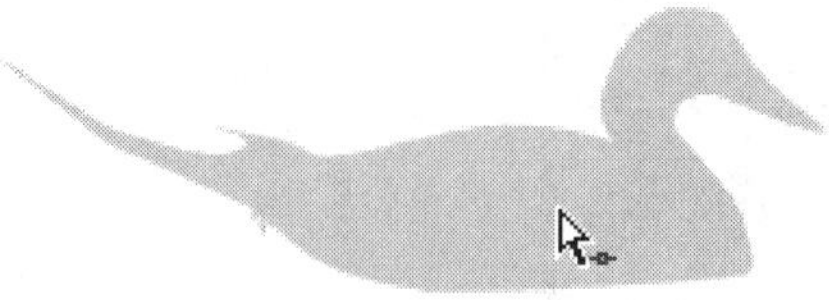

4➤ If you click on a path or another geometric object with the ***Pen-selection*** *tool…*

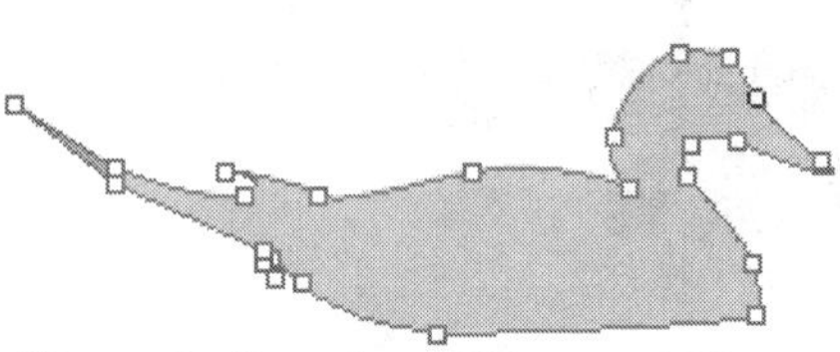

5➤ …all of its ***points*** *will become visible.*

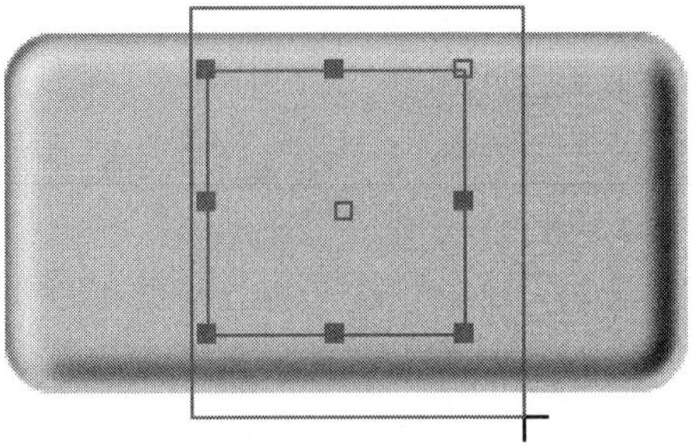

1➤ *A button that's hidden behind another object is selected using the **Drag-selection** tool.*

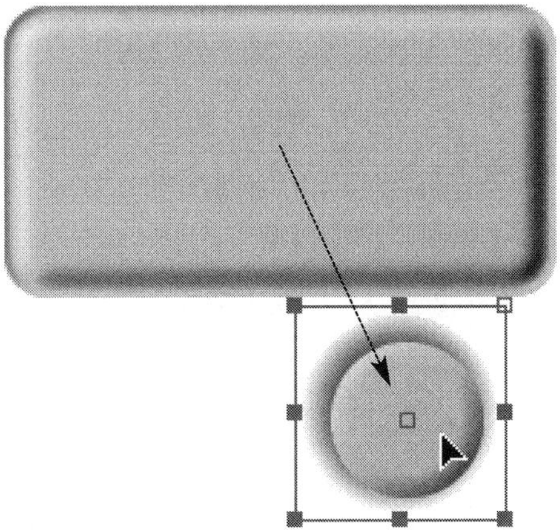

2➤ *The newly selected object is moved using the same tool.*

To select all the objects in a composition:

Choose Edit menu > Select All (Command-A/Ctrl-A). This command works with any tool selected.

In order to select an object that's completely obscured by another object, without the Drag-selection tool, you'd have to move the top object out of the way to get to the hidden one. The Drag-selection tool gets right to the object you want to select.

To select a hidden object:

1. Choose the Drag-selection tool (U).
2. Drag a marquee **completely** over the area where the object you want to select is located (Fig. 1). If multiple objects are stacked behind each other in the same spot, they will all become selected.
3. *Optional:* Drag the object (Fig. 2).

Sometime you might get an urge to see your objects in all their naked glory without their accoutrements (selection border, handles).

To hide object edges:

Choose View menu > Hide Object Edges (Command-H/Ctrl-H).

To deselect individual objects:

1. Choose the Selection tool (V), Drag-selection tool (U), or Subgroup-selection tool (A).
2. Shift-click on individual objects to deselect just those objects.

To deselect all objects:

Choose any selection tool, then click on a blank area of the composition where there are no objects.
or
Choose Edit menu > Deselect All (Command-Shift-A/Ctrl-Shift-A).

Scaling

In this section, you'll learn how to scale (resize) an object using the handles on its selection border. We're teaching you this basic skill early in the book because we know you'll find a need to use it on a regular basis.

Scaling, like the other transform properties, can be undone at any time—and not just via the Undo command. To read more about this feature and about other methods for transforming objects, see page pages 113–116.

Note: When vector shapes are scaled up or down they remain crisp. When bitmap image shapes are enlarged, on the other hand, they develop jaggies (become pixelated).

To scale or rotate an object by dragging:

1. Select an object using any selection tool except the Pen-selection tool.
2. To **scale** the object horizontally and vertically, drag any corner handle except the upper right corner handle (the pointer becomes a four-way arrow), then drag the handle (Figs. 1–2).

   Hold down **Shift** while dragging to constrain the object's width and height proportions.

   To scale only the horizontal or vertical dimension, drag any **side** handle (the pointer becomes a two-way arrow) (Figs. 3–4).

   By default, objects scale from their center. To scale from a selection handle of your choosing, **Option-drag/Alt-drag** the handle that's opposite from the one you want to remain stationary (e.g., if you drag the upper left handle, the lower right corner will remain stationary).
3. To **rotate** the object, drag the upper right corner handle in a circular direction (Figs. 5–6).

➤ Hold down Command/Ctrl to use the scale function when dragging the upper right corner handle, which is normally used for rotating.

➤ To un-rotate a rotated object, enter an angle of 0 on the Transform palette.

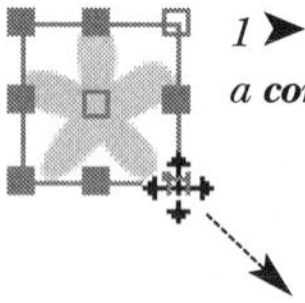

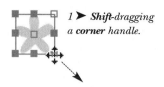

*1 ➤ **Shift**-dragging a **corner** handle.*

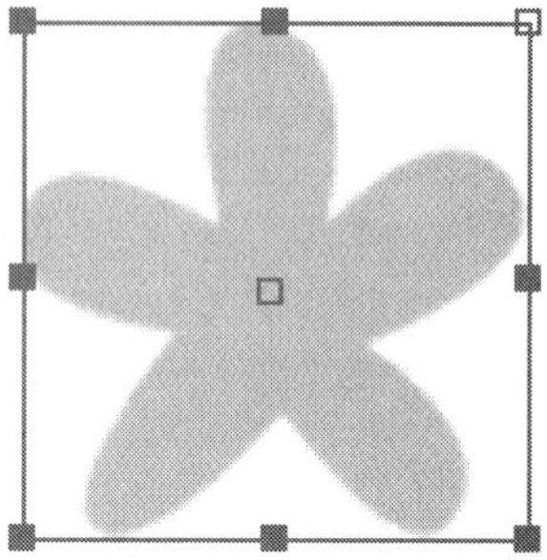

2 ➤ The object is enlarged.

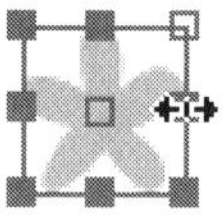

*3 ➤ Dragging a **side** handle.*

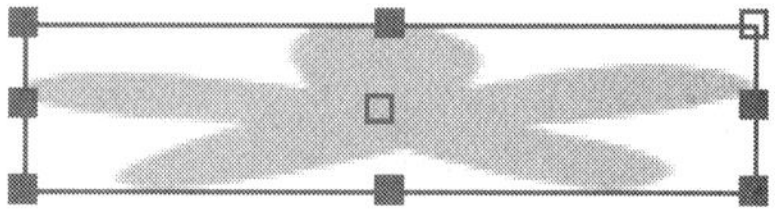

4 ➤ The object's proportions change.

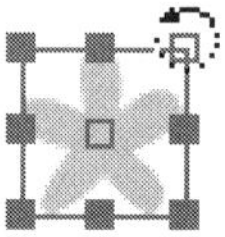

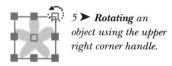

*5 ➤ **Rotating** an object using the upper right corner handle.*

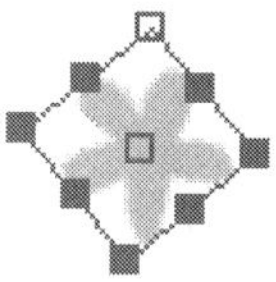

6 ➤ The object is rotated.

More ways to move

- Use the **Transform palette** to move a whole object to an exact location on the *x/y* axes (see page 114).
- Use the **Layer-offset tool** to move an individual object layer by dragging (see page 70).
- Use the **Layer palette** to move an object layer by entering precise X Offset and/or Y Offset values (see page 70).

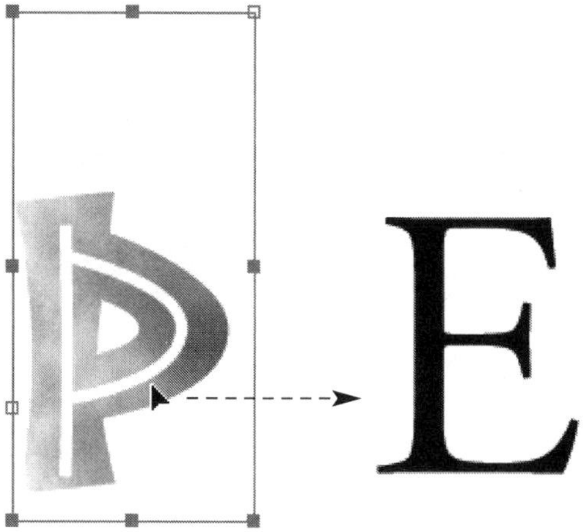

*1 ➤ **Moving** an object by **dragging** it.*

2 ➤ The object is moved to a new location.

Moving

In these instructions, you'll move an entire object with all its layers.

To move an object:

METHOD 1 (nudging)

1. Choose any selection tool (except the Pen-selection tool) or choose the Transform tool (E), then select the object.
2. Press an arrow key to move the object one pixel at a time. Hold down Shift as you press an arrow to move the object 10 pixels at a time.

METHOD 2 (dragging)

1. Choose the Selection or Subgroup-selection tool or choose the Transform tool (E).
2. To move a geometric object with a Fill property or to move an image object, drag from anywhere inside the object (Figs. 1–2). If it has an Outline property (a geometric or type object), drag the outline. Don't drag a handle.

- Shift-drag to constrain the movement to the horizontal or vertical axis.
- Option-drag/Alt-drag to drag a copy of an object.
- Be careful not to move an object's center point when you're using the Transform tool (unless that's what you want to do!).

METHOD 3 (hidden object)

1. Choose the Drag-selection tool (U).
2. Drag a marquee **completely** over the area where the object you want to select is located. If multiple objects are stacked behind each other in the same spot, they will all become selected.
3. Drag the selected object.

Using aliases and duplicates

In LiveMotion, when you make an alias of an object, it becomes an equal partner with its parent object; they become co-aliases. Any style or shape changes that are made to any alias are duplicated automatically in all of the other aliases it is linked to. If you make an alias for a text object and then edit the words in that object or change their typographic attributes, those changes will also occur in all its other aliases.

Why make aliases instead of using the Duplicate command? Three good reasons: Because using aliases helps to reduce the file size of a composition; it speeds up screen redraw; and it speeds up editing.

To make an alias of an object:

METHOD 1

1. Select an object.
2. Choose Edit menu > Make Alias (Command-M/Ctrl-M).
   or
   Windows only: Right-click in the composition window and choose Make Alias from the context menu.

   The alias will land right on top of the original object (now its co-alias).

METHOD 2

1. Choose any selection tool (except the Pen-selection tool) or choose the Transform tool (E).
2. Option-Shift-drag/Alt-Shift-drag an object (the pointer will turn into a double arrowhead) (Figs. 1–3).

➤ If Object menu > Maintain Alignment is turned on and you edit text that's grouped with an object, that object will resize, as needed, to accommodate the new text, and any aliases that are associated with that object will also resize. See page 59.

If you unlink an alias and then edit the object, it will no longer change or be affected by its former alias(es) in any way.

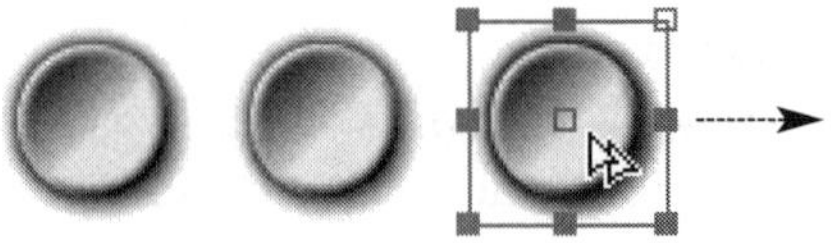

*1 ➤ An object is dragged with **Option-Shift/ Alt-Shift** held down.*

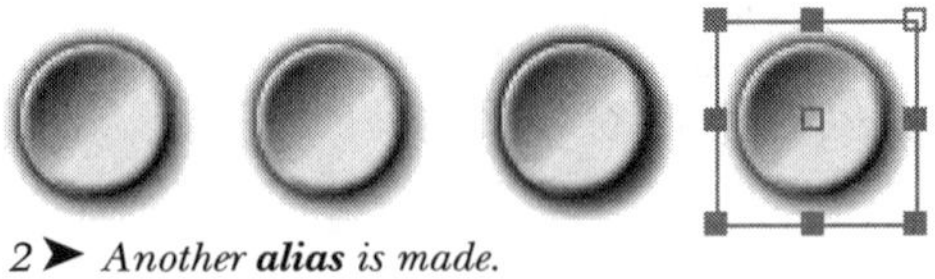

*2 ➤ Another **alias** is made.*

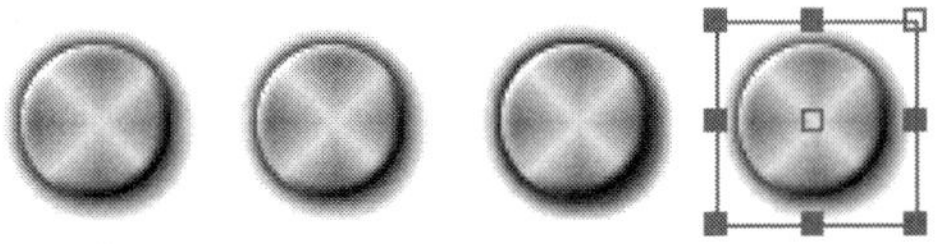

3 ➤ Then the gradient in of one of the aliases is changed. The other aliases follow suit.

Relinking

After you break an alias, you can convert the object back into an alias again by choosing Edit menu > Undo > **Undo Break Alias** (that is, if it's still available on the submenu) or by selecting the object and one or more of its former aliases and choosing Edit menu > **Make Alias** again.

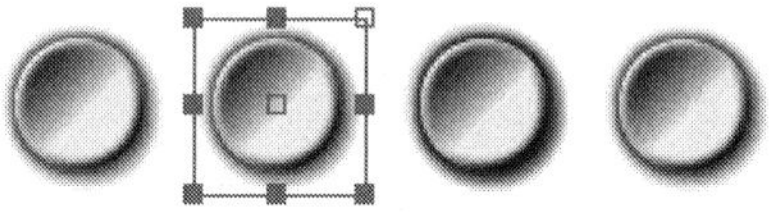

1 ➤ Select the alias you want to unlink, then choose Edit menu > ***Break Alias****.*

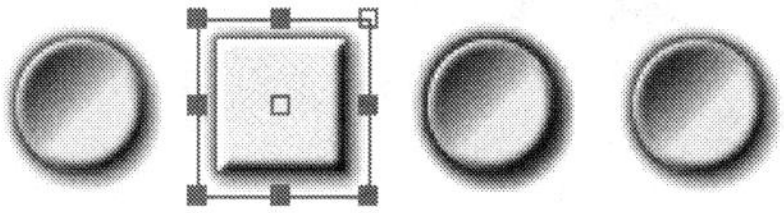

2 ➤ When that object is edited, only that object changes; the other objects are still aliases.

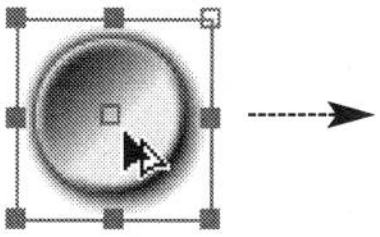

3 ➤ ***Option-drag/Alt-drag*** *the object you want to duplicate.*

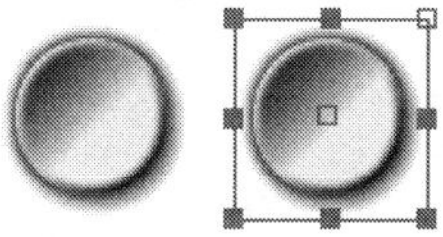

4 ➤ A duplicate is made.

To break an alias link:

1. Choose a selection tool (V, A, or U) or the Transform tool (E).
2. Select one of the aliases you want to unlink.
3. Choose Edit menu > Break Alias (Command-Option-M/Ctrl-Alt-M).
   or
   Windows only: Right-click in the composition window and choose Break Alias from the context menu (Figs. 1–2).

Note: Before duplicating an object, read about aliasing, which is sometimes preferable.

To duplicate an object:

METHOD 1

1. Choose a selection tool.
2. Click on the object you want to duplicate.
3. Choose Edit menu > Duplicate (Command-D/Ctrl-D).
   or
   Windows only: Right-click in the composition window and choose Duplicate from the context menu.

   The duplicate will land right on top of the original object.

METHOD 2

1. Choose a selection tool.
2. Option-drag/Alt-drag the object you want to duplicate (Figs. 3–4).

➤ Hold down Shift while dragging to constrain the object to the horizontal or vertical axis. Just be sure to press Option before Shift, otherwise you'll create an alias instead of a duplicate.

Grouping

When objects are grouped together, they can be moved as a cohesive unit, yet each item in the group remains editable. The objects will keep their original stacking order relative to the other objects in the group.

Note: Any transform commands that are applied to a group affect all the objects in the group. Multiple groups (or groups and individual objects) can be nested into a larger group.

To group objects:

1. Choose a selection tool, then marquee or Shift-click all the items to be grouped (Fig. 1).
2. Choose Object menu > Group (Command-G/Ctrl-G) (Fig. 2).

Use this technique if you want to edit the attributes or characters of a text object in a group.

To select the topmost text object in a group:

1. Choose the Selection tool.
2. Double-click the group. Neat trick.

To select a grouped object, you can use the Subgroup-selection tool, but we think it's easier to just hold down the "A" key to access that tool temporarily.

To select a grouped object:

1. Choose the Selection tool.
2. Hold down the "A" key as you click on the group, subgroup (nested group), or object you want to select (Fig. 3). To select an object within a subgroup, click on the subgroup, then click again to select the individual object.

*1 ➤ **Select** the objects to be grouped.*

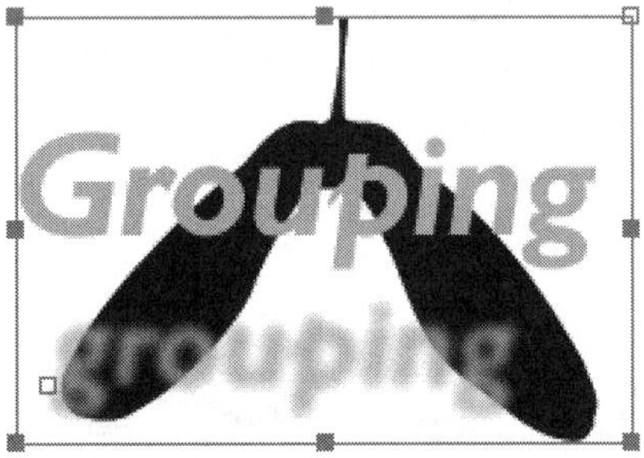

*2 ➤ After choosing the **Group** command. A selection box surrounds a group when it's selected with the **Selection** tool.*

*3 ➤ Use the **Subgroup-selection** tool to select individual objects or nested subgroups within a group.*

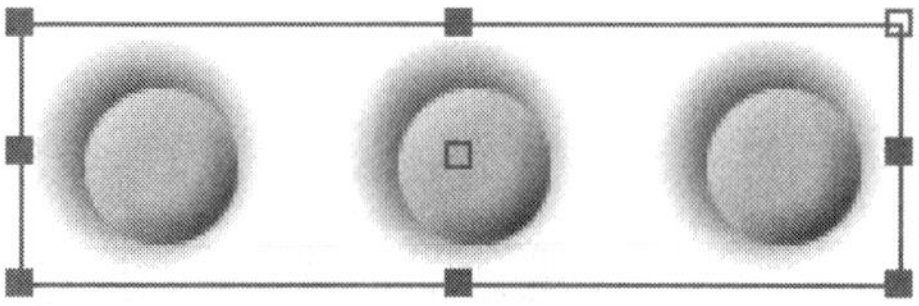

1 ➤ A **group** is selected using the Selection tool. A selection box surrounds the entire group.

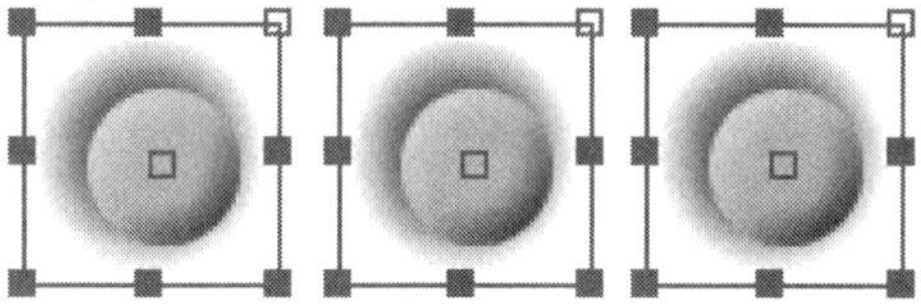

2 ➤ After the **Ungroup** command is chosen, the individual objects become selected.

3 ➤ The rectangular object and the type object are grouped together, and then **Maintain Alignment** is turned on.

4 ➤ The text is changed, and the button automatically **resizes** to accommodate the additional characters.

To ungroup objects:

1. Choose a selection tool, then click on the group (Fig. 1).
2. Choose Object menu > Ungroup (Command-U/Ctrl-U) (Fig. 2).

Let's say you've got some text that's grouped together with an object and you change its attributes (e.g., font, size, tracking) or add or delete characters. Chances are, it will no longer fit properly over the object. Ah! You remembered to turn on the Maintain Alignment command. The object magically resizes to accommodate the text.

To turn on Maintain Alignment:

1. Choose the Selection tool (V), then click on a group that includes a text object (Fig. 3).
2. Choose Object menu > Maintain Alignment.
3. To see how this feature works, add a few characters to the text (Fig. 4). To do this, choose the Selection tool, then double-click on the group to open the Type Tool dialog box.

➤ To turn Maintain Alignment off, re-select the same object, then re-choose the command.

➤ To use the Maintain Alignment command when performing batch HTML replacement, see page 262.

Restacking

Each new object you create in a LiveMotion composition is stacked above all the existing objects in the composition, regardless of its location on the *x/y* axes. That includes new objects created by any means, whether by drawing, duplication, placing from another application, pasting, making an alias, creating text, or placing as a shape from the Library palette.

The stacking scheme can be changed for any object or group, though. The Bring to Front command brings an object (or group) to the very front of the entire composition; Send to Back sends the object to the very back. The Bring Forward and Send Backward commands move an object one level at a time. If you restack an object in a group, it will remain in the group.

To restack objects:

1. Choose a selection tool (V, A, or U) or the Transform tool (E), then click on the object or group whose stacking position you want to change (Fig. 1).
2. Choose a command from the Object menu > Arrange submenu:

   Bring to Front (Command-Shift-]/ Ctrl-Shift-]) (Fig. 2).
   or
   Bring Forward (Command-]/Ctrl-]).
   or
   Send Backward (Command-[/Ctrl-[).
   or
   Send to Back (Command-Shift-[/ Ctrl-Shift-[).

➤ Windows only: You can also access the Arrange submenu by Right-clicking in the composition window.

➤ In addition to restacking whole objects, you can also restack individual layers within an object. To restack a layer, drag it upward or downward on the Object Layers palette. You'll read more about layers in the next chapter.

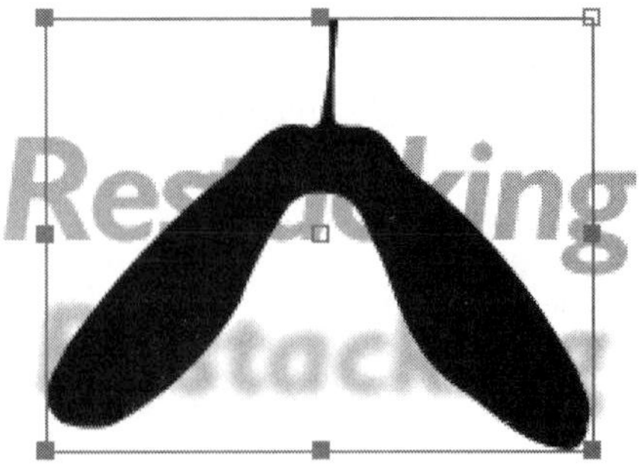

1 ➤ The maple seed object is selected.

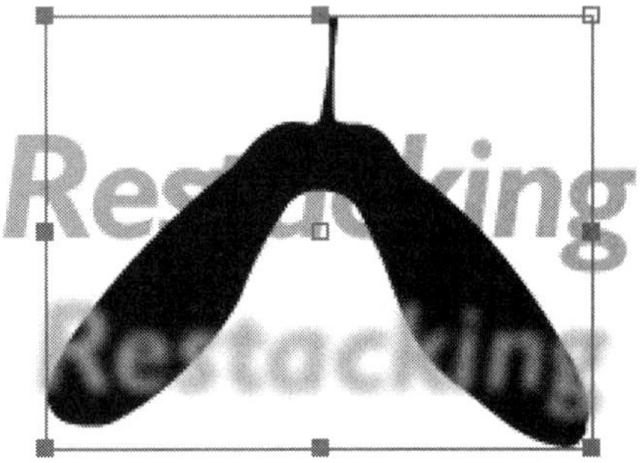

*2 ➤ After choosing **Send Backward**, the seed object moves back one **layer**.*

*3 ➤ After choosing **Send to Back**, the seed object moves to the back of the **entire composition**.*

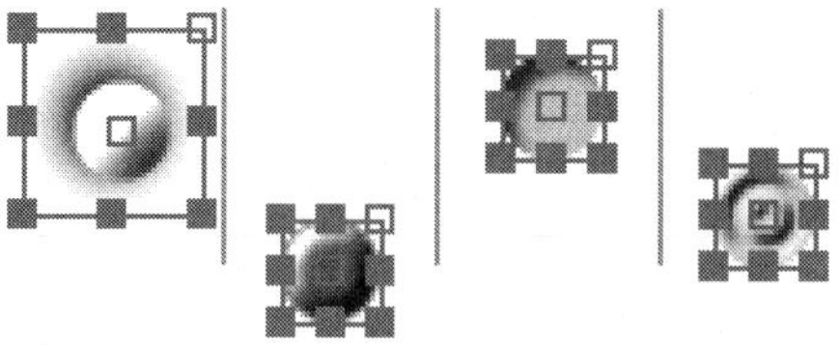

1 ➤ *Four button objects are selected.*

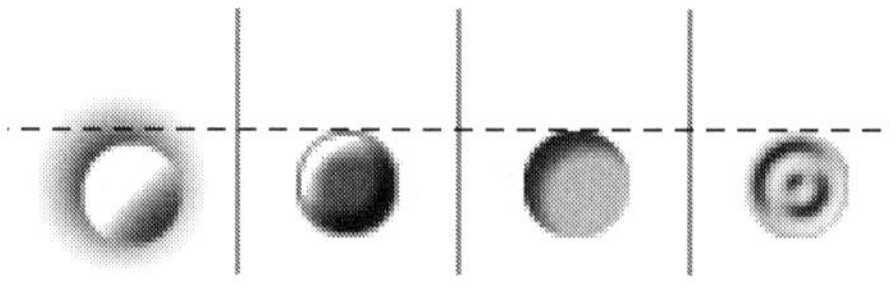

2 ➤ *After choosing Object menu > Align >* ***Vertical Centers****. Note: Read the second tip on this page.*

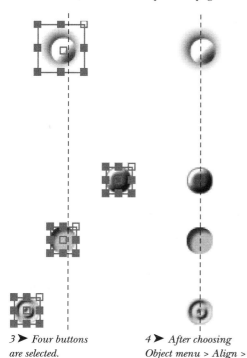

3 ➤ *Four buttons are selected.*

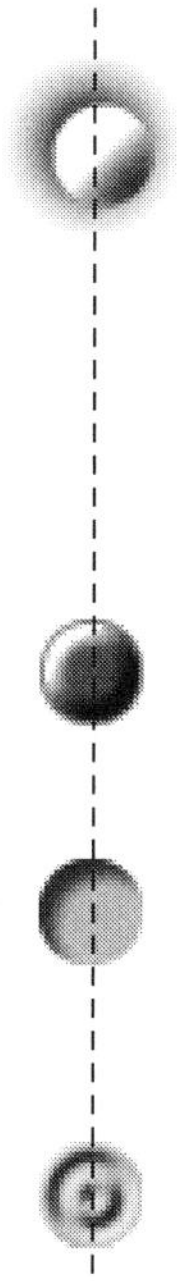

4 ➤ *After choosing Object menu > Align >* ***Horizontal Centers****.*

Aligning

The Align commands are indispensable for aligning a row or column of buttons, bullets, text blocks, or other objects. You could line up objects manually to a guide, but why not use a command that does the job perfectly? It's not that we don't trust our "eye," it's just that we like to know things are exactly where we want them to be. And besides, the Align commands do the job faster.

If you're accustomed to aligning or distributing via a palette, having to choose those commands from a menu will feel a bit cumbersome, but don't let that turn you off.

To align objects:

1. Choose a selection tool.
2. Select more than one object (or group) by Shift-clicking or by dragging a marquee completely around them (Fig. 1).
3. Choose Object menu > Align > Left, Right, Top, Bottom, Horizontal Centers, Vertical Centers, or Centers (Figs. 2–6). Study the icons on the Align submenu—they'll clue you in as to what the command does.

➤ Once your objects are aligned and/or distributed, group them together so their relationships remain fixed.

➤ Each object is lined up according to the width of its widest layer, even if that layer contains a soft shadow. If some objects have a shadow and others don't, they won't look like they're aligned correctly. Use your eye or a ruler guide to adjust any objects that look askew (see "To use ruler guides" on the following page). Another workaround is to hide the wider layer before using the Align command, then redisplay the layer.

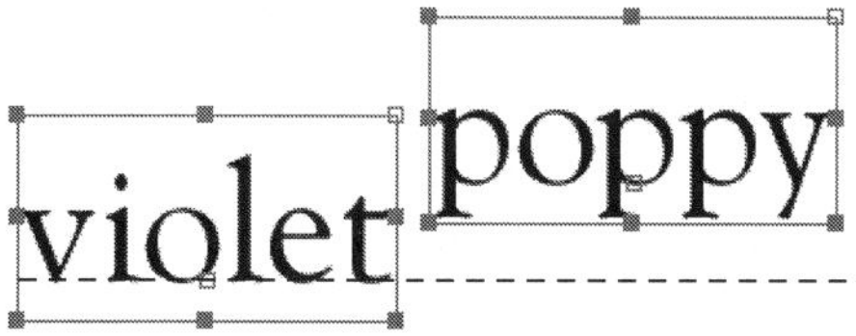

5 ➤ *Two text objects are selected, then Object menu > Align >* ***Bottom*** *is chosen.*

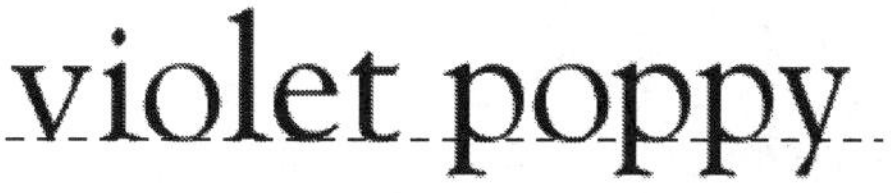

6 ➤ *The baseline of the "poppy" object aligns with the baseline of the bottommost object "violet."*

In LiveMotion, distributing doesn't involve handing things out or scattering things around, it involves equalizing the spacing between three or more objects. Depending on which Distribute command you choose, the topmost and bottommost (or leftmost and rightmost) objects will remain stationary and the objects in between will be spaced apart equally between them. Try distributing a row or column of buttons or text objects.

To distribute objects:

1. Select three or more objects and/or groups by Shift-clicking them or drawing a marquee completely around them (Fig. 1).
2. Choose Object menu > Distribute > Horizontal or Vertical (Fig. 2).

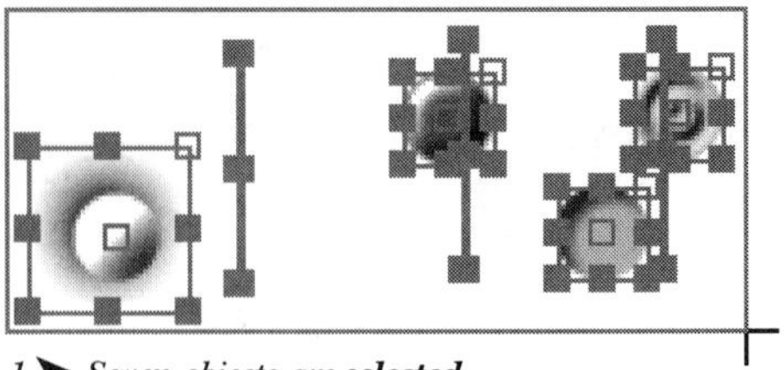

*1 ➤ Seven objects are **selected**.*

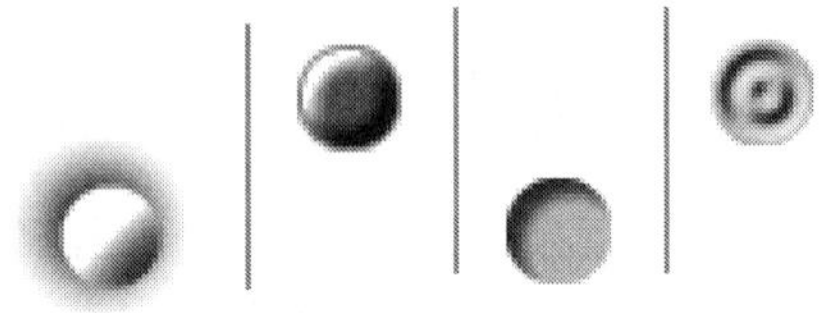

*2 ➤ After choosing the **Distribute Horizontal** command.*

We usually use the Align and Distribute commands or the X and Y fields on the Transform palette to align objects precisely, but sometimes you might need to do things "by eye," especially if the objects have soft edges. That's where ruler guides come in handy.

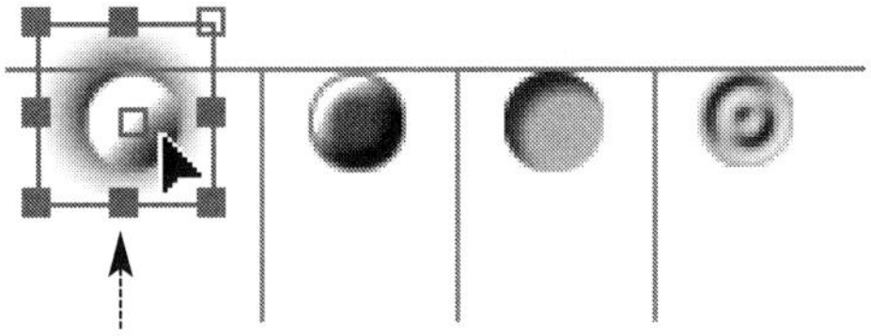

3 ➤ An object is dragged upward to a ruler guide.

To use ruler guides:

1. If the rulers aren't visible, choose View menu > Show Rulers (Command-R/ Ctrl-R) (Fig. 3). Also make sure View menu > Show Guides has a check mark.
2. If you want the edges or anchor points of objects to snap to ruler guides as they are moved near the guides, toggle the View menu > Snap To Guides feature on, if it isn't already on.
3. Drag a guide from the horizontal or vertical ruler into the composition window. Now try dragging an object near a guide, just for the heck of it.

➤ To lock all guides in place so you don't inadvertently move them, choose View menu > Lock Guides.

➤ To remove a guide, drag it back over the ruler, then let go. We know of no command that deletes them all at once. To hide all the guides, choose View menu > Hide Guides.

Handy dandy shortcuts

Show/Hide Grid	Command-'/Ctrl-'
Show/Hide Rulers	Command-R/Ctrl-R
Show/Hide Guides	Command-;/Ctrl-;
Snap To Guides	Command-Shift-;/Ctrl-Shift-;
Lock Guides	Command-Option-;/Ctrl-Alt-;

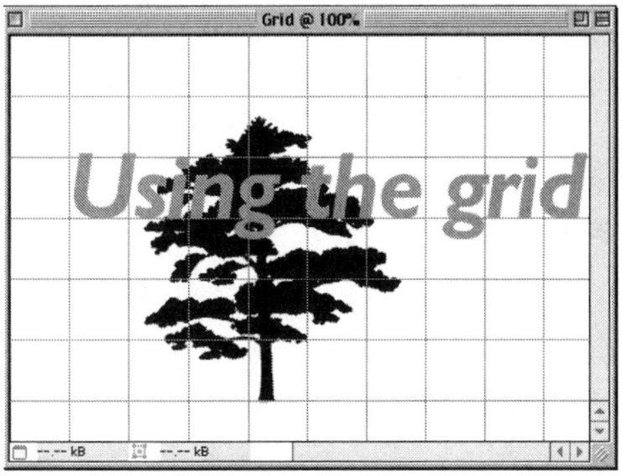

*1➤ The **grid** is used to map out an arrangement of objects.*

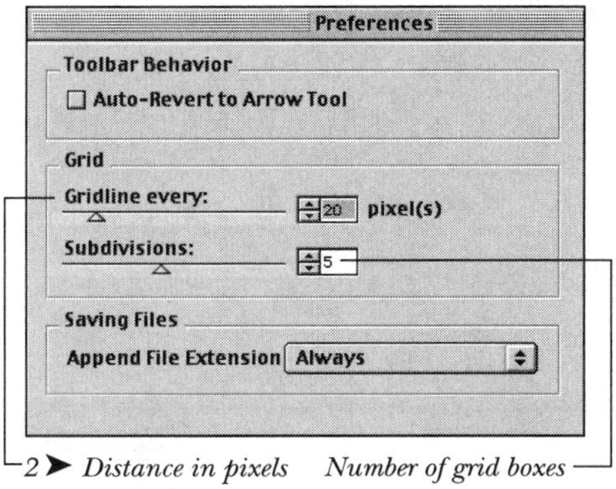

*2➤ Distance in pixels between the **Gridlines** (the lighter blue lines).*

*Number of grid boxes between **Subdivisions** (the slightly darker lines).*

The grid is like electronic graph paper—graph paper with magnetism. If you turn on the Snap To Grid function, any object you drag near a grid line will snap to the line.

To use the grid:

1. To make the grid appear, choose View menu > Show Grid (Command-'/Ctrl-') (Fig. 1).
2. *Optional:* To use the grid's snap-to feature, make sure View menu > Snap To Grid has a check mark (Command-Shift-'/Ctrl-Shift-').
3. *Optional:* To change the grid spacing, choose Edit menu > Preferences (Command-K/Ctrl-K), then change the Grid: Gridline every [ ] pixels value and/or the Subdivisions value (Fig. 2). The new values will take effect in the composition window while the dialog box is open. *Note:* The difference between the gridlines and the subdivisions is so subtle it's almost impossible to distinguish—at least on our monitors.

Pasting

You may already be a whiz at cutting and pasting whole objects or groups in other applications. If not, here are the basic facts:

- The Cut, Copy, Paste, and Paste Special commands all use the Clipboard, a temporary storage area in memory.
- The previous contents of the Clipboard are replaced each time you choose Cut or Copy.
- The same Clipboard contents can be pasted repeatedly.
- You can copy and paste objects from one composition window to another—even between some applications.

To cut and paste an object or a group:

1. Choose a selection tool.
2. Select the object or group to be cut or copied.
3. Choose Edit menu > Cut to cut the object (remove it to the Clipboard) (Command-X/Ctrl-X or Shift-Del) (Fig. 1). Or in Windows only: Right-click in the composition window and choose Cut from the context menu.
   or
   Choose Edit menu > Copy to put a copy of the object onto the Clipboard (Command-C/Ctrl-C or Ctrl-Ins). Or in Windows only: Right-click in the composition window and choose Copy from the context menu.
4. Click in a different composition window, if desired, then choose Edit menu > Paste (Command-V/Ctrl-V or Shift-Ins) (Fig. 2). The object will reappear smack in the center of the window.

Pasting is so special

The **Paste Special** commands have the power to copy individual attributes or components from one object to another, such as an object's fill, transform, or properties settings. We discuss the Paste Special commands whenever they seem relevant to a particular topic. Look up "Paste Special" in the index if you want to see a listing. If you fall in love with these commands, write an e-mail to Adobe and ask them to add them to your other favorite applications. (Hey, it never hurts to ask. Not that long ago, Elaine called up a publisher and asked them if she could write a book on QuarkXPress...)

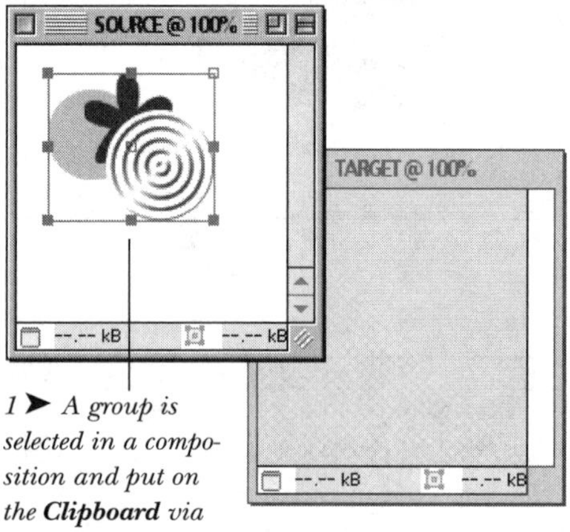

*1 ➤ A group is selected in a composition and put on the **Clipboard** via Edit menu > **Copy**.*

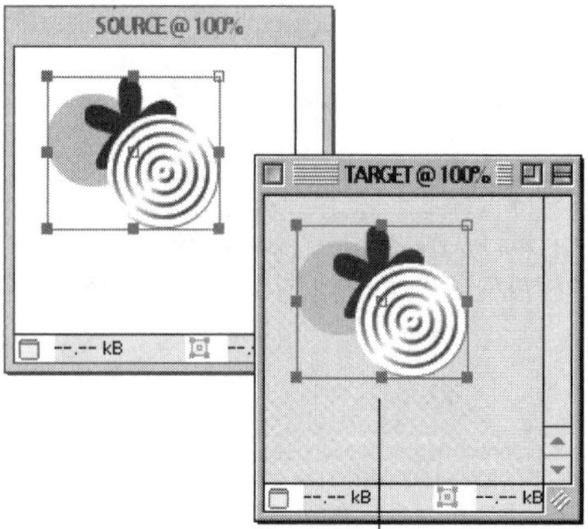

*2 ➤ Another composition is made active, then Edit menu > **Paste** is chosen.*

Layers & Styles 5

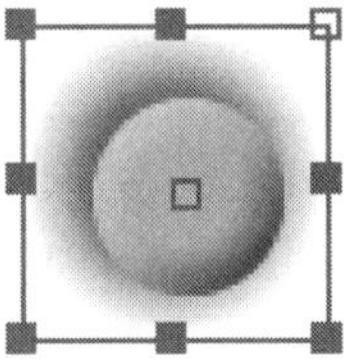

*1 ➤ This object has **two layers**. The top layer has an emboss effect (3D palette), and the bottom layer was widened and softened to create a shadow.*

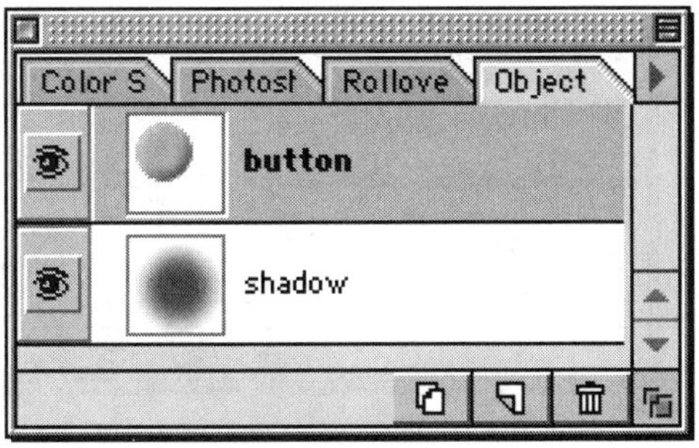

*2 ➤ Thumbnails and names for the object's layers appear on the **Object Layers** palette.*

Creating layers

IN LIVEMOTION, each object automatically has one layer; up to 99 more layers can be added. The layers for an object, called "object layers," conform to the shape of, and belong only to, that object—not to the entire rectangular-shaped composition. The layers for a flower-shaped object, for example, will also be shaped like a flower. (Layers in Photoshop or Illustrator, by comparison, always match the dimensions of the entire rectangular canvas.)

Since each object layer in LiveMotion functions independently of the other object layers, a layer can be offset from the other layers and different attributes can be applied to it (e.g., color, texture, gradient, opacity, and distortion and 3D effects). Multiple layers can also be saved as a style. This is a tremendously flexible system, since you can apply attributes to different layers of an object and edit them independently.

The **Object Layers** palette is used to select, create, duplicate, restack, delete, hide, and show layers (Figs. 1–2). This palette lists only the layers for the currently selected object. If more than one object is selected, the palette will show only the layers for the topmost selected object. The palette is blank when no objects are selected.

➤ You'll need to keep the Object Layers palette open for the instructions in this chapter.

The **Layer** palette, illustrated on page 9, is used to change an individual layer's location relative to its object's other layers, its width, the softness of its edges, and its fill type (color, image, background, or texture).

Each newly created layer is automatically placed directly behind the currently selected layer, and is assigned a black fill. Individual layers can be modified and styled using palettes such as Adjust, 3D, Textures, Distort, and Gradient. To learn how to apply color and work with all those palettes, read Chapter 6, Embellish.

To create a new layer:

1. Choose a selection tool (A, V, or U) or the Transform tool (E), then select the object to which you want to add a layer.
2. Click the layer name below which you want the new layer to appear (you can restack it later).
3. Click the New Layer button on the Object Layers palette (Command-L/Ctrl-L) (Figs. 1–2). To rename the new layer, double-click the layer name.
4. Edit the new layer, if desired. For example, you could make it wider and softer via the Layer palette. To read more about layer editing, see the sidebar. And remember, changes are always editable and reversible.

To select a layer:

1. Choose a selection tool, then select an object in the composition window.
2. Click a layer name on the Object Layers palette.
   or
   Use a Select Layer shortcut: Command-1/Ctrl-1 for Layer 1, Command-2/Ctrl-2 for Layer 2, and so on, up to Layer 5. The numbers refer to the position of the layers in the object, with 1 being the topmost—not necessarily the layer names.
   or
   Windows: Right-click in the composition window and choose from the Select Layer submenu on the context menu (only layers one through five will be listed).

To learn more about editing layers

Offset	page 70
Width	page 71
Soften	page 72
Recolor	page 87
Change opacity	page 73
Apply a texture	page 124
Apply a 3D effect	page 94
Apply a tint	page 93

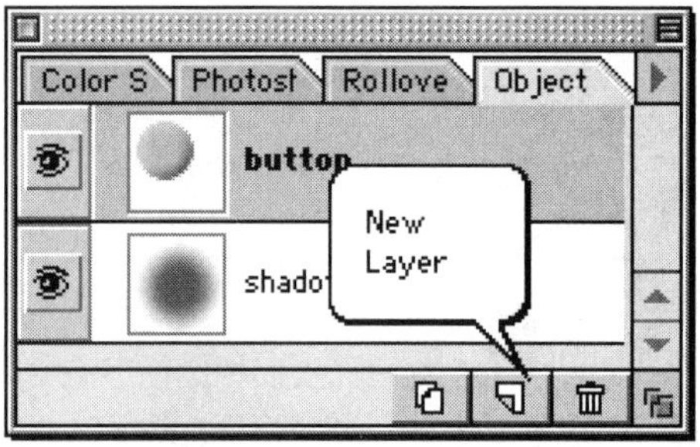

*1 ➤ Select an object in the composition, then click the **New Layer** button on the **Object Layers** palette.*

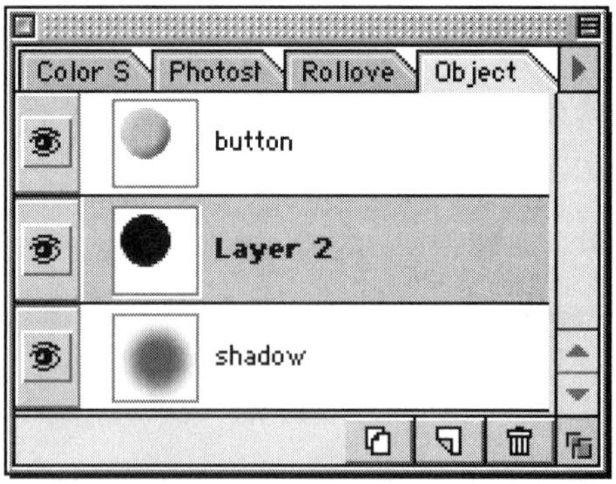

*2 ➤ The **new layer** appears, with a **black** fill.*

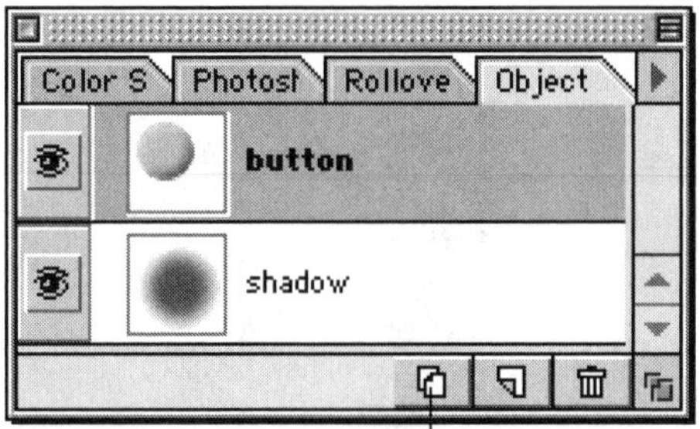

*1 ➤ Click the layer name you want to duplicate, then click the **Duplicate Layer** button.*

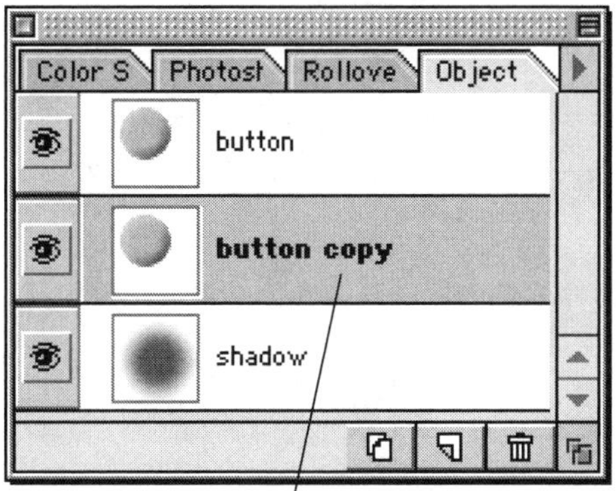

*2 ➤ The **duplicate** layer appears on the palette.*

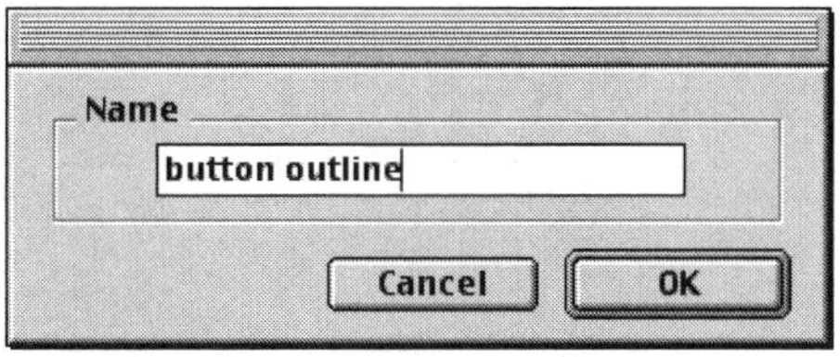

*3 ➤ Double-click a layer to **rename** it.*

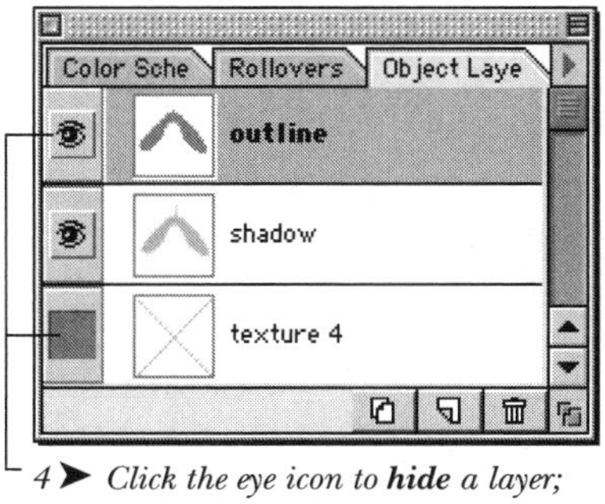

*4 ➤ Click the eye icon to **hide** a layer; click the gray box to **redisplay** it.*

A duplicate layer will have the exact same attributes as the original from which it is duplicated.

To duplicate a layer:

METHOD 1

1. On the Object Layers palette, click on the name of the layer you want to duplicate (Fig. 1).
2. Click the Duplicate Layer button on the palette (Fig. 2).
   or
   Choose Layer menu > Duplicate Layer.
   or
   Windows: Right-click in the composition window and choose Duplicate Layer from the context menu.

➤ You can't duplicate a layer by dragging its name over the New Layer or Duplicate Layer button (as you can in Photoshop and Illustrator).

To rename a layer:

1. Double-click a layer name on the Object Layers palette.
2. Change the layer name, then click OK (Return/Enter) (Fig. 3). Be as descriptive as possible, especially if you've got a rotating team of elves working on the same project.

Sometimes things just get in the way. The eye icon works like a switch for flicking the display of individual layers on and off.

To hide or show a layer:

On the Object Layers palette, click on the eye icon to the left of a layer thumbnail to hide that layer (Fig. 4). The objects on that layer will no longer be visible in the composition.

Click on the gray box to the left of a layer thumbnail to show the layer again and redisplay the objects on the layer.

When you restack a layer, it shifts position in relation to the other layers in that object—not in relation to other objects in the composition.

To restack a layer:

1. Choose a selection tool (A, V, or U), then select the object whose layers you want to restack (Fig. 1).
2. Drag a layer name upward or downward on the Object Layers palette.

   MacOS: Release the mouse when a blue highlight appears in the desired position for the layer you're restacking. If you drag downward, the layer will stack below the layer with the blue highlight; if you drag upward, the layer will stack above the layer with the blue highlight. If you restacked a layer that's visible, the object's appearance will change (Figs. 2–4).

➤ If you insist on doing things the hard way, you could choose Layer menu > Arrange > Bring to Front, Bring Forward, Send to Back, or Send Backward instead.

1 ➤ The original stacking order.

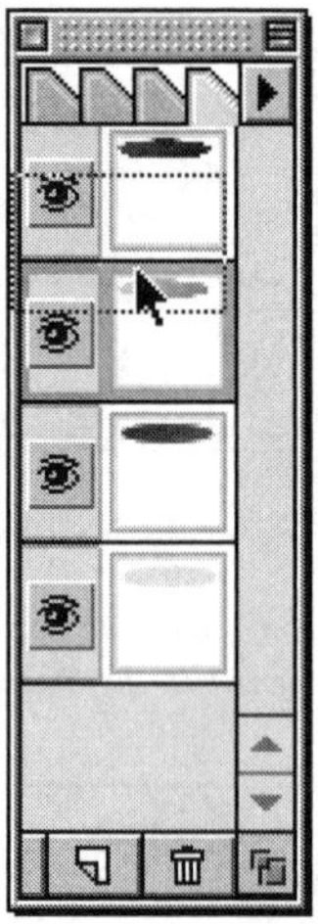

2 ➤ Moving the lighter and smaller layer ***upward***.

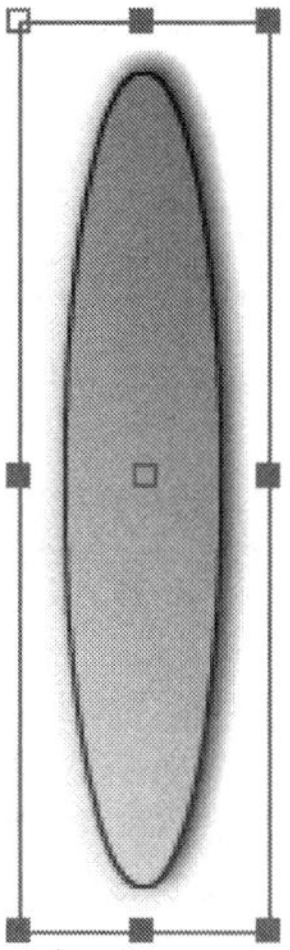

3 ➤ The result.

4 ➤ The lighter layer is now on ***top***.

To delete a layer:

1. Choose a selection tool (A, V, or U), then select the object from which you want to delete a layer.
2. On the Object Layers palette, click the name of the layer that you want to delete. Only one layer can be selected at a time.
3. Click the Delete Layer (trash) button on the palette.

   or

   Choose Layer menu > Delete Layer.

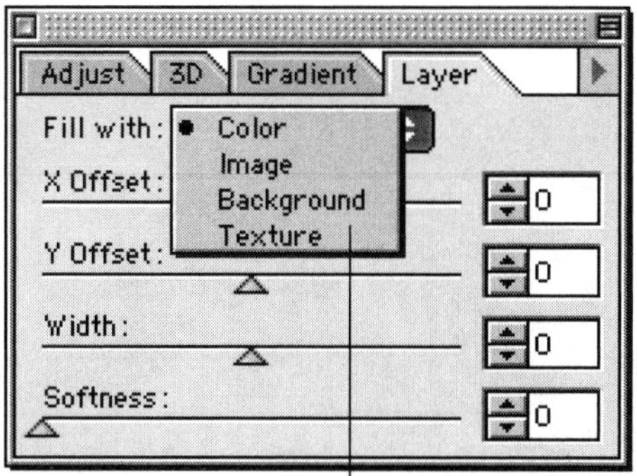

1 ➤ Choose a ***Fill with*** *option for an object layer.*

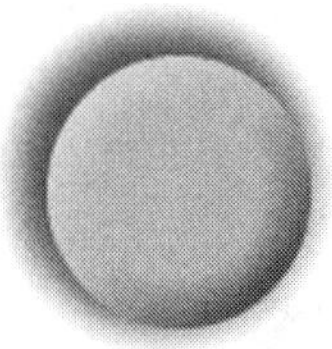

2 ➤ Fill with: ***Color****.*

3 ➤ Fill with: ***Color*** *(in this case a gradient).*

4 ➤ Fill with: ***Image****.*

5 ➤ Fill with: ***Background****.*

6 ➤ Fill with: ***Texture****.*

Working with layers

The **Layer palette** is used to precisely control the *x-y* (horizontal/vertical) location of the currently selected layer relative to the overall object, to modify its width or the softness of its edges, or to cycle through its different fill options. First, the fill options.

The "Fill with" pop-up menu on the Layer palette has a better memory than we do. It remembers which color, image, and texture was last applied to each layer, and it retains all this information even after you perform other operations, or even save, close, and reopen the file. You can cycle through the different fill options whenever you like.

To cycle through fill options for a layer:

1. Choose a selection tool, then select the object layer whose fill you want to change.
2. Click a layer on the Object Layers palette.
3. If you haven't already done so, just to see how this feature works:

   Apply a solid or gradient color fill to the layer (see pages 87 and 91).
   and
   Copy an image object then choose Edit menu > Paste Special > Paste Image; or use File menu > Replace to fill the layer with the image (see page 104).
   and
   Apply a texture to the layer via the Textures palette (see page 124).
4. From the "Fill with" pop-up menu on the Layer palette (Fig. 1), choose:

   Color to reapply the last solid color or gradient that was applied to that layer (Figs. 2–3).

   Image to redisplay the last image that layer was filled with (via Paste Image or Replace) (Fig. 4). (If no image, then the last-applied color will be reapplied.)

   Background to make that layer transparent. Choose for the top layer (100% opacity) to make all the layers transparent.

   Texture to reapply the last texture that was applied to that layer (Fig. 6).

You can use the Layer palette or the Layer Offset tool to offset a layer up to 50 pixels in any direction. By offsetting a layer and then softening its edges, you can create a nice drop shadow (see also the following page).

To offset a layer:

METHOD 1 (entering values)

1. Choose a selection tool (A, V, or U), then select the object whose layer you want to offset.
2. On the Object Layers palette, click the name of the layer that you want to offset.
3. On the Layer palette, move the X Offset slider or enter the number of pixels you want the layer to move (-50–50). A negative value will move the layer to the left; a positive value will move the layer to the right.
4. Move the Y offset slider or enter the number of pixels you want the layer to move (-50–50). A negative value will move the layer upward; a positive value will move the layer downward.

METHOD 2 (dragging)

1. Choose a selection tool, then select the object whose layer you want to offset (Fig. 1).
2. On the Object Layers palette, click the name of the layer that you want to offset.
3. Choose the Layer Offset tool (O).
4. Carefully position the pointer over an area of the object that contains color (the pointer will become a four-headed arrow), then drag the layer in the composition window (Figs. 2–3). The X Offset and Y Offset values on the Layer palette will update to reflect the layer's new position.

1 ➤ The original object.

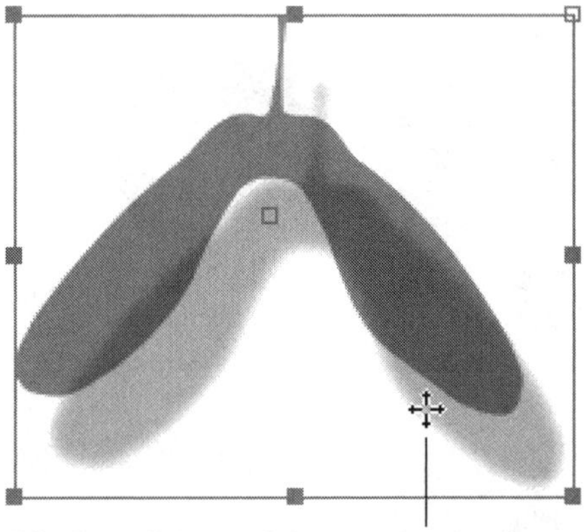

*2 ➤ Layer 2 is moved downward and to the right using the **Layer Offset** tool.*

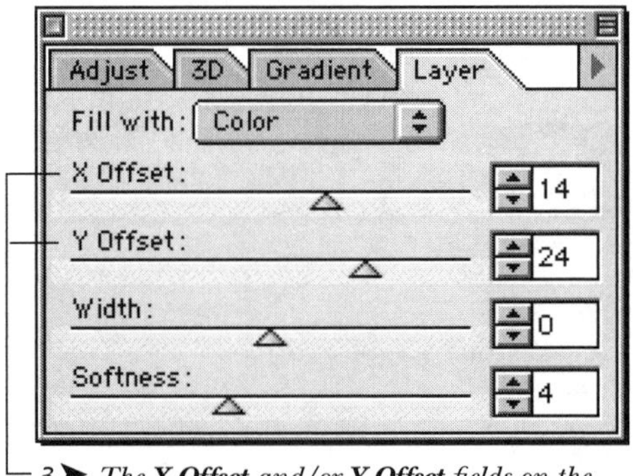

*3 ➤ The **X Offset** and/or **Y Offset** fields on the **Layer** palette control the **position** of a layer relative to the other layers in the **same object**.*

The whole thing

To scale an **entire** object and **all** its **layers**, select the object, then drag a selection handle (see page 54) or change its width and/or height values using the Transform palette (see page 114).

You can also use the Layer palette to widen an individual layer within an object. The name of this slider is confusing; it actually resizes a whole layer inward or outward in all directions from its center.

Since an object can have a fill **or** an outline, not both, you can create the illusion of an outline for an object by enlarging one of its underlying layers or by shrinking its topmost layer. To create a glow around an object, increase both the Width and Softness of one of its lower layers (see also the next page).

To change the width of a layer:

1. Choose a selection tool, then select the object whose layer you want to scale (Fig. 1).
2. On the Object Layers palette, click on the name of the layer that you want to scale (Fig. 2).
3. On the Layer palette, move the Width slider (-10–10). A positive value will enlarge the layer; a negative value will shrink the layer (Figs. 3–4).

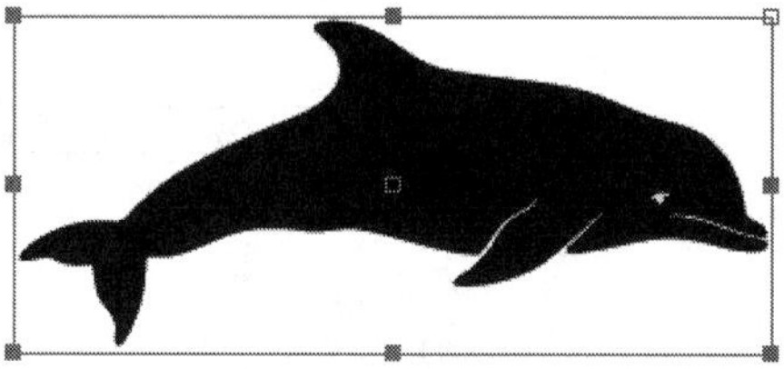

1 ➤ The original object.

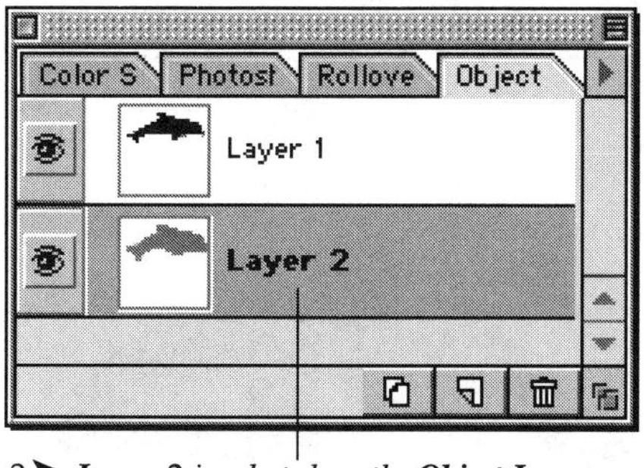

*2 ➤ **Layer 2** is selected on the **Object Layers** palette.*

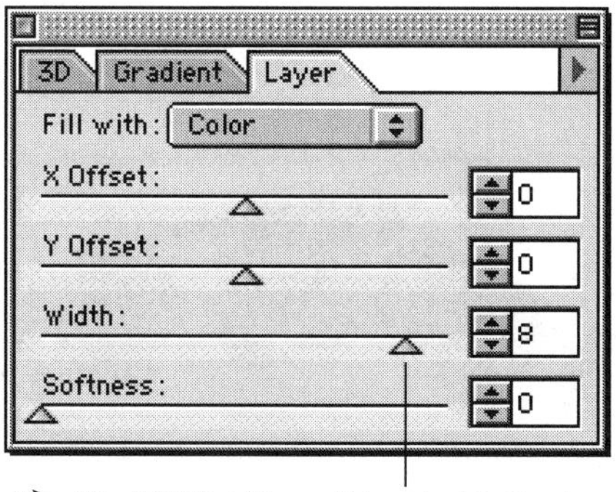

*3 ➤ The **Width** of Layer 2 is raised to 8 using the **Layer** palette.*

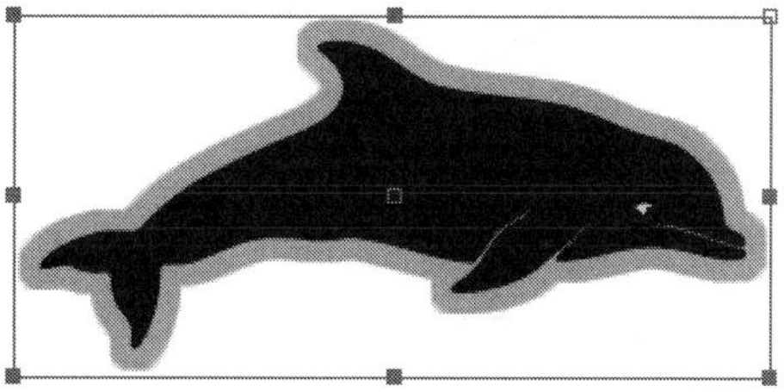

*4 ➤ Now Layer 2 is **wider** than layer 1.*

Changing layer opacity

This is the way to create a soft drop shadow.

To soften the edge of a layer:

1. Choose a selection tool, then select the object whose layer you want to soften (Fig. 1).
2. On the Object Layers palette, click on the name of the layer that you want to soften (Fig. 2).
3. On the Layer palette, move the Softness slider (0–10). 0 will produce a hard edge; 10 will produce a soft, feathered edge (Figs. 3–4). Now, to lighten the layer, see the next page. To make it larger or smaller, see the previous page. To offset it (Fig. 5), see page 70.

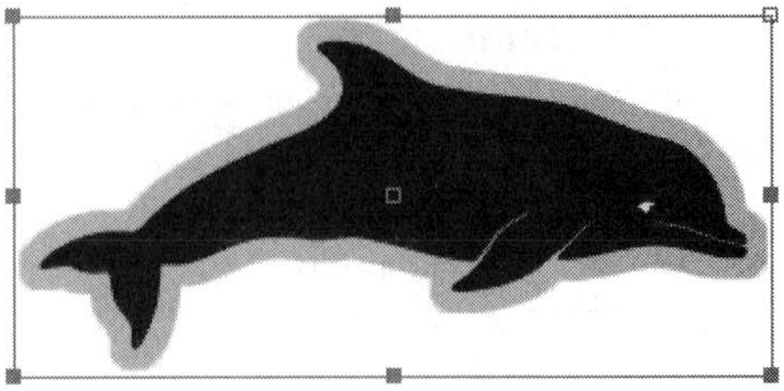

1 ➤ *Layer 2 is **wider** than layer 1.*

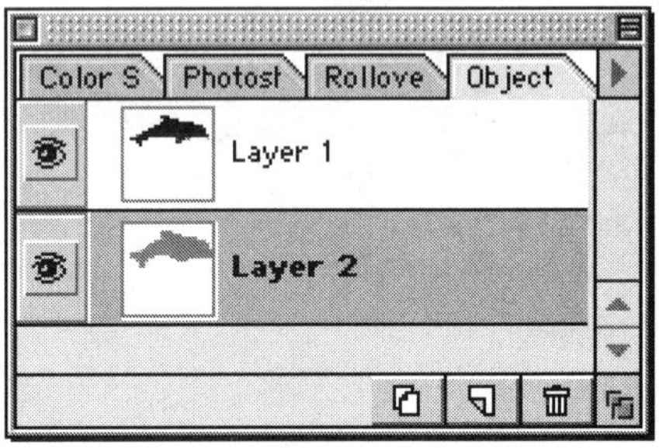

2 ➤ *Layer 2 is selected.*

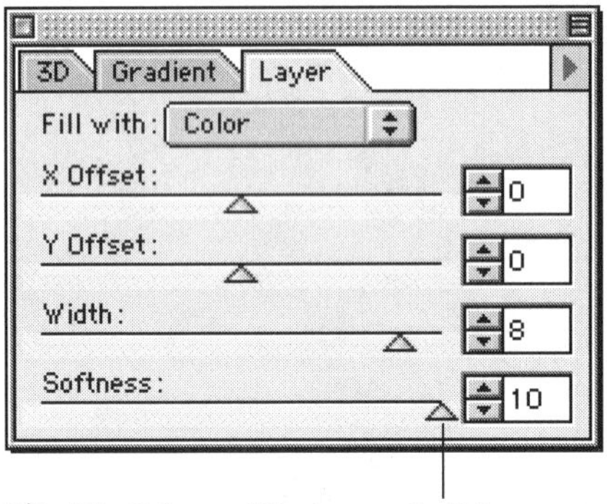

3 ➤ *The **Softness** slider is moved all the way to the right on the **Layer** palette.*

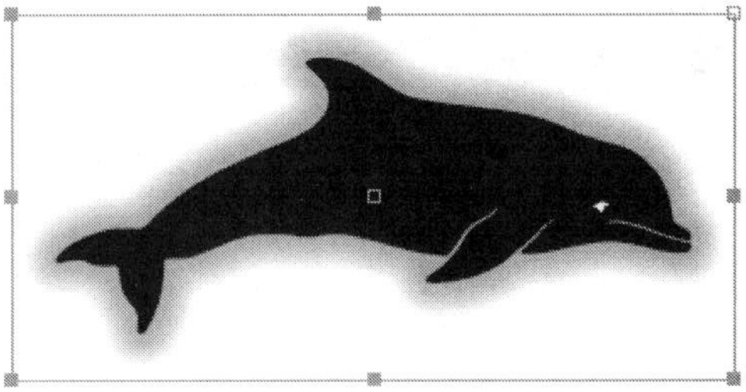

4 ➤ *Layer 2 is now **softened**.*

5 ➤ *Finally, the **X Offset** and **Y Offset** values are raised to move the shadow to the right and downward.*

1 ➤ *The original two-layer object.*

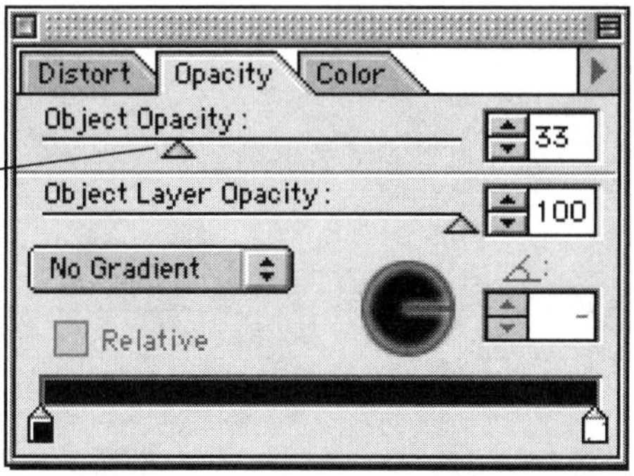

2 ➤ *The **Object Opacity** slider on the **Opacity** palette controls the opacity of **all** an object's layers.*

3 ➤ *The **opacity** of the **entire object** is lowered.*

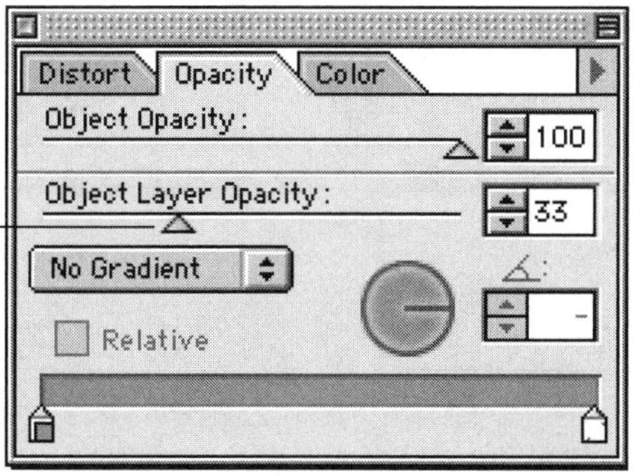

4 ➤ *The Object Opacity is restored back to 100, and then the **Object Layer Opacity** is lowered only for the **topmost layer**—not the shadow layer.*

In LiveMotion, you can change the opacity (transparency) for one layer at a time or you can change the opacity of all an object's layers at once. When a whole **object** has a low opacity, you'll be able to see through it to underlying **objects**. When a **layer** has a low opacity, you'll only be able to see through it to underlying **layers**. Both types of opacity—object opacity and layer opacity—can be adjusted or restored to full strength at any time.

To change the opacity of a whole object (all its layers):

1. Choose a selection tool (A, V, or U), then select the object whose opacity you want to change (Fig. 1).
2. Show the Opacity palette (Window menu > Opacity).
3. Move the Object Opacity slider or enter a value (0–100) (Figs. 2–3). The higher the opacity, the more opaque the color.
4. Make sure No Gradient is chosen from the pop-up menu.

To change the opacity of one layer:

1. Choose a selection tool (A, V, or U), then select the object that contains the layer whose opacity you want to change (Fig. 4).
2. On the Object Layers palette, click on a layer.
3. On the Opacity palette, move the Object Layer Opacity slider or enter a value (0–100) (Fig. 5).

5 ➤ *Only the opacity of the **top layer** is changed.*

This method for making a layer's opacity fade smoothly and gradually across an object can be edited or removed at any time.

To change the opacity of a layer using a gradient mask:

1. Choose a selection tool, click on an object, and choose a layer for that object (Fig. 1).
2. From the pop-up menu on the Opacity palette (not the Gradient palette!), choose Linear, Burst, Double Burst, or Radial (Fig. 2).
3. Click the opacity gradient start marker (the left marker) under the gradient bar on the Opacity palette, and note the Object Layer Opacity value for that marker; then do the same for the end (right) marker (Fig. 3). If both markers have a value of 100, change one of them to 0.
4. *Optional:* To change the angle for the gradient mask, move the dial; or click the up or down arrow; or enter a value in the Angle field (Fig. 4).
5. *Optional:* Move the start or end marker toward the middle of the bar to adjust where and how abruptly the fadeout occurs. You can change the opacity and location of either marker.

➤ To prevent the gradient mask from rotating if the object is rotated, choose Object menu > Transform > Shape Transforms, uncheck the Relative box on the Opacity palette, then Rotate the object. (Reselect Shape Transforms when you're ready to turn it off.)

➤ To flip the transparent and opaque parts of the layer, click each opacity marker and reverse its opacity value (e.g., change 0% to 100%). The white marker will turn black; the black marker will turn white.

Restoring opacity

Choose **No Gradient** from the Opacity palette to make the opacity uniform again.

1 ➤ The original object.

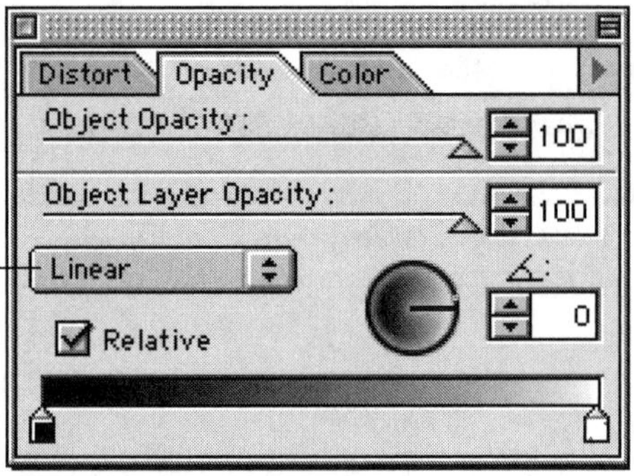

*2 ➤ A **gradient type** (Linear) is chosen from the pop-up menu on the **Opacity** palette.*

*3 ➤ The type object gradually becomes **less opaque** from left to right.*

*4 ➤ The gradient **angle** is changed to -90. Now the gradient runs from top to bottom instead of left to right.*

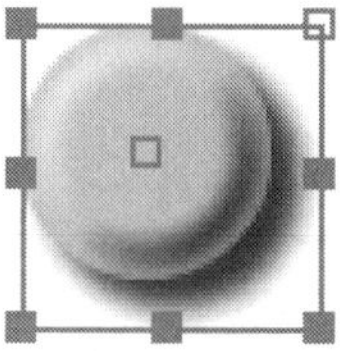

1 ➤ The original object.

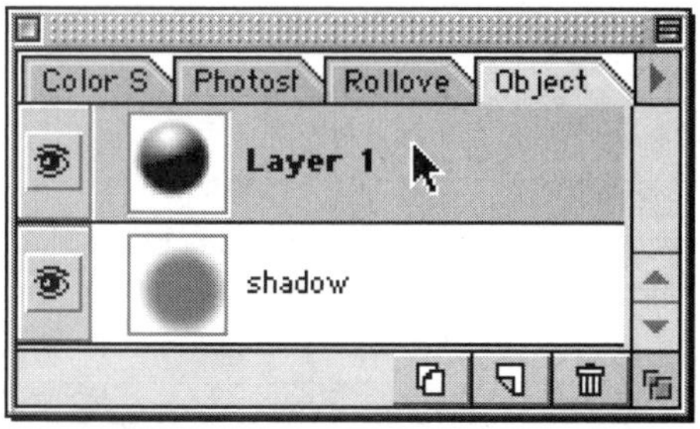

2 ➤ ***Layer 1*** *is chosen.*

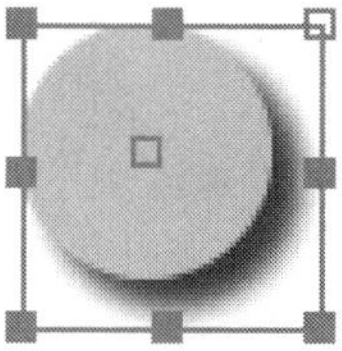

3 ➤ The topmost layer is restored to a ***plain*** *state. It's filled with the current Foreground color automatically.*

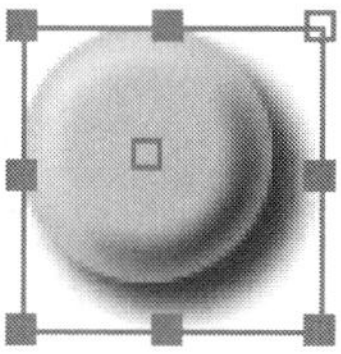

4 ➤ The topmost ***layer*** *of this object is copied to the* ***Clipboard****.*

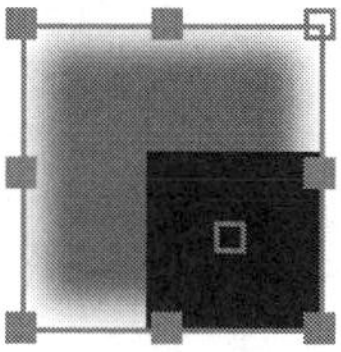

5 ➤ A layer on another object is selected.

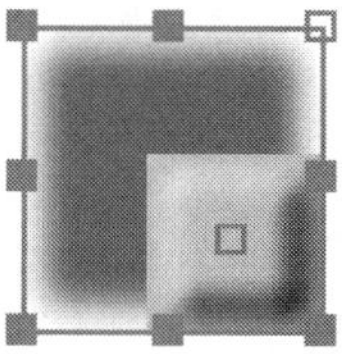

6 ➤ Edit menu > ***Paste Special*** *>* ***Layer*** *is chosen. The original layer attributes are replaced by the pasted layer attributes.*

Removing attributes

The Clear Layer Attributes command restores the default Layer, Adjust, Distort, 3D, Texture, and Gradient palette settings to a layer. This command *can* be undone.

To restore a layer to its plain, unadorned state:

1. Select an object and select the layer from which you want to remove attributes (Figs. 1–2)
2. Choose Layer menu > Clear Layer Attributes (Fig 3.). The layer will be filled automatically with the current Foreground color. The Object Layer Opacity will be restored to 100%; the Object Opacity won't change. The Layer and Adjust palette settings will default to 0; the Distort and 3D palettes will be reset to None; and the Gradient palette will be reset to No Gradient.

Copying attributes

In these instructions, you'll learn how to copy and paste attributes from one object to another.

Note: Once you've got a set of attributes you're happy with, we recommend that you save it as a style (see the following page). Then you can use it to apply attributes quickly without relying on the Clipboard. Also, it will remain on the Styles palette even after you quit/exit and re-launch LiveMotion.

To copy layer attributes from one object to another:

1. Choose a selection tool, then select the object whose layer attributes you want to copy (Fig 4).
2. On the Object Layers palette, click the layer whose attributes you want to copy.
3. Choose Edit menu > Copy (Command-C/ Ctrl-C).
4. Select the object and the layer to which you want to apply the copied attributes (Fig 5).
5. Choose Edit menu > Paste Special > Layer (Fig. 6).

Using styles

In LiveMotion, a style is a set of layer attributes. Those attributes include Color, Distort, 3D, Adjust, Gradient, Layer, Opacity, Textures, and Photoshop Filters palette settings. A style can also contain multiple layers, animation instructions, and rollovers.

The same style can be assigned to as many objects as you like in any composition. This is obviously a great timesaver. And since you can apply the same style to multiple objects, styles also help to ensure consistency from one object to the next or even between compositions, an important consideration when you're designing repetitive elements for Web pages.

You can use a predefined style from the Styles palette or, better yet, you can create your own styles. To create your own style, you'll create layer effects for an object and then create a new style based on that object. Even after it has been assigned a style, an object can be custom-modified to give it a distinctive look.

Note: Unlike styles in a word processing or layout application, when you edit a style, those changes won't appear in objects to which the style is already applied.

First, acquaint yourself with the Styles palette.

To choose a display mode for the Styles palette:

From the Styles palette menu, choose a display mode:

Swatches View to display styles as swatch thumbnails without names.

Preview View to display a list of names and a large thumbnail only for the currently highlighted style (Fig. 1).

Name View to display small thumbnails and names for all the styles (Fig. 2).

To narrow down the selection of swatches that are displayed on the palette, uncheck any of the four buttons in the lower left corner of the palette.

What a style can't store

These object characteristics **cannot** be stored as a style:

- Type specifications
- An object's location in the composition
- Transformations applied to an object (rotation, scaling, skewing)
- Properties of a geometric object (whether it's a Rectangle, Rounded Rectangle, Ellipse, Polygon, or Path, and its outline properties
- A Web palette URL attached to an object

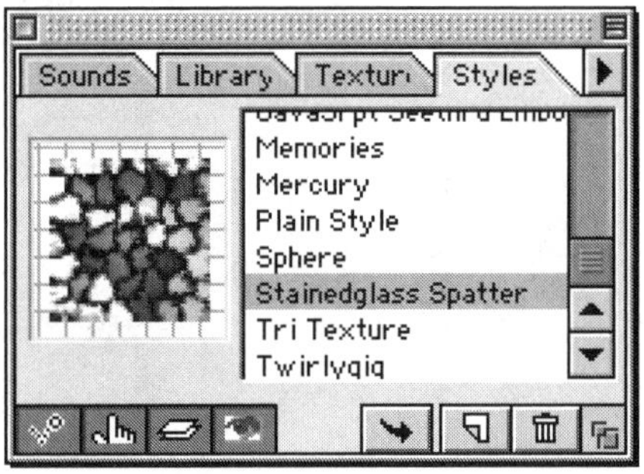

*1 ➤ The **Styles** palette in **Preview View**.*

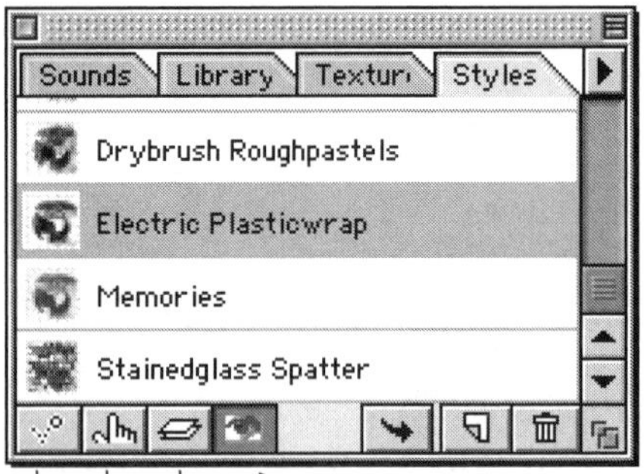

*2 ➤ Use these buttons to narrow down or expand the number of object **categories** that are displayed on the **Styles** palette.*

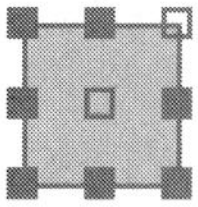

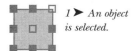

1 ➤ An object is selected.

*2 ➤ A style swatch (or name) is clicked on on the **Styles** palette, then the **Apply Style** button is clicked.*

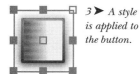

3 ➤ A style is applied to the button.

A style can be applied to any type of object—geometric, text, or image. Only one style can be applied per object. When a style is applied to an object, any and all existing layers and layer attributes are **removed** from that object! Reread the last sentence.

Note: To save a whole object, including its shape and object type and any applied styling, rollovers, or animations, use the Library palette (see pages 49–50).

To apply a style to an object:

METHOD 1 (clicking)

1. Choose a selection tool (V, U, or A), and select the object or objects in the composition window to which you want to apply a style (Fig. 1).
2. Show the Styles palette (Window menu > Show Styles).
3. Double-click a style swatch or name.
   or
   Click a style swatch or name, then click the Apply Style button at the bottom of the palette (Figs. 2–3).

METHOD 2 (dragging)

1. Show the Styles palette (Window menu > Show Styles).
2. Drag a style swatch or name over a selected or unselected object. Release the mouse when the object's selection border appears. The object will become selected, if it wasn't selected already.

Use either of these two methods to copy an object's current attributes and paste it into another object. Those attributes don't have to be saved to the Styles palette in order to do this.

Note: As when a new style is applied, using the Paste Style command causes all previously applied layers and layer attributes to be **removed**!

To copy styling from one object to another:

METHOD 1 (Clipboard)

1. Choose a selection tool (V, U, or A).
2. Select the object whose style you want to apply to another object (Fig. 1).
3. Choose Edit menu > Copy.
4. Select the object to which you want to apply the copied style (Fig 2.).
5. Choose Edit menu > Paste Style (Command-B/Ctrl-B) (Fig. 3).
   or
   Windows: Right-click in the composition window and choose Paste Style from the context menu.

   If you copied more than one object to the Clipboard, only the style of the frontmost object on the Clipboard will be pasted.

METHOD 2 (Eyedropper)

1. Select the object to which you want to **apply** the copied style.
2. Choose the Eyedropper tool (I). 
3. Shift-click on the object whose style you want to **copy**.

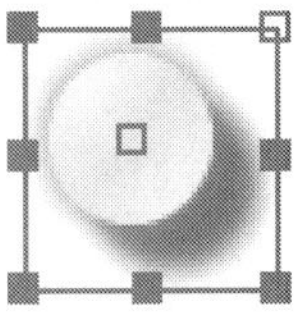

1 ➤ An object is copied.

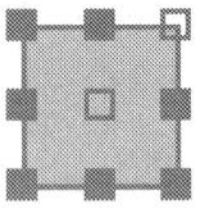

2 ➤ A different object is selected.

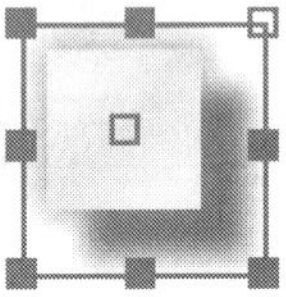

*3 ➤ Edit menu > **Paste Style** is chosen. The attributes from the first object are pasted into the second object.*

Get organized

If you find yourself creating a lot of styles, organize them into separate folders inside the Adobe LiveMotion > Styles folder on your hard drive. The folders can be labeled by style type, client name, task name, etc. All style files residing in this folder, whether on the first level or in subfolders, will appear on the Styles palette under the file name after launching LiveMotion. Each LiveMotion file you save into the Styles folder should contain only one styled object, since only the topmost object's style will be listed on the palette.

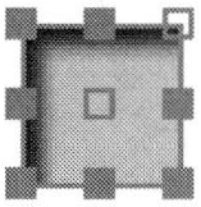

1 ➤ Select an object whose attributes you want to save as a style.

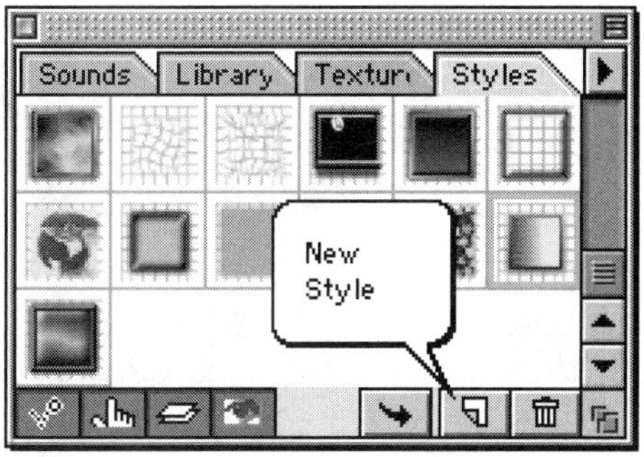

2 ➤ The ***New Style*** *button is clicked on the* ***Styles*** *palette.*

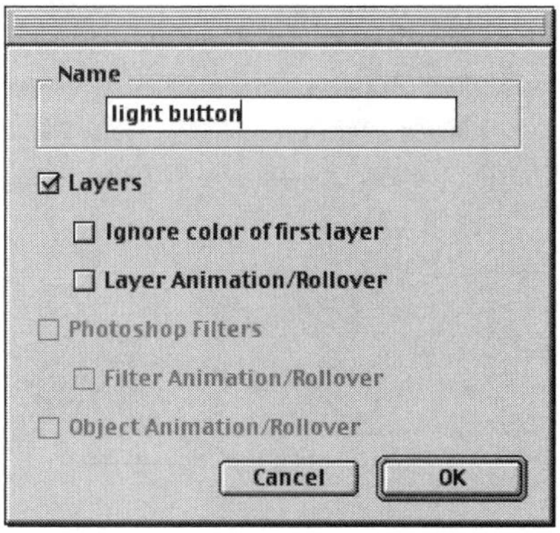

3 ➤ Give the new style a ***descriptive name****.*

If you save an object's attributes as a style, you can then reuse the style in any LiveMotion composition or even share it with a LiveMotion buddy on another platform. An object's type and shape aren't saved in a style.

To save an object's attributes as a style:

1. Create an object and assign attributes to it (e.g., color, texture, opacity). Make sure the object is selected (Fig. 1).
2. Show the Styles palette (Window menu > Styles).
3. Click the New Style button at the bottom of the palette (Fig. 2).
   or
   Drag the object onto the Styles palette.
   Note: If you can't seem to drag the object onto the Styles palette, make sure the palette isn't overlapping the composition window. Bug.
4. Type a name for the new style (Fig. 3). Make it short but descriptive. The ".liv" extension will be added automatically.
   Note: Don't use a name that starts with "p." That way, you'll be able to type "p" to select the Plain Style quickly whenever you need to.
5. *Optional:* Check the "Ignore color of first layer" box to save the style without a fill in its topmost layer. When you apply a style for which this option is turned on, the style won't change the fill of the object to which it is applied. With this option unchecked, the fill attributes of the style's first layer will take precedence.
6. Click OK (Return/Enter). The new style will appear on the Styles palette.

➤ Another way to save a style is to drag a LiveMotion file icon directly from the Desktop into the Styles folder inside the LiveMotion application folder. The style won't appear on the Styles palette until you re-launch the application. *Note:* The style must have the ".liv" extension to be used on both the MacOS and Windows platforms.

When you modify a style, the objects to which that style is currently applied **won't update** to reflect the change. That's the way it's designed to work.

To modify a saved style:

1. Choose a selection tool (V, U, or A), then select any object (Fig. 1).
2. To the selected object, apply the style you want to modify (Fig. 2).
3. Modify the object so it has the new characteristics that you want to re-save in the style (Fig. 3).
4. Drag the object onto the Styles palette (Fig. 4).
5. Enter the **same** name exactly, letter for letter, to overwrite the existing style (Fig. 5).
6. Click OK (Return/Enter), then click Replace.

➤ If you inadvertently overwrite one of the default LiveMotion styles, you can reinstall it from the LiveMotion CD-ROM installer disk.

1 ➤ Select any ol' object.

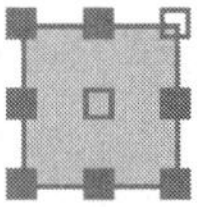

*2 ➤ To the selcted object, **apply** the style that you want to modify.*

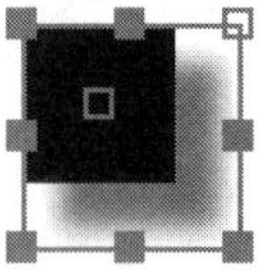

*3 ➤ **Modify** the object so it has the desired style attributes.*

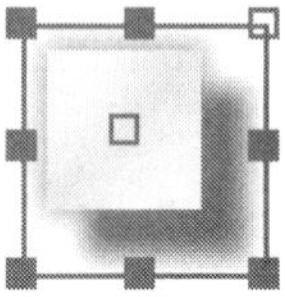

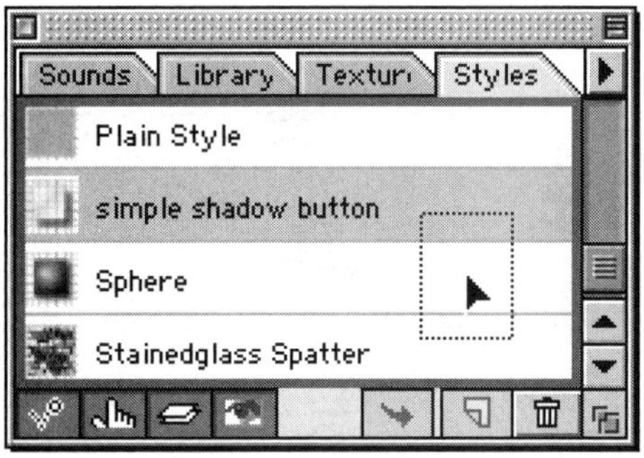

*4 ➤ **Drag** the object onto the **Styles** palette.*

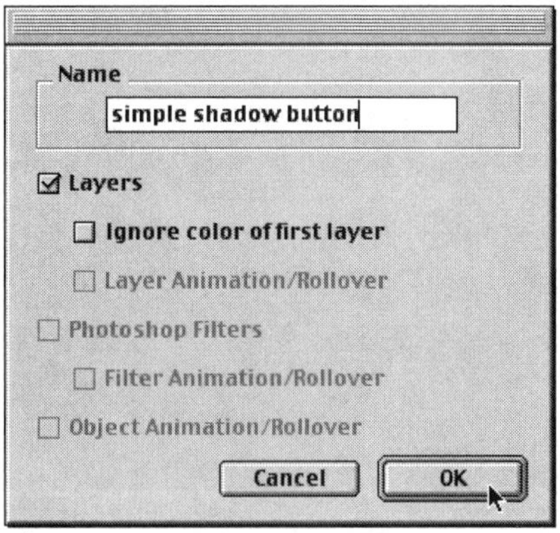

*5 ➤ Enter the style's **original name** exactly.*

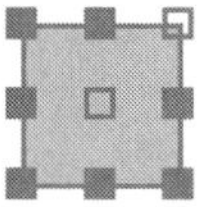

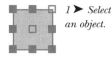

1 ➤ Select an object.

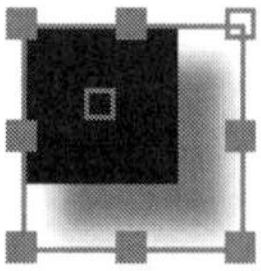

2 ➤ To the selected object, ***apply*** *the style that you want to create a variation of.*

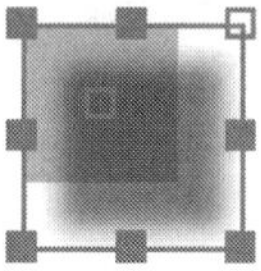

3 ➤ The object's topmost layer is made semi-transparent.

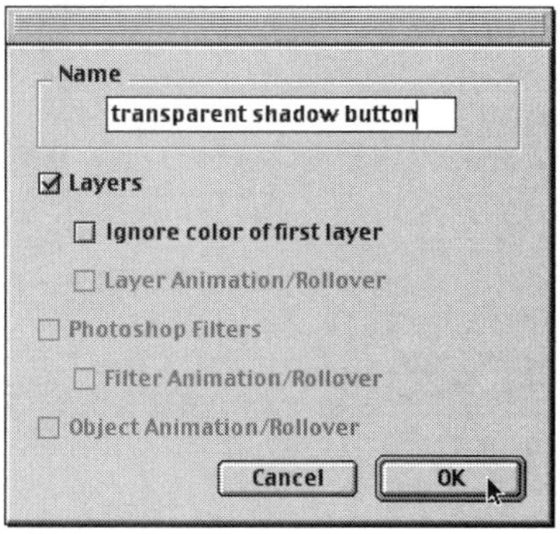

4 ➤ The style name is changed from "simple shadow button" to "transparent shadow button."

Follow these instructions if you've got a style that you think is terrific, but you want to create another version of it—maybe change the opacity or color of one of its layers. It's easier to use an existing style as a starting point than it is to create a new one from scratch.

To create a new style based on an existing style:

1. Choose a selection tool (V, U, or A), then select any object (Fig. 1).
2. To the selected object, apply the style from which you want to spawn a variation (Fig. 2).
3. Modify the object so it has the new characteristics that you want to save as a style (Fig. 3).
4. Click the New Style button at the bottom of the Styles palette.
5. Type a **new** name for the style or change the existing name (Fig. 4). Make sure you don't leave it as is or you'll save over the existing style. Don't use a name that starts with "p" (you'll see why on the following page).
6. Click OK (Return/Enter).

When you remove a style from an object, the attributes of the style are removed from the object.

To remove a style from an object:

1. Choose a selection tool (V, U, or A), then select the object from which you want to remove the style (Fig. 1).
2. On the Styles palette:

   Double-click the Plain Style.
   or
   Click in the palette scroll list, type a "p," then click the Apply Style button (Figs. 2–3). If any of the styles start with the letter "p," you may need to type a few more letters to get to the Plain Style.

Note: When you remove a Style from the Styles palette, the actual style file is removed from the Styles folder on your hard drive. If it's a default style, you can reinstall it from the LiveMotion CD-ROM install disk. Otherwise, you're outta luck—you can't undo the Delete Style operation.

To remove a style from the Styles palette:

1. On the Styles palette, click on the style swatch or name that you want to remove.
2. Click the Delete Style (trash) button at the bottom of the palette.
3. Click Delete (or click Cancel if you get cold feet).

➤ LiveMotion updates the list of styles on the Styles palette when the program is launched and whenever a style is added to or deleted from the Styles palette.

➤ Styles are stored in the Adobe LiveMotion folder > Styles folder, and they carry the ".liv" extension to signify they are LiveMotion files.

➤ You can also permanently remove a style by dragging it from the Styles folder into the Desktop trash.

A softer approach

To remove a style from the list without permanently deleting it, drag it from the Styles folder into another folder. Move it back in when you need to use it.

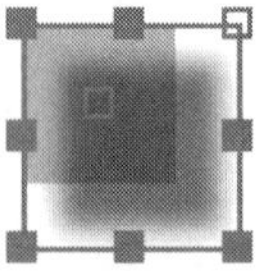

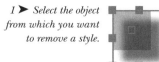

1 ➤ Select the object from which you want to remove a style.

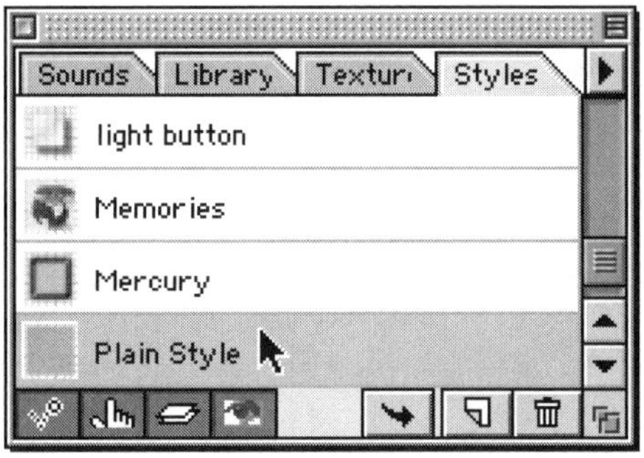

*2 ➤ Double-click the **Plain Style** on the **Styles** palette.*

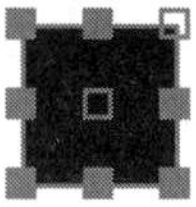

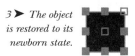

3 ➤ The object is restored to its newborn state.

Embellish 6

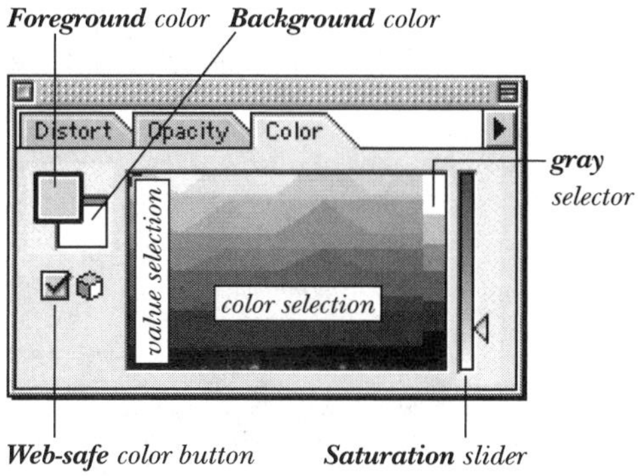

1 ➤ ***Saturation** View is organized by the purity (strength) of color (the presence or absence of gray).*

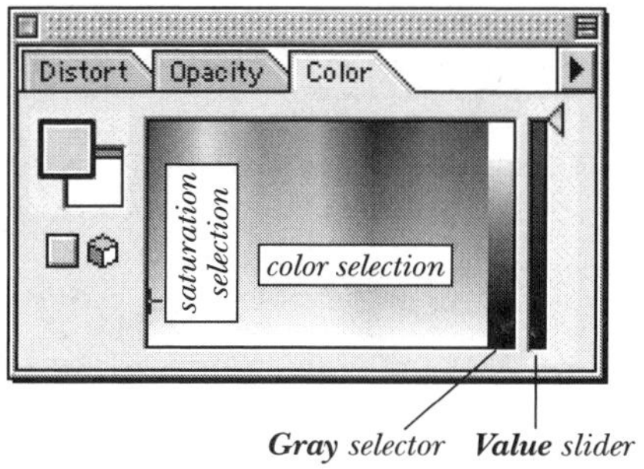

2 ➤ ***Value** View is organized by the lightness or darkness of color (the amount of black or white).*

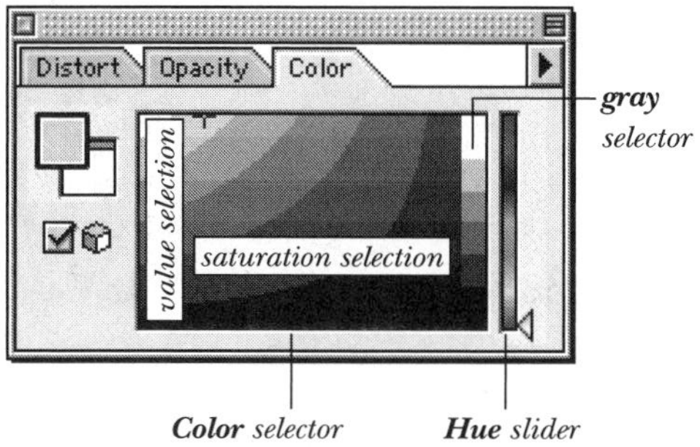

3 ➤ ***Hue** View is organized by the location of colors on the color wheel.*

Applying color

YOU'VE CREATED some objects and your composition looks, well, ho-hum. Here's your chance to stir things up, add some excitement. Objects can be embellished using any one or combination of these features:

- ➤ **Color** palette
- ➤ **Eyedropper** and **Paint Bucket** tools
- ➤ **Color Scheme** palette
- ➤ **Gradient** palette
- ➤ **Opacity** palette
- ➤ **Adjust** palette
- ➤ **Textures** palette (see Chapter 10)
- ➤ **3D** palette
- ➤ **Distort** palette
- ➤ **Photoshop Filters** palette (see pages 108–109)

Color for the Web

When it comes to color, Web designers have to work under some constraints, albeit different constraints than print-based designers work under. Before you learn how to play with all the buttons and dials on the Color and Color Scheme palettes, you'll need to learn a few rules and regulations.

Since you're creating elements for online output (a Web page), you won't be using process (CMYK) or spot colors (e.g., Pantone), nor will you be preparing your files for color separation. You will be working exclusively with combinations of **RGB** (red, green, and blue) colors, which are the colored lights that your computer monitor beams out at you. There are six **View** choices on the LiveMotion Color palette menu**: Saturation, Value, Hue, HSB, RGB,** and **CIE L**. The first four Views represent different ways to use the HSB color model; RGB and CIE L are their own color models. In LiveMotion, all the Views boil down to the same thing: RGB. That's because your artwork will never leave the on-screen environment. (Actually, all Web pages are ultimately translated into something called hexadecimal code, but you don't need to worry about that when you're using LiveMotion.)

Now, everything sounds fine and dandy until you learn that color display can vary dramatically among browsers, between the Mac OS and Windows platforms, and from monitor to monitor. The operating systems and browsers (e.g., Netscape Navigator, Netscape Communicator, Microsoft Internet Explorer) have only 216 colors in common. If you use a color that isn't available on all the browser palettes, the browser will substitute the nearest Web-safe equivalent color for the missing one, or it will dither (substitute) colors to simulate the missing color. This can make your graphics look quite different than you intended. For flat colors, your best bet is to choose from the 216 Web-safe colors. Click the **Web-safe color** button on the LiveMotion Color palette to limit the palette to only these colors (Fig. 2).

Textures and other bitmap images that contain gradual tonal changes (e.g., Photoshop images) fall into a different category. Dithering is acceptable in these types of images because it's less noticeable. (When you apply solid colors to objects in another application with the intention of importing them into LiveMotion, though, you should use a Web-safe color palette.) On pages 103 and 196, we discuss how to prepare Photoshop images for the Web. In Chapter 16, Export, we discuss how to optimize Web graphics so they will download as quickly as possible.

Another issue to be concerned with when you're choosing colors for a Web page is the fact that images look **darker** on a **Windows** machine than on a **Mac OS** machine due to the difference in gamma between the two platforms. In order to compensate for this discrepancy, you should be careful to avoid

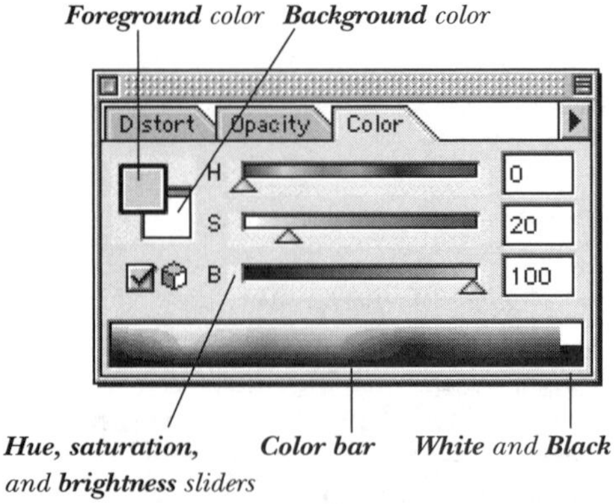

*1 ➤ **HSB** View is organized by a color's hue, saturation, and brightness values.*

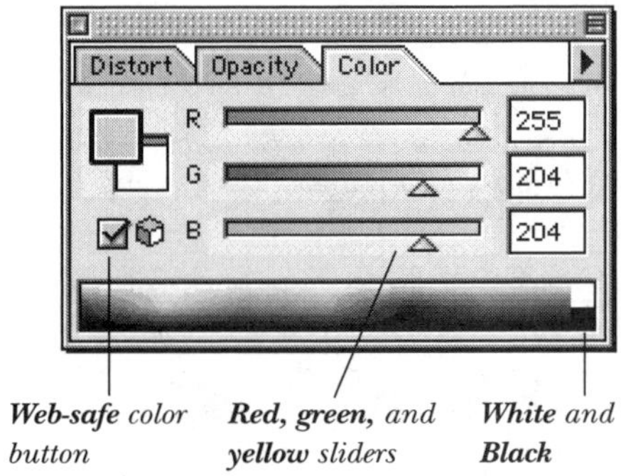

*2 ➤ **RGB** View is organized by the red, green, and blue additive colors. This is the model that's used to display color on a computer screen.*

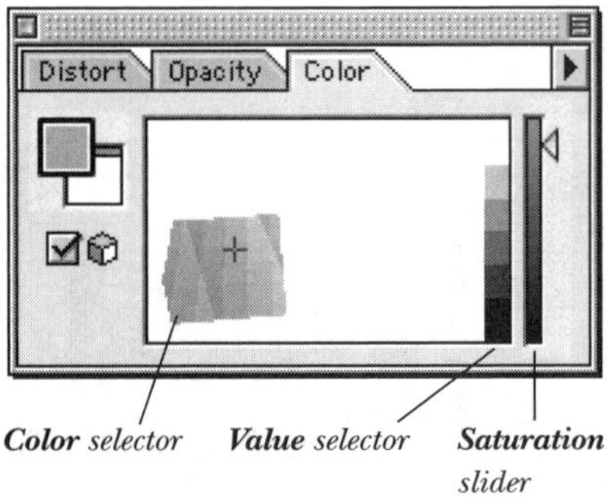

*3 ➤ **CIE L** View is organized by the gamut of visible colors that color monitors can display.*

Understanding color depth

Color depth (bit depth) is the number of bits used to represent the color of each pixel in an animation or still image. A **1-bit** image contains only black and white pixels; an **8-bit** image can contain a maximum of 256 colors; a **24-bit** image can contain a maximum of 16.7 million colors (also called "32-bit color" or "True Color"). Color depth is controlled by the amount of video RAM mounted on the video display card and the pixel resolution chosen for the card.

Why not create only 24-bit images for 24-bit monitors, since such images will be the sharpest and the smoothest and will have the most pleasing and accurate colors? Because many viewers use 8-bit monitors. As a Web designer, you can gear your artwork for the high-end viewer and accept the fact that your work will look especially poor on an 8-bit monitor or you can compromise and design with both 8-bit and 24-bit monitors in mind.

creating any dark or murky objects in LiveMotion. And to ensure that your judgments are sound, don't forget to preview your artwork in both browsers. If you have both platforms in your office, great. If not, we'll show you how to simulate both platform environments in Chapter 16. If your artwork looks a little on the dark side on a Windows machine or when viewed using a simulation of the Windows gamma, you should lighten it up. And make sure your graphics have a decent amount of contrast to help ensure that they look bright and sparkly—not dull—on the Web page.

- All images become 72 ppi resolution when they're imported into LiveMotion.
- LiveMotion's 3D, Distort, Tint (Adjust palette), and Gradient features can generate non-Web-safe colors and thus cause some dithering (color substitutions) to occur in the browser. Dithering is most noticeable in solid color areas and least noticeable in continuous-tone images. A dithered gradient may have noticeable bands of color instead of smooth color transitions. Objects with soft edge properties are exported from LiveMotion in a bitmap format, not a vector format. In this case, dithering won't be objectionable. You'll use the Export palette with its preview option to judge the best export format. And of course, preview your artwork in the browsers (yes, we know we're repeating ourselves).

A geometric object can be filled completely with a solid Foreground color, a gradient, or a texture, or it can be turned into an outline in which only the perimeter of the shape is filled with a color, a gradient, or a texture. This is an either/or situation—an object can't be an outline and have a fill simultaneously, and it affects all of an object's layers. We'll show you how to apply a texture or a gradient to a Fill or an Outline shape later on in this chapter.

Note: For now, the object will be filled with the current Foreground color, if Color is currently chosen from the "Fill with" drop-down menu on the Layer palette for the currently selected layer. To learn how to choose colors, see the following page.

To switch between the Fill and Outline properties:

1. Choose a selection tool, then select a geometric object (an object that was created using the Rectangle, Ellipse, Rounded Rectangle, Polygon, or Pen tool). The Fill and Outline options are not available for image or text objects.
2. Show the Properties palette (Window menu > Properties) (Fig. 1).
3. Click **Fill** to fill the object with the current Foreground color (Fig. 2).
   or
   Click **Outline** to turn the geometric shape into a ring or a donut (Fig. 3). The Outline option will make the center of the object's layers transparent. Move the Width slider to change the width of the outline in ¼-pixel increments (0–200).

➤ You can use Edit menu > Paste Special > Paste Properties to paste Properties palette settings from one object to another.

An outline is not a stroke

The Outline option on the Properties palette creates a shape with a **hole** in the center, like a donut or a ring. If you want to apply a stroke color to an object, add a new layer and **widen** the **layer** by an amount equal to the desired "stroke" width (see page 71).

*Change an **Ellipse** to a **Rectangle**, or vice versa, via this drop-down menu*

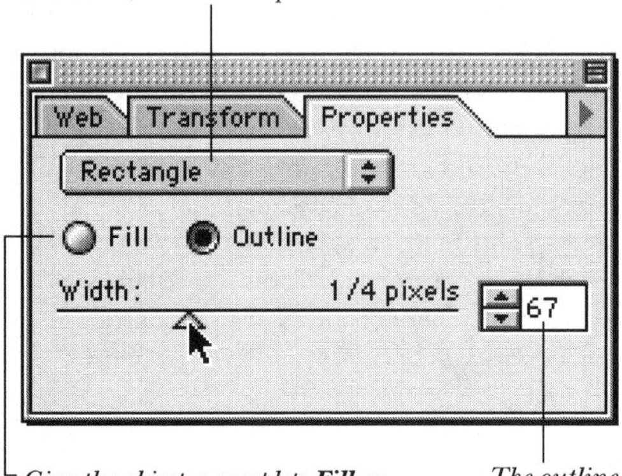

*Give the object a complete **Fill** or turn it into an **Outline** donut.*

*The outline **Width***

*1 ➤ The Properties palette when a **geometric** object is selected.*

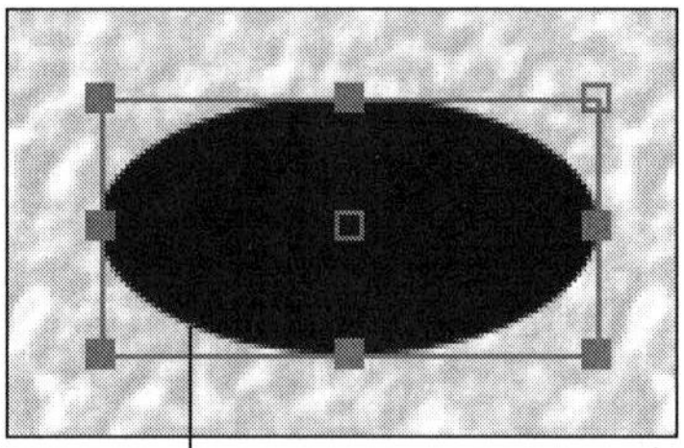

*2 ➤ This object has a **Fill** property.*

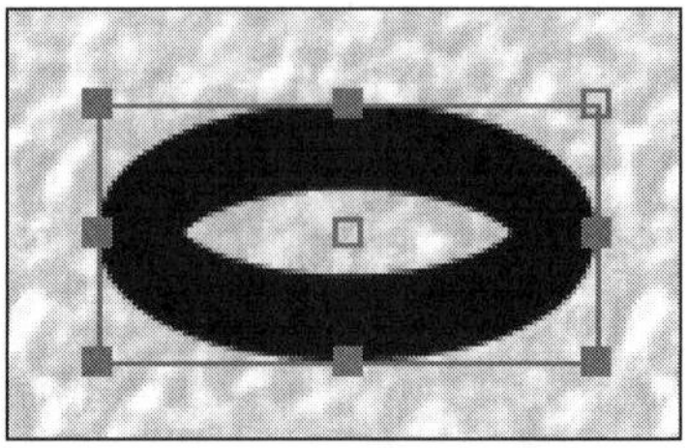

*3 ➤ Now the object has an **Outline** property.*

Understanding CIE L

The Color palette's CIE L View represents the gamut of visible colors that color monitors can display. As you move the vertical Saturation slider in CIE L View, the number and distribution of available colors changes. For example, reds are only available at medium saturation, while blue-greens are only available at high saturation. Out-of-gamut colors are represented by white (thus the white background on the Color palette).

***Foreground** color box* ***Background** color box* *1 ➤ Choose a **View** (color model) for the palette*

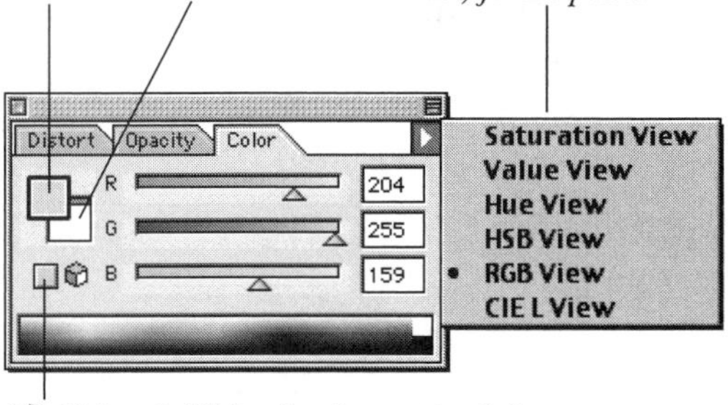

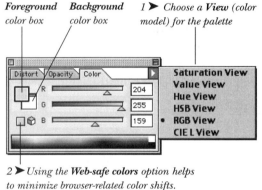

*2 ➤ Using the **Web-safe colors** option helps to minimize browser-related color shifts.*

At the bottom of the Toolbox and on the left side of the Color palette, you'll see two color boxes. The box in the upper left is the current **Foreground** color, which is applied to objects. The box on the lower right is the **Background** color, which is applied to the background of the overall composition.

To apply a solid color using the Color palette:

1. Show the Color palette (Window menu > Color).
2. Choose a selection tool, click on an object (not a texture or a placed image), choose a layer, then click the Foreground color box on the Color palette.
   or
   Click the Background color box on the Color palette.
3. If the selected layer is already filled with a texture or an image, choose Color from the "Fill with" drop-down menu on the Layer palette to restore its fill to a solid color. (If it contains a gradient, changing the Foreground color will change the starting color in the gradient.)
4. Choose a View (color model) for the Color palette from the palette menu (see the figures on pages 83–84) (Fig. 1).
5. Check the Web-safe colors box to force the palette display to only the 216 Web-safe colors (Fig. 2).
6. If the palette is in RGB or HSB View, drag the color sliders; or enter values in the fields adjacent to the sliders; or click on the color bar at the bottom of the palette.

   If the palette is in Saturation, Value, Hue, or CIE L View, move the vertical slider first, then click in the large rectangle.

➤ To lower the opacity of an object or a layer, use the Opacity palette. To lighten a color, use the Brightness slider on the Adjust palette.

➤ To recolor a layer containing a texture or a placed image, choose a color, then move the Tint slider on the Adjust palette.

Here we decribe how to use yet another of the selective Paste Special commands: Paste Fill. This command pastes the color, texture, or gradient attributes of a cut or copied object layer onto the selected layer of the currently selected object. It doesn't matter whether the object has a Fill or an Outline property.

To copy and paste fill attributes:

1. Choose a selection tool (V, U, A), select an object whose fill attributes you want to duplicate in another object, and don't forget to choose a layer for that object (Fig. 1).
2. Choose Edit menu > Copy (Command-C/ Ctrl-C). (Choosing Edit menu > Cut would remove the object.)
3. Select an object (or objects) and an object layer to which you want to apply the copied fill attributes (Fig. 2).
4. Choose Edit menu > Paste Special > Fill (Fig. 3). Or Right-click in the composition window and choose Paste Special > Fill.

➤ If more than one object was copied to the Clipboard, the fill attributes of the frontmost of the selected objects will be pasted.

*1➤ The object whose fill attributes are to be **copied** is selected, then Edit menu > **Copy** is chosen.*

*2➤ The object to which the copied attributes are to be **applied** is selected.*

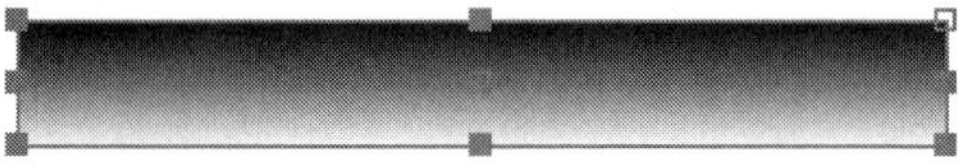

*3➤ Edit menu > **Paste Special** > **Fill** is chosen.*

The Eyedropper can be used simply to sample an existing color in your composition for use as a Foreground or Background color or it can be used to sample and apply color simultaneously. We'll show you how to do both. (To use the Eyedropper to sample and apply styles, see page 78.)

To sample a color using the Eyedropper:

1. If you want to apply the sampled color to an object, choose a selection tool, select the object, and select a layer for that object.
   or
   If you only want to sample a color (not apply it), deselect all objects (Command-Shift-A/Ctrl-Shift-A).

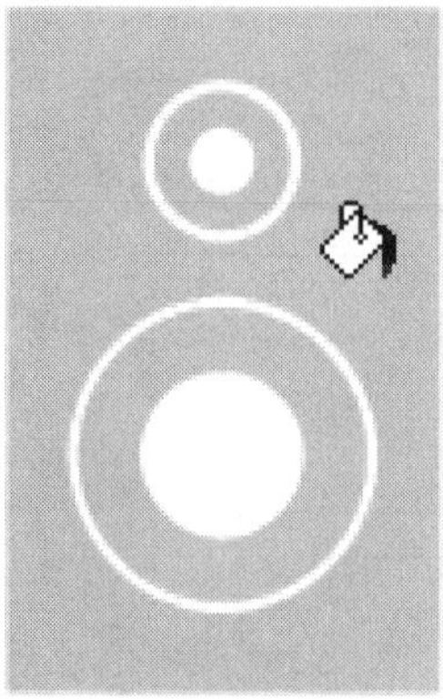

*1 ➤ After sampling or choosing a color, the **Paint Bucket** tool is positioned over the object to be recolored.*

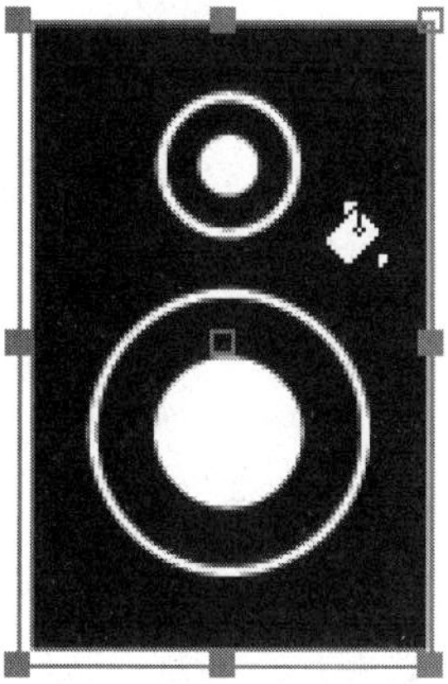

*2 ➤ After clicking with the Paint Bucket tool, the current **Foreground** color is applied to the object.*

2. Click the Foreground or Background color box on the Toolbox or the Color palette.
3. Choose the Eyedropper tool (I).
4. To sample a color, click or drag anywhere in the composition window. The sampled color will appear on Foreground or Background color box, whichever was selected for step 2, and in any objects that were selected.

➤ To sample a color on an layer other than an object's topmost layer, select the object first, choose the layer that contains the color you want to sample, then click on the object.

➤ To sample a color from outside LiveMotion, drag with the Eyedropper tool from a LiveMotion composition window to a spot on the Desktop or into an open window in another application.

To apply a solid color using the Paint Bucket:

1. Click the Foreground color square on the Toolbox or the Color palette, then choose a color using the Eyedropper tool or the Color palette.
2. Choose the Paint Bucket tool (K).
3. Click on an object. The color will be applied to the object's topmost layer (Figs. 1–2). The object doesn't have to be selected first—that's the whole reason for using the Paint Bucket tool.

➤ Click with the Paint Bucket on the background of the composition to apply the current Foreground color to the background.

Let's say you've created some terrific shapes, but you really don't know where to start as far as picking colors for them. The Color Scheme palette simplifies color selection by creating arrangements of swatches that work well together, like an interior decorator would compile an assortment of fabric or paint swatches for a client. The arrangements range from light to dark, vibrant to subtle.

To apply a color scheme:

1. Show the Color Scheme palette (Window menu > Color Scheme).
2. If the Lock button is pressed (dark), click it to unlock the palette (Fig. 1).
3. To establish a starting color for the Color Scheme palette, choose a color using the Eyedropper tool or the Color palette. That color and related colors will appear on the Color Scheme palette.
4. From the menu at the right side of the palette, choose the Triangles or Honey Comb swatches arrangement (Fig. 2).
5. Choose the number of colors you want the palette to display (2–6).
6. Select the object(s) and an object layer to which you want to apply a color.
7. Click a swatch on the Color Scheme palette or at the bottom of the Toolbox (Fig. 3).

   Note: Each time you click a swatch, the palette becomes locked.
8. Just to experiment, click any of the dots on the circle on the left side of the dialog box, or rotate the circle. The colors on the swatches will shift.

   and/or

   Click a different color wheel relationship button. The dots represent the basic hues. The first button distributes the colors equally around the color wheel; the other buttons collect the colors into primary or complementary color groups. The button choices will vary depending on how many colors the palette is currently displaying.

Trust thy self (or thy friend)

Color preferences are very subjective. Color combinations that appeal to an Adobe programmer may not look harmonious to you. Trust your instincts or those of a designer whose skills you have confidence in. And by all means **preview** it in the browsers!

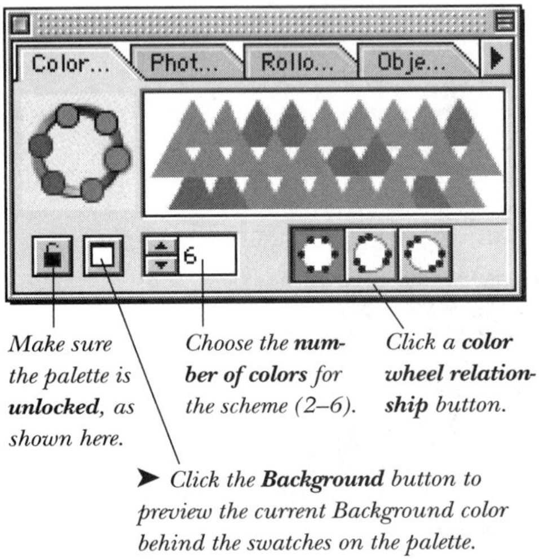
Color...
Phot...
Rollo...
Obje...
6
*Make sure the palette is **unlocked**, as shown here.*
*Choose the **number of colors** for the scheme (2–6).*
*Click a **color wheel relationship** button.*
➤ *Click the **Background** button to preview the current Background color behind the swatches on the palette.*

*1 ➤ The **Color Scheme** palette in **Triangles** view.*

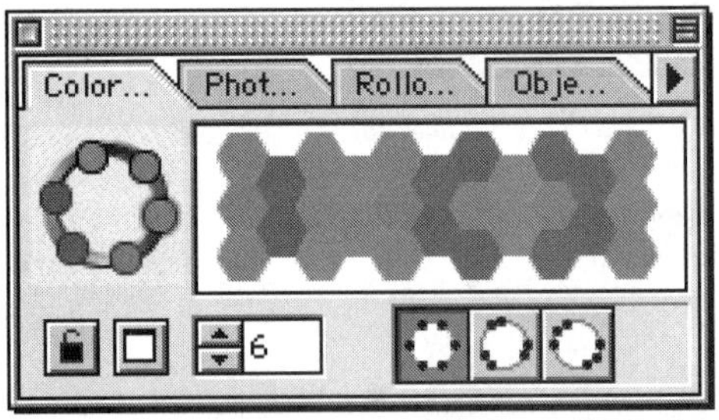
Color...
Phot...
Rollo...
Obje...
6

*2 ➤ The **Color Scheme** palette in **Honey Comb** view.*

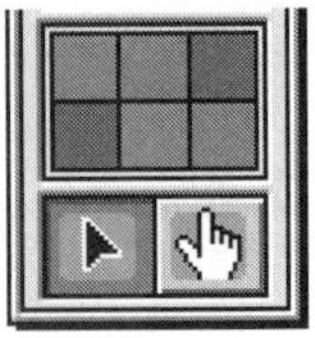

*3 ➤ The **Color Scheme swatches.***

1 ➤ Choose a ***gradient type*** *from the pop-up menu.*

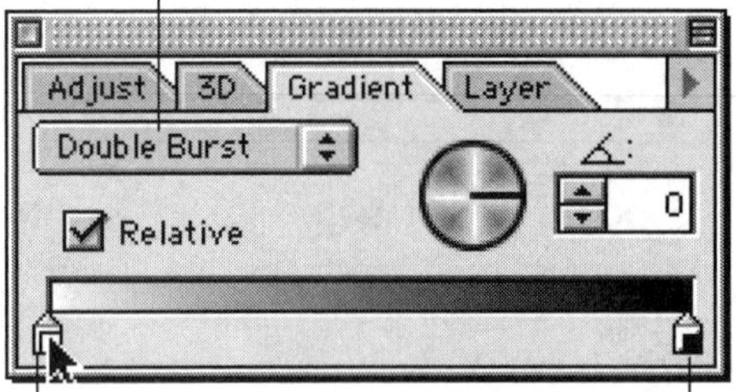

Click the ***start*** *marker and choose a color.*

Then click the ***end*** *marker and choose a color.*

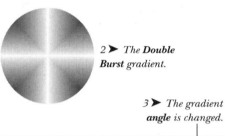

2 ➤ The ***Double Burst*** *gradient.*

3 ➤ The gradient ***angle*** *is changed.*

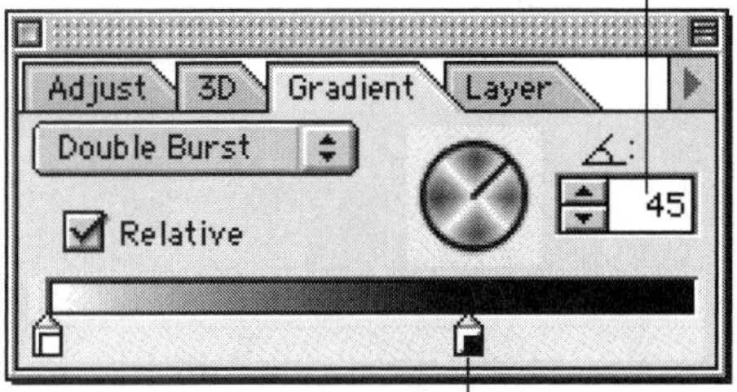

4 ➤ And the right marker is moved to the left.

5 ➤ After changing the gradient ***angle*** *and moving the right marker.*

6 ➤ To create this object, a texture was applied to layer 1, a linear gradient was applied to layer 2 (90°), and the opacity of layer 1 was lowered.

A gradient is a soft blend from one color to another. Gradients help to give objects depth and volume. In LiveMotion you can create a gradient using only two colors. You can use two different hues or you can use different saturation or brightness levels of the same color.

Note: To minimize download stress, make your gradient objects small. And make them vertical—not horizontal. Vertical gradients download faster. When you export a gradient, use the SWF or JPEG format, but not GIF.

To apply a gradient:

1. Choose a selection tool, click on an object, and choose a layer for that object.
   or
   Select the background by clicking the Background color box on the Toolbox or the Color palette.
2. Show the Gradient palette (Window menu > Gradient), then choose a gradient type from the pop-up menu: Linear, Burst, Double Burst, or Radial (Figs. 1–2).
3. Click the color gradient start marker under the gradient bar (Fig. 1), then choose a starting color for the gradient via the Color palette (or click on a color in the composition window with the Eyedropper tool).
4. Click the color gradient end marker under the gradient bar, then choose an ending color.
5. *Optional:* Change the gradient angle by dragging the bar in the preview circle; by clicking the up or down arrow; or by entering an angle (Fig. 3).
6. *Optional:* Move the left and/or right marker to change the location where that color begins (Figs. 4–6).

➤ To prevent the gradient from rotating if the object is rotated, choose Object menu > Transform > Shape Transforms, uncheck the Relative box on the Gradient palette, then Rotate the object. (Reselect Shape Transforms when you're ready to turn it off.)

➤ On a 256-color (8-bit) display, gradients will have noticeable color bands.

Adjusting color

In LiveMotion, the Adjust palette is used for making basic brightness, contrast, or saturation adjustments to object or background colors. Because these changes are made via a palette, they're super-easy to readjust.

Note: Use the Adjust palette to color adjust a texture, gradient, bitmap image, or other continuous-tone area. You can use the Adjust palette to adjust a solid color, but you can just as easily apply different solid color via the Color palette.

To adjust a color's brightness, contrast, or saturation:

1. Choose a selection tool, click on an object, and choose a layer for that object (Fig. 1).
2. Show the Adjust palette (Window menu > Adjust) (Fig. 2).
3. Do any of the following:

   Change the Brightness (-255–255). The higher the Brightness, the lighter the color (the more white it contains) (Fig. 3).

   Change the Contrast (-128–128) (Fig. 4).

   Change the Saturation (-128–128). The higher the Saturation, the more pure the hue (the less gray it contains).

➤ Hot tip: To ensure that an object's color is still Web-safe after adjusting its Brightness, Contrast, or Saturation, select the object, check the Web-safe color box on the Color palette, choose the Eyedropper tool (I), then click on the object.

1 ➤ The original ***placed*** *image.*

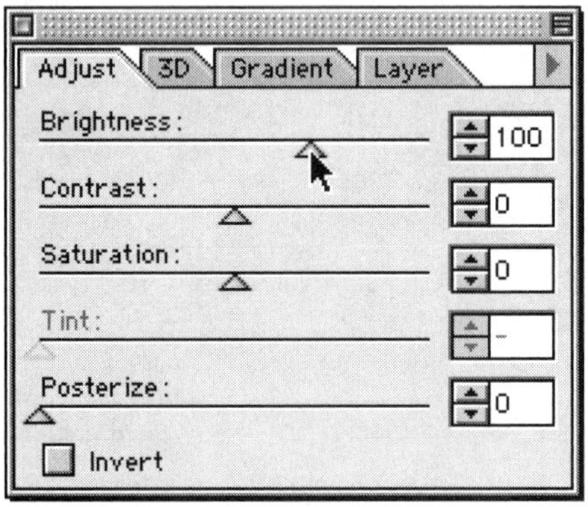

2 ➤ The ***Adjust*** *palette is used as a color adjustment tool.*

3 ➤ After increasing the image ***Brightness*** *to 67.*

4 ➤ After increasing the image ***Contrast*** *to 119.*

*1 ➤ The original **placed** image.*

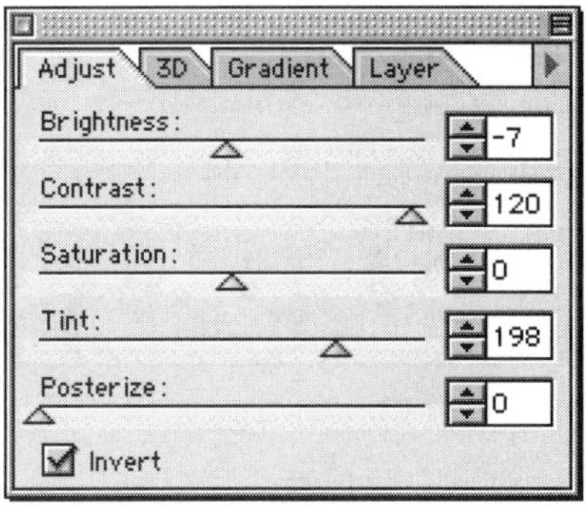

*2 ➤ The **Adjust** palette.*

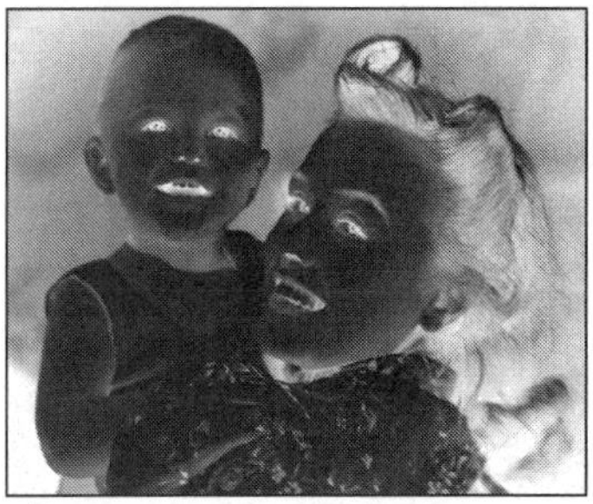

*3 ➤ After the **Invert** box is checked.*

*4 ➤ The original image, after **Posterizing** to 6 levels.*

A tint can be applied to an image object or to a texture in an object or the background, but not to a solid color or a gradient. *Note:* To switch between the fill options for a layer, use the "Fill with" pop-up menu on the Layer palette.

To apply a tint:

1. Choose a selection tool, click on an object, and choose a layer of that object.
2. Click the Foreground color box on the Color palette or the Toolbox, then choose a Foreground color using the Color palette or the Eyedropper tool.
3. Show the Adjust palette (Window menu > Adjust).
4. Change the Tint value (0–255 percent). The higher the Tint value, the more of the current Foreground color will be **added** to the object's fill (Fig. 2).

➤ Try also raising or lowering the Saturation of the object or the layer.

The Posterize command reduces the number of color values in an object. The Invert command converts each color into its opposite, thus creating the appearance of a film negative.

To posterize or invert colors:

1. Choose a selection tool, click on an object, and choose a layer for that object (Fig. 1).
2. Show the Adjust palette (Window menu > Adjust).
3. Check the Invert box to convert each object color into its opposite color on the color wheel (e.g., red will become cyan) (Figs. 2–3).
   and/or
   Choose a Posterize value (1–30). The object's color values will be reduced to exactly that number (Fig. 4).

Applying 3D effects

Depth, softness, and lighting are the elements that create an illusion of three dimensionality. These properties can be customized for each of the four preset 3D effects.

To apply 3D effects:

1. Select an object and a layer for that object.
2. Show the 3D palette (Window menu > 3D).
3. From the pop-up menu, choose **Cutout**, **Emboss**, **Bevel**, or **Ripple** (**None** applies no effect) (Figs. 1–10).
4. Choose a **Depth** value (0–40 pixels) for the distance between the edge of the layer and the most intense part of the effect. Try a low Depth for an edge Bevel; try a high Depth for a pyramid bevel.
5. Choose a **Softness** value (0–10). The higher the Softness, the greater the gaussian blur (smoothing) of the effect.
6. Choose an overall **Lighting** value (0–200). The higher the Lighting value, the greater the contrast in value.
7. Choose an **angle** for the light: click on the circle; move the dial; enter an angle; or click the up or down arrow. 0° lights an object from the right; 90° lights it from the top; 180° lights it from the left; and 270° lights it from the bottom.
8. Choose an **Edge** setting: Straight, Button, Plateau, or Ripple. This option is not available for the Cutout effect.
9. Choose a **Light** type:

   Normal to apply neutral lighting, highlights, and shadows.

   Light Only to apply only neutral lighting and highlights but no shadows.

   Dark Only to apply only neutral lighting and shadows but no highlights.

Pasting light and volume

Use Edit menu > **Paste Special** > **Effect** to paste 3D palette settings from one object to another. The objects will have the same amount of three dimensionality and will be lit from the same angle.

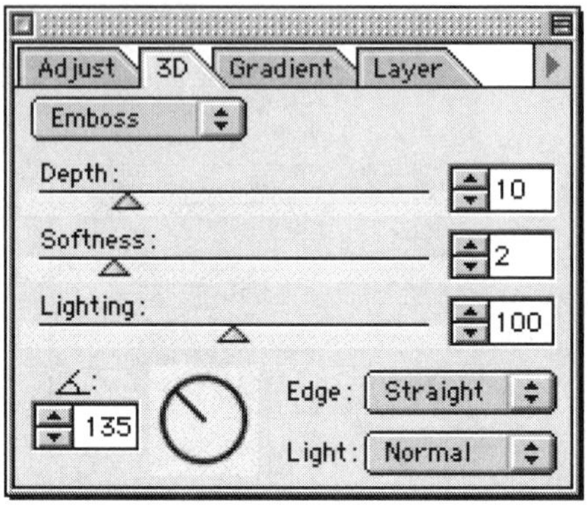

*1 ➤ The **3D** palette.*

*2 ➤ **Emboss**, Edge: **Straight**.*

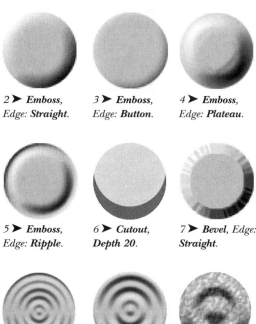

*3 ➤ **Emboss**, Edge: **Button**.*

*4 ➤ **Emboss**, Edge: **Plateau**.*

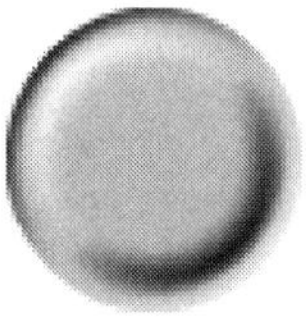

*5 ➤ **Emboss**, Edge: **Ripple**.*

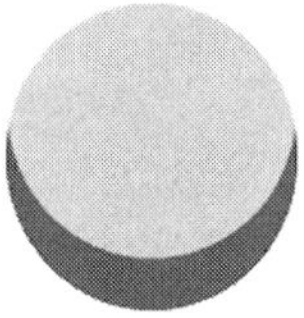

*6 ➤ **Cutout**, **Depth 20**.*

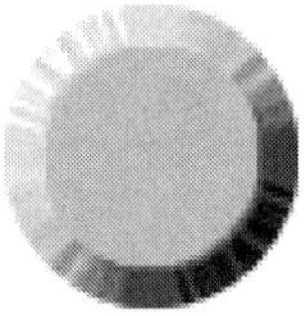

*7 ➤ **Bevel**, Edge: **Straight**.*

*8 ➤ **Ripple**, **Depth 6**.*

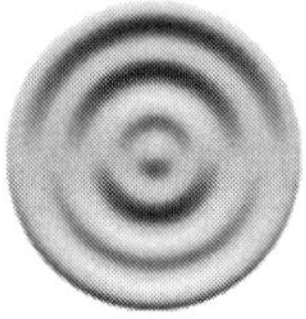

*9 ➤ **Ripple**, **Depth 9**.*

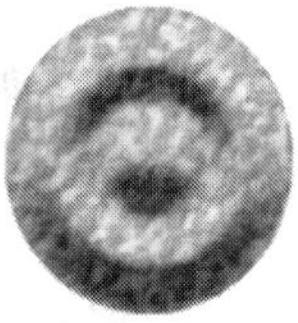

10 ➤ A Ripple layer (layer opacity lowered) on top of a texture layer.

1 ➤ *The original object.*

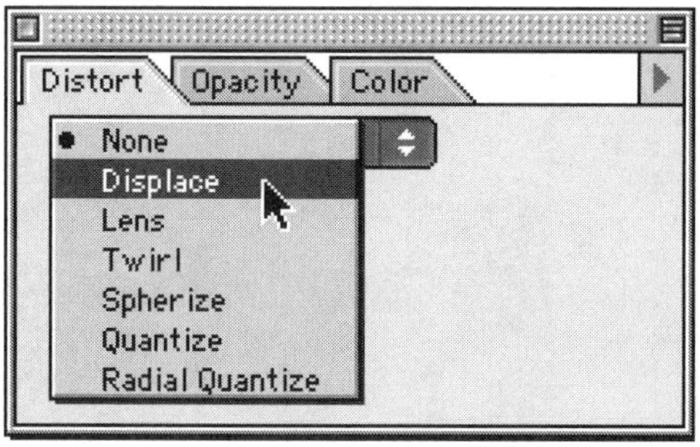

2 ➤ *Choose a distortion type from the **Distort** palette.*

3 ➤ ***Displace.***

Applying distortion

The Distort palette is used to apply various image-editing effects to a placed bitmap image, a texture fill or outline, or a background texture. The Distort commands have no effect on solid colors. Twirl and Spherize are worth trying on a gradient.

To apply distortion:

1. Select a placed bitmap image (Fig. 1).
   or
   Select an object and a layer that contains a texture fill or outline.
   or
   Click the Background color square on the Color palette or the Toolbox to distort a background gradient or texture.
2. Show the Distort palette (Window menu > Distort).
3. From the pop-up menu, choose one of the following (Fig. 2):

   Displace to shift the fill (Fig. 3). Choose a Distance in pixels for the degree of displacement, and choose an Angle.

   Lens to magnify or shrink the fill (Fig. 4). Change the Angle to rotate the texture or image.

   Twirl to twirl the fill around the vortex like a tornado (Fig. 5). Move the Turns slider further from zero to intensify the effect or closer to zero to lessen the effect. A positive Turns value will produce a clockwise twirl; a negative Turns value will produce a counterclockwise twirl. Change the Band Size to make the swirls more or less delineated.

(Continued on the next page)

4 ➤ ***Lens.***

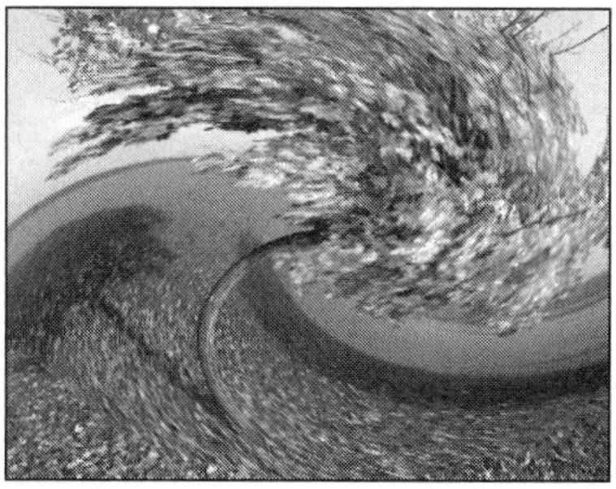

5 ➤ ***Twirl.***

Spherize to wrap the fill onto a sphere (Fig. 1). Change the Magnification to change the degree to which the image or texture is enlarged in the center of the sphere. Change the Amount to lessen or intensify the degree of distortion.

Quantize to fracture the fill into mosaic-like tiles (Fig. 2). The higher the Size value, the larger the tiles.

Radial Quantize to fracture the fill into concentric bands radiating outward from the center (Fig. 3). The higher the Size value, the wider and more obvious the bands and the more distorted the image or texture.

None applies no effect.

➤ To make a fish-eye "lens" to use as a still image or an object in an animation (e.g., in the tutorial that starts on pages 156–157), first create a circle object and apply a Drop Shadow style to it. Choose Fill with: Background on the Layer palette. On the Distort palette, choose Twirl: Turns 10–17, Band Size 0, or choose Spherize: Magnification: 120, Amount: 25. You can also apply a 3D Emboss to the object to accent its edges. Place the circle on top of an image object (choose Arrange menu > Bring to Front, if necessary). Move the circle object back and forth across the image object to see how the "lens" effect works (Fig. 4).

1 ➤ Spherize.

2 ➤ Quantize.

3 ➤ Radial Quantize.

4 ➤ A moveable "lens."

Text 7

Creating text for the Web

IN LIVEMOTION, you can create text that runs horizontally or vertically. The typographic attributes of an existing text object (e.g., font, point size, kerning, alignment) can be easily edited any time via the Type tool dialog box or the Properties palette.

In addition to editing typographic attributes, you can also edit the object attributes of type. For example, you can add layers to a text object, apply a style to it, transform it, or recolor it (Fig. 1).

Creating text for online viewing poses different challenges than creating text for print output. Here are some tips for choosing typographic attributes to help you make your Web pages as legible as possible:

Size matters
Use a larger point size than you would normally choose for print output. Between 10 and 15 points is generally a good size range to work with for body copy.

Serif or sans serif
Choose sans serif fonts for longer text passages and serif fonts for headlines and other short passages. In LiveMotion, you'll primarily be creating short passages.

Fonts
Choose typefaces that are easy to read. For legibility's sake, the less uniform the characters, the better. That means clearly defined ascenders and descenders and distinct character shapes. Save that delicate script face for your friend's bridal shower invitation.

Knowing where to click
Back in the early days of Web design (say, a few years ago), hypertext links were traditionally denoted with underlining. Nowadays

(Continued on the next page)

Typography lingo

Points are the measurement units that are used to measure type sizes in LiveMotion. Twelve points equals one **pica**; six picas equals one inch. The letter "p" is used to denote picas (4p5 would signify four picas and five points). In a 72-ppi image, one point is equal to $^1/_{72}$ of an inch.

Serif fonts have little lines that project from each character; **sans serif** fonts have none. The type you're reading is sans serif (Myriad Roman). The main body type in the column to the right is a serif font (New Baskerville).

Anti-aliasing is the addition of pixels along the edges of shapes or text characters to reduce their jagginess (stair-stepped-ness) and make them look smoother. LiveMotion automatically turns on anti-aliasing for type. There is some debate about whether anti-aliasing is desirable or not for text that's going to be displayed on a Web page. We think it should be turned off only for small type, but then you shouldn't be creating small type for Web pages anyway—it's too hard to read.

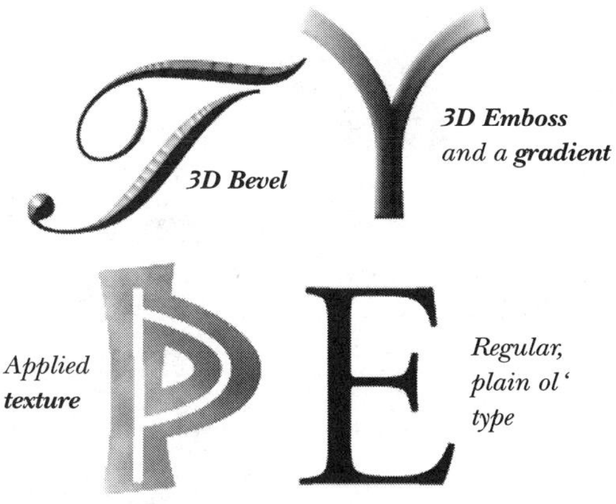

1 ➤ A text object can be embellished like any other object.

other methods are used, such as larger point sizes or boldface (as well as graphic markers like buttons or rollovers). Italics, all caps, and small caps are hard to read (both in print and on the Web), so use them in small quantities, if at all.

Letterspacing
Be careful not to track characters too tightly, or they will be hard to read. In fact, a little extra positive tracking can help make text easier to read in a browser (not so for print output). You cannot kern between a pair of characters in LiveMotion; you can only track a whole text object.

Column width
Avoid making columns of text that span the whole browser window. Reading across a wide span is tiring, especially on screen. The smaller the point size, the narrower the column should be.

Embellishing
When you're ready to embellish the text, don't sacrifice legibility for the sake of a favorite special effect. Legibility and artistry should go hand in hand. In fact, they are the trademarks of all successful graphic design, whether on screen or in print.

Preview preview preview
Preview your composition online in all the major browsers (e.g., Internet Explorer and Netscape Communicator). In LiveMotion, use File menu > Preview In. Pretend you're the viewer, and ask yourself, is the interface easy to use? Are the text objects easy to read? It's annoying enough to have to wait for images to download. Don't add text that's a struggle to read to the mix!

➤ Look for OpenType in the near future. It's a text file format developed by Adobe and Microsoft that allows fonts to be embedded right onto Web pages. With OpenType, viewers will be able to see Web pages in the designer's font of choice, not in a substitute font.

Are fonts needed?

In order to choose a particular font in LiveMotion, it must be installed in your system. Let's say you style text in a particular font in LiveMotion, but that font is unavailable when you reopen the file. LiveMotion will substitute another font when the document is reopened (you'll get an alert dialog box), and that substitution will become permanent as soon as you resave the file. If you make a font available after LiveMotion is already launched, you must relaunch the application in order to make LiveMotion recognize it.

But what happens to your text when it gets to the browser? The font you used is embedded into the export file and will display correctly when the HTML file is loaded even if it's unavailable in the viewer's system. (See also "OpenType" on this page.)

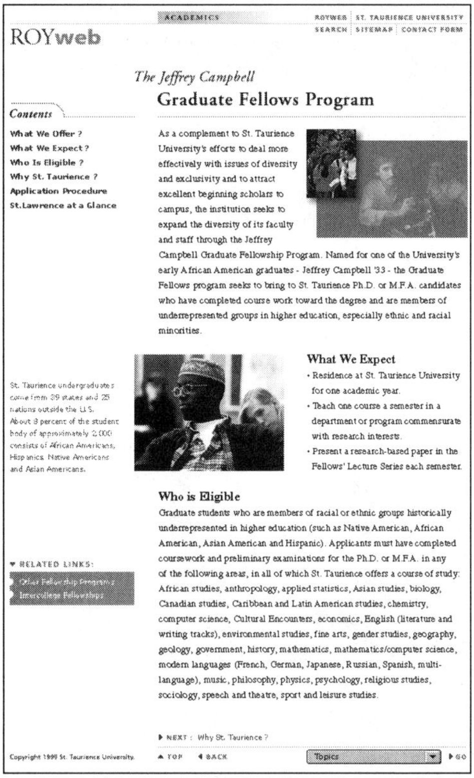

Web site designed by Newfangled Graphics

Selecting text in the Type Tool dialog

- ➤ Drag over the text you want to select
- ➤ Click at the beginning of the string of words that you want to select, then Shift-click at the end of the string
- ➤ Double-click within a word to select only that word
- ➤ Use Command + A to select all the text in the dialog box (Macintosh only)

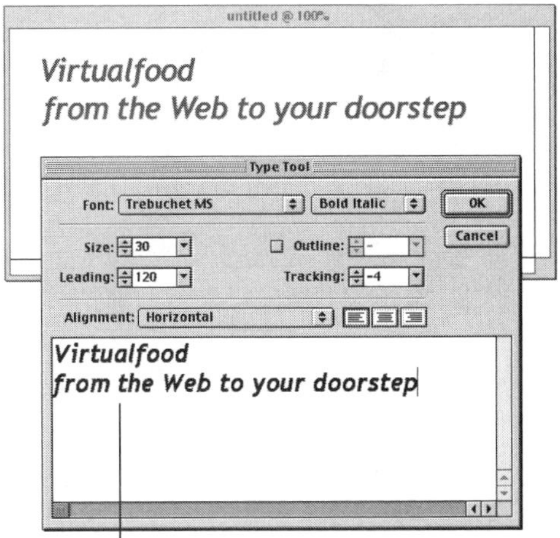

1 ➤ The only typographic attribute that will preview in the dialog box is the font. Watch the ***preview*** *in the* ***composition*** *window instead.*

2 ➤ ***Alignment: Horizontal, left.***

3 ➤ ***Alignment: Horizontal, right.***

To add text to a composition:

1. Choose the Type tool (T) **T**.
2. Click on a blank area of the composition. The text object can be moved later on.
3. Type into the large field in the dialog box (Fig. 1). Press Return/Enter, when necessary, to create a line break as you type. Click the up or down arrow to navigate upward or downward through lines of text.

   If you make a mistake, click directly to the right of the character you want to remove, then press Delete/Backspace. Or select a text string, then press Delete/Backspace.
4. As you choose attributes in the Type Tool dialog box, watch as the text previews in the composition window, not in the dialog box:

   Font (typeface design) and **style** for that font, if available (e.g., the Myriad font in the Bold Italic style).

   Size (1–999 points).

   Leading (the vertical spacing between baselines for multiple lines of text, measured as a percentage of the point size).

   Tracking, the horizontal letterspacing between each character in the text object (-50–5000 of an em space). The higher the tracking value, the wider the spacing.

   Alignment, choose an orientation option from the pop-up menu, then click the left, center, or right button (Figs. 2–3).

   Optional: Check the **Outline** box, then enter a width (1–100 in quarter-pixel units). Outline works only for TrueType and PostScript fonts. The characters will have a stroke and a transparent fill.
5. Click OK (or press Enter on the keypad only).

➤ You can drag-and-drop text into a LiveMotion composition or copy and paste it from another LiveMotion composition. A text object from another application will become an image object in LiveMotion, which means its typographic attributes will no longer be editable; it will only be editable as a graphic.

You can't change the font, point size, or other attributes of individual characters or words in a text block—it's all or nothing. If you need mixed attributes, create separate text objects for them.

To edit a text object:

METHOD 1

Use this method to edit the text itself and/or change its typographic attributes.

1. Choose the Type tool (T), then click **directly** on a type character.
   or
   Choose the Selection tool (V), then double-click the text object.
   or
   Click the text object, then press Return/Enter.
2. To change typographic attributes, follow step 4 on the previous page.

   To add or delete characters, use the standard word processing moves: click to create an insertion point; press Delete to delete the currently selected text or the character to the left of the insertion point. To select text for editing, see the sidebar on the previous page.

METHOD 2

Use this method if you only need to change typographic attributes.

1. Choose the Type tool or a selection tool.
2. Click on the text object.
3. Change any type attributes using the Properties palette (Window menu > Properties) (Fig. 1).

➤ To move a text object, treat it like any other LiveMotion object.

To resize text interactively:

1. Choose a selection tool (V, U, or A).
2. Click on the text.
3. Drag a corner handle (except the handle in the upper right corner) inward or outward (the pointer will become a four-headed arrow). Shift-drag to constrain the proportions of the text (Figs. 2–4).

Asian fonts

Japanese, Korean, or Chinese double-byte text can be created if the proper system software and LiveMotion module is installed. Double-byte text must be created in its own object; it cannot be mixed with English text.

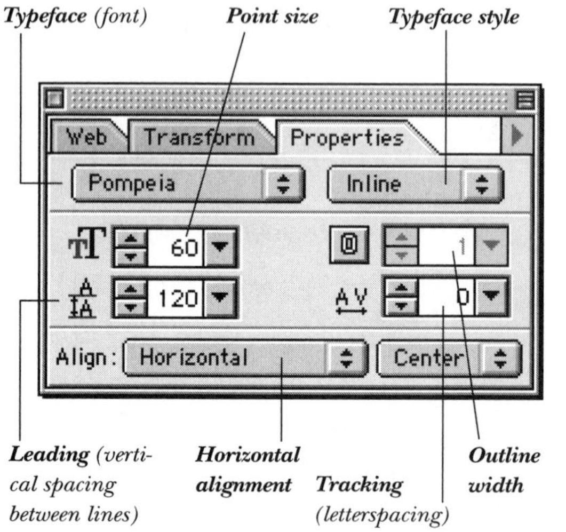

*1 ➤ The **Properties** palette when a **text** object is selected.*

2 ➤ Dragging a corner handle of a text object.

*3 ➤ The text will resize **proportionally** if you hold down **Shift** as you drag.*

*4 ➤ Dragging a side handle upward **without** holding down Shift. The text is extended (it's now wider than it is tall).*

Acquire Images 8

1 ➤ *The original object.*

2 ➤ *After using the* ***Replace*** *command, the new object (a flower image) replaces the original object. The 3D Bevel and shadow layer from the original object are preserved, but not the shape.*

3 ➤ *After using the* ***Place as Texture*** *command on the original object, the texture is applied to the object's selected layer (in this case, the topmost). The original object's shape, 3D Bevel, and shadow layer are preserved.*

Acquiring images

AS WE SAID EARLIER, three types of objects are created in LiveMotion: geometric objects, text objects, and image objects. In this chapter we focus on the methods used for acquiring imagery from other applications. In most cases, imported graphics become image objects in LiveMotion, regardless of whether they were vector or bitmap objects in their original application. Exceptions are noted.

These are the methods for acquiring images in LiveMotion:

The commands under the **Import** submenu are used to scan directly into LiveMotion from a TWAIN-compatible device. The object becomes an image object.

The File menu > **Place** command embeds an image from another application into a LiveMotion composition. The imported image becomes an image object.

The File menu > **Replace** command replaces an object in a LiveMotion composition with the imported image. The style of the original LiveMotion object is applied to the replacement object (Figs. 1–2).

The File menu > **Place as Texture** command places an image as the overall background texture in a LiveMotion composition or as a replacement fill in a selected object's selected layer (see page 126).

The Edit menu > **Paste** command pastes imagery into a LiveMotion composition via the Clipboard (the Copy or Cut command). If you paste an object from another application, it will become an image object. If you paste solely within LiveMotion, the object type won't change.

(Continued on the next page)

Each of the Edit menu > **Paste Special** commands pastes a particular category of attributes. In this chapter we discuss the Paste Image command. Other Paste Special commands are discussed elsewhere in this book.

Use File menu > **Place as Sequence** to import a series of consecutively numbered files generated in a 3D modeling or animation program for use as an animation sequence (see page 194).

And finally, the **drag-and-drop** method can be used to drag a file icon directly into a LiveMotion composition window. Any file that can be imported via the Place command can also be acquired using drag-and-drop.

Placing

The Place command will place a vector or bitmap graphic into the current LiveMotion composition as a new image object. File formats that can be placed include EPS, sequenced EPS, GIF, animated GIF, Illustrator up to version 8, JPEG, PICT (Mac OS), PNG, TIFF, Photoshop (PSD), and LiveMotion. You cannot place or replace a CorelDraw, Macromedia FreeHand, or (WMF) Windows Metafile. Illustrator 9 objects can be drag-and-dropped or copy/pasted into LiveMotion.

Note: Only files in RGB or grayscale mode can be placed (not files in CMYK, Bitmap, Indexed, or Lab color mode).

To place a file into a LiveMotion composition:

1. With a LiveMotion file open, choose File menu > Place (Command-I/Ctrl-I).
2. *Optional:* Click Show Preview, if the file preview is hidden.
3. Locate and highlight the name of the file you want to place, then click Open (Return/Enter) (Figs. 1–2).

➤ If a file name fails to appear on the scroll list in the Place dialog box, it means the file is saved in a format that LiveMotion cannot place. Go back to the program in which the image was created, re-save it in one of the formats listed above, then try placing it again.

LiveMotion to LiveMotion

You can place one LiveMotion file into another LiveMotion file. The file will place as a group of objects. You can build a complex composition using smaller parts from other compositions this way.

*1 ➤ A file is located in the **Place** dialog box.*

*2 ➤ The **placed image** appears in the center of the LiveMotion composition window.*

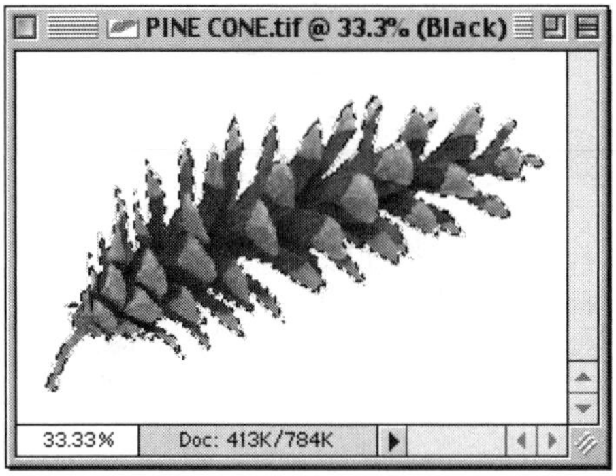

*1➤ The image is selected in Photoshop, and saved as an **alpha channel** (Select menu > Save Selection).*

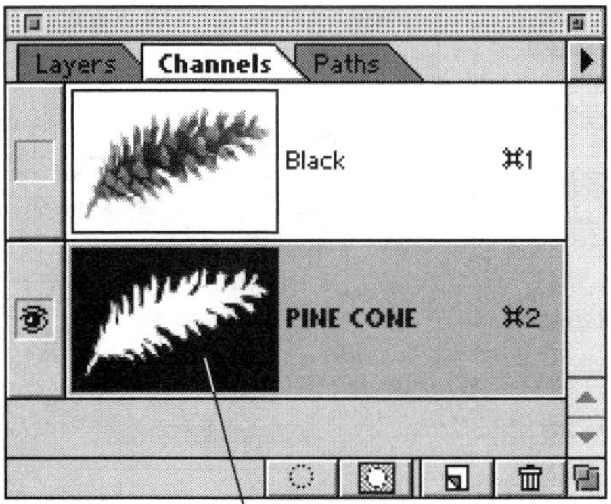

*2➤ This is what the alpha channel looks like on the Photoshop **Channels** palette.*

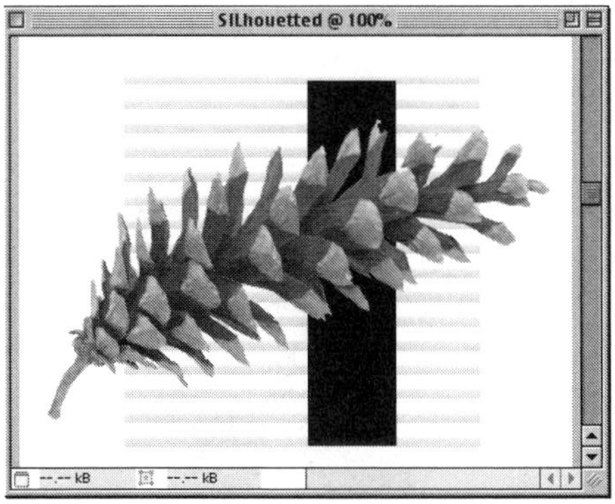

*3➤ The pine cone image is placed into LiveMotion. Its **background** is **transparent**, so other LiveMotion objects are visible underneath it.*

Photoshop to LiveMotion

In order for LiveMotion to place or replace a Photoshop image, do the following in Photoshop:

- Make sure the image has a **non-transparent Background layer**, not a Layer 0. (Choose Layer menu > New > Background if you need to create the background layer.) The file can contain multiple layers.
- Create an **alpha channel** if you want to silhouette any shapes. Make sure the alpha channel has a black background and a white silhouette (Figs. 1–3).
- If the file is in a **color mode** other than RGB (e.g., CMYK color or Indexed color), convert it to RGB.
- A **multi-layered** file from Photoshop or another application will be flattened into a one-layer object when it's placed in LiveMotion. Once it's placed, though, you can use Object menu > Convert Layers Into > Objects or Group of Objects to convert each layer into a separate object (see pages 192–193).
- When a layered Photoshop file is placed into LiveMotion as a composite, **one-layer** object, all opacity, adjustment layer, layer effect, layer mask, and blending mode effects are preserved. If you apply any Convert Layers Into command to the placed file, however, those effects will be nullified. If you need to preserve effects on a placed image, leave the object as one layer in LiveMotion—don't convert it into separate objects. You'll have more flexibility if you apply effects in LiveMotion rather than in Photoshop (e.g., opacity changes, opacity masks, shadows, 3D).
- **Filters** can be applied in either Photoshop or LiveMotion. Photoshop offers more filters than LiveMotion, but in LiveMotion you have the power to hide or remove individual filter effects.

Replacing

The Replace command places vector or bitmap graphics onto the currently selected layer of the currently selected object. The replacement image is sized automatically to fit within the current selection border of the selected layer and the object's contour is changed to fit within the shape of the newly placed imagery. Replace converts **all** objects, whether vector or bitmap, into **image** objects.

The main reason to use the Replace command instead of another import method is that when it's used to fill an existing LiveMotion object with new imagery, the object's original styling is preserved. This speeds up updating when you need to edit image objects. Say, for example, you import a Photoshop image into LiveMotion and then apply a style and a texture to it. If you edit the image in Photoshop and then Replace it in LiveMotion, the original style and texture will apply to the new image.

Note: LiveMotion can only Replace files in the EPS, sequenced EPS, GIF, animated GIF, Illustrator (8.0 and earlier), JPEG, PICT (Mac OS), PNG, TIFF, Photoshop (PSD), and LiveMotion format.

To replace an object with a placed image:

1. Select the object or objects that you want to replace with an image and choose a layer (Fig. 1).
2. Choose File menu > Replace (Command-Shift-I/Ctrl-Shift-I).
3. Locate and highlight a file name, then click Open (Return/Enter) (Figs. 2–3). Any transformations, effects, or styles that were previously applied to the selected layer will be applied to the replacement image.

➤ If a file name fails to appear in the Place dialog box, then the file is saved in a format that LiveMotion cannot place. Re-save it in the EPS, TIFF, GIF, JPEG, PNG, PICT (Mac OS), or Photoshop format, then try placing it again.

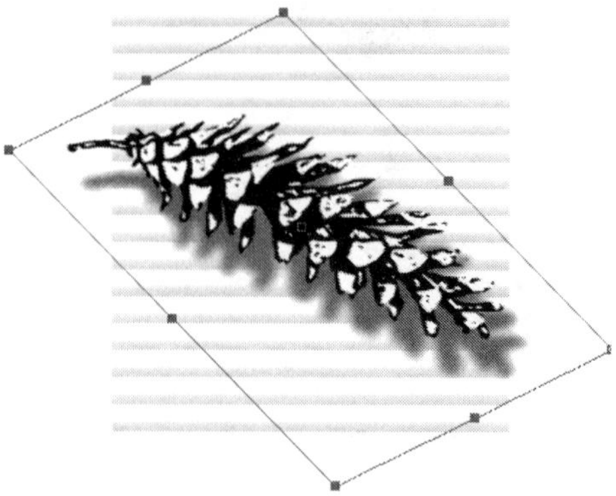

1 ➤ An object is selected. This object was skewed and rotated; the Object menu > Filters > Sketch > Stamp filter was applied to it; and a shadow layer was added (widened, softened, and offset).

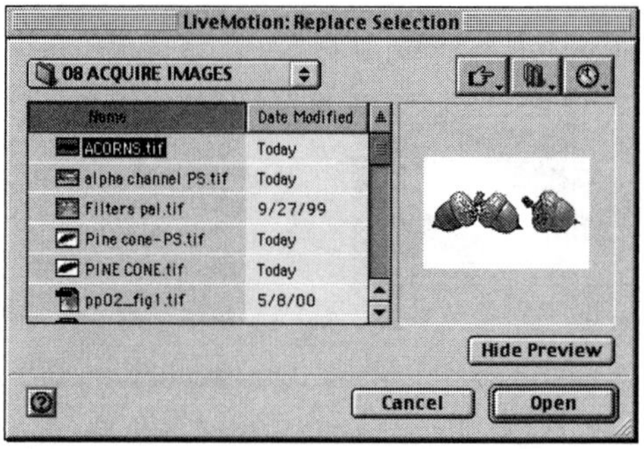

*2 ➤ A file is located in the **Replace Selection** dialog box.*

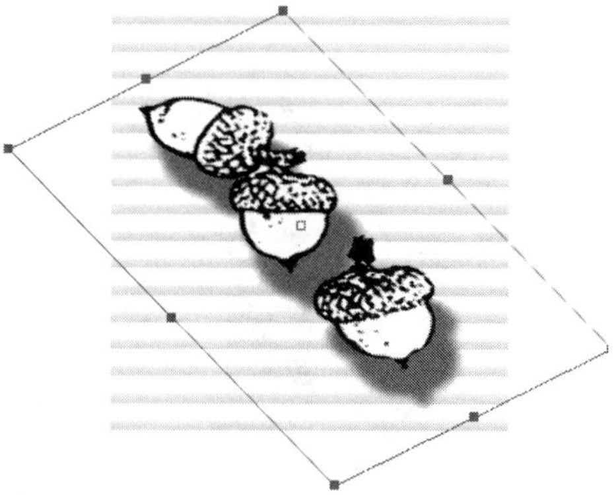

*3 ➤ The selected object is **replaced** with another image. The transform, filter, and layer effects from the pine cone are applied to the replacement object (the acorns).*

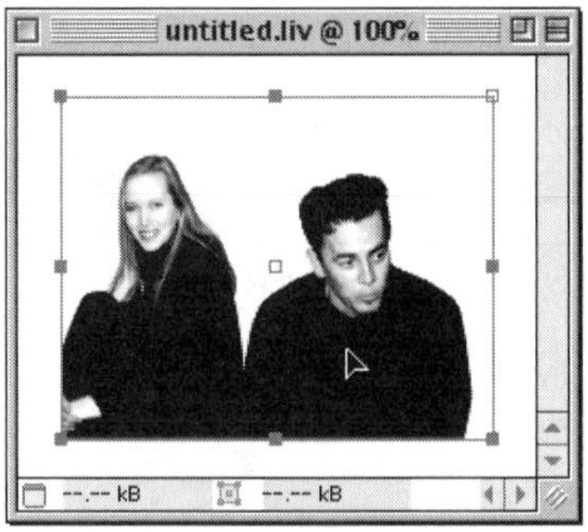

1 ➤ An image object is copied in a composition.

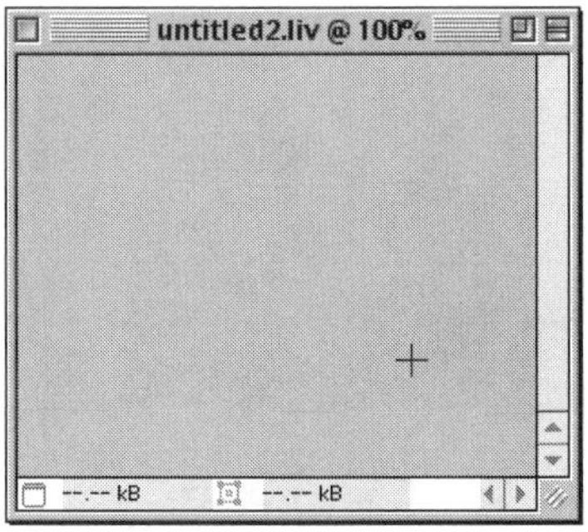

2 ➤ The pointer clicks in another composition window.

*3 ➤ After choosing Edit menu > **Paste**.*

Using the Clipboard

The Paste command pastes the contents of the Clipboard (an area of temporary memory) into a LiveMotion composition as an object. The Clipboard can be used to copy an object between LiveMotion compositions or from another application into LiveMotion.

LiveMotion will paste the following file formats: EPS, PICT (Mac OS), ASCII, RTF, and Photoshop (PSD). You can even copy text from a page layout program and paste it into LiveMotion, where it will become a new, editable text object.

To paste an image as a new object:

1. In a LiveMotion composition or in a window in another application, select the object or objects you want to copy (in a bitmap application, create a selection) (Fig. 1).
2. Choose Edit menu > Copy (Command-C/ Ctrl-C).
3. Click in the LiveMotion composition window into which you want to paste the copied object (Fig. 2).
4. Choose Edit menu > Paste (Command-V/ Ctrl-V) (Fig. 3).

➤ If you copy and paste a selection from Photoshop, it will become an image object in LiveMotion. Alpha channels from a Photoshop image won't paste, though. If you need to import an object with an alpha channel in order to give it a transparent background in LiveMotion, use the Place command instead.

The Paste Image command can be used to paste an image from another program directly into a selected layer of a Live Motion object. The Paste command, in comparison, produces a new object.

Note: When you use the Paste Image command, the shape of the object into which you paste will change to that of the pasted image; the contour of the original LiveMotion object will be lost. The pasted object will turn into an image object, if it isn't already.

To paste an image into an existing object:

1. Select the object or objects that you want to copy in a vector application or create a selection in an image-editing application (Fig. 1).
2. Choose Edit menu > Copy (Command-C/Ctrl-C).
3. Click in the LiveMotion composition window into which you want to paste the copied object.
4. Select an object and choose a layer for that object (Fig. 2). (If you don't do this, the image will be pasted as a new object.)
5. Choose Edit menu > Paste Special > Paste Image.
   or
   Windows only : Right-click in the composition window and choose Paste Special > Paste Image. The image will be cropped, if necessary, to fit within the current object layer's selection border (Fig. 3).
6. *Optional:* If the pasted image is cropped by the object, you can move the image inside the box or enlarge the box using the Crop tool.

➤ Use Paste Image to rasterize a LiveMotion object so that Photoshop filters or a Tint can be applied to it.

One at a time

A LiveMotion object can only hold one pasted image at a time. If you paste an image onto a layer and then paste another image into another layer in the same LiveMotion object, the first image you pasted will also be replaced by the new one. To layer multiple images, use the Paste Special > Paste Texture command on individual selected layers.

1 ➤ An object is selected and copied.

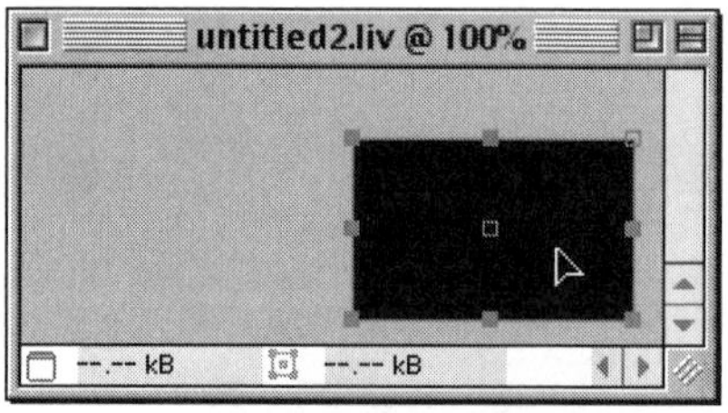

2 ➤ An object is selected in another composition.

*3 ➤ Edit menu > **Paste Special** > **Paste Image** is chosen. The image is cropped automatically.*

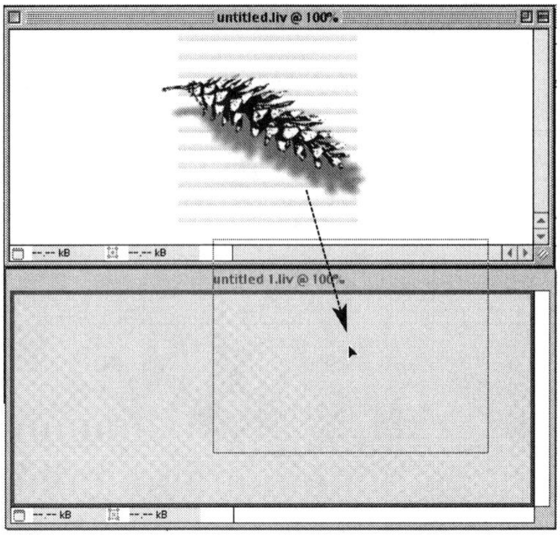

1 ➤ *If you* ***drag*** *an object or group from one LiveMotion composition to another...*

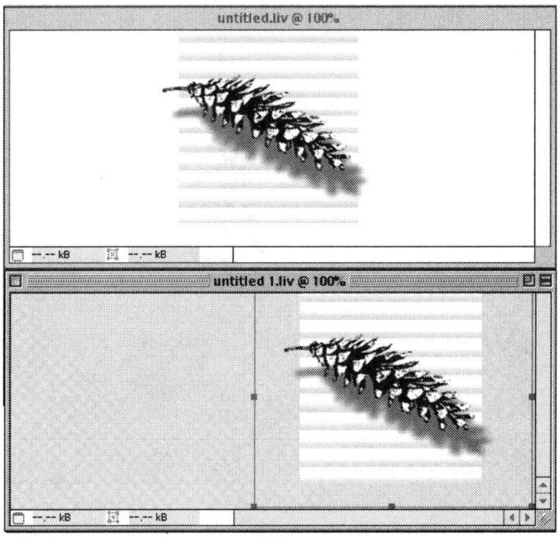

2 ➤ *...a* ***copy*** *of the object or group is made automatically.*

Drag-and-drop

Any file that can be acquired via the Place or Paste command can also be acquired via the drag-and-drop method. There are many ways to use drag-and-drop:

- ➤ Drag-and-drop an object or objects from one **LiveMotion** window into another LiveMotion window (Figs. 1–2).
- ➤ Drop an object from an open document window in another application right on **top** of a LiveMotion object. The dropped image will replace the existing object.
- ➤ Drop **text** from another application into a LiveMotion composition window. It will become a new image object (not a text object). Text from Microsoft Word version 98 or later will drop as a text object.
- ➤ Drop a LiveMotion **file icon** from the Desktop into an open LiveMotion composition window. The composition you drag and drop will be placed as a group.
- ➤ Drag-and-drop a LiveMotion object into another application (e.g., Adobe Photoshop, Adobe Illustrator, or Microsoft Word).

To drag-and-drop an image:

1. Move and/or resize the source and destination windows so they're both visible on screen.
2. Choose a selection tool, then in LiveMotion or in another application, select the object or objects you want to drag-and-drop.
3. Drag the desired object into a LiveMotion window. The object will be copied automatically. Not everything in life is complicated.

Photoshop filters

Photoshop filters can only be applied to placed bitmap image objects. Once a filter is applied to an object, the filter name will be listed on the Photoshop Filters palette when that object is selected. You can apply an unlimited number of filters to the same object. In fact, you can achieve some beautiful effects by combining them. Are you ready for the fun part? Filter effects are editable after they're applied, and each filter can be turned off and on individually (see the following page).

To apply a Photoshop filter:

1. Select the placed bitmap image or images to which you want to apply a filter (or filters) (Fig. 1).
2. Choose a filter name from the Object menu > Filters submenu.
   or
   Windows only: Right-click in the composition window and choose from a submenu on the Filters menu.
3. Choose settings for the filter (Fig. 2). (For an illustrated compendium of Photoshop filters, see our Photoshop or Illustrator Visual QuickStart Guide. Maybe a ratty old copy of one of those books is lying around your office somewhere.)
4. Click OK (Return/Enter) (Fig. 3). The filter name will appear on the Photoshop Filters palette (Fig. 4).

Do it again

To apply the last-applied filter to a different object, select the object and then choose Filter menu > **Apply Last Filter** (Command-F/Ctrl-F).

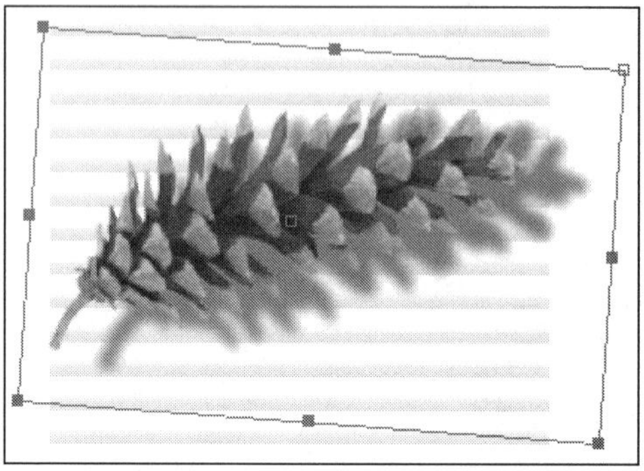

*1 ➤ An **image** object is selected.*

*2 ➤ The **Stamp filter** is applied.*

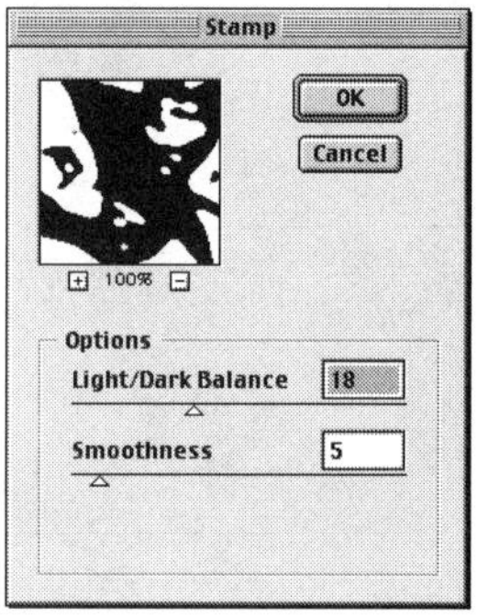

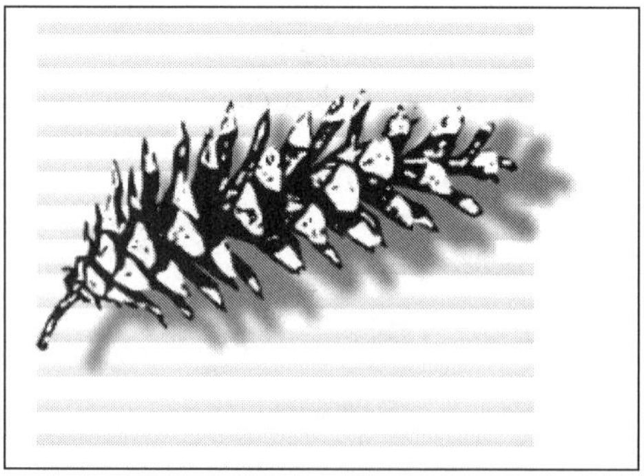

*3 ➤ After applying the **Stamp** filter.*

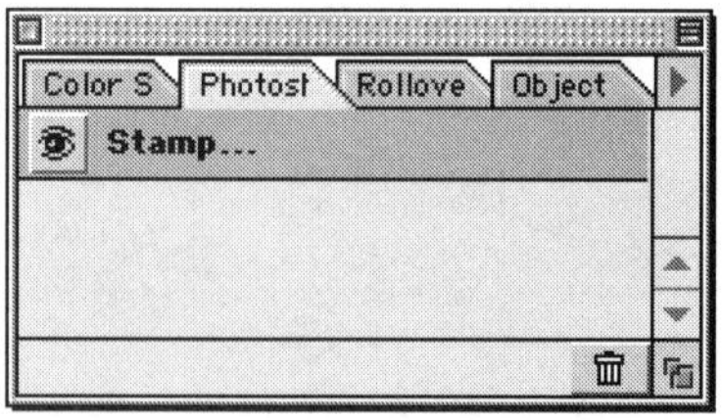

*4 ➤ "Stamp" appears on the **Photoshop Filters** palette. (Note: If the Photoshop Filters palette is still in its default group, you won't see the full palette name at the top; you will only see "Photosh.")*

*1 ➤ The **Grain** and **Accented Edges** filters are applied to this object.*

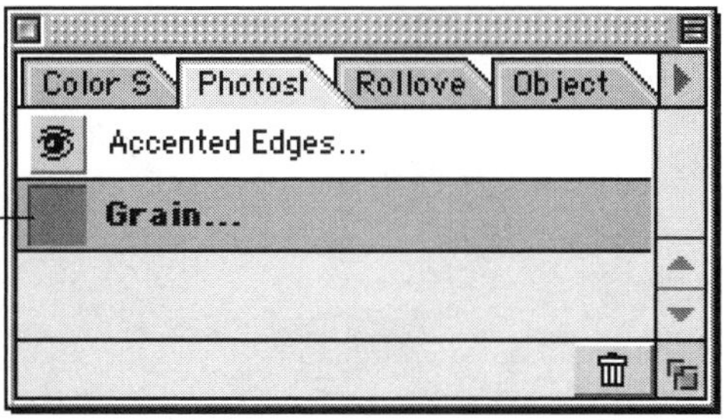

*2 ➤ The **Grain** filter effect is turned **off**.*

*3 ➤ The **Accented Edges** filter is still in effect.*

Here's the fun part we mentioned before: You don't have to undo an applied filter and then reapply it in order to adjust settings for it. All you have to do is double-click the filter name on the palette and fiddle with the dials.

To change the way a filter is applied:

1. Select the image to which the filter you want to edit is already applied.
2. Show the Photoshop Filters palette, then double-click the filter name on the Photoshop Filters palette.
3. Adjust the settings, then click OK (Return/Enter).

Here's another great feature of the Photoshop Filters palette: You can turn any individual, applied filter completely on or off faster than you can say "LiveMotion."

To turn a filter effect on or off:

1. Select the image to which the filter you want to turn on or off is applied (Fig. 1).
2. On the Photoshop Filters palette, click the eye icon next to the filter name (the eye will disappear) (Figs. 2–3). Click in the same spot to restore the filter effect (the eye will reappear). This may take a few seconds to process, even on a fast machine.

To remove a filter effect altogether:

1. On the Photoshop Filters palette, select the name of the filter that you want to delete.
2. Click the Delete Filter (trash) button.

Using alpha channels

Here's a theoretical dilemma. You've got a picture of a cow with a landscape behind it that you created in Photoshop. You want to drop the original background out so you can place the cow on top of a textured or solid-colored background in your LiveMotion composition. Who you gonna call?

Nobody. Select the cow, save the selection as an alpha channel, save the file, then place the image in LiveMotion. (Does "alpha channel" sound like something from Star Trek? Sorry to disappoint. It's just a grayscale channel that's used for saving selections and creating transparency.) Finally, choose Use Alpha Channel from the Properties palette. LiveMotion will drop out the landscape using the image's alpha channel.

➤ When you create an alpha channel for an image in Photoshop, make sure the alpha thumbnail on the Channels palette shows a white image on a black background.

Solution number two: Have LiveMotion build an alpha channel for an image object. Caveat: LiveMotion can do this only if the background in the image object is white or very light. Warning: Build Alpha From Image will probably change the current light and dark values in the image object. This diminishes its usefulness, to say the least.

To use an alpha channel with an image object:

1. Select an image object.
2. Show the Properties palette (Window menu > Properties).
3. On the Alpha Channel pop-up menu:

   Use Alpha Channel will be chosen automatically if the placed image was saved with an alpha channel in its original application (Figs. 1–3). *Note:* This option can be turned off if you don't need it and turned back on any time you need it (see the last tip on the following page).

   or

   Build Alpha From Image should be chosen if you want LiveMotion to create an

*1 ➤ Choose **Alpha Channel: Use Alpha Channel** or **Build Alpha From Image**.*

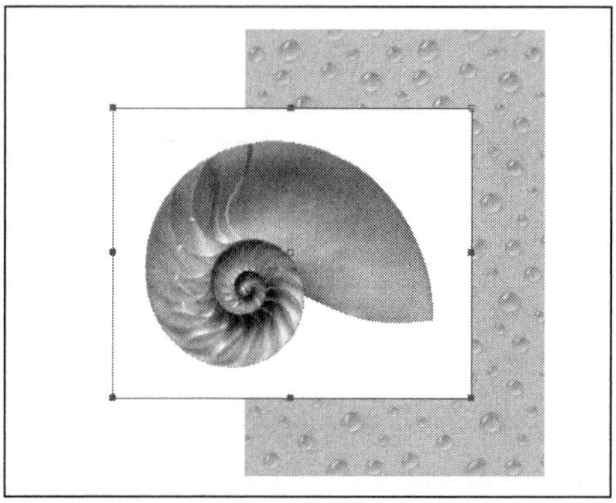

*2 ➤ **No Alpha**. The white area of the image obscures the gray pattern bar behind it, which is another object in the LiveMotion composition.*

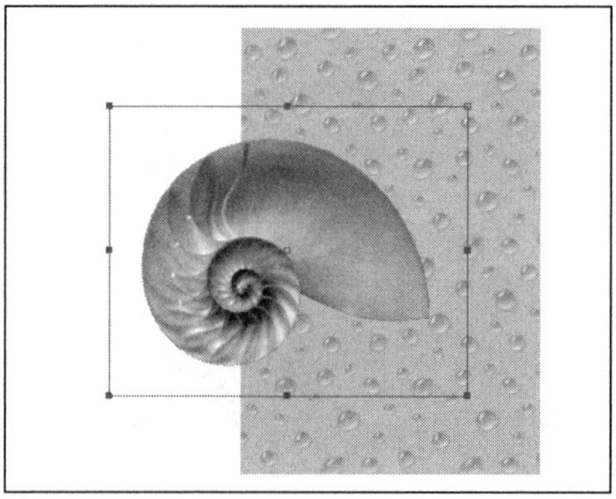

*3 ➤ **Use Alpha Channel** (in this case, the channel that was saved with the shell image in Photoshop). The background of the shell image becomes transparent.*

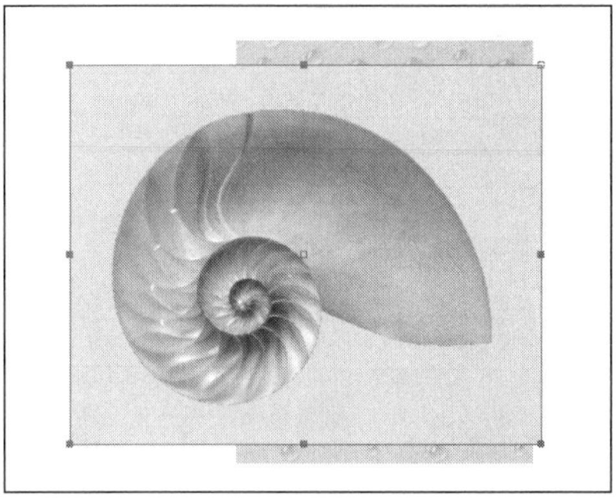

*1a ➤ The background of this placed image is **12% gray**.*

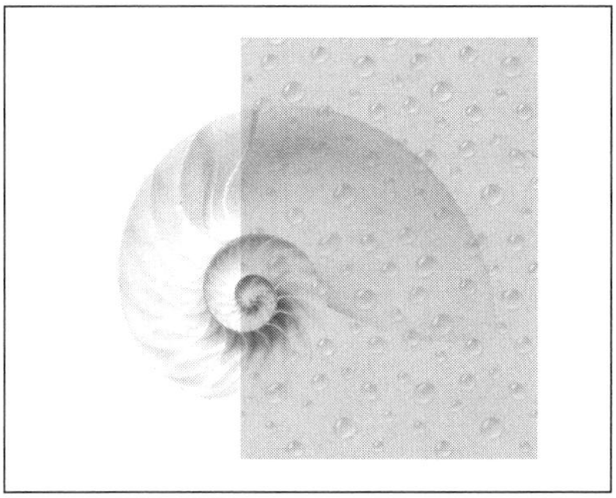

*1b ➤ The **Build Alpha From Image** option dropped the gray out—and also changed the luminosity values in the image.*

alpha channel for the image object (Figs. 1a–2b). LiveMotion will create the channel based on the object's luminosity (lightness) values. In order to do this, it maps each color in the image object to a corresponding value on a theoretical grayscale ramp. High color values (values near the white end of the black-to-white ramp) will become transparent; midtones will become semi-transparent; dark tones will remain opaque. Choose this option to have LiveMotion remove a white or very light background from an image object.

➤ Choose Alpha Channel: No Alpha to have LiveMotion ignore any alpha channel that was saved with a placed image. The whole placed image will be visible.

*2a ➤ The background of this placed image is **29% gray**.*

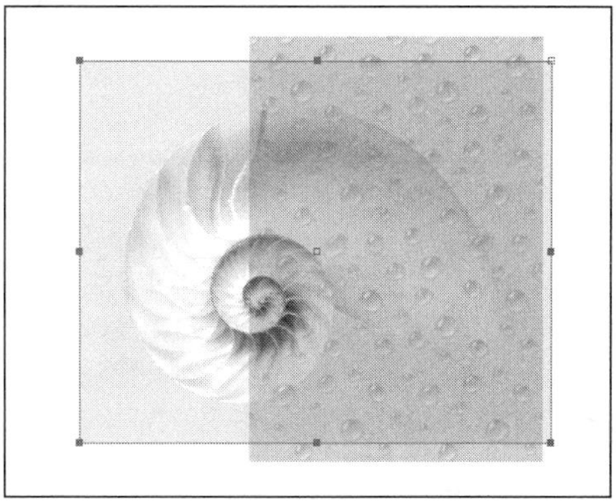

*2b ➤ After choosing **Build Alpha From Image**. The **gray doesn't drop out** and the luminosity values in the image are altered. This is a lose-lose situation.*

Scanning

We'll be honest with you. We're not wild about the idea of scanning directly into LiveMotion. It's direct and it's fast, but scans usually need tonal and color cast adjustments, color correction, sharpening, or retouching, and LiveMotion lacks features for performing most of those tasks. You can use LiveMotion's Adjust palette to adjust an image object's brightness, contrast, or saturation, but that's about it. (The Tint slider on the Adjust palette, by the way, is used for applying a tint, not for color correction.) Pixel editing just isn't LiveMotion's forté.

So what's the alternative? Scan the image in another application, touch it up, make it look nice (e.g., in our old friend Photoshop), and then import it into LiveMotion as a bitmap image object. Follow the instructions below only if you lack access to another application for scanning.

Note: In order to scan into LiveMotion, the scanner's own LiveMotion compatible plug-in module must be in the Plug-ins folder inside the Adobe LiveMotion folder or the scanner must support the TWAIN specifications and interface. The TWAIN module is automatically installed in the Plug-ins > Acquire Export folder when LiveMotion is installed.

To choose a TWAIN scanning module the first time you scan in LiveMotion:

1. Choose File menu > Import > Twain-Select Source (MacOS)/TWAIN_32 Source (Windows).
2. Choose a TWAIN device (the scanner), then click OK/Select.

To scan using a TWAIN scanner:

1. Choose TWAIN-Acquire (MacOS)/ TWAIN_32 (Windows).
2. Pre-scan, crop, and scale the image following your scanner manufacturer's guidelines; set the scanning resolution; then scan the image.

Plugging in

- The Import submenu will list whichever import plug-ins are currently residing in the Plug-ins > Acquire Export folder inside the Adobe LiveMotion folder. Each plug-in is designed to be used for a particular file format.
- If you need to install a plug-in, be aware that some plug-ins can be dragged directly into the Plug-ins folder while other plug-ins must be installed using their own installers in order to become available in LiveMotion.
- If your scanner doesn't have a LiveMotion-compatible driver, scan the image in another application, then place it or copy-and-paste it into LiveMotion.

Edit Objects 9

1 ➤ *The original object.*

2 ➤ *The object* ***flipped horizontally***.

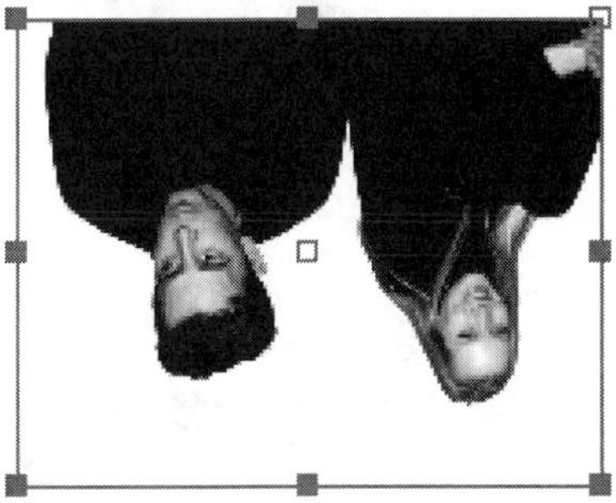

3 ➤ *Figure 2* ***flipped vertically***.

Transforming objects

THE BASIC TRANSFORMATION operations are scale, flip, move, rotate, horizontal skew, and vertical skew. Transformations can be applied using the Transform palette, a selection tool, the Transform tool, or commands on the Object menu > Transform submenu. Layer attributes are preserved when an object is transformed.

You can flip an object or multiple objects, but not a group. (You can ungroup, flip, and then regroup, however.)

To flip an object:

1. Choose the Selection tool, and select the object or objects you want to flip.
2. Choose Object menu > Transform > Flip Horizontal and/or Flip Vertical (Figs. 1–3).

➤ To undo either or both flip commands if you've performed subsequent editing steps, select the object and choose either command again, or use the Edit menu > Undo submenu.

The Transform palette displays location, width, height, rotation, horizontal skew, and vertical skew information for a selected object. The palette can also be used to transform selected objects by entering values into those fields.

Note: The Transform palette only accepts whole numbers—no decimal points.

To reposition, scale, rotate, or skew an object using the Transform palette:

1. Show the Transform palette (Window menu > Transform) (Fig. 1).
2. Select an object or objects using any selection tool.
3. When you do any of the following, you can press Tab to move from field to field or press Shift-Return/Shift-Enter to apply a transformation and leave the current field highlighted.

   Enter a higher value in the **X** field or click the up arrow to move the object horizontally to the right; enter a lower X value or click the down arrow to move the object to the left.

   Enter a higher value in the **Y** field or click the up arrow to move the object downward; enter a lower value or click the down arrow to move the object upward (yup, that's right).

   To scale the object, enter new values in the **width** and/or **height** field or click either up or down arrow (Figs. 2–3). *Note:* To scale proportionally, drag a selection border handle with a Selection tool and Shift held down instead (see pages 54 and 115).

   To **rotate** the object, enter a rotation angle; or click the up/down arrow; or drag the radial dial clockwise or counterclockwise (Fig. 4).

   To **skew** the object **horizontally** to the right, enter a positive Horizontal Shear value or click the up arrow (Fig. 5). To skew to the left, enter a negative value or click the down arrow.

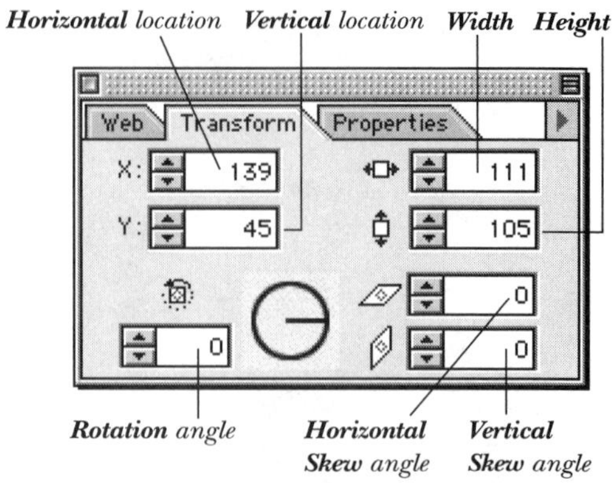

*1 ➤ The **Transform** palette.*

2 ➤ The original object.

*3 ➤ The original object's **width** is decreased.*

*4 ➤ The original object is **rotated**.*

*5 ➤ The original object is **skewed horizontally**.*

To **skew** the object **vertically** upward, enter a positive Vertical Skew value or click the up arrow. To skew the object downward, enter a negative Vertical Skew value or click the down arrow.

4. To exit the palette: Press Return/Enter or click anywhere in the composition.

When an object is selected, its selection border is visible. You can use the corner and side handles on the selection border to transform an object.

To scale or rotate an object by dragging (selection tool):

1. Select an object using a selection tool.
2. To **scale** (resize) the object:

   To scale the object horizontally and vertically, position the pointer over any corner handle except the upper right corner handle (the pointer becomes a four-way arrow), then drag the handle (Fig. 1).

   Hold down Shift while dragging to constrain the object's width and height proportions.

   To scale only the horizontal or vertical dimension, drag any side handle.

   To scale the object from a corner handle instead of the center, hold down Option/Alt while dragging the opposite handle. (Shift has no effect when Option/Alt is held down.)
3. To **rotate** the object, position the pointer over the upper right corner handle (the pointer will become a rotate arrow), then drag in a wide circle (Fig. 2). Hold down Shift while dragging to constrain the rotation to a multiple of 15°. You can watch the Angle field on the Transform palette as you drag.

➤ Hold down Command/Ctrl to rotate an object while dragging any corner handle except the upper right one or to scale an object while dragging the upper right corner handle.

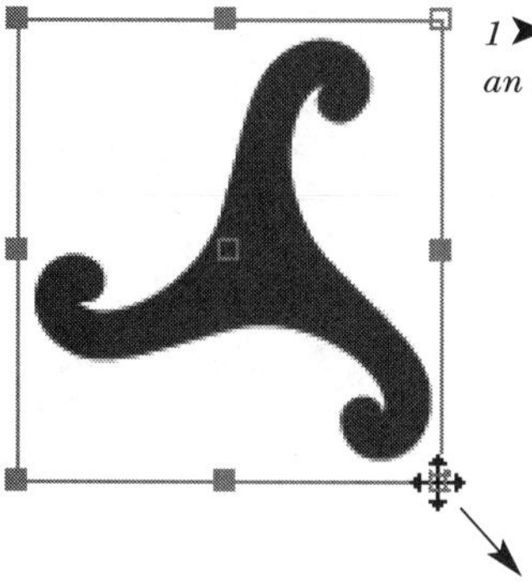

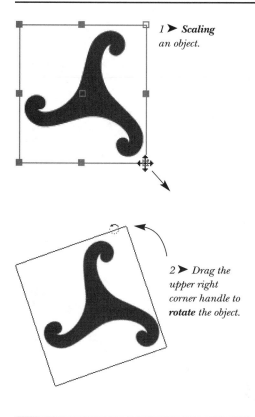

*1 ➤ **Scaling** an object.*

*2 ➤ Drag the upper right corner handle to **rotate** the object.*

Off center

All transformations are calculated from an object's **anchor point**, whether the transformation is performed via the Transform palette, a selection tool, or the Transform tool. By default, the anchor point is located in the center of an object, but it can be moved by dragging it using the **Transform** tool (E) (Figs. 3–4). *Note:* Moving the anchor point will also cause a **texture** fill to shift within the object!

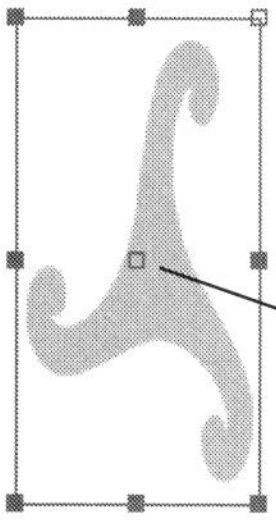

*3 ➤ The **default** location of the **anchor point**.*

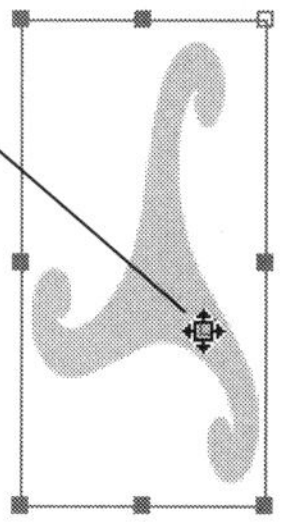

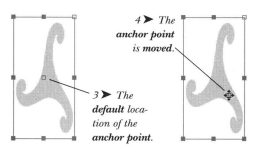

*4 ➤ The **anchor point** is moved.*

An object can be skewed vertically and/or horizontally.

To skew an object by dragging (selection tool):

1. Choose a selection tool, then select the object that you want to skew (Fig. 1). You can use a Library shape, just for practice.
2. To skew the object along the vertical (*y*) axis, move the pointer over the left or right side handle, hold down Command/Ctrl (the pointer will become a skew arrow pointer), then drag the handle upward or downward (Fig. 2).
   and/or
   To skew the object along the horizontal (*x*) axis, move the pointer over the top or bottom side handle, hold down Command/Ctrl (the pointer will become a skew arrow pointer), then drag the handle to the left or the right (Fig. 3).

➤ You can also skew an object via the Transform palette (see page 114).

To skew or rotate an object using the Transform tool:

1. Choose the Transform tool (E).
2. Select the object that you want to skew or rotate.
3. Drag **any** side handle to skew the object.
   and/or
   Drag **any** corner handle to rotate the object.

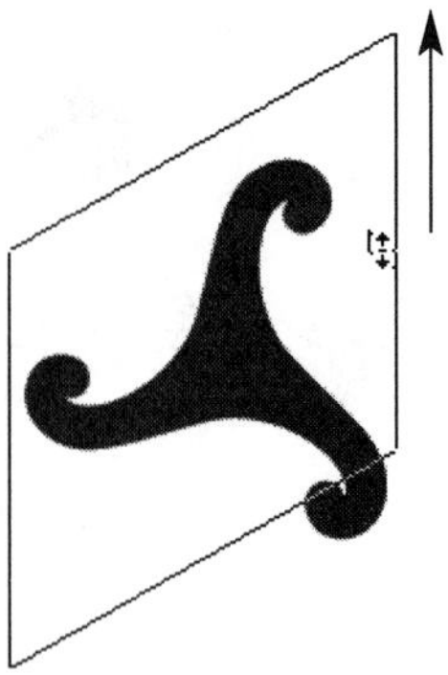

*1 ➤ **Skewing vertically.***

*2 ➤ The **skewed** object.*

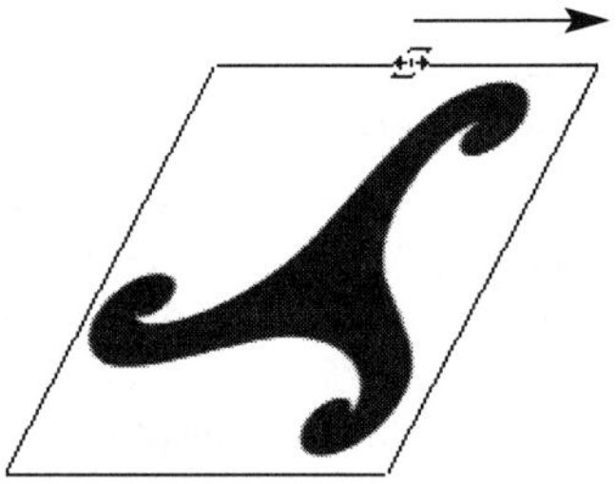

*3 ➤ **Skewing** the original object **horizontally**.*

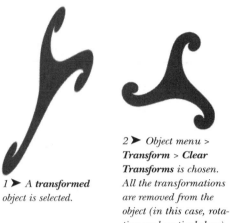

1 ➤ A ***transformed*** *object is selected.*

2 ➤ Object menu > ***Transform*** *>* ***Clear Transforms*** *is chosen. All the transformations are removed from the object (in this case, rotation and vertical skew).*

3 ➤ An object is copied.

4 ➤ Another object is selected.

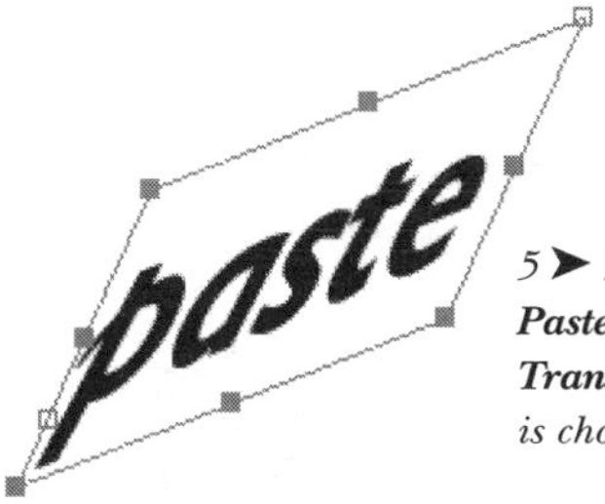

5 ➤ Edit menu > ***Paste Special*** *>* ***Transformations*** *is chosen.*

If you make a mistake while transforming an object, you can undo using the Edit menu > Undo submenu—that is, if the command you want to undo is still listed there. You can also correct or change a transformation another way. Since LiveMotion remembers the transformations that are currently applied to each object, they can be undone individually by resetting the value for that particular transformation on the Transform palette or they can be undone collectively using the Clear Transforms command.

To remove all transformations from an object:

1. Choose a selection tool, then select the object from which you want to remove all transformations (Fig. 1).
2. Choose Object menu > Transform > Clear Transforms (Fig. 2). *Note:* This command won't restore an object's center point to its original location.

Some features take us a while to warm up to, while others become useful and part of our working vocabulary the instant we get to know them. The Paste Special commands fall into the latter category. In these instructions, you'll learn how to use the Paste Special > Transformations command, which isolates, copies, and pastes only transformations from one object to another. None of an object's other attributes are pasted (e.g., color or distortion).

To copy and paste transformations:

1. Select the object that contains the transformations you want to copy (Fig. 3). *Note:* The scale value won't be copied.
2. Choose Edit menu > Copy (Command-C/ Ctrl-C).
3. Select the object to which you want to apply the copied transformations (Fig. 4).
4. Choose Edit menu > Paste Special > Transformations (Fig. 5).
   or
   Windows only: Right-click in the composition window and choose Paste Special > Transformations.

Combining objects

If you've worked with the Pathfinder commands in Adobe Illustrator, the Combine commands in LiveMotion will seem instantly familiar. Like the Pathfinders, they create a new object from two or more selected and overlapping objects. They combine or remove areas that do overlap or areas that don't overlap. Thus from simple objects you can produce more complex object contours, shapes, or cutouts.

You can combine any type of object: geometric, text, or image. The final object may be a different type than the original objects (e.g., a geometric object will turn into either a path or an image object). It depends on what type of object you start with and which command you use.

To combine two or more objects:

1. Select two or more objects that have some amount of overlap (Fig. 1).
2. From the Object menu > Combine submenu, choose one of the following:

   Unite joins the outer edges of selected objects into one combined object. The layers and layer attributes (and thus the style) of the backmost object are preserved and are applied to the new object. The fill of the backmost object's layer 1 is preserved (Fig. 2). A path object results.

   Unite with Color joins the shapes of selected objects into one combined object. The objects won't change in appearance, but the united object will only have one layer (Fig. 3). Use the Subgroup selection tool to select its individual components. An image object results.

➤ To select and modify an individual object within a Unite with Color object, choose the Subgroup selection tool, click on the larger shape, then click on the smaller shape or the cutout. To edit or restyle type, double-click instead.

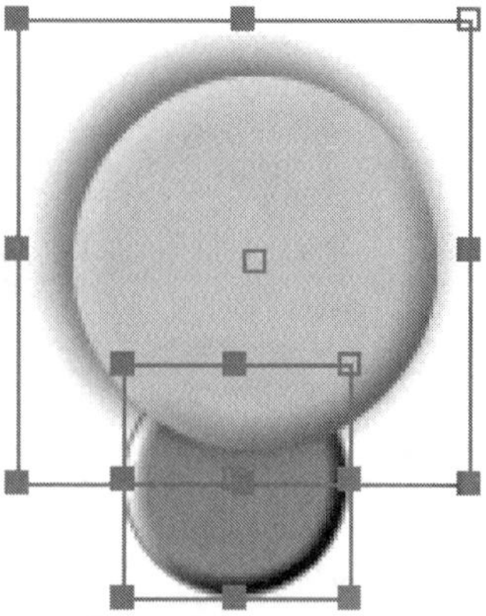

1 ➤ The original objects.

*2 ➤ **Unite**.*

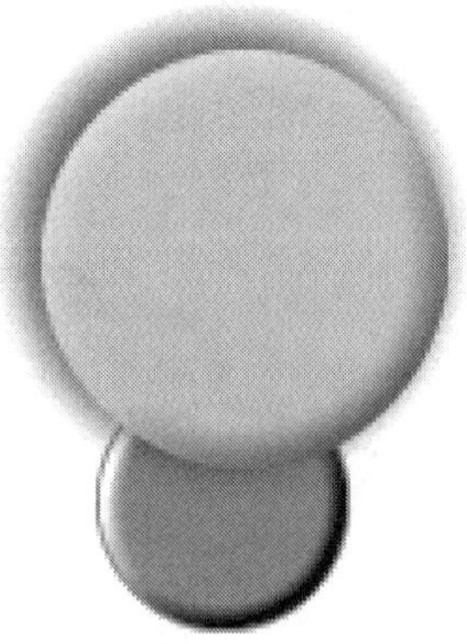

*3 ➤ **Unite with Color**.*

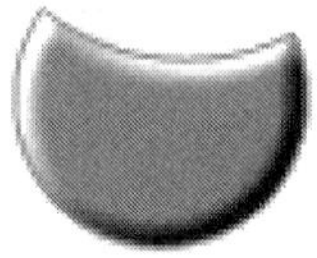

1 ➤ *Minus Front.*

2 ➤ *Intersect.*

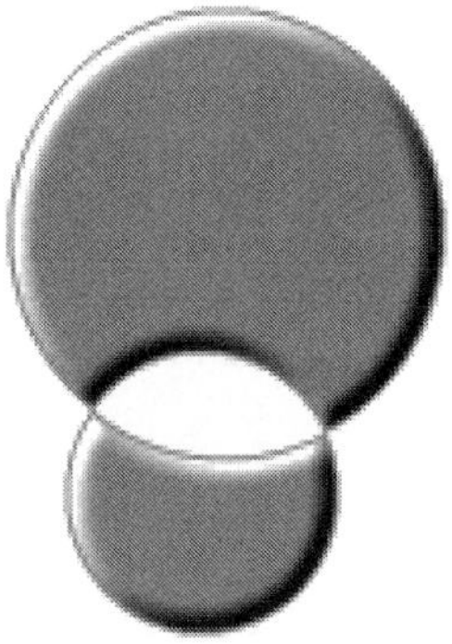

3 ➤ *Exclude.*

Minus Front subtracts the frontmost selected object(s) from the backmost object's top layer. It's as if the upper object's shape is cutting through the backmost object. The layers and layer attributes (and thus the style) of the backmost object are preserved and are applied to the new object (Fig. 1). A path object results.

Intersect deletes all non-overlapping areas from the original, overlapping, selected objects. The layers and layer attributes of the backmost object are preserved and are applied to the new object. In order to apply this command, the selected objects must overlap partially, but not completely (Fig. 2). A path object results.

Exclude makes areas where an even number of selected objects overlap transparent and fills areas where an odd number of objects overlap with the color of the backmost object (Fig. 3). The layers and layer attributes of the backmost object are preserved and are applied to the new object. A path object results.

Note: If a smaller object is positioned completely on top of another object instead of partially overlapping it, Exclude will work like Minus Front.

➤ Sometimes it's easier and faster to use a Combine command to create a complex path shape from simple shapes than it is to use the Pen tool. You can use the Pen-selection tool to reshape the path objects that result.

➤ On the Timeline (animation) editor, combined Unite with Color objects are assigned the name "combination." Geometric objects that are combined are assigned the name "geometric."

The Uncombine command can be used on a file even after it has been saved, closed, and reopened.

To uncombine a Unite with Color object:

1. Use the Selection tool to select an object that was created using the Combine command (Fig. 1).
2. Choose Object menu > Uncombine. The original objects will reappear (Fig. 2).

➤ If you uncombine an object to which a shape has been applied, the shape will be restored.

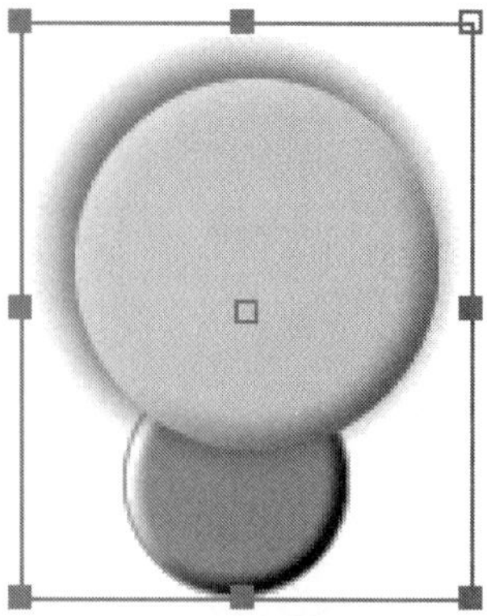

1➤ *The combined,* ***Unite with Color*** *object.*

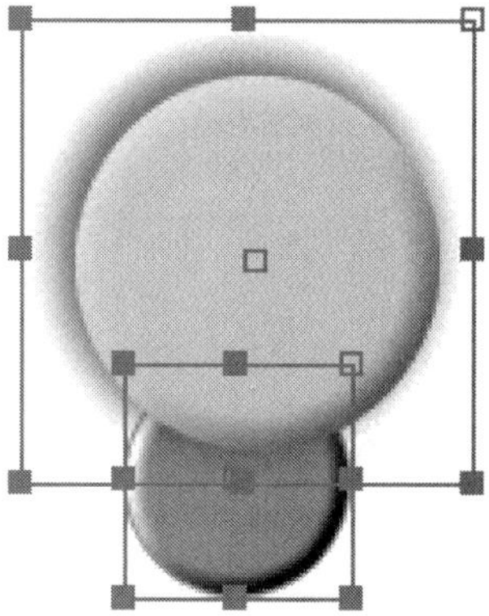

2➤ *The objects* ***uncombined****.*

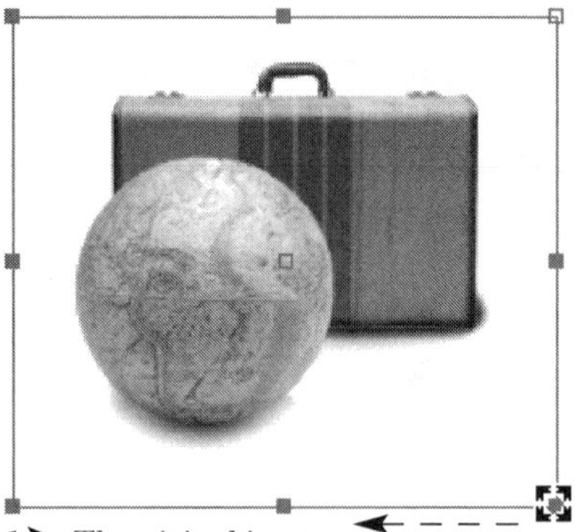

1 ➤ *The original image.*

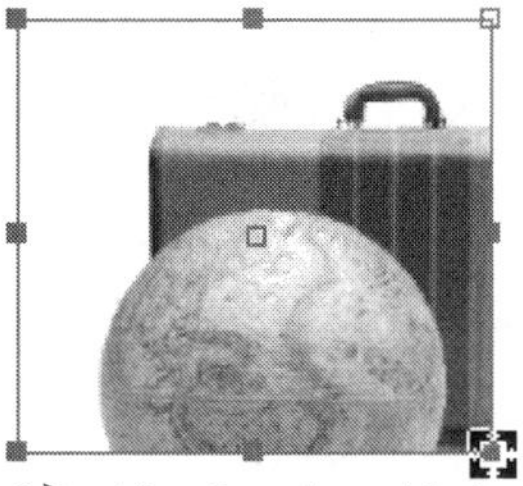

2 ➤ *After dragging with the Crop tool, the **visible** area of the object is **reduced**.*

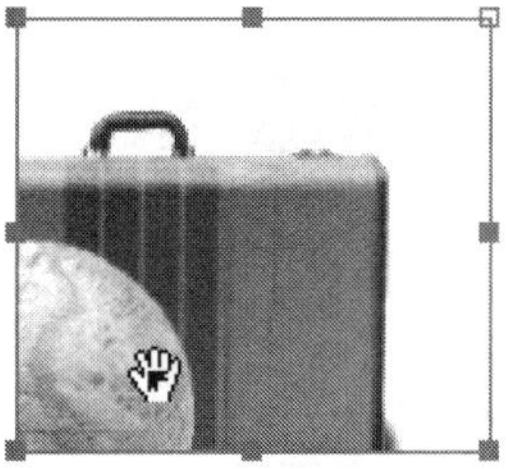

3 ➤ *Since this object is an image object, we were able to use the Crop tool as a **Hand** tool to reposition the image inside the selection border.*

Cropping

The Crop tool is used to shrink an object's selection border, and thus reduce how much of the object is visible. The hidden parts of the object are preserved; they just remain hidden until the object is un-cropped. Un-cropping (also done with the Crop tool) expands the object's selection border and makes the hidden areas visible again.

Note: The Crop tool can't be used to change the dimensions of an object or the composition.

To crop an object:

1. Select the object to be cropped (Fig. 1).
2. Choose the Crop tool (C).
3. To crop the object in only one dimension, move the pointer over one of the object's side selection handles (the pointer will become two corner brackets).
   or
   To crop the object in two dimensions, move the pointer over a corner handle (the pointer will become four brackets).
4. Drag the handle (Fig. 2).
5. *Optional:* If the selected object is an image object, you can reposition the image within the crop boundaries after cropping. Position the Crop tool pointer over the image (the pointer will become a hand icon with a bracket), then drag (Fig. 3). Pause to allow the screen to redraw.

➤ Double-click the Crop tool to show the Transform palette, then watch the X, Y, width, height values change as you crop.

To un-crop an object:

1. Select the cropped object.
2. Choose the Crop tool (C).
3. Drag a selection handle. The hidden areas will become exposed. You won't be able to drag the handle beyond the object's original size.

➤ The Crop tool can be used to un-crop an object even after the file has been saved, closed, and reopened.

Using mattes

In order to understand how mattes work in LiveMotion, envision the kind of matte that's used to frame a photograph or a drawing. A matte in LiveMotion, like a cardboard matte, controls how much of an image is visible, except in this case you have a virtually unlimited range of matte shapes to work with—from geometric to irregular. And like a cardboard matte, a LiveMotion matte has no effect on the image itself. Try placing a rectangular image into LiveMotion (e.g., a Photoshop image), and then change the active matte to make the image show through an opening of a different shape. Have some fun with this.

To apply a matte to an image object:

METHOD 1 (Library palette)

1. Select the image object to which you want to apply a matte (Fig. 1). You can use an object that was created in another application (e.g., Illustrator, Photoshop).
2. Show the Library palette.
3. Click a shape on the Library palette to use as the matte.
4. Click the Make Active Matte button at the bottom of the Library palette.
   or
   Show the Properties palette, then drag the Library swatch or name over the Active Matte thumbnail on the Properties palette (Fig. 2). The image object's contour will become the shape of the current Active Matte, and "Active Matte" will appear automatically on the Alpha Channel pop-up menu. Resize the image object, if desired (Figs. 3–4).

METHOD 2 (Paste Active Matte)

1. In the composition window, select an image object (shape) that has the contour that you want to use as a matte.
2. Choose Edit menu > Copy.
3. Select the object to which you want to apply the matte.
4. Choose Edit menu > Paste Special > Paste Active Matte. Note the Active Matte thumbnail on the Properties palette.

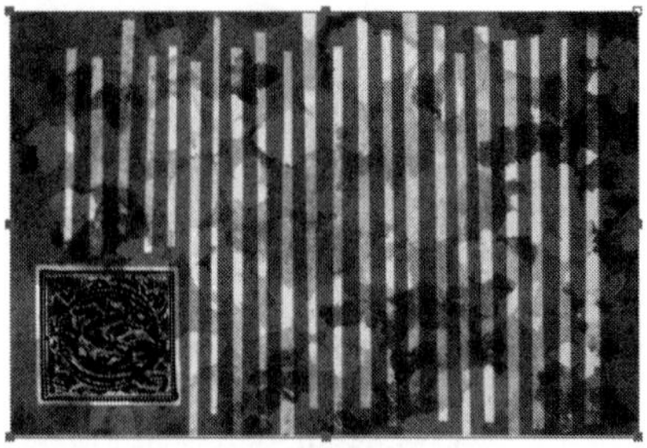

*1 ➤ An **image** object is selected.*

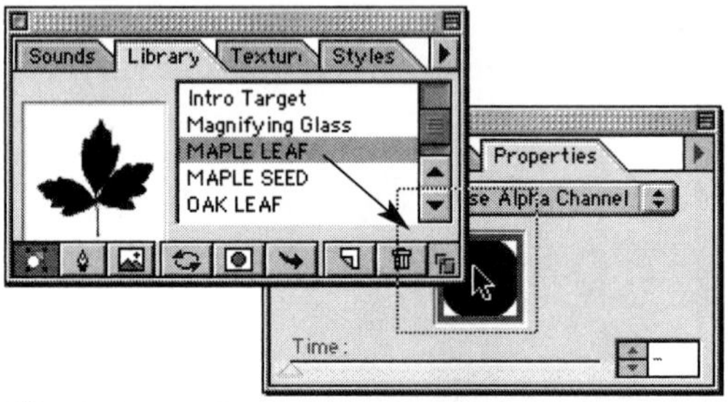

*2 ➤ A shape is dragged from the **Library** palette over the **Active Matte** thumbnail on the **Properties** palette.*

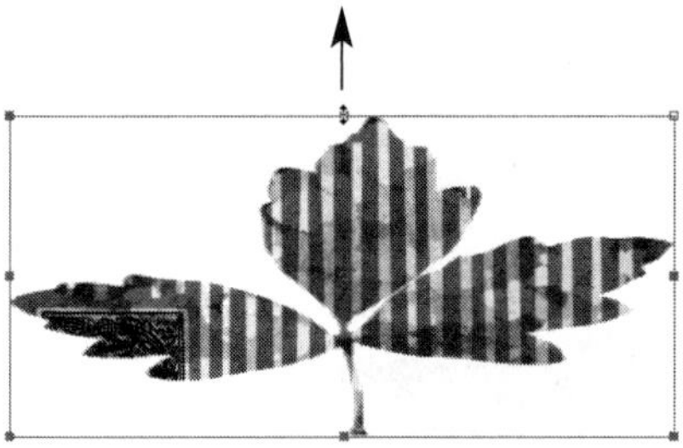

*3 ➤ The maple leaf shape acts as a **matte** for the image object. As the box is resized (the top handle is dragged upward)...*

4 ➤ ...the Library object matte is un-smushed.

Textures 10

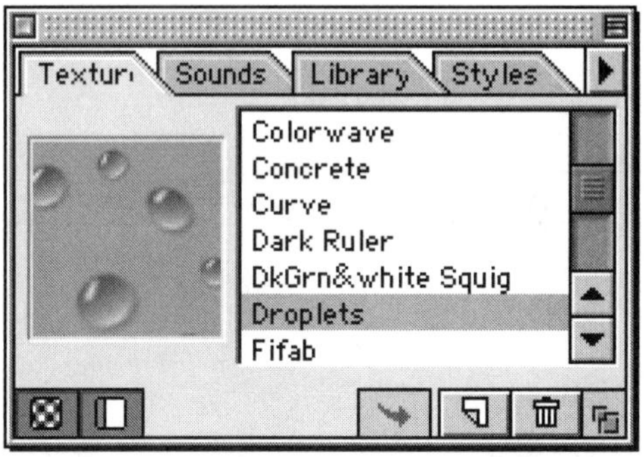

1 ➤ *The **Textures** palette in **Preview** view.*

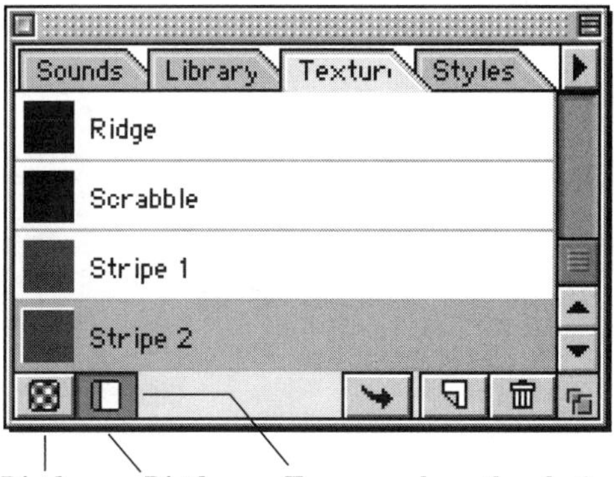

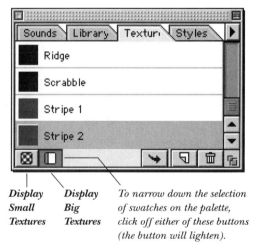

Display Small Textures ***Display Big Textures*** *To narrow down the selection of swatches on the palette, click off either of these buttons (the button will lighten).*

2 ➤ *The **Textures** palette in **Name** view.*

Applying textures

IN LIVEMOTION, a texture is not something scratchy or smooth that you can feel with your fingertips. A texture is a bitmap image that's applied to an object layer or used as a background fill. Depending on the size of the image you're using, the texture may or may not repeat as a tile pattern. You can use any of the textures that install with the application or you can create your own textures using your own bitmap images. Once a texture has been added to the Textures palette, it can be used in any LiveMotion composition.

There are several ways to apply a texture:

➤ Via the **Textures palette** (to an object or to the background) (see page 124)

➤ Via the **Place as Texture** command (to an object or the background) (see page 126)

➤ Via the Paste Special > **Paste Texture** command (see page 125)

➤ By **dragging** an image file from the Desktop to a layer on the **Object Layers** palette (see page 124)

Start by familiarizing yourself with the Textures palette.

To choose a display mode for the Textures palette:

From the pop-up menu at the right side of the Textures palette, choose:

Swatches View (swatches only).
or
Preview View (a listing of all the names, with a large swatch only for the currently selected texture) (Fig. 1).
or
Name View (a name and a small swatch for each texture) (Fig. 2).

To apply a texture via the Textures palette:

METHOD 1 (layer or background)

1. Choose a selection tool, click on an object, and choose a layer for that object (Fig. 1).
   or
   To apply the texture to the background, click the Background color box on the Toolbox or the Color palette.
2. Show the Textures palette (Window menu > Textures).
3. Click on a texture swatch or type a texture name, then click the Apply Texture button at the bottom of the palette (Return/Enter) (Figs. 2–4).
   or
   Double-click a texture name or swatch.
   or
   Drag a texture name or swatch onto a layer on the Object Layers palette.

➤ To blend two textures, apply two different textures to two different layers in the same object, and then lower the opacity of the texture layer that's on top (Fig. 5).

METHOD 2 (layer or background)

1. To apply a texture to an object, you don't have to select it.
   or
   To apply a texture to the background, deselect (Command-Shift-A/Ctrl-Shift-A).
2. Drag a texture name or swatch from the Textures palette over an object or onto the background in the composition.

METHOD 3 (layer only)

1. On the Desktop, open the directory/folder that contains the bitmap image file that you want to use as a texture.
2. Select an object in the LiveMotion composition, and resize the composition window, if necessary, so you can still see the bitmap file on the Desktop.
3. Show the Object Layers palette (Window menu > Object Layers).
4. Drag the image file from the Desktop onto a layer on the Object Layers palette.

1 ➤ The original object.

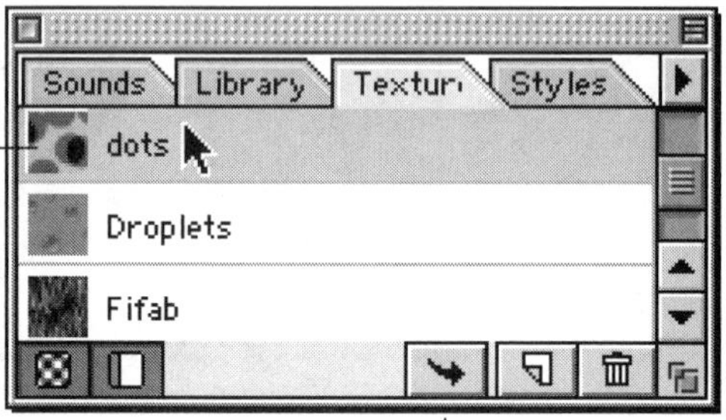

*2 ➤ **Highlight** a texture name (or swatch).*

*3 ➤ Then click the **Apply Texture** button.*

*4 ➤ The **texture** image fills the object.*

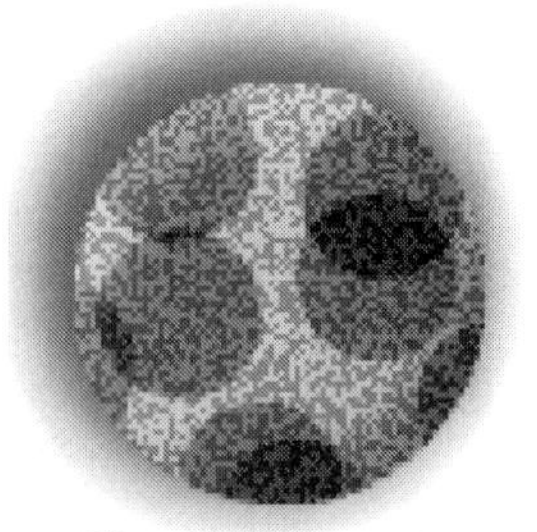

5 ➤ The opacity of the top texture layer is lowered, another layer is added below it, and a noise texture is applied to the new layer.

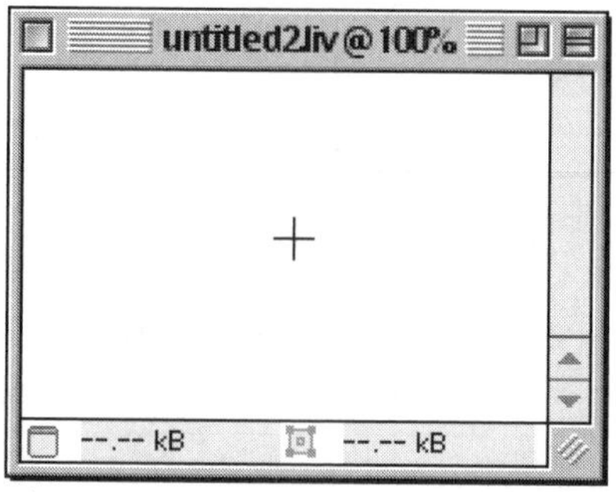

*1 ➤ Click in the composition window into which you want to paste the copied image. To paste into the **background**, make sure no objects are selected.*

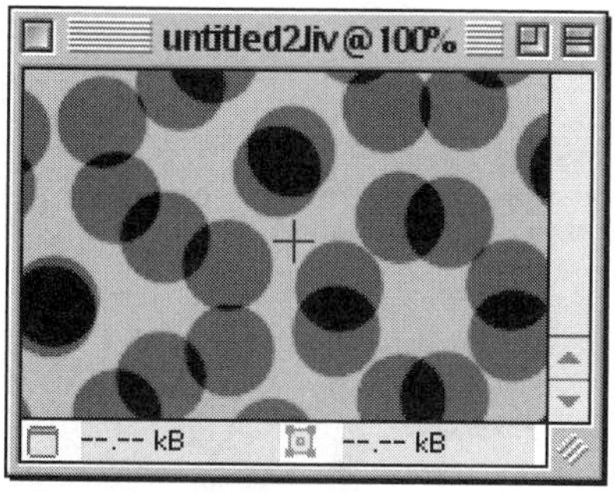

*2 ➤ After choosing Edit menu > **Paste Special** > **Paste Texture**, the texture appears in the **background**.*

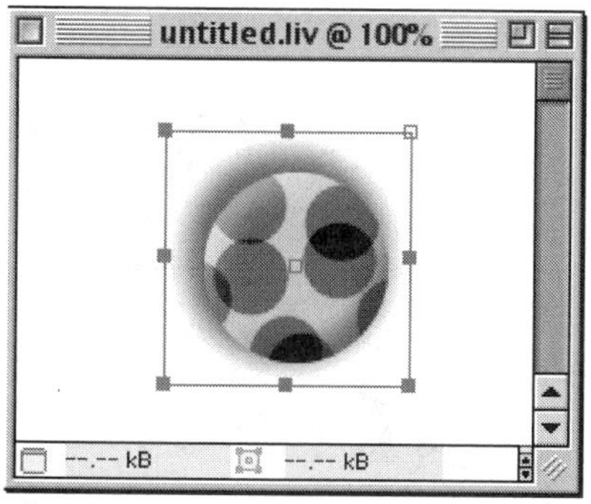

*3 ➤ If you select an object and then choose Edit menu > **Paste Special** > **Paste Texture**, the texture will only appear inside the **object**.*

The Paste Texture command is used to copy a texture layer attribute from one object to another.

To paste an image as a texture:

1. In LiveMotion, select a placed image that you want to use as a texture.
   or
   Select an area of an image in a bitmap application (e.g., Adobe Photoshop).
2. Choose Edit menu > Copy (Command-C/ Ctrl-C).
3. Click in the composition window into which you want to paste the copied object (Fig. 1).
4. To paste the image or texture into the background of the composition, deselect all objects (Command-Shift-A/ Ctrl-Shift-A or click on a blank area of the composition window).
   or
   If you want to paste the texture into an object, select that object and choose a layer on the Object Layers palette.
5. Choose Edit menu > Paste Special > Paste Texture.
   or
   Windows only: Right-click in the composition window and choose Paste Special > Paste Texture.

   If an object was selected for step 1, the copied image will be pasted onto the selected layer of the currently selected object (Figs. 2–3). The type and shape of the object into which the image is pasted will be preserved. The image will be cropped by the object's shape, but it will keep its original size.

   If no object is selected, the texture will paste onto the background. If the image is smaller than the dimensions of the composition, it will repeat as a tile, if necessary, in order to fill the background.

➤ Paste Texture can be used to paste different images onto different layers of the same object, while maintaining the object's shape. Experiment with changing the object layer opacities.

If an object layer is selected, the Place as Texture command will place an image file as a texture fill within that object's shape. If no object is selected, the texture will fill the background of the composition instead. Place as Texture won't change the shape of an object or an object's type (geometric, text, image), nor will it change any styling on the current layer.

Note: If you use the Paste Texture or Place as Texture command to add a texture image to the background of a composition, the image will tile, if necessary, to fill the background.

To place an image as a texture:

1. To place a texture in an object, select the object and choose a layer on the Object Layers palette (Fig. 1).
   or
   To fill the background of the composition with a texture, deselect all objects (Command-Shift-A/Ctrl-Shift-A or click on a blank area of the composition).
2. Choose File menu > Place as Texture.
3. Locate and highlight a file name (Fig. 2). MacOS: Check the Show Preview box, if the preview is currently hidden.
4. Click Open (Return/Enter). If you selected an object, the new imagery will now fill the selected layer; any preexisting layer attributes will be preserved (Fig. 3).

   If no objects were selected, the placed imagery will fill the background as a texture (Fig. 4).

➤ To remove a texture and restore a solid fill to an object, choose Fill with: Color from the Layer palette.

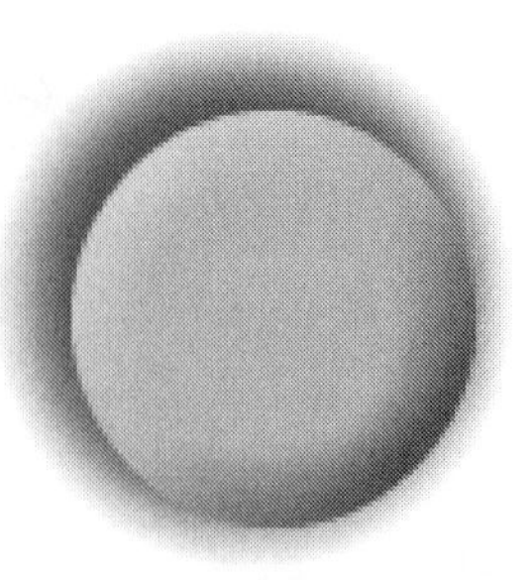

1 ➤ The original object has an emboss effect and a shadow layer.

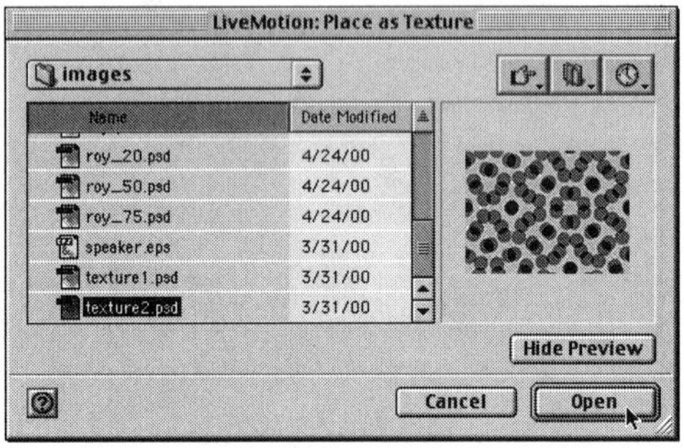

*2 ➤ Choose a file in the **Place as Texture** dialog box, then click **Open**.*

3 ➤ The texture appears inside the object; the object's original styling is preserved.

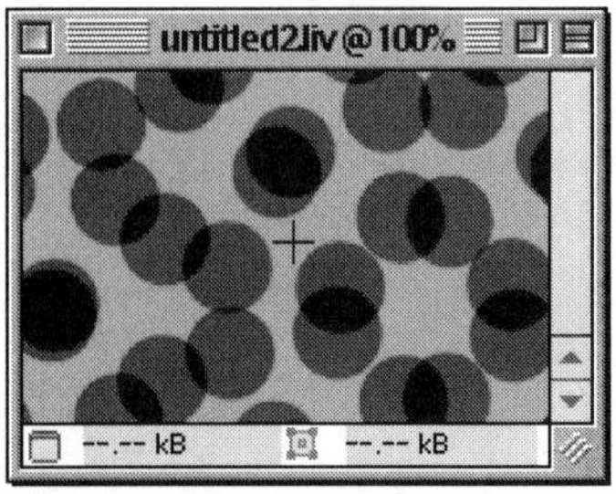

*4 ➤ If you deselect all objects before you place a texture, the texture will fill the **background**.*

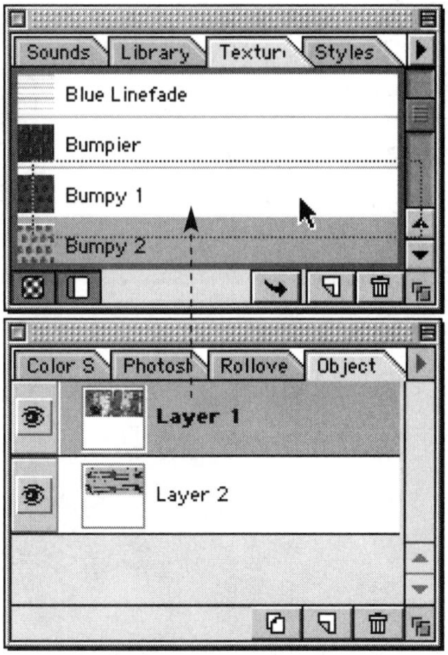

1 ➤ To save a texture, ***drag*** *from an object to the* ***Textures*** *palette.*

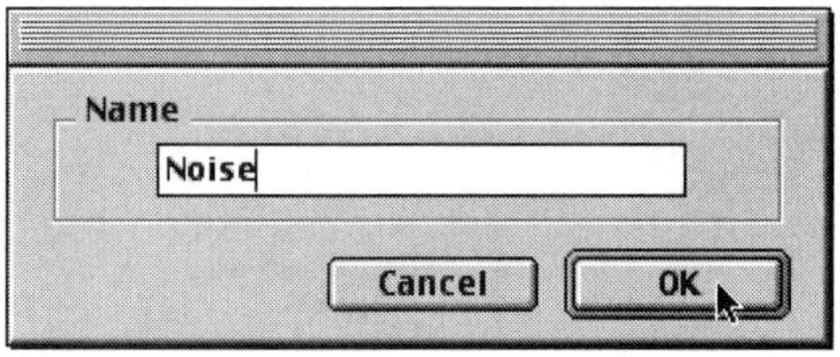

2 ➤ Assign a descriptive ***name*** *to the texture.*

If you add a texture to the Textures palette, you'll then have the option to reuse it in the same composition or in another composition. Skim through the four methods below, then use whichever one seems most appropriate.

To add a texture to the Textures palette:

METHOD 1

1. Select the object and object layer that contains the texture you want to save.
2. Drag from the object or from the Object Layers palette onto the Textures palette (Fig. 1). (Make sure the palette doesn't overlap the composition window.)
3. Enter a name for the new texture, then click OK (Return/Enter) (Fig. 2).

METHOD 2

On the Desktop, move the texture image file into the Textures folder inside the LiveMotion application folder, rename the file, if desired, then relaunch LiveMotion.

METHOD 3

1. Click the New Texture button at the bottom of the Textures palette.
2. Locate the texture image file, then click Open.
3. Enter a name for the new texture, then click OK (Return/Enter).

METHOD 4

1. On the Desktop, open the directory/ folder that contains the texture image file.
2. Click back in the LiveMotion composition window.
3. Drag the texture image file onto the Textures palette.
4. Enter a name for the new texture, then click OK (Return/Enter).

➤ Be careful: If you enter a name that matches an existing texture and then click Replace, you'll replace the old texture with the new one.

➤ If you like subtle textures, try the Ultimate Symbol WebPage Graphics CD (ultimatesymbol.com).

To remove a texture swatch from the Textures palette:

1. On the Textures palette, click on the texture name or swatch that you want to delete.
2. Click the Delete Texture (trash) button on the palette, then click Delete (Fig. 1). The texture file will be deleted from your system.

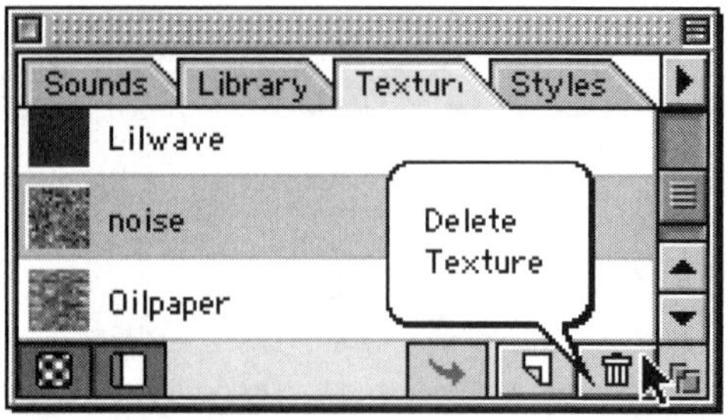

1➤ *Click the **Delete Texture** button.*

To reposition a texture within a layer:

1. Choose the Selection tool (V).
2. Command-drag/Ctrl-drag the object's anchor point (center point). Any textures that have been pasted or placed on any of the object's layers will move as you drag (Figs. 2–3).

➤ To restore the anchor point to the center of the object, choose Object menu > Transform > Reset Anchor Point. The texture will shift back to its original location.

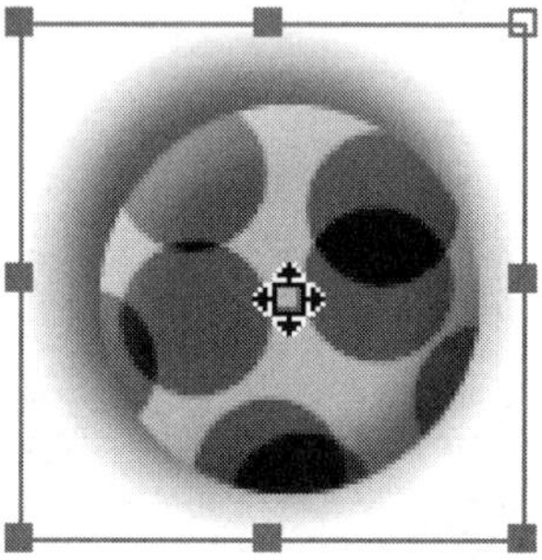

2➤ *To move a texture inside an object, **Command-drag/Ctrl-drag** the object's **anchor point**.*

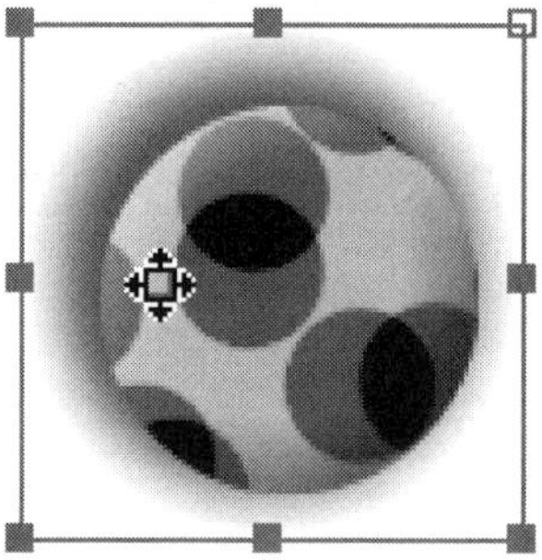

3➤ *The **pattern** and the anchor point are **moved**.*

Backgrounds 11

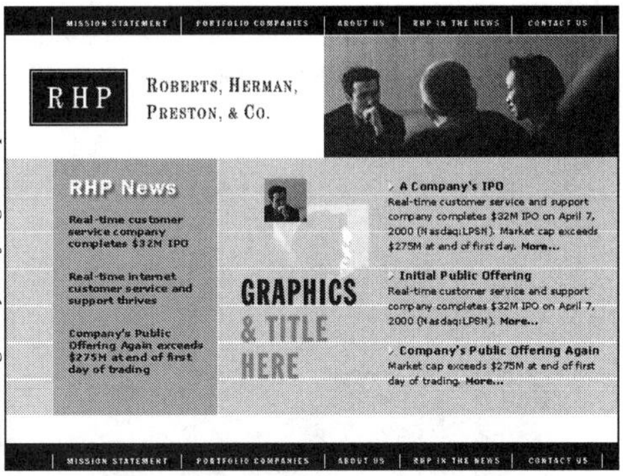

Web site designed by Newfangled Graphics

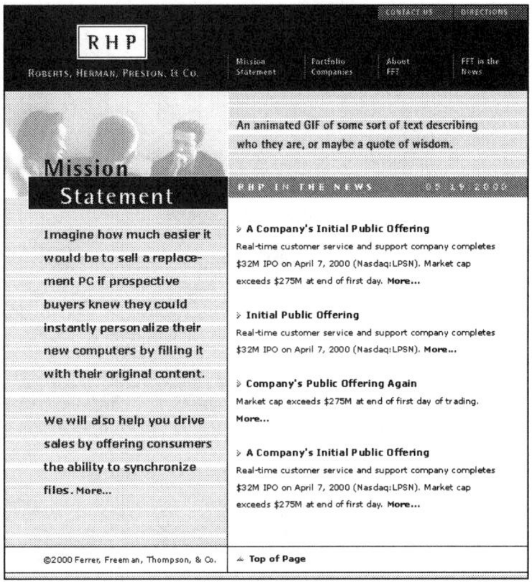

Creating backgrounds

BACKGROUNDS COUNT. In fact, the background of a Web page occupies the largest land mass, and thus can have the largest impact. In Chapter 10, you learned how to apply textures to objects and backgrounds. In this chapter, we focus on other ways to fill up backgrounds, namely, single-color backgrounds, two-color backgrounds, backgrounds made using shapes, and background images. The Color palette is used to create solid-color backgrounds, whereas a tiling technique is used to produce two-color backgrounds.

When you choose a color (or colors) for a background, consider how that color will contrast with objects in the composition. Most compositions include text, for which readability is always a top priority. If your text and background colors are very close in hue or saturation, they will lack contrast between them and the text will be a strain to read.

Instead, choose a background color (hue) that contrasts with the text so the text stands out. Or make the background considerably lighter or darker than the text and the other objects in the composition. You can do this by choosing a lighter or darker color from the Color palette. Be sure to preview the whole composition in the most popular browsers before you commit yourself to a particular color combination.

(To paste an image as a texture background, see page 125. To place an image as a texture background, see page 126.)

There's no law that says your background has to contain all the colors of the rainbow. In fact, if a Web page contains imagery or animation, a simple background will provide a nice respite from all the activity. Even more important, a solid-color background will download faster than a background that contains a texture or a gradient.

To create a solid-color background:

1. Show the Color palette. Check the Web-Safe color box if it's not already checked (it's next to the cube icon).
2. Click the Background color square on the Toolbox or the Color palette (Figs. 1–3). Any selected objects will deselect automatically.
3. Use the Color palette to mix a new background color (Fig. 4).
   or
   Choose the Eyedropper tool (I), then click on an object in the composition window or on a color anywhere on the Color palette. This is an easy way to match the background to an existing object.
4. Click the Foreground color square to reactivate it.

➤ To sample a color outside LiveMotion, choose the Eyedropper tool, then press the mouse and drag from inside the LiveMotion composition window to anywhere else on your screen (even another application window).

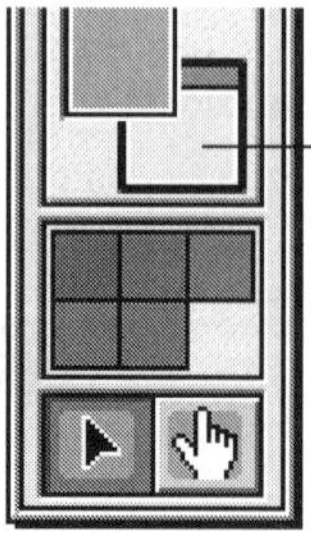

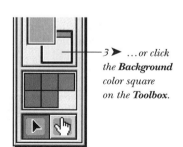

3➤ *...or click the* ***Background*** *color square on the* ***Toolbox****.*

Color in quantity

When you're choosing colors for a background, remember that color in a large quantity looks more intense than color in a smaller, concentrated area. If you've ever chosen the wrong paint color for a room, you know exactly what we mean. If you want knock-your-socks off color, fine. If you want something subtle, tone it down a bit more. P.S. It's okay to use white as a background color.

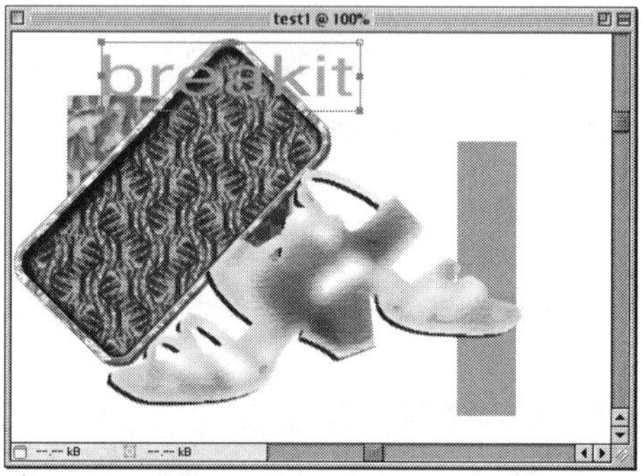

1➤ *The original composition.*

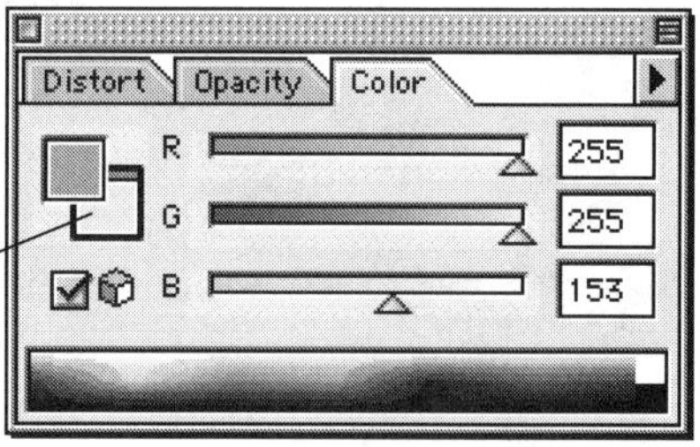

2➤ *Click the* ***Background*** *color square on the* ***Color*** *palette...*

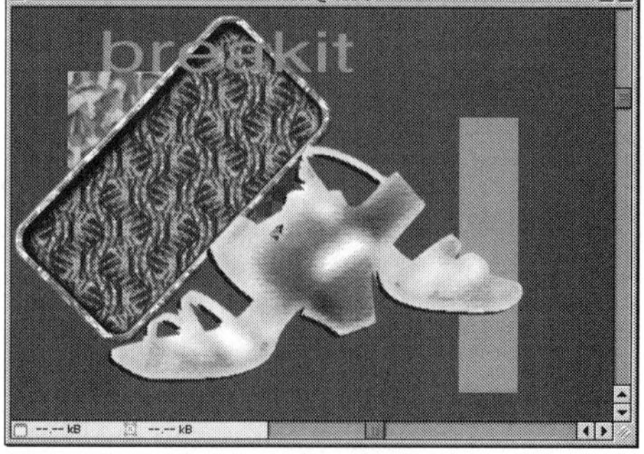

4➤ *The background is recolored..*

Sizing guidelines

When you create a background tile, you need to consider the maximum pixel dimensions of the standard-size monitor at a default resolution (e.g., 640 x 480 or 832 x 624 pixels). We recommend that you design for a 800 x 600 pixel area. The area beyond the 800-pixel width will be seen without scrolling on a 20" monitor, but not on a 17" monitor. Visitors (ourselves included) don't like to scroll sideways. To change a file's dimensions, use Edit menu > Composition Settings (Command-Shift-N/ Ctrl-Shift-N).

If you choose tile dimensions that accomodate the largest monitors, on the other hand, the tile won't repeat where you don't want it to. To do this, make your tile the maximum 1024-pixel width for a vertical stripe effect or the maximum 1024-pixel height for a horizontal stripe effect. A design of this size may look off balance on a smaller monitor, though.

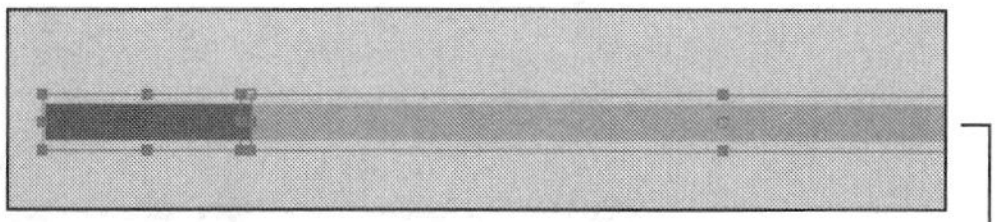

1 ➤ Both rectangles extend beyond the composition to prevent any background color from showing through.

2 ➤ This two-color tile background resulted from exporting, then ***placing****, the file shown in the previous figure.*

In order to create a two-color background tile, you'll need to follow these three basic steps:

➤ First, create and align two color objects. You can create stripes, a rectangular color block inside a larger rectangle, a square inside another square, or any other configuration.

➤ Second, export the file that contains the objects as GIF or JPEG.

➤ Third, open another file, then use File menu > Place as Texture to place the file as a background into that composition.

To create a two-color tile using two rectangles:

1. Choose Edit menu > Composition Settings, enter a width (see the sidebar for guidelines), make the height between 4 and 20 pixels, then click OK. Enlarge the composition window so some gray is showing.
2. Choose the Rectangle tool (M), then draw two rectangles. Extend the rectangles beyond the edge of the composition to prevent any background color from showing. Note the object's height on the Transform palette.
3. Apply a different color to each rectangle (Fig. 1).
4. Use the Selection tool (V) to move the objects, if necessary, so they slightly overlap (Fig. 1). This will prevent the background color from showing between the rectangles in the tile.
5. Save this original file in LiveMotion format for possible reediting at a later time.
6. Follow the steps on the following page to export the file for use as a tile (Fig. 2).

➤ A GIF export sometimes renders a blank background as black or an odd color. To cover any exposed background areas to prevent this from happening, create a white or colored rectangle and send it to the back.

➤ Windows: If you encounter a problem creating the tile, try matching the object height to the composition height.

Before you can get a new tile design onto a Web page, you have to use the Export palette to optimize it and then use the Export or Export Selection command to save the optimized version of it. Once you do that, you're ready to place it as a texture.

To export a tile file:

1. Follow the steps on the previous page (or create some other kind of composition to use as a tile), and leave the tile file open (Fig. 1).
2. Choose Export: Trimmed Composition, uncheck the Make HTML box, then click OK. No additional HTML header is required, since the exported tile file won't become a separate HTML page—it will merely be placed into another LiveMotion file.
3. Show the Export palette (Fig. 2), and check the Preview box.
4. Choose GIF from the topmost pop-up menu and check the Preview box.
   and
   For a file containing multiple colors, move the Colors slider to 2, 4, or 8—whichever looks best in the preview.
   and
   Choose the Web Adaptive palette from the second pop-up menu.
   and
   Deselect the Include Transparency Information, Dither, and Interlace buttons.

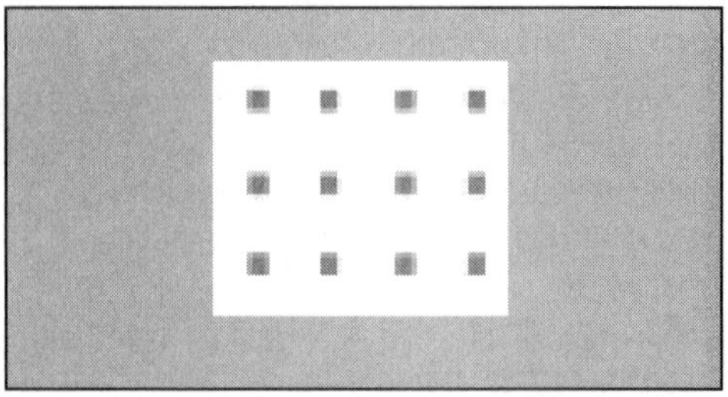

1 ➤ To create this tile image, a grid of squares was created in Illustrator and imported as an image object (shown here at 200% view). A large white rectangle was then placed behind it. The width and height (Composition Settings) were reduced to crop the image object to produce an evenly spaced tile pattern.

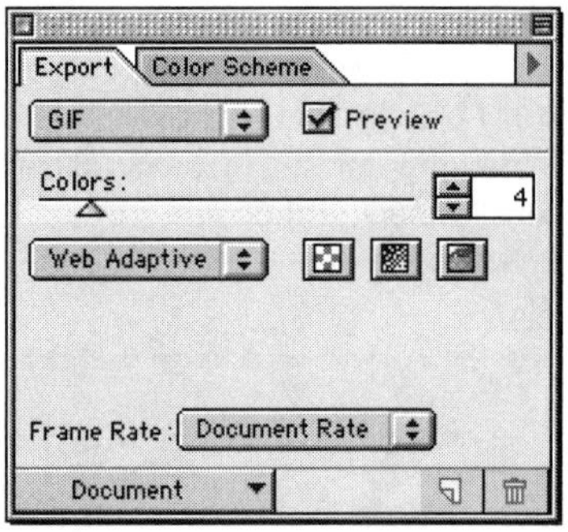

*2 ➤ The **Export palette** is used to choose **optimization** settings.*

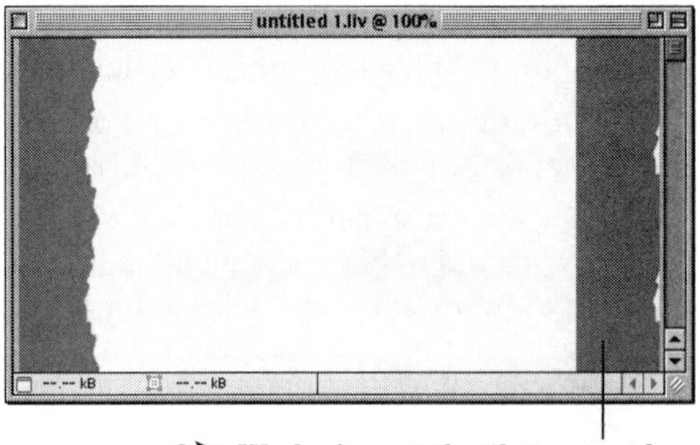

3 ➤ We don't want the tile to repeat here.

Do the tiles look funny?

After performing all the steps on this page and the next page, does the tile repeat where you don't want it to—at the right or bottom edge of the composition window into which it is placed (Fig. 3)? If so, increase the width and/or height of the original file and the tile objects, then re-export it. Is the white background showing between the tiles? Reposition the objects in the original tile file, then re-export it.

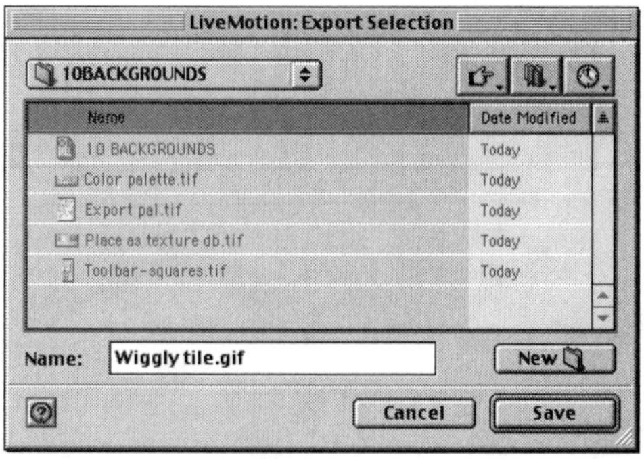

*1 ➤ The **Export** or **Export Selection** dialog box is used to save the tile using the current **Export palette** settings.*

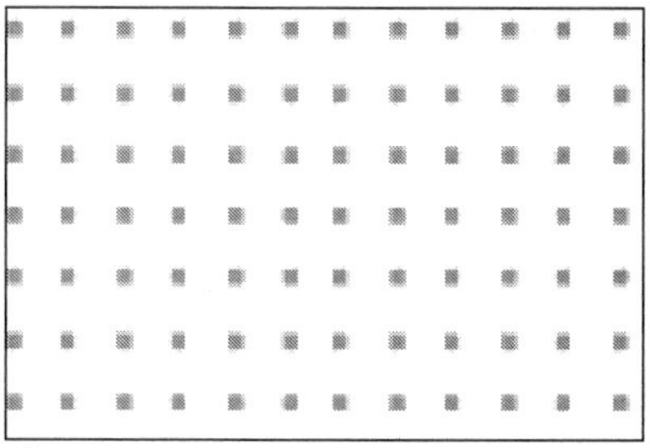

*2 ➤ After placing the file as a background texture using the **Place as Texture** command.*

5. Choose File menu > Export (Command-E/ Ctrl-E), enter a file name, choose a location in which to save the file, then click Save (Fig. 1).
or
Select the tile objects in the composition, choose File menu > Export Selection, enter a file name, choose a location in which to save the file, then click Save.

➤ Beware! If you use File menu > Export again now, you won't get back to the Save dialog box—you'll save right over the last file you just exported! To create a variation on an existing tile, use File menu > Export As instead.

6. To use the exported file as a background, create or open another composition, then use the File menu > Place as Texture command in the new composition (see page 126) (Fig. 2).

Some other tile ideas

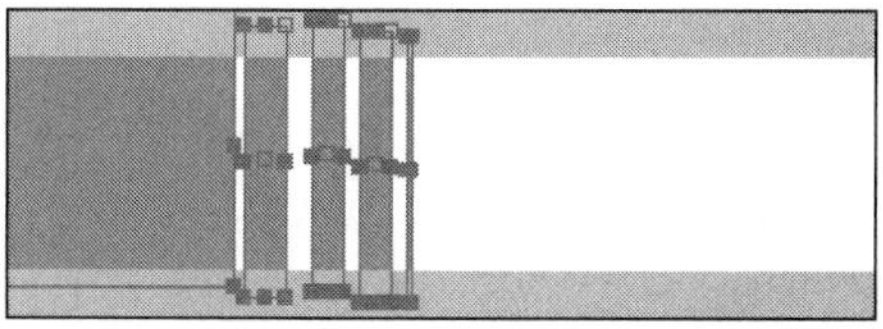

3 ➤ An enlarged view of the original objects.

*4 ➤ The **horizontal** tile file **placed** as **texture**.*

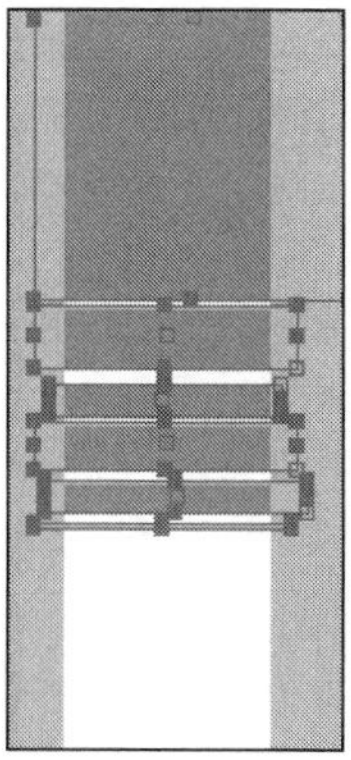

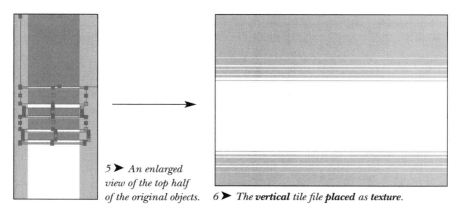

5 ➤ An enlarged view of the top half of the original objects.

*6 ➤ The **vertical** tile file **placed** as **texture**.*

Some other tile ideas *(Cont'd)*

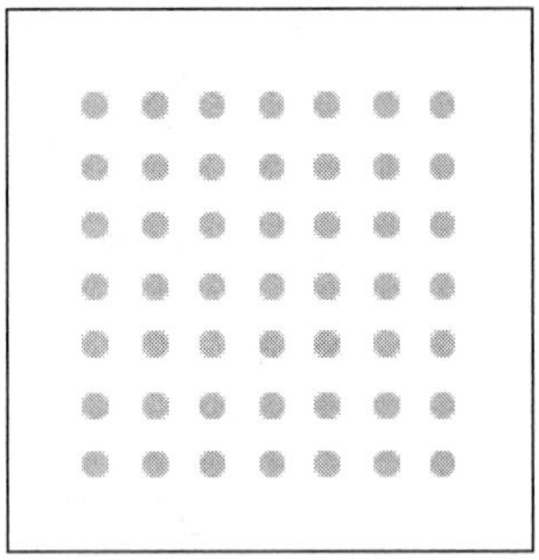

1 ➤ These dots were created in ***Illustrator*** *and imported as an image object. A large white rectangle is sent to the back.*

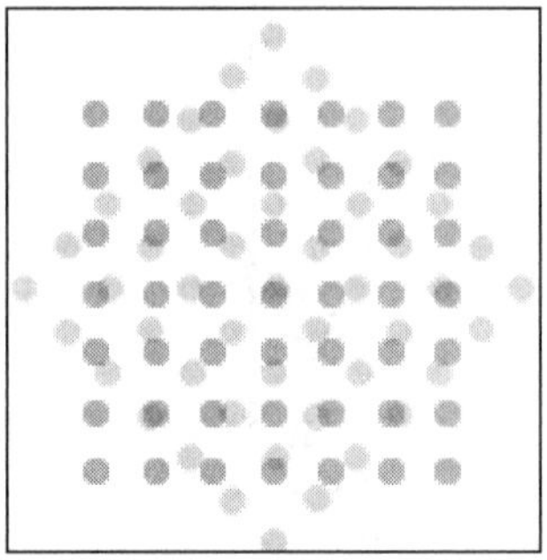

2 ➤ The image object is ***duplicated*** *and* ***rotated*** *45°. Its* ***Object Opacity*** *is set to 50%.*

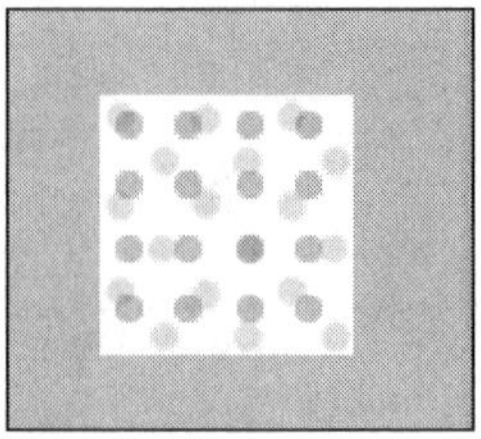

3 ➤ The ***width*** *and* ***height*** *of the composition is* ***reduced*** *to crop the object into an evenly spaced tile.*

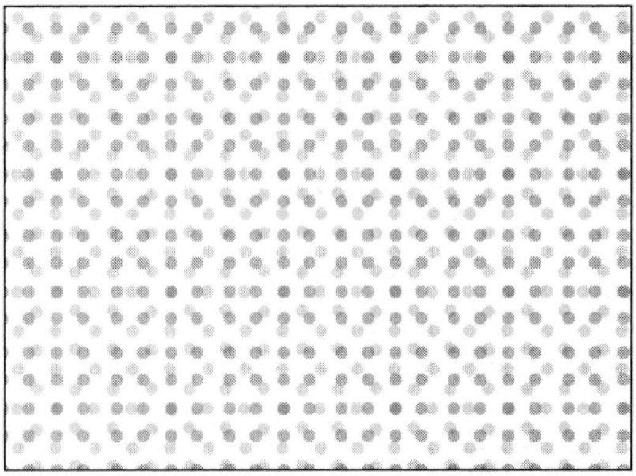

4 ➤ After exporting the tile file as a ***GIF****, then using* ***Place as Texture*** *to place it as a tiled background in another LiveMotion file.*

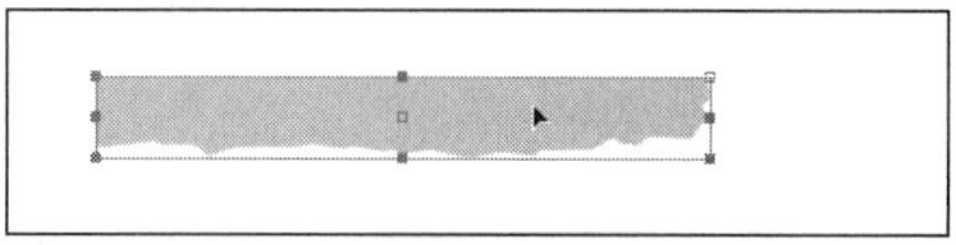

1 ➤ *This is the Navbar torn paper 111 object from the default LiveMotion **Library** palette.*

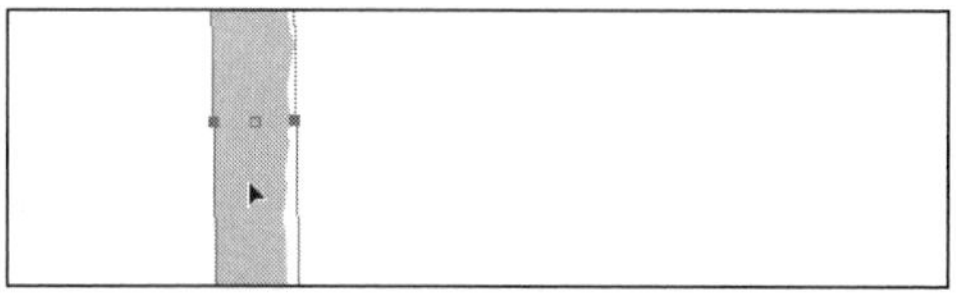

2 ➤ *The object is **rotated** and repositioned.*

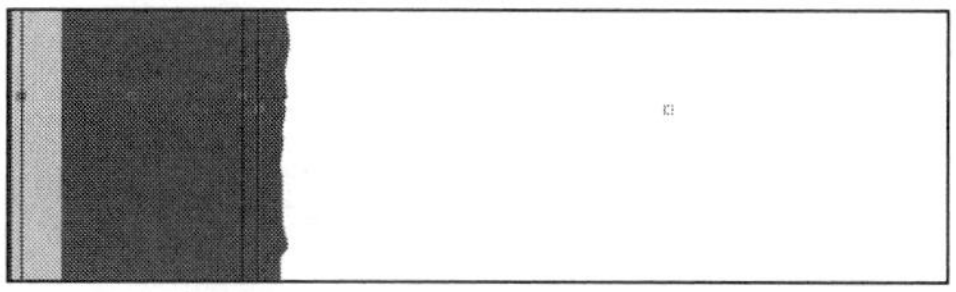

3 ➤ *This is a closeup of the tile objects. An overlapping rectangle in the same color as the library object is drawn to its left. A white rectangle, sent to the back, is used to fill the space on the right. Then, the file is exported as an eight-color GIF.*

4 ➤ *Finally, the Navbar tile file is **placed** as a **texture**.*

More suggestions for backgrounds

- ➤ To create an object with an irregular edge, use a Photoshop filter or a Distort effect in Adobe Illustrator. Save the file, then File menu > Place or Copy-and-Paste the object into LiveMotion. Finally, follow the steps on page 131 to use the object to create a two-color tile.
- ➤ Use the Library palette to place a shape with a curved, wavy, or torn edge into a LiveMotion composition (e.g., try the Navbar 2 torn paper Library shape). Use the selection handles to enlarge and/or rotate the object, then use this object as one of the two rectangles in the steps on page 131 (Figs. 1–4).
- ➤ If you use a tile object that has a texture fill, you may get an unsightly seam between the tiles when the texture is placed as a background in a composition. To avoid this problem, choose a texture that doesn't have a noticeable edge when it repeats and/or soften the edge of the tile via the Softness slider on the Layer palette to make the seam less noticeable.
- ➤ To make objects with soft edges fade smoothly into the background and prevent halos from appearing on its edges when it's viewed in a browser, export the entire composition (tiled background and objects) as a JPEG or SWF, then place it in a Web layout program. This works even for text objects.

To use a dimmed image as a background:

1. Choose Edit menu > Composition Settings (Command-Shift-N/Ctrl-Shift-N).
2. Enter 1024 for both the Width and Height, then click OK (Return/Enter).
3. Place a large image that has a limited number of colors—a monochromatic or two-tone image. Leave blank space around it so the image won't repeat in a large-sized browser window, and yet will look balanced in a normal-sized browser window. The fewer the colors the image contains, the better the image will compress and the smaller will be its export file size. The smaller its file size, the faster it will download on the Web (Fig. 1).

   To reduce the number of colors or gray-scale levels in the image, you can use the Posterize command in Photoshop before you import it or you can use the Posterize slider on the Adjust palette in LiveMotion after it's imported.

   To dim the image, use the Levels dialog box in Photoshop or lower the Contrast and raise the Brightness using the Adjust palette in LiveMotion.
4. Follow the instructions on page 132 to export the file as a tile (Fig. 2).

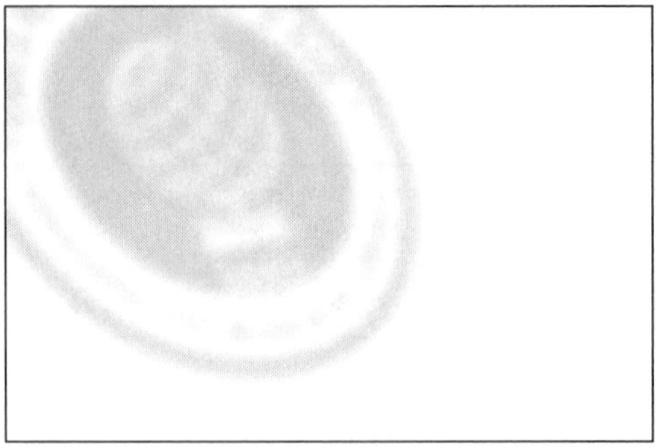

1 ➤ A large, faint image is placed into a LiveMotion composition.

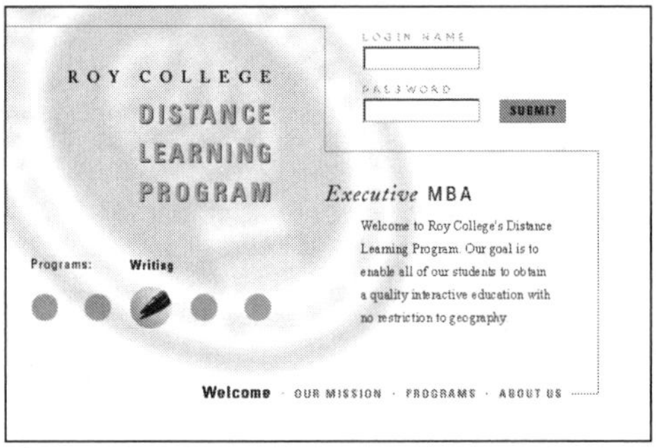

Web site designed by Newfangled Graphics

2 ➤ Other elements are built on top of it.

Rollovers 12

What a rollover looks like

From a design point of view, a rollover is simply a collection of object states, each with a different appearance. Virtually anything that can be done to an object can be applied to a rollover state, such as:

- A change in object's **hue** (e.g., red to green), **brightness**, or **saturation**
- The application (or removal) of a **tint** to an image object or a texture fill
- A change in a layer's **fill with, X offset, Y offset**, **width**, or **softness** setting
- A change in a layer's **opacity**
- The application (or removal) of a **texture, distort, drop shadow, glow**, **gradient**, or **3D** effect
- The application of a **Photoshop filter** to an image object
- The **substitution** (replacement) of one image for another
- The emergence of a **second object** (this is called a remote or secondary rollover)
- The playing of a **sound**
- The playing of an **animation** (see pages 217–225)

Basic rollovers

A ROLLOVER IS A CHANGE that happens to an object on screen when the mouse is moved over it or clicked on it. A "classic" rollover is a button that changes color when the mouse is over it (called the Over state) and then changes to another color, changes to another shape, or undergoes some other change when the mouse button is clicked (called the Down state). In LiveMotion, states are assigned to an object via the Rollovers palette.

Technically, what happens "backstage" is that LiveMotion exports each of an object's rollover states as a separate image. The browser then substitutes a rollover image for the original image to produce the rollover effect.

Rollovers are fun and entertaining. But more important, rollovers are used as visual clues for online viewers so they will know where to click to make additional information display on screen or to activate a link to another Web page or another site. This chapter inclues everything from generic instructions for basic rollovers to four tutorials that will give you the opportunity to practice your new skills. Rollovers aren't just fun to use—they're also fun to create.

In LiveMotion you can choose from preset styles with built-in rollovers that automatically apply a different color or effect to each of the button states (Normal, Over, and Down). Or you can bypass the preset styles and create your own object property changes for each state. First, the presets.

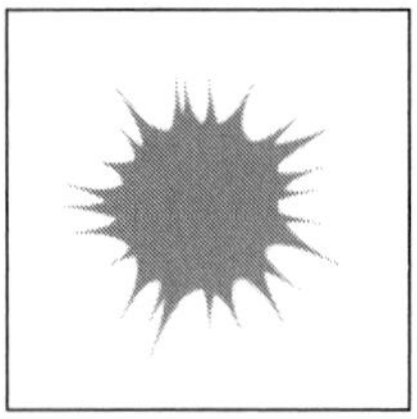

1 ➤ We chose this object from the Library palette to use for a rollover.

To create a rollover using a preset style:

1. Create and select the object that you want to use for the rollover (Fig. 1). It can be any type of object, even a text object.
2. Show the Styles palette, and choose Preview View from the palette menu. Make sure the View Styles With Rollovers button at the bottom of the palette is pressed, and un-press the other buttons (Fig. 2).
3. Click a style name, then click the Apply Style button.
4. Show the Rollovers palette. The Normal and Over states will be listed; there may also be a Down state. Click on the Over thumbnail or on the blank area around the "over" pop-up menu (Fig. 3), then choose a color for the Over state using the Color palette (see page 87).
5. If there's a Down thumbnail, click on it, then choose a new color for that state (Fig. 4).
6. Click the Preview mode button at the bottom of the Toolbox (Q). 
7. To preview the rollover, move the pointer over the button. If the rollover has a Down state, click on the button, then move the mouse away from the object. Click the Edit mode button at the bottom of the Toolbox when you're finished admiring your handiwork (Q). 

➤ When a Down state is previewed in the browser, the object is temporarily assigned the URL for adobe.com. (To preview a composition in the browsers, see page 150.) To prevent this from happening, enter your own URL in the URL field on the Web palette or just enter "#".

2 ➤ Apply a rollover style from the Styles palette.

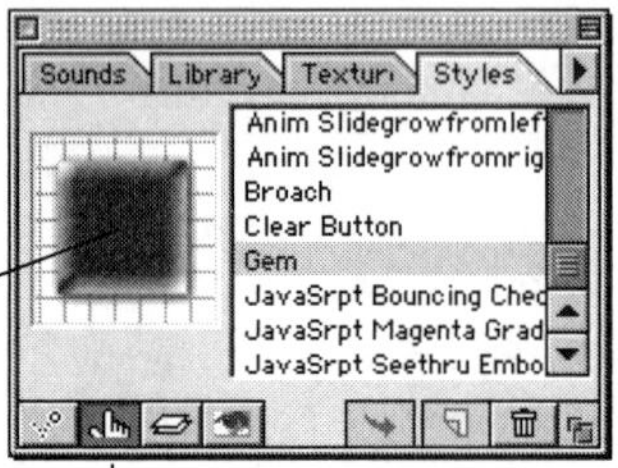

***View Styles With Rollovers** is the only button that's pressed.*

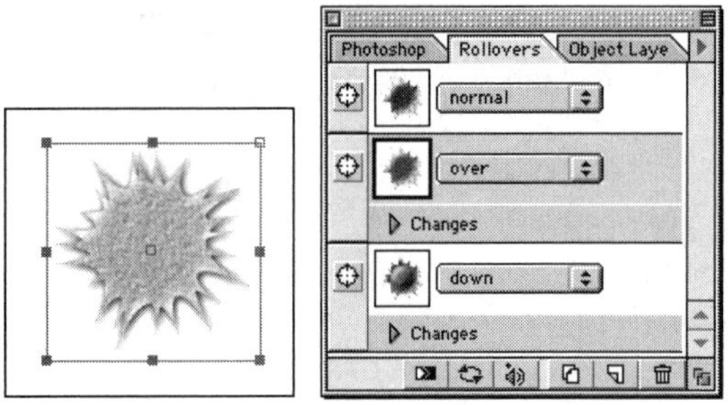

*3 ➤ Click the **Over** thumbnail (or click the blank area around the "over" pop-up menu) to select that state.*

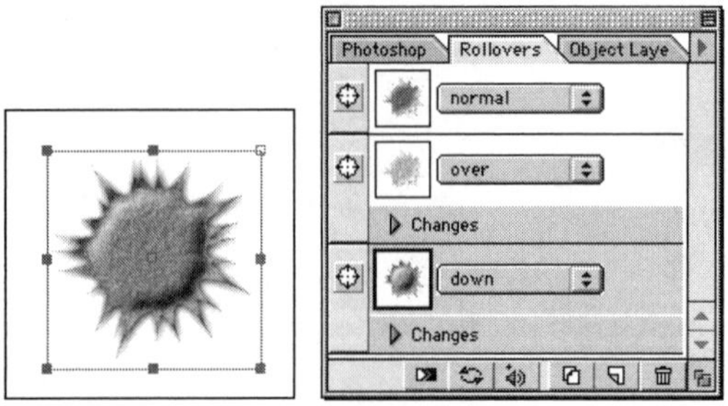

*4 ➤ Click on the **Down** thumbnail (or click the blank area around the "down" pop-up menu) to select that state.*

Rollover color

The Adjust palette is especially handy for creating rollovers that invoke color changes. Just make sure the Over or Down state object's hue, saturation, contrast, or tint differs noticeably with that of the Normal state object or the rollover won't look like a rollover. For example, to change the Over or Down state, you could:

- Deeply **Saturate** or desaturate it
- Make it a much lighter or darker **Tint**
- Apply a **combination** of adjustments to it (e.g., change its **hue** via the Color palette and change its **Brightness** and/or **Contrast** via the Adjust palette). Be creative!

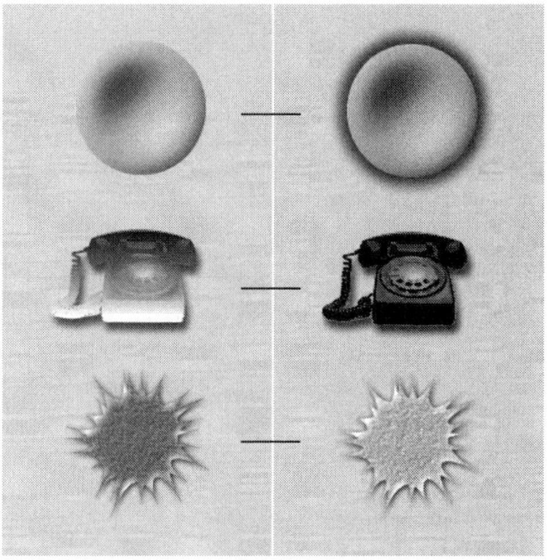

*1 ➤ **Normal** states on the left; **Over** states on the right.*

If you're satisfied using Adobe's preset effects, fine and dandy. If you're not, here's how to make a more personalized rollover. In these instructions, you'll work with two rollover states: Normal and Over.

To create a customized rollover:

1. Create and select the object that you want to use for the rollover. It can be any type of object.
2. Show the Rollovers palette.
3. Click the New Rollover State button at the bottom of the palette to create an Over state.
4. With the Over state selected, make an alteration to the object. Your options here are almost infinite, and of course you can combine many of these changes. Here are some suggestions:

   Change the object's **hue** (e.g., red to green or dark red to light green).

   Adjust the **Brightness** or **Saturation** of the object's color using the Adjust palette. Apply a **Tint** via the Adjust palette to an image object or texture fill.

   Change one of the object layer's Layer palette settings (**Fill with, X Offset, Y Offset, Width,** or **Softness**).

   Apply a **texture, distort, drop shadow, glow,** or **3D** effect.

   Change the **Object Layer Opacity** of one of the object's layers.
5. Watch the composition window as you click between the Normal and Over states on the Rollovers palette (Fig. 1).
6. To preview the rollover, click the Preview mode button at the bottom of the Toolbox (Q). Move the pointer over the button, then away from it.
7. Click the Edit mode button at the bottom of the Toolbox when you're done previewing (Q).

- Don't confuse the Object Layers palette with the Rollovers palette!
- Windows: You may need to deselect all objects before using the "Q" shortcut to enter Preview mode.

Tutorial 1

Now you're ready to work with three rollover states: Normal, Over, and Down. In these instructions, you'll create a button that becomes three-dimensional when the mouse is over it (the Over state), and then looks like it's been pressed down when the mouse clicks on it (the Down state). These are mere suggestions to get you started. Be creative!

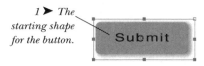

1 ➤ The starting shape for the button.

The separate text object on top of the button won't be affected by the rollover. Our object also has a light gray shadow layer (X Offset 4, Y Offset 2, Wiidth 2, Softness 6).

Create a 3D button

1. Select a geometric object to use for the rollover, and show the Rollovers palette (Fig. 1).
2. Show the 3D palette.
3. Choose Emboss from the drop-down menu. Set the Depth to 1, the Softness to 0, the Lighting to 92, and the Angle to 135 (Fig. 2).
4. On the Rollovers palette, click the New Rollover State button twice to create an Over state and a Down state.
5. Click on the Over state. On the 3D palette, set the Depth to 10 and the Lighting to 158 (Fig. 3).
6. Click on the Down state. On the 3D palette, set the Depth to 6, the Angle to 320, and the Lighting to 120. Choose white as the object color from the Color palette (Fig. 4).
7. Click the Preview mode button at the bottom of the Toolbox (Q). Move the pointer over the object, then click on it. Click the Edit mode button at the bottom of the Toolbox when you're done previewing (Q). ▲

*2 ➤ The **3D** palette setup for the button's **Normal** state.*

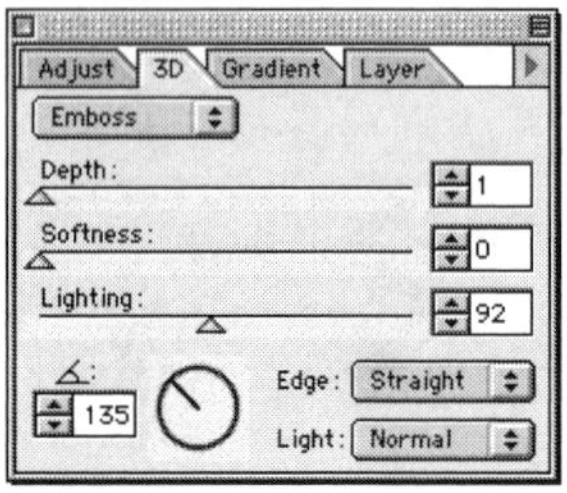

*3 ➤ After clicking the **Over** state and changing **3D** palette settings.*

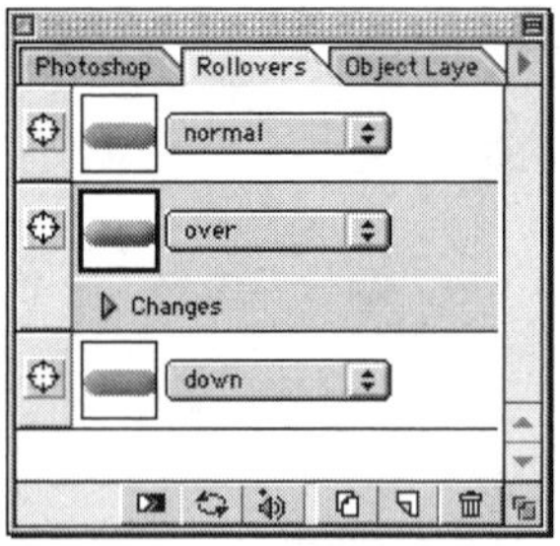

*4 ➤ After clicking the **Down** state and changing **3D** and **Color** palette settings.*

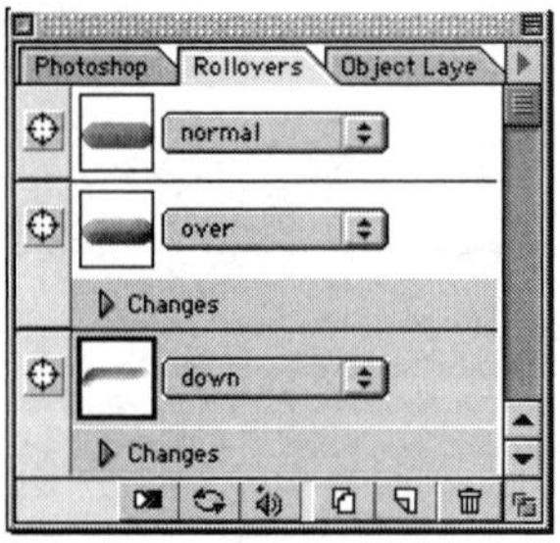

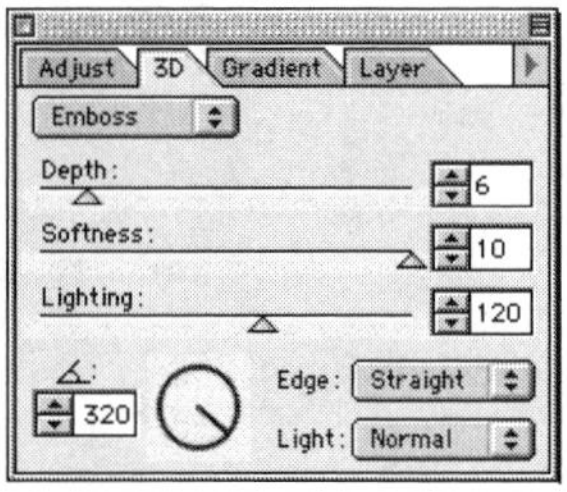

1 ➤ *The original image object to be used for the rollover.*

2 ➤ *The **object** is flipped **horizontally**.*

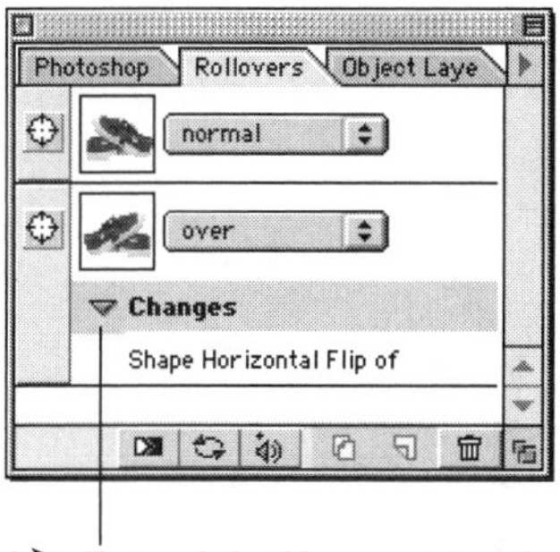

3 ➤ *Expand the **Changes** triangle on the **Rollovers** palette to display a list of the changes made to that state.*

4 ➤ *The phone object was imported as a two-layer file, and each layer was made into a **separate object** in LiveMotion. Only the receiver layer was scaled for the Over state.*

Here, instead of using type or a geometric object for a rollover, you'll use an image object. (To create a rollover using two image objects, see the instructions on the following page.)

To create a rollover using one image object:

1. Place an image object into a LiveMotion composition (Command-I/Ctrl-I), scale the image to the desired size, and keep the object selected (Fig. 1).
2. Click the New Rollover State button on the Rollovers palette to create an Over state.
3. With the Over state still selected, make a change to the object. Start by choosing Object menu > Transform > Flip Horizontal to flip the image (Figs. 2–3). You could also enlarge it, rotate it, recolor it, desaturate it, steam it, roast it, or sauté it. Use your imagination.
4. Click the Preview mode button at the bottom of the Toolbox (Q), preview the rollover, then click back on the Edit mode button (Q).

➤ You can make an object look modular by converting the object into layers in Photoshop and then working with one of the layers. To do this, divide the image into two separate layers in Photoshop, import the file into LiveMotion, convert the layers into separate objects (see page 192), and position them to recreate the "whole" image. Finally, for the Over state, transform one of the converted objects (Fig. 4).

In these instructions, instead of editing the same object for the Over state, you'll make a whole new object appear for the Over state. You can make a gorilla turn into a kangaroo or you can do something tasteful. We offer two methods for doing this.

To create a rollover using two different image objects:

METHOD 1

1. Place two objects into a composition. Position the one you want to use for the the Normal state in the desired location. The other object can be placed anywhere in the composition, since it's going to be deleted later (Fig. 1).
2. Select the image object you want to use for the Over state, then choose Edit menu > Copy.
3. Select the image object you are using for the Normal state.
4. Click the New Rollover State button on the Rollovers palette to create an Over state (Fig. 2).
5. Choose Edit menu > Paste Special > Paste Image. If you copy and paste a bitmap image, the image will be scaled automatically to fit the selection border of the selected object (Fig. 3); a pasted Illustrator object won't be scaled.
6. Select, the original image you used for step 2, then delete it.
7. Click the Preview mode button at the bottom of the Toolbox (Q), preview the rollover (Fig. 4), then click back on the Edit mode button (Q).

➤ If you want to make further changes to either state, select the state and apply individual attributes. Don't apply a style, because a style will change all the states!

METHOD 2

1. Select an image object.
2. On the Rollovers palette, click the New Rollover State button to create an Over state.

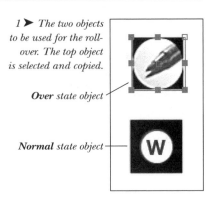

1 ➤ The two objects to be used for the roll-over. The top object is selected and copied.

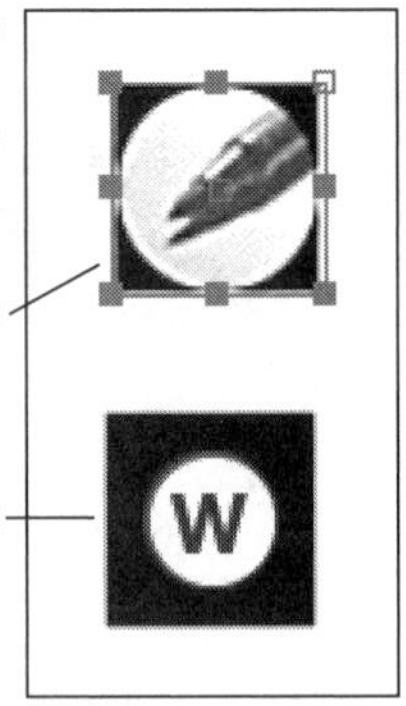

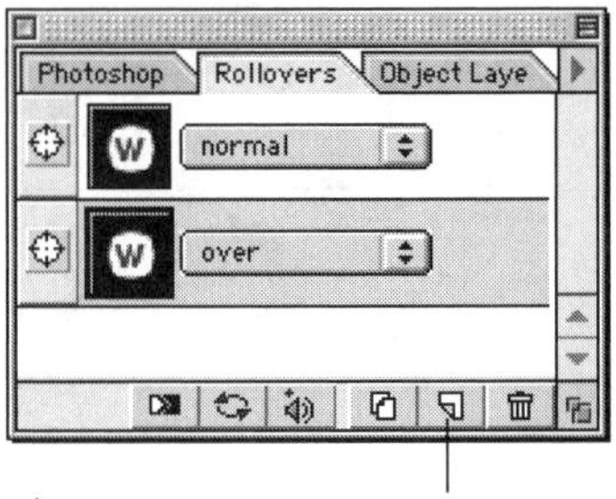

*2 ➤ The **New Rollover State** button is clicked on the **Rollovers** palette to create an Over state.*

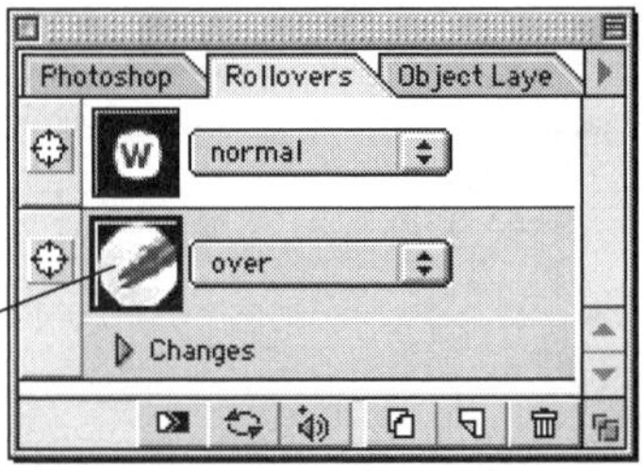

*3 ➤ After using Paste Special > **Paste Image** on the object that has the Over state.*

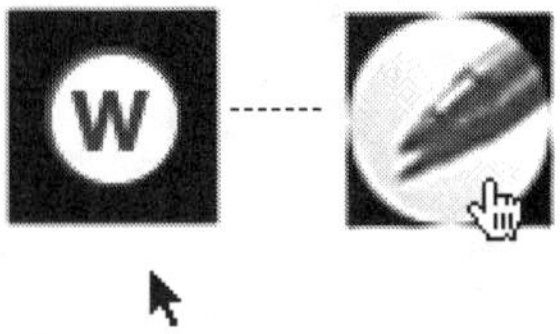

*4 ➤ The **rollover** in action.*

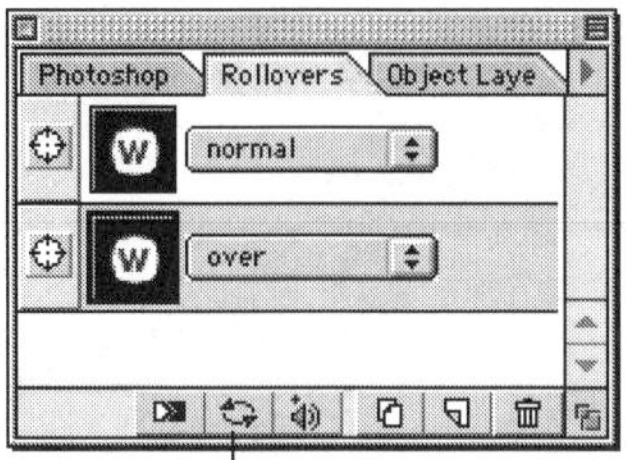

*1 ➤ The **Replace Image** button at the bottom of the **Rollovers** palette is clicked.*

2 ➤ This is the image object (Layer 1) to be used for the rollover.

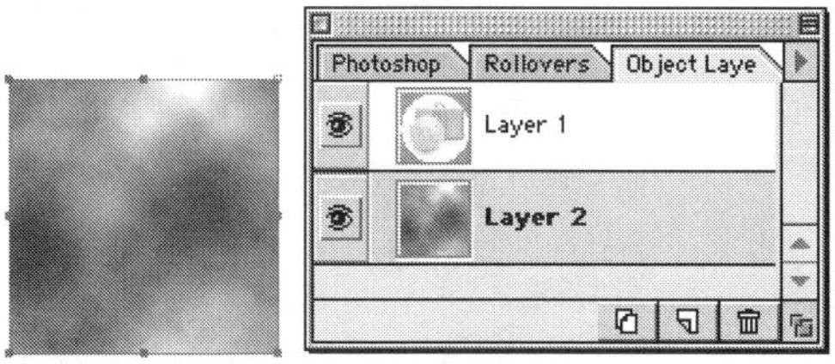

*3 ➤ Another image object is copied and pasted into the new Layer 2 (Object Layers palette) using Paste Special > **Paste Texture**.*

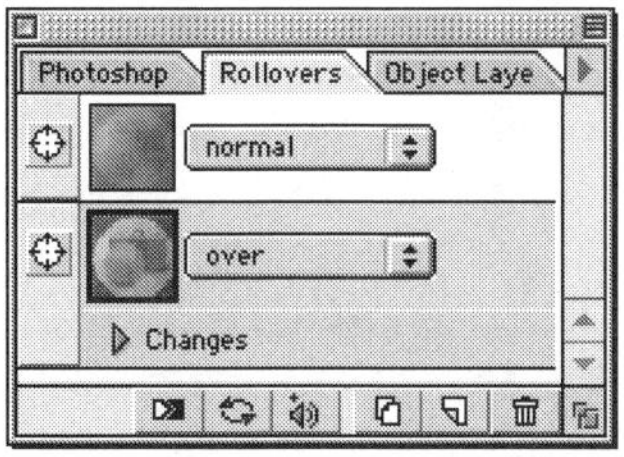

*4 ➤ The **Over** state is created.*

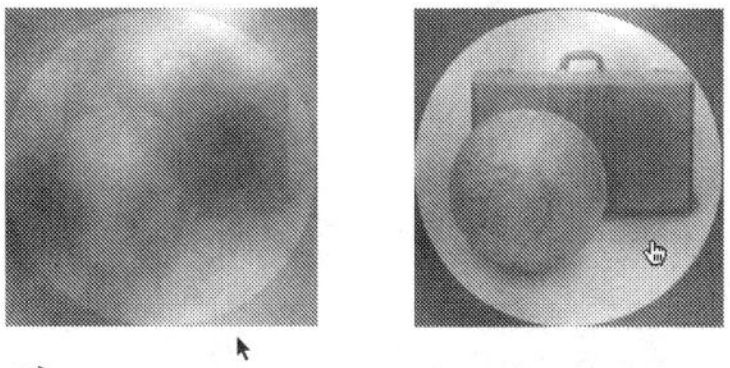

*5 ➤ The **Object Layer Opacity** for Layer 1 changes from 8 for the Normal state to 40 for the Over state.*

3. Click the Replace Image button at the bottom of the Rollovers palette (Fig. 1).
4. Locate the image file for the Over state, then click Open. If you open a LiveMotion file, all the objects in that file will be imported.
5. Preview the rollover.

To hide an image, then make it appear for the Over state:

1. Select an image object (Fig. 2).
2. On the Object Layers palette, select the topmost layer, then click the New Layer button.
3. Use the Color palette to apply a color to the new layer.
   or
   Use the Textures palette to apply a texture to the new layer.
   or
   Copy another image object, select the new layer, then choose Edit menu > Paste Special > Paste Texture (Fig. 3).
4. Reselect the topmost layer (the image or texture layer).
5. On the Opacity palette, lower the Object Layer Opacity to 8.
6. Click the New Rollover State button on the Rollovers palette to create an Over state (Fig. 4), and keep the Over state selected.
7. On the Opacity palette, raise the Object Layer Opacity for Layer 1 to the desired level.
8. Click the Normal state and then the Over state to view the effect. Or click the Preview mode button, move the mouse over the object, then move it away from the object (Fig. 5).

To delete a rollover state:

1. On the Rollovers palette, click on the state you want to delete.
2. Click the Delete Rollover State (trash) button at the bottom of the palette. You won't get a warning prompt, so be careful.

Tutorial 2

Use an embossed button in a rollover

1. Create a document 200 pixels high by 200 pixels wide. Choose the Ellipse tool (L). Show the Transform palette, then draw a circle 100 pixels in width and height.
2. Show the 3D palette. Choose Ripple from the pop-up menu. Set the Depth to 37, the Softness to 4, the Lighting to 100, the Edge to Ripple, and the Angle to 135° (Figs. 1–2). *Note:* You'd use a lower Depth setting for a smaller object.
3. Click the Background color square on the Color palette, then choose a dark color.
4. Select the button object. Show the Layer palette, and choose Fill with: Background (Fig. 3).
5. Show the Object Layers palette. Click the New Layer button, double-click the new layer, rename it "glow," and click OK. Leave the glow layer selected.
6. Choose a light gray from the Color palette for the Glow layer (R, G, and B all 204). Show the 3D palette, and choose None from the pop-up menu.
7. Show the Rollovers palette. Click the Duplicate Rollover State button to create the Over state.
8. Make sure the Glow layer is selected on the Object Layers palette.
9. Show the Layer palette. Choose Fill with: Color, set the Width to 6, and set the Softness to 9 (Fig. 4).
10. Show the Rollovers palette. Click the Duplicate Rollover State button to create the Down state (Fig. 5).
11. On the Object Layers palette, select Layer 1.
12. On the 3D palette, make the Angle 230°.
13. Click the Preview mode button at the bottom of the Toolbox (Q), move the pointer over the button, click on it, then move the pointer away. Click the Edit mode button when you're done (Q).▲

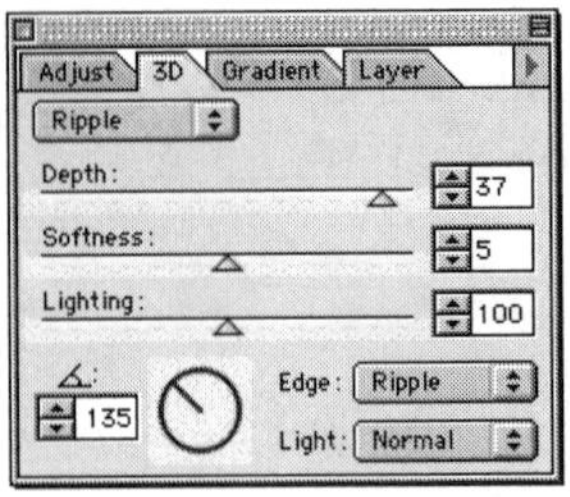

*1➤ The **3D palette** settings for the **button** object.*

*2➤ The **button** object with the **3D Ripple** effect.*

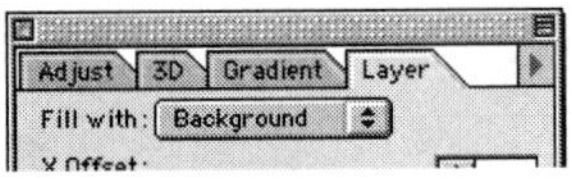

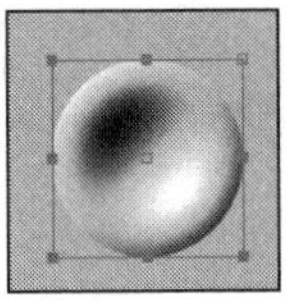

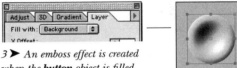

*3➤ An emboss effect is created when the **button** object is filled with **Background**.*

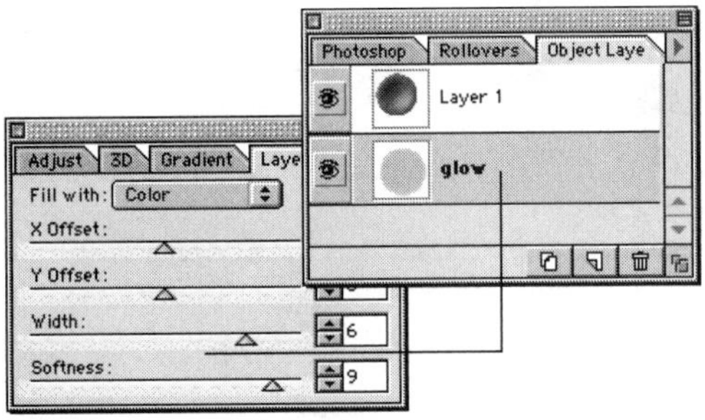

*4➤ **Layer** palette **Width** and **Softness** values are used to produce a glow effect on the "glow" layer.*

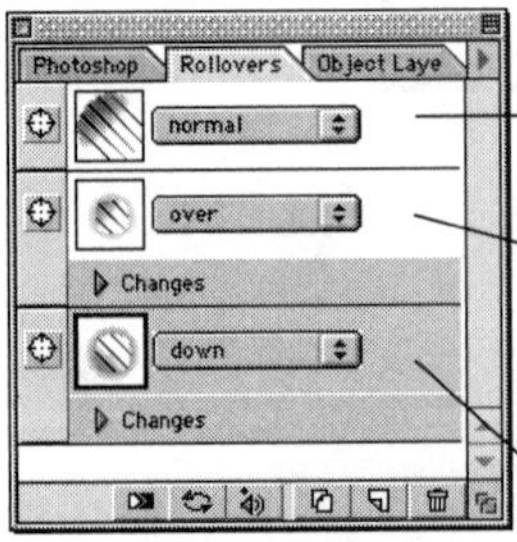

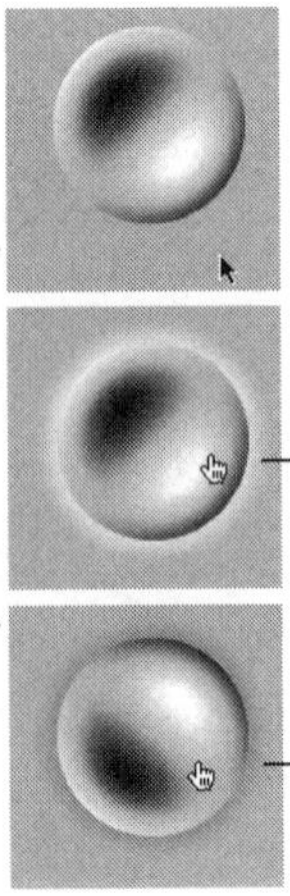

*5➤ The **three states** on the Rollovers palette and on the object.*

***Glow** effect from the Layer palette.*

***Angle** change from the **3D** palette.*

1 ➤ We chose this image object to become a remote object. It will be controlled by a button object.

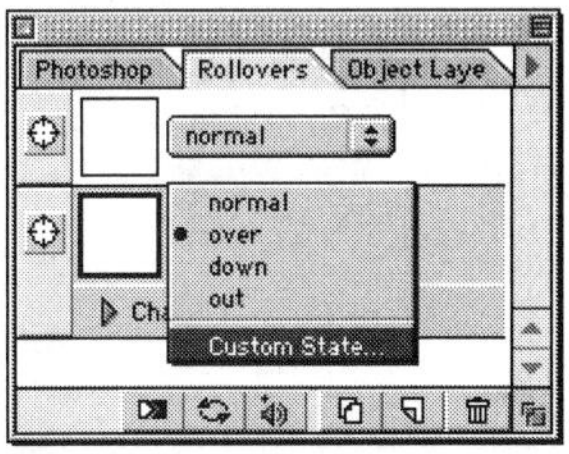

*2 ➤ Press on the pop-up menu for the over state and choose **Custom State**.*

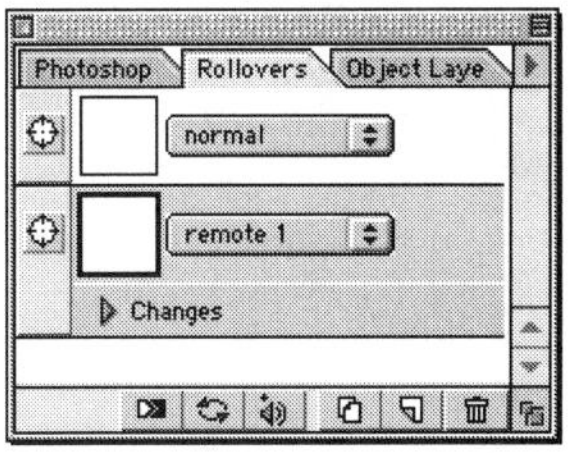

*3 ➤ The new **remote 1** state.*

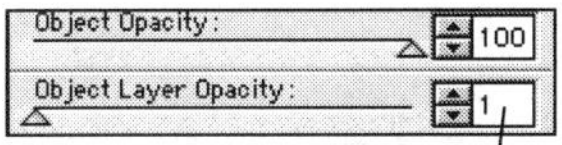

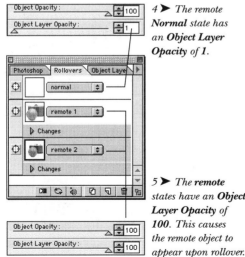

*4 ➤ The remote **Normal** state has an **Object Layer Opacity** of **1**.*

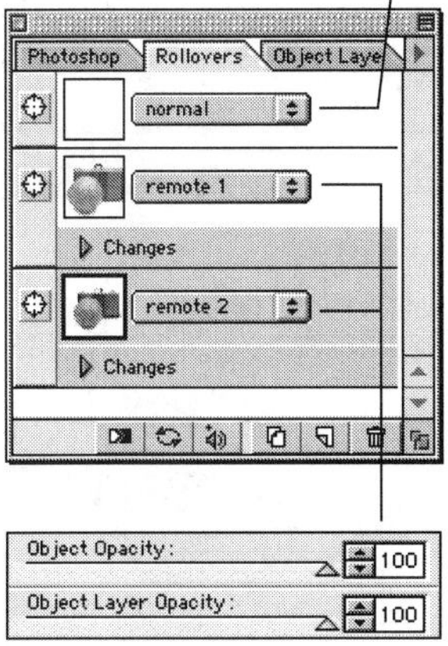

*5 ➤ The **remote** states have an **Object Layer Opacity** of **100**. This causes the remote object to appear upon rollover.*

Tutorial 3

Not enough excitement for you? Make your rollovers work harder. In this tutorial, you will create a remote (or secondary) rollover that occurs when a primary rollover is activated. Examples of remote rollovers are: a button triggers the display of an image; a thumbnail of an image triggers the display of a larger version of the same image; or an image triggers the display of type.

Create a remote rollover

CREATE TARGET STATES FOR A REMOTE OBJECT

1. Create a one-layer text, image, or geometric object to be the remote object the rollover triggers (Fig. 1), and select it using the Selection tool (V).
2. Click the New Rollover State button on the Rollovers palette to create an Over state for the remote (target) object. This object will become the target for another rollover object.
3. From the pop-up menu for the Over state, choose Custom State, enter a name (e.g., "remote 1"), then click OK (Figs. 2–3).
4. To create another target state, click the New Rollover State button again to create the Over state.
5. From the pop-up menu for the Over state, choose Custom State, enter a name (e.g., "remote 2"), then click OK. Custom States are listed in alphabetical order.
6. *Optional:* If you're using an image object, choose a color from the Color palette.On the Adjust palette, move the Tint slider to around 200. A tinted version of the image will display for the remote 2 state (target Down state). A Changes list will now appear below the Down state. Expand the list to see the property changes.
7. Click on the target Normal state. On the Opacity palette, move the Object Layer Opacity slider to 1 (Fig. 4). (To select this now-invisible object, marquee the whole thing with the Selection tool.)

(Continued on the next page)

8. For the remote 1 (Over) and remote 2 (Down) state, reset the Object Layer Opacity slider to 100 (Fig. 5, previous page). Continue with the remaining steps.
9. *Optional:* Click the Down state and change the object's appearance.

Now that you've created target states for a remote object, it's time to target the remote object to the rollover object.

TARGET A REMOTE OBJECT TO THE ROLLOVER OBJECT

1. Create a button rollover object with Over and Down states (instructions are on page 140), and leave the object selected (Figs. 1–2). This is a separate object from the one you just created.
2. Drag the Target (leftmost) icon from the button's Normal state on the Rollovers palette over the remote object in the composition window. Release the mouse when the target object's selection border appears (Fig. 3). Win: Reselect the button.
3. Make sure Normal is chosen from the nested target state's pop-up menu (Fig. 4).
4. Drag the Target (leftmost) icon from the Over state on the Rollovers palette over the remote object in the composition window. Release the mouse when the target object's selection border appears. Win: Reselect the button.
5. On the Rollovers palette, a nested target state with its own pop-up menu will display below the Over state. Choose Remote 1 from the target pop-up menu.
6. Drag the Target (leftmost) icon from the Down state over the remote object in the composition window. Release the mouse when the target object's selection border appears. Win: Reselect the button.
7. From the nested target state's pop-up menu, choose Remote 2 (Fig. 5, opposite page).
8. Deselect all objects.
9. Click the Preview mode button (Q). Move the pointer over the button object, then click on it. Click the Edit mode button when you're finished (Q).▲

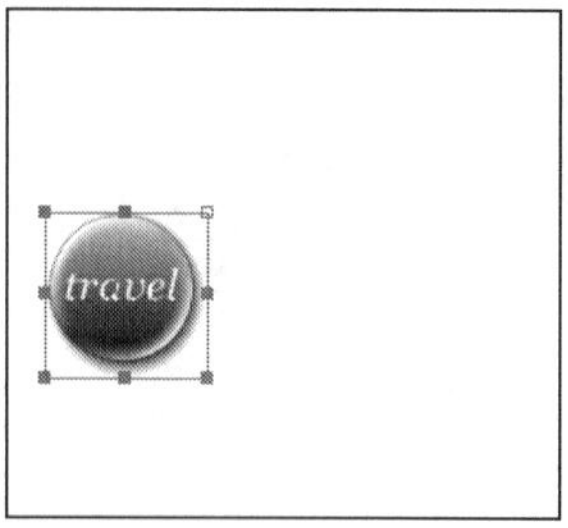

*1 ➤ The **button** object. (We added a text object on top of the button.)*

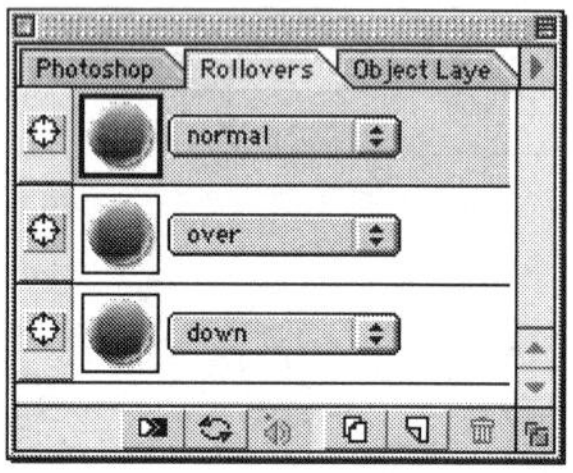

2 ➤ An Over and Down state are created for the button object.

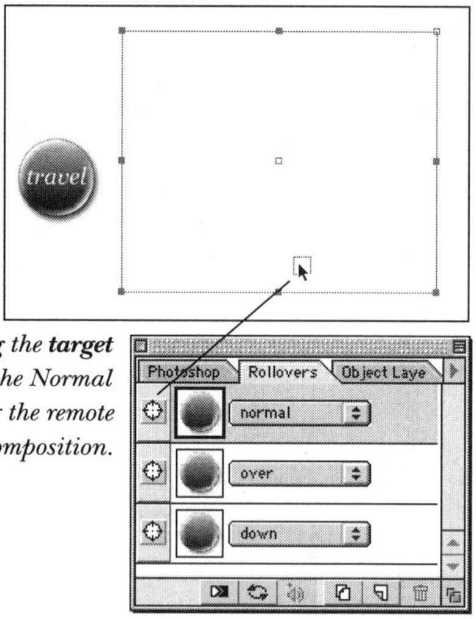

*3 ➤ Drag the **target** icon from the Normal state over the remote object in the composition.*

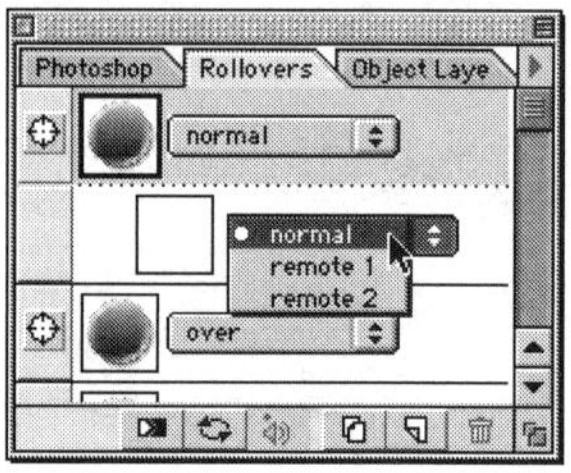

*4 ➤ Choose **normal** from the **nested target state** pop-up menu.*

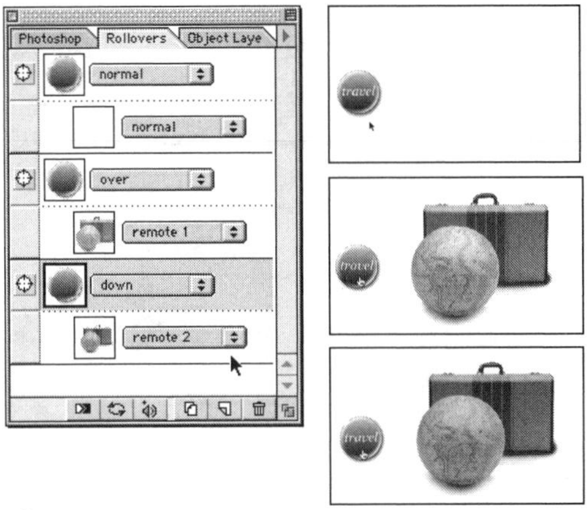

5 ➤ After dragging the Over and Down state target icons and ***linking*** *them to* ***remote 1*** *and* ***remote 2****, respectively. Now the rollover can be previewed.*

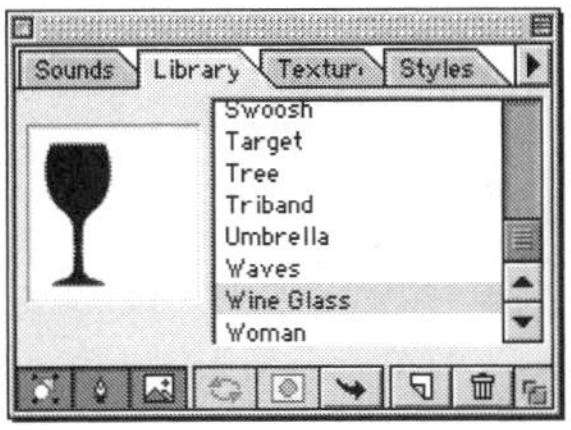

1 ➤ Drag a shape from the ***Library*** *palette.*

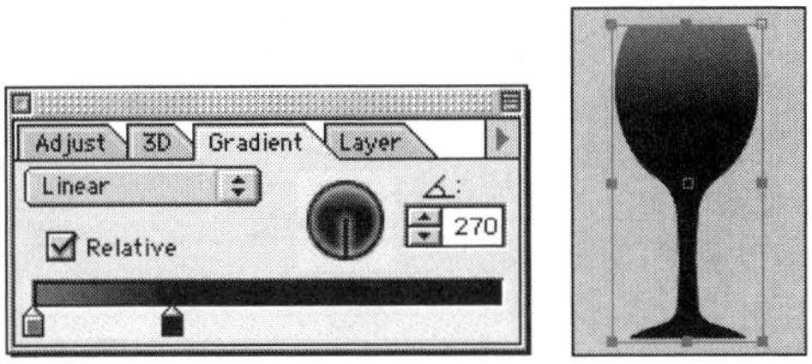

2 ➤ Apply a ***gradient*** *with these settings to the shape.*

Tutorial 4

In these instructions you'll use a gradient that gradually changes color in a remote rollover object.

A moving gradient in a remote rollover

CREATE THE REMOTE OBJECT

1. Drag a shape from the Library palette into the composition window or draw a new shape (Fig. 1), and make it any color except black.
2. On the Gradient palette, choose Linear from the drop-down menu. Set the Angle to 270. Move the color gradient end marker so it's about a quarter of an inch away from the color gradient start marker (Fig. 2).
3. On the Rollovers palette, click the Duplicate Rollover State button.
4. From the pop-up menu for the Over state, choose Custom State, type "gradient 1," then click OK (Fig. 3).
5. On the Gradient palette, move the color gradient end marker all the way to the right. Move the color gradient start marker so it's about a quarter of an inch from the left edge of the gradient bar (Fig. 4).
6. On the Rollovers palette, click the Duplicate Rollover State button again.

(Continued on the next page)

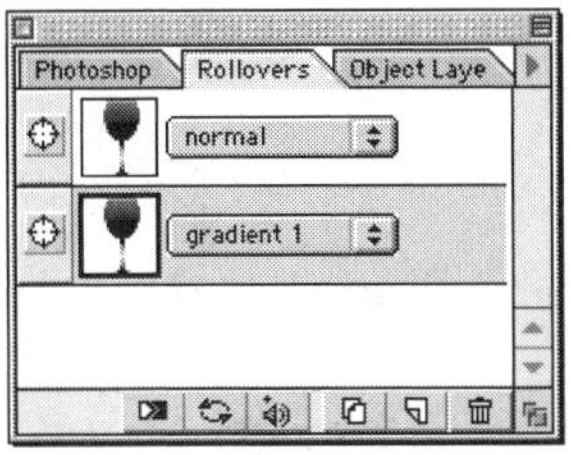

3 ➤ Create a new rollover state. choose Custom State, and rename it "gradient 1."

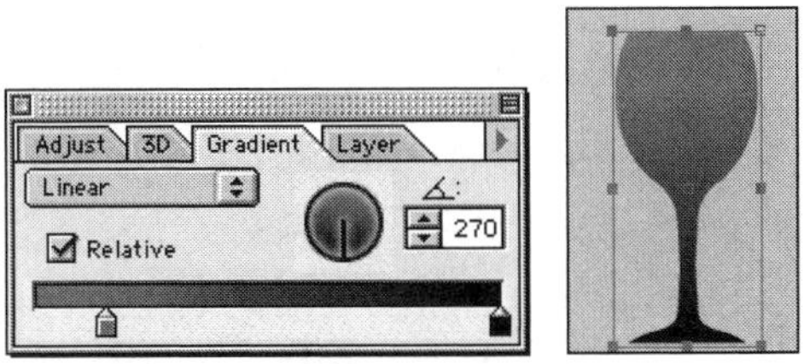

4 ➤ Assign these gradient properties to the gradient 1 rollover state.

7. From the pop-up menu for the Over state, choose Custom State, enter "gradient 2," then click OK (Fig. 1).
8. On the Gradient palette, move the color gradient start marker so it's positioned about two-thirds of the way across the length of the gradient bar to the right (Fig. 2).
9. On the Adjust palette, set the Brightness to 14.

CREATE THE BUTTON AND TARGET THE REMOTE OBJECT

1. Create a separate button (Fig. 3), and add an Over rollover state and a Down rollover state to it.
2. On the Rollovers palette, drag the Target icon for the Normal state over the remote object. Make sure Normal is chosen from the Target state pop-up menu (Fig. 4).
3. Drag the Target icon for the Over state over the remote object. Choose "gradient 1" from the Target state pop-up menu.
4. Drag the Target icon for the Down state over the remote object. Choose "gradient 2" from the Target state pop-up menu (Fig. 5).
5. Deselect all objects (Command-Shift-A/Ctrl-Shift-A).
6. Click the Preview mode button on the Toolbox (Q). Move the pointer over the button, then click. Click the Edit mode button when you're done previewing (Q).

➤ Be sure to assign a custom name to each state as you create it. Remember, the states are listed alphabetically.▲

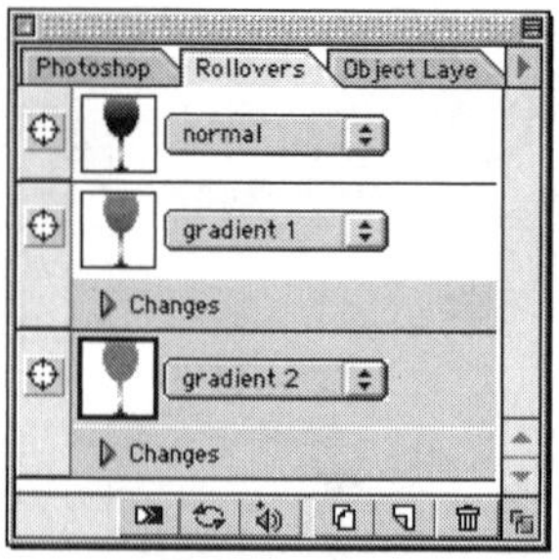

1➤ Create a new rollover state, choose Custom State, and rename it "gradient 2."

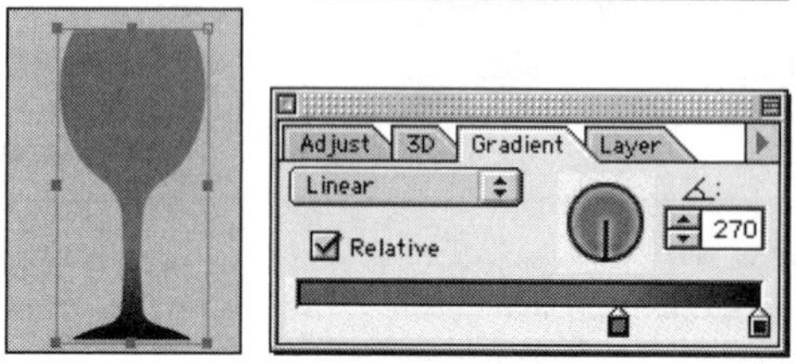

*2➤ Assign these **gradient** properties to the gradient 2 rollover state.*

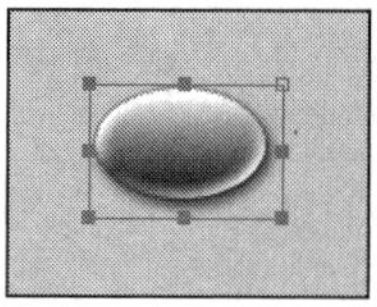

3➤ This is the button object that will trigger the rollover.

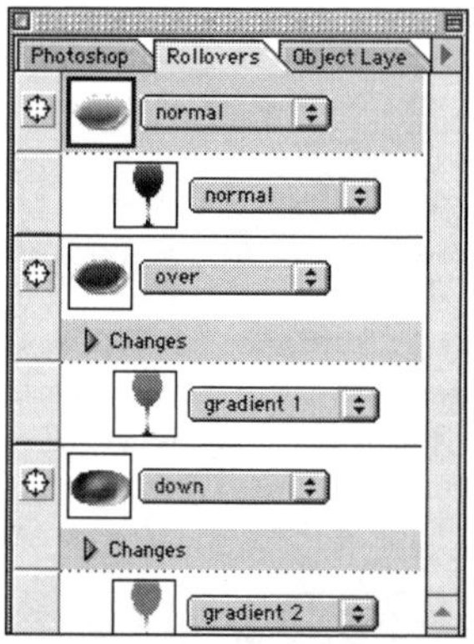

*5➤ The **Rollovers** palette after dragging all three target icons and choosing the appropriate remote state from each target state pop-up menu.*

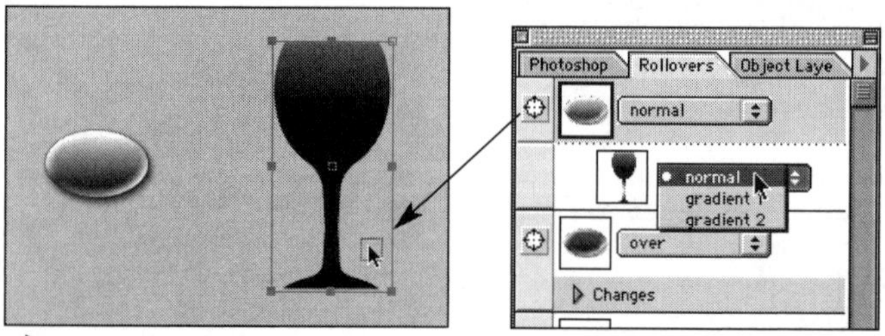

*4➤ Drag the Normal state **target** icon over the **remote** object, then choose **normal** from the target state pop-up menu.*

*1 ➤ The rollover object to which a **sound** will be attached.*

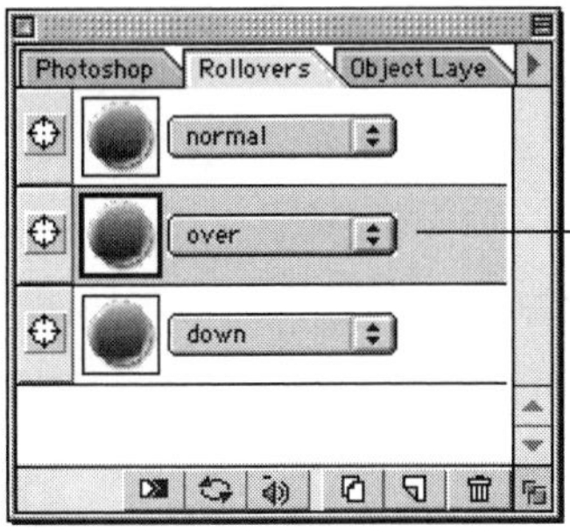

*2 ➤ Choose the object's **Over** state on the **Rollovers** palette.*

*3 ➤ Choose a sound on the Sounds palette, then click the **Apply Sound** button.*

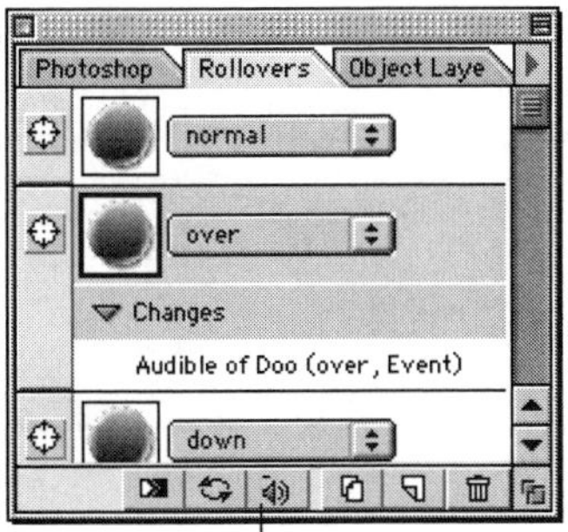

*4 ➤ The attached sound appears on the **Changes** list on the **Rollovers** palette, and the Sound button has a **minus** sign.*

Using sound

Sounds can be used to grab a viewer's attention and literally amplify areas of a Web page. Sounds can be attached to the Over, Down, and Out states, but not to the Normal state. (Read more about sounds on pages 188–189.)

To attach a sound to a rollover:

1. Create and select a rollover object that has at least an Over state (Fig. 1).
2. On the Rollovers palette, select the Over state (Fig. 2).
3. Show the Sounds palette.
4. Click on a sound, then click the Apply Sound button at the bottom of the Sounds palette. (Fig. 3) A tiny "-" (minus sign) will appear on the Sound button on the Rollovers palette instead of a "+" (plus sign). (Fig. 4)
5. *Optional:* Click on the Down state on the Rollovers palette, then repeat the previous step.
6. Click the Preview mode button (Q), roll over the button, then click on it. Click the Edit mode button when you're finished previewing (Q).

   Note: If you apply a sound to both the Over and the Down states, when you release the button from the Down state, the Over state sound will be repeated.

➤ If you forget which sound was applied to which state, expand the Changes list for a state—the name of the sound will be listed as an "Audible" property (Fig. 4).

➤ Use the SWF format to export objects with attached sounds.

To remove a sound from a rollover state:

1. On the Rollovers palette, select the state from which you want to remove a sound.
2. Click the Sound button.

Previewing rollovers

To preview a rollover in the browser:

1. Show the Export palette (Fig. 1).
2. Check the Preview box. The composition display will now reflect the current export settings.
3. Choose GIF from the topmost pop-up menu. Watch the screen preview as you move the Colors slider to the lowest possible number before the colors in image and gradient objects start to degrade. Next, choose Web Adaptive from the palette pop-up menu. And finally, for objects that include an alpha channel, make sure the Include Transparency Information button is pressed. Leave the Dither and Interlace options off.
   or
   Choose SWF from the topmost pop-up menu, and and choose JPEG or Truecolor from the second pop-up menu.
4. Choose Edit menu > Composition Settings (Command-Shift-N/Ctrl-Shift-N).
5. If you chose GIF for step 3, choose AutoLayout from the Export pop-up menu (Fig. 2).
   or
   If you chose SWF for step 3, choose Export: Entire Composition and check the Make HTML box.
6. From the File menu > Preview In submenu, choose a browser.
7. Move the pointer over the button in the browser, then click on it if the rollover has a Down state. Close the browser window and click back in LiveMotion when you're done previewing. For more about export, see Chapter 16.

➤ Don't group or overlap a button or remote object with any other objects in a composition. Grouping and overlapping will prevent a rollover exported as GIF from functioning in the browser. Grouping and overlapping won't adversely affect rollovers exported as SWF.

AutoSlice or AutoLayout?

Both AutoSlice and AutoLayout will generate an HTML file for the exported rollover and a folder containing an image for each state. AutoSlice will position all the images along the left edge of the browser window, whereas AutoLayout will preserve the current layout in the browser by exporting the composition in an HTML table. The HTML code controls when the various rollover image states that are exported as slices will display.

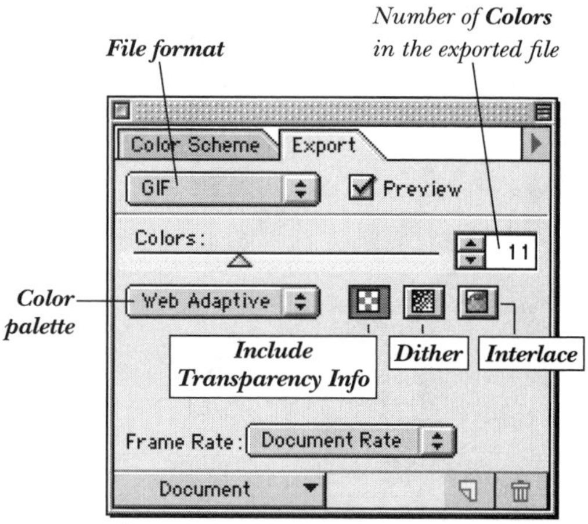

*1 ➤ The **Export** palette is used to **optimize** individual objects or a whole composition.*

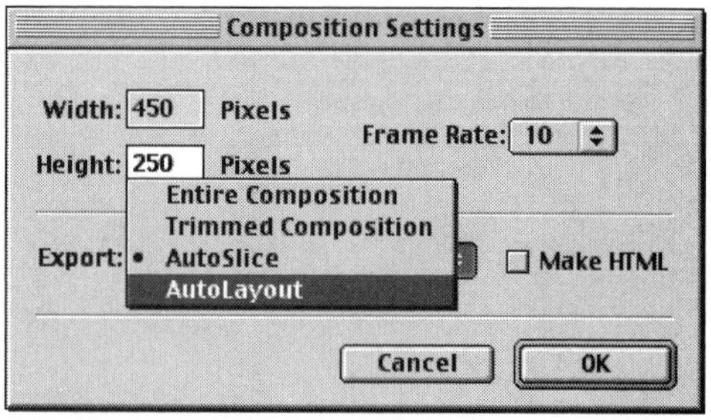

*2 ➤ The **Composition Settings** dialog box is used to choose **Export** settings.*

Animation 13

A tutorial approach

When we approached writing this important chapter, we thought it would be easier for our readers to learn animation techniques using tutorial exercises than using our usual all-purpose instructions. Once you've run through the tutorials, try creating some animations using your own formulations.

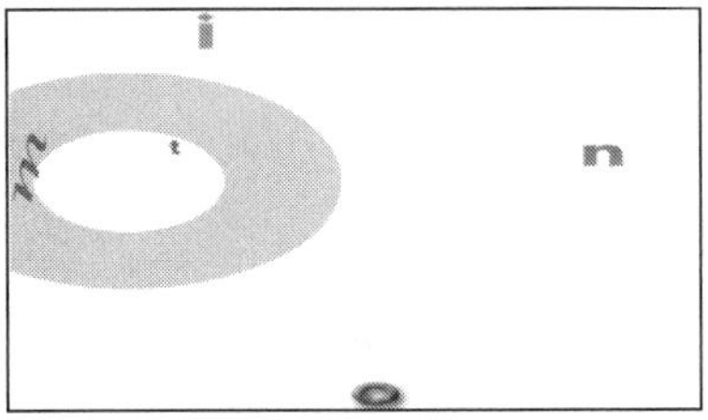

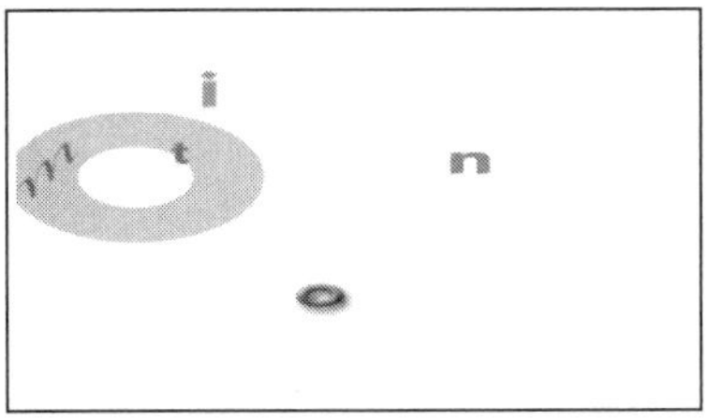

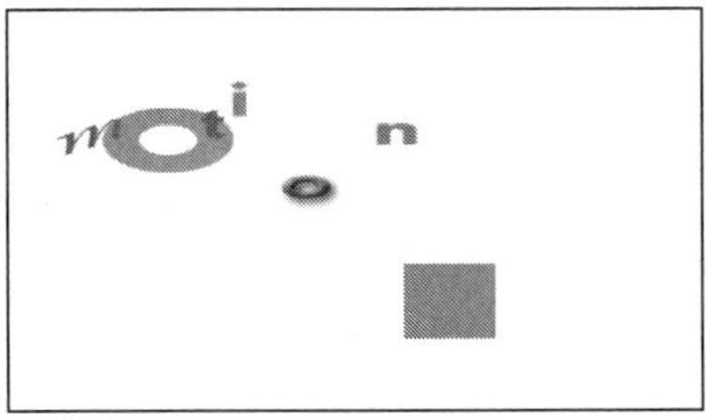

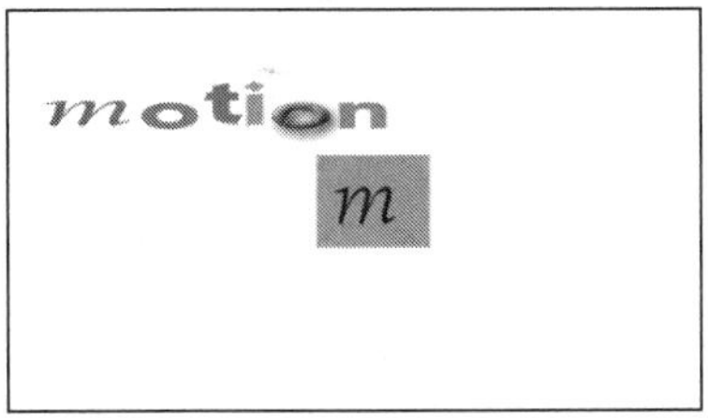

Animation basics

What is animation?

SIMPLY PUT, ANIMATION is the movement of objects or words across a computer screen or a video monitor. Many types of animations can be produced using LiveMotion. For example, you can:

- Make an object **move** across a Web page. An object can move from side to side, from top to bottom, or diagonally. In a more complex animation, you could make more than one object move; make an object move and also change in scale; or make an object move and rotate simultaneously.
- Make an object or objects **fade in** or **fade out** gradually. A more complex fade-in or fade-out would be to make two objects fade simultaneously—one fades out as the other fades in. A fade-in or fade-out can also be combined with movement.
- **Replace** one object with another object. One object disappears and another object takes its place. A more complex replacement would be a gradual fade from one object into another object instead of an abrupt change.
- **Transform** an object via animation (e.g., scale, rotate, skew, or a combination thereof).
- Change an object's **color** via animation. A tint could be applied or removed or an object's saturation or brightness could be altered. A more complex color animation would be to have the angle of a gradient change over time.

How is an animation produced?

In LiveMotion, animations for a Web page can be produced using any or all of the objects currently in a composition. You can animate entire objects or you can be more specific and animate individual object layers.

The Timeline editor is the workhorse palette that you'll use for all your animations. Let's take a look at it. Open a composition that contains some objects, then choose Timeline menu > **Show Timeline Window** (Command-T/Ctrl-T) (see the next page). (Adobe AfterEffects people: No, it's not your imagination, the LiveMotion **Timeline editor** looks and works a lot like the Time Layout editor in AfterEffects.)

Using the Timeline editor, you can control how long individual objects will appear on screen, whether for the entire duration of the composition or only a portion thereof. You can make individual objects enter or exit at any time during an animation. An object's duration is represented by the **duration bar** on the Timeline editor.

To create an animation, first you'll decide when and for how long you want an object to display on screen. After choosing a particular point in time, you'll establish a **property** setting for an object using one of the palettes. When you do this, a **keyframe** appears in the Timeline editor (take a peek at pages 154 and 156).

A palette setting will remain constant throughout a composition until you establish a different setting for the same property at another point in time. This is done by editing the selected object property using a palette at another point in time. This, in turn, creates another keyframe. LiveMotion will create a series of steps between the properties so they flow smoothly from one to the other—that's how digital animation works!

You can also create **time-independent** objects that have their own duration and play separately from the main composition. You can make a time-independent object **loop** or you can set a **behavior** to make the object play or stop to allow for visitor interaction.

Check it out!

To see the completed tutorial animations from this book and a few others we've thrown in just for the sheer thrill of it, visit:

www.peachpit.com/vqs/livemotion/

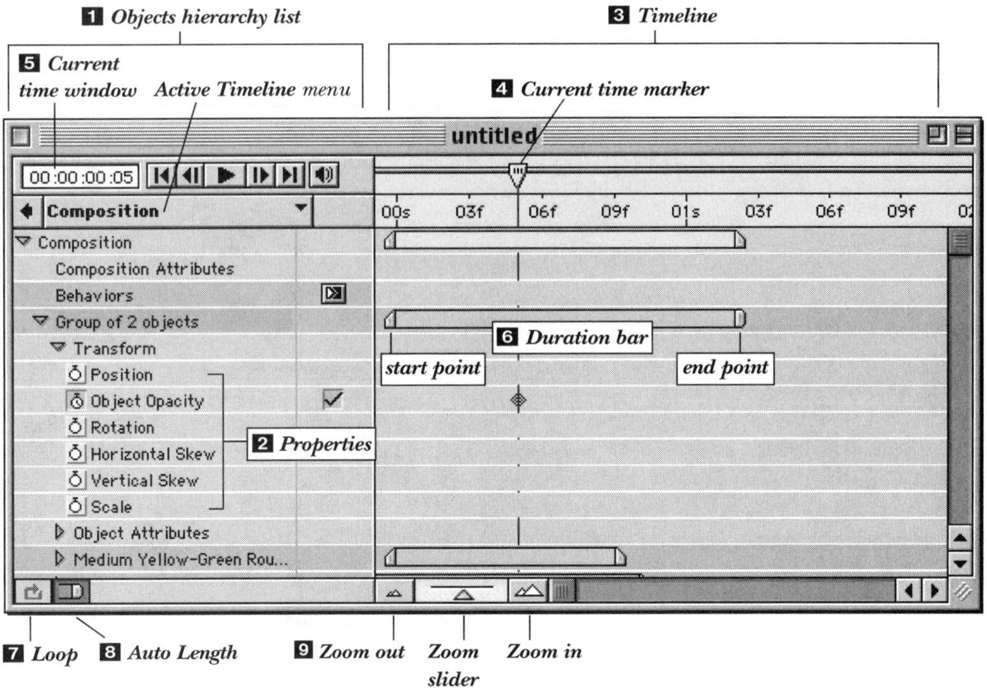

1 The **objects hierarchy list** displays the descriptive names of all the objects in a composition from top to bottom in the front to back order in which they appear in the composition. Click the triangle to the left of a name to expand that object's list and access the Transform, Object Attributes, and Layer **properties** for that object **2**. The properties are an object's attributes, such as its current position, scale, opacity, color, gradient, etc. Animations are created by setting and changing object properties over a specific time period. Click a triangle again to collapse the list.

3 The tick marks on the **timeline** signify time intervals. The red vertical line is called the **current time marker** (or CTM, for short) **4**. It designates the frame that's currently being worked on and it shows which keyframes align with the current frame. Drag the CTM or click on the timeline to move the marker and its vertical line to a new point in time.

5 The **current time window** shows the time location of the current time marker in hours, minutes, seconds, and frames. Frames are counted in portions of a second, since LiveMotion plays back animations on a frames-per-second basis.

6 Each object has its own **duration bar**, which represents that object's temporal relation to other objects in the animation. Each duration bar has a start point and an end point.

7 Looping is the continuous repetition of an animation. The **Loop** button toggles looping on and off for the entire composition or for individual objects that have been made time-independent.

8 With the **Auto Length** button pressed, a selected object's duration bar end point moves as the composition duration bar end point is moved. When this button is not pressed, the duration bar will remain stationary as the composition duration end point is moved.

9 If your animation is longer than several seconds, you can click the **Zoom out** button or drag the **Zoom** slider to the left to view more of the total timeline. Click the **Zoom in** button or drag the slider to the right to magnify part of the timeline.

(Continued on the next page)

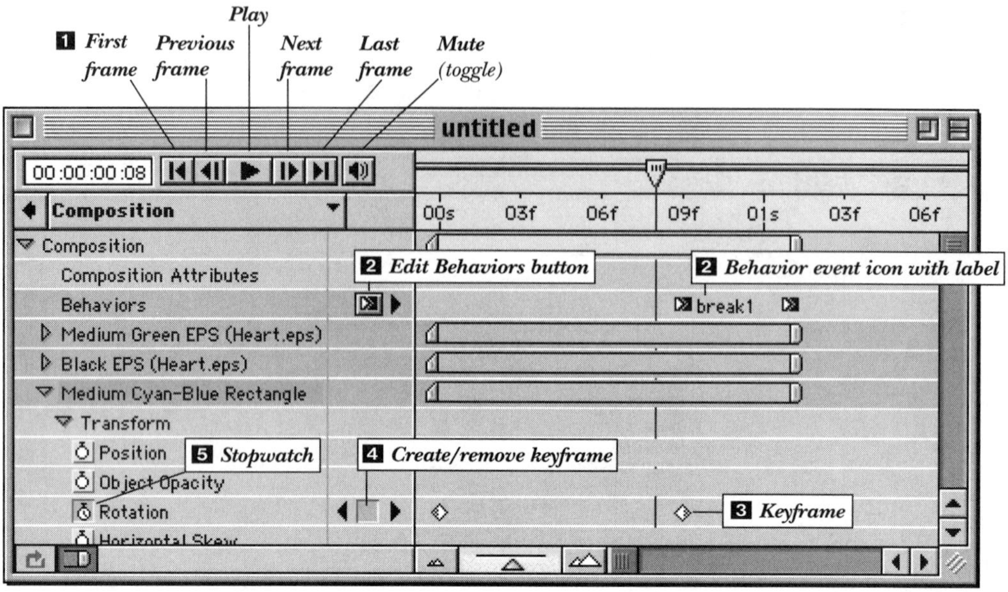

1 The **First Frame** button restores the current time marker to the beginning of the composition.

The **Previous Frame** button moves the current time marker back one frame.

The **Play** button plays the composition starting from the position of the current time marker.

The **Next Frame** button moves the current time marker forward one frame.

The **Last Frame** button moves the current time marker to the end of the composition.

The **Mute** button toggles the audio playback on or off in a composition that contains a sound object.

2 Behaviors are commands that change the normal linear playback of an animation and allow for viewer interactivity. Choose a point in time, then click the **Create/Edit Behaviors** button to create a behavior event on the behaviors track. Behavior events can be edited and repositioned.

3 When a change is made to an individual property on the timeline, a **keyframe** appears in the row for that property. Keyframes can be set for any object on the objects heirarchy list, and for any given time frame, you can set as many separate property keyframes as you want. A **Create/remove keyframe** box will also appear for any object property that has a keyframe **4**.

5 Click the **stopwatch** to establish a current palette setting as an initial setting for that object property. This creates a keyframe.

Timing shorthand

In this chapter, you'll be instructed to move the **current time marker** to specific locations on the timeline. If we write "01s-04f," for example, it means move the marker to 01 seconds, 4th frame.

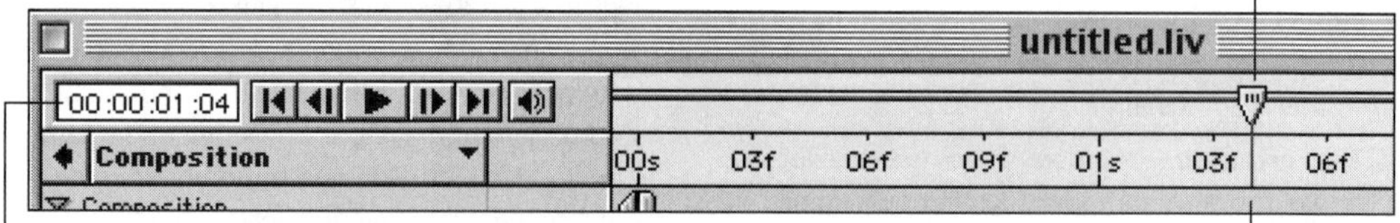

The equivalent time readout displays in the current time window ←→ Current time marker position

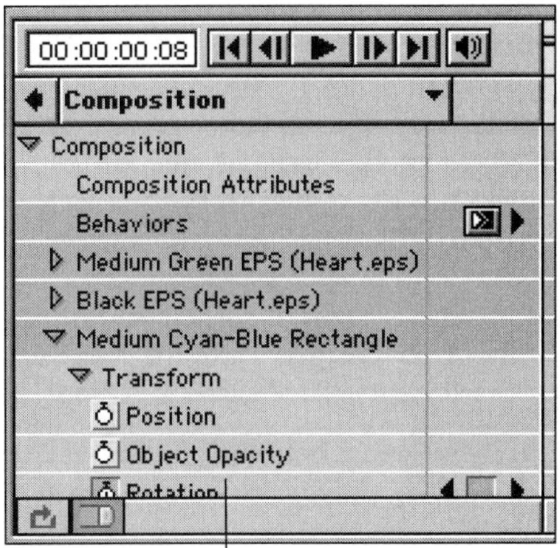

1 ➤ *Object properties*

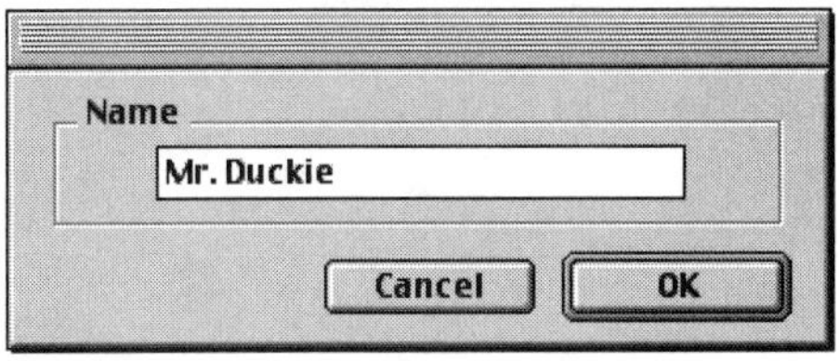

2 ➤ ***Renaming*** *an object.*

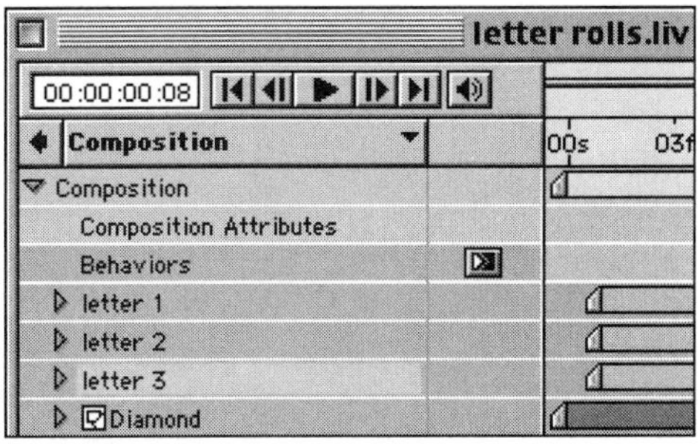

3 ➤ ***Restacking*** *an object using Bring Forward.*

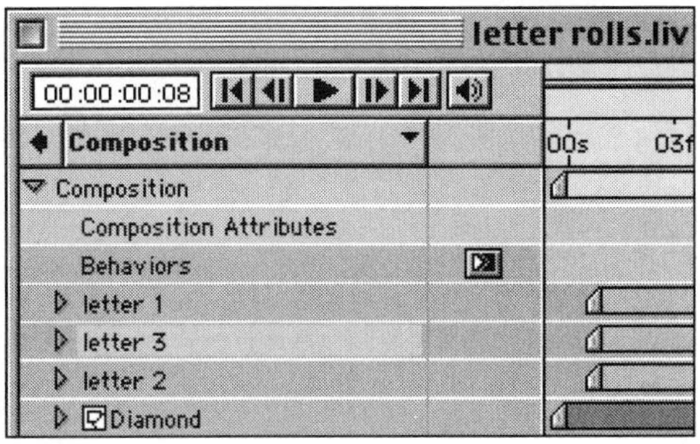

4 ➤ *Letter 3 is moved forward* ***one level.***

Using the Timeline editor

Now let's learn how to work with the Timeline editor. Open or create a composition that contains a few assorted objects. And keep the editor open for all the instructions in this chapter (Timeline menu > Show Timeline Window).

To hide or show object categories and properties:

Click the triangle to the left of an object name to expand that object's list of properties.

Click the triangle to the left of a Transform category, Object Attributes category, or Layer name to expand that list (Fig. 1). Click a downward-pointing triangle to contract a list.

To rename an object:

1. Click an object name on the objects hierarchy list.
2. Press Return/Enter.
3. Rename the object, then click OK (Return/Enter) (Fig. 2).

To restack an object on the list:

1. Click an object name on the objects hierarchy list.
2. Choose Object menu > Arrange > Bring to Front, Bring Forward, Send to Back, or Send Backward. Both the composition and the objects hierarchy list will update to reflect the new stacking order (Fig. 3–4).

To select or deselect an object on the list:

To select an object, click on the object name or on any property listed under the object name.

or

To deselect all objects, click in the gray area below or to the left of the list; or click on a blank area in the composition window; or use the Command-Shift-A/Ctrl-Shift-A shortcut.

Tutorial 1

Make an object move across the screen

This first tutorial involves manually repositioning and scaling an object. You will learn how to set keyframes for the Transform > Position and Scale properties.

CREATE AN OBJECT

1. Choose Edit menu > New (or choose Edit menu > Composition Settings to work with an existing composition).
2. Enter a Width of 580 and a Height of 250 pixels; make the Frame Rate 15; choose Export: Entire Composition; check the Make HTML box; then click OK (Fig. 1).
3. Show the Transform palette. Choose the Ellipse tool (L), then Shift-drag a circle 100 x 100 pixels in size (watch the width and height fields on the Transform palette as you drag).
4. Keep the object selected, and choose a color on the Color palette.
5. Show the Gradient palette, and choose Linear from the pop-up menu. Recolor the gradient, if desired.
6. Choose Timeline menu > Show Timeline Window. Now follow the next set of instructions to make the circle move.

CHANGE THE OBJECT'S POSITION OVER TIME

1. Choose the Selection tool (V), then move the circle to the left-hand side of the composition (Fig. 2).
2. Click Ellipse on the Timeline editor's objects hierarchy list, press Return/Enter, type the name "circle," then click OK.
3. Click the triangle for the circle object to expand that object's list, then click the triangle for the Transform category (Fig. 3).
4. Click the stopwatch next to Position (Fig. 4). This will insert a keyframe (diamond-shaped icon) for the object's current position at the left side of the composition at the current time, which at the moment is zero (00s).

Remember these rules!

Rule 1: You must click the **stopwatch** to establish both a current palette setting for an object property and a keyframe **before** you advance the time marker to set another keyframe for that property. No additional keyframes can be created unless you click the stopwatch.

Rule 2: You must reposition the **current time marker before** you make a property change to an object. If you don't reposition the marker, you will alter the property's existing keyframe at the current time position. This is a common error budding animators make.

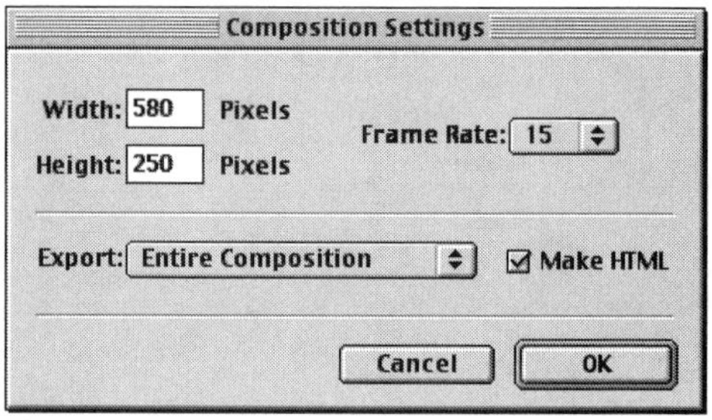

*1 ➤ **Composition Settings** dialog box.*

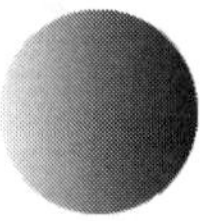

2 ➤ The object positioned at the left side.

3 ➤

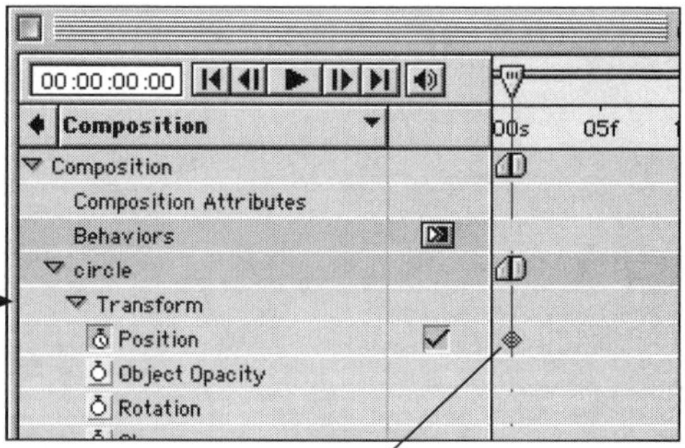

*4 ➤ A **Position keyframe** is set.*

Extending the duration

If you extend the duration of a composition, the duration of any existing objects on the Timeline whose end points line up with the composition's end point will also be extended. This is because the **Auto Length** option is turned on by default.

After step 5 on this page, you could have manually extended the composition's duration by dragging the end point of the composition's duration bar to a new time position (the pointer becomes a two-way arrow when it's over a start or end point). However, we think it's easier to gauge time on the timeline if you first move the current time marker to a specific time position, as in our instructions.

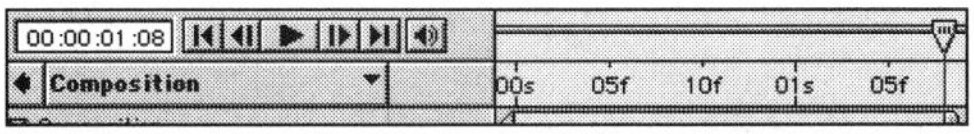

1 ➤ Position the current time marker...

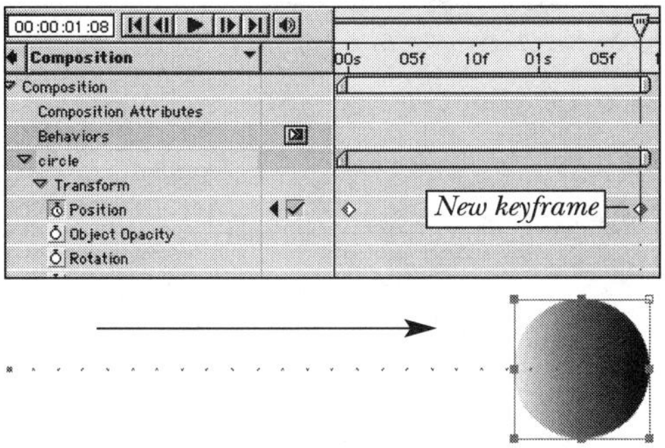

2 ➤ ...then move the object to the right. A new keyframe will result.

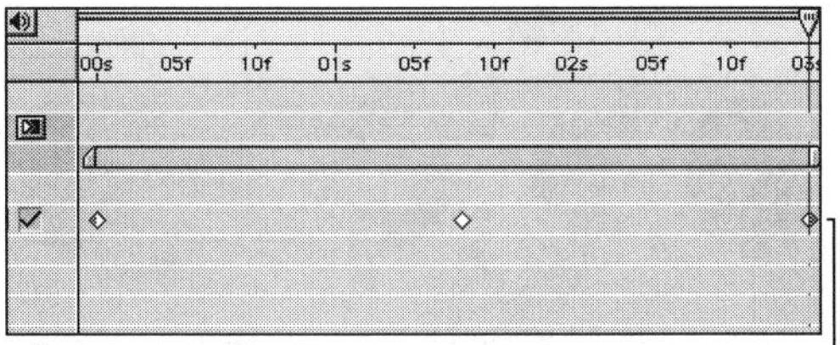

3 ➤ The current time marker is moved, then the object is moved back to the left. Another new keyframe results.

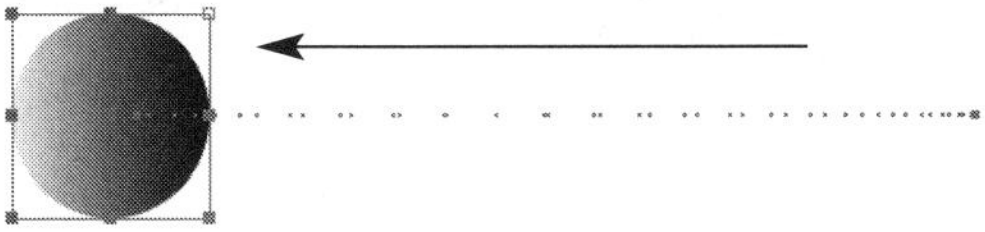

5. Drag the current time marker to the 01s-08f mark. The time display window will read "01.08" (Fig. 1).
6. Click in the composition window. Start dragging the still-selected circle to the right side of the composition, then hold down Shift to constrain the movement. Release the mouse, then release Shift. In the Timeline editor, a keyframe will automatically be created for the object's new position at the new time. Note that the duration bars of the composition and the object now span from 00s to 01s-08f (Fig. 2).
7. Click back in the Timeline editor, then click in the gray area below the objects hierarchy list to deselect the object.
8. Click the First Frame button at the top of the Timeline editor.
9. Click the Play button to preview the animation. Save the file.

MAKE THE OBJECT MOVE BACK TO ITS STARTING POSITION

1. In the Timeline editor, move the current time marker to the 03s mark (scroll the Timeline window, if necessary).
2. Click in the composition window. Start dragging the selected circle back to its starting place at the left side of the composition, then hold down Shift. Release the mouse, then release Shift. In the Timeline, a keyframe will be created for the circle at its new position and new time (Fig. 3).
3. Click in the Timeline editor, then click in the gray area below the objects hierarchy list to deselect the object.
4. Click the First Frame button, then click the Play button. The circle will move from left to right, then back again.

   Congratulations! You created an animation. Keep the composition open and follow the instructions on the next page to make the object come forward and then recede.

(Continued on the next page)

This is a continuation of the instructions on the previous page.

MAKE AN OBJECT COME FORWARD AND RECEDE VIA A SCALE CHANGE

1. In the Timeline editor, move the current time marker back to 00s.
2. Expand the Transform category list, then click the stopwatch next to Scale to establish a starting size. A keyframe icon will appear on the scale row in the Timeline (Fig. 1).
3. Move the current time marker to the 01s-08f mark. Check the blank box in the Create/Remove keyframe column in the Scale property row to maintain the same scale for this time period (Fig. 2).
   and
   Move the current time marker to the 03s mark.
   and
   Check the blank keyframe box again to set another keyframe for the same scale (Fig. 3).
4. Move the current time marker until the circle is in the middle of the composition (around the 00s-09f mark).
5. Click in the composition window, and make sure the circle is still selected. Drag the upper left selection handle diagonally inward while holding down Shift. Shrink the circle to about half its size (Fig. 4).
6. Click in the Timeline editor. Move the current time marker to the right to where the circle is in the middle of the composition (around the 02s-06f mark).
7. Click in the composition window. Select the circle, then drag its upper left selection handle diagonally outward while holding down Shift until the circle is roughly double in size (Fig. 5). Deselect.
8. Click in the Timeline editor.
9. Click the First Frame button, then click the Play button. The object will appear take a circular path as it recedes, then move forward again. Save the file.▲

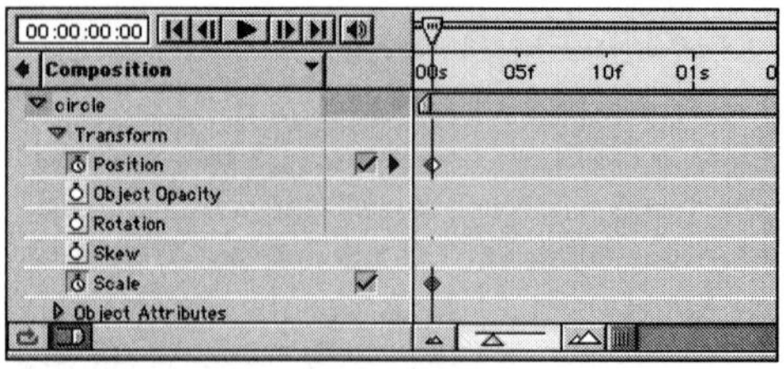

*1 ➤ Set a keyframe for **Scale**.*

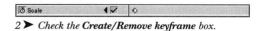

*2 ➤ Check the **Create/Remove keyframe** box.*

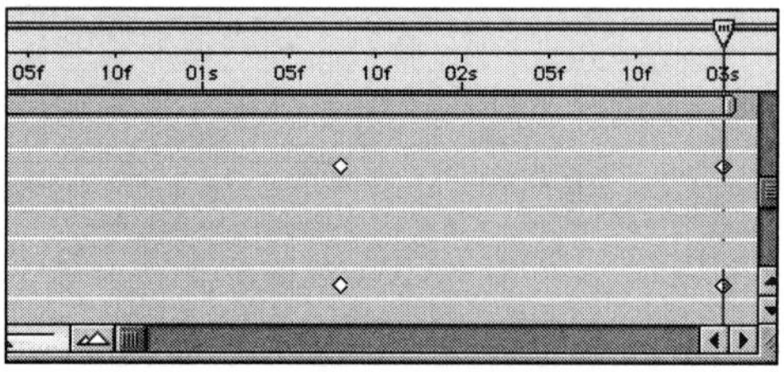

*3 ➤ Set the third keyframe for **Scale**.*

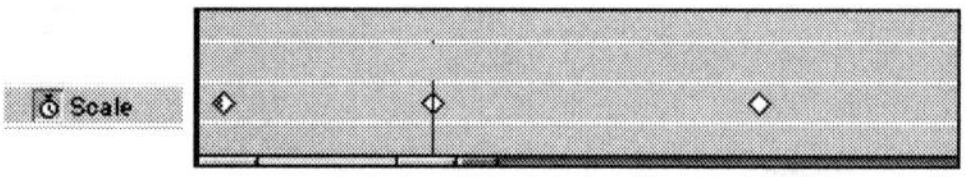

4 ➤ Create a new keyframe for Scale by scaling the object down at 00s-09f.

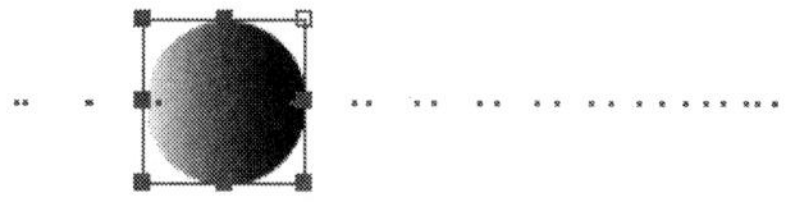

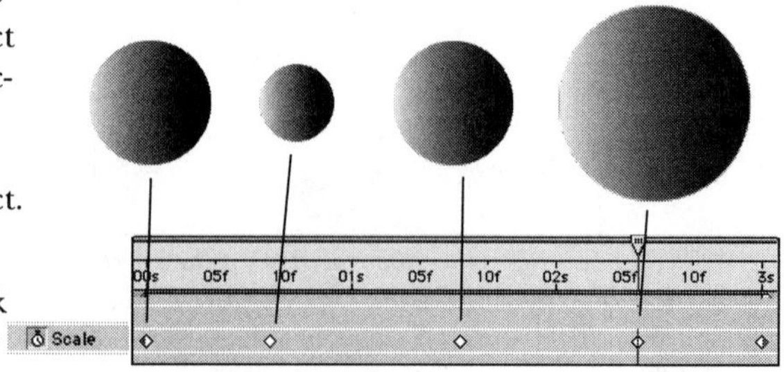

5 ➤ The 4 Scale keyframes and the corresponding object size.

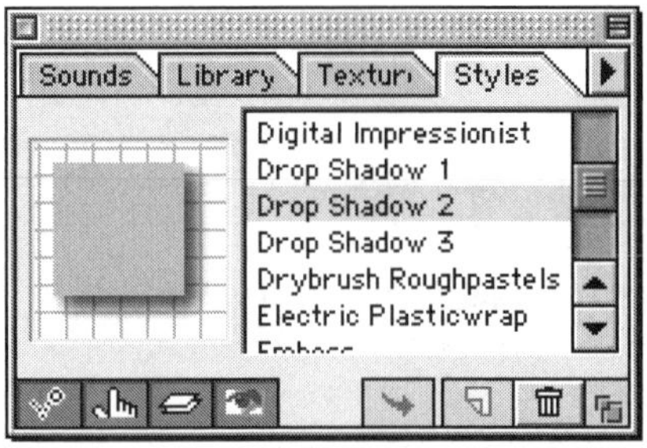

1 ➤ *Choose the style from the Styles palette.*

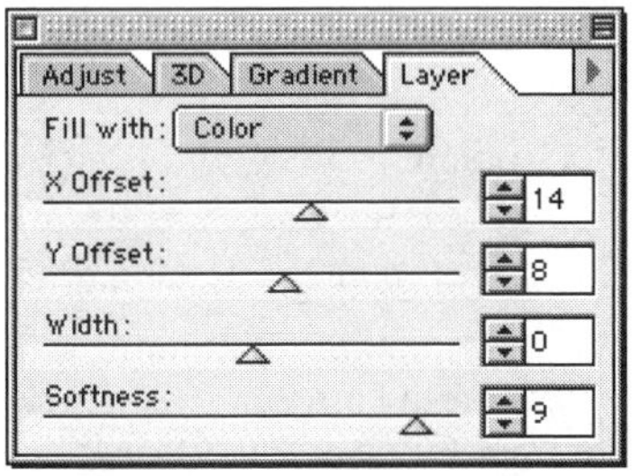

2 ➤ *Choose Layer palette settings.*

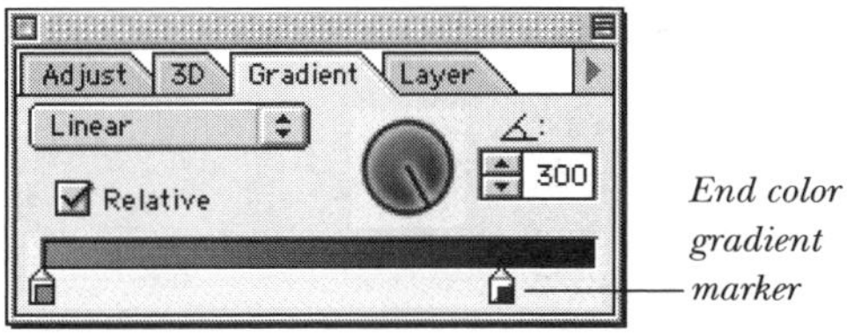

3 ➤ *The* ***gradient*** *properties you choose will be listed as Color Gradient Type, Color Gradient Angle, etc. on the Timeline.*

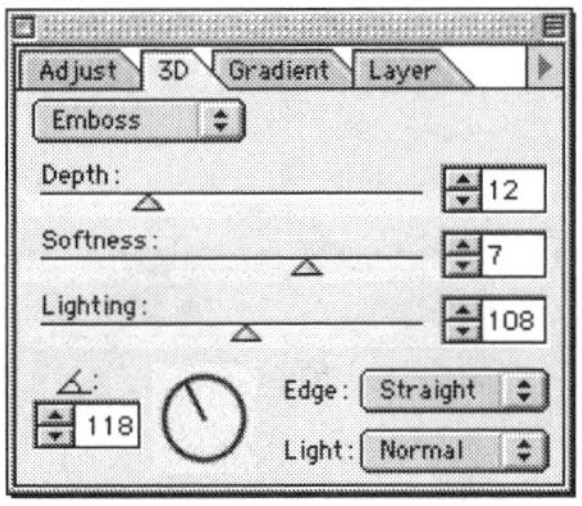

4 ➤ *The* ***3D*** *properties you choose will be listed as Effect, Effect Depth, etc. on the Timeline.*

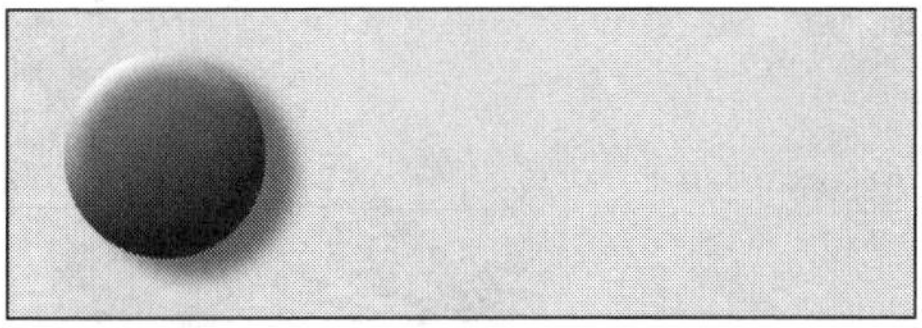

5 ➤ *The resulting object.*

Tutorial 2

In this tutorial, you'll modify various layer properties using several palettes, including Opacity, Color, and 3D. You'll offset a drop shadow, add a 3D effect, change the angle of the effect, change the angle of a gradient, and add a text fade-in.

Assign object property changes and a fade-in

CREATE AN OBJECT FOR ANIMATION

1. Choose File menu > New (Command-N/Ctrl-N). Choose a width of 500 and a height of 250 pixels; make the Frame Rate 15; Choose Export: Entire Composition; check the Make HTML box; then click OK.
2. Choose the Ellipse tool (L), then Shift-drag a circle 110 pixels wide and high (watch the Transform palette).
3. Using the Styles palette, apply the Drop Shadow 2 style to the object (Fig. 1). On the Object Layers palette, click the shadow layer. On the Layer palette, change the X Offset to 14, the Y Offset to 8, and the Softness to 9 (Fig. 2). On the Opacity palette, make the Object Layer Opacity 56.
4. Choose the Selection tool (V), move the object to the left side of the composition, and leave it selected. Click back on Layer 1 on the Object Layers palette, then choose a mid-range reddish-orange from the Color palette.
5. Show the Gradient palette, then choose Linear from the pop-up menu.
6. *Optional:* Click the end color gradient marker, then choose a dark color for the ending gradient color.
7. Move the dark end color gradient marker to the left about a quarter of an inch to lengthen the dark part of the gradient.
8. Set the gradient Angle to 300° (Fig. 3).
9. Show the 3D palette. Choose Emboss from the pop-up menu; make the Depth 12; make the Softness 7; make the angle 118°; and make the Lighting 108 (Figs. 4–5). Save the file.

(Continued on the next page)

Now you'll move the object's drop shadow to the left and move the highlight to the right.

MOVE THE OBJECT'S LIGHT SOURCE

1. Show the Timeline editor (Command-T/ Ctrl-T).
2. *Optional:* Click the ellipse object name on the objects hierarchy list, press Return/Enter, type "logo shape," then click OK.
3. On the Timeline, move the current time marker to 02s-08f.
4. Drag the end point of the composition duration bar to the current time marker's vertical red line (Fig. 1). The composition and the logo shape will now have a duration of 02s-08f.
5. Move the current time marker to 00s. Expand the logo shape list and the shadow (layer) list.
6. Click the stopwatch in the Offset property row. A new keyframe will appear in that row (Fig. 2).
7. Move the current time marker to 01s. Show the Layer palette, then move the X Offset to -8. A new keyframe will appear in the Offset row (Fig. 3).
8. Move the current time marker back to 00s. Collapse the shadow list and expand the Layer 1 list.
9. Click the stopwatch for Color Gradient Angle and for Effect Angle.
10. Move the current time marker to 01s.
11. Show the Gradient palette, and set the Color Gradient angle to 260°.
12. Show the 3D palette, and set the Effect Angle to 32° (Fig. 4).
13. Click to the left of the logo shape name to deselect it.
14. Click the First Frame button, then click the Play button. Or click the Preview mode button at the bottom of the Toolbox. Click the Edit mode button when you're finished. Save your file.

(Continued on the next page)

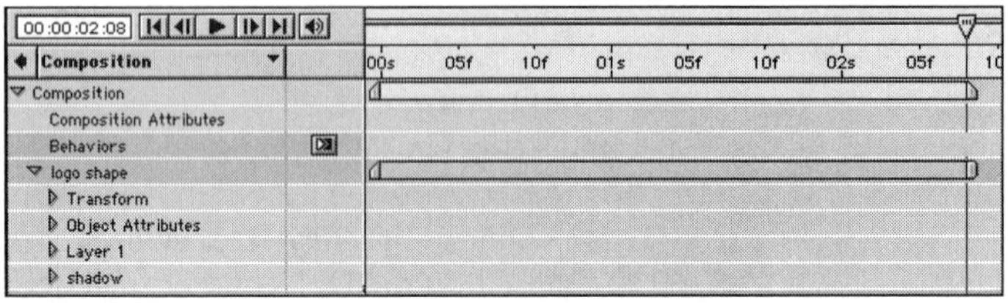

1 ➤ Set the **composition duration**.

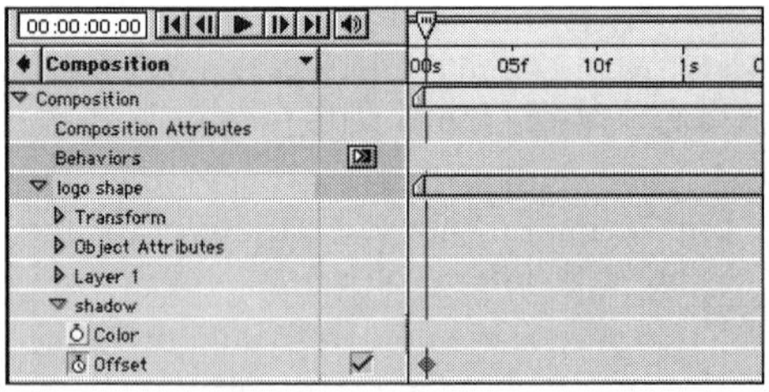

2 ➤ Set the **first Offset keyframe**.

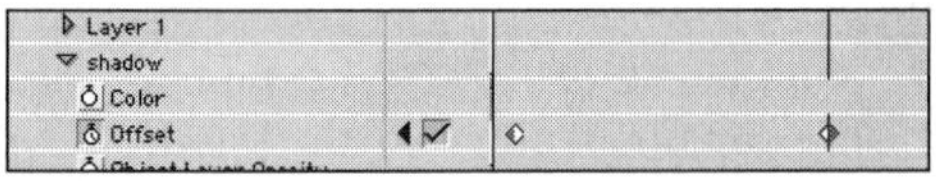

3 ➤ Set the **second Offset keyframe**.

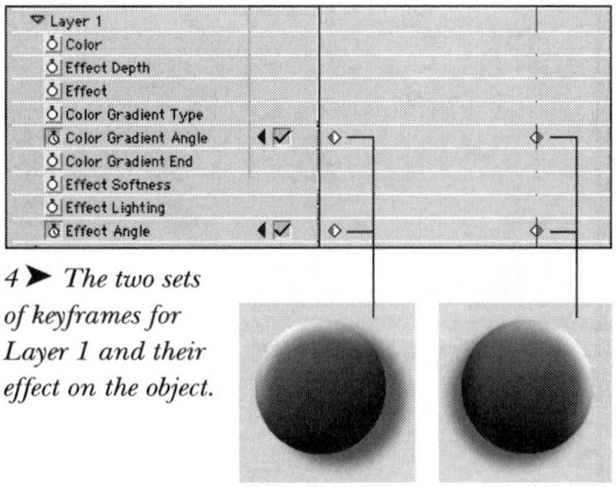

4 ➤ The two sets of keyframes for Layer 1 and their effect on the object.

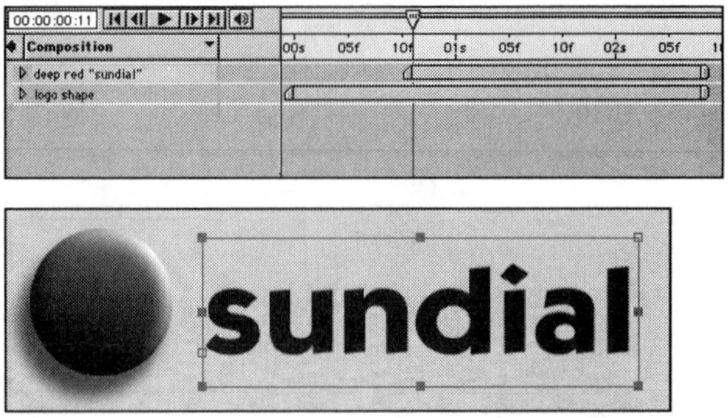

1 ➤ Create the text object at 00s-11f.

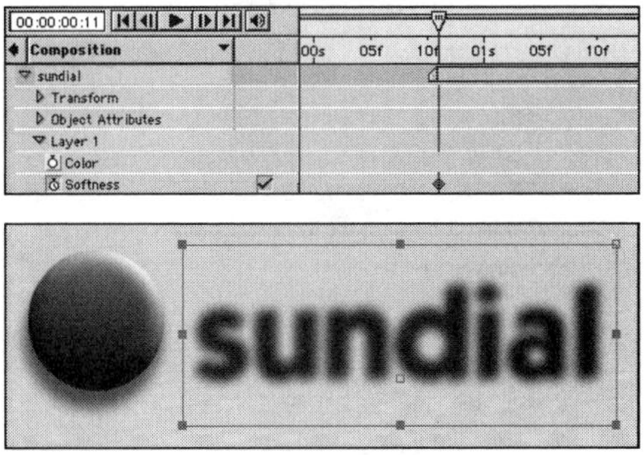

2 ➤ Set a Softness keyframe for the text object.

3 ➤ Set a keyframe to remove the Softness from the text object.

In this continuation of Tutorial 2, you'll create some text and use one of three methods to make the text appear in the middle of the animation.

CREATE A TEXT FADE-IN

1. On the Timeline editor, move the current time marker to 00s-11f. This will establish the start point for the text duration at the desired time. The end point for the text object will be the current end of the composition's duration.
2. Choose the Type tool (T). Click to the right of the logo shape object in the composition window.
3. Type the word "sundial."
4. Choose a font (we chose ITC Kabel Bold), choose a size of 90 points, choose Alignment: Horizontal, Center, then click OK.
5. With the text still selected, choose a medium red from the Color palette.
6. Position the text to the right of the logo shape (fig. 1).

SET UP THE TIMELINE EDITOR

1. On the Timeline editor, click on the new text name.
2. Press Return/Enter, type the name "sundial," then click OK.
3. Show the Layer palette, and set the layer Softness to 7.
4. On the Timeline editor, make sure the current time marker is at 00s-11f.
5. Expand the sundial list and the Layer 1 list.
6. Click the stopwatch next to Softness to set the starting softness value (fig. 2).
7. Move the current time marker to 01s-11f.
8. On the Layer palette, set the Softness to 0. A keyframe will be created for the ending softness value (fig. 3).

(Continued on the next page)

Now you'll use scaling and object opacity to make the text scale up as it fades in (method 1) or make the text fade in from its edges (method 2).

SCALE THE TEXT...

1. Make sure the current time marker is at 01s-11f.
2. Expand the Transform list under the sundial list.
3. Click the stopwatch next to Scale to set the final text size (Fig. 1). Now you'll work backwards in time to animate the scale change.
4. Move the current time marker to 00s-11f.
5. Choose the Selection tool, and make sure the text object is selected.
6. Drag a corner selection handle diagonally inward, hold down Shift, then keep dragging inward. Make the text very small. A keyframe will be created for the change in scale (Fig. 2).
7. Click in the Timeline editor.
8. Click First Frame, then click Play.

...AND MAKE THE TEXT FADE IN

1. On the Timeline editor, select the sundial text object. Move the current time marker to 00s-11f.
2. Show the Opacity palette, and set the Object Opacity slider to 0 (Fig. 3).
3. On the Timeline editor, expand the Transform list under the sundial object list. Click the stopwatch for Object Opacity to set the starting opacity.
4. Move the current time marker to 01s-11f.
5. On the Opacity palette, set the Object Opacity slider back up to 100. A keyframe will be created for the property change (Fig. 4).
6. Click to the left of the sundial name to deselect it.
7. Click First Frame, then click Play (Fig. 5).

➤ When you make an object appear using both a scale enlargement and an opacity reduction, it's easier to do the scale

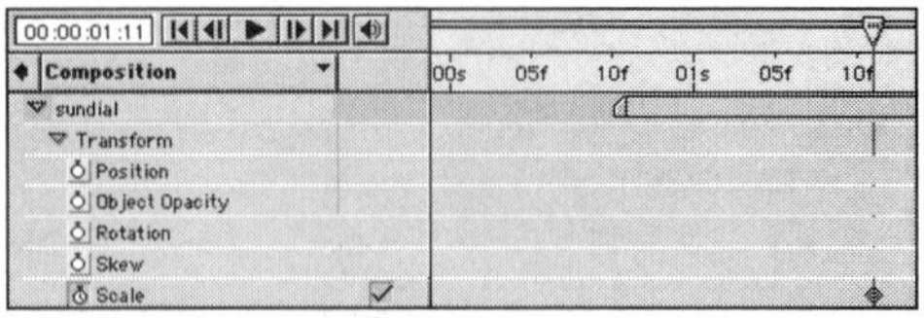

1 ➤ Set a keyframe for the ***final scale.***

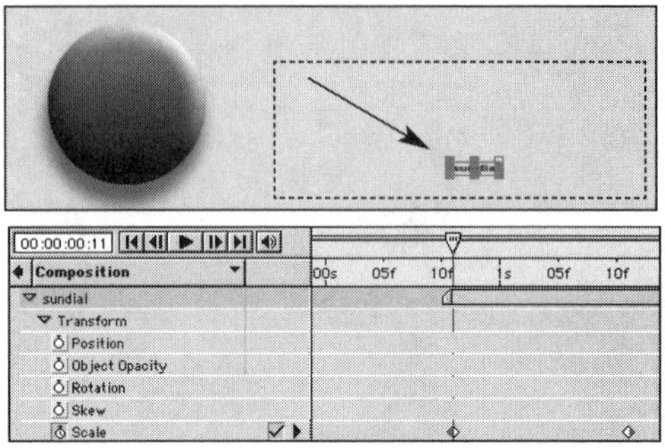

2 ➤ Scale down the object at a new time to create a second ***scale keyframe.***

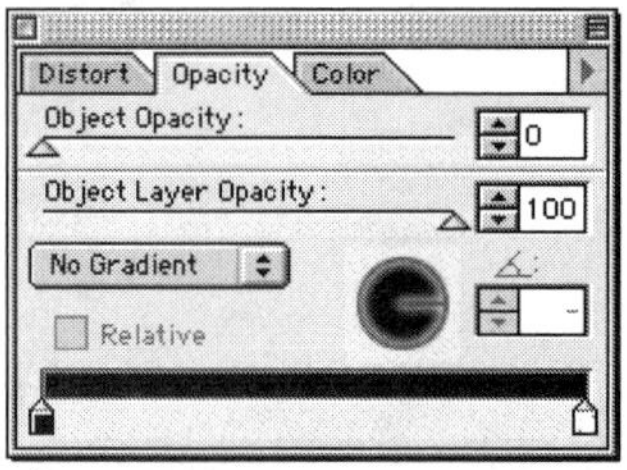

3 ➤ The ***Object Opacity*** *property is set to 0.*

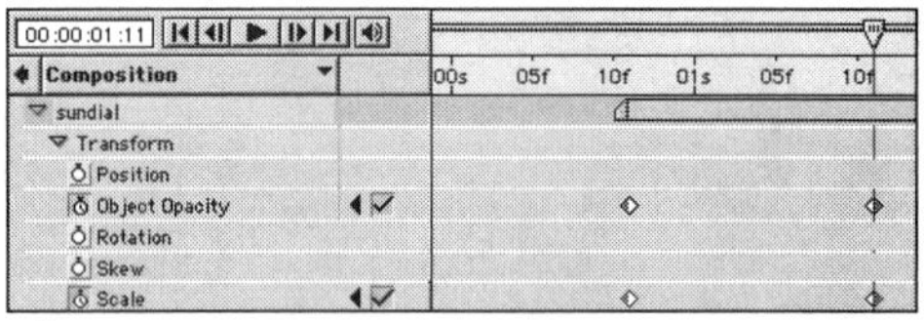

4 ➤ The sundial object now has two keyframes for Object Opacity to produce the fade-in.

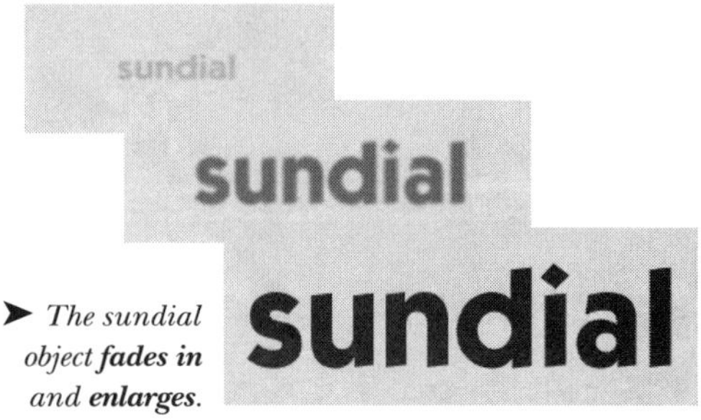

5 ➤ The sundial object ***fades in*** *and* ***enlarges.***

1 ➤ The Object Opacity property is set to 25.

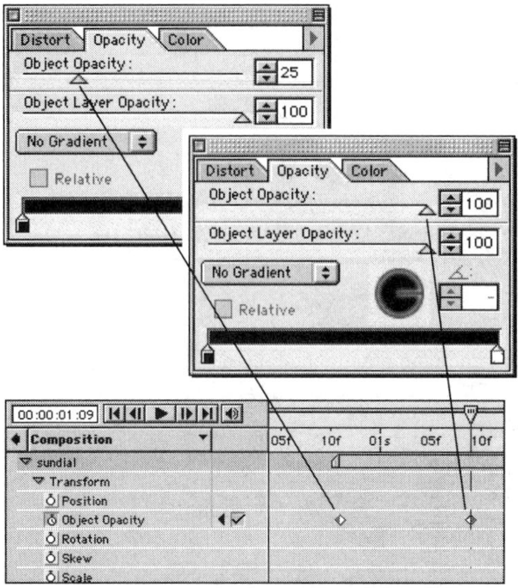

2 ➤ The current time is moved and the Object Opacity property is set to 100.

3 ➤ The text object is at its final size at the second Scale keyframe.

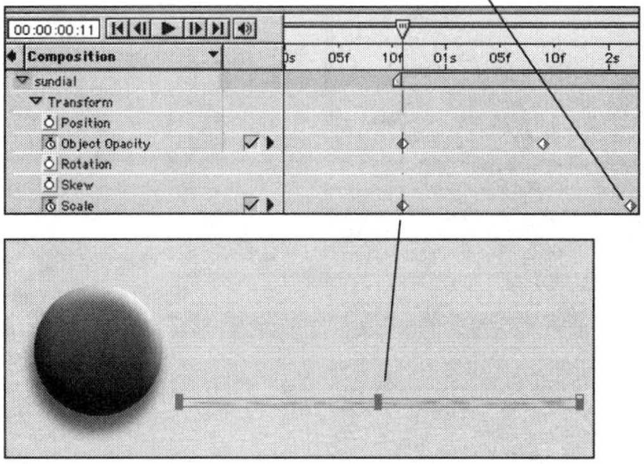

4 ➤ The text object is vertically scaled down at the first Scale keyframe.

keyframes before the opacity reduction keyframes. That way, the object will be easier to see and select in the composition window.

As a variation, we will now scale the text vertically and make it fade in from its edges using an opacity mask. We will also produce a shadow reflection of the text.

OR FADE TEXT IN FROM ITS EDGES...

1. If you followed the previous steps, you will first have to remove some existing property keyframes. To do this, expand the sundial list and the Transform list. Click the stopwatch next to Scale, and click the stopwatch next to Object Opacity. All the keyframes for those properties will be deleted. Leave the Softness keyframes as is.
2. Now you'll change the overall object opacity in order to make the text fade in gradually. On the Timeline editor, move the current time marker to 00s-11f.
3. Click "sundial" on the objects list. Expand the Transform list.
4. Show the Opacity palette, then move the Object Opacity slider to 25.
5. Click the Object Opacity stopwatch (Fig. 1).
6. Move the current time marker to 01s-09f and move the Object Opacity slider to 100 (Fig. 2).

...AND SCALE THE TEXT

1. Move the current time marker to 02s-02f.
2. Click the stopwatch for Scale (Fig. 3).
3. Move the current time marker to 00s-11f.
4. In the composition window, drag the text object's top center selection handle downward until the object is about 6 pixels in height (note the height value on the Transform palette) (Fig. 4).
5. Move the current time marker back and forth slowly to preview the changes.

(Continued on the next page)

Next, you'll make a layer fade in from its edges using an opacity gradient mask.

CHANGE THE OPACITY OF TEXT USING AN OPACITY GRADIENT

1. Move the current time marker back to 00s-11f (Fig. 1).
2. Click on sundial. On the Opacity palette, choose Burst from the pop-up menu.
   and
   Click on the opacity gradient start marker (left marker), then move the Object Layer Opacity slider to 1. The marker should now be white.
   and
   Click the opacity gradient end marker (right marker), then move the Object Layer Opacity slider to 100. The marker should now be black.
   and
   Move the opacity gradient start marker (left marker) to the right until it almost touches the opacity gradient end marker (Fig 2). This will increase the amount of white in the gradient and hide the layer.
3. Click the stopwatch for Layer 1 > Opacity Gradient Start to set a keyframe for the position of the left marker (Fig 3).

   The other Opacity palette properties (Opacity Gradient Type, Object Layer Opacity, End Object Layer Opacity, and Opacity Gradient Angle) will remain constant, so they don't need keyframes.

   Note: You'll see two markers below the opacity gradient bar—the opacity gradient start marker and the opacity gradient end marker. You can assign a different Object Layer Opacity to each marker (select the marker, then move the slider). On the Timeline editor list, the opacity gradient start marker's opacity keyframes will be in the Layer 1 > Object Layer Opacity property row (Fig. 4) and the opacity gradient end marker's opacity keyframes will be in the Layer 1 > End Object Layer Opacity property row (Fig. 5).

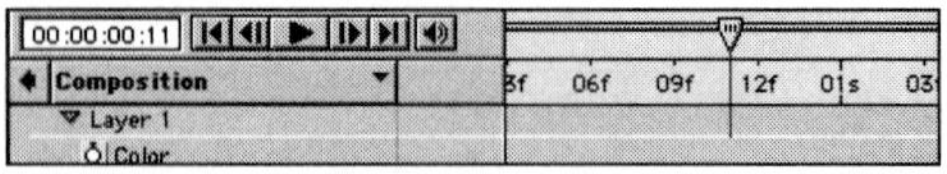

1 ➤ The current time marker set to 00s-11f.

2 ➤ The opacity gradient start marker (left marker) is dragged to the right. The Object Layer Opacity field is set for either the left or the right marker, whichever is selected.

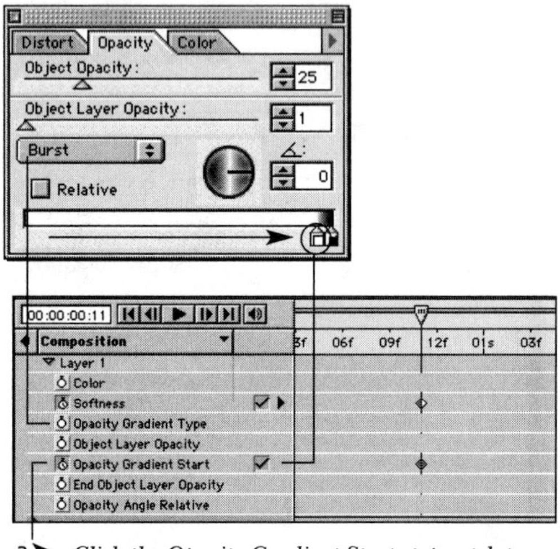

3 ➤ Click the Opacity Gradient Start stopwatch to set a keyframe for that property at the time marker's current position.

***Opacity** palette*

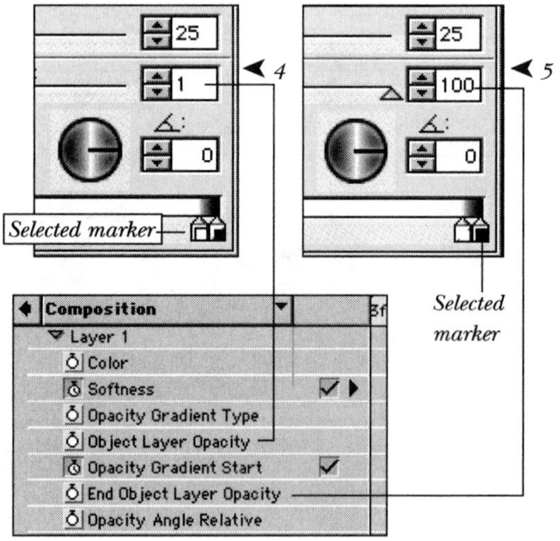

4. Move the current time marker to 01s-14f (scroll in the timeline, if necessary).
5. On the Opacity palette, drag the opacity gradient start marker (the left marker) all the way to the left. A new keyframe icon will appear (Fig. 1).
6. Drag the current time marker back and forth slowly to preview the changes in the text object (Fig 2).

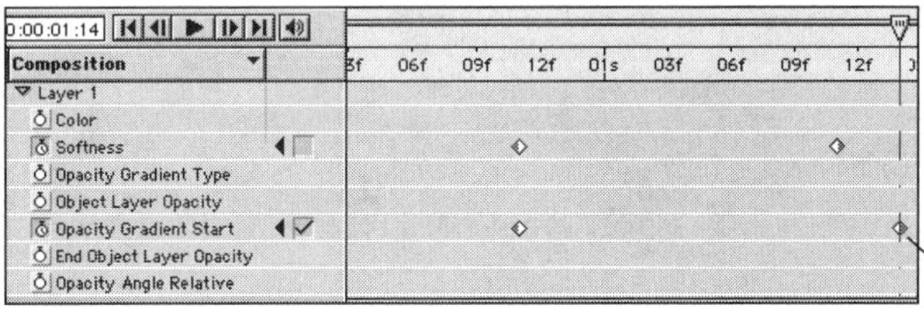

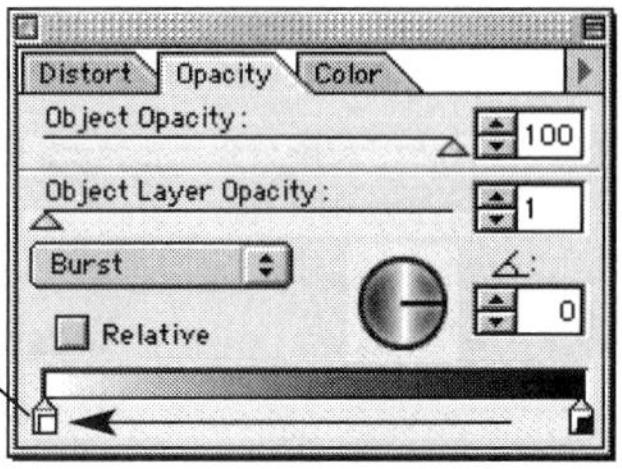

1 ➤ *Drag the* ***Opacity Gradient Start*** *marker (the left marker) back to the left. This will set a new keyframe for that property row.*

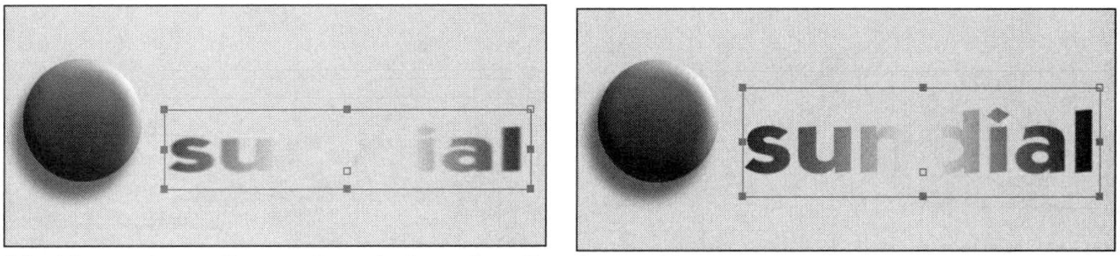

2 ➤ *The* ***opacity gradient mask*** *recedes inward to allow the text object to appear.*

3 ➤ *The text object after Flip Vertical.*

CREATE A SHADOW REFLECTION FOR THE TEXT OBJECT

1. In the Timeline editor, click on sundial. Move the current time marker to 01s-09f.
2. Choose Edit menu > Duplicate. Leave the duplicate selected.
3. Choose Object menu > Transform > Flip Vertical (Fig. 3).
4. In the Timeline, click the new sundial object name, press Return/Enter, rename it "sundial shadow," then click OK.

(Continued on the following page)

The duplicate contains all the original animation instructions; we just need to change the duplicate into a soft shadow object.

CREATE A SOFT SHADOW OBJECT

1. On the objects hierarchy list, click on "sundial shadow."
2. On the Color palette, make R, G, and B 102.
3. On the Layer palette, set the Softness to 8.
4. Expand the sundial shadow list and its Transform list.
5. The current time marker should be over the second keyframe in the Object Opacity row (at 01s-09f).
6. On the Opacity palette, set the Object Opacity to 65.
7. Expand the Layer 1 list, then click the Softness stopwatch to remove any keyframes from that property.
8. On the Layer palette, set the Softness to 9.
9. Click the Preview mode button on the Toolbox (Fig. 1). Click the Edit mode button when you're finished previewing. Save your file. ▲

Tutorial 3

Make an object change colors over time

1. Choose File menu > New (or Edit menu > Composition Settings).
2. Enter a Width and Height of your choosing; make the Frame Rate 15; choose Export: Entire Composition; check the Make HTML box; then click OK.
3. Create an object, then assign a color to it using the Color palette.
4. With the object selected, display the Timeline editor (Command-T/Ctrl-T).
5. Select the object on the objects hierarchy list.

Hue isn't all

When you change object colors for animation, consider shifting just one of a color's attributes. For example, you could choose HSB View on the Color palette and change only a color's saturation (S) or brightness (B) while keeping the hue (H) constant. Or try moving the Brightness or Saturation slider on the Adjust palette.

1 ➤ The final view in the animation.

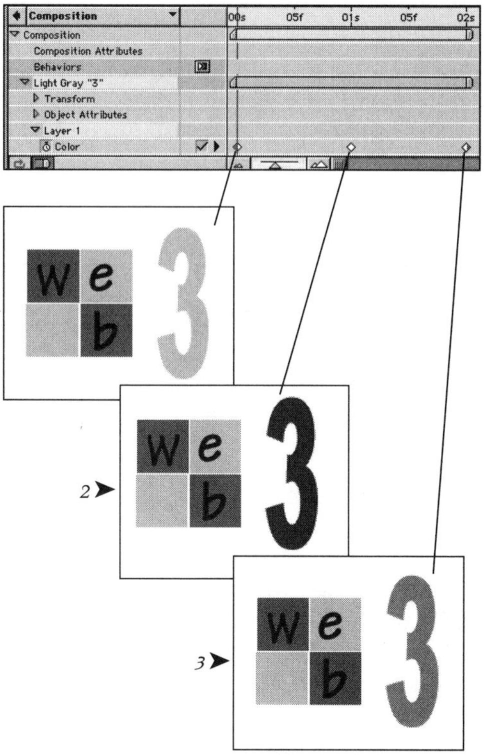

1➤

2➤

3➤

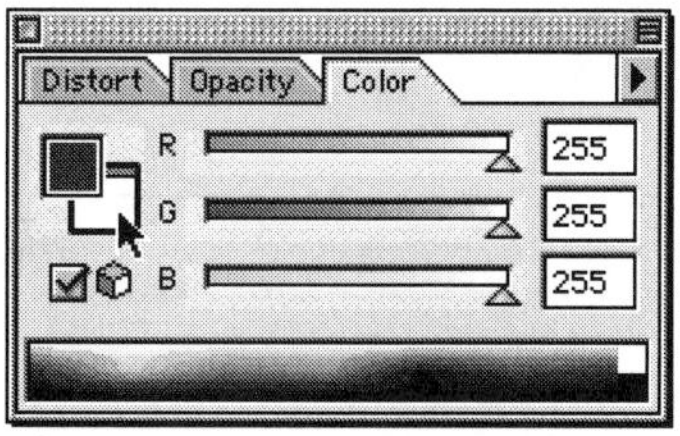

4➤ *Click the Background color box and choose a color on the Color palette.*

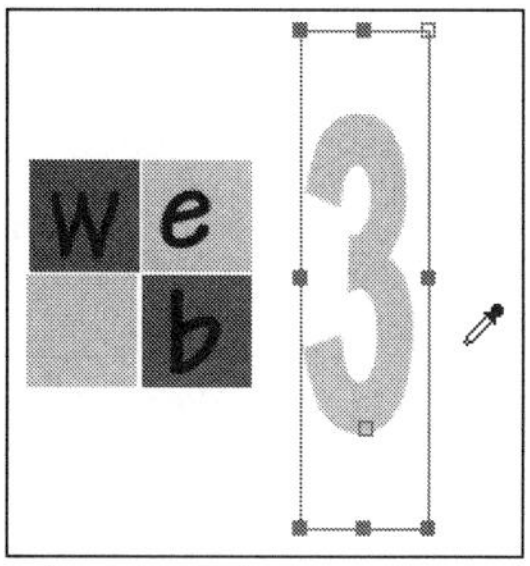

5➤ *Select the object to be recolored, then click on the Background with the Eyedropper tool.*

6. Press Return/Enter, type a name for the object, then click OK.
7. Expand that object's list and the Layer 1 list.
8. Click the stopwatch next to the Color property to set a keyframe for the current color (Fig. 1), then move the current time marker to 01s.
9. Choose a new color from the Color palette. A new keyframe will be created automatically (Fig. 2).
10. Move the current time marker to 02s, then choose yet another color from the Color palette. Another new keyframe will be created automatically (Fig. 3).
11. Deselect the object on the Timeline editor. Click First Frame, then click Play to preview the animation.

Here's a nice variation on the previous set of instructions.

TO USE COLOR CHANGE TO MAKE AN OBJECT FADE INTO THE BACKGROUND

1. Follow steps 3–9, starting on the previous page.
2. Click the Background box on the Color palette, then choose a color from the palette (Fig. 4).
3. Select the object. Move the current time marker to 02s.
4. Choose the Eyedropper tool (I), then click on the background in the composition window (Fig. 5). That color will automatically be applied to the selected object and a keyframe will be created in the Color property row.
5. Deselect the object.
6. Click First Frame, then click Play to preview the animation. The object will change colors and then fade into the background color. ▲

Tutorial 4

In this tutorial you will change an ellipse into a circle, create a shadow for the circle, and make type expand outward toward the viewer.

Change an object's shape

1. Choose File menu > New or Edit menu > Composition Settings.
2. Enter a Width of 500 and a Height of 250; make the Frame Rate 15; choose Export: Entire Composition; check the Make HTML box; then click OK.
3. Choose the Ellipse tool (L). Show the Transform palette, and watch the palette as you Shift-drag a circle with a width and height of 122 pixels in the middle of the composition window.
4. Apply a medium dark color to the circle (or choose Linear from the pop-up menu on the Opacity palette to apply a gradient). Choose the Selection tool (V), then move the circle to the middle of the composition.
5. Set the Layer palette Softness to 1 (Fig.1).
6. Display the Timeline editor (Command-T/Ctrl-T). Select the ellipse object on the objects hierarchy list.
7. Press Return/Enter, rename the object "oval," then click OK.
8. Move the current time marker to 01s-02f.
9. Expand the Oval list and then the Transform list.
10. Click the stopwatch for Position to set a keyframe for the current position. Also click the stopwatch for Scale (Fig. 2).
11. Expand the Layer 1 list, then click the stopwatch for Softness.
12. Now you'll work backwards in time to create the animation. Move the current time marker back to 00s (Fig. 3).
13. Choose the Selection tool (V), click in composition window, and make sure the oval object is selected.

Another way

The Shape Resize property can also be used to set keyframes for shape changes. However, using the Scale property will result in a smaller export file when the SWF format is used.

1 ➤ The circle object.

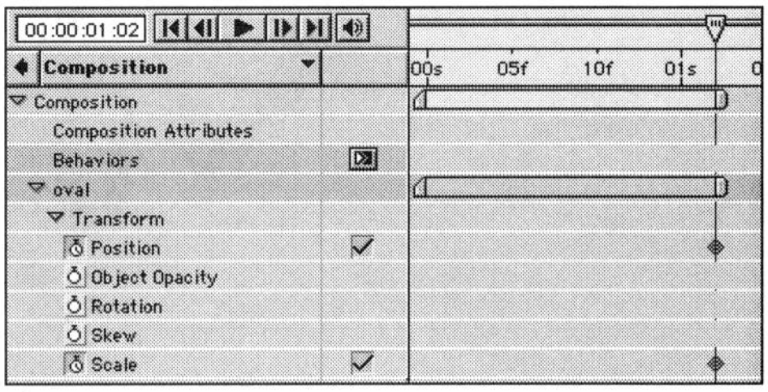

2 ➤ Set keyframes for the Position and Scale properties.

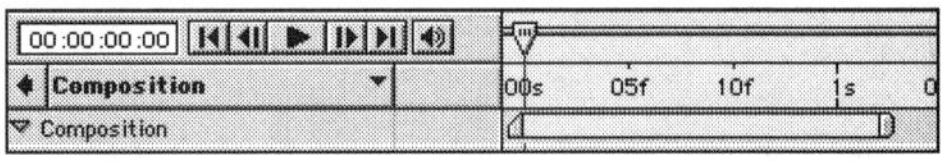

3 ➤ Move the current time marker to 00s.

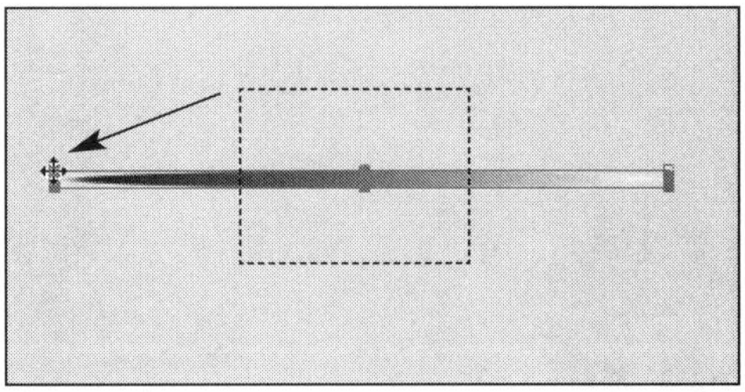

4 ➤ Drag a corner selection handle to create a long, thin oval.

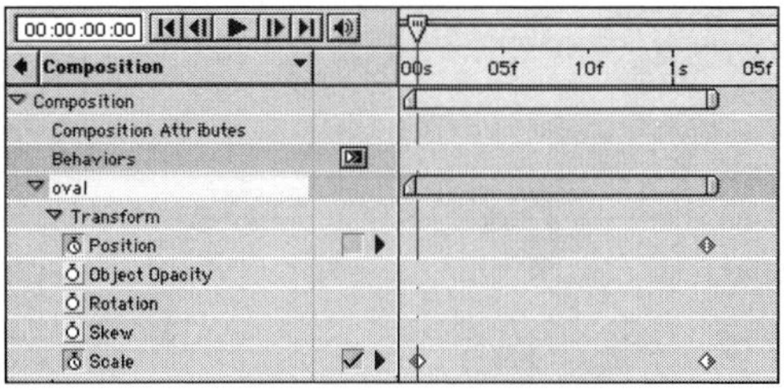

1 ➤ A new keyframe for Scale is created when the circle is re-scaled.

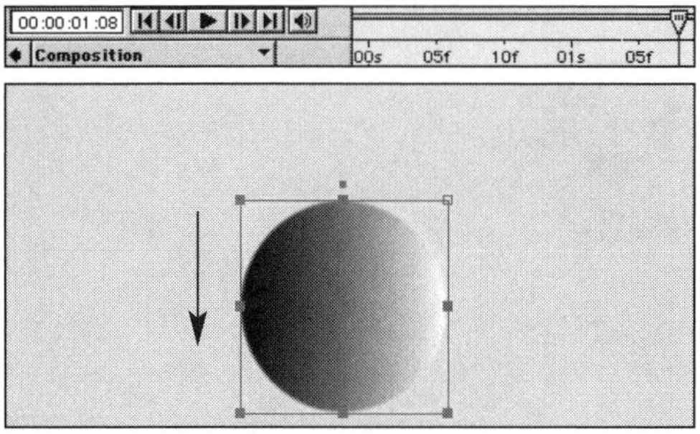

2 ➤ Move the circle object downward.

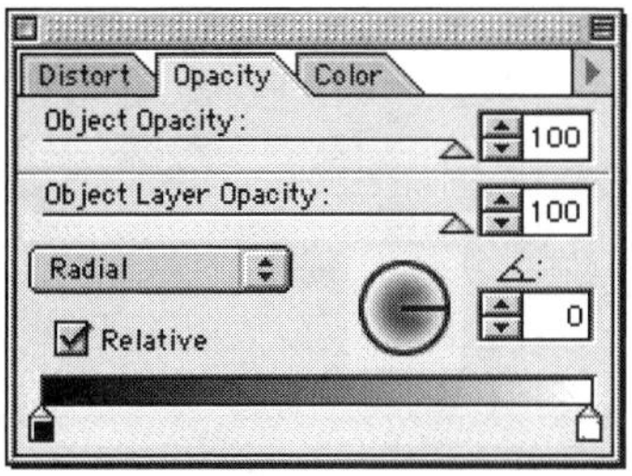

3 ➤ Set the Opacity palette to Radial for a gradient shadow appearance.

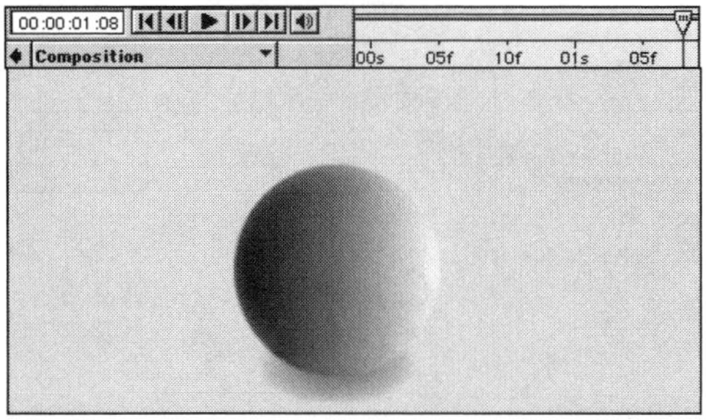

4 ➤ The shadow object is sent behind the circle, and the Radial opacity and softness properties are applied to it.

14. Drag a corner selection handle (not the upper right handle) outward to create a long, thin oval approximately 330 pixels wide and 6 pixels high (Fig. 4, previous page). A new keyframe will be created for Scale (Fig. 1, this page).
15. Click the oval name on the objects hierarchy list, then change the Softness to 4 on the Layer palette.

MAKE THE CIRCLE MOVE DOWNWARD

1. Move current time marker to 01s-08f.
2. Click in the composition window, then drag the ellipse toward the bottom of the window (Fig 2). (You already set a position keyframe for the oval at 01s-02f, otherwise you would have to set a keyframe before moving the oval.)
3. Click on a blank area of the objects list, click the First Frame button, then click the Play button to preview the animation. Save the file.

CREATE A SHADOW SHAPE

1. Move the current time marker to 01s-08f.
2. Use the Ellipse tool (L) to create an oval. Using the Transform palette, make the ellipse approximately 108 pixels wide and 60 pixels high. Set the R, G, and B to 102 on the Color palette.
3. Position the new ellipse so it slightly overlaps the bottom of the circle. Choose Object menu > Arrange > Send to Back (Command-Shift-[/Ctrl-Shift-[).
4. On the Opacity palette, choose Radial from the pop-up menu (Fig. 3).
5. Set the Layer palette Softness to 7 (Fig. 4).
6. On the objects hierarchy list, select the new ellipse shape. Press Return/Enter, type the name "shadow," then click OK.
7. Expand the shadow object's list, expand the Transform list, then click the stopwatch for Object Opacity and for Scale.

(Continued on the next page)

8. Move the current time marker back to 00s. Drag the shadow object's duration bar start point to 00s.

9. Click in the composition window and make sure the shadow object is selected.

10. Drag a corner selection handle outward to make the oval wider and thinner (width about 330, height about 28) (Fig. 1). Its position property won't change. A new keyframe will be created for Scale.

11. Using the Opacity palette, change the shadow's Object Opacity to 30. A keyframe will be created for this property.

12. Click on a blank area of the objects list, click the First Frame button, then click the Play button to preview the animation (Fig. 2). Save the file.

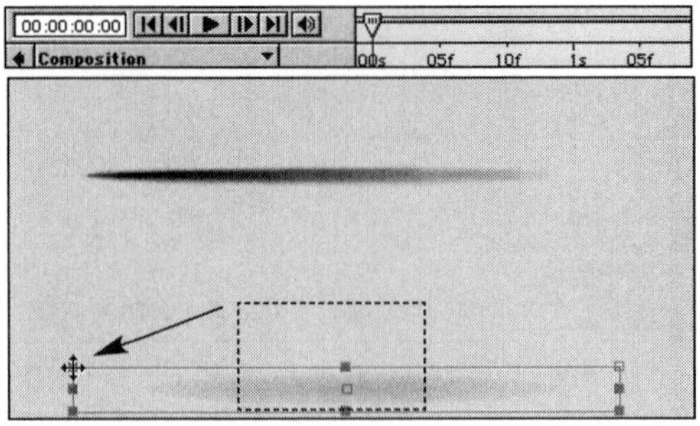

1 ➤ Drag a corner selection handle to create a long, thin shadow object.

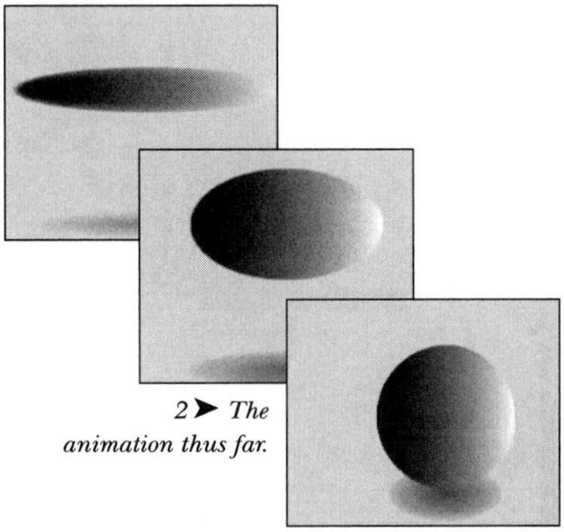

2 ➤ The animation thus far.

MAKE TEXT APPEAR IN FRONT OF THE CIRCLE OBJECT

1. Move the current time marker to 01-09f.

2. Choose the Type tool (T). Click in the composition window, then type the word "globe.com".

3. Choose a Font; a type Size of 48 points; Alignment: Horizontal and Center; then click OK.

4. Choose a color for the type.

5. Move the current time marker for the type to 03s-10f. Extend the text object's duration bar so it touches the time marker line (scroll the Timeline window, if necessary). Move the current time marker to 02s.

6. On the Opacity palette, set the Object Opacity to 85.

7. On the Layer palette, set the Softness to 1. You will reset this later.

8. Choose the Selection tool (V), then position the type about a half-inch above the top edge of the circle object and center the type over the circle object (Fig. 3).

9. Expand the globe.com object list and the Transform list, then click the

3 ➤

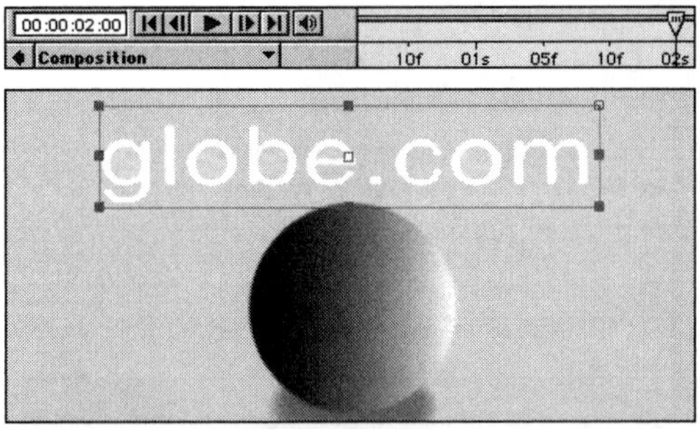

4 ➤

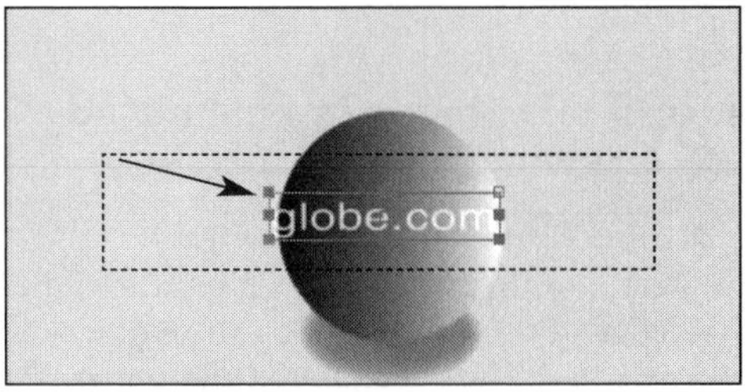

1 ➤ *The text object scaled down.*

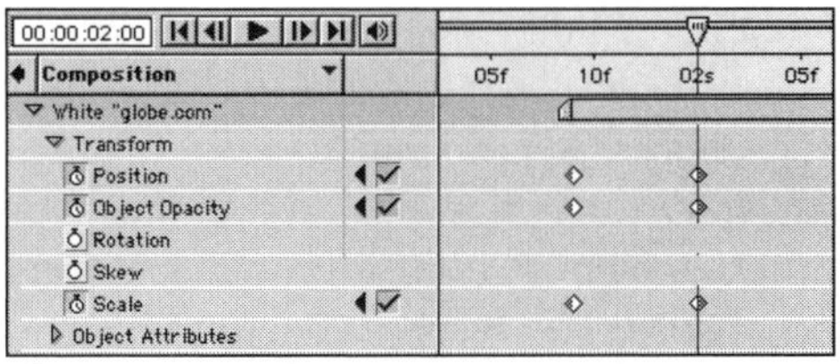

2 ➤ *The Transform keyframes for the text object.*

3 ➤ 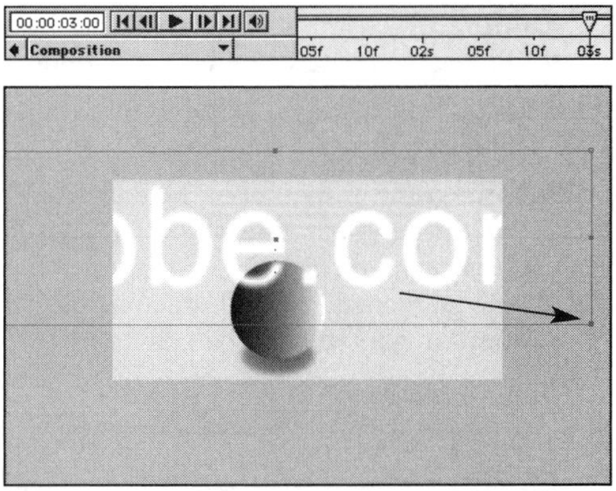

4 ➤ 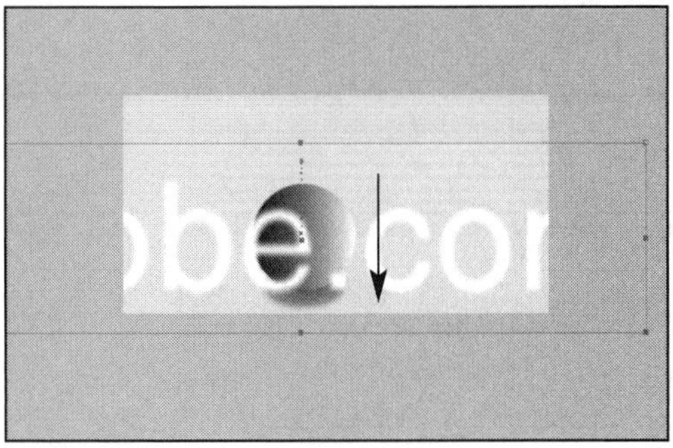

stopwatches for Position, Object Opacity, and Scale. Expand the Layer 1 list and click the stopwatch for Softness. Keyframes will be created.

10. Move the current time marker to 01s-09f.

11. Click on the text object in the composition window. Shift-drag it downward so it's centered on the circle object (Fig. 4, previous page).

12. Shift-drag a corner selection handle (not the upper right handle) inward to make the type smaller. Its bounding box should fit within the circle shape (Fig. 1).

13. Set the Layer palette Softness to 5.

14. Set the Opacity palette Object Opacity to 10.

15. Move the current time marker to 02s.

16. Select the globe.com object, then make the Softness 0 on the Layer palette. This will modify the existing keyframe.

17. Save the file (Fig 2).

STRETCH OUT THE GLOBE.COM TYPE

1. Position the current time marker at 03s.

2. Click in the composition window. Drag the window resize button to enlarge the window beyond the background border.

3. Drag the corner selection handle for the text object outward horizontally until the type extends beyond the edge of the background (Fig. 3).

4. Set the Layer palette Softness to 1 or 2.

5. Set the Object Opacity on the Opacity palette to 15.

6. Drag the stretched text object downward so it's in front of the circle object (Fig. 4).

Keyframes were created for the text object properties (Position, Object Opacity, Scale, and Softness).

7. Click on a blank area of the objects hierarchy list, click the First Frame button, then click the Play button to preview the animation. Save the file. You're done! ▲

Tutorial 5

Sequence the appearance and disappearance of text objects in a banner ad

CREATE THE TEXT

1. This animation is modeled for a standard full-size banner ad. Choose File menu > New (or Edit menu > Composition Settings). Enter a Width of 468 pixels and a Height of 60 pixels; make the Frame Rate 15; choose Export: Entire Composition; check the Make HTML box; then click OK.
2. Choose the Type tool (T).
3. Click in the composition window. Choose a Font; a type Size of around 25 points; and Alignment: Horizontal and Center. Enter the text "Hey, you". This is object 1.

   Now create three more text objects to hold the following phrases: "Are you game?" (object 2), "Roll on over and" (object 3), and "click here!" (object 4). Increase the type size for each successive text object, reselecting the Type tool each time. Don't worry about the placement of the text objects yet.
4. Apply the same color to objects 1, 2, and 3. Apply a brighter color to object 4 (the "click here" text).
5. Move object 1 to the left edge of the composition. Move object 4 to the right edge of the composition. Move object 2 just to the left of center. Move object 3 just to the right of center (Fig. 1). They will partially overlap.
6. Choose Edit menu > Select All to select all the text objects (Command-A/Ctrl-A).
7. Choose Object menu > Align > Bottom.
8. If the rulers aren't showing, choose View menu > Show Rulers. Drag a guide from the horizontal ruler and position it at the baseline of one of the text objects.
9. Deselect all, then select each text object one at a time and use the arrow keys to align each text baseline with the guide.
10. Display the Timeline editor. Move the current time marker to 03s.
11. Position the end point of the composition duration bar (the white bar) so it touches the vertical line of the current time marker (Fig. 2). All the text object's duration bars will also be extended.

1 ➤ The text objects placed and aligned in the composition.

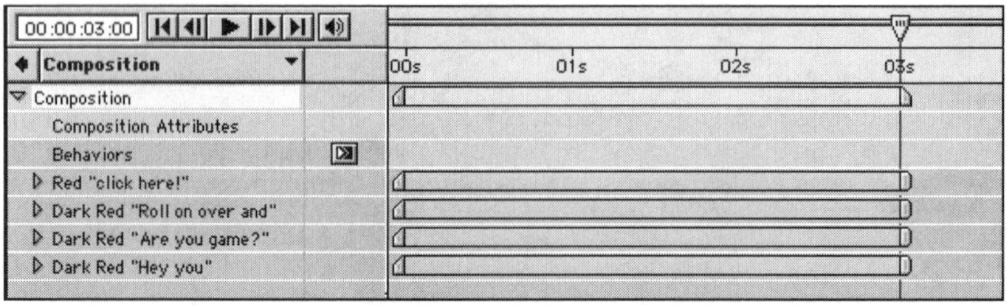

2 ➤ The text object's duration bars are the same length as the composition duration bar.

SEQUENCE THE APPEARANCE OF THE TEXT OBJECTS

1. Move the current time marker to 00s-06f. Drag the duration end point of object 1 ("Hey you") so it touches the vertical time marker.
2. Move the current time marker to 00s-11f. Drag the duration start point of object 2 so it touches the vertical time marker.
3. Move the current time marker to 01s-05f. Drag the duration end point of object 2 so it touches the vertical time marker.
4. For object 3, set the duration start point to 01s-09f and the duration end point to 02s-02f.
5. For object 4, set the duration start point to 02s-06f and leave the duration end point as is.
6. Click First Frame, then click Play. Save your file (Fig. 1).

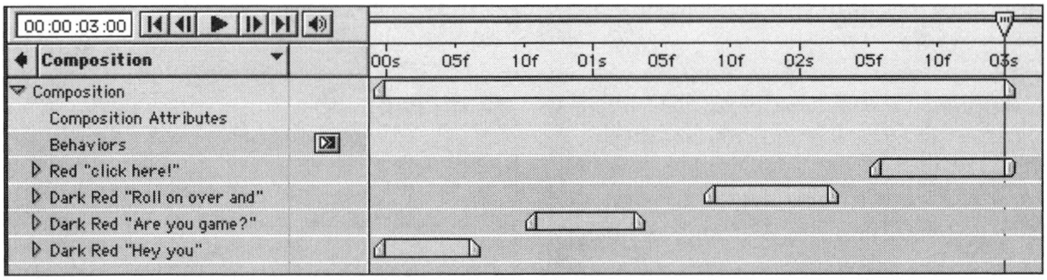

1 ➤ The text objects are sequenced in a stairstep pattern so each object appears at a different time. The duration bars don't overlap.

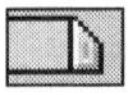 *Auto Length off*  *Auto Length on*

The end points of the duration bars for the first three text objects aren't rounded. This is because Auto Length is automatically turned off for duration bars that are manually lengthened or shortened.

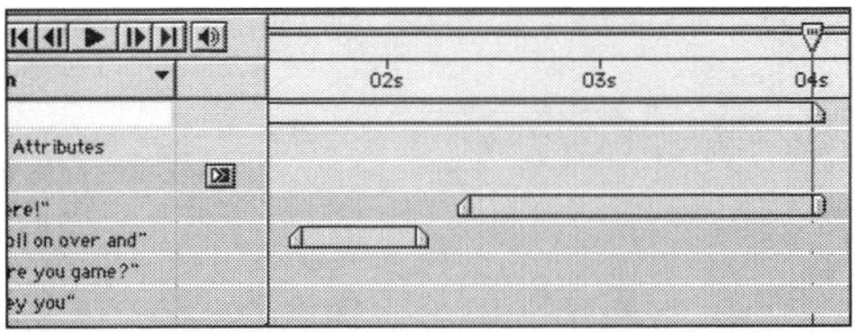

2 ➤ The composition duration is extended to 04s. If you turn on the Auto Length feature for the "click here" object, its duration will automatically match that of the composition.

To make the ad more entertaining, you can incorporate fade-ins and fade-outs for the first two text objects. This will require resetting the Object Opacity for those objects and also extending their duration bars so they overlap slightly. In order to do this, you will have to lengthen the duration of the entire composition.

MAKE THE TEXT FADE IN AND OUT

1. In the Timeline editor, move the current time marker to 04s.
2. Move the end point of the composition duration bar (the white bar) so it touches the vertical time marker. *Note:* The end point of the "click here!" object should also move. If it doesn't, select the object and click the Auto Length button (Fig. 2).
3. Move the current time marker to 00s.
4. Click on "Hey you" on the Objects hierarchy list.
   then

(Continued on the next page)

On the Opacity palette, set the Object Opacity to 0.
then
Expand the "Hey you" object list. Expand the Transform list, then click the stopwatch for Object Opacity.
then
Move the current time marker to 00s–5f.
then
On the Opacity palette, set the Object Opacity to 100. A keyframe will be created.
then
Move the current time marker to 01s-03f.
then
Drag the "Hey you" object duration bar end point so it touches the vertical time marker. Click the current time marker.
then
On the Opacity palette, set the Object Opacity to 0 (Fig. 1). A keyframe will be created (Fig. 2).

Note: If the Opacity palette fields are empty, move the current time marker over the object's duration bar first, then work with the palette.

5. Click the "Are you game?" object on the objects hierarchy list.
then
Move the current time marker to 01s.
then
Drag the duration bar start point so it touches the vertical time marker.
then
On the Opacity palette, set the Object Opacity to 0.
then
On the objects hierarchy list, click the stopwatch for Transform > Object Opacity.
then
Move the current time marker to 01s-06f. Move the duration end point so it touches the vertical time marker. Click the current time marker.
then
On the Opacity palette, set the Object Opacity to 100.
then

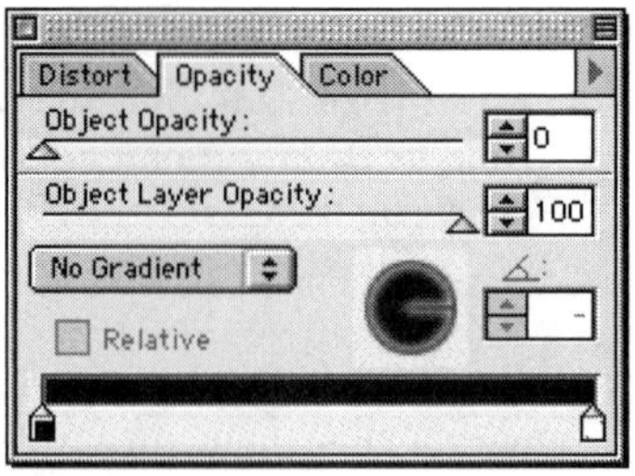

1➤ The object opacity for the first text object set to 0.

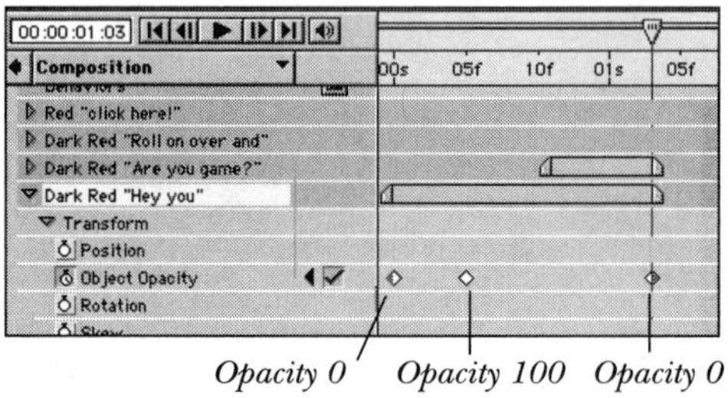

2➤ The first text object with the 3 keyframes to control object opacity.

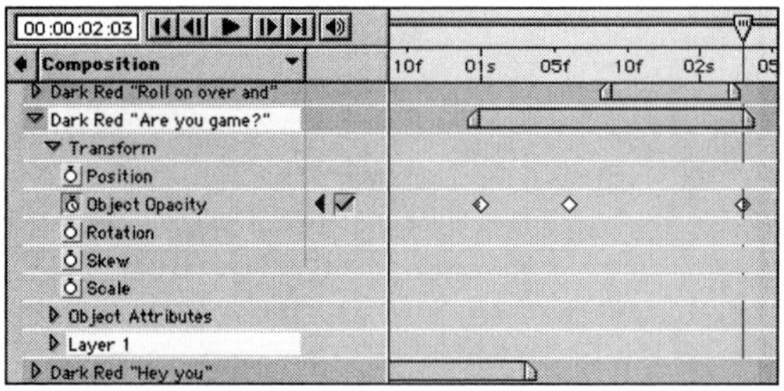

3➤ The second text object with the 3 keyframes to control object opacity.

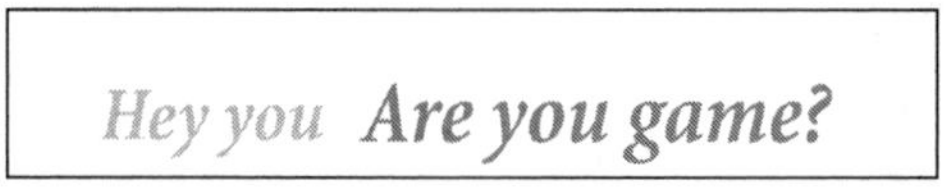

4➤ One text object fades out while the next fades in.

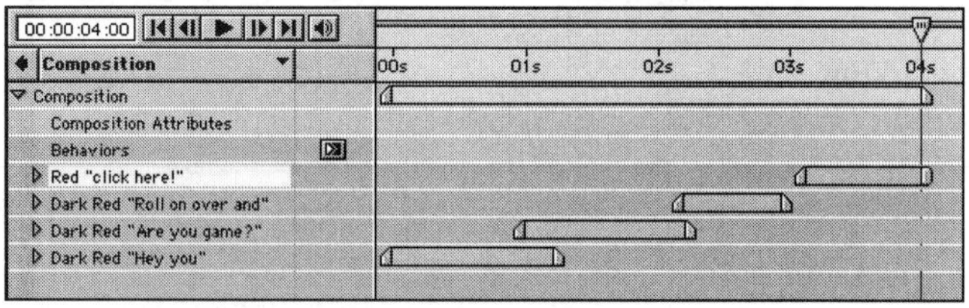

1 ➤ The final positions of the object duration bars on the Timeline. Objects whose bars overlap will be seen at the same time in the composition.

2 ➤ The final sequence of text objects.

Move the current time marker to 02s-03f.
then
Drag the end point of the duration bar so it touches the vertical time marker.
then
On the Opacity palette, set the Object Opacity to 0 (Figs. 3–4, previous page).

Note: If the Opacity palette fields are empty, move the current time marker over the object's duration bar first, then work with the palette.

6. Click the "Roll on over and" object on the objects hierarchy list. We won't change the opacity for the next two text objects.
then
Move the current time marker to 02s-14f.
then
Drag the duration bar end point so it touches the vertical time marker.
then
Move the current time marker to 02s-03f.
then
Drag the duration bar start point so it touches the vertical time marker.
then
Click the "click here!" object on the objects hierarchy list.
then
Move the current time marker to 03s-02f.
then
Drag the duration bar start point so it touches the vertical time marker. The end point is already positioned correctly (Figs. 1–2).

7. Click First Frame, then click Play. Save your file. ▲

Working with keyframes

Here are some basic techniques for working with keyframes and object lists on the Timeline editor. They will help speed up the animation production and editing process.

To set the same property keyframe for multiple objects:

1. Position the current time marker at the desired time spot.
2. Shift-select more than one object on the objects hierarchy list whose duration bars are currently touching the vertical line of the current time marker (Fig. 1).
3. Click a stopwatch for a property on an object's list on the objects hierarchy list (Fig. 2). That stopwatch will be clicked, if it's available, for all the currently selected objects on the list. Beware! Clicking a stopwatch for one selected object may cause the similar stopwatch for another selected object to become "unclicked."
4. Move the current time marker, then change a property in any of the palettes (Fig. 3). A new keyframe will be created for all the selected objects on the objects hierarchy list (Fig. 4).

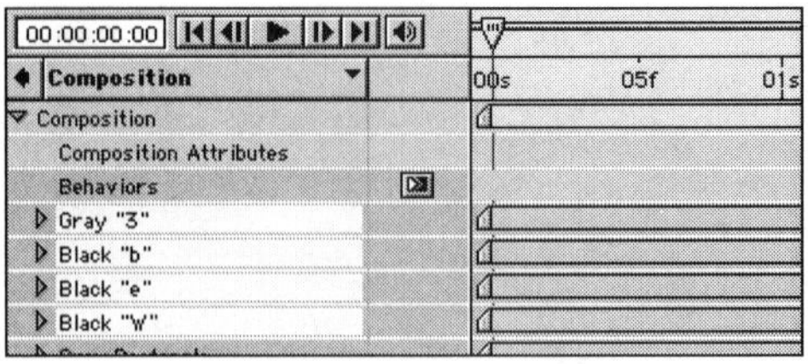

1 ➤ Shift-select multiple objects on the objects hierarchy list.

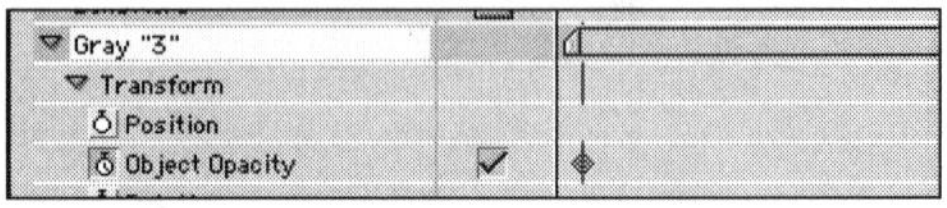

2 ➤ Click the stopwatch for the property to be changed.

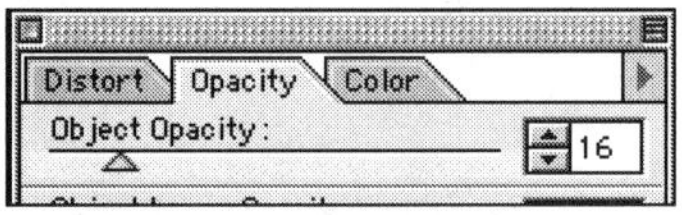

3 ➤ We moved the time marker, then lowered the Object Opacity value for the selected objects.

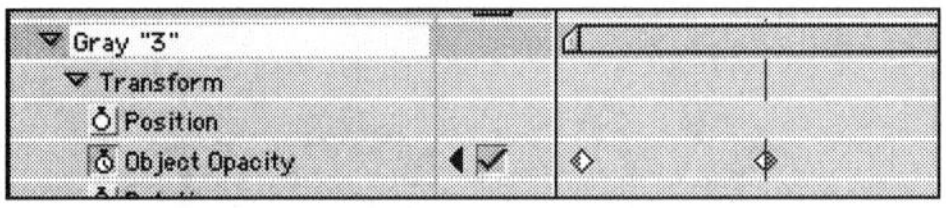

4 ➤ The Opacity palette change creates a new keyframe in each selected object's list. All of the selected objects are modified.

Keyframe icons can be repositioned on the timeline at any time. Repositioning a property keyframe will cause that property change to occur at a new time.

To move keyframes:

Drag a keyframe icon in the Timeline to a new position.

or

Shift-click multiple keyframes or choose the Drag-selection (U) or Selection (V) tool and draw a marquee around multiple keyframes (Fig. 5). The keyframes can be in the same row or in different rows. Then drag one of the selected keyframes. The other selected keyframes will follow suit (Fig. 6).

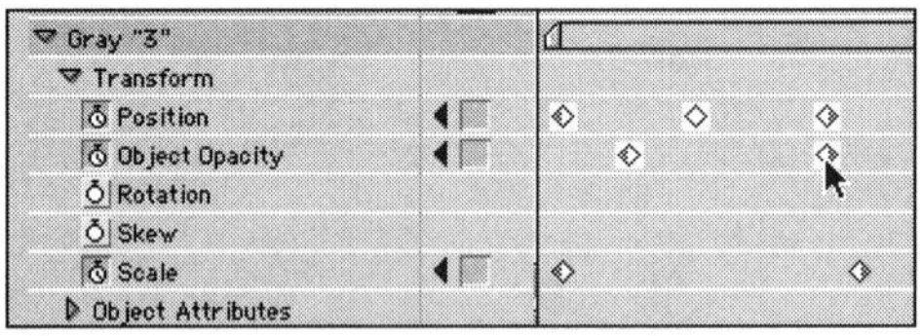

5 ➤ Select several keyframes in one or more rows.

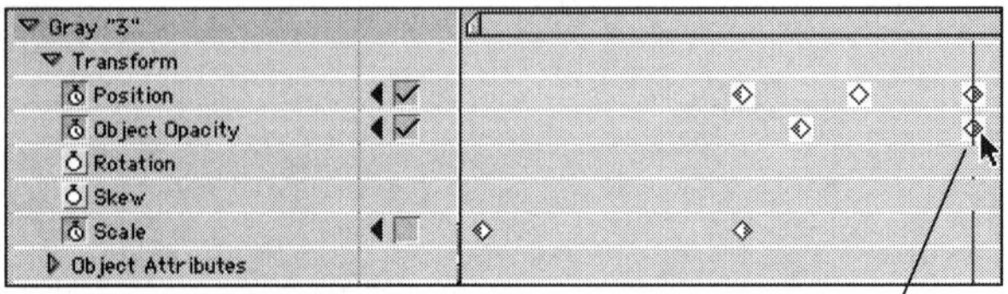

6 ➤ Drag the keyframes horizontally to a new position.

Quick dupe

To duplicate an object to use again in an animation, select the object in the composition, copy it, move the current time indicator to a new location, then paste the copy into the composition.

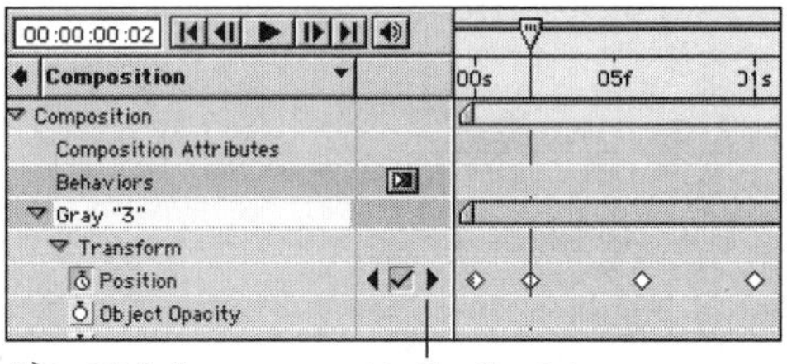

1 ➤ Click the arrow next to the Create/remove keyframe box.

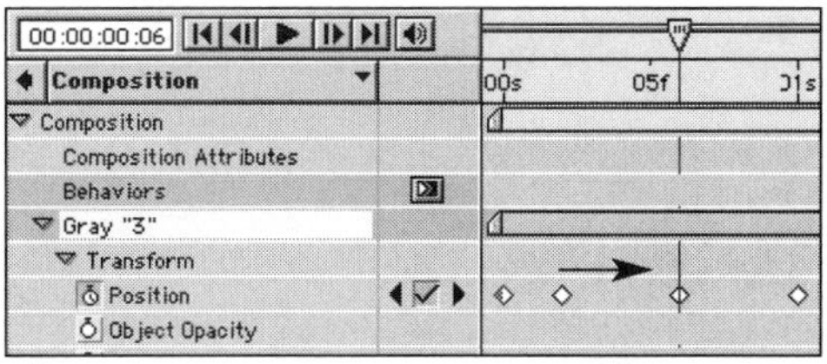

2 ➤ The current time marker moves to the next keyframe.

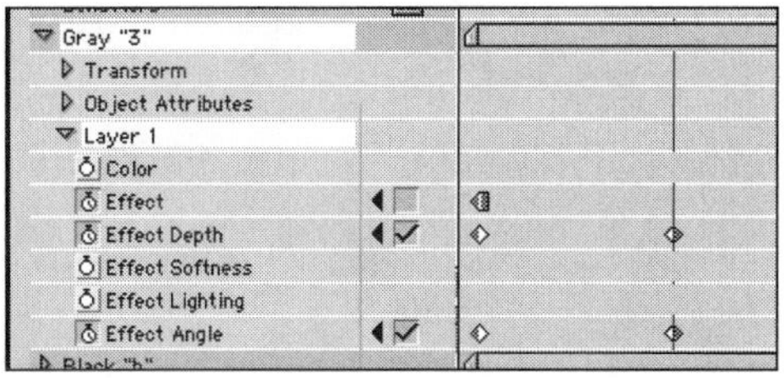

3 ➤ The Gray "3" object keyframes are copied...

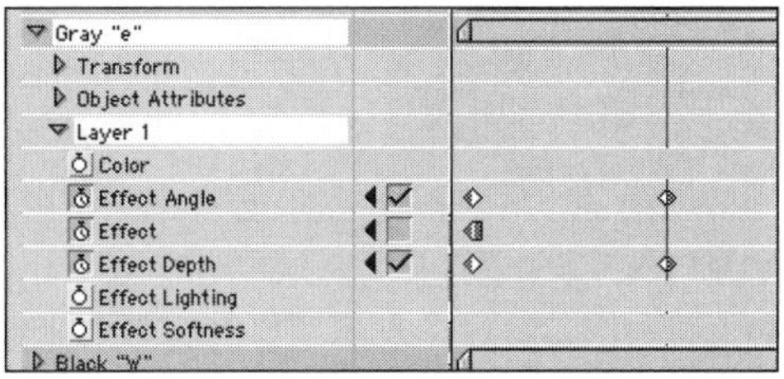

4 ➤ ...and pasted into the Gray "e" object.

➤ To re-sequence a property change, you can swap keyframes. To reverse an animation effect, drag each keyframe to the other keyframe's original position on the timeline (not on top of each other.)

To navigate between keyframes:

Wherever you see a keyframe, you'll also see a check box in the Create/remove keyframe column next to the objects hierarchy list (Fig. 1). You'll also see an arrowhead to the left or the right of the check box. Click the left (previous) or right (next) arrowhead to move the current time marker from one keyframe to the next (Fig. 2).

Properties listed on an object's Layer list can be copied and pasted to other objects.

To copy and paste layer property keyframes:

1. Click an object name on the objects hierarchy list (Fig. 3).
2. Choose Edit menu > Copy.
3. Select another object on the objects hierarchy list.
4. Choose Edit menu > Paste Style (Command-B/Ctrl-B). Layer properties from the original object will now also apply to the new object (Figs. 4–5).

➤ To paste Transform property keyframes, choose Edit menu > Paste Object Animation.

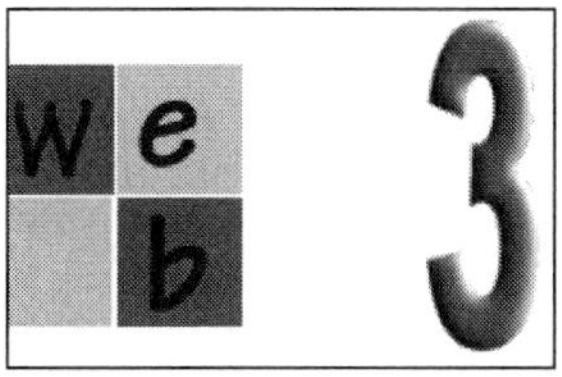

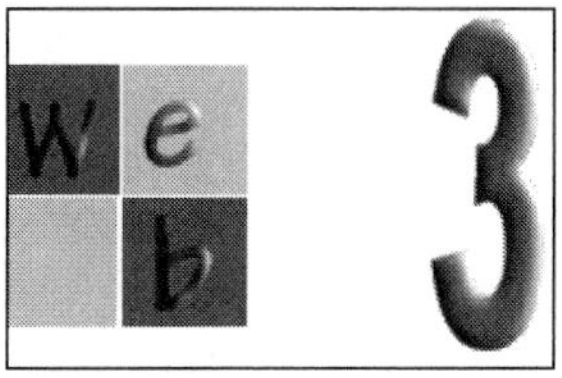

5 ➤ The 3D effects from the number 3 are copied to the letter objects.

There may be some point during an animation when you want a changing object property to stop changing temporarily. To extend the current value of an object property, all you have to do is create another keyframe with the same value.

This technique works well if you want an object that is moving or fading to hold its current position or current opacity level for a brief period of time. It won't work if you are adding a keyframe between two existing keyframes.

To add a keyframe with the same value as the previous keyframe:

1. Click on an object property on the object's list (e.g., Scale). Set a keyframe for that property either by clicking the stopwatch to create the initial keyframe or by checking the Create/remove keyframe box.
2. Move the current time marker to a new position (Fig. 1).
3. Check the Create/remove keyframe box. A keyframe with the same property value as the previous keyframe will be created (Fig. 2).

To delete one keyframe:

Click the keyframe icon in the Timeline, then press Delete/Backspace.

or

Position the current time marker on the keyframe icon, then uncheck the Create/remove keyframe box.

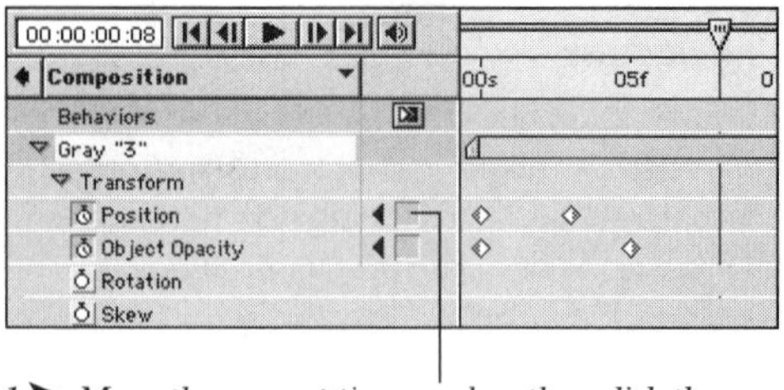

1 ➤ Move the current time marker, then click the Create/remove keyframe box.

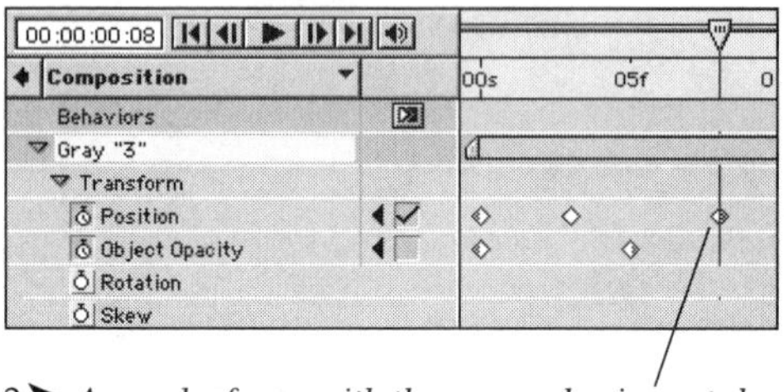

2 ➤ A new keyframe with the same value is created.

Preview preview

To preview your animations, choose each browser from the File menu > **Preview in** submenu. Compare the differences between Netscape Navigator or Communicator and Internet Explorer.

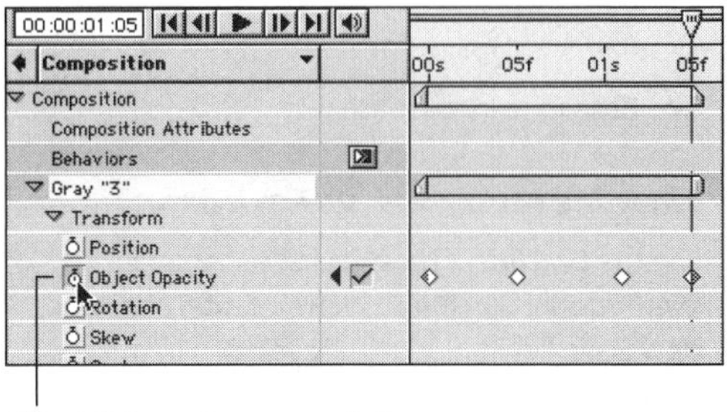

1 ➤ Click on the stopwatch for a property row.

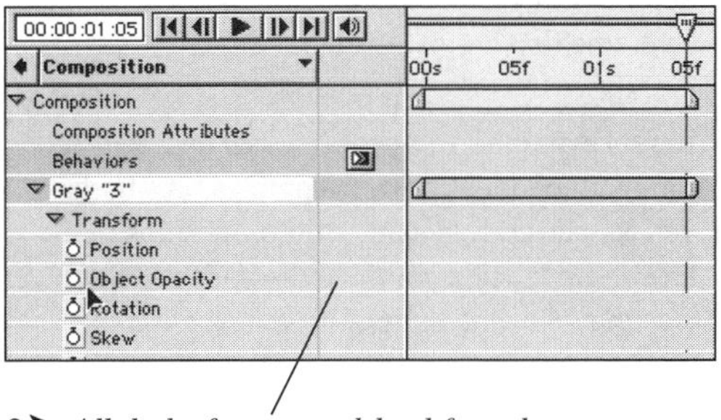

2 ➤ All the keyframes are deleted from that row.

To delete all the keyframes for a property:

Click the stopwatch for the property from which you want to delete all the keyframes (Fig. 1). The keyframes for that property will be removed (Fig. 2), and the object will take on whatever properties are applied for the current time position, except for scale; the object will be restored to its original size.

➤ To restore the deleted keyframes, choose Edit menu > Undo.

Beware! When an object is deleted from the objects hierarchy list, it is also deleted from the composition!

To delete an object from the objects hierarchy list:

1. Click on the name of the object you want to delete.
2. Press Delete/Backspace.

You can choose from five different transition (interpolation) options for a selected keyframe: Linear, Auto Bezier, Hold Keyframe, Ease In, and Ease Out. These options modify the transition of a property value as it passes through a keyframe change during the animation playback.

To set a keyframe transition option:

1. Click a keyframe or Shift-click several keyframes.
2. Choose a command from the Timeline menu:

   Linear produces a straight-line motion path with abrupt spacial position changes. For temporal (time) transitions, Linear produces sharp property transitions.

   Auto Bezier is the default option for spacial and temporal property value changes. It produces either curved motion paths or smooth property transitions. This option is best used for animating position changes.

   Hold Keyframe produces no transition stages. An object will simply hold to its current spatial position or property value and then abruptly change position or values when the next keyframe is encountered. Use this option to create a quick, dramatic property change.

   Ease In and **Ease Out** produce a more gradual change in property values as the object approaches or leaves a selected keyframe, slowing the rate of change. Ease In affects values as the object approaches the keyframe; Ease Out affects values as the object leaves the keyframe. These options create the most realistic motion because objects in the real world don't move at a constant rate.

➤ To turn off a checkmarked option, choose it again. A keyframe must be either Linear or Auto Bezier.

What the symbols mean

- Starting keyframe
- Ending keyframe
- Hold Keyframe
- Ease In
- Ease Out
- Both Ease In and Ease Out

Timeline menu > New Keyframe

Use the Timeline > New Keyframe commands (New Position keyframe, New Rotation keyframe, New Scale keyframe, New Opacity keyframe, and New Anchor Point keyframe) to set keyframes for these properties for the currently selected object or objects at the current time. The commands automatically set a stopwatch for the first keyframe that is created in that property's row.

The New Keyframe commands can also be used to set keyframes on a property row for a selected time-independent object, regardless of whether you are currently viewing the composition timeline or the timeline for the independent object (see the following page). This will save you the trouble of switching between timeline views.

Nesting animations

An object with an independent timeline is also called a **nested animation routine**. A nested animation routine has its own time scheme within the larger composition, its own objects hierarchy list, and its own duration bar. A composition can contain more than one nested animation routine, and they can be viewed when needed.

The names of time-independent objects that are nested within other time-independent objects will appear on the **Active Timeline** menu at the top of the objects hierarchy list in the order in which they were nested. The Composition will always be listed at the bottom of this list. Use this menu or click the arrow to the left of the menu to navigate upward or downward through nested timelines.

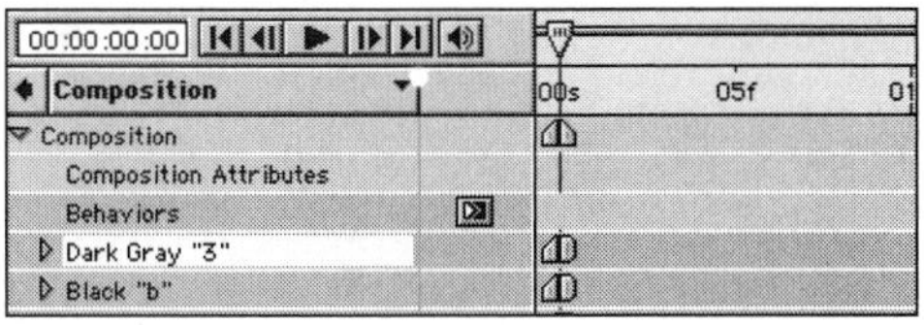

1 ➤ The object that is to be made time-independent is selected.

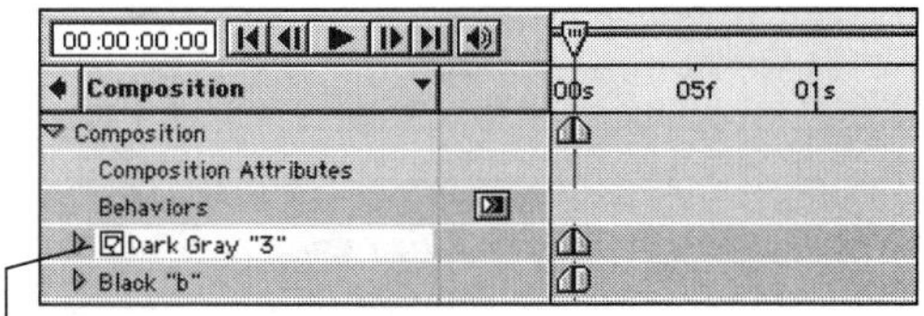

2 ➤ The object is now time-independent and an icon displays next to its name.

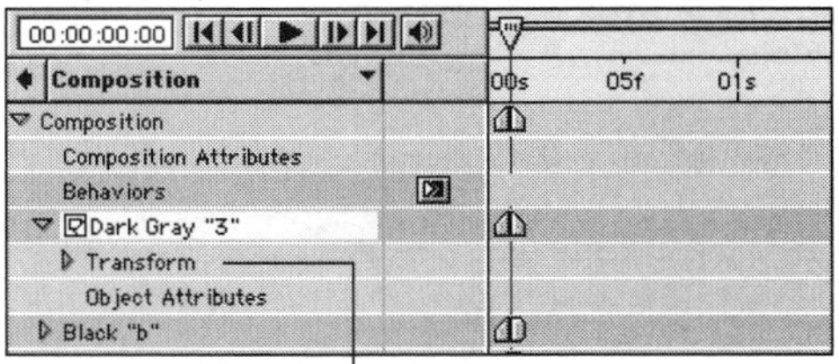

3 ➤ The transform properties can be edited in the main composition timeline (note the expansion arrow). Object Attributes and Layer properties can be edited only in the independent timeline.

Tutorial 6

In this exercise, you'll learn how to make an object cycle through an animation independent of the duration of the main composition. These nested, self-contained animations with their own timelines are a vehicle for dazzling special effects.

To make an animated object loop independently:

1. Position the current time marker at 00s.
2. Create some objects. One of the objects will be animated. Move it away from the other objects in the composition.
3. Show the Timeline editor (Command-T/Ctrl-T), then select the object to be animated by clicking its name on the objects hierarchy list or by clicking on the object in the composition window (Fig. 1).
4. Choose Timeline menu > Time Independent. Now the object's time duration will be separate from the time duration of the main composition. An icon will display to the left of the name of the now-independent object and its duration bar will be gray (Fig. 2).
5. Leave all the duration bars as is (including the composition bar). The start and end points will be touching, which means they have a one-frame duration.

   Note: You can't view or edit any of the Object Attributes or Layer properties while a time-independent object is being viewed on the main composition timeline. These properties are located in the independent timeline. You can edit Transform properties, however, because these properties affect the entire object, not just an individual layer or attribute. These properties are located in and controlled by the timing of the main composition (Fig. 3).
6. Double-click the independent object to be animated. This will bring up that object's independent Timeline. The

(Continued on the next page)

object's name will appear at the top of the objects hierarchy list and on the Active Timeline pop-up menu (Fig. 1). You can now edit Object Attributes and Layer 1 properties.

7. Expand the Layer 1 list.

8. On the Opacity palette, set the Object Layer Opacity to 0.

9. Click the stopwatch next to Object Layer Opacity (Fig. 2).

10. Move the current time marker to 01s.

11. On the Opacity palette, set the Object Layer Opacity to 100. The object's duration end point will extend automatically to the vertical marker (Fig. 3).

12. Click First Frame, then click Play. There will now be a Layer 1 fade-in. Other layers, if any, will remain visible.

13. To return to the main composition view, choose Composition from the Active Timeline menu above the objects hierarchy list or click the left-pointing arrow to the left of the active timeline name (Figs. 4–5).

14. *Optional:* To make the object animation loop, click the object name, then click the Loop button at the bottom of the Timeline editor.

15. Click to the left of the objects hierarchy list to deselect all objects.

16. Click the Preview mode button at the bottom of the Toolbox. The animation will loop independently from all the other objects. Click the Edit mode button when you're done. (Click Preview mode again to restart the animation.)

Note: An independent timeline animation will play only while its independent timeline is displayed or when you click Preview mode.

➤ To release an object from being time-independent, select the object, then reselect Timeline menu > Time Independent to uncheck the option. The layer properties will now be editable in the next higher level of timelines (Composition being the highest level). ▲

1 ➤ The name of the selected time-independent object appears on the active timeline menu.

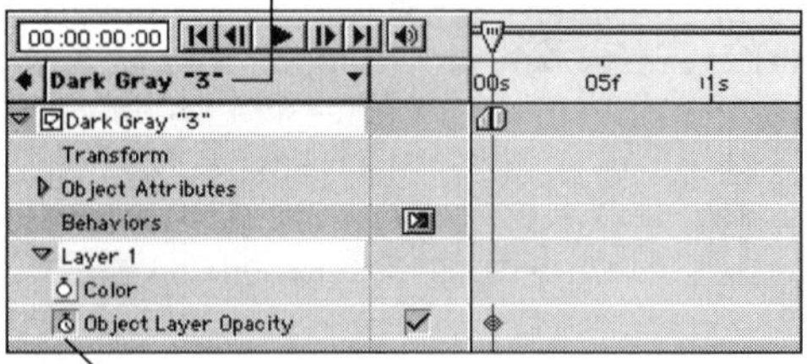

2 ➤ This is the independent timeline for the Dark Gray "3" object. The Layer 1 > Object Layer Opacity stopwatch is clicked to create a keyframe.

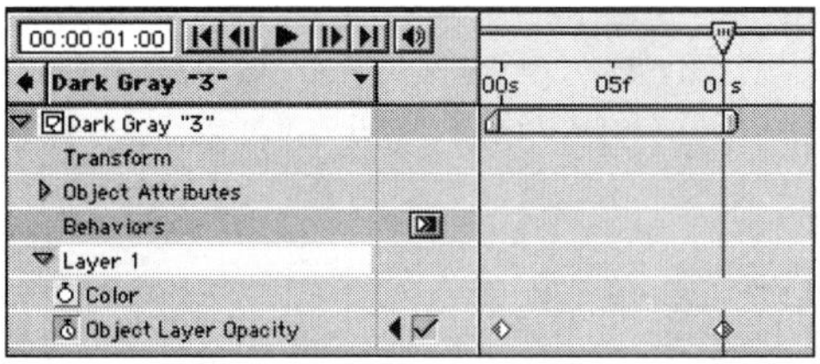

3 ➤ At 01s, the Object Layer Opacity value is changed to 100 and a new keyframe is created.

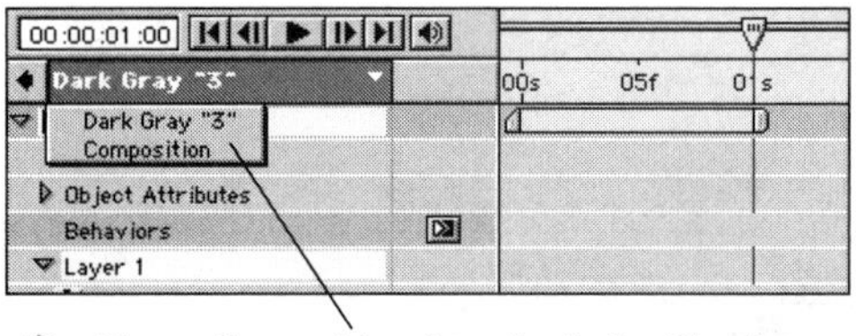

4 ➤ Choose Composition from the Active Timeline menu to return to the composition timeline (or choose a different name, if any, on the menu to return to that timeline level).

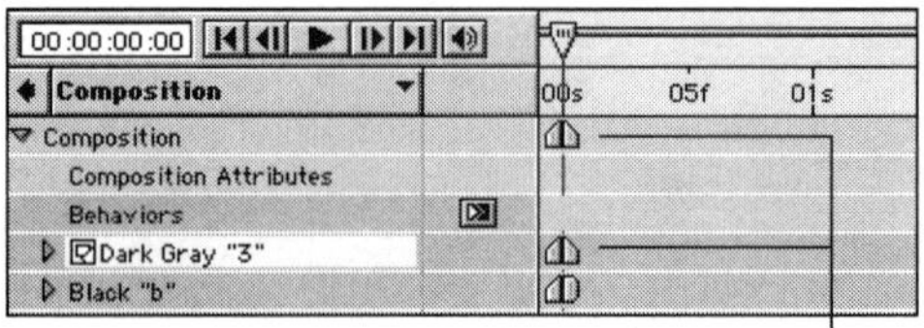

5 ➤ The composition timeline now displays. The time-independent object will have the same duration as the composition in this timeline. The object's real duration is set in its independent timeline.

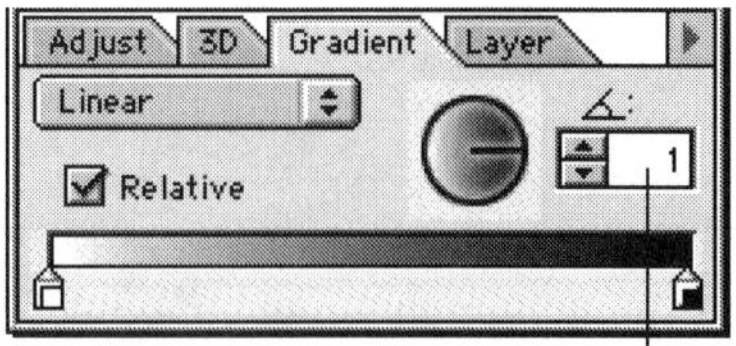

1 ➤ *The Gradient palette, with an angle of 1.*

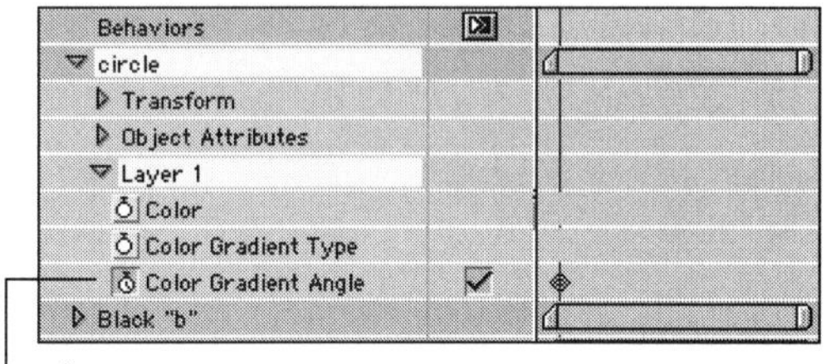

2 ➤ *Click the stopwatch for the Color Gradient Angle property to set the first keyframe.*

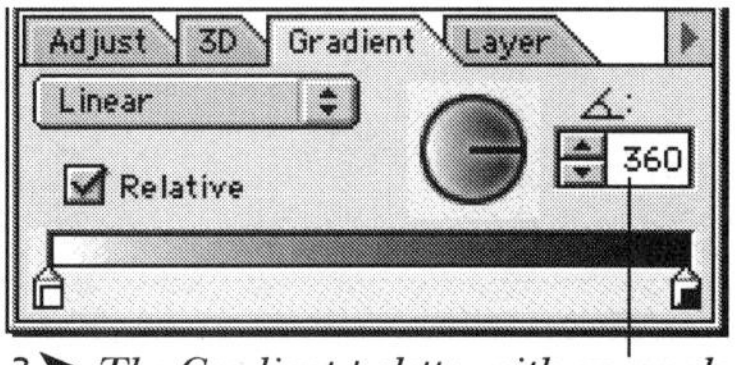

3 ➤ *The Gradient palette, with an angle of 360.*

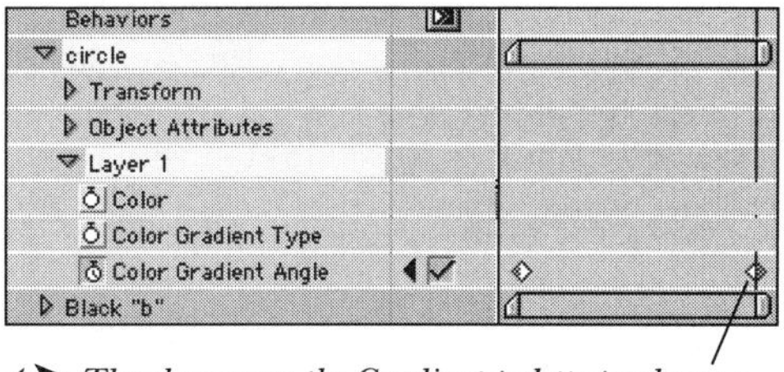

4 ➤ *The change on the Gradient palette produces a new keyframe.*

5 ➤ *The rotating gradient.*

Tutorial 7

In this exercise, you will learn how to make a gradient spin around inside an object.

Rotate a gradient inside an object

1. Choose Edit menu > New or Edit menu > Composition Settings. Enter a Width and Height; choose 15 as the Frame Rate; choose Export: Entire Composition; check the Make HTML box; then click OK.
2. Show the Transform palette, choose the Ellipse tool (L), then drag while holding down Shift to create a circle with a width and height of 96.
3. Apply a color to the object, then move it to one side of the composition window.
4. On the Gradient palette, choose Linear from the pop-up menu to produce a gradient from a color to black.
   and
   Click the upward-pointing arrow next to the Angle field to create an angle of 1 (Fig. 1). (This will force the Color Gradient Angle property to appear on the Layer 1 list.)
5. Show the Timeline editor, then click the object on the objects hierarchy list.
6. Press Return/Enter, type the name "circle," then click OK.
7. Expand the object's list and the Layer 1 list.
8. Click the stopwatch for Color Gradient Angle to set a keyframe (Fig. 2).
9. Move the current time marker to 01s.
10. On the Gradient palette, enter 360 in the Angle field, then press Return/Enter (Fig. 3). A new keyframe will be created (Fig. 4).
11. Click to the left of the objects hierarchy list to deselect the object.
12. Click First Frame, then click Play (Fig. 1).

    Save your file, then follow the next set of instructions to turn the Gradient Angle rotation into a looping animation.

(Continued on the following page)

As a variation on the instructions on the previous page, we'll show you how you can make the gradient in the circle rotate continuously, independent from other objects.

MAKE THE GRADIENT IN THE CIRCLE OBJECT ROTATE IN AN INDEPENDENT LOOP

1. Select the circle object on the objects hierarchy list.
2. Choose Timeline menu > Time Independent to make the object into an independent character.
3. Select the now independent object on the hierarchy list.
4. Click the Loop button at the lower left corner of the Timeline editor (Fig. 1).
   or
   Choose Timeline menu > Loop.

   Either way, the Loop icon will display next to the object name.
5. Click on the left side of the objects hierarchy list to deselect all objects.
6. Click the Preview mode button at the bottom of the Toolbox. Click the Edit mode button when you're done previewing.

➤ By entering a multiple of 360 in the Angle field, you will cause the gradient to spin around that many times during the object's independent timeline loop. For example, if you enter 1440, the gradient will rotate four times within the one-second time duration.

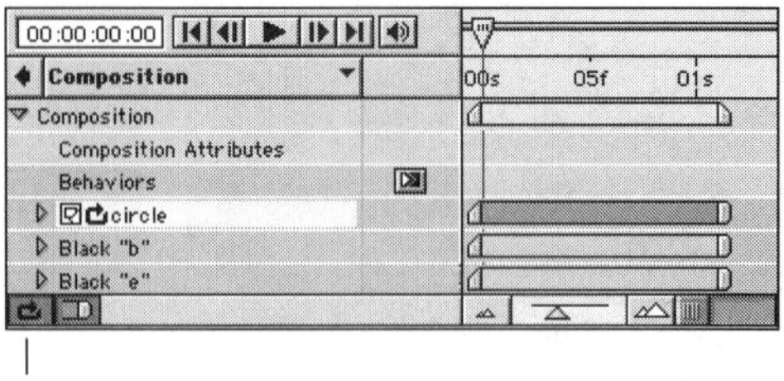

1 ➤ The Loop button was clicked on to make the circle object loop independently of the composition. Notice the loop icon next to the circle name.

In Sync

In the main composition timeline view, if you extend the duration bar of an independent timeline object, faint vertical lines will appear (Fig. 2). These lines show when the loop will repeat within the main composition duration. Use these lines to line up (sync) the loop repeats to other keyframe changes of other objects in the timeline.

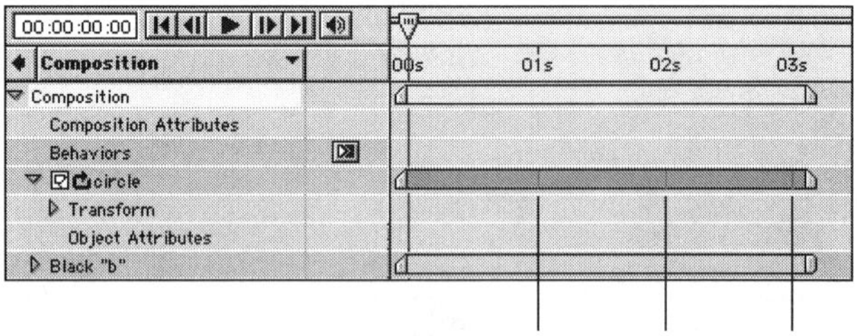

*2 ➤ Faint vertical lines on the duration bar of the circle object mark when the **loop** will **repeat** within the main composition duration.*

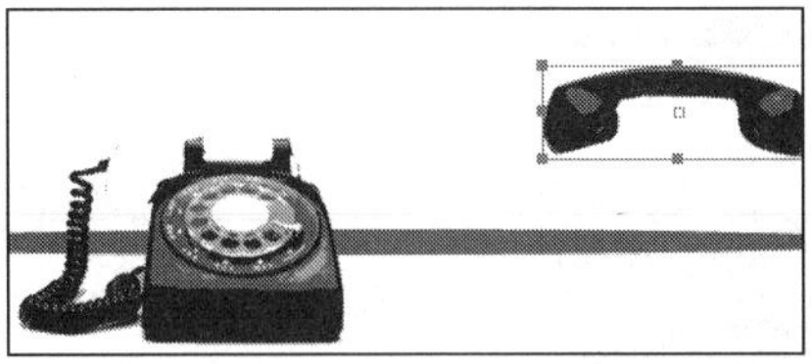

1➤ *The receiver object is selected. It will be animated using rotation and movement.*

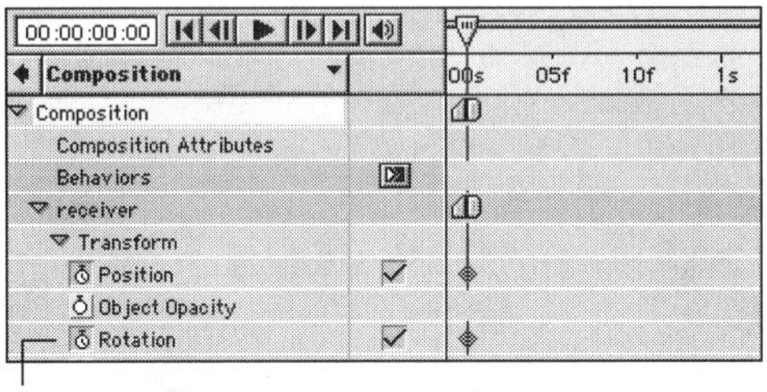

2➤ *Click the stopwatch to set a keyframe for Rotation and optionally, Position.*

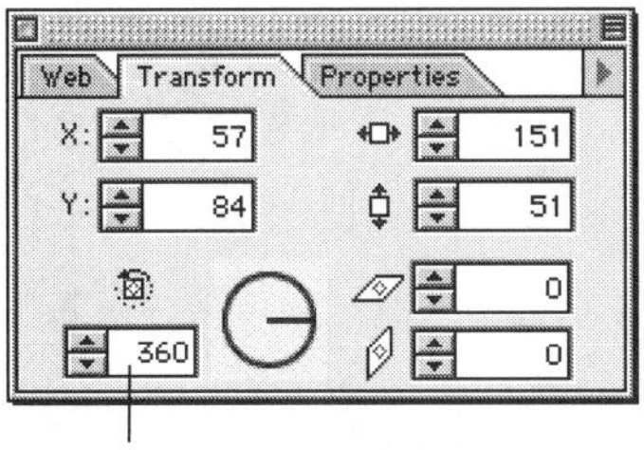

3➤ *At 01s, set the Transform palette > Rotation Angle to 360.*

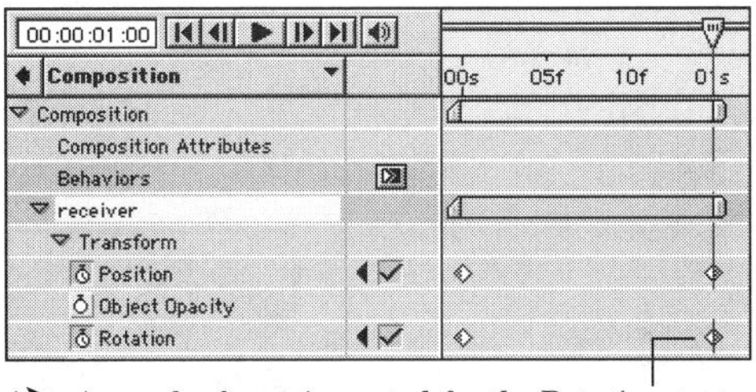

4➤ *A new keyframe is created for the Rotation property. We also repositioned our object at this time frame.*

The Transform > Rotate property is used to rotate an entire object. This is a continuation of Tutorial 7.

ROTATE AN IMAGE OBJECT

1. In the Timeline editor, move the current time marker to 00s. Choose File menu > Place to place an image at this point on the timeline.
2. Scale and position the object appropriately in the composition (Fig. 1).
3. Click the new object's name on the objects hierarchy list, press Return/Enter, rename the object, then click OK.
4. Expand the object's list and the Transform list. Click the Rotation stopwatch to set a starting keyframe (Fig. 2).
5. *Optional:* If you plan to move the object, click the Position stopwatch to set a starting keyframe.
6. Move the current time marker to 01s.
7. On the Transform palette, enter 360 in the Rotation Angle field, then press Return/Enter (Figs. 3–4). Enter a multiple of 360 to rotate the object more than once.
8. *Optional:* If you set a Position keyframe in step 5, drag the object to another position in the composition. A keyframe will be created.
9. Click first Frame, then click Play; or click the Preview mode button. Save the file.

➤ To learn how to make a rollover trigger an animation, see pages 221–224.

➤ You will not be able to make object rotation in an independent loop because the Rotation property is still within the main composition timeline. Learn about a "Group of 1" workaround for this limitation on page 206. ▲

Saving animations

If you save an animated object and all its animation effects to the Library palette, it can then be placed into any composition.

To save an animation object in the Library palette:

1. Show the Library palette.
2. Select an animation object in the composition or in the Timeline editor. It can be a time-independent object or group.
3. Drag the object from the composition window onto the Library palette (Fig. 1). (Bug: Make sure the Library palette doesn't overlap the composition window.)
4. Type a name for the object, then click OK (Figs. 2–3).

➤ To place the object into another LiveMotion composition, open a new file, select the object on the Library palette, then either click the Place Object button or drag the object into the composition window.

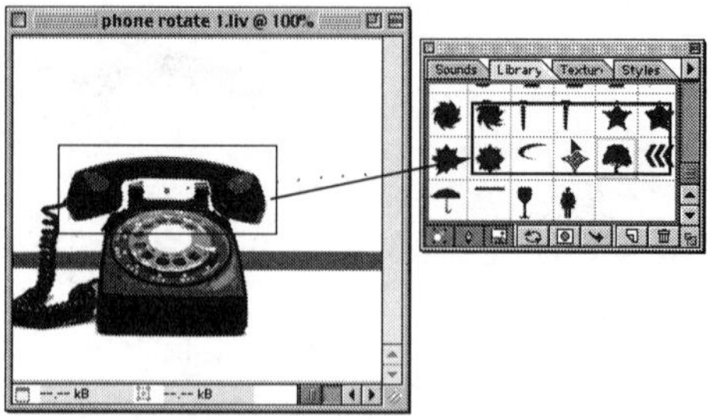

1 ➤ The receiver object is dragged onto the Library palette.

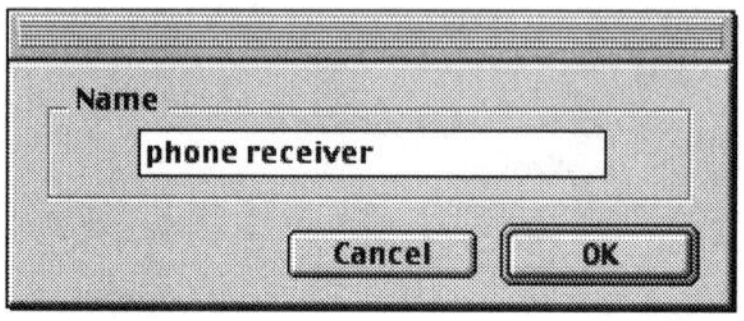

2 ➤ The object is named.

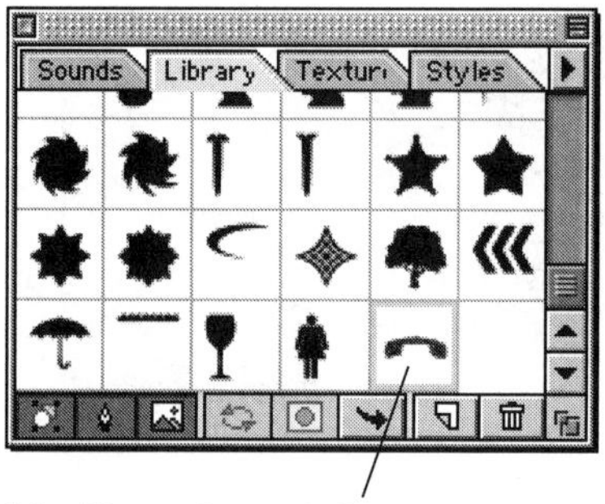

3 ➤ The newly saved object appears on the Library palette.

An animation is really just a collection of instructions that are applied to an object. The instructions track changes in property values over time. They can be saved to the Styles palette because, like styles, they are actually separate from any object they are applied to. An animation style can be applied to any object.

Note: Saving an animation to the Styles palette saves only the animation instructions that are applied to the object—not the object itself.

To save animation effects to the Styles palette:

1. Show the Styles palette.
2. Drag an animation object from the composition window onto the Styles palette (Fig. 4). (Bug: Make sure the Styles palette doesn't overlap the composition window.)

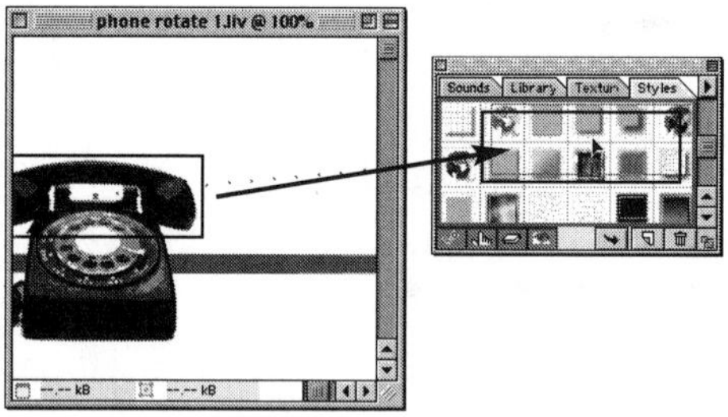

4 ➤ The receiver object is dragged onto the Styles palette.

Exporting animations

Be sure to test each animation you create in order to see which Export palette settings will produce the smallest possible file size and still produce acceptable results in the browsers. You can use either the GIF or the SWF (Flash) file format. Read about the Export palette in Chapter 16.

1 ➤ Name the object for saving into the Styles palette.

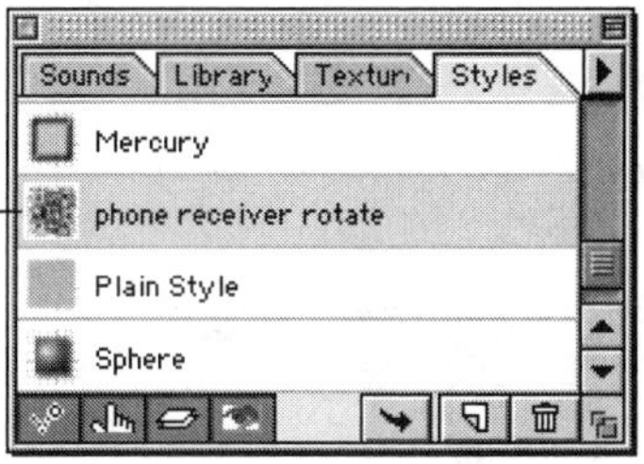

2 ➤ The new object appears on the Styles palette.

3. Enter a name for the new style.

4. Choose options for how the style will be saved:

Layers saves layer effects in the style. The next two options become accessible when this option is chosen.

When **Ignore color of first layer** is checked, the Layer 1 color of the current object is not saved as part of the style, which means the style won't change the Layer 1 color of objects to which it is applied. Don't check this option if the first layer of the object whose style you're saving contains a color gradient.

Layer Animation/Rollover saves layer animation properties, rollover states, and property changes as part of the style.

Photoshop Filters saves any Photoshop filters that were applied to an image object as part of the style. Filter Animation/Rollover becomes available when this option is chosen.

Filter Animation/Rollover saves in the style any animation or rollover effects based on filter usage.

Object Animation/Rollover saves any animation or rollover effects based on object manipulation.

5. Click OK (Figs. 1–2).

Note: To apply a saved animation style to an object, use one of the usual methods for applying a style: Select the object, click the style name on the Styles palette, then double-click the style name; or click the Apply Style button; or drag the style onto the object.

Adding sound

Sounds add a whole new dimension to Web pages. Sounds can be fun, beautiful, or irritating, but they're hard to ignore. LiveMotion supports the .aif, .av, QuickTime, and .wav sound file formats.

To add sound to an animation:

1. If the sound you want to use is not already on the Sounds palette, drag the sound file icon from the Desktop into the Sounds palette. Or, in the Mac OS Finder or in Windows Explorer, drag the sound file you want to use into the Adobe LiveMotion > Sounds folder, then relaunch LiveMotion.
2. Position the current time marker at the time when you want the sound to occur.
3. Show the Sounds palette. Click a sound icon, then drag the sound icon from the palette into the composition window or into the Timeline to place the sound in the main composition (Figs. 1–2).

   or

   In the Timeline editor, double-click a time-independent object, position the current time marker, then drag the sound icon onto the time-independent Timeline or onto the object in the composition window to place the sound in that independent timeline.

   The sound will automatically be added to the timeline as a separate object at the current time marker position.
4. Position the sound duration bar and adjust the start and end points. Shorten the duration to truncate the sound; lengthen the duration to cause the sound to loop. The delicate vertical lines that appear on the duration bar mark where the sound is repeated (Fig. 3).

   To sync a sound with an object change or motion, reposition or extend the sound duration bar so its vertical line aligns with the frame where the object change or motion occurs.

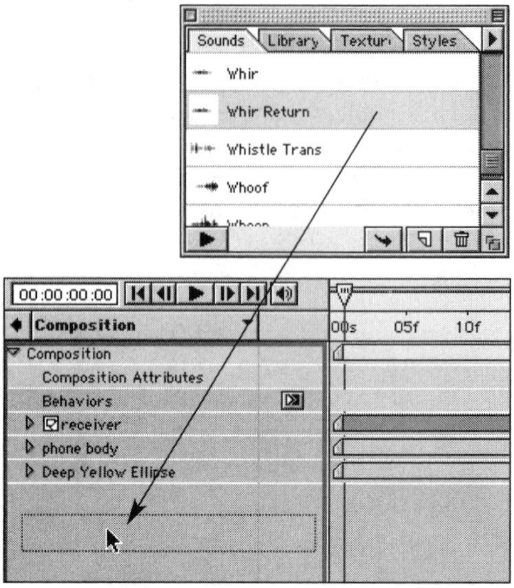

1 ➤ *Drag a sound icon into the Timeline.*

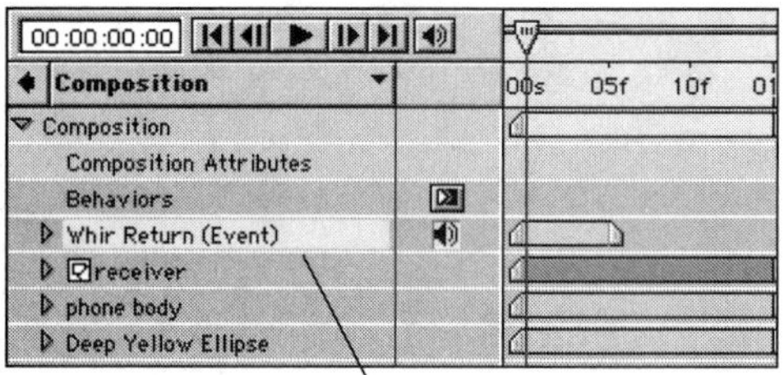

2 ➤ *The new sound object appears on the Timeline.*

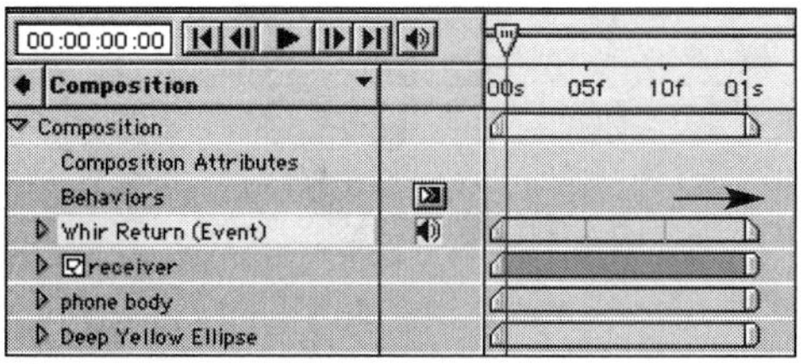

3 ➤ *The sound object's duration is increased. The thin vertical lines mark where the sound repeats.*

Sound options

These Sound options are available on the pop-up menu on the Properties palette:

Event Sound
The sound will play after it has downloaded and will be stored in memory for reuse. Use this option for a sound that plays more than once at separate points on the timeline.

Solo Event Sound
The sound will play in response to a mouse event, but all other playbacks of this sound will stop once the sound is played. This will prevent the sound from playing several times if the button to which it is attached is clicked on repeatedly.

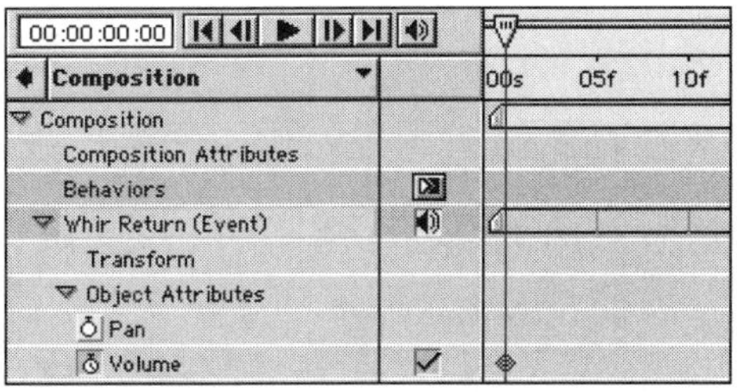

1 ➤ The sound object's list is expanded and a keyframe is set for ***Volume****.*

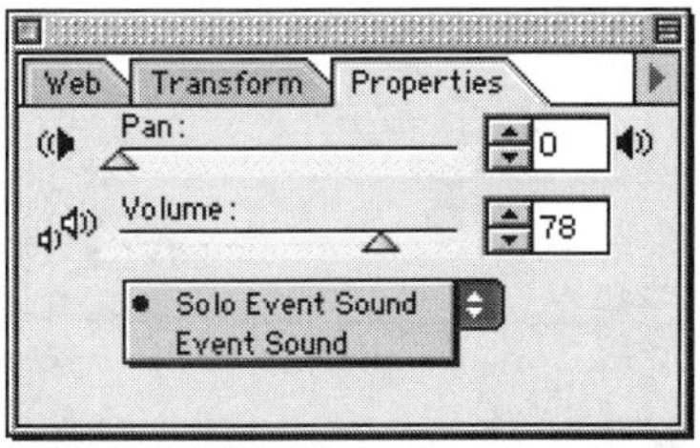

2 ➤ Use the ***Properties*** *palette to adjust* ***sound properties****.*

5. *Optional:* Expand the Object Attributes list under the sound object name to access the Pan and Volume sound properties. Pan causes the sound to move from the left stereo channel to the right stereo channel. Volume controls the loudness of the sound (Fig. 1). Use the Properties palette to change the current values for these properties (Fig. 2). Set keyframes to animate these properties as you would for any property. Align the sound keyframes with object change keyframes to have pan and/or volume changes sync with object transitions.
6. Choose an option from the pop-up menu on the Properties palette (see the sidebar).

➤ All sounds that are added to a composition become objects in the timeline (with the exception of a sound that is attached to a selected rollover state other than Normal via the Rollovers palette).

➤ Additional sound files are contained in the Adobe LiveMotion > Goodies > Sounds folder.

➤ All sounds from LiveMotion are exported to the MP3 format, but LiveMotion can't import MP3 sounds.

Properties and palettes

Illustrated below are properties on the Timeline and corresponding fields on the 3D, Gradient, and Distort palettes.

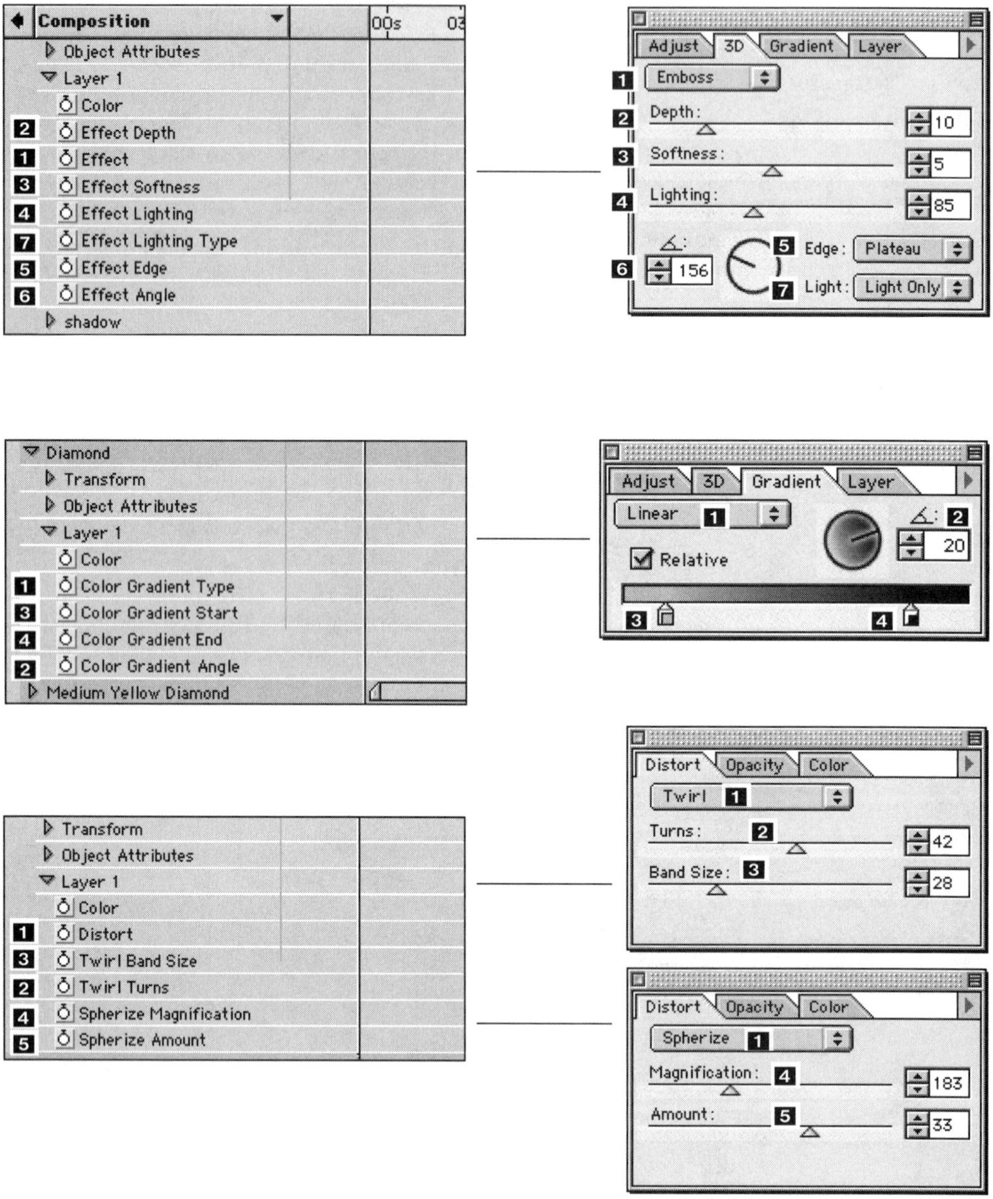

More Animation 14

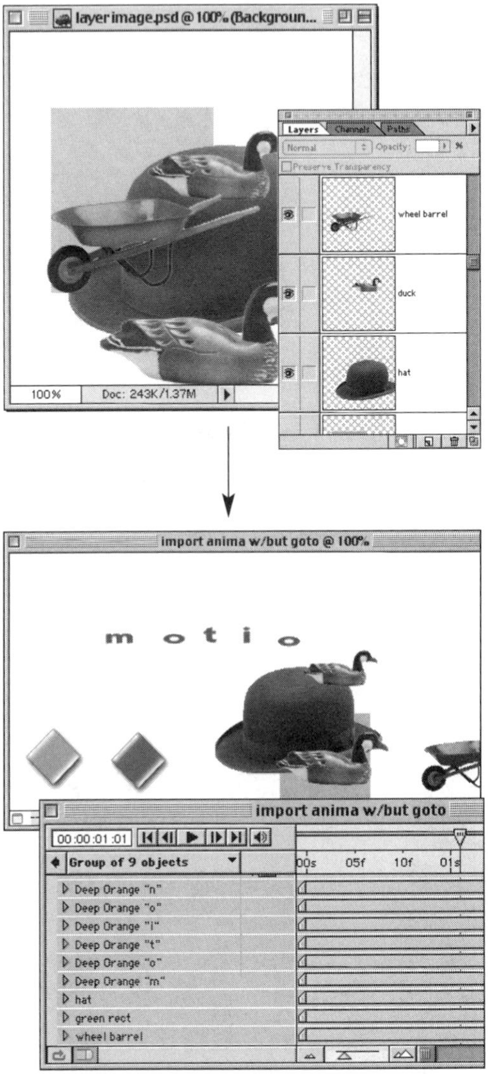

1 ➤ A layered Photoshop file was placed into LiveMotion. The placed layers were then converted into individual objects. The "layer" objects can be animated like any LiveMotion object.

Converting layers

IN THIS CHAPTER you'll learn more advanced animation techniques. First we'll show you how you can use Photoshop or Illustrator as the source application for animation objects.

In Photoshop, you can place different images on different layers and then use the program's industrial-strength image editing techniques to modify them. The layers can then be used as building blocks for an animation in LiveMotion.

In Illustrator 9, you can make several copies of a vector shape, change the contour of each copy incrementally, and then save each copy to a separate layer using the Release to Layers command. Or you can use Illustrator's Blend tool to produce a progression of shapes, which can then be used as separate objects or frames in LiveMotion.

One way to get a Photoshop or Illustrator file that contains multiple layers into LiveMotion is via the **Place** command. Another route is to **drag-and-drop** a **layer** from a Photoshop or Illustrator document window into a LiveMotion composition window. And a third route is to drag-and-drop an Illustrator or Photoshop **file icon** from the Desktop into a composition window.

Once a layered file has been placed or dropped into LiveMotion, you can then use the **Convert Layers Into** command to convert the layers either into separate objects or into a sequence of frames on one object layer. Any of the individual objects that result from such a conversion can then be selected in the Timeline editor (Fig. 1).

(Continued on the next page)

To top it all off, using the **Edit Original** command, any object (or frame) that's been placed or dropped into LiveMotion can be opened and edited in its original application (actually, you'll be working off a copy of the original file). When the newly edited copy is saved in its original application, it automatically updates in LiveMotion. This means that you have all the professional Photoshop and Illustrator tools at your disposal to revise a LiveMotion animation quickly.

➤ For better export to SWF (Flash) format, make object opacity changes in LiveMotion, not in Illustrator.

➤ In order to preserve objects or layers with blending modes from Photoshop or Illustrator, bring them in as one object in LiveMotion. Converting layers to separate objects causes any blending mode settings to be ignored.

To use Illustrator or Photoshop layers in LiveMotion:

1. In Illustrator or Photoshop, create a series of shapes to be used in an animation sequence. Don't group the shapes. Place each shape on its own layer, and save the file (Fig. 1).
2. In LiveMotion, show the Timeline editor (Command-T/Ctrl-T) and position the current time marker where you want the animation to start.
3. Choose File menu > Place (Command-I/Ctrl-I). Locate and highlight the Illustrator or Photoshop file, then click Open (Return/Enter) (Fig. 2).
4. From the Object menu > Convert Layers Into submenu, choose one of these commands:

   Objects to convert the layers into individual Timeline objects. They will all be positioned at the current time (Fig. 3). (*Note:* If you want to group objects into an independent timeline, Shift-select them on the objects hierarchy list, then choose Timeline menu > Make

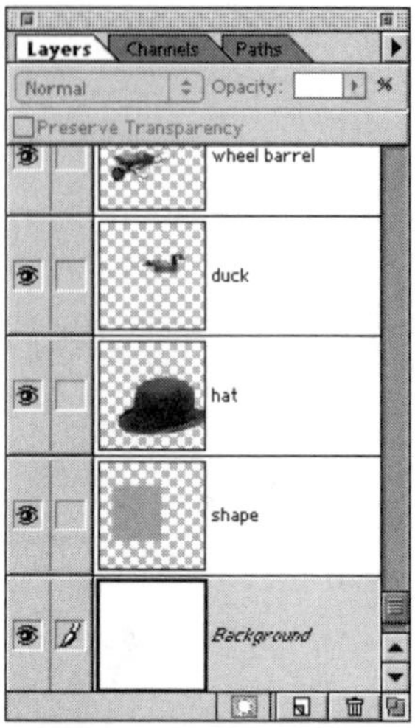

*1 ➤ The Layers palette in **Photoshop**, showing the individual layers.*

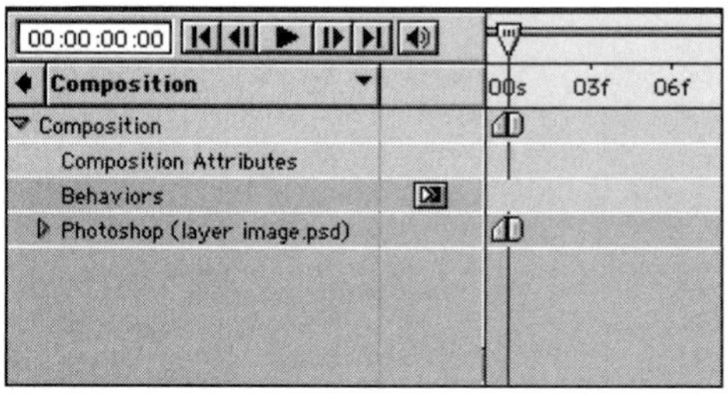

*2 ➤ This is how the LiveMotion **Timeline** looks after a layered Photoshop file is **placed**.*

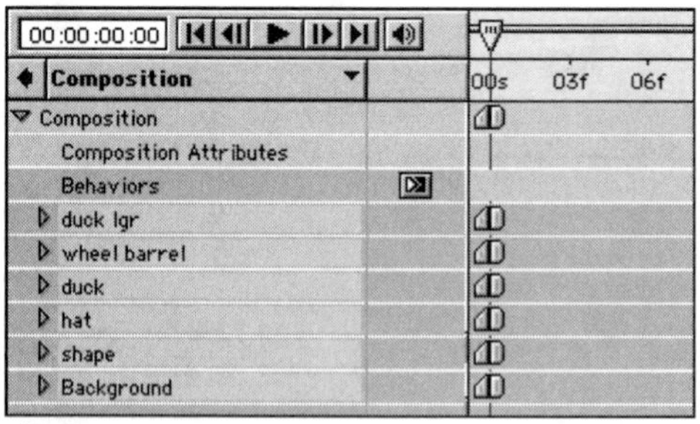

*3 ➤ After choosing Object menu > Convert Layers Into > **Objects**.*

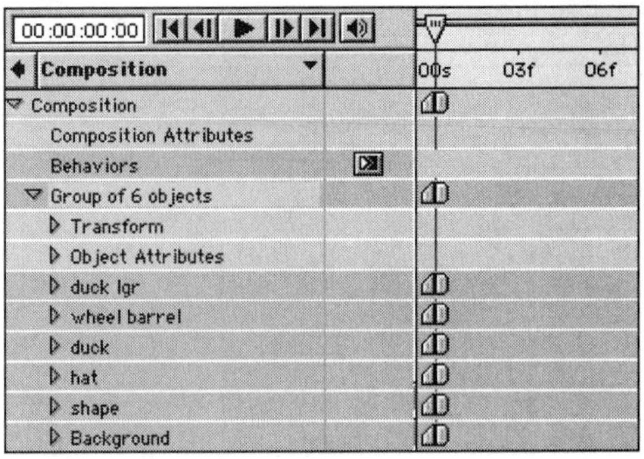

1 ➤ *After choosing Object menu > Convert Layers Into >* ***Group of Objects.***

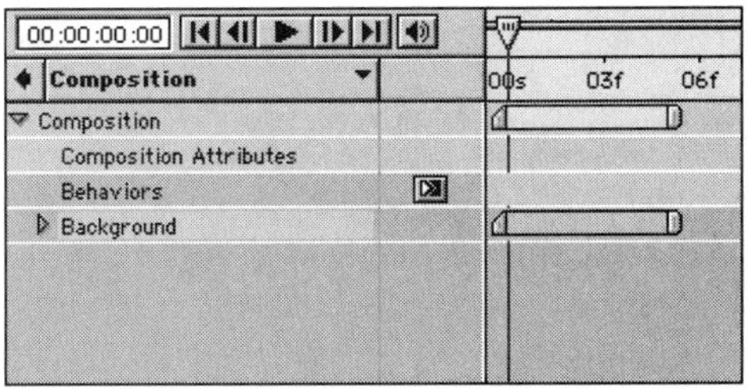

2 ➤ *After choosing Object menu > Convert Layers Into >* ***Sequence.***

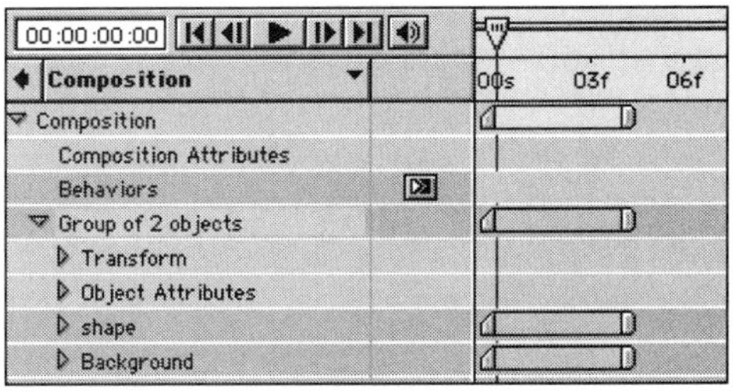

3 ➤ *After choosing Object menu > Convert Layers Into >* ***Sequence with Background.***

Independent Timeline Group (Command-Shift-G/Ctrl-Shift-G).)

Choose **Group of Objects** to have LiveMotion group the newly converted objects for you (Fig. 1). You can then create your own time-independent group animation on the Timeline. (*Note:* If the group is to be used in a loop animation, choose Timeline menu > Time Independent to make the group display as an independent timeline. An icon will display to the left of the group name to signify that it's an independent timeline.)

Sequence to convert the layers into individual frames within a single Timeline object. The object will be assigned the name of whichever layer frame is currently displayed (Fig. 2). Each layer will automatically have a duration of one frame in the Timeline. The object's default duration will be determined by the number of layers that are converted to frames. You can change the frame display rate for the object (see page 198).

Sequence with Background to convert the layers into a group of two objects. (Expand the Group list to reveal the two objects (Fig. 3)). The Layer 0 or Background object on the list will contain the bottommost Illustrator or Photoshop layer, and it will behave like any ordinary image object. The Layer 1 or layer name object will contain all the other Illustrator or Photoshop layers, which will have been converted into a progression of frames. The frame display rate for this object can also be changed (see page 198). By default, the background object will have the same duration as the multi-frame object.

Use LiveMotion's Place Sequence command to acquire a series of files containing sequential object changes from an external application so they can be used in an animation.

To place images as a sequence:

1. With a LiveMotion file open, position the current time marker where you want the start point to occur for the placed object (Fig. 1).
2. Choose File menu > Place Sequence (Command-Option-Shift-I/Ctrl-Alt-Shift-I).
3. Locate and highlight the first name in the sequence of files you want to place, then click Open. A new object will appear in the center of the composition and on the Timeline editor.

   Like the Convert Layers Into > Sequence command, Place Sequence will cause two Object Attributes > Object Time property keyframes to be generated (Figs. 2–3). These keyframes control the duration of the sequential images. The sequence is controlled by the Properties palette.
4. *Optional:* Reposition and/or scale the object. If the object's linework looks too thin, increase its weight using the Width slider on the Layer palette.
5. *Optional:* To change the duration of the sequence, follow the steps on page 198.

➤ Make sure the composition duration bar is long enough to show the complete sequence of frames.

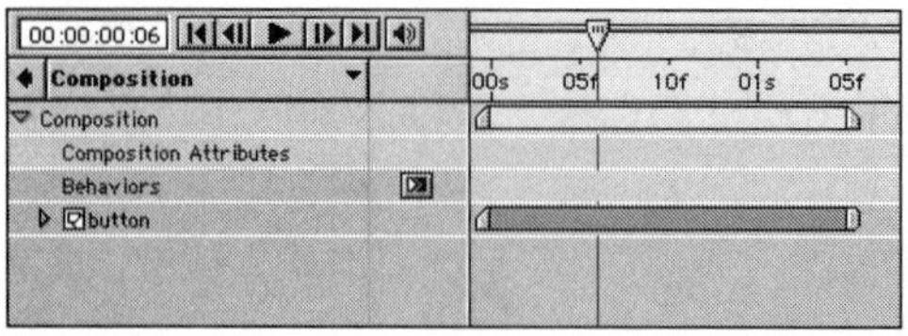

1 ➤ Position the current time marker to set the ***start*** *point for the object that will be placed.*

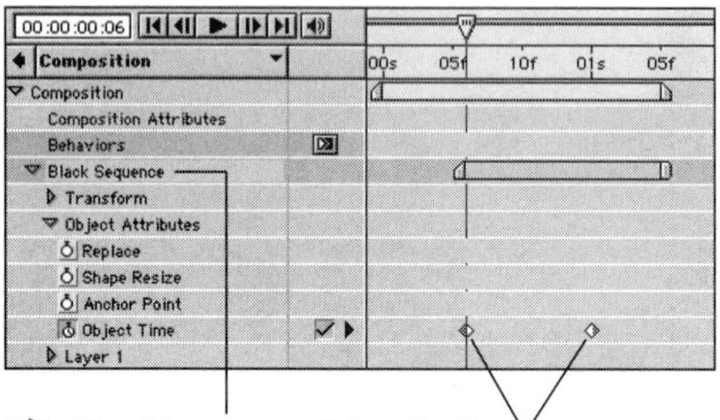

2 ➤ The object generated from the place sequence command has two ***Object Time*** *keyframes.*

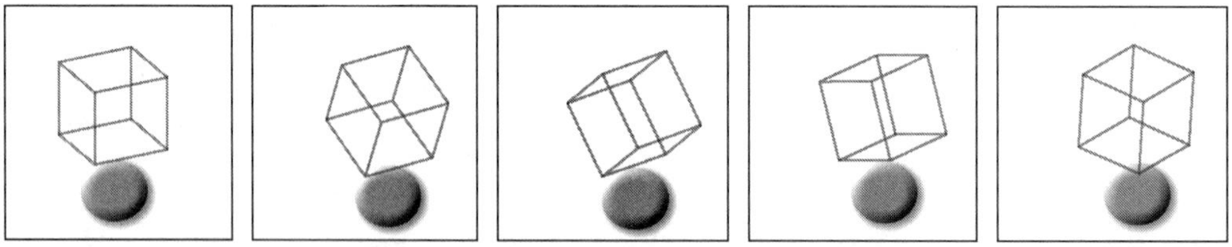

3 ➤ This sequence of files was produced using ***Adobe Dimensions****. To do this yourself, use the Dimensions Generate Sequence command on a Dimensions object or objects. When prompted, save the sequence of files in Adobe Illustrator format. In LiveMotion, use the Place Sequence command to place the numbered files in the proper numeric order.*

1 ➤ *The **Time** slider on the **Properties** palette.*

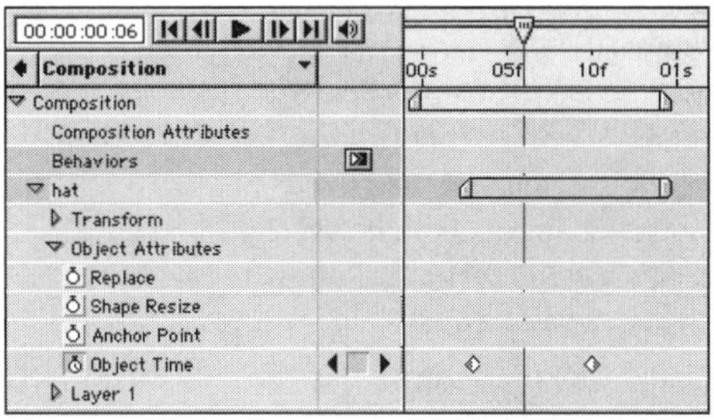

2 ➤ *Drag the current time marker through a **frame sequence**.*

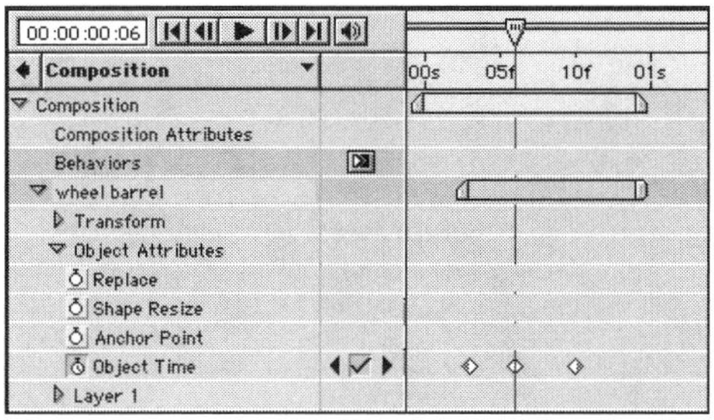

3 ➤ *When the frame sequence is changed using the Time slider on the Properties palette, a new keyframe is created in the **Object Time** property row at the current time.*

Re-sequencing frames

When a layered file is placed into LiveMotion and then converted into a sequence, a Time slider appears on the Properties palette (Fig. 1). This slider can be used to change the sequence in which frames play back. As the current time marker is moved through the frame object's duration, the Time slider moves by increments through the frame numbers. If you position the current time marker at a given point within the frame sequence and then drag the Time slider or click on a slider arrow, the frames will play back in a different order.

For example, let's say you move the current time marker through a nine-frame sequence (frame 0, frame 1, frame 2, frame 3...) (Fig. 2), stop at frame 3, and then click the Time up arrow on the Properties palette to progress to frame 7. If you then move the current time marker again, frame 8 will display next, but frames 4, 5 and 6 will no longer display. A keyframe will be created in the Object Attributes > Object Time row to mark the re-sequencing (Fig. 3). This can be confusing, and we're not suggesting that you re-sequence frames this way. We just want you to be careful not to re-sequence frames inadvertently using the Properties palette. It's easier to restack original layers in their original application and then re-import them as a fresh frame sequence than it is to try to re-sequence frames in LiveMotion using the Timeline and Properties palettes.

If you inadvertently click a Time arrow on the Properties palette and thus re-sequence some frames, just delete the resulting new keyframe(s) between the start and end keyframes on the Object Attributes > Object Time row. Be careful not to delete the start and end keyframes! Use Undo to restore them if you do.

Preparing Photoshop or Illustrator artwork for LiveMotion: a few tips

- In Illustrator 9, instead of leaving shapes as separate **sublayers** within one layer, use the **Release to Layers** command to put each shape on its own layer. Then you'll be able to convert layers into objects in LiveMotion and it will be easier to edit the individual shapes using LiveMotion's Edit Original command.
- In Illustrator, each **group** of objects is stacked on its own layer. LiveMotion can't ungroup an Illustrator group, so while still in Illustrator, ungroup the objects and choose the **Release to Layers** command to distribute the individual objects to separate layers (Figs. 1–2), then import the objects into LiveMotion.
- In Photoshop, make sure the file has a **white background layer** that contains no imagery (put the imagery on other layers). When you place and convert the layers in LiveMotion, the Photoshop background will become an opaque white object. Deleting this white object won't affect other converted objects.
- Objects that are converted in a LiveMotion composition keep their **stacking order** from their original application. The lowest (backmost) layer will become the lowest object on the objects hierarchy list, and so on. Think ahead: Restack objects in their original application before placing them.
- If you're going to convert imported layers into more than one **time-independent** group in LiveMotion, don't cram all the shapes into one Illustrator or Photoshop file. Instead, use Copy and Paste to divide a sequence of shapes into **separate files**. Place and convert each file individually in LiveMotion, then select the new layers from the placed file on the timeline and make them a time-independent group. The converted objects will have a logical, clean organization on the objects hierarchy list.

Reshaping using Illustrator

If you want to animate a transition from one shape into another, first use the Blend tool in Adobe Illustrator to create intermediate steps between two existing shapes (Fig. 1). Double-click the Blend tool, choose Spacing: Specified Steps, and enter the number of intermediate steps you want Illustrator to create.

While you're still in Illustrator, decide on the final stacking order of the objects for the LiveMotion composition. To reverse the stacking order of the resulting blend objects, choose Object menu > Blends > Reverse Front to Back. Use Object menu > Expand, ungroup the blend, then put each intermediate shape on its own layer (Fig. 2). If you're using Illustrator 9, choose Release to Layers from the Layers palette menu.

Finally, place the Illustrator file into LiveMotion, then convert the layer to a sequence of frames or to separate objects whose duration you will sequence yourself.

*1 ➤ An **Illustrator blend** created using six steps.*

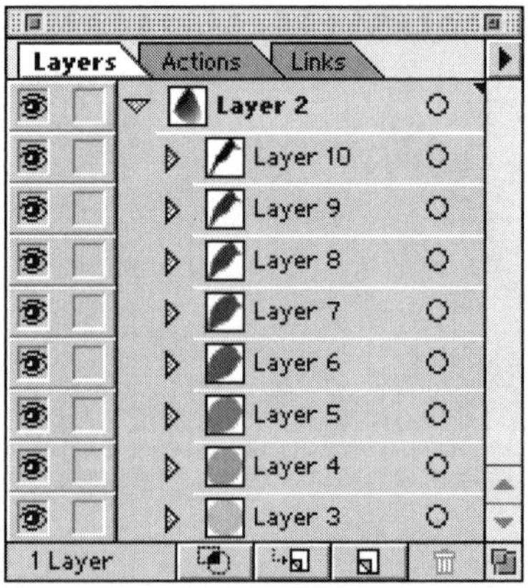

*2 ➤ The **Layers** palette in Illustrator after releasing the blend object to **separate layers**.*

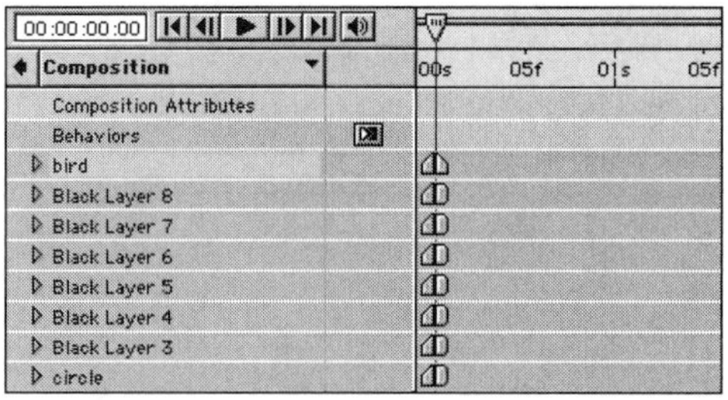

1➤ The blend layers placed and converted into objects in LiveMotion.

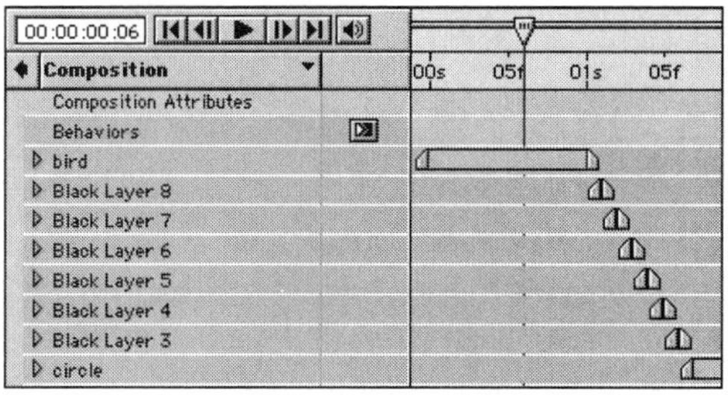

2➤ The object duration bars are in a stairstep arrangement. Since each object occupys a different frame interval, they will be seen one at a time.

➤ You must save **Illustrator 9** files in **Illustrator 8** format in order to **place** them into version 1.0 of LiveMotion. Illustrator 9 files can be copy/pasted or drag-and-dropped into LiveMotion.

Now that you know how to import layers and convert them into separate objects, you need to learn how to move their duration bars in the timeline to create a time-based sequence.

To use Convert Layers Into Objects on the Timeline:

1. Follow the steps on page 192 to convert individual Illustrator or Photoshop layers into objects. All the new objects will have a one-frame duration and will occupy the same point on the Timeline (Fig. 1).
2. Reposition the duration bars and/or the duration start and end points of each object so they form an animation sequence. *Note:* For a basic sequence, you could keep the durations to one frame each and stairstep the duration bars so each bar occupies a different frame interval on the Timeline (Fig. 2). With the duration bars in this configuration, each object will appear for a split second during playback in an orderly, top-to-bottom or bottom-to-top sequence (Fig. 3).
3. *Optional:* Extend the duration of any object to make it linger for a longer time in the playback sequence.

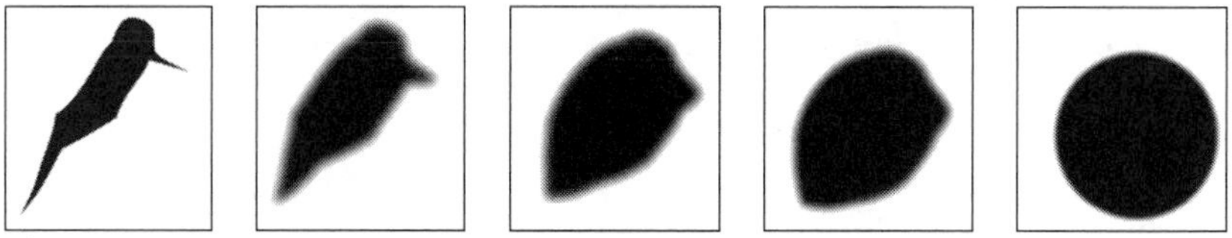

3➤ When the animation is played, the bird transforms into a circle.

To change the playback duration of layers converted to a frame sequence:

1. Follow the steps on pages 192–193 to convert individual Illustrator or Photoshop layers into a sequence of frames (use Sequence or Sequence with Background).
2. Show the Timeline editor (Command-T/Ctrl-T). The frames should be contained in one new object.
3. Expand that new object's list and expand the Object Attributes list.
4. The Object Time property has two keyframes, and they coincide with the display of the first and last frames (Fig. 1). Drag the keyframes closer together to shorten each frame's duration or farther apart to lengthen each frame's duration (Fig. 2).

   Note: The duration bar for the object that contains the frames must be at least as long as the duration between the keyframes. If the bar is shorter, the frame playback will be truncated (Fig. 3). If the bar is longer, the last frame will display for the remainder of the object's duration.
5. *Optional:* Change any of the Transform or Layer 1 properties for all the frames by setting keyframes and altering palette values over time.

➤ To recolor all the frames, select the object that contains the frames, show the Adjust palette, choose a color from the Color palette, then move the Tint slider. Or show the Layer palette, choose Fill with: Color, then choose a color. The color will be applied to all the frames. In some frames, the color may fill the entire selection border.

➤ See the fourth tip on page 196.

➤ If you used Convert Layers Into > Sequence with Background, the background object won't have an Object Attributes > Object Time property because the object doesn't change.

Previewing a frame sequence

To preview the individual frames, show the **Properties** palette, then click the up and down arrows to sequence through the frame progression (the first frame is number 0). You can also preview frames by dragging the current time marker.

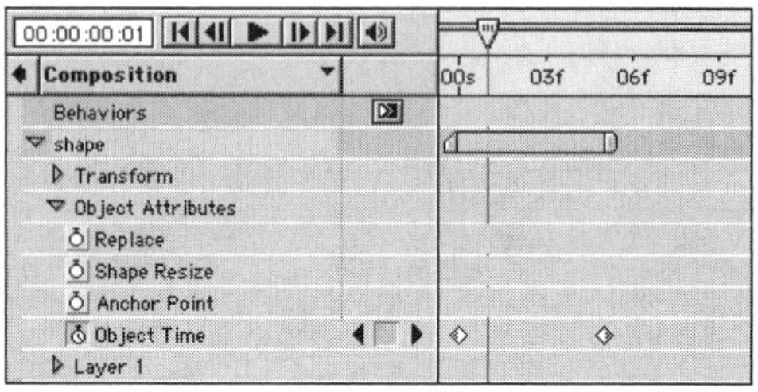

1 ➤ This is the default position of the keyframes for the first and last frames of the frame sequence.

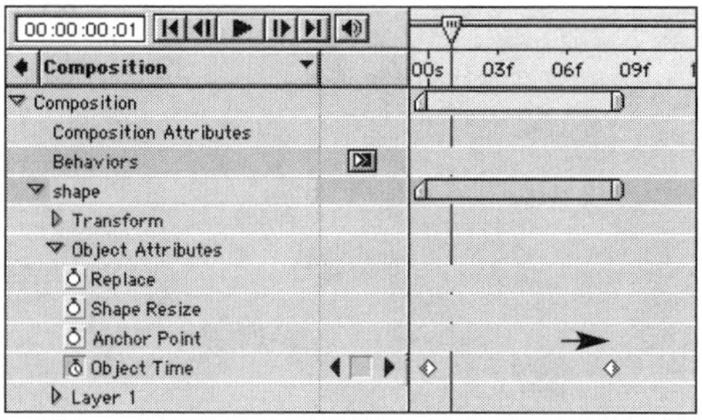

2 ➤ The last keyframe is dragged to the right to lengthen each frame's duration.

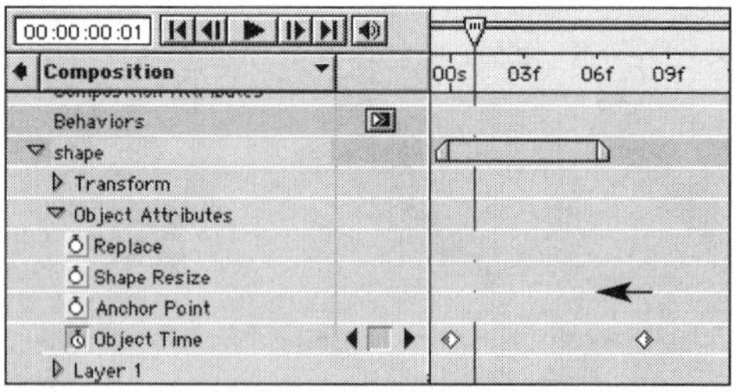

3 ➤ The object duration end point is dragged to the left. This shortens the sequence duration and truncates the last frames.

Lost your link?

If the Edit Original command is dimmed, it may be because the link between LiveMotion and the external program is broken. Open the Adobe LiveMotion > Helpers > Graphics folder (for Photoshop) or the Vector Editors folder (for Illustrator), then double-click the program alias or shortcut. If the program launches, the link is intact. If it doesn't, follow the operating System info to relink an alias or shortcut.

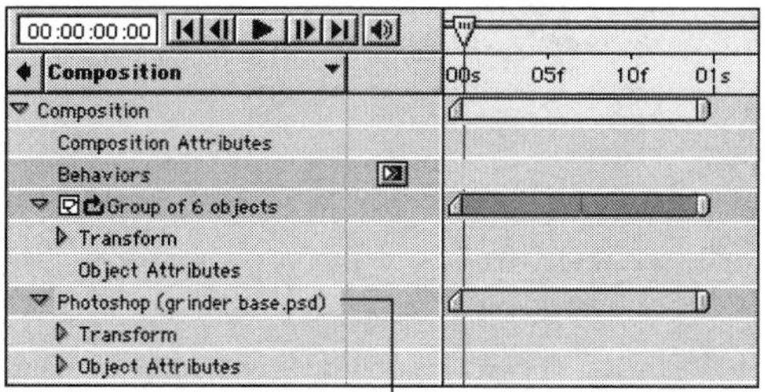

*1 ➤ An **image object** imported from Photoshop (with its original name unchanged) is selected on the **Timeline**…*

2 ➤ …and in the composition.

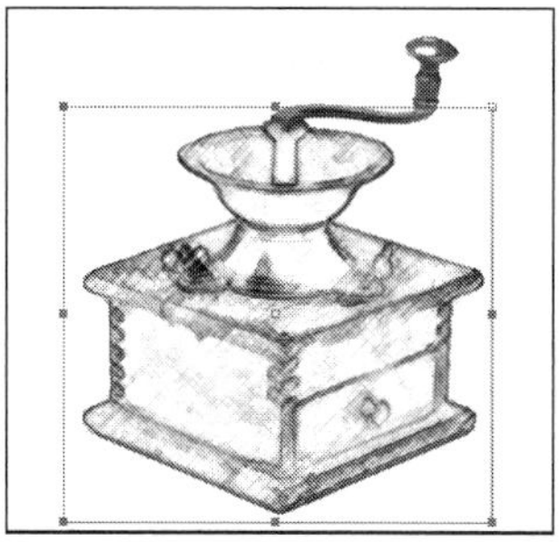

*3 ➤ The image object is edited and saved in Photoshop, and it **updates** in LiveMotion.*

Editing objects

Let's say you've got an imported object in LiveMotion that you want to revise, but it's already been converted into objects or a sequence. Using the Edit Original command, you can edit the shape in its original application (Photoshop or Illustrator) and then replace it in LiveMotion either for one point in time or for the entire animation.

To edit shapes using Edit Original:

1. Open a file that contains a placed image or an animation that was created by converting layers into objects or frames.
2. Position the current time marker so the object or frame that you want to edit is displayed, then select the object on the objects hierarchy list. A selection border will display in the composition window (Figs. 1–2).
3. Choose Edit menu > Edit Original (Command-Shift-M/Ctrl-Shift-M). A copy of the object's file will open in its original application (e.g., Illustrator or Photoshop). The original, external file won't be changed.
4. Edit the object or image as desired, then save the file. Don't change the name for this internal copy of the file.
5. Switch back to LiveMotion. The object will update in the composition (Figs. 3–4). Pre-existing object properties are preserved.

➤ If you use Edit Original on a sequence of converted layers from Photoshop, all the frames in the sequence will change, even if you set a Replace keyframe (see the next page). In this scenario, we recommend that you use Convert Layers Into > Objects instead.

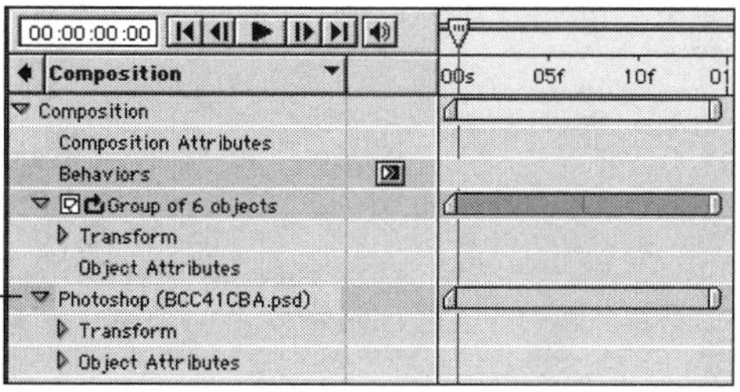

4 ➤ The object name on the Timeline now reflects the name of the internal copy.

Let's say you've placed an object into a LiveMotion animation and its duration is longer than one frame. You then decide to edit the object—but only for a portion of its duration. If you set the Replace property before you use Edit Original to edit the object in its original application, you can control at which point in time the edit will apply.

To use Edit Original for only a portion of an object's duration:

1. Expand the object's list on the Timeline and expand its Object Attributes list.
2. Click the stopwatch next to Replace to set a keyframe for the current object (Fig. 1).
3. Position the current time marker at the time where you want the object to be edited.
4. Choose Edit menu > Edit Original (Command-Shift-M/Ctrl-Shift-M).
5. In the external application, edit the shapes or image, then save the file.
6. Switch back to LiveMotion to view the updated object. A new Replace keyframe will be created at the current time to signify that the object was replaced (Fig. 2).
7. *Optional:* Repeat steps 3–6 to edit the object further.
8. Preview the animation (Fig. 3).

Illustrator to LiveMotion

If you place into LiveMotion an Illustrator file that has multiple objects on one layer, the size of the LiveMotion file will increase each time you use Edit Original. That's because all the shapes on the imported and corrected layer will be replaced, whether they are edited or not. This increase in size will have an impact when you export the file, particularly if you use the SWF format.

What should you do instead? Divide the Illustrator shapes onto separate layers. Then, when you use Edit Original, the LiveMotion file will stay the same size because only that one layer will be replaced.

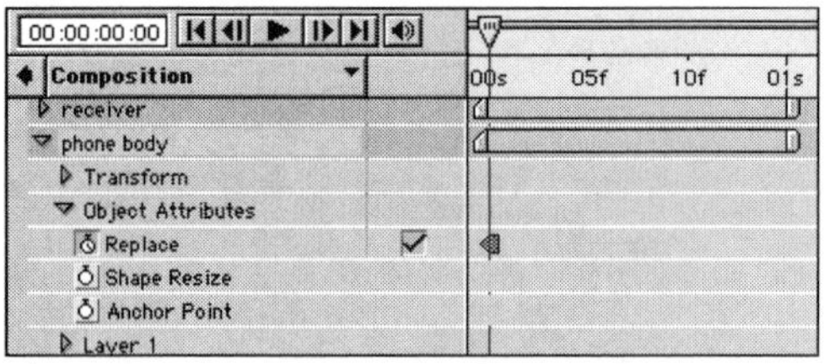

*1 ➤ Click the **Replace** stopwatch to set a keyframe.*

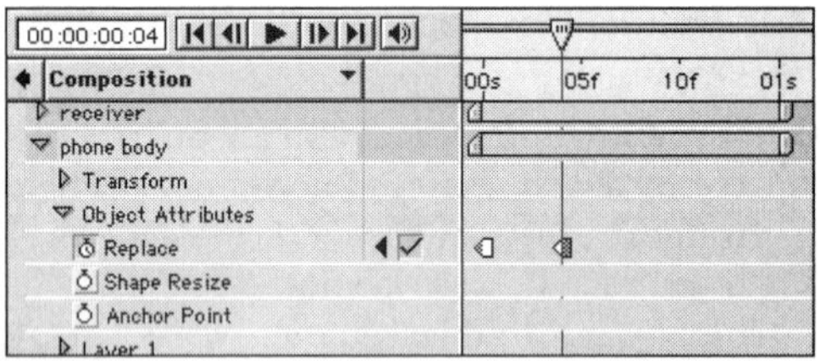

*2 ➤ Move the time marker, then use **Edit Original**. When you return to LiveMotion, a new keyframe will be created and the new edits will take effect at that point in time.*

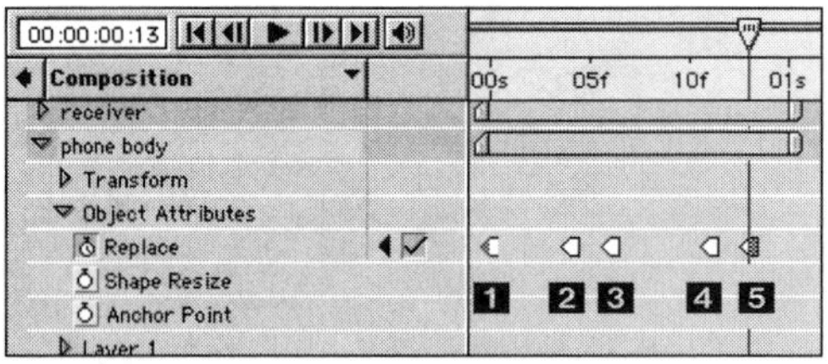

*3 ➤ The object now has **five** Replace keyframes. Keyframes two through five mark the points where edits were made to the image in Photoshop.*

Group 'em

Use the Group command on a word or a string of words so they will stay together if you restyle or reposition them. To make property changes to a whole group, click the group name on the Timeline, then set keyframes for the group's Transform properties.

1 ➤ *The original text object.*

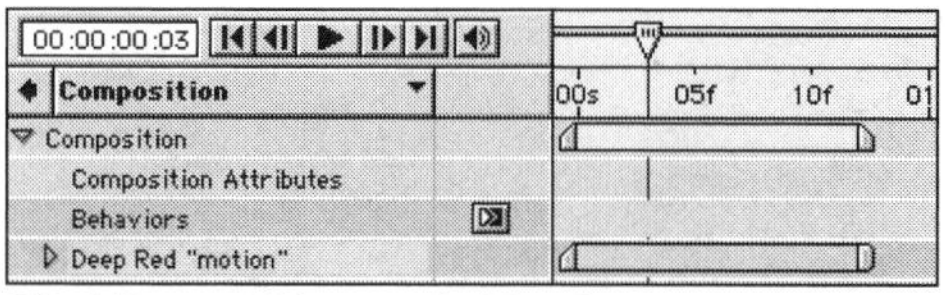

2 ➤ *The* ***text object*** *on the Timeline.*

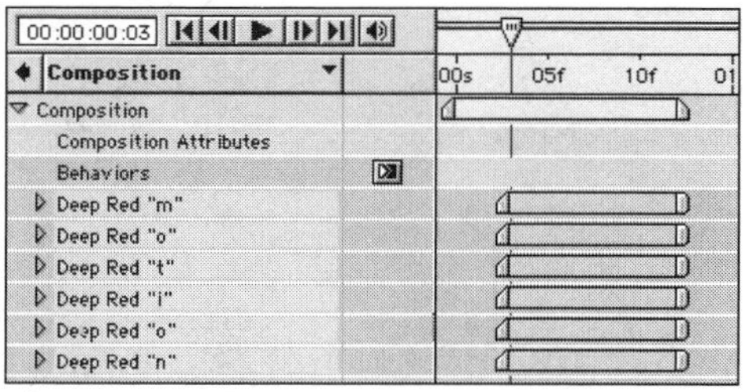

3 ➤ *After using* ***Break Apart Text****, each letter is now a separate text object.*

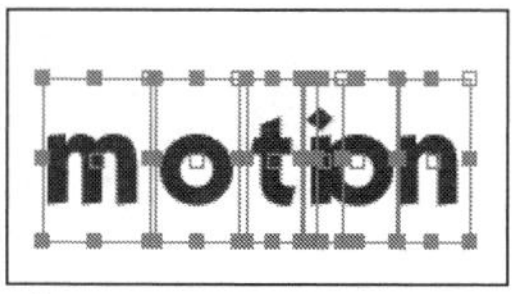

4 ➤ *The selected letter objects.*

5 ➤ *The final position of the letter objects at 01s-01f.*

Breaking apart text

Have you ever seen an animation in which individual letters fly together to form a word formation? You can do this and other special text effects in LiveMotion. You'll start by using the Break Apart Text command, which breaks a text object into individual letter objects. Then you can restyle the individual letter objects separately or use them at different times in an animation.

To break a text object into individual letter objects:

1. Create a text object, position it in the composition, and keep it selected (Fig. 1).
2. Show the Timeline editor (Command-T/Ctrl-T).
3. Choose Object menu > Break Apart Text. Each letter will now be listed on the objects hierarchy list as a separate object (Figs. 2–4). All the letter objects will be selected.
4. Deselect, then click a letter object on the objects hierarchy list.
5. Move the current time marker to the desired time, and change object properties as you would for any object. In addition, you can set keyframes at different times to change any of the text properties on the Object Attributes list for each letter object, such as Font, Text (for changing the current text character), Text Size, Justification, or Text Style.

Believe it or not, it's easier to work backwards to make letters fly into a word formation than it is to work forwards. You will establish the final positions for the letters first.

To make letters form a word in an animation:

1. Follow the instructions above to break text apart, then position the current time marker at the ending time for all the letter movements (Fig. 5).

(Continued on the next page)

2. Make sure all the letter objects are in their final positions (not their starting positions). The letter objects are probably already positioned correctly.
3. Set a Transform > Position keyframe for each letter object (Fig. 1).
4. Move the current time marker backwards in time to the position from which the letters will start moving.
5. Move each letter object away from its final position to its start position (Figs. 2–3). Set additional keyframes for any desired turn or bend in its motion path.

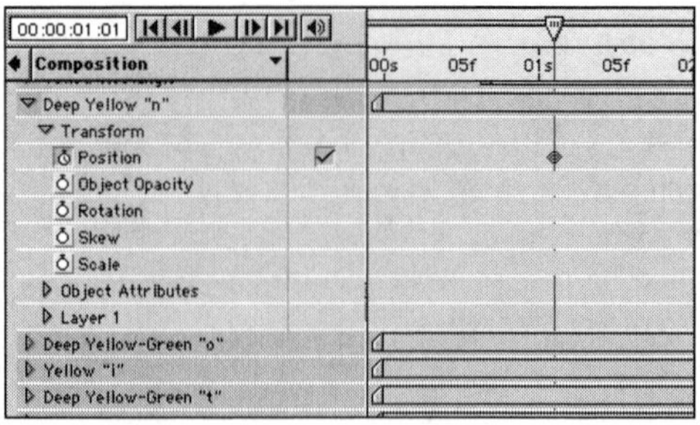

1 ➤ A keyframe is set for the letter object's final position.

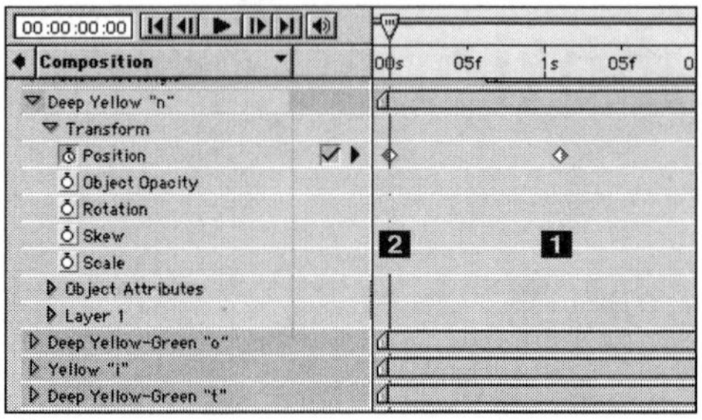

2 ➤ A keyframe is set for the letter object's start position.

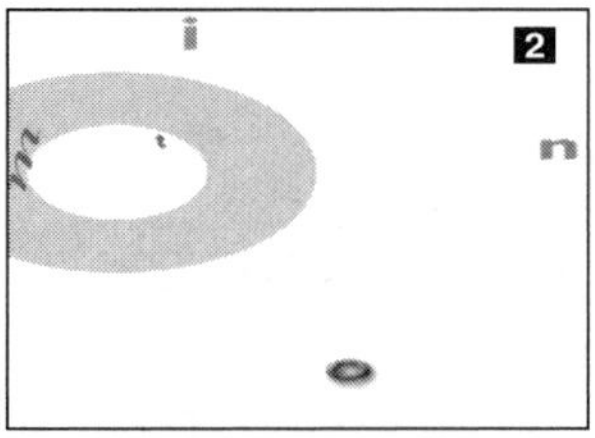

*3 ➤ The position of the letter objects at **00s** 2. The **Scale** and **Rotation** properties were altered for some letters.*

Since each text object occupies one position in the Timeline editor, you can use the Text property to quickly cycle through a list of characters in an object. (This way, you won't need to position several object duration bars in the Timeline.) You can keep the letter object's color, font, and size constant or you can change any or all of those attributes for any or all of the Text keyframes.

To cycle through characters in one text object:

1. Create a text object, and keep it selected. It can consist of one character (or one character in a broken-apart text object), a word, or a phrase.
2. On the Timeline, position the current time marker at a frame over the object's duration.
3. Expand the text object's list. Click the stopwatch for the text object's Object Attributes > Text property (Fig. 4).
4. Advance the time marker forward one frame.
5. Choose a selection tool, then double-click the text object.
6. Change the character(s), then click OK.
7. Repeat steps 4–6 to cycle through more characters in the text object (Figs. 5–6).

4 ➤

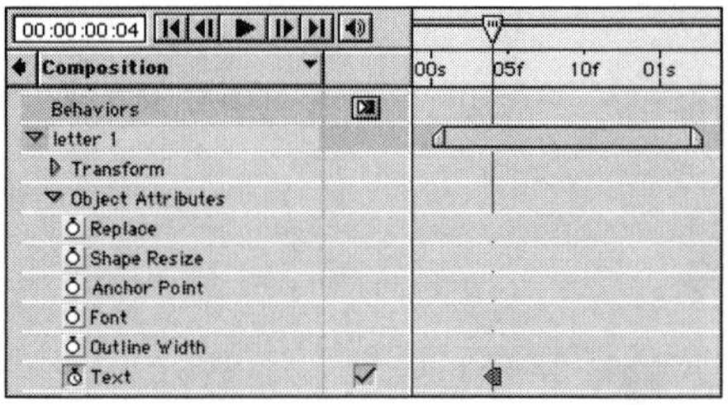

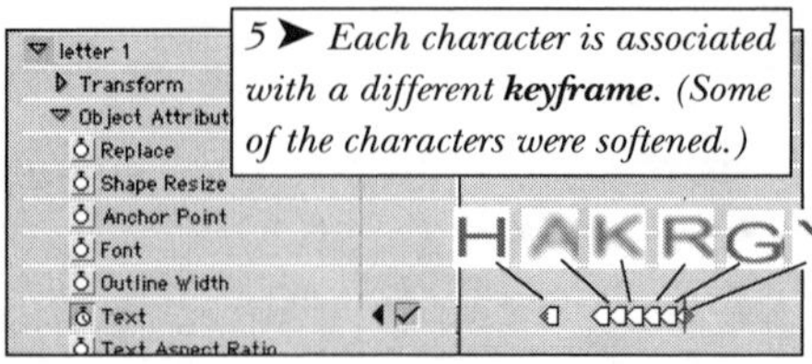

*5 ➤ Each character is associated with a different **keyframe**. (Some of the characters were softened.)*

6 ➤ Each of the three separate text objects cycle through various characters. "HEY" turns into "YOU".

1 & 2 ➤ Objects are selected in the composition and on the Timeline.

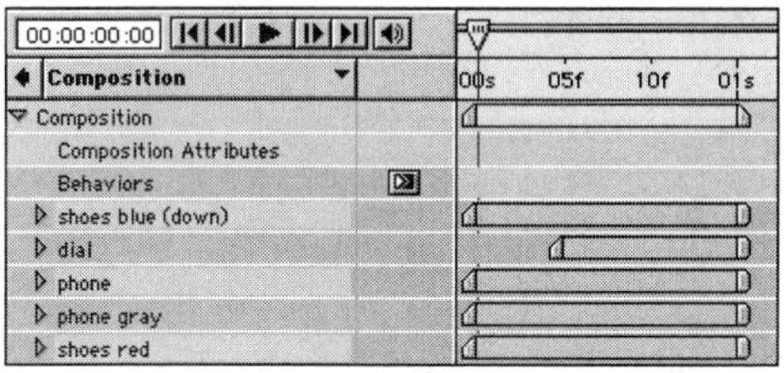

2 ➤

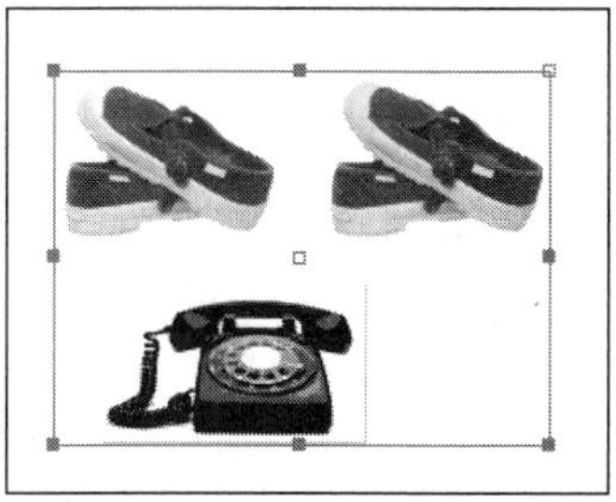

*3 ➤ The **new group** is selected in the composition and on the Timeline.*

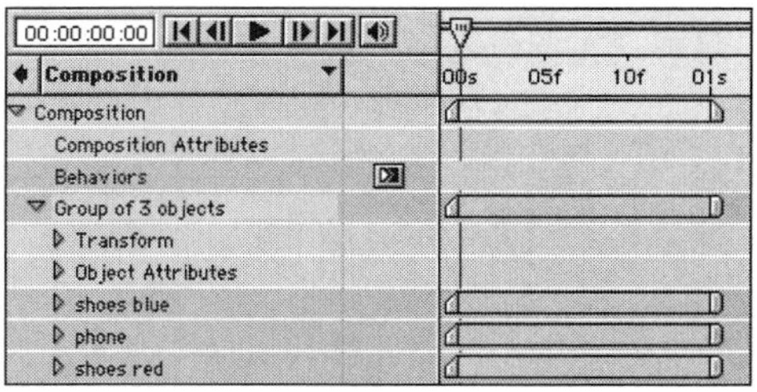

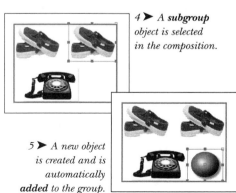

*4 ➤ A **subgroup** object is selected in the composition.*

*5 ➤ A new object is created and is automatically **added** to the group.*

Grouping objects for animation

Why group objects together? Well, for one thing, to streamline your work. If you change a group's scale, position, or rotation, that property change will affect all the objects in the group. Properties for individual layers within a group always remain editable.

To group objects for an animation:

1. Create or import several object shapes to be used for the animation, and move them to their starting locations in the composition window.
2. Shift-select the objects in the composition window (Fig. 1).
   or
   Shift-select object names on the objects hierarchy list in the Timeline (Fig. 2).
3. Choose Object menu > Group (Command-G/Ctrl-G). "Group of [ ] objects" will appear on the list (Fig. 3).
4. To make property changes to all the objects in the group simultaneously, use the Transform or Object Attributes list directly under the group's hierarchy list.
   or
   To make property changes to any individual object in the group, use the Transform, Object Attributes, or Layer list under that individual object's name.

To add a new object to a group:

1. Select an object in the group using the Subgroup selection tool (A) or by clicking the object name on the objects hierarchy list (Fig. 4).
2. Create a new object (Fig. 5). The new object will automatically become a part of the group.

To add an existing object to a group:

1. Select the object that you want to add to a group.
2. Choose Edit menu > Cut or Copy.
3. Choose the Subgroup selection tool (A), then select an object in the group to which you want to add the object.
4. Choose Edit menu > Paste.

In these instructions, you will learn how to create a group within a larger animation that has its own independent timeline.

To create a group with an independent timeline:

METHOD 1

1. Shift-select objects on the objects hierarchy list to be made into an independent group.
2. Choose Timeline menu > Make Time Independent Group (Command-Shift-G/Ctrl-Shift-G). "Group of [ ] objects" with a time-independent icon will appear in the main timeline. Double-click this group object to view its timeline (Fig. 2).

METHOD 2

1. Select an existing group on the objects hierarchy list.
2. Choose Timeline menu > Time Independent.
3. Double-click the group name on the objects hierarchy list to display the group's independent timeline.

➤ If you choose Make Time Independent Group for an existing group, the result will be an independent group of 1 in the main timeline. Double-click this "Group of 1 objects" to display its independent timeline. The original group will now be listed on the hierarchy list of the independent timeline.

To release a group from being an independent timeline object:

1. Click the group name on the objects hierarchy list.
2. Re-choose Timeline menu > Time Independent.
3. *Optional:* To ungroup the objects, choose Object menu > Ungroup (Command-U/Ctrl-U).

Building nests

The group whose timeline you make independent can itself contain objects whose timelines are already independent. When you're working with an independent timeline, click on the Active Timeline drop-down menu to see how many levels down the current timeline is nested relative to the main composition and use the same menu to navigate through the chain of nested levels back to the main composition (Fig. 1).

1➤ The Active Timeline menu showing two ***nesting*** *levels.*

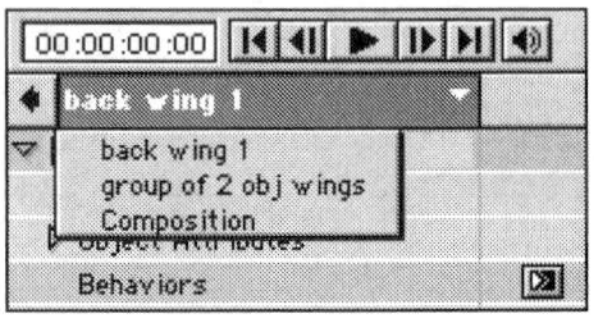

Nesting parts of an animation

Make a bird-shaped object.

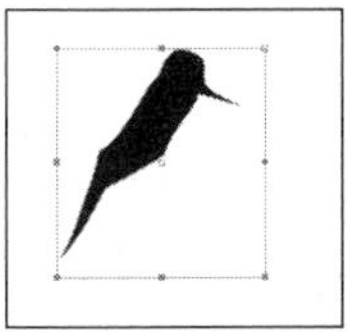

Make each wing a separate object. Duplicate each wing, then rotate the duplicates. You now have two wings in the up position and two wings in the down poition.

2➤

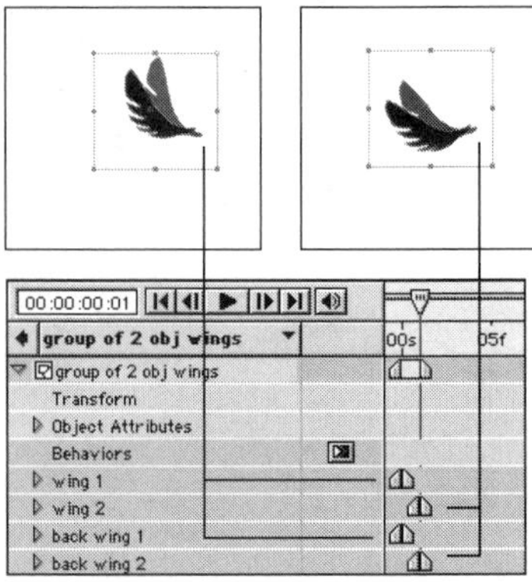

Timeline menu > ***Make Independent Timeline Group*** *is used to convert the selected wing objects into a time-independent group. A flapping wings effect is created by controlling when the up and down wings are visible.*

(Bird illustrations continue on the next page)

Work smart

If you're constructing a complex animation that contains a lot of objects and groups, first create and save each portion of the animation in a separate LiveMotion file. Second, create a final file in which to gather all the elements. And third, File menu > Place each of the individual LiveMotion files that you created into that final composition. Each placed file will display on the Timeline editor as a group.

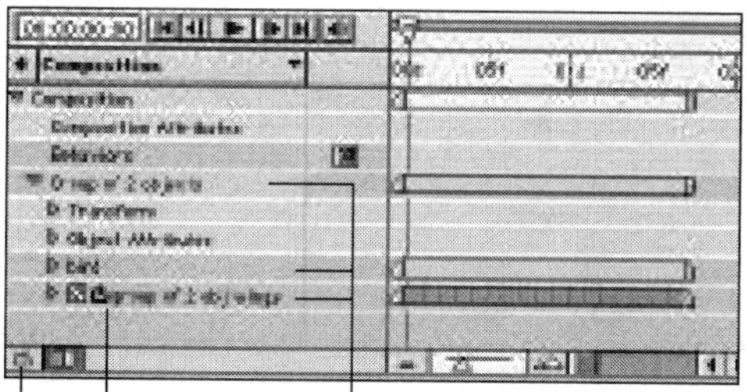

3 ➤ ***Looping*** *is turned on for the time-independent group of wings.*

The independent wings group is grouped with the bird object.

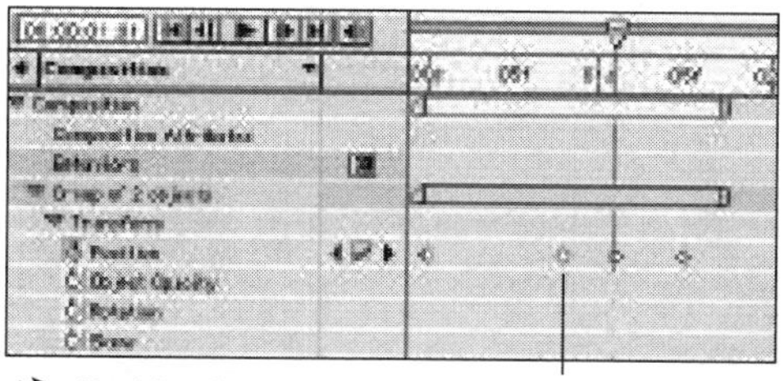

4 ➤ ***Position*** *keyframes are set for the new, larger group. The wing group (flapping wings) will loop as it and the bird shape move together through the composition.*

The loop command causes an animation to repeat in a continuous, uninterrupted cycle. In these instructions, you will assign the loop option to a group that has been converted into an independent timeline. The power of nesting and grouping is that an animation can loop independently and be grouped with other objects to create a more complex animation.

To make a group of animated objects loop:

1. Select an existing Group layer on the objects hierarchy list in the main Composition timeline.
2. Position the current time marker so it rests on a portion of the group's duration bar.
3. Click the Loop button in the lower left corner of the Timeline editor (Fig. 3).
   or
   Choose Timeline menu > Loop.

➤ The group will now loop even if the composition's duration is only one frame. If the composition duration is longer than one frame, you can extend the group's duration bar to control the number of loops in the animation. Each loop will be designated by a faint vertical bar on the group's duration bar.

➤ To preview the looping, click the Preview mode button at the bottom of the Toolbox. Click the Edit mode button when you tire of watching it.

Note: Looping can't be previewed by clicking the Play button on the Timeline.

If an object with an independent timeline is nested within the main composition timeline, the object's Transform properties will still be listed in, and controlled by, the main composition timeline. In that scenario, the object's Transform properties can't loop separately from the time flow of the main composition. If, however, you convert the object or group into an independent timeline group of one, you will be able to edit its Transform properties separately from the main composition.

To make an object's Transform properties independent:

1. Select an object or group on the objects hierarchy list (Fig. 1).
2. Choose Timeline menu > Make Time Independent Group (Command-Shift-G/ Ctrl-Shift-G). The new group will now be called "Group of 1 objects" (Fig. 2). The Transform list for the original object or group will be completely nested within the new group of 1 timeline and will no longer be connected directly to the main composition timeline (Fig. 3).

➤ To make the Transform properties loop, click the independent group of 1 name, then click the Loop button at the bottom of the Timeline.

The Group of 1 object will now play as an independent animation while other objects come and go in the main composition (Fig 4–5).

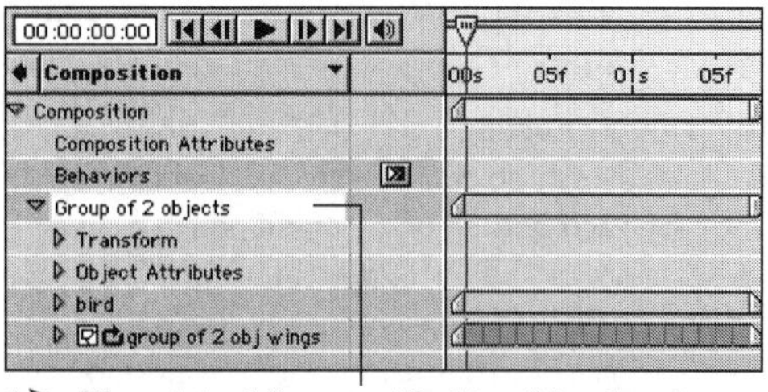

1 ➤ The original "group of 2 objects" is selected.

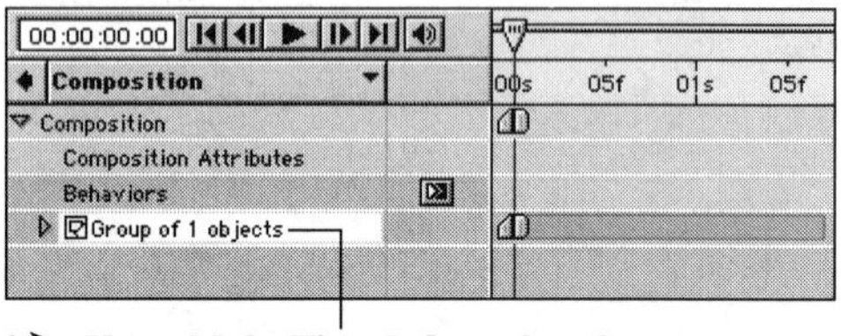

*2 ➤ Using **Make Time Independent Group** creates a Group of 1 object.*

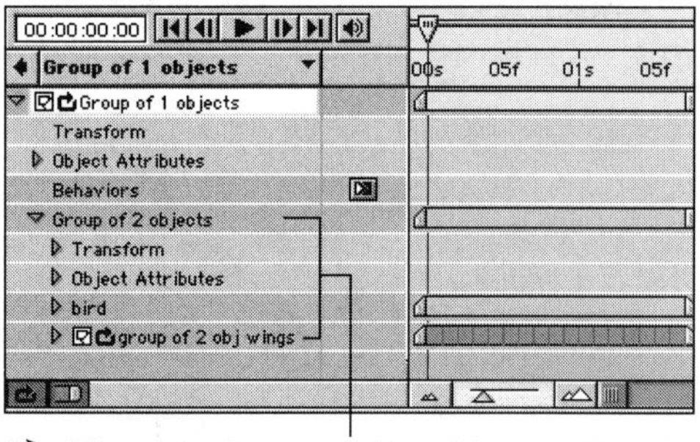

3 ➤ The original group of objects (shown in Fig. 1) is now nested within the Group of 1 objects. View these objects by double-clicking the Group of 1 name.

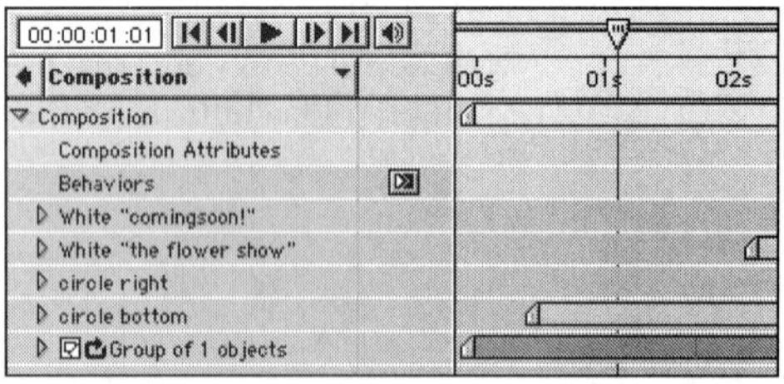

4 ➤ The Group of 1 object will now play as an independently looping animation. Other objects can be created in the composition timeline to appear with the Group of 1 object.

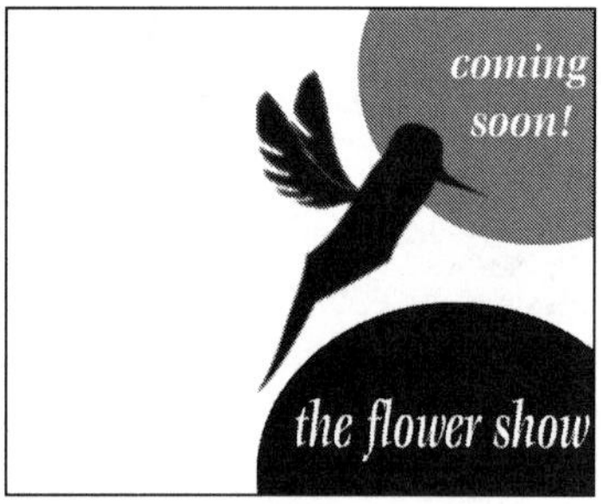

5 ➤ The Group of 1 object (the animated bird) will fly continuously while other objects in the composition appear and disappear.

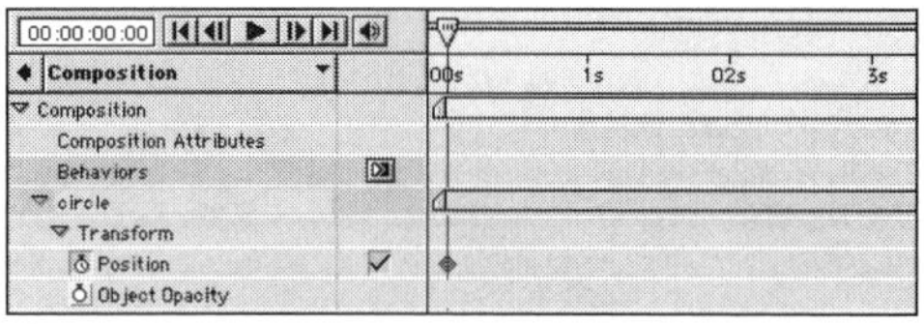

*1 ➤ Click the **Position** stopwatch to set a starting keyframe.*

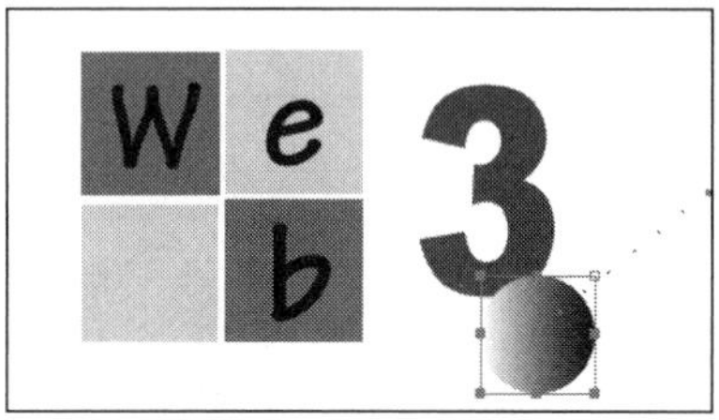

*2 ➤ The selected object is dragged to a new position. The **motion path** now displays...*

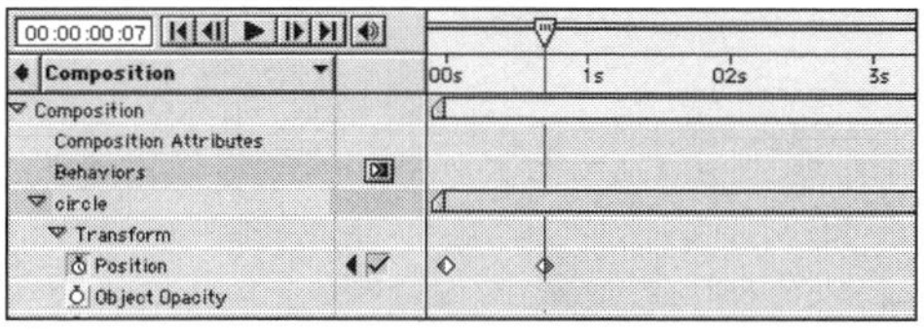

*3 ➤ ...and a new **keyframe** is created.*

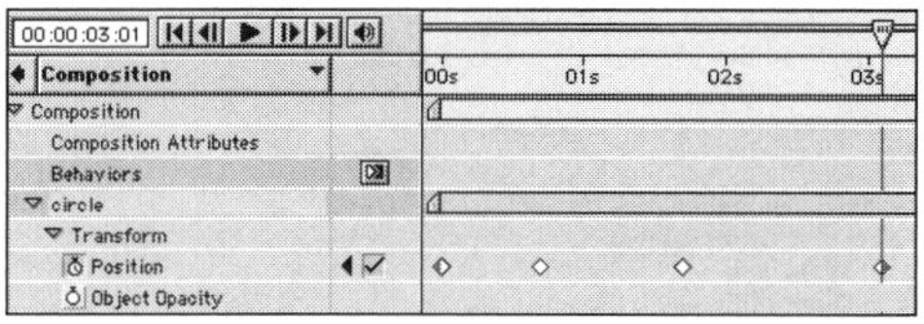

*4 ➤ This is the full set of **Position** keyframes.*

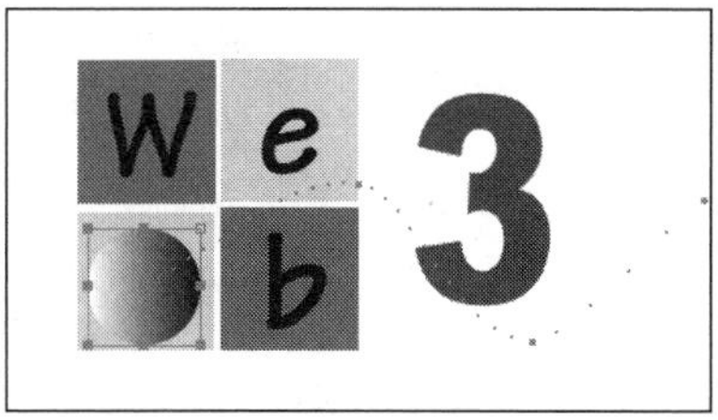

5 ➤ This is the object's complete motion path. The circle bounces once.

Using motion paths

Do you want to give an object rhythm? Make it dance, fly, swerve, or hop? You can't create this kind of movement in one step. Instead, you have to move the object in increments, creating a Position keyframe each time you want it to change direction. The route the object follows is called its motion path.

To create a motion path for an object:

1. Select an object.
2. Make sure View menu > Preview Motion Path is on (has a checkmark) (Command-Shift-H/Ctrl-Shift-H).
3. On the Timeline editor, expand the object's list and the Transform list.
4. Move the current time marker to the desired starting time.
5. Click the Position stopwatch or check the Create/remove keyframe box for Position to set a Position keyframe for the object (Fig. 1).
6. Move the current time marker to another point in time.
7. Drag the object to a new position. The dotted line that connects the object to its original position as you drag is its motion path (Figs. 2–3). The farther you drag the object for each keyframe, the faster the object will move.

   The small square at the start and end of the dotted line marks where the object's anchor point was located when that keyframe was created.
8. Continue to reposition the time marker and move the object to set other position keyframes. A keyframe will be set automatically each time you move the current time marker and then move the object (Figs. 4–5). The keyframe square that appears on the dotted line for each keyframe will help you visualize where the object changes direction in its motion path.
9. *Optional:* To reshape the motion path, see the following page.

If you want an object's motion path to have a wider curve, a more abrupt peak, or some other shape, you have to adjust it manually.

To reshape a motion path:

1. Follow the steps on the previous page to create a motion path with several keyframe squares, and select the object.
2. Make sure View menu > Preview Motion Path is turned on (has a checkmark) so the motion path is visible.
3. To move the object at an existing keyframe, move the current time marker over one of the Position keyframes. The object's anchor point will align with the keyframe square on the motion path.
   or
   To move the object along its motion path, move the current time marker (Fig. 1).
4. Drag the object to change the curvature of its path. The line seqment will be reshaped between the previous and next keyframe squares (Fig. 2). A new motion path square and Position keyframe will be added.
5. Repeat steps 3 and 4 to modify other segments on the motion path (Figs. 3–4).

➤ To delete an existing keyframe square, click the keyframe icon on the Timeline, then press Delete/Backspace.

1 ➤ Move the current time marker to move the object along its motion path.

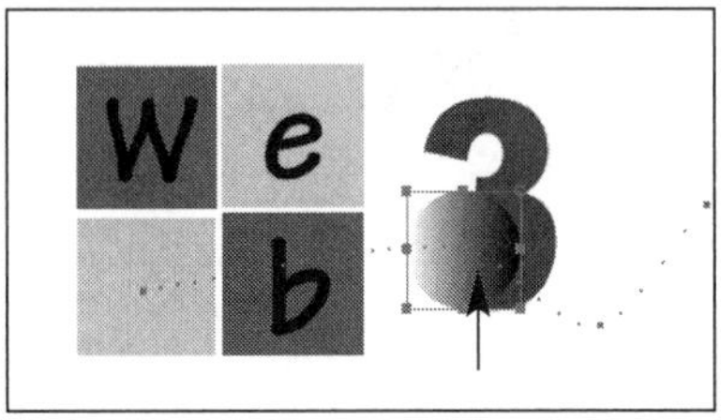

2 ➤ Drag the object to a new position. A keyframe will be created.

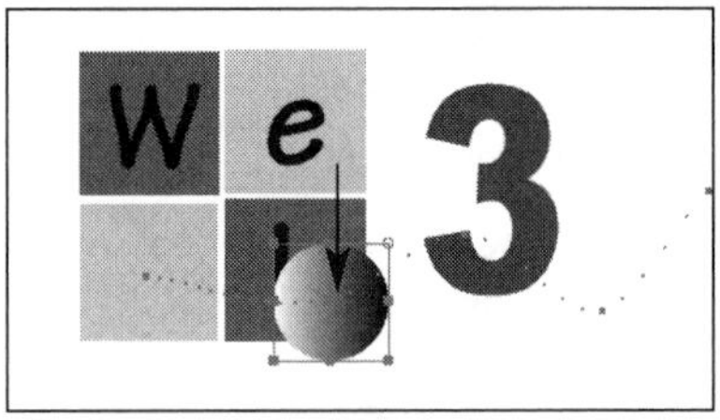

3 ➤ Continue moving the time marker and dragging the object to reshape the motion path.

4 ➤ The reshaped motion path now has six keyframes and the circle object bounces twice.

Changing speed

To change the speed at which an object travels from one keyframe to the next, position the object's anchor point over a square, then drag the object farther away from or closer to the previous square or the next square. The longer the segment between squares, the faster the object will move between them. Each dot on the motion path represents a frame on the Timeline. The larger the segment, the fewer the dots, and thus the quicker the movement.

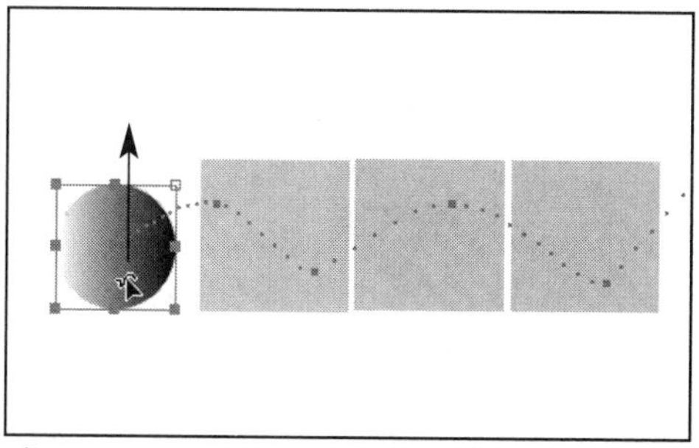

1➤ *Command-Option-drag/Ctrl-Alt-drag the object.*

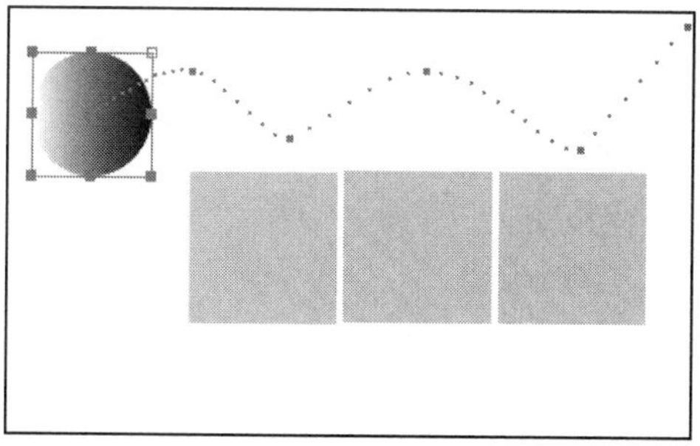

2➤ *The object and its motion path are repositioned.*

To reposition an object with its motion path:

1. Select the object in the composition window.
2. Command-Option-drag/Ctrl-Alt-drag the object. The object and its motion path will move to the new location; its path shape and position keyframe time locations will stay the same (Figs. 1–2).

To insert a pause into an object's continous motion:

1. Click a Position keyframe.
2. Choose Timeline menu > Hold Keyframe. The object will remain at the hold keyframe until the current time marker passes over that object's next position keyframe. The object will move to that keyframe position without any of the in-between frames that would create the appearance of smooth motion (Fig. 1).

➤ Reselect the checked Hold Keyframe option if you want to turn it off.

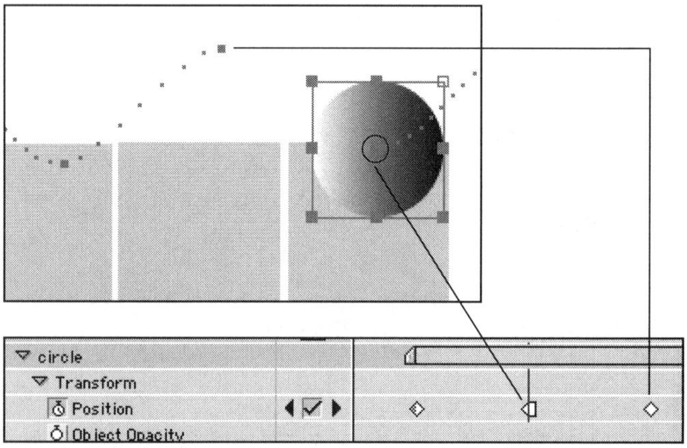

*1 ➤ A **hold** keyframe is created for the object. Note that there are no dots on the motion path between the hold and the next keyframe.*

Timeline shortcuts

Note: The Timeline window must be active!

	Mac OS/Win
Make animation play or stop	Spacebar
Move time marker ahead one frame	Page Down
Move time marker ahead ten frames	Shift-Page Down
Move time marker back one frame	Page Up
Move time marker back ten frames	Shift-Page Up
Move to beginning of timeline	Home
Move to end of timeline	End

Auto Bezier or Linear

By default, the Auto Bezier option, which smooths curves, is turned on for all position keyframes. To turn it on for any existing keyframes, Shift-select the keyframes, then choose Timeline menu > **Auto Bezier**.

To convert an Auto Bezier path into a straight (Linear) path, select the object that has a motion path, expand the object's Transform list to view its Position property keyframes, Shift-select the keyframes, then choose Timeline menu > **Linear**. The segments between motion path squares will be straight; the keyframe locations won't change.

Setting the render size

When LiveMotion exports an animation, it converts images and soft-edged objects into a stream of bitmap images, and they are rendered at screen resolution. Any Transform properties are computed after the object's layer properties are rendered. If you display an object at actual size and then enlarge it, its resolution will be lowered and it will become pixelated.

To prevent an object from becoming pixelated, first choose the point in the animation where the object is at its largest size, then choose the Make Actual Size command. LiveMotion will recalculate and render the object's actual size based on its largest screen size. *Note:* Unfortunately, this process also increases an object's output size.

To set the render size of a bitmap object:

1. Select an object in an animation that is scaled up over time (Shrinking an object won't cause it to become pixelated.)
2. Position the current time marker where the object is at the preferred final scale.
3. Choose Object menu > Transform > Make Actual Size (Option-S/Alt-S). The object may look sharper. This is its new default actual size.

➤ If you scale a text object in an animation and the object looks blurry at its normal size, select the object at that point in time and choose Make Actual Size to resharpen it.

Tutorial

In this tutorial, we'll show you how to create a spinning top using some of the shapes and textures that ship with LiveMotion. You will use the Top Object is Mask command, which clips the underlying objects into the contour of the topmost shape. This command can be used to clip a gradient or texture into any shape. In an animation, it can be used to move objects inside another shape. In these instructions, it will be used to clip textures inside a spinning top shape. The Paste Object Animation command will also be used to copy and paste Transform keyframes from one object to another.

To create a spinning top using a mask:

CREATE THE OBJECT

1. Choose File menu > New, enter a Width of 450 and a Height of 230, Set the Frame Rate to 15, choose Export: Entire Composition, check the Make HTML box, then click OK.
2. Display the Timeline editor.
3. Choose the Rectangle tool (M). Draw a rectangle with a width of 426 and a height of 86 (use the Transform palette). Click on the Timeline editor. Press Return/Enter and rename the object "rectangle bottom."
4. Duplicate the rectangle (Command-D/ Ctrl-D), move the duplicate, click on the Timeline editor. Press Return/Enter and rename the object "rectangle top."
5. Choose the Polygon tool (N). On the Properties palette, set the Sides to 4.
6. Drag a diamond shape with a width of 91 and a height of 127. Move the diamond to the left of the center of the composition (Fig. 1).
7. Select the rectangle bottom. Display the Color palette, then choose a light color.
8. Show the Gradient palette. Choose Linear from the drop-down menu and set the Angle to 270°.
9. Show the Adjust palette. Set Posterize to 12 (Fig. 2).

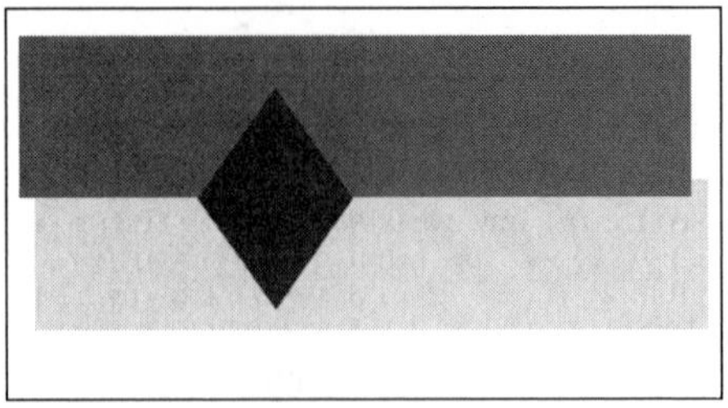

1➤ The rectangle and diamond objects in the composition.

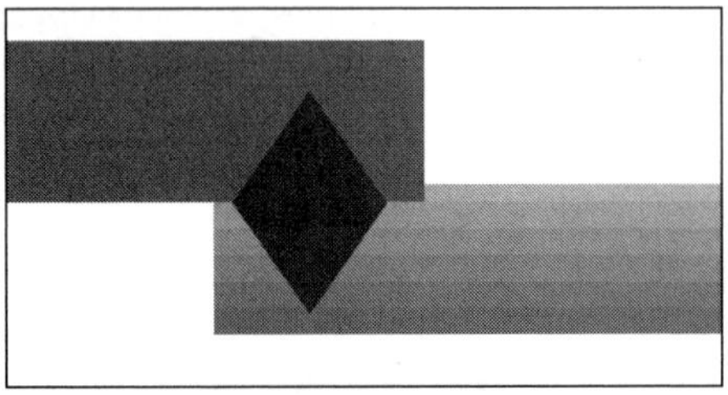

2➤ The bottom rectangle with a gradient and a posterize effect.

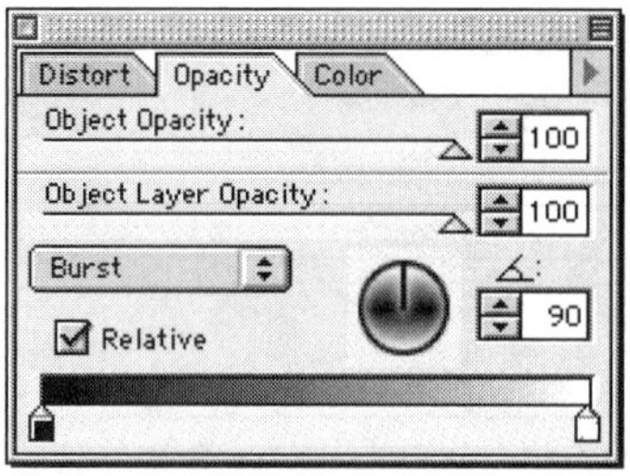

1 ➤ The **Opacity** palette settings for the top rectangle.

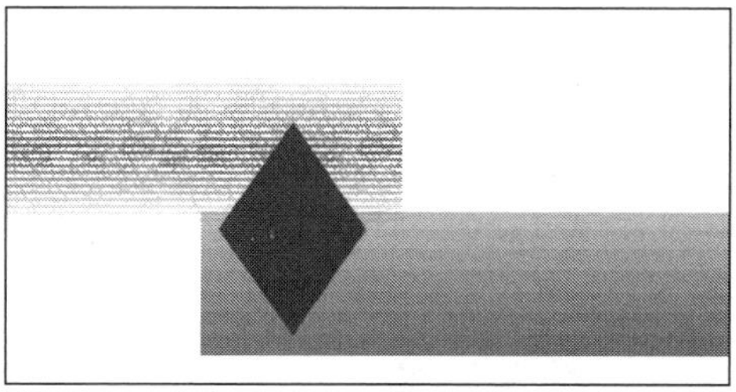
2 ➤ The rectangle and diamond objects in the composition.

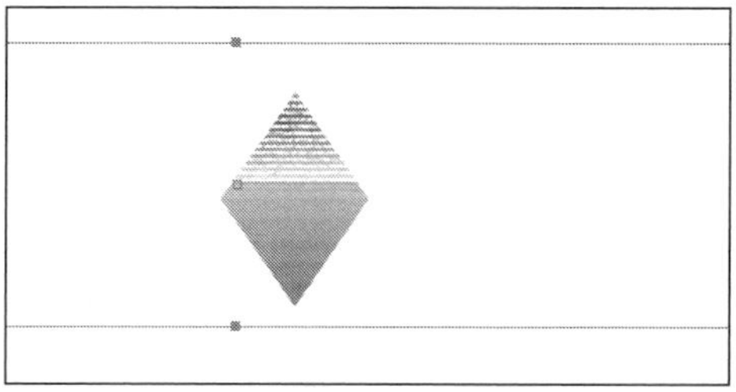
3 ➤ The objects are **grouped** and **Top Object Is Mask** command applied.

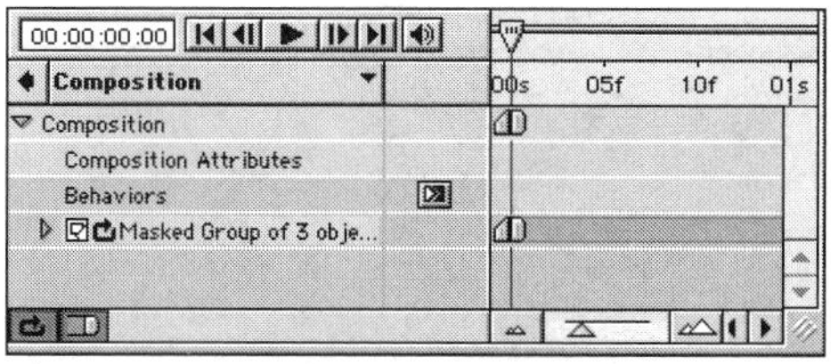

4 ➤ The **Masked Group** object is made **Time Independent** and **looping** is turned on.

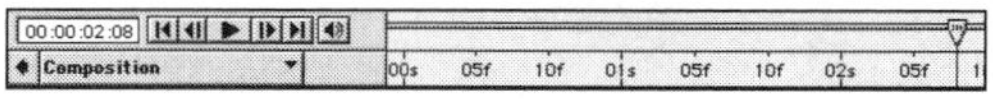

5 ➤ The current time marker at 02s-08f.

10. Select the top rectangle. Show the Textures palette. Choose the "Badreception" texture, then click the Apply Texture button.

11. Show the Opacity palette. To soften the transition between the top and bottom shapes, choose Burst from the drop-down menu and set the Angle to 90° (Fig. 1).

12. Position the bottom rectangle so its left edge is just visible to the left of the diamond object and its top edge rests just above the middle of the diamond.

13. Position the top rectangle so its right edge is just visible to the right of the diamond and its bottom edge is just below the middle of the diamond. The two rectangles will now overlap slightly (Fig. 2).

14. Select all the objects.

15. Choose Object menu > Group (Command-G/Ctrl-G).

16. Choose Object menu > Top Object Is Mask. The textures in the rectangles will now be visible only through the diamond (Fig. 3). Save your document.

ANIMATE THE RECTANGLES FOR THE SPIN EFFECT

1. Click the "Masked Group of 3 objects" on the Timeline.

2. Choose Timeline menu > Time Independent to give the group its own timeline. Click the Loop button in the lower left corner of the Timeline (Fig. 4).

3. Double-click the Masked Group, then click on "rectangle top" in the independent timeline.

4. Expand the object's list, expand the Transform list, then click the stopwatch for Position to set a starting keyframe.

5. Move the current time marker to 02s-08f (Fig. 5). Shift-drag the top rectangle to the right until its left edge almost touches the diamond shape (Fig. 1, next page).

(Continued on the next page)

6. Move the current time marker to 00s.
7. Select the bottom rectangle. Expand the object's list and the Transform list, then click the stopwatch for Position to set a starting keyframe.
8. Move the current time marker to 02s-08f. Shift-drag the rectangle to the left until its right edge almost touches the diamond shape (Fig. 2).
9. Click First Frame, then click Play. Save your document.

Follow the next set of instructions to make the diamond top move and bob around.

ANIMATE THE DIAMOND SHAPE AND SET POSITION KEYFRAMES

1. On the Timeline, move the current time marker to 00s.
2. Select the diamond name. Expand its list and expand the Transform list.
3. Click the stopwatch for Position.
4. Move the current time marker to 00s-08f, then check the Create/remove keyframe box to set another keyframe for the current position.
5. Move the current time marker to 01s-03f. Increase the X value on the Transform palette by 30 (Fig. 3).
6. Move the current time marker to 01s-11f. Check the blank Create/remove keyframe box to set another keyframe for the current position.
7. Move the current time marker to 02s-03f. Decrease the X value on the Transform palette by 30 to return the object to its starting position (Fig. 4).

SET ROTATION KEYFRAMES

1. Move the current time marker to 00s.
2. Click the stopwatch for Rotation.
3. Move the current time marker to 00s-03f. On the Transform palette, click the Rotation field down arrow to set the angle to -4 (Fig. 1, next page).
4. Move the current time marker to 00s-06f. On the Transform palette, click the

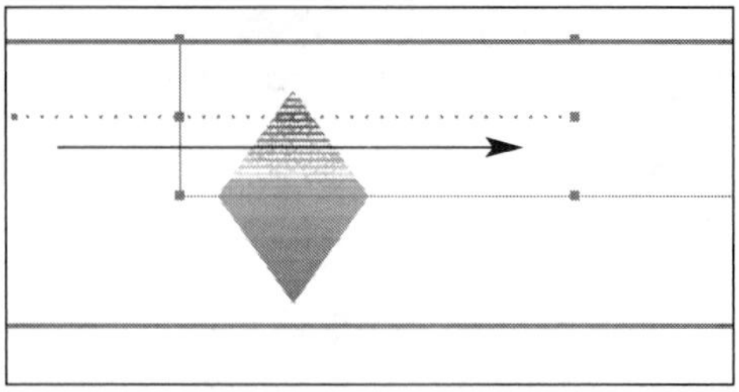

1 ➤ The rectangle top object is dragged to the right.

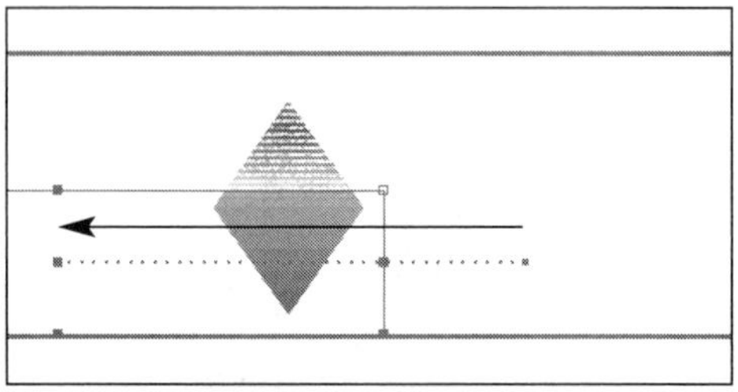

2 ➤ The rectangle bottom object is dragged to the left.

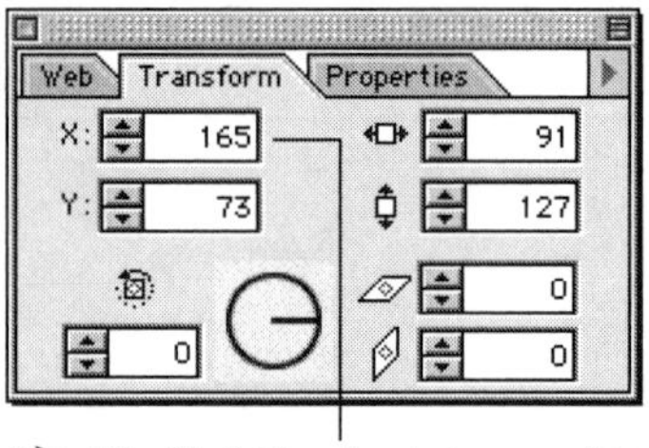

*3 ➤ The **X:** field value is increased to move the Diamond object to the **right**.*

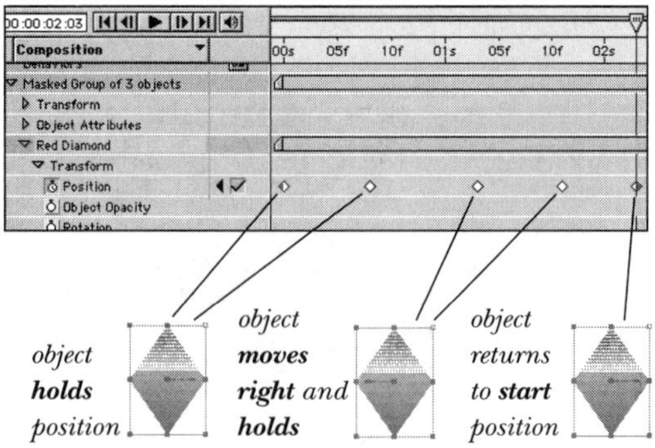

*4 ➤ The **Position** keyframes for the Diamond object.*

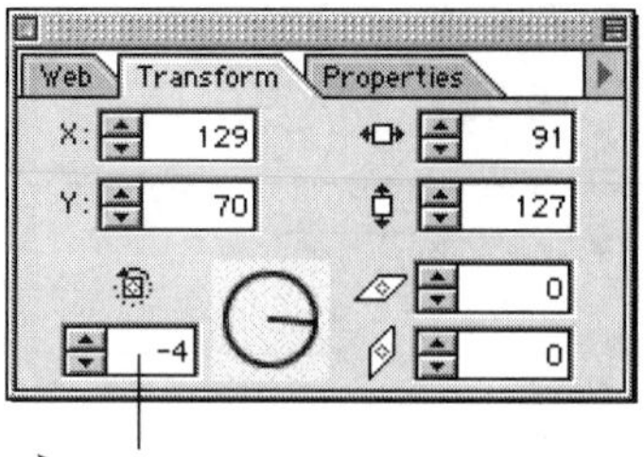

1 ➤ *The **Rotation** is set to -4 to tilt the Diamond object to the right.*

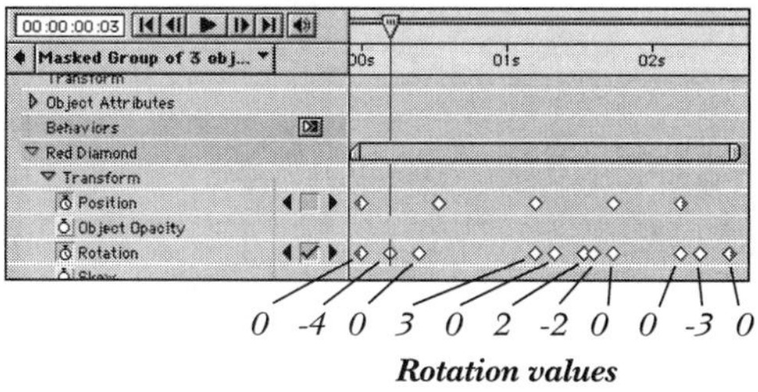

2 ➤ *The **Rotation keyframes** for the Diamond object.*

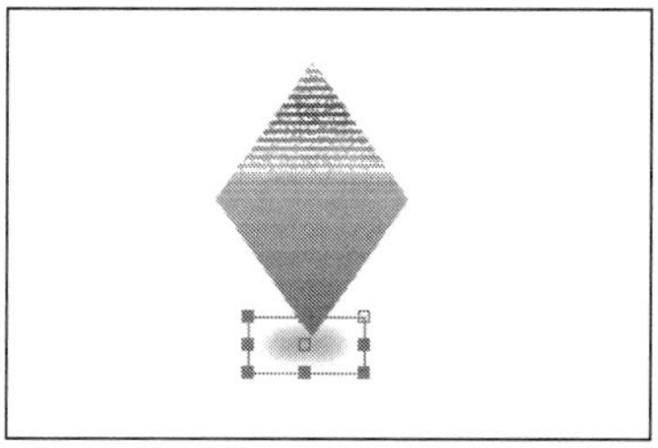

3 ➤ *The shadow object is **positioned, colored, softened,** and lowered in **opacity**.*

5. Use these time and Rotation angle values to set new keyframes (Fig. 2):

Time	Angle
01:03	3
01:05	0
01:08	2
01:09	-2
01:11	0
02:03	0 (check the keyframe box for Rotation)
02:05	-3
02:08	0

6. Click the Preview mode button at the bottom of the Toolbox. Click the Edit mode button when you're done previewing. Save your document, and continue with the remaining instructions.

In the final part of this exercise, you'll copy and paste the diamond's Transform keyframes to create a shadow shape that follows the spinning top.

CREATE A SHADOW FOR THE SPINNING TOP

1. On the Timeline, choose Composition from the Active Timeline drop-down menu to return to the main composition timeline. Deselect all objects.
2. Choose the Ellipse tool (L). Drag a small ellipse (width 55, height 25).
3. Position the ellipse at the bottom point of the diamond.
4. Show the Color palette, then choose a light gray (R, G, and B of 102).
5. Show the Opacity palette, then set the Object Opacity to 43.
6. Show the Layer palette, then set the Softness to 9 (Fig. 3).
7. Double-click the Masked Group on the Timeline, click the Diamond object, then choose Edit menu > Copy.
8. Click the left-pointing arrow next to the Active Timeline drop-down menu to return to the main composition timeline.

(Continued on the next page)

9. Select the gray ellipse. Choose Edit menu > Paste Object Animation.
10. Expand the gray ellipse list and its Transform list to verify that all the diamond keyframes were copied to the ellipse object (Fig. 1).
11. Click the Preview mode button on the Toolbox. Click the Edit mode button when you're done.

Things are working fine, except for one detail: The shadow isn't looping with the spinning top.

MAKE THE SHADOW AND TOP LOOP TOGETHER

1. Make sure you're in the main Composition timeline.
2. Click the gray Ellipse object name, then Shift-select the Group of 3 objects name (Fig. 2).
3. Choose Timeline menu > Make Time Independent Group (Command-Shift-G/ Ctrl-Shift-G). The shadow and the top objects now share the same independent timeline. The top objects will keep their own nested, independent timeline.
4. With the Group of 2 objects selected, click the Loop button in the lower left corner of the Timeline. The shadow and top will now loop together (Fig. 3).
5. Click the Preview mode button on the Toolbox. Click the Edit mode button when you're done. Save your file. ▲

➤ The main composition timeline currently has a one-frame duration. To add other non-time-independent objects, extend the composition's duration—the duration bar for the Group of 2 objects will extend automatically.

➤ To create a logo, you could add a stationary text object on the right side of the composition at the one-second mark.

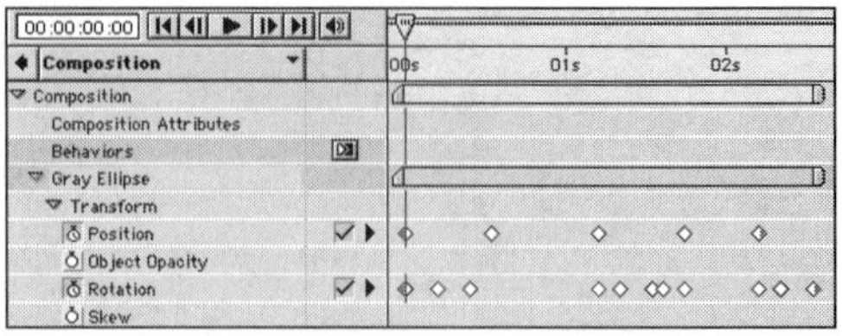

1 ➤ *The **Position** and **Rotation** keyframes are copied to the Ellipse (shadow) object.*

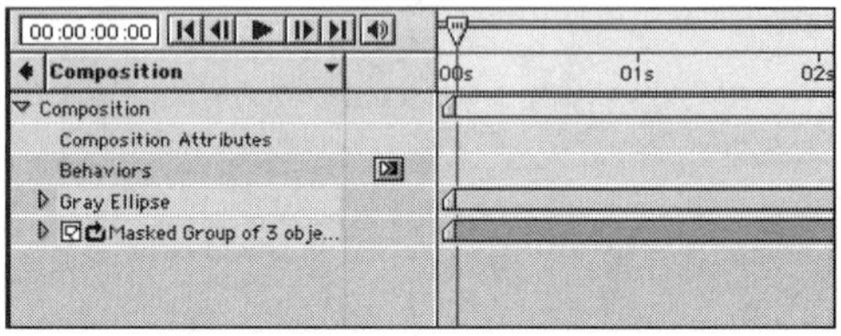

2 ➤ *The **Ellipse** and **Masked Group** objects are selected in the Timeline so that the Make Time Independent Group command can be applied.*

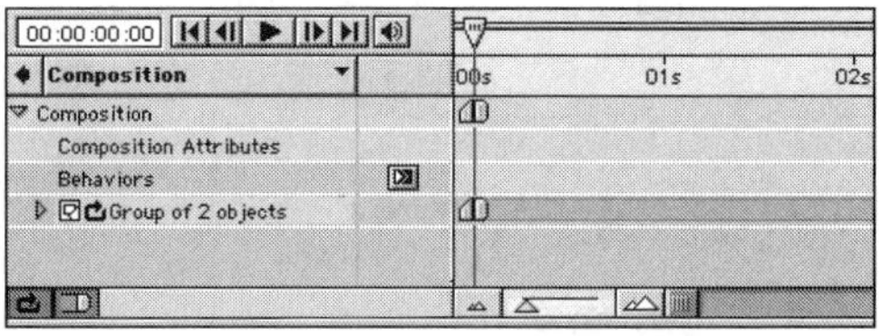

3 ➤ ***Looping** is turned on for the new time-independent group object. Note that the composition and object durations are now only one frame long. Even if the composition duration is extended and new objects are added, the Group of 2 objects will continue to loop during, and at the end of, the composition.*

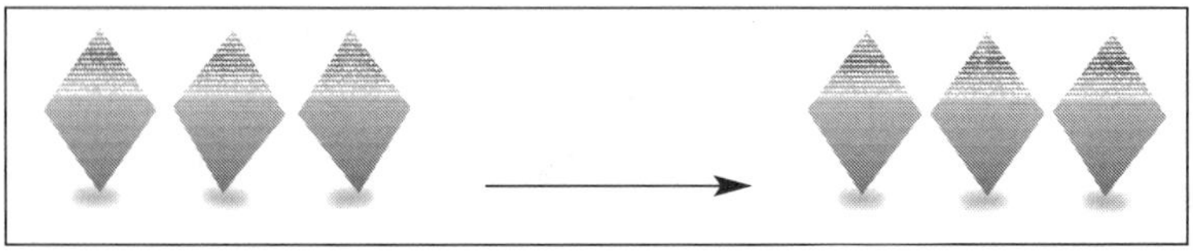

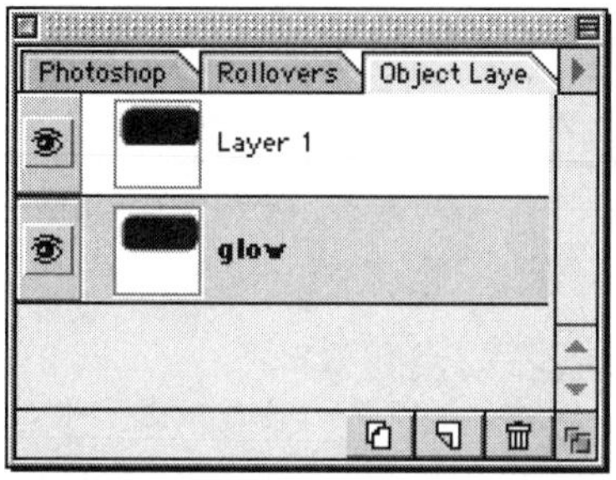

*1 ➤ The **Object Layers** palette showing the new glow layer.*

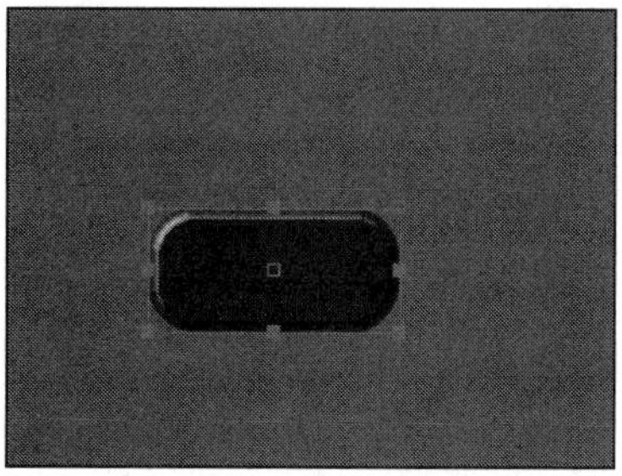

*2 ➤ The button object. The glow layer will only be visible when a **rollover** occurs.*

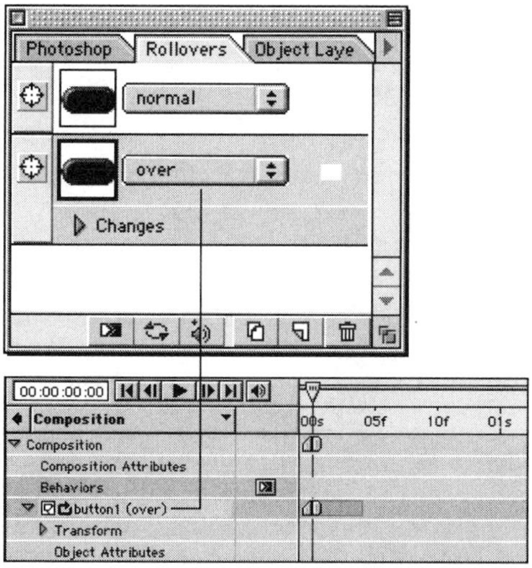

*3 ➤ The button object has become **time-independent**. When the **Over** state is selected on the Rollovers palette, the word "(over)" appears next to the button name on the objects hierarchy list.*

Using rollovers with animation

Animations created using the Timeline editor can be combined with individual rollover states to produce eye-catching results.

Tutorial 2

Animate a button object using a color change and a glow effect

CREATE THE BUTTON AND THE ROLLOVER STATES

1. Choose Edit menu > Composition Settings (Command-Shift-N/Ctrl-Shift-N) or File menu > New. Enter a Width and Height, set Frame Rate to 15, choose Export: Entire Composition, check the Make HTML box, then click OK.
2. *Optional:* To make a dark background, click the Background color square on the Color palette, then choose a dark color from the color bar.
3. Create a button object. Apply an Emboss effect (3D palette) and a deep orange color (R: 204, G: 51, B:0 on the Color palette).
4. On the Adjust palette, set the Brightness to -100.
5. On the Object Layers palette, click the Duplicate Layer button. Double-click the new layer, enter "glow," then click OK (Figs. 1–2).
6. On the Layer palette, set the Width to -2 and the Softness to 1.
7. Show the Timeline editor (Command-T/Ctrl-T). Click the orange shape on the objects hierarchy list, press Return/Enter, type "button 1," then click OK.
8. On the Rollovers palette, click the Duplicate Rollover State button. Note that on the objects hierarchy list in the Timeline, the word "(over)" displays next to the button 1 name whenever the Over state is selected (Fig. 3).

(Continued on the next page)

The button is now time-independent from the main composition timeline because it has multiple states. It now has its own timeline.

9. Click the Normal state on the Rollovers palette, then choose Timeline menu > Loop.

CREATE THE NORMAL STATE ANIMATION

1. In the Timeline editor, double-click the button 1 name. You are now viewing the independent timeline for the Normal state. Click the Layer 1 name and expand the Layer 1 list, then click the stopwatch for Brightness.
2. Move the current time marker to 00s-10f. On the Adjust palette, set the Brightness to -25.
3. Move the current time marker to 01s-06f. Extend the object's duration bar to the current time marker. On the Adjust palette, set the Brightness back to -100 (Figs. 1–2).
4. On the Timeline editor, click the Play button to preview the animation.
5. Click the arrow to the left of the active timeline name to return to the main Composition list and timeline. Select button 1.

➤ You can make a color change instead of a Brightness change. To do this, ignore step 3 above, click the Layer 1 > Color stopwatch, and change the object's color instead of Brightness for steps 2–4, above.

CREATE THE OVER STATE ANIMATION

1. On the Rollovers palette, click on the Over state.
2. On the Timeline editor, double-click button 1 (over) to view the independent timeline for the Over state.
3. Click the glow name and expand the glow layer. Click the stopwatch for Softness and for Width Adjustment (Fig. 3).
4. From the Color palette menu, choose HSB View (Fig. 4). Use the sliders to

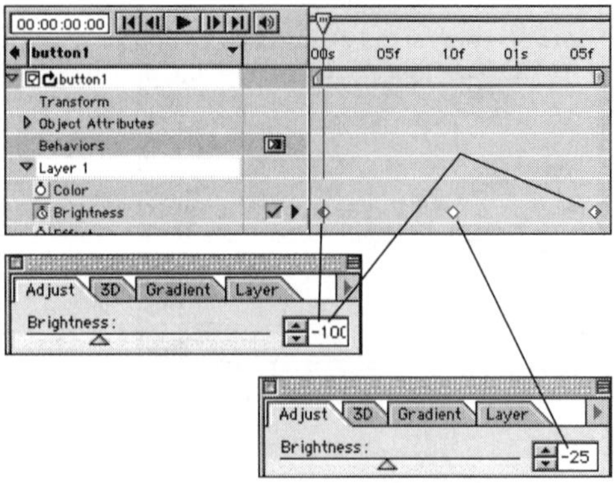

*1 ➤ The object's **Brightness** is changed from -100 (00s) to -25 (00s-10f), then back to -100 (01s-06f).*

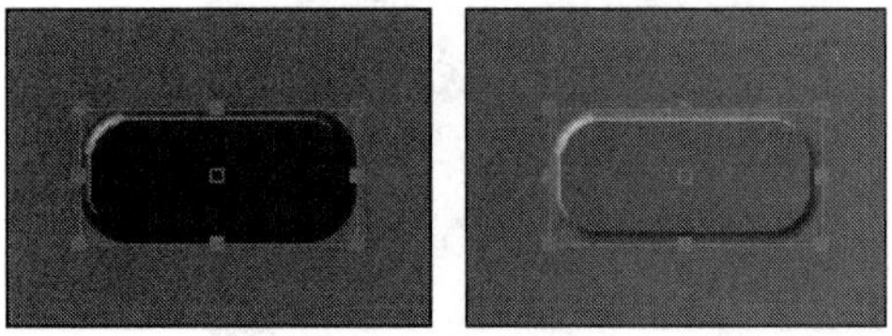

*2 ➤ The object at lower and higher **Brightness** values.*

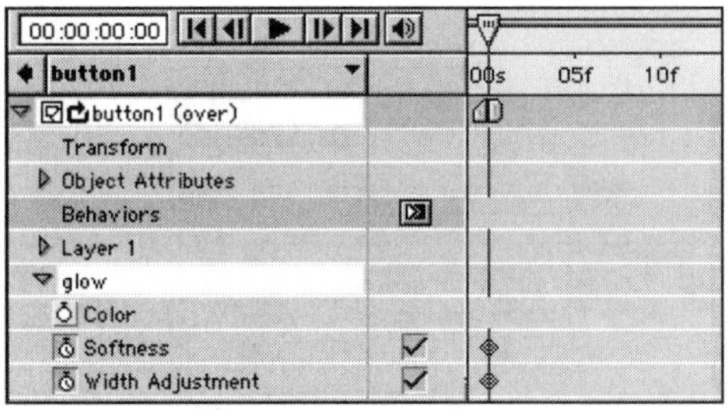

*3 ➤ **Keyframes** are set for the glow layer's **Softness** and **Width Adjustment** properties.*

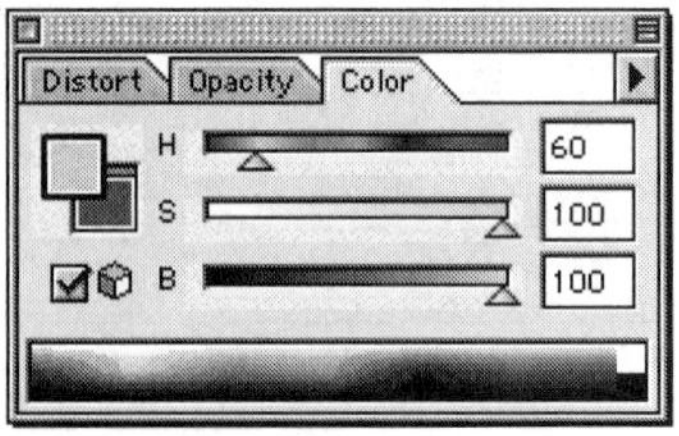

*4 ➤ The **Color** palette in **HSB** View. This view is convenient for changing a color's saturation or brightness.*

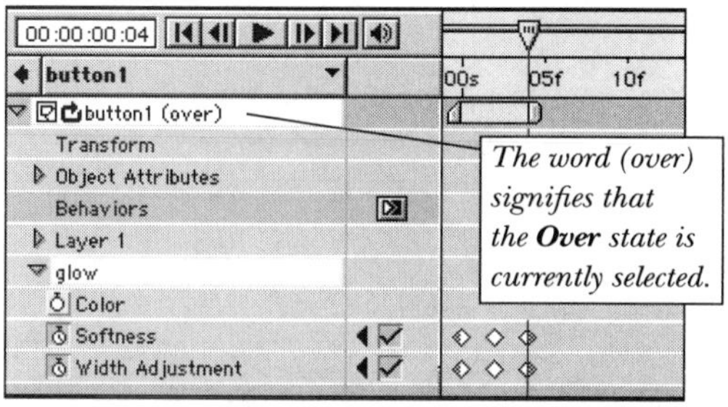

1 ➤ *Additional keyframes are set for the glow layer* ***Softness*** *and* ***Width Adjustment*** *properties. The glow layer now expands and softens, and then it returns to its initial softness and width.*

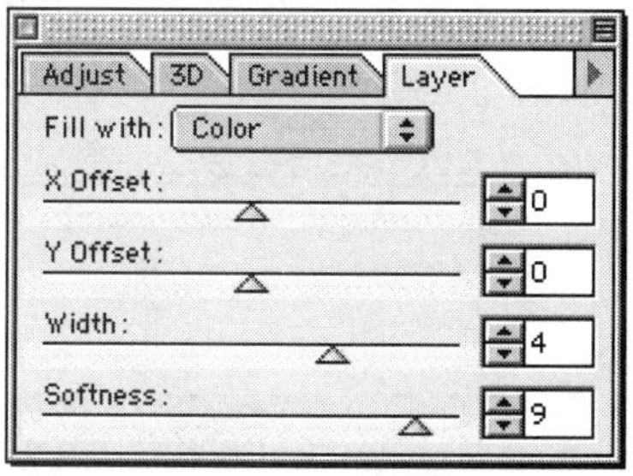

2 ➤ *Layer palette settings for the glow layer* ***Softness*** *and* ***Width Adjustment*** *keyframes at 00s-02f.*

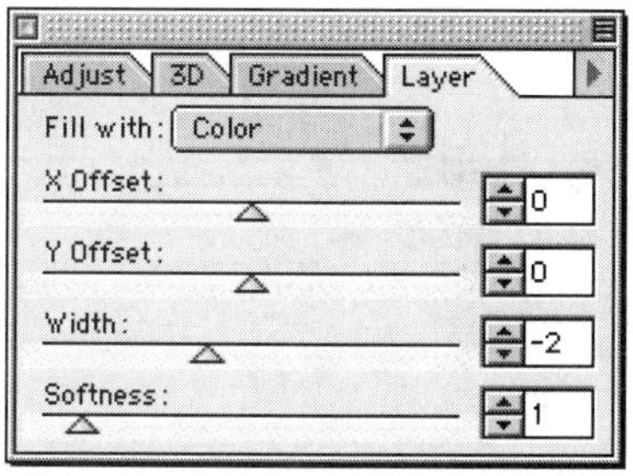

3 ➤ *Layer palette settings for the glow layer* ***Softness*** *and* ***Width Adjustment*** *keyframes at 00s-04f.*

create a light, saturated color, then switch the palette back to RGB View.

5. In the Timeline editor, move the current time marker to 00s-02f. On the Layer palette, set the Width to 4 and the Softness to 9.
6. Move the current time marker to 00s-04f. On the Layer palette, set the Width back to -2 and the Softness to 1 (Figs. 1–3).
7. Click Play to view the Over animation. Select button 1 (over) at the top of the objects hierarchy list, then click the Loop button in the lower-left corner of the Timeline editor to make the Over state loop.
8. Click the arrow to the left of the active timeline name to return to the Composition view.

➤ If you don't want the glow effect to be animated, don't move the time marker for step 5 (just change the properties), and ignore step 6.

(Continued on the next page)

CREATE THE DOWN STATE

1. Select button 1. On the Rollovers palette, click the New Rollover State button to create a Down state (Fig. 1).
2. On the Adjust palette, set the Brightness to -50.
3. *Optional:* Double-click button 1 (down) on the objects hierarchy list to view the Down timeline, and create property changes over time for this state (Figs. 2–3).

PREVIEW THE COMPLETE ROLLOVER ANIMATION

1. Click the Preview mode button at the bottom of the Toolbox.
2. Move the pointer over the button object in the composition window, then click on the button.
3. Click back on the Edit mode button at the bottom of the Toolbox. Save your file. ▲

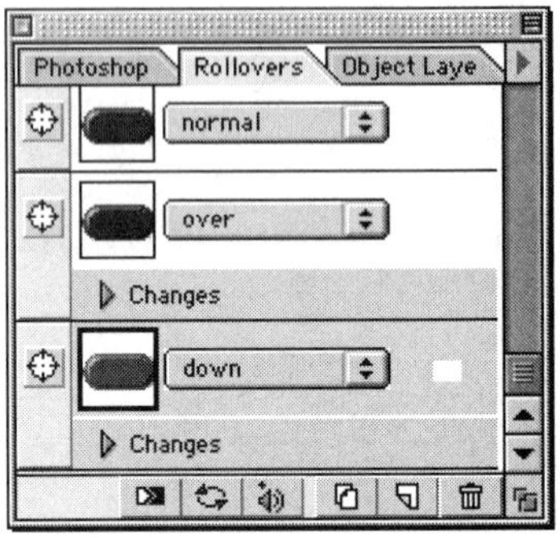

*1 ➤ The **Rollovers** palette showing the new **Down** state.*

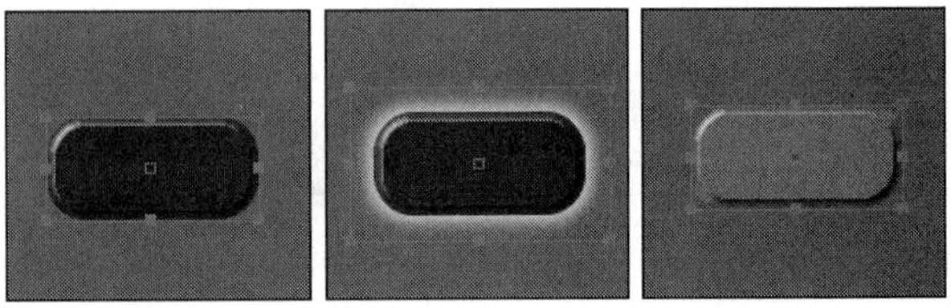

*2 ➤ The object in the **Normal, Over** and **Down** states.*

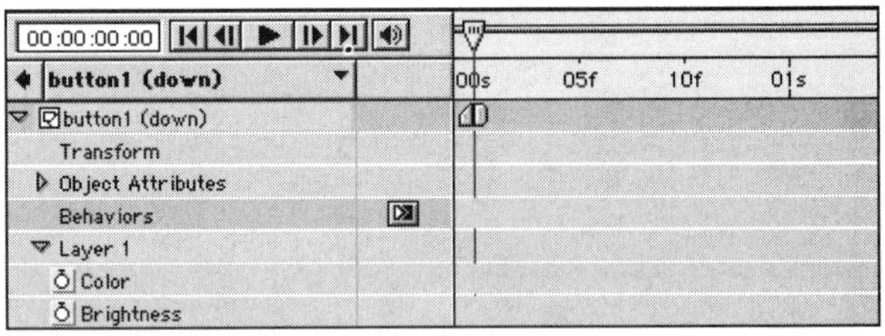

3 ➤ This is the time-independent timeline for the Down state. Currently, the state is only one frame in duration, but you could lengthen the duration bar for button 1 (down) and create layer property changes for the button over time.

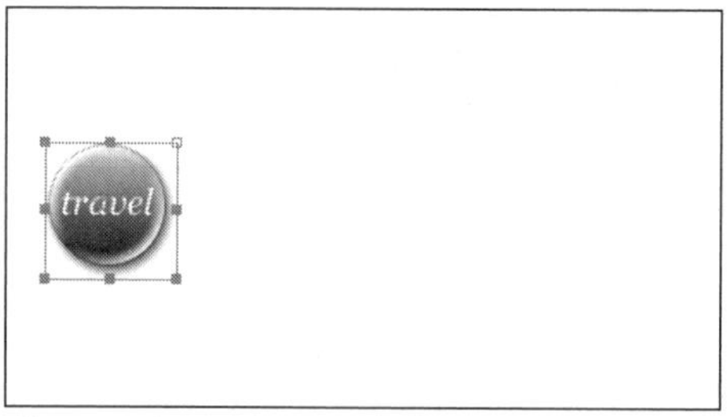

1 ➤ *The **circle** object. We also put a separate **text** object on top of the circle object.*

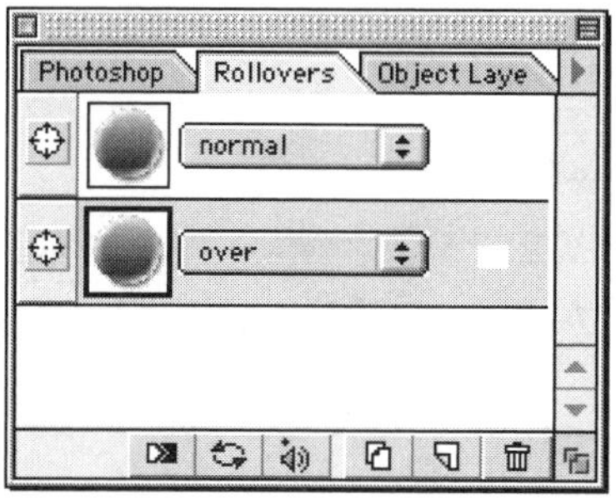

2 ➤ *A new **Over** state is created for the circle object.*

3 ➤ *The **remote** object.*

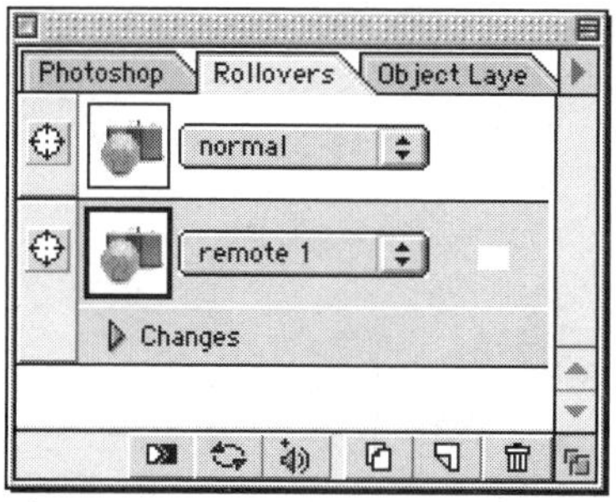

4 ➤ *A new **custom** state is created for the **remote** object.*

Tutorial 3

Create a rollover that triggers an animation effect in a remote object

CREATE THE BUTTON OBJECT AND REMOTE OBJECT

1. Choose Edit menu > Composition Settings or File menu > New. Enter a Width and Height, set the Frame Rate to 15, choose Export: Entire Composition, check the Make HTML box, then click OK.
2. Create a circle object (Fig. 1). Apply a style or manually adjust any of the properties, if desired.
3. On the Rollovers palette, click the Duplicate Rollover State button to create the Over state (Fig. 2).
4. For the remote object, create a text object or import an image to create an image object.
5. With the remote object selected, on the Rollovers palette, click the Duplicate Rollover State button. Choose Custom State from the Over state pop-up menu, type "remote 1," then click OK (Figs. 3–4). Adding a state to an object makes it time-independent automatically.

(Continued on the next page)

CREATE THE ANIMATION

1. Show the Timeline editor (Command-T/ Ctrl-T).
2. Click the circle object name. Press Return/Enter, type "button," then click OK.
3. Click the remote object name. Press Return/Enter, type "object A," then click OK (Fig. 1).
4. On the objects hierarchy list, double-click the object A name to view its independent timeline.
5. On the Rollovers palette, select the remote 1 state. Note how the object A (remote 1) layer is now visible. This a clue to let you know which rollover state you're animating and which independent timeline you're in (Fig. 2).
6. Set the current time marker to 00s.
7. On the Opacity palette, set the Object Layer Opacity to 0. On the objects hierarchy list, expand Layer 1. Click the stopwatch next to Object Layer Opacity.

   Note: The Object Opacity property can't be used to control the fade effect. That property affects all the object states and not just a single state. In this case, we only want to change the opacity of the Over state.
8. Move the current time marker to 00s-07f.
9. On the Opacity palette, set the Object Layer Opacity back to 100. A new keyframe will be created (Fig. 3).
10. Drag the current time marker back and forth to preview the fade-in. Move the time marker back to 00s.
11. If object A has any other layers (e.g., a shadow layer), repeat steps 6–10 to modify the object layer opacity for those layers as well.
12. *Optional:* Perform other layer property changes to object A while it's in the remote 1 state. Remember to click a stopwatch first to set a starting value for any property you change.

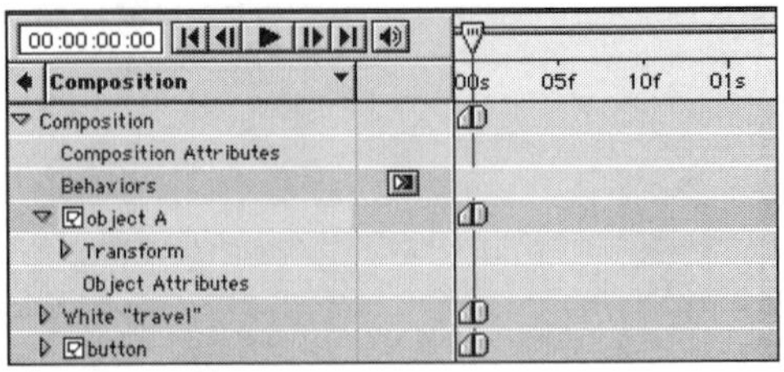

1 ➤ The Timeline editor with the two time-independent objects (and our text object).

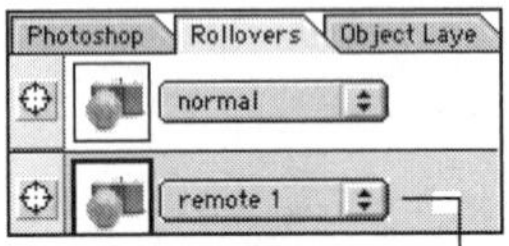

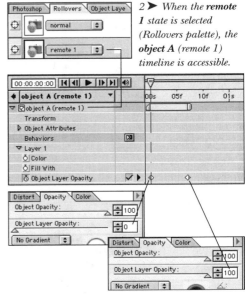

*2 ➤ When the **remote 1** state is selected (Rollovers palette), the **object A** (remote 1) timeline is accessible.*

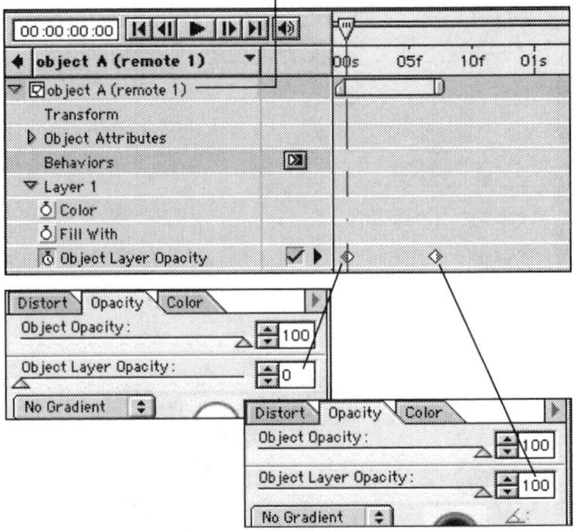

*3 ➤ The two **keyframes** for object A and their respective **Object Layer Opacity** values.*

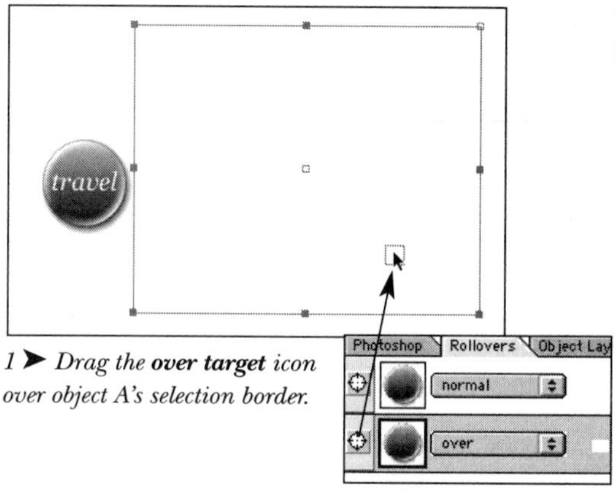

1 ➤ *Drag the **over target** icon over object A's selection border.*

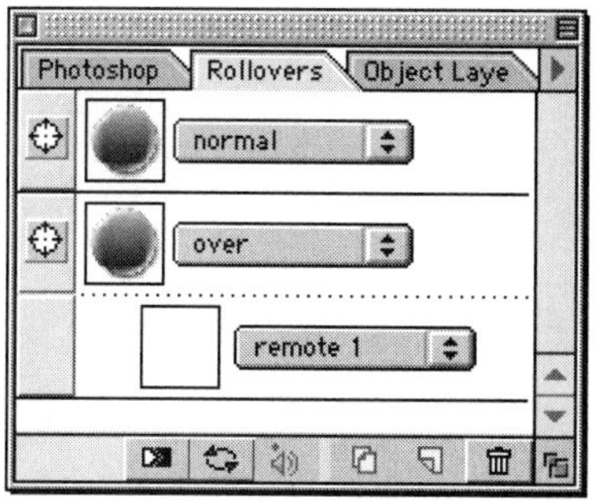

2 ➤ *The Rollovers palette after targeting the button **over** state to object A's **remote 1** state.*

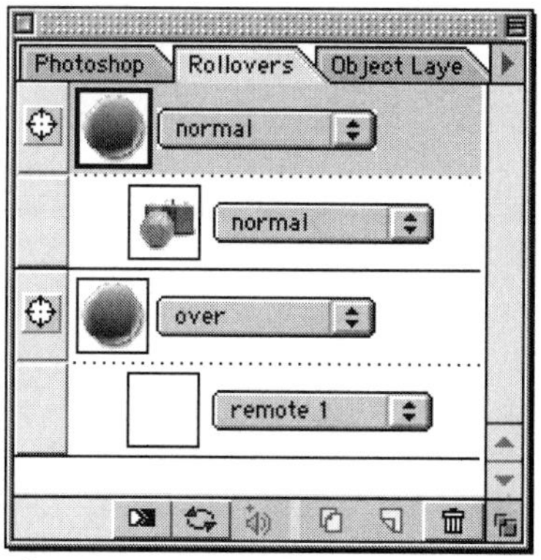

3 ➤ *The Rollovers palette after targeting the button **normal** state to object A's **normal** state.*

TARGET THE REMOTE OBJECT TO THE BUTTON OBJECT

1. Leave object A's remote 1 layer selected on the Rollovers palette.
2. Return to the main Composition list, then select the button name on the objects hierarchy list.
3. On the Rollovers palette, drag the target icon for the Over state over object A in the composition window. Release the mouse when the selection border appears (Fig. 1). Make sure remote 1 is chosen on the target state pop-up menu (Fig. 2).
4. Drag the target icon for the Normal state (button object) over object A in the composition window. Release the mouse when the selection border appears. From the target state pop-up menu on the Rollovers palette, choose Normal (Fig. 3).
5. Click the Preview mode button at the bottom of the Toolbox. Move the mouse over the button to preview the animated fade-in. Click the Edit mode button when you're done. Save your file.

The last step is to make the Normal state invisible (see the following page).

(Continued on the next page)

MAKE THE NORMAL STATE INVISIBLE

1. Double-click object A to display its timeline.
2. On the Rollovers palette, select the Normal state for object A. The timeline is now the Normal state timeline—not remote 1 (Fig. 1).
3. Click on Layer 1. On the Opacity palette, set the Object Layer Opacity to 0 (Fig. 2). This will make the Normal state invisible. The Normal state displays when the mouse is *not* over the button.

   Repeat this step for any other layers in object A, if there are any.
4. Leave the object duration bar as is (a one-frame duration) for the Normal state. You needed to create a duration only for the remote 1 state.
5. Click the arrow to the left of the Active timeline menu to return to the Composition list.
6. Click the Preview mode button at the bottom of the Toolbox. Move the mouse over the button to preview the animated fade-in (Fig. 3). Click the Edit mode button when you're done. Save your file. ▲

*1 ➤ With the **normal** state chosen, you can work on object A's "normal" Timeline.*

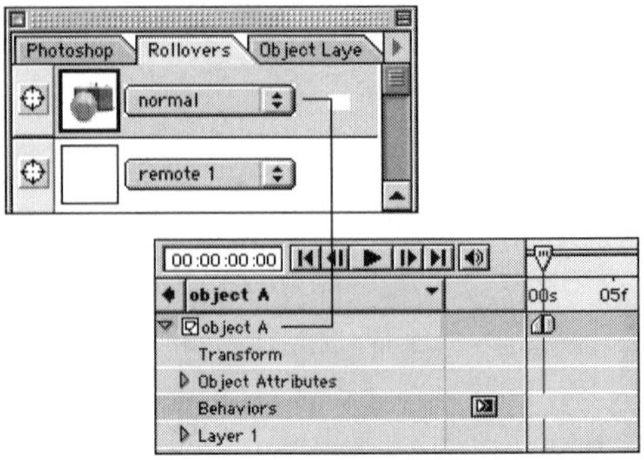

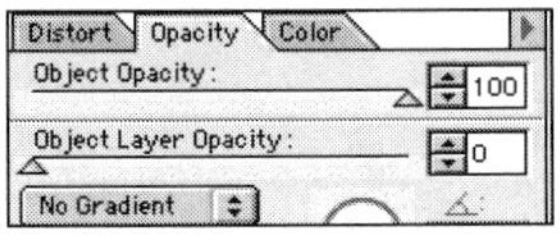

*2 ➤ Set the **Object Layer Opacity** to 0 for object A.*

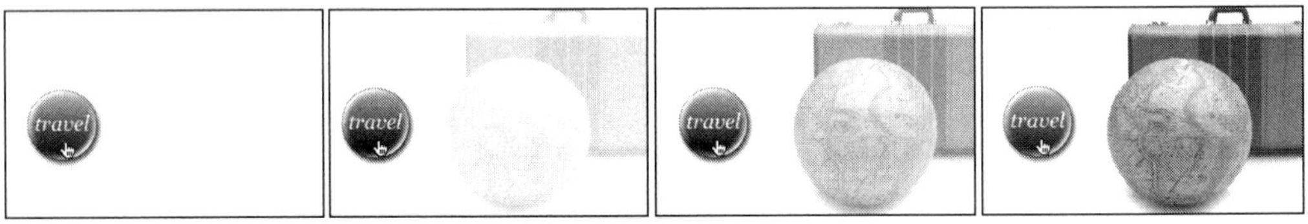

*3 ➤ The **finished** rollover animation.*

1 ➤ *The text objects are aligned within the composition.*

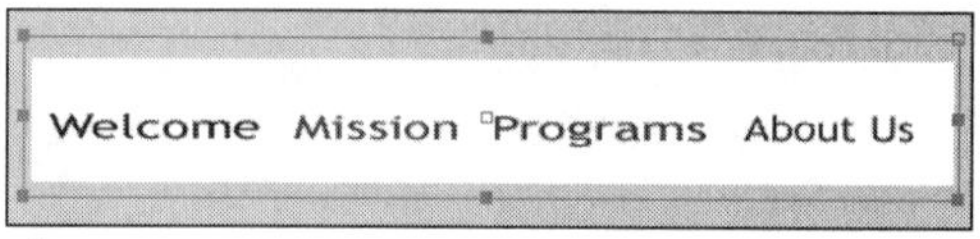

2 ➤ *A rectangle is created and sent to the back.*

Tutorial 4

Create a text navigation bar that fades in

1. Choose Edit menu > Composition Settings (Command-Shift-N/Ctrl-Shift-N). Enter a Width of 460 and a height of 60, choose a Frame Rate of 10, choose Export: Entire Composition, check the Make HTML box, then click OK.
2. Create several text objects for the various services or pages that will be offered at your site. For Type properties, try a Size of approximately 16 to 20 points and choose Align: Horizontal, Center. Apply the same color to all the objects.

   Place the first object you create at the left side of the composition. Place the next object you create to the right of the first one, etc. Place the last object you create at the far right side of the composition. This step is important for establishing the proper stacking order in the composition and on the Timeline editor list.
3. Select all the text objects (Command-A/Ctrl-A). Choose Object menu > Align > Vertical Centers and choose Object menu > Distribute > Horizontal. The objects are now centered horizontally and vertically in the composition (Fig. 1).
4. Select the Rectangle tool (M), then draw a rectangle that is slightly larger than the size of the composition. Choose Object menu > Arrange > Send to Back (Fig. 2).
5. Apply a color to the rectangle object that contrasts well with the text.
6. *Optional:* With the rectangle object selected, show the Gradient palette. Choose Linear from the pop-up menu; click the dark color gradient end marker, then click on White or a very light color on the Color palette.
7. Show the Timeline editor (Command-T/Ctrl-T).

(Continued on the next page)

8. Move the current time marker to 03s-03f. Drag the out point of the composition duration bar so it touches the vertical time marker. The duration for all the other objects will be extended automatically (Fig. 1).
9. Move the current time marker to 00s. Select and expand the rectangle object list then expand the Transform list.
10. On the Opacity palette, set the Object Opacity to 0. On the Timeline editor, click the stopwatch for Object Opacity.
11. Move the current time marker to 00s-08f. On the Opacity palette, set the Object Opacity to 100. A keyframe will be created (Fig. 2).
12. Move the current time marker to 01s-07f. Click on the text object layer at the top of the objects hierarchy list. Drag the start point of its duration bar so it touches the vertical time marker.
13. Move the current time marker to 00s-05f. Click on the text object layer at the bottom of the objects list. Position its duration bar in point so it touches the vertical time marker.
14. Drag each subsequent text object's start point to make a stairstep sequence between the lowest and highest text object layers in the timeline (Fig. 3). This sequencing will cause each text object to appear in a staggered sequence from left to right in the composition window. This is why the object stacking order was important.
15. Click the First Frame button, then click the Play button.

You will now create properties and rollover states for the first text object. Later, you will copy and paste these changes to the other text objects.

MAKE THE FIRST TEXT OBJECT FADE IN USING SCALING AND SOFTENING

1. Select the bottommost text object on the objects hierarchy list. Position the current time marker at this object's start

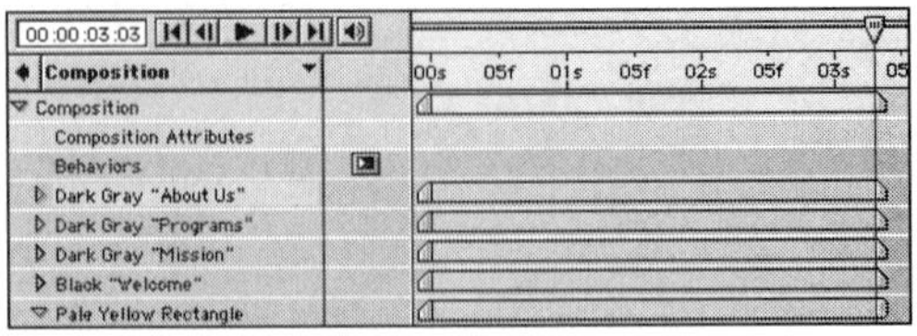

*1 ➤ Extend the composition **duration bar**. The text object duration bars will also extend automatically.*

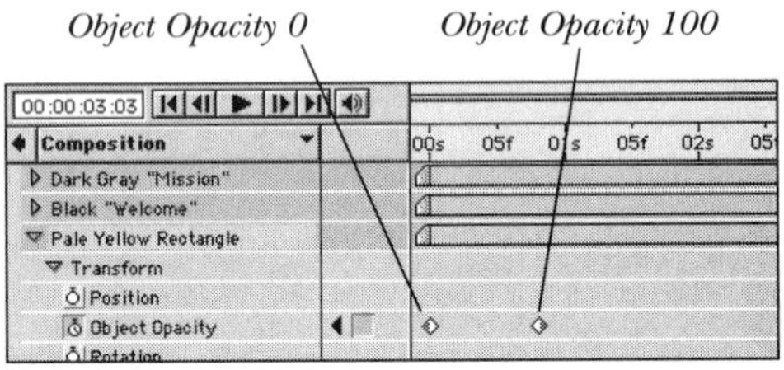

*2 ➤ Set **Object Opacity** keyframes for the Rectangle object to make it fade in.*

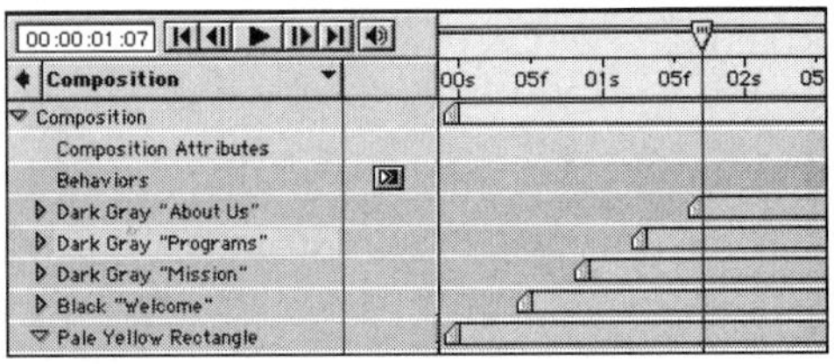

3 ➤ The duration bars are lined up in a stairstep formation.

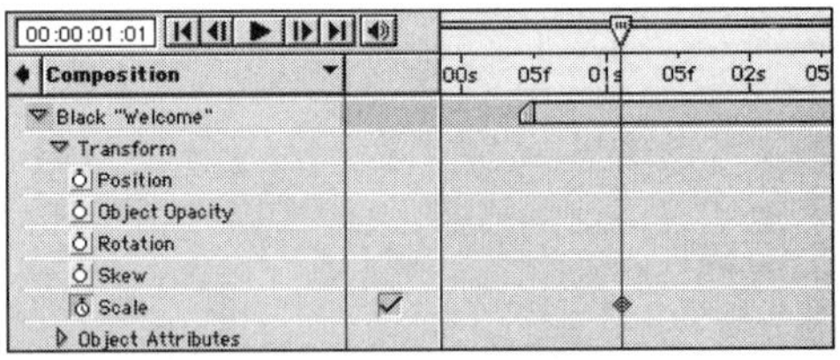

*4 ➤ Click the **Scale** stopwatch to create a keyframe for the text object's current size.*

*1 ➤ Drag a handle of the text object to enlarge it. This will create a **Scale** keyframe at the current time.*

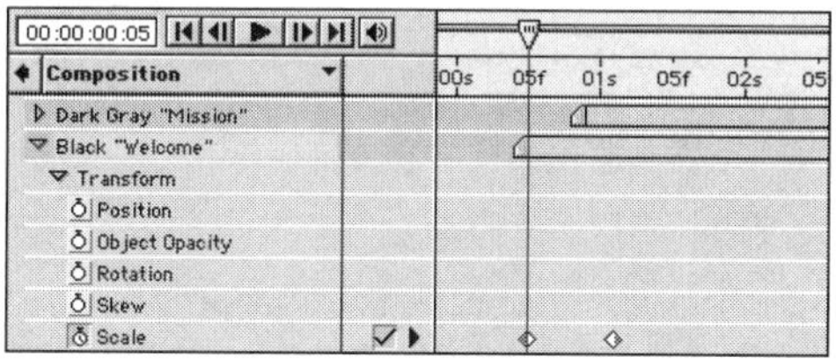

*2 ➤ The text object now has **two Scale** keyframes. The object will scale **down** during playback.*

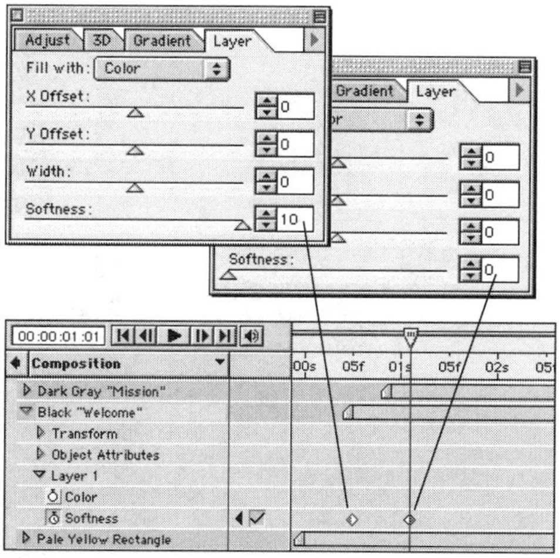

*3 ➤ Two **Softness** keyframes have been created for the text object. The object will sharpen as it scales down.*

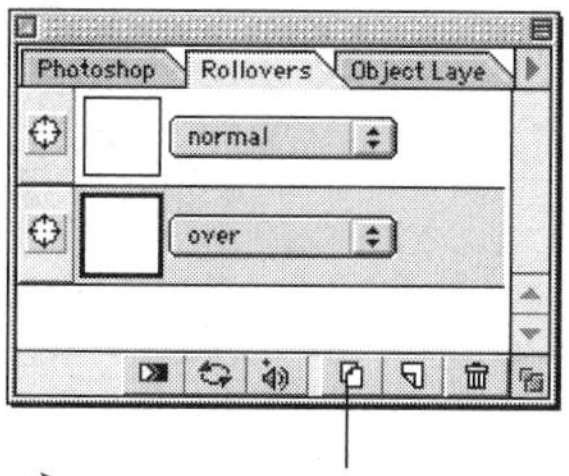

*4 ➤ Click the **Duplicate Rollover State** button to create an **Over** state.*

point. Then position the time marker 6 frames to the right, in this case at 01s-01f.

2. Expand the list for this text object. Expand the Transform list. Click the stopwatch for Scale to set an ending scale keyframe (Fig. 4, previous page). You will now work backwards in time to create the animation.
3. Reposition the current time marker to the start point of the text object.
4. Click in the composition window. Resize the window so there is at least an inch of gray backdrop showing. Drag the object's upper-left selection handle diagonally outward while holding down Shift to proportionately scale the object boundary about a quarter of an inch beyond the edge of the canvas (Figs. 1–2).
5. On the Layer palette, set the Softness to 10. Click the stopwatch by the object's Layer 1 > Softness property (Fig. 3).
6. Reposition the current time marker to the second Scale keyframe. (Try clicking the next keyframe arrow in the keyframe column by the Scale property to advance.) On the Layer palette, set the Softness to 0 (Fig. 3). Drag the current time marker back and forth over the timeline to preview the animation.

CREATE ROLLOVERS FOR THE FIRST TEXT OBJECT

1. Select the bottommost text object on the objects hierarchy list. Move the current time marker to 01s.
2. Show the Rollovers palette. Click the Duplicate Rollover State button to create an Over state (Fig. 4). Remember that by creating another state, the object has become a time-independent object automatically. Each state on the Rollovers palette will have its own timeline view on the Timeline editor.
3. Using the Color palette, change the color of the object. (We chose a medium blue R: 0, G: 102, B: 255.) Yes, the text is blurry. We'll fix that next.

(Continued on the next page)

4. Leave the Over state selected on the Rollovers palette. On the Timeline, double-click the "[your text object name]" (over) layer to display the Over state timeline (Fig. 1).
5. Expand the Layer 1 list.
6. Click the Softness stopwatch. This will remove the Softness property.
7. On the Layer palette, set the Softness to 0.
8. Click the Auto Length button at the bottom of the Timeline editor. The object now has a one-frame duration (Fig. 2).
9. Leave the (over) timeline displayed and don't move the time marker.

➤ Don't have the Normal state selected when you double-click the object name to remove the Layer 1 Softness keyframes (step 4, above). If you do, the text object won't sharpen as it scales down. Because the text object has multiple states (Normal, Over, etc.), it has multiple timeline views. A Transform property (Scale) is viewed in and controlled in the main timeline view. A layer property (Softness), on the other hand, is viewed in and controlled by the timeline view for the state (e.g., Normal, Over). When that state is selected on the Rollovers palette, you can access its timeline.

➤ You won't be able to select other Rollover states for an object unless the current time marker is over that object's duration bar in the main composition timeline.

ASSIGN A URL AND A DOWN STATE TO THE FIRST TEXT OBJECT

1. Show the Web palette. Assign a link by entering the URL into the URL field. Enter "#" if you don't have a link but you want to test the animation in a browser. This will override Adobe's default URL (Fig. 3).
2. On the Rollovers palette, click the Duplicate Rollover State button to create the Down state (Fig. 4).
3. Choose a bright color from the Color palette. (We chose R: 255, G: 51, B: 0.)

*1 ➤ The word "(over)" signifies that the **Over** state is selected on the Rollovers palette.*

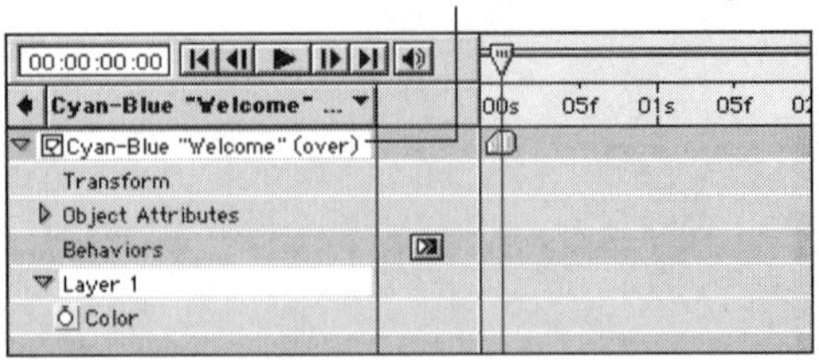

*2 ➤ With the object's (over) timeline displayed, set the **Softness** to **0**. This will cause the object's Over state to look sharp (2a), not blurry (2b).*

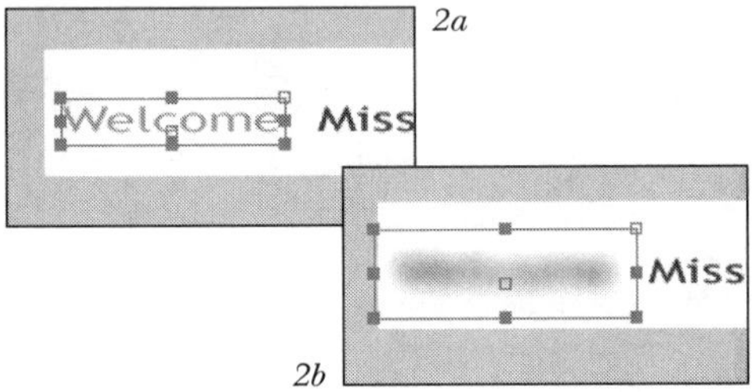

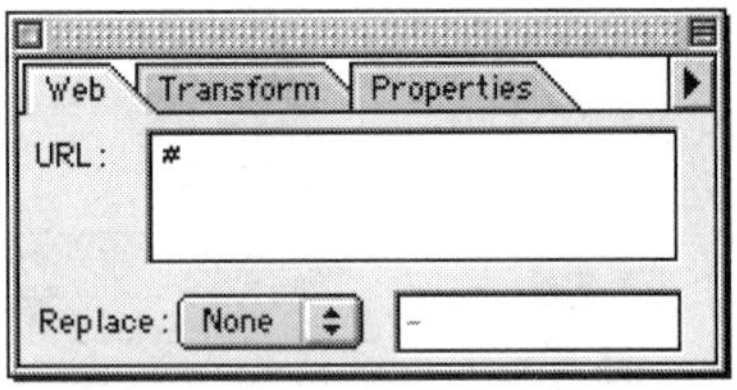

*3 ➤ On the **Web** palette, enter a **URL** or enter "#" to override Adobe's default URL.*

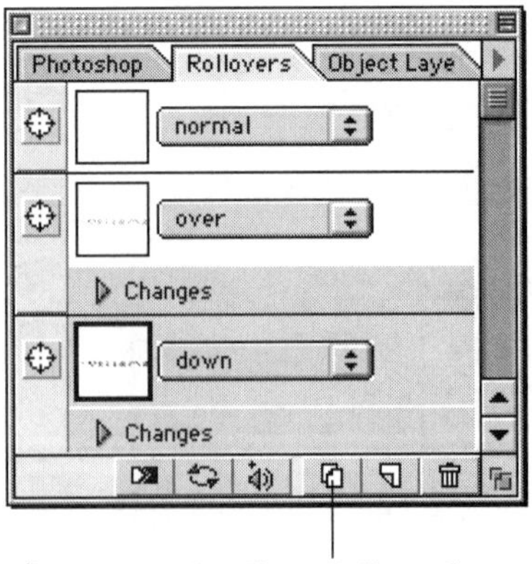

*4 ➤ Click the **Duplicate Rollover State** button to create a **Down** state.*

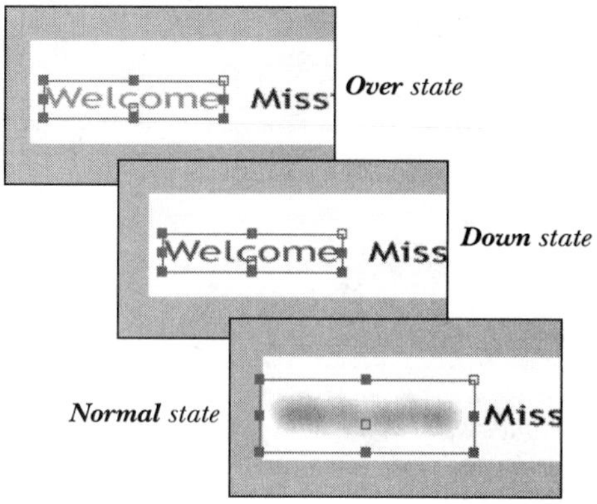

1 ➤ *The text object with its three rollover states:* ***Over, Down,*** *and* ***Normal****. An Out state is needed to prevent the text from blurring when the rollover ends.*

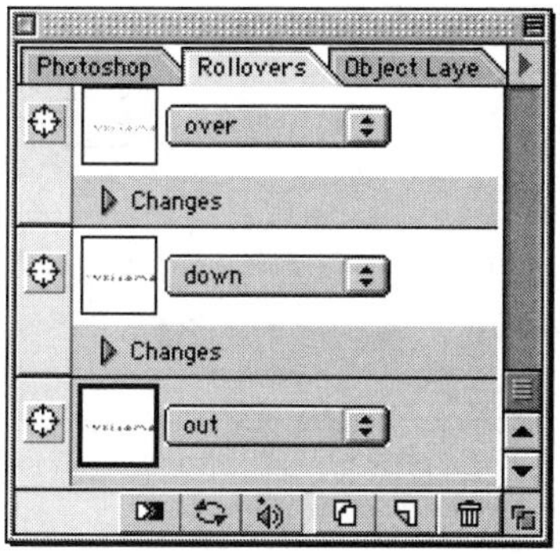

2 ➤ *Click the Duplicate Rollover State button to create an* ***Out*** *state. The Out state has no Softness change, so the text stays sharp.*

3 ➤ *The* ***Out*** *state.*

4. Leave the (down) timeline displayed. Don't move the time marker.

Note: If we stop now, there will be a lingering problem after the rollover is completed: The program will play the Normal state animation in which the soft text becomes sharp (Fig. 1).

We need one more state—the Out state—in order to restore the text object's original color and sharpness after a rollover without the softness change. The Out state occurs when the mouse is moved away from the object.

CREATE THE OUT STATE FOR THE FIRST TEXT OBJECT

1. Show the Rollovers palette. Click the Duplicate Rollover State button to create the Out state (Fig. 2).
3. Choose the original text color (from the Normal state) from the Color palette (Fig. 3).
4. Click the arrow to the left of the active timeline name to return to the main composition timeline.
5. Click the Preview mode button at the bottom of the Toolbox. Move the pointer into the composition window and roll over the text entry you modified. Click the Edit mode button to stop the preview. Save your file.

Next, you will copy and paste the changes you just made to the other text objects.

COPY THE ROLLOVERS AND PROPERTY CHANGES TO THE OTHER TEXT OBJECTS

1. On the objects hierarchy list, click the name of the text object you just modified.
2. Position the current time marker anywhere over that object's duration bar.
3. Choose Edit menu > Copy (Command-C/ Ctrl-C).
4. Click the next higher object name on the list.
5. Position the current time marker anywhere over that object's duration bar.

(Continued on the following page)

6. Choose Edit menu > Paste Style. The Rollover states will be copied.
7. Choose Edit menu > Paste Object Animation (Fig. 1). The scale and softness changes will be copied.
8. Repeat steps 4–7 for all the remaining text objects.
9. Click the Preview mode button on the Toolbox. Roll the mouse over the text in the composition window, then click on it (Fig. 3). Click the Edit mode button when you're done previewing. Save your file.

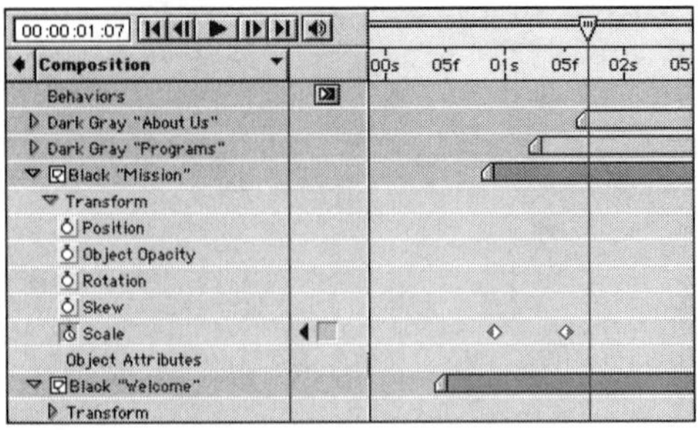

1 ➤ *After using **Paste Style** and **Paste Object Animation**, the next text object now contains the same keyframe properties.*

EXPORT THE TEXT NAVIGATION ANIMATION

1. Show the Export palette.
2. Choose these Export palette settings: SWF file format, Truecolor, Color Resolution 8, Opacity Resolution 6, and Frame Rate: Document Rate (Fig. 2).
3. Choose File menu > Preview in, Internet Explorer. When you're done previewing, choose File menu > Preview in > Netscape Communicator. Don't forget to preview your animations in both major browsers!
4. Click back in the LiveMotion composition and save your file.
5. Choose File menu > Export As, choose a location in which to save the file, enter a new name or leave the default name as is, then click Save. ▲

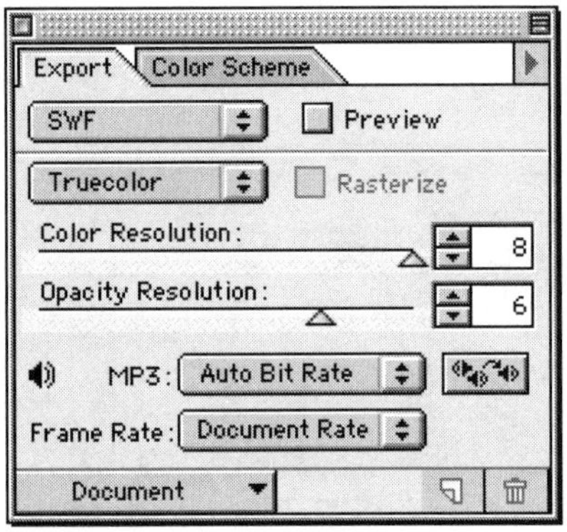

2 ➤ *We used these **Export** palette settings to **preview** and **export** the animation.*

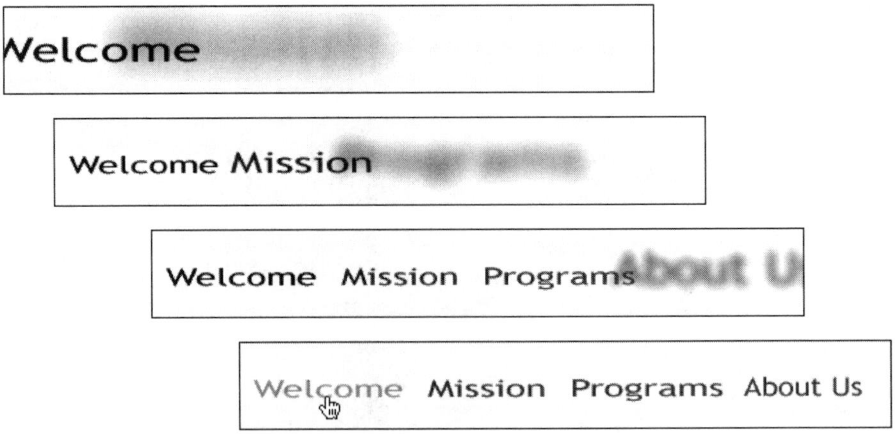

3 ➤ *The **finished** animation.*

Behaviors 15

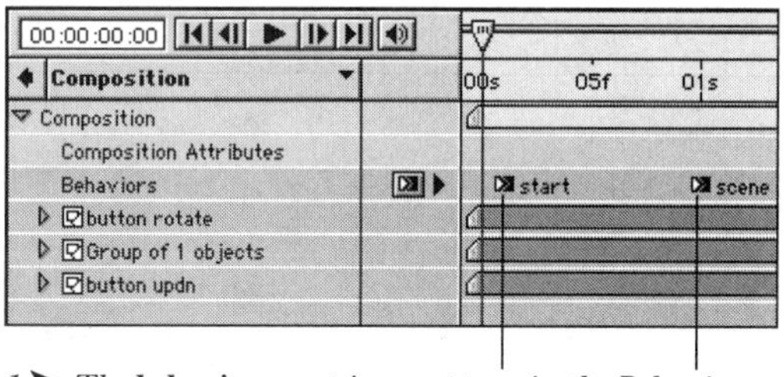

1 ➤ *The* ***behavior event*** *icons appear in the Behaviors row on the Timeline. The events displayed here have behavior event labels that can be targeted by the Go To Label navigation behavior to move to their positions on the timeline.*

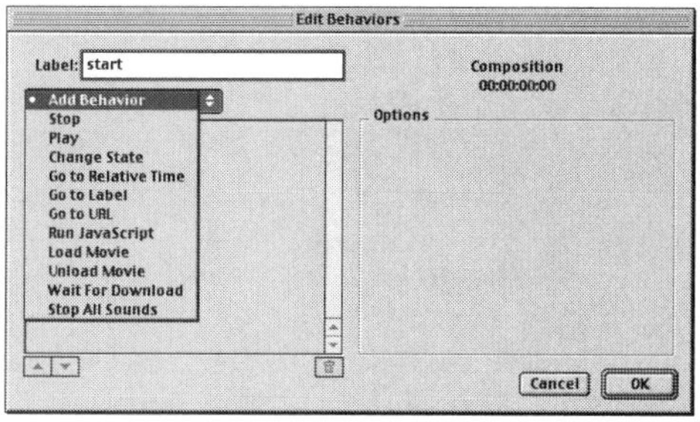

2 ➤ *Behaviors are added to a behavior event using the* ***Edit Behaviors*** *dialog box.*

Behaviors basics

BEHAVIORS ARE COMMANDS that control the playback of an animation. They tell an animation to play, stop, repeat specific frames, go to a specific frame in the Timeline, or even download a movie file to play in the current animation. A behavior can be positioned so it occurs when a certain frame in the animation is reached or a behavior can be instructed to execute when the viewer interacts with a rollover object. Behaviors have a lot of power.

Behavior commands aren't visible on the objects hierarchy list of the Timeline. What is visible is a behavior event icon (Fig. 1) which signifies that a behavior command or commands (Fig. 2) are present at that particular point in the timeline.

Before you do the three tutorials in this chapter, please read through this brief overview of how behaviors work.

Behaviors that navigate the timeline
Behaviors make it possible to play back an animation in a non-linear fashion. For example, if a user mouses over a rollover object that has a behavior attached to one of its states, a behavior can move the current time marker to a different part of the timeline. At that point, another behavior can be used to either restore the time marker to the same starting point on the timeline or go to another point on the timeline.

Behavior event labels
The first step in creating behavior events that control navigation in an animation is to create behavior event labels. Labels mark specific frames on the timeline. These event labels are used by the navigation behaviors

(Continued on the next page)

to move through the animation. We will show you how to create behavior event labels in this chapter.

➤ Behavior events can be placed in an independent timeline. First double-click the time-independent object on the objects hierarchy list to open its timeline, then create the behavior events.

Behavior events in object states

To enable a user to control the playback of an animation, you can attach behavior events to specific object rollover states. When a user interacts with the object, the behavior commands are executed. You'll learn how to create an object state behavior event in Tutorial 1 in this chapter.

➤ An object state behavior event does not appear on the Timeline, and cannot be used by the navigation behaviors. Therefore, these behavior events cannot be assigned a label.

➤ To edit a behavior event that's attached to an object state, you must first position the current time marker over that object's duration bar in the timeline. That way, you'll be able to select object states on the Rollovers palette.

Control behaviors

The simplest control behaviors that you can add to an animation are Stop and Play. Stop stops the playing of an individual object animation or the entire composition. Play plays an individual object animation or the entire composition. We will show you how to create Stop and Play behavior events.

➤ A Target pop-up menu will be available in the Edit Behaviors dialog box for control behaviors like Stop, Play, and Change State (Fig. 1). Only time-independent objects or the Composition will appear on this menu. Objects that are not time-independent are controlled by the composition and therefore cannot be directly targeted or controlled by behaviors.

The Change State behavior

If you create a behavior event anywhere in the timeline and then choose the Change

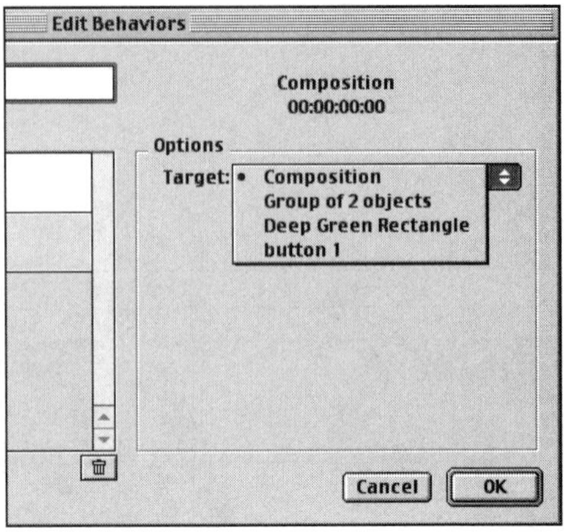

*1 ➤ The **Target** pop-up menu in the Edit Behaviors dialog box is available for some behaviors.*

State behavior, an object with more than one state will automatically change to another of its states without requiring any user interaction.

In the Edit Behaviors dialog box, choose the Change State behavior from the Add Behavior pop-up menu, choose an object with multiple states from the Target pop-up menu, then choose the state to be changed to from the State pop-up menu. After a few frames, you can create another behavior event, then choose Change State to restore the button to its normal state. This behavior could be used to visually alert the viewer that a button has other states so the viewer knows to interact with the button.

The Change State behavior can also be used to change an object's appearance in an animation. To do this, either create another object state with property changes for that state or substitute another image altogether (see page 142). The changes will be visible while the Change State behavior executes.

When the Change State behavior is executed in an animation, only behavior events that are attached to other states for that object will execute; behavior events that are attached to the state you change to won't execute.

Navigation behaviors

The "Go to" behaviors are used to help the viewer navigate within the timeline of the current animation or to navigate to a different Web page or site.

Go to Label moves the current time marker to a specific behavior event label in the main timeline or in any independent timeline.

Go to Relative Time moves the current time marker forward or backward by the number of frames specified when this behavior is chosen.

➤ Both the Go to Label and Go to Relative Time behaviors merely move the time marker. They do not cause the animation to resume playing.

Go to URL links to a specified Web URL when the animation is viewed in a browser.

Next, we offer three tutorials that will help you learn how to use behaviors. In the first tutorial, you will create a button that plays an animation when it is rolled over. In the second tutorial, you will create an animation that plays, pauses, and then continues with the next scene when a button is clicked. And in the third tutorial, you will create buttons that play separate time-independent object animations.

Tutorial 1

To create a button-controlled animation

CREATE THE OBJECTS AND THE ANIMATION

1. Choose File menu > New (Command-N/Ctrl-N), enter a Width and Height; make the Frame Rate 15; choose Export: Entire Composition; check the Make HTML box; then click OK.
2. Create a button shape and move it to one side of the composition. Create three other objects for the animation and move them to the other side of the composition.
3. Show the Timeline editor (Command-T/Ctrl-T). Select and rename each animation object individually (see page 155).
4. Select the objects to become animation loops. Choose Timeline menu > Time Independent. Each object now has its own timeline (Fig. 1).
5. Drag the composition duration bar end point to 01s. Move the start point of each animation object away from 00s so that no objects are viewed at the first frame of the animation (Fig. 2). The objects can enter the composition any time at or after frame 00s-02f.
6. Animate each object. For example, you could make an object move across the composition (see pages 156–157); make another object enlarge while increasing in Object Opacity from 0% to 100%; then make a third object rotate back and forth (see pages 162 and 185).

1 ➤ The Timeline with two time-independent objects and their respective timelines.

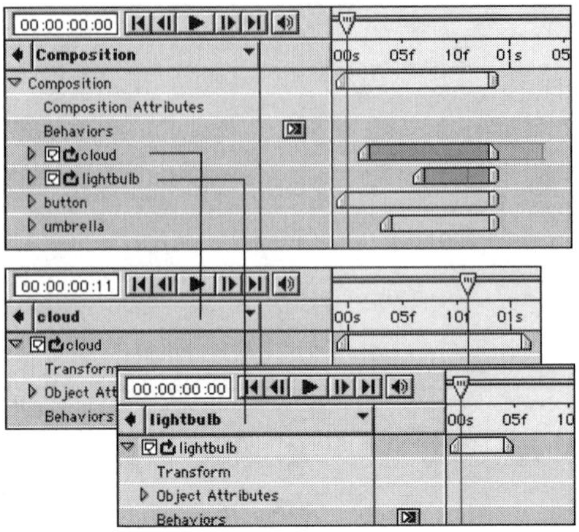

The cloud and lightbulb objects are both time-independent loops. The display of the bottom layer of the cloud object cycles on and off; colors cycle in the light bulb.

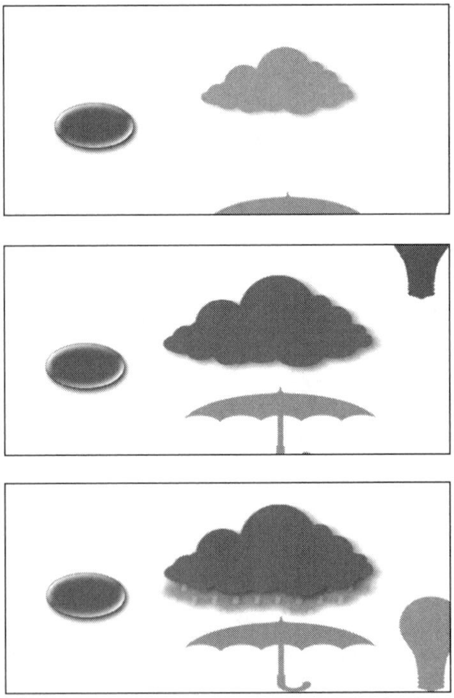

2 ➤ The animated objects in action. The cloud scales up and its opacity increases; its bottom layer is shown and then hidden; the umbrella moves up and scales up; the light bulb moves down along a curved path, then cycles between a dark and a light color.

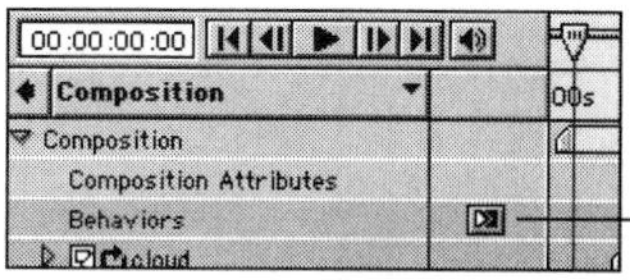

1 ➤ ***Behaviors*** *button*

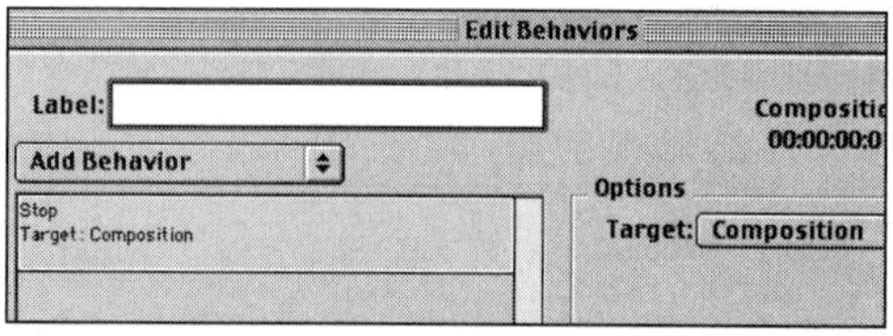

2 ➤ *The* ***Edit Behaviors*** *dialog box with the* ***Stop*** *behavior targeting the Composition.*

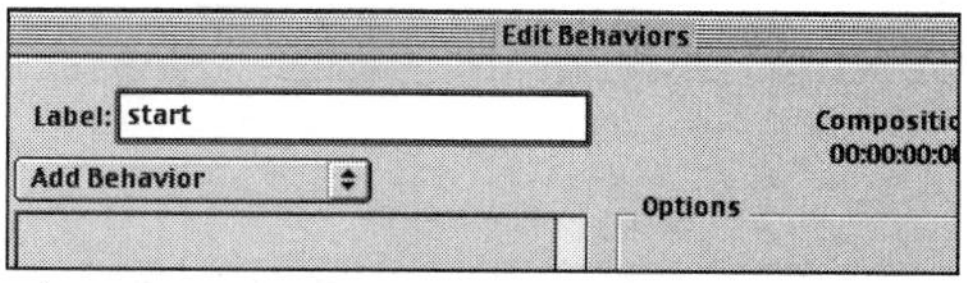

3 ➤ *Enter "start" as the* ***Label*** *in the Edit Behaviors dialog box.*

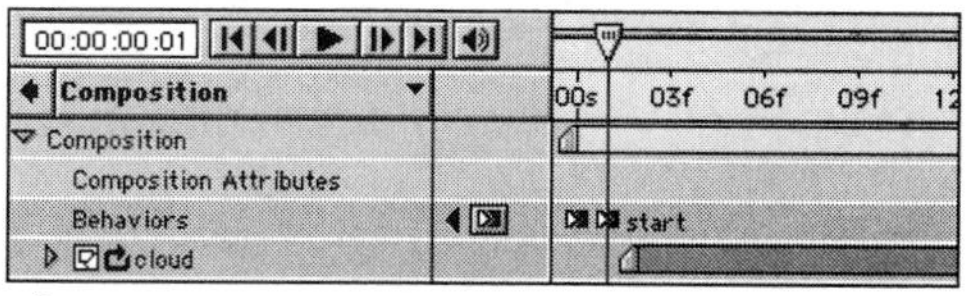

4 ➤ *The initial* ***Stop*** *behavior event and "****start****" behavior event label on the timeline.*

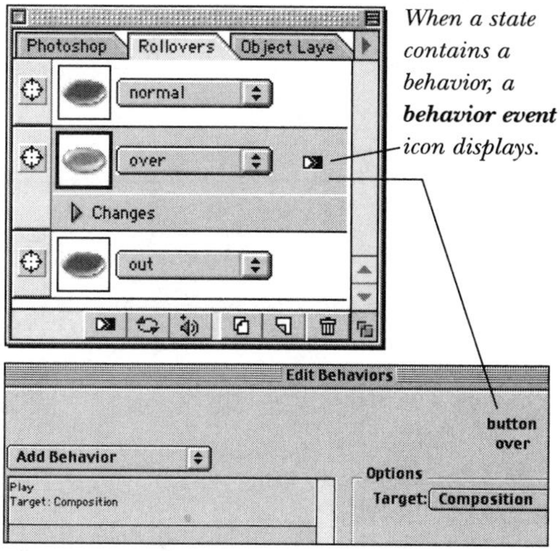

5 ➤ *The* ***Play*** *behavior is attached to the* ***Over*** *state.*

CREATE BEHAVIOR EVENTS FOR THE OBJECT STATES

1. Navigate back to the main composition timeline. Move the current time marker to 00s, then click the Behaviors button for the composition (Fig. 1).
2. In the Edit Behavior dialog box, choose Stop from the Add Behavior pop-up menu, choose Composition from the Target pop-up menu (Fig. 2), then click OK.
3. Move the current time marker to 00s-01f.
4. Click the Behaviors button, type the word "start" in the Label field, then click OK. A behavior event named "start" will appear on the Behaviors track (Figs. 3–4).
5. Select the button object. On the Rollovers palette, click the New Rollover State button to create an Over state.
6. Click the Edit Behaviors button at the bottom of the Rollovers palette.
7. Choose Play from the Add Behavior pop-up menu, choose Composition from the Target pop-up menu, then click OK (Fig. 5). Now the compositon and all animated objects within the composition will play back during the Over state.
8. Click the New Rollover State button to create a Down state, then choose Out from the state pop-up menu.
9. Click the Edit Behaviors button on the Rollovers palette.
10. Choose Go To Label from the Add Behavior pop-up menu, choose Composition from the Target pop-up menu, and choose start from the Label pop-up menu (Fig. 1, next page). Click OK.
11. Click the Preview mode button at the bottom of the Toolbox, then roll over the button. Click the Edit mode button when you're done. Save your file.

The animation will stop at frame 00s and will only proceed if the user rolls over the button object. The Over state

(Continued on the next page)

tells the composition to play. The Out state (mouse no longer over the object) tells the animation to go back to start and wait for a rollover.

The Out state does not cause the playback to go back to frame 00s, where the Stop behavior is located. The Stop behavior is used only at the start of the animation.

You've just created an interactive loop. ▲

➤ Don't forget to choose Export palette settings (try SWF format) and then test the animation using Preview In [browser].

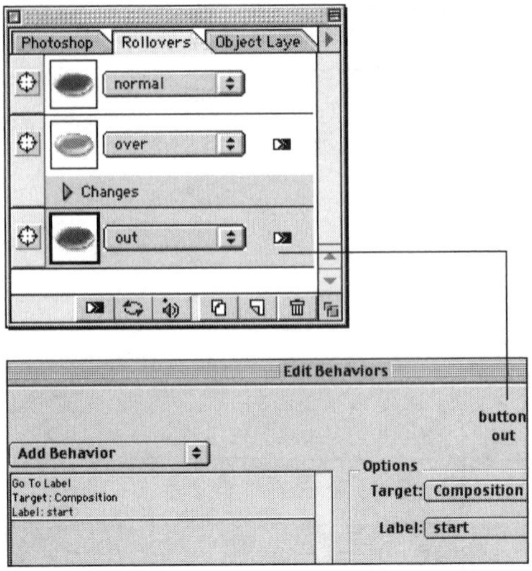

*1 ➤ The **Go To Label** behavior is attached to the Out state.*

Moving, deleting, and editing behavior events

To reposition a behavior event:

1. On the Timeline editor, click on the behavior event that you want to move.
2. Drag the event icon to a new position on the timeline (Fig. 2).

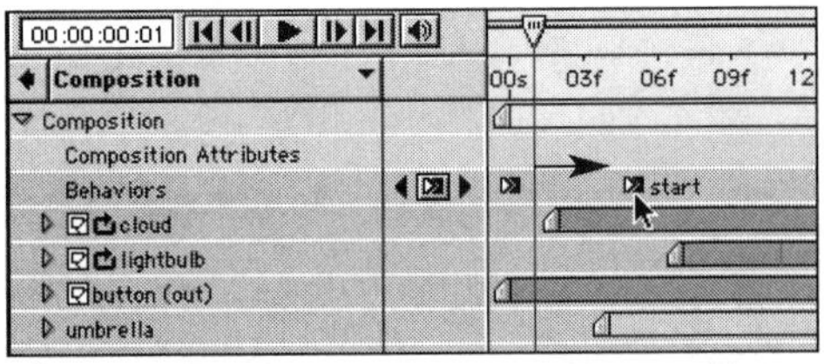

2 ➤ Drag a Behavior event icon to a new position.

To delete a behavior event:

1. On the Timeline editor, click on the behavior event that you want to delete.
2. Press Delete/Backspace.

➤ To remove an added behavior from the behavior list window in the Edit Behaviors dialog box, click the behavior you want to remove, then click the trash button in the dialog box (Fig. 3).

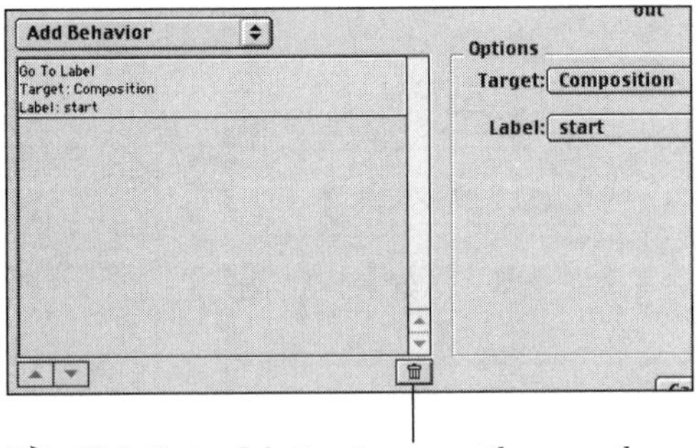

*3 ➤ Click the trash button to **remove** the currently highlighted behavior.*

To edit an existing behavior event:

1. On the Timeline editor, double-click a behavior event. (Open any independent timeline first, if necessary, to display the behavior event.)
   or
   Choose a rollover state on the Rollovers palette, then click the Edit Behaviors button at the bottom of the palette.
2. Make changes in the Edit Behaviors dialog box, then click OK.

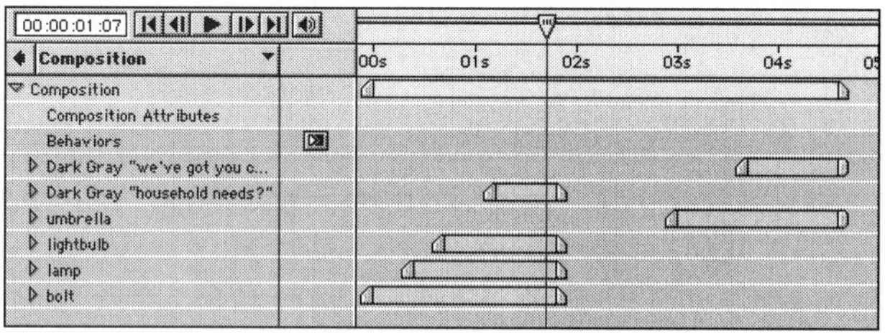

1 ➤ The objects for the animation are arranged in two separate areas of the timeline, with a time gap between them. The objects for the second animation start at the next full-second frame mark (03s), in our example.

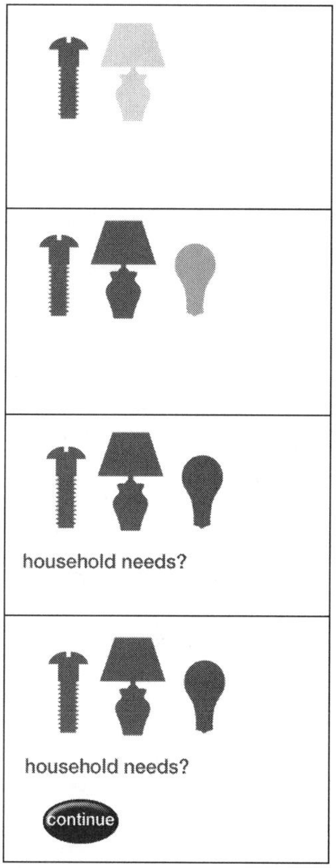

2 ➤ Our animation sequence for the first part of the timeline.

Tutorial 2

Create separate animation scenes

In this tutorial, you will attach a Go To Label behavior to a button's Down state. Clicking the button will enable a visitor go to the next scene in the animation timeline.

CREATE THE ELEMENTS OF ANIMATION

1. Create a composition with objects to be used in an animation or import two existing LiveMotion animation files using File menu > Place.
2. Show the Timeline editor (Command-T/ Ctrl-T).
3. Extend the composition duration bar to create enough time to play two consecutive animations, one after the other.
4. Position the duration bar start and end points for some of the objects (or for an animation group) so they occur within the first two or three seconds.

   Position the duration bar start and end points for the remaining objects (or animation group) so they occur within the last two or three seconds (Fig. 1).
5. Leave a time gap of approximately one second in the timeline to create a break between what will become scene 1 and scene 2. Start scene 2 objects at the next full-second frame mark on the timeline (Fig. 1). The time gap will only contain the composition duration bar and any background objects you may want to remain visible for the entire animation.

   The amount of time you allocate for the gap isn't important. One or two frames

(Continued on the next page)

would also work. We just happen to like having scene 2 start when the frame count starts again at 0f.

6. Create animations with the objects in the first part of the timeline (Fig. 2, previous page).
7. Create animations with the object in the second part of the timeline (Fig. 1).
8. *Optional:* Create any objects that will remain visible for the entire animation, and drag their duration bars so they're the same length as the composition.
9. Create a button object. Set its duration end point so it's at the end of the first part of the animation on the timeline. Move its start point to a few frames before the end point (Fig. 2).
10. Click the button object on the objects hierarchy list, press Return/Enter, type "button 1," then click OK.
11. Create a text object that contains the word "continue." Position and scale the text object so it fits over the button you created in step 9 (Fig. 2, previous page).

CREATE BEHAVIOR EVENTS FOR THE ANIMATION

1. Move the current time marker to 00s.
2. Click the Behaviors button for the composition, enter "scene 1" in the Label field, then click OK.
3. Move the current time marker to the end of the first animation part, then click the Behaviors button. Enter the word "stop1," choose Stop from the Add Behavior pop-up menu, choose Composition from the Target pop-up menu, then click OK (Fig. 3).

   The composition playback will stop at this point, due to the behavior event you just added. Next, to make the composition playback resume, you will attach a behavior event to the Down state for button 1.
4. Move the current time marker to the start of the second animation part. Click

1 ➤ Our animation sequence for the second part of the timeline.

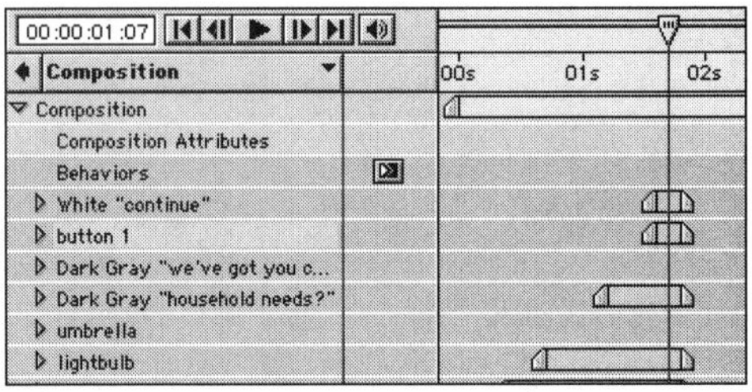

2 ➤ The button object and the "continue" text object are positioned at the end of the first animation.

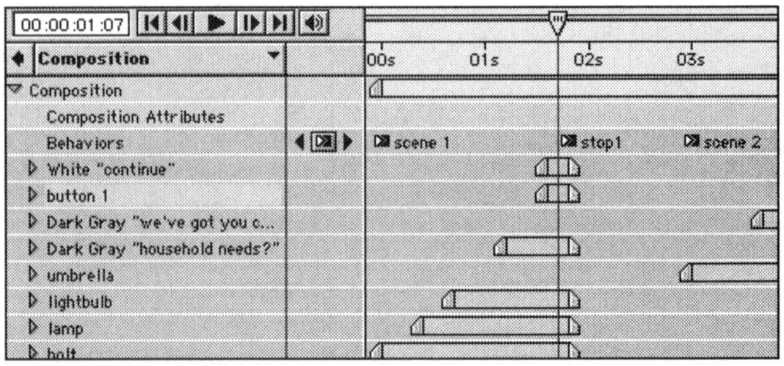

3 ➤ The stop1 behavior event contains the Stop behavior; the other two event labels are used by the Go To Label behavior.

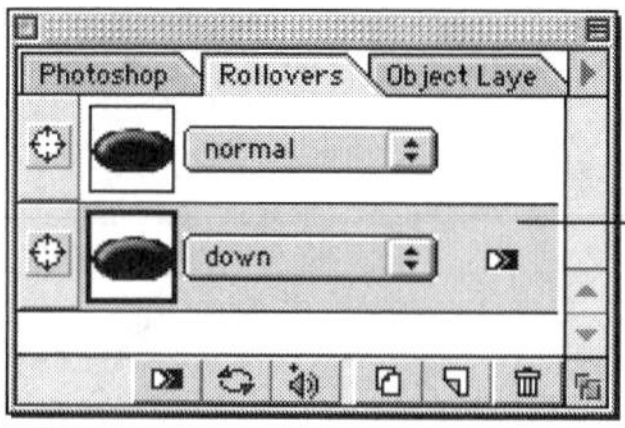

1➤ *The Down state on the Rollovers palette.*

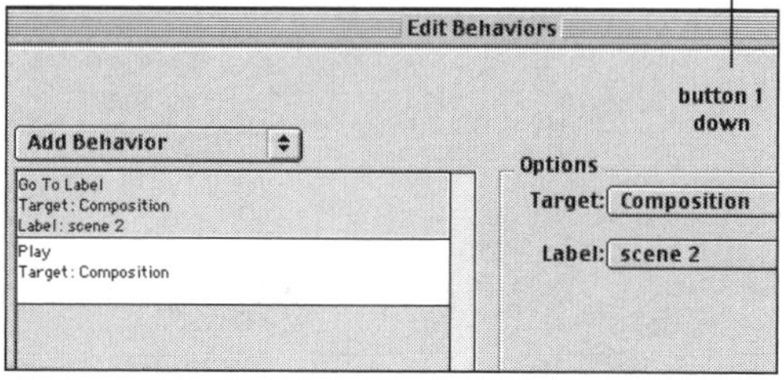

2➤ *Two behaviors are attached to button 1's Down state.*

3➤ *In Preview mode, click on the button 1 object in the composition to activate the Go To behavior that's attached to its Down state. The animation will advance from the stop1 label to the scene 2 label. The Play behavior will cause the second part of the animation to start playing.*

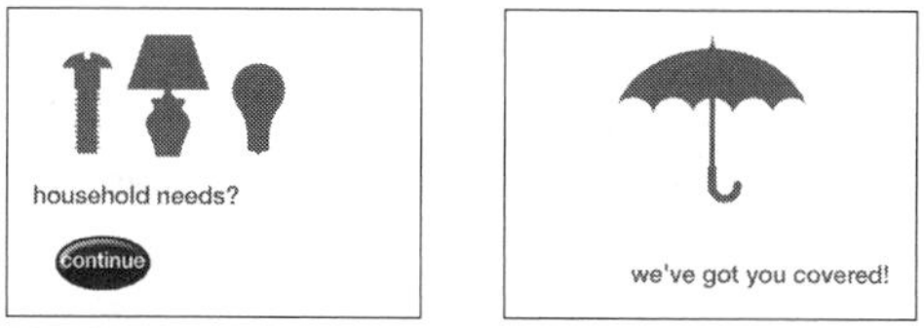

The first part of the animation ends here.

The second part of the animation starts here.

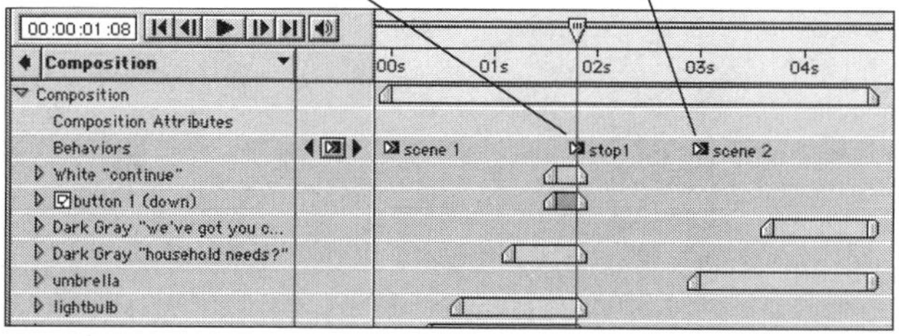

the Behaviors button, enter "scene 2" in the Label field, then click OK.

5. Position the current time marker over the button 1 duration bar and select the button 1 name on the objects hierarchy list.
6. Show the Rollovers palette, then click the New Rollover State button.
7. Choose Down from the state pop-up menu.
8. Click the Edit Behaviors button at the bottom of the Rollovers palette (Fig. 1).
9. Choose Go To Label from the Add Behavior pop-up menu, choose Composition from the Target pop-up menu, then choose scene 2 from the Label pop-up menu (Fig. 2).
10. Choose Play from the Add Behavior pop-up menu, then choose Composition from the Target pop-up menu (Fig. 2). If necessary, click the down arrow at the bottom of the behavior list window to move the Play behavior below the Go To Label behavior on the list.

    The Play behavior only works when it's placed after the Go To behavior on the behavior list. A Go To navigation behavior will only reposition the current time marker. A Play behavior is needed to make the composition resume playing; a separate Play behavior is needed to make an independent object start playing.
11. Click the Preview mode button at the bottom of the Toolbox. When the animation stops, click the Continue button (Fig. 3). Click the Edit mode button when you're done. Save your file. ▲

Tutorial 3

Make two buttons play separate animations using behavior events

In this tutorial, you will create two buttons. Each button will play and stop a separate time-independent object—not the whole composition.

CREATE THE OBJECTS

1. Create two button objects. Position them near one edge of the composition.
2. Show the Timeline editor (Command-T/Ctrl-T).
3. Select and rename each object on the objects hierarchy list (call them "button 1" and "button 2" or some other names so you will be able to tell them apart).
4. Move the current time marker to about 00s-05f. Create some objects and change their properties to make them into a collection of animated objects (Figs. 1–2). Select all the animation objects on the objects hierarchy list (not the buttons!), then choose Timeline menu > Make Time Independent Group (Command-Shift-G/Ctrl-Shift-G)(Fig. 3).
   or
   Import an existing LiveMotion animation file using File menu > Place, then, with the imported group selected, choose Timeline menu > Time Independent.
5. Rename the group "group animation 1." The objects are now an independent group. First, this will help to keep them organized. Second, it will remove the objects and their Transform properties from the main composition timeline so they aren't controlled by the main composition. And third, it will make it possible to use behaviors to target the group.
6. Move the current time marker to approximately 01s-05f. Create more objects and change their properties to make them into animated objects, or import another LiveMotion animation file (Fig. 4). The first and second animations don't have to be the same length.

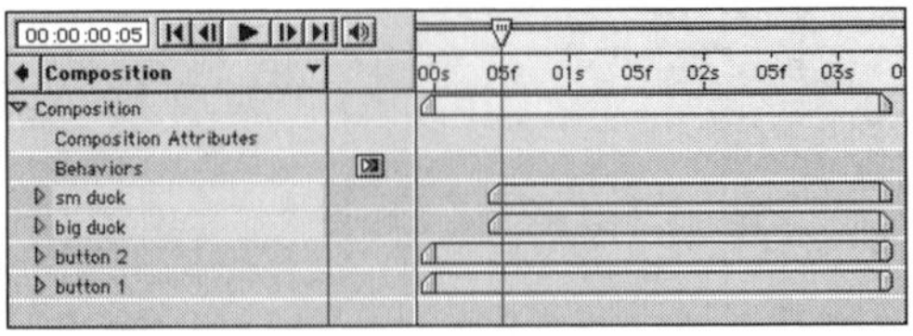

1 ➤ Two objects are created for animation 1.

2 ➤ The animation 1 objects move toward each other, then away from each other.

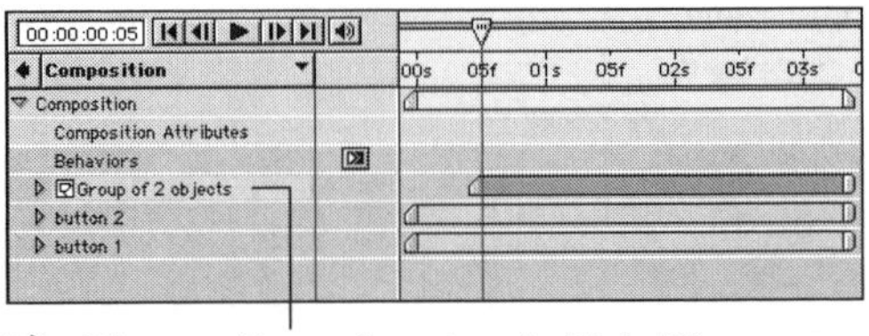

3 ➤ The two objects after using the Make Time Independent Group command.

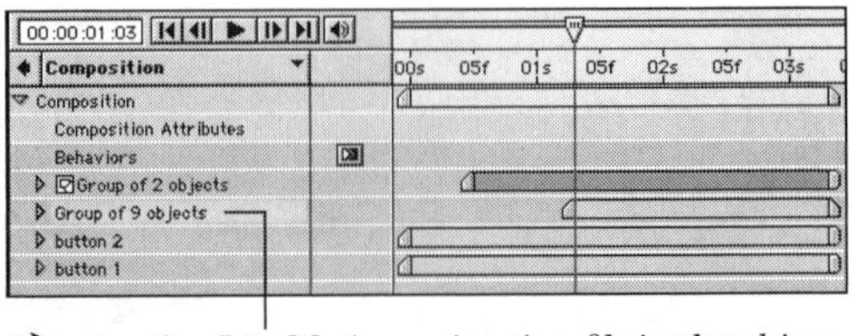

4 ➤ Another LiveMotion animation file is placed into the composition. The file comes in as a group.

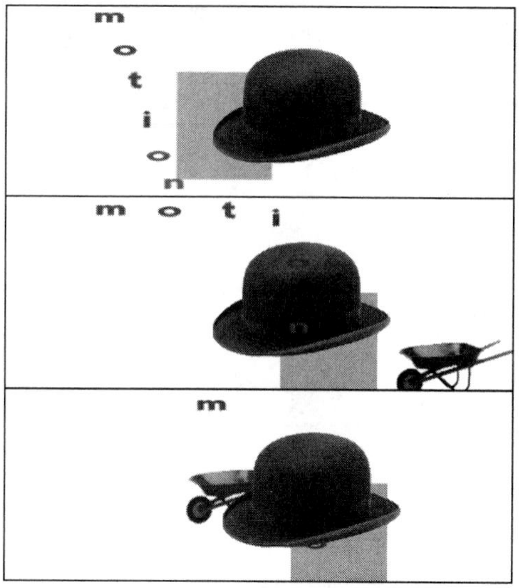

1 ➤ *The group animation 2 objects either remain stationary or move across the screen.*

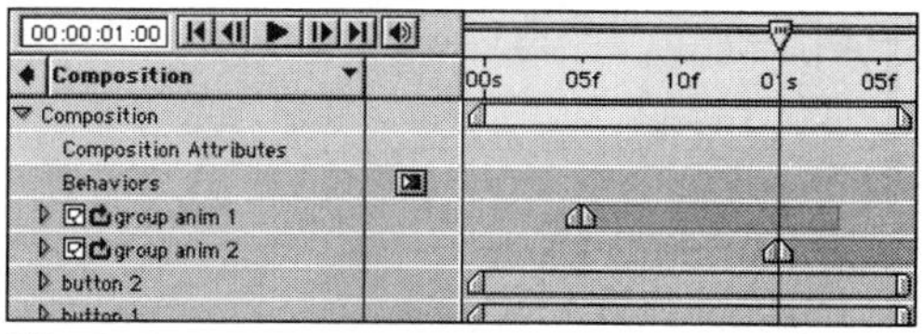

2 ➤ *Both animation groups are now time-independent objects, and looping is turned on for both. Since they are time-independent loops, the group's duration can be reduced to just one frame.*

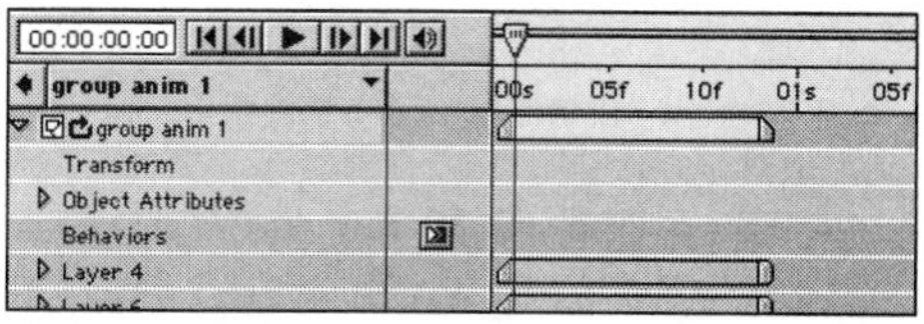

3 ➤ *Double-click a group name to reveal its timeline so you can edit the existing animation loop.*

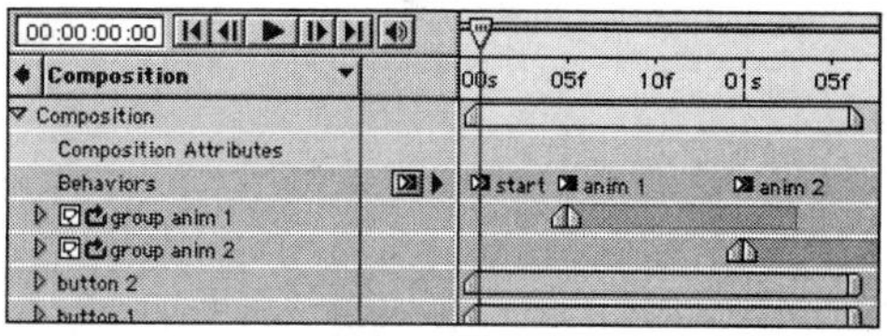

4 ➤ *The three behavior event labels on the timeline.*

7. Select all the new animation objects on the objects hierarchy list (not the buttons or group animation 1!). Choose Timeline menu > Make Time Independent Group (Command-Shift-G/Ctrl-Shift-G). *Note:* If the objects are already grouped, choose Timeline menu > Time Independent instead. Rename the group "group animation 2" (Fig. 1).
8. Shrink the duration bar of the group animation 1 object down to one frame, and move it to 00s-05f. Click the Loop button on the Timeline editor to make the group loop.
9. Shrink the duration bar of the group animation 2 object down to one frame, and move it to around 01s. Click the Loop button to make the group loop.

   The timeline should now have four objects: two buttons and two independent-looping groups. The duration of the button object should be the same as the duration of the composition (Figs. 2–3).

ATTACH BEHAVIOR EVENT LABELS TO THE TIMELINE

1. Move the current time marker to 00s. Click the Behaviors button, enter "start" in the Label field, then click OK.
2. Position the current time marker on the group animation 1 object. Click the Behaviors button, enter "anim 1" in the Label field (or another appropriate name), then click OK.
3. Position the current time marker on the group animation 2 object. Click the Behaviors button, enter "anim 2" in the Label field (or another appropriate name), then click OK (Fig. 4).

ATTACH BEHAVIOR EVENTS TO THE BUTTONS

1. Select the button 1 object name.
2. Show the Rollovers palette, then click the New Rollover State button. Make property changes, if desired, to mark the change of state.

(Continued on the next page)

3. Select the Over state on the Rollovers palette, then click the Edit Behaviors button.
4. Add a Go To Label behavior, Target: Composition, Label: anim 1.
5. Add a Play behavior, Target: group animation 1, then click OK (Fig. 1).
6. Click the New Rollover State button at the bottom of the Rollovers palette, then choose Out from the state pop-up menu.
7. Click the Edit Behaviors button on the Rollovers palette, then add a Stop behavior, Target: group animation 1.
8. Add a Go To Label behavior, Target: Composition, Label: start, then click OK (Fig. 2).
9. Select button 2, and repeat steps 2–9 above, but with the following modifications: step 4, add a Go To Label behavior, Target: Composition, Label: **anim 2**; step 5, add a Play behavior, Target: **group animation 2**; step 7, add a Stop behavior, Target: **group animation 2**.

PREVENT THE COMPOSITION AND OBJECTS FROM PLAYING AT THE START

1. Double-click the "start" behavior event.
2. Add a Stop behavior, Target: Composition.
3. Click OK (Fig. 3).
4. Click the Preview mode button at the bottom of the Toolbox, then roll over the buttons to preview the separate animations. Click the Edit mode button when you're done. Save your file!

The animation is fine, except for one detail. When you roll off a button, the independent animations are not going back to their starting point. If you like this "continue from" feature—great. If not, you can use a behavior event to instruct the animations to go back to the start of their time-independent timelines.

"REWIND" THE ANIMATION LOOPS

1. Double-click the group animation 1 object.

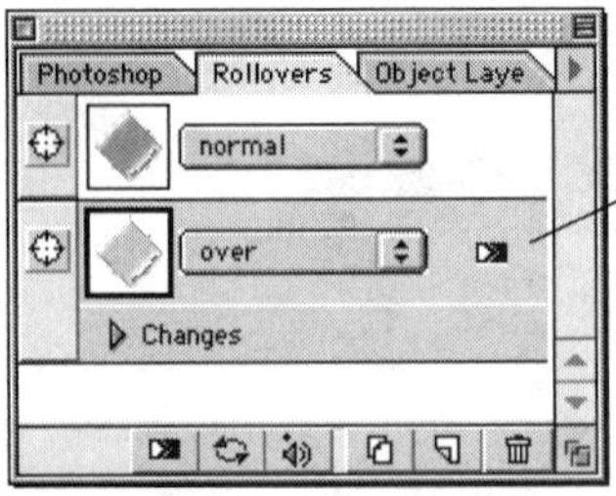

An Over state is created on the Rollovers palette.

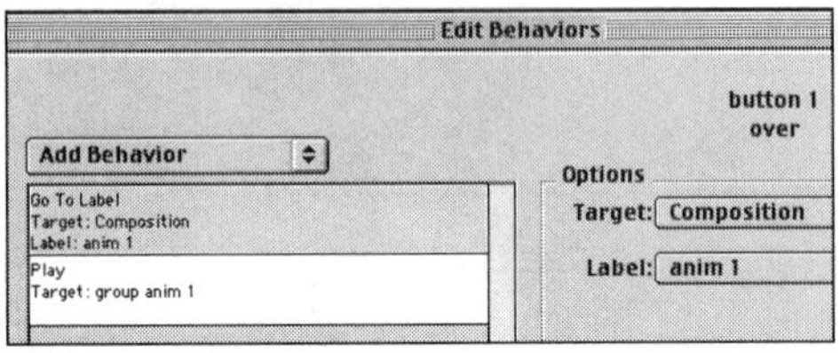

1 ➤ The Go To Label and Play behaviors are attached to the Over state.

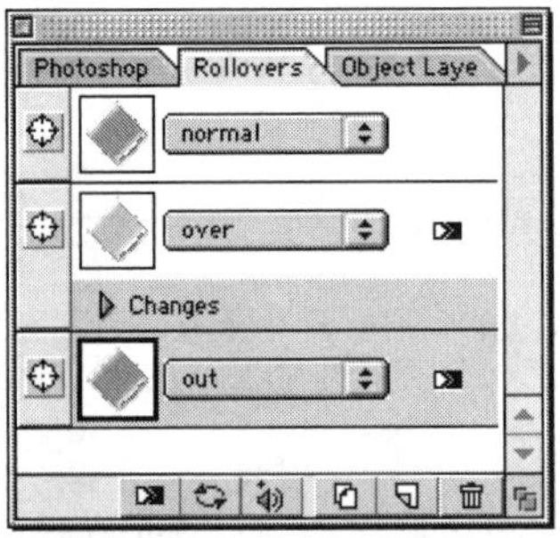

2 ➤ An Out state is created on the Rollovers palette. The Stop and Go To Label behaviors are attached to the Out state.

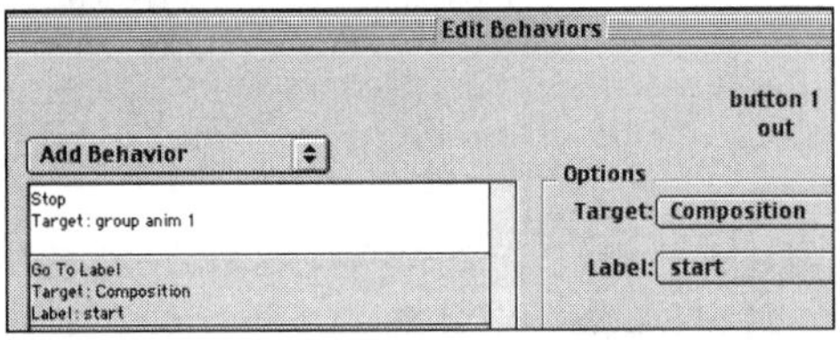

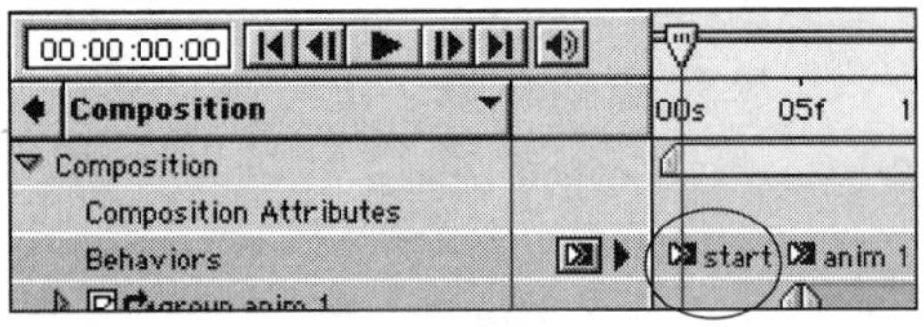

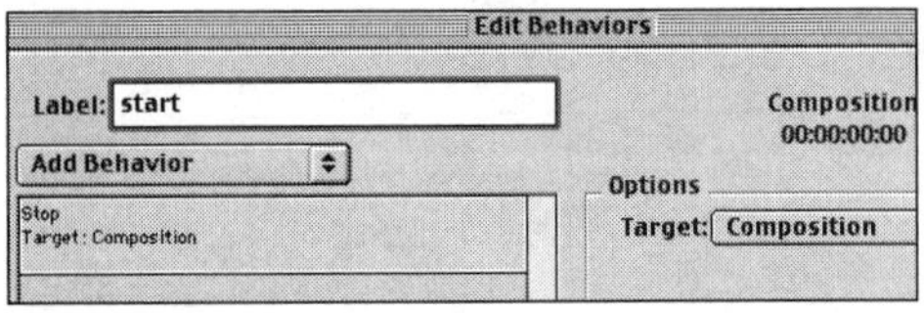

3 ➤ Double-click the start behavior event label. Add a Stop behavior in the Edit Behaviors dialog box.

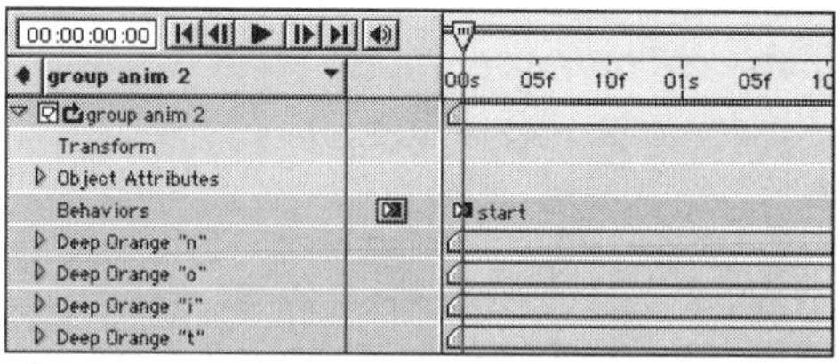

1 ➤ Create a behavior event label at 00s on a time-independent group's timeline.

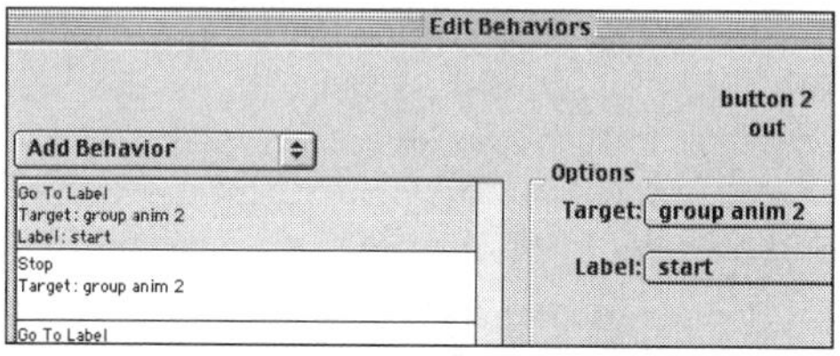

2 ➤ Click the Out state for the button that controls the play of the animation, click the Edit Behaviors button, add a Go To Label behavior, then Target the group, Label: start (the new label you just created).

2. On its timeline, move the timeline marker to 00s. Click the Behaviors button on the timeline.
3. Enter "start" in the Label field, then click OK (Fig. 1). *Note:* It's okay if two labels have the same name, as long as they are in different timelines.
4. Navigate back to the main composition timeline, then click button 1 on the list.
5. On the Rollovers palette, click the Out state, then click the Edit Behaviors button on the same palette.
6. Add a Go To Label behavior, Target: group animation 1; Label: start, then click OK (Fig. 2).
7. Double-click the group animation 2 object. Repeat steps 2–6 for group animation 2 and button 2 with the following modification: step 4, click on **button 2** on the list; step 6, add a Go To Label behavior, Target: **group animation 2**, Label: start. Now the tutorial is really and truly finished. ▲

➤ If you change the name of a group object on the objects hierarchy list, any behaviors that targeted the old name will automatically target the new name.

If you change the name of a behavior event label on the timeline, though, any existing Go To Label behaviors will not automatically target the new name. You need to update the Label: pop-up menu in the Edit Behaviors dialog box that's being used by those behaviors.

The other navigation behaviors listed on the Add Behavior pop-up menu are Go To Relative Time and Go To URL.We'll show you how to use both.

To add the Go to Relative Time behavior:

1. In an animation, position the current time marker (or double-click an independent object and position the current time marker), then click the Behaviors button.
   or
   On the Rollovers palette, click a state other than Normal, then click the Edit Behaviors button.
2. In the Edit Behaviors dialog box, choose Add Behaviors: Go To Relative Time.
3. Choose Composition or an independent object from the Target pop-up menu to use the timeline for either one as the reference point for the time movement.
4. Choose Forward or Backward from the Time pop-up menu for the direction of movement.
5. Enter the number of frames you want to move in the Frame(s) field.
6. Click OK.

To add a Go to URL behavior:

1. In an animation, position the current time marker, then click the Behaviors button.
   or
   On the Rollovers palette, select an object state other than Normal, then click the Edit Behaviors button.
2. In the Edit Behaviors dialog box, choose Go To URL from the Add Behaviors pop-up menu.
3. Enter the URL in the URL field.
4. Enter which browser frame the URL link will load into or choose a standard frame (_parent, _top, _self, or _blank) from the pop-up menu, then click OK.

Advanced behavior: Load Movie

Use the **Load Movie** behavior to load external movies into the current animation when they're viewed online. The external movie can be a LiveMotion file exported in **SWF** format or an animation file saved in SWF format from another application.

The external file can be located at another Web address. In this case, enter the entire **URL** for the file in the Edit Behaviors dialog box. You can also use a relative URL to load a SWF file that resides in the same folder as the current exported LiveMotion animation file. In this case, enter the entire file name in the Edit Behaviors dialog box.

Click **Replace** to make the imported movie replace the existing animation. The current animation will stop immediately when the movie loads and starts playing. Or click Append to layer the imported movie onto the existing animation.

With Append chosen, enter a number in the **Layer** field to make the imported movie fit into any existing stack of other imported movies. If you choose a layer number that is already occupied by an imported movie, the existing imported movie will be replaced by the incoming movie.

To preview this behavior, you must export the LiveMotion animation file in SWF format and then open that SWF file in a browser. (Don't just use LiveMotion's Preview In command.) In order for this behavior to work, the Flash plug-in must be installed for your browser.

Export 16

Two ways to export

To export an entire **composition**, use File menu > **Export** or **Export As**. You can choose different optimization settings for individual objects within a composition (see pages 251–257).

To export an object (or objects), select it (or them), then use File menu > **Export Selection** (see page 258).

Exporting LiveMotion files

YOU'VE CREATED A MASTERPIECE, but it won't be of much use until it's optimized and exported. Then it will be ready for a Web page design program (e.g., Adobe GoLive or Macromedia).

LiveMotion gives you many options for optimization and export. In the optimization process, you will choose a file format and various settings for that particular format. The export step is simply a save operation using those optimization settings. You can export your composition as a single file or you can export objects individually with different optimization settings.

LiveMotion will create an HTML file that will arrange the various elements of your composition in an HTML table so it will look the same in a Web browser as it did when you created it in LiveMotion. You can easily copy that HTML code and paste it into a Web page design program like Adobe GoLive or Macromedia Dreamweaver or you can import the exported file into the site folder of either of those programs.

You can also use LiveMotion to create rollovers and image maps. The program will generate the appropriate HTML file to make interactivity possible.

If you have a large number of graphics to create, you can also use LiveMotion to batch-generate them, saving you time and trouble.

- ➤ Even after you've exported your files for the Web, you'll want to be sure to save your original .liv file for future revisions.
- ➤ When you create a new document, the composition dialog box asks how you want to export the file. Don't worry—you can change these values later.

File types

Web browsers can't read the LiveMotion native .liv file format. So when you're ready to export your work, LiveMotion will allow you to choose from a variety of file types that browsers can read.

SWF *(pronounced "swiff")*
The SWF format is an animated graphics format that can be read by browsers in which the Flash plug-in is installed. Although many Web users already have the plug-in, if you use this format, you may want to include in your animation a link to Macromedia, where Web viewers can download the plug-in.

The SWF format saves information as vector images, and works well for images with sharp areas of definition and solid colors. However, many animations contain objects that aren't vectors. In this case, the SWF file will generate a series of JPEG, GIF, or PNG images and embed those images within the SWF file.

SVG
(Not yet available.) The Scalable Vector Graphics format is another vector format that will allow for such features as editable and searchable text; millions of colors; fills; gradients; animation; filters; raster and vector objects; and—because it is based on XML (Extensible Markup Language)—interactivity. SVG graphics should also render correctly if Web viewers wish to print them out. The SVG format can be read by browsers in which the SVG Viewer plug-in is installed. This format has been presented to the World Wide Web consortium for approval, and should be approved and available by year end.

JPEG *(pronounced "jaypeg")*
The JPEG format uses 24-bit color, and can therefore reproduce millions of colors. It works best for continuous-tone graphics with gradations of color, such as photos. It is a lossy compression scheme; some information is thrown away during compression.

The JPEG format is not a good choice for images that need consistent color and sharp

What is dithering?

Dithering is the side-by-side placement of two color pixels to create the impression of a third color. This technique is similar to the pointillist technique used by artists like Georges Seurat.

Dithering usually works best in continuous-tone images, like photographs. But in flat-color images, the results can be awful. If a browser can't display a particular color in your image, it will try to create that color with dots of color that the browser can produce. For this reason, it's often advisable to stick to the 216 Web-safe colors that all browsers can display, particularly for flat colors that dominate an image.

*1 ➤ You can choose from these six **file formats** on the **Export** palette pop-up menu.*

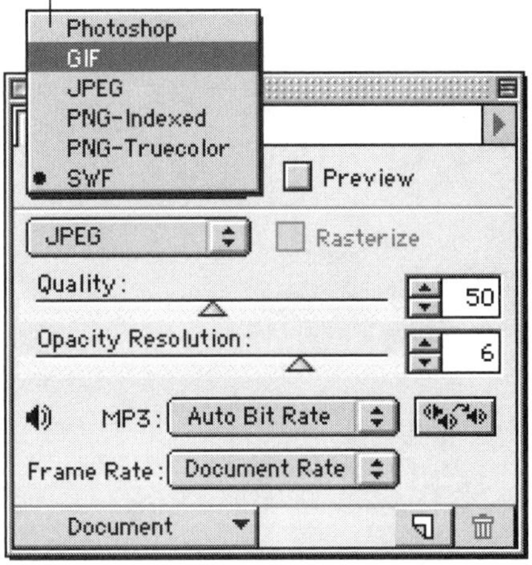

Plugging in

Keep in mind that not all your Web viewers will have the requisite plug-ins for viewing SWF, PNG, or SVG graphics. Although the Flash plug-in in particular is very popular, some users would sooner visit another site than take the time to download a new plug-in. To make your site accessible to the greatest number of people, consider creating an alternate version of your site using only the GIF or JPEG image format.

edges. For example, if you need the solid white tones in your image to remain solid white, don't save it as a JPEG. This format produces artifacts that can show up as smudges or miscolored pixels.

The JPEG file format doesn't support object animation. However, JPEG objects can be used in an animation which is then exported as a SWF. The JPEG object will be embedded into the SWF file.

Also remember that because JPEGs use 24-bit color, Web surfers who have monitors that can only produce hundreds or thousands of colors may notice dithering effects.

➤ Always export JPEG files from the original LiveMotion file. Every time you export a JPEG file, you lose information, so you should avoid re-importing and re-exporting JPEG images.

GIF *(pronounced "giff" or "jiff")*
The GIF formats works well for compressing images that contain solid areas of color or type. It supports 8-bit indexed color and a total of 256 colors. GIF supports one level of transparency if you are using an active matte or an alpha channel. With one level of transparency, a pixel can either be fully opaque or fully transparent. This format also supports animations. It is appropriate for small-scale animations, but for larger animations, the SWF format is preferable because it will often yield a smaller file size than GIF. The GIF format is lossless, so a GIF can be reimported and exported without losing image information.

PNG-INDEXED *(pronounced "ping")*
Also called PNG-8, the PNG-indexed format is similar to GIF in that it also supports 8-bit color and a lossless compression method. PNG-Indexed supports one level of transparency if you are using an active matte or an alpha channel. The PNG-Indexed format doesn't support animation, but like JPEG, PNG-Indexed objects can be embedded into a SWF file. The PNG-Indexed format

(Continued on the next page)

is currently supported by Internet Explorer 4.0 and 5.0. Earlier versions of Internet Explorer and Netscape Navigator versions 2.0 and later are supported via a plug-in.

PNG-TRUECOLOR

Like the JPEG format, the PNG-Truecolor format supports 24-bit color. But unlike JPEG, it uses a lossless compression method, meaning you can save and resave the same file without degrading image quality.

PNG-Truecolor works well for photographs and other images that contain a wide spectrum of color. It supports 256 levels of transparency. With 256 levels of transparency, each pixel can be anywhere from completely opaque to completely transparent, with 254 levels in between. Small bitmaps (smaller than 100 x 100 pixels) tend to compress efficiently using PNG-Truecolor. For larger bitmaps, JPEG usually works best. Like PNG-Indexed and JPEG, the PNG-Truecolor format doesn't support animation, but PNG-Truecolor objects can be embedded into a SWF file.

See the PNG-Indexed section for a list of browsers that support PNG-Truecolor.

PHOTOSHOP

When you choose this format, LiveMotion exports your work as a flattened bitmap image in Photoshop format. This format is useful if you want to create a supplementary, non-Web project based on your LiveMotion artwork (e.g., a printed brochure).

Bitmaps and vectors

Most object types will export as vector. These object types will export as bitmap:

- placed image object
- an object containing more than one layer
- texture on an object layer
- 3D effect on an object layer
- Double-burst gradient on an object layer

Small is best

At least for the time being, most Web viewers will access the Web site you're designing via a 56K modem. If the site takes too long for them to download, they will probably get restless and exit before they have a chance to glean any pearls of wisdom. A 100kb file takes 20 seconds to download on a 56K modem. **Keep your files small!**

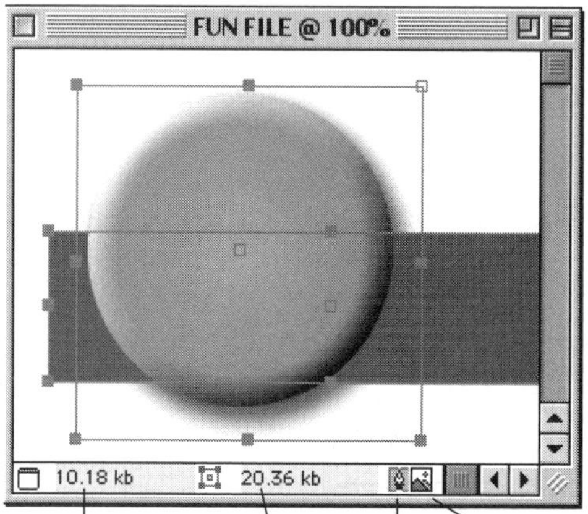

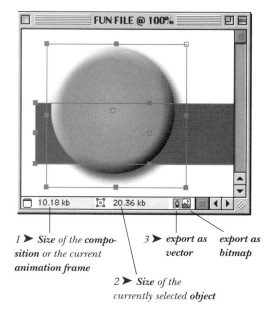

1 ➤ ***Size*** *of the* ***composition*** *or the current* ***animation frame***

2 ➤ ***Size*** *of the currently selected* ***object***

3 ➤ ***export as vector*** ***export as bitmap***

Previewing

You can preview how your composition will look in a Web browser, as well as view how any changes will affect file size, image quality, and download time, in Active Export Preview Mode.

Note: Although all the LiveMotion commands and tools function normally in Active Preview Mode, this mode also causes the program to run more slowly. For this reason, you're better off creating your composition with this feature turned off; turn it on only when needed.

To work in Active Export Preview mode:

Choose View menu > Active Export Preview (Command-9/Ctrl-9), or check the Preview box on the Export palette. If you look in the bottom-left corner of any LiveMotion composition/application window, the readout on the left is the size of the overall composition (Fig. 1).

If an object or group is currently selected (Selection tool or Subgroup selection tool), a size readout for that object or group will appear to the right of the composition size readout (Fig. 2). Selected objects have a red highlight border while Active Export Preview mode is on.

And finally, if an object is currently selected and SWF is chosen as the format on the Export palette, an icon will appear next to the above-mentioned readouts. The icon indicates whether the object will be exported as a bitmap object or vector object. If more than one object is selected and both icons appear, it means that at least one of the objects will export as bitmap and at least one of the objects will export as vector (Fig 3).

➤ If an object is currently selected and the object size readout is 0 bytes, try clicking Preview off and then on again or nudge the object to update the readout.

Exporting

Once your LiveMotion composition is finished and you have decided how you want to optimize the elements within it, you have a number of choices for bringing your file into an HTML document.

Choose from these options in the Composition Settings dialog box (Fig. 1):

Entire Composition exports the composition as one file.

➤ To export **animations**, the SWF format with the Entire Composition option and the Make HTML box checked would be our first choice. If for some reason you decide to export an animation as a GIF, choose Entire Composition for that format as well.

Trimmed Composition exports the smallest area encompassing all the objects in the composition. This option can reduce the file's final export size because it trims off unnecessary areas in the composition.

AutoSlice exports each object or group of objects as a separate image slice and creates an images folder and an HTML file (except if you choose the SWF format). Use this option to export objects or a group as separate image slices arranged in a column—not in the current layout. The exported image slices can be rearranged in a Web page design program (e.g., GoLive). If you export using AutoSlice and the SWF format, the entire composition will export—not individual objects.

AutoLayout slices a composition on export and preserves its layout in an HTML table in an HTML file. A separate images folder is also generated. Keep in mind that if you use this function with a GIF, JPEG, PNG-Indexed, or PNG-Truecolor file, the topmost object in a slice determines the slice's composition settings. Use this option when exporting a GIF file. In a Web page design program (e.g., GoLive), the export file will display as image slices arranged in an editable HTML table.

To HTML or not to HTML

You can choose whether to create an HTML file when you select Entire Composition or Trimmed Composition. If your composition contains elements that need HTML in order to function properly (such as an image map or a rollover), you should create an HTML file. Choosing AutoSlice or AutoLayout will always generate an HTML page whether the Make HTML box is checked or not.

Read the readout

If Entire Composition is chosen with the GIF or JPEG format, only a single GIF or JPEG file will be exported, so only a composition size readout will display at the bottom of the composition/application window.

If Entire Composition is chosen for the SWF format, an object size readout (greater than zero) will display, because you can choose object settings for each object in the composition for a SWF.

If AutoLayout is chosen with the GIF, JPEG, or PNG format, an object size readout will display because you can choose settings for each object that is placed into an exported HTML layout table.

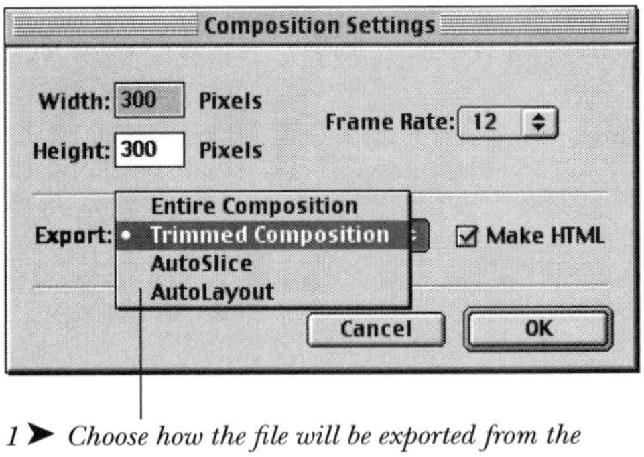

1 ➤ Choose how the file will be exported from the ***Export*** *pop-up menu in the* ***Composition Settings*** *dialog box. This setting can be changed at any time.*

Color palettes

If you have chosen to export your composition or any object as a **GIF**, **PNG-Indexed**, or **SWF** with an Indexed Color file, you will need to choose a color palette. The color palette determines which colors will be available for your image to use.

PERCEPTUAL
Creates a custom palette by giving priority to colors to which the human eye is most sensitive. Use when you want the most accurate color and you aren't concerned about Web-safe color.

SELECTIVE
Creates a custom palette that uses the colors that appear most often in the image. This option can be used for images for which the perceptual color palette would also be appropriate.

WEB ADAPTIVE
Creates a custom palette by shifting image colors to Web-safe colors.

WEB
Uses the 216 Web-safe colors that appear on all Windows and Mac platforms. Use this option when you want colors to render accurately on the Web, and you have mostly solid blocks of color, as this option doesn't reproduce subtle gradations very well.

WIN
Uses the Windows system's default 8-bit color palette. Use this option only if all the site's visitors will be on a Windows system.

MAC
Uses the Mac OS system's default 8-bit color palette. Use this option only if all the site visitor's will be on a Mac.

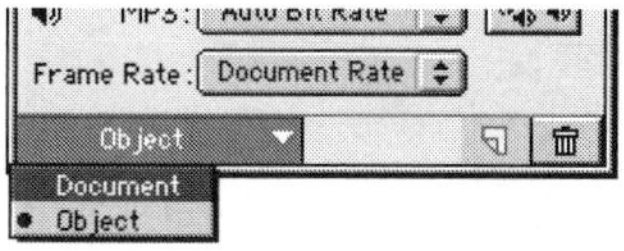

*1 ➤ Choose **Document** from the drop-down menu.*

Starting on this page and continuing through page 257, we show you how to choose Export palette settings for the GIF, PNG-Indexed, JPEG, PNG-Truecolor, and SWF file formats.

To export a GIF or PNG-Indexed file:

1. Open the Export palette by choosing File menu > Export Settings (Command-Option-Shift-E/Ctrl-Alt-Shift-E) or by choosing Window menu > Export.
2. Check the Preview box to turn on Active Export Preview mode so you can see how different settings will affect file sizes.
3. First, to choose settings for the entire composition, leave Document as the choice on the drop-down menu at the bottom of the palette (Fig. 1). (You can choose settings for individual objects later.)
4. Choose GIF or PNG-Indexed from the topmost pop-up menu (Figs. 2–3, next page).
5. Choose a color palette for the object or composition from the next pop-up menu (see the sidebar).
6. To specify how many colors you want the optimized image to contain, choose a Colors value (2–256). Larger values increase file size, but might be necessary for the image to display well.

➤ Shift-drag the Colors slider to force it to snap to commonly used color depth values.

7. Press the Include Transparency Info button to include in export any alpha channel or active matte that is used to produce object transparency in the file.
8. *Optional:* Press the Dither button. Dithering can improve the appearance of gradations, but it can also make an image look dotty. It also increases the file size.
9. *Optional:* Press the Interlace button if you'd like viewers to see a low-resolution version of the image while the higher-resolution version is downloading.

(Continued on the next page)

10. If you are exporting an animated GIF, choose a Frame Rate (see the sidebar).
11. *Optional:* To choose optimization settings for an object (or objects) that differ from the document settings, select that object (or objects) in the composition, click the Create Object Settings button at the bottom of the palette (Fig. 1), then choose settings by following steps 4–10 on the previous page.
12. *Optional:* Choose optimization settings for other objects, as in the previous step. Click the Create Object Settings button each time before choosing settings.

    Note: To change the composition settings at any time, choose Document from the drop-down menu. If you reselect an object, choose Object from the drop-down menu to view its settings.
13. To actually export the file, choose File menu > Export (Command-E/Ctrl-E).
    or
    If the file has already been exported and you don't want to write over the exported file, choose File menu > Export As.
14. Enter a file name, choose a location in which to save the exported file, then click Save (Return/Enter).

➤ To delete a selected object's individual export settings, click the Delete Object Settings (trash) button (Fig. 1).

Choosing a frame rate

The frame rate controls how quickly the frames in your exported animation will display in a browser. The faster the frame rate, the smoother your animation will appear. If you choose to animate your document **Keyframes only**, only the Keyframes in your timeline will be animated—no in-between frames will be included. The animation will play back with abrupt transitions.

If you choose **Document Rate**, your animation will play at the rate chosen for the current document. All in-between frames will be included in playback, allowing for smooth transitions.

You can also choose a regular frame rate between 8 and 40 frames per second to play the animation back at a different rate than the one in which it was authored. The higher the frame rate, the faster the animation could potentially play back, but the larger will be its export file size and the longer will be its download time. The animation and all the parts within it will play only at one rate.

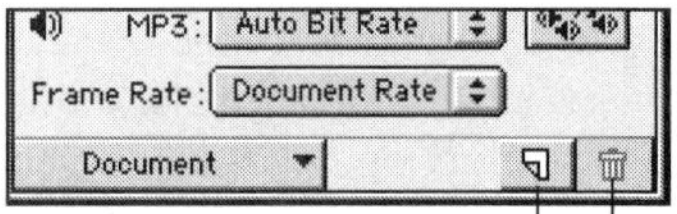

*1➤ Click the **Create Object Settings** button.*

*Click the **Delete Object Settings** button to remove the current settings from the selected object.*

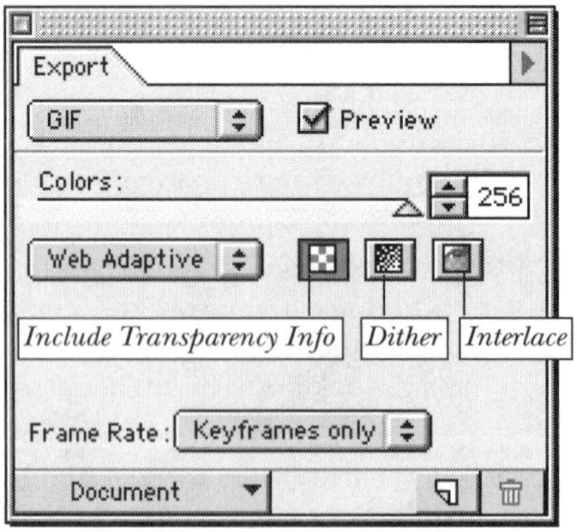

*2➤ The **Export** palette with **GIF** chosen as the file format. (The **Include Transparency Info** button is pressed.)*

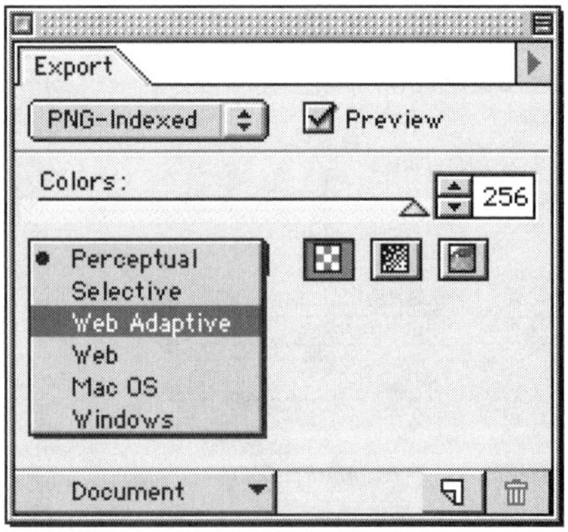

*3➤ The **Export** palette with **PNG-Indexed** chosen as the file format. The color palette pop-up menu is currently displayed.*

1 ➤ *The **Export** palette with **JPEG** chosen as the file format.*

To export a JPEG file:

1. Show the Export palette.
2. Check the Preview box to turn on Active Export Preview mode so you can see how different settings will affect file sizes.
3. Choose JPEG from the topmost pop-up menu (Fig. 1).
4. First, to choose settings for the entire composition, leave Document as the choice on the drop-down menu at the bottom of the palette. (You can choose settings for individual objects later.)
5. Choose a Quality value (0–100) to specify image quality. The higher the quality, the larger the file size.

   ➤ Shift-drag the Quality slider to snap it to increments of 10.
6. *Optional:* Check the Progressive box to export the image as a progressive JPEG. This way, viewers can see a low-resolution version of the image before the final image downloads completely.
7. *Optional:* Check the Reduce Chroma box to create a smaller JPEG file. This option discards every other pixel in the color range, but it usually doesn't visibly affect image quality. If it does, try raising the Quality.
8. *Optional:* Check the Optimized box to create a custom compression table for the image. The resulting file will be slightly smaller, but it will take longer to compress.
9. *Optional:* To choose optimization settings for an object that differ from the document settings, select that object in the composition, click the Create Object Settings button at the bottom of the palette, then choose settings by following steps 5–8, above (Fig. 1).
10. To choose optimization settings for other objects, select them one by one. Click the Create Object Settings button each time and choose settings as per the instructions above.

(Continued on the next page)

Note: To change the composition settings at any time, choose Document from the drop-down menu. If you reselect an object, choose Object from the drop-down menu to view its settings.

11. To actually export the file, choose File menu > Export (Command-E/Ctrl-E).
    or
    If the file has already been exported and you don't want to write over the exported file, choose File menu > Export As.
12. Enter a file name, choose a location in which to save the exported file, then click Save (Return/Enter).

To export a PNG-Truecolor file:

1. Show the Export palette.
2. Check the Preview box to turn on Active Export Preview mode so you can see how different settings will affect file sizes.
3. Choose PNG-Truecolor from the top-most pop-up menu (Fig. 1).
4. First, to choose settings for the entire composition, leave Document as the choice on the drop-down menu at the bottom of the palette. (You can choose settings for individual objects later.)
5. Press the Include Transparency Info button to include in export any alpha channel or active matte that was used to produce object transparency in the file.
6. *Optional:* Press the Interlace button to export an image that will first load at a low resolution and increase in quality as the image continues to download.
7. *Optional:* To choose optimization settings for an object that differ from the document settings, select that object in the composition, click the Create Object Settings button at the bottom of the palette, then choose settings by following steps 3–6, above.
8. To choose optimization settings for other objects, select them one by one. Click the Create Object Settings button

Fresh start

To delete a selected object's current export settings, click the **Delete Object Settings** (trash) button on the Export palette.

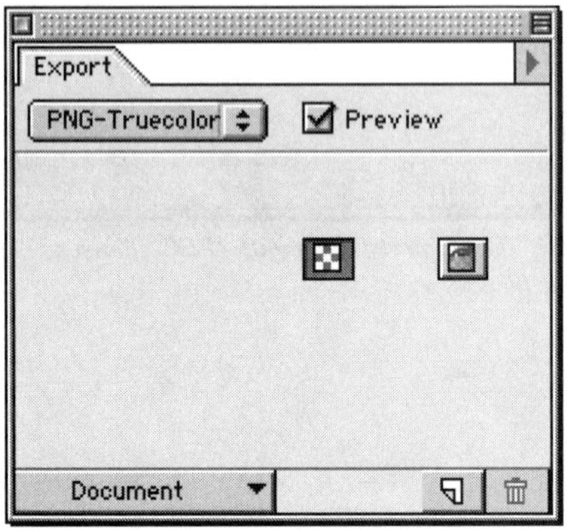

*1 ➤ The **Export** palette with **PNG-Truecolor** chosen as the file format.*

each time and choose settings as per the instructions above.

Note: To change the composition settings at any time, choose Document from the drop-down menu. If you reselect an object, choose Object from the drop-down menu to view its settings.

9. To actually export the file, choose File menu > Export (Command-E/Ctrl-E).
or
If the file has already been exported and you don't want to write over that exported file, choose File menu > Export As.

10. Enter a file name, choose a location in which to save the exported file, then click Save (Return/Enter).

To export a SWF file:

1. Show the Export palette.
2. Check the Preview box to turn on Active Export Preview mode so you can see how different settings will affect file sizes (Fig. 1).
3. Choose SWF from the topmost pop-up menu.
4. First, to choose settings for the entire composition, leave Document as the choice on the drop-down menu at the bottom of the palette. (You can choose settings for individual objects later.)
5. Choose the JPEG, Indexed, or Truecolor image format option for bitmapped images that your SWF file will embed.
6. If you chose **JPEG**, choose a Quality (0–100). The higher the Quality, the larger the file size. Specify the opacity resolution by dragging the slider or entering a value between 0 and 8 in the text box. High values will increase the quality of the image's colored areas. Smaller values will result in a smaller file size, but may cause color banding and a loss of transparency.
   or
   If you chose **Indexed**, choose your compression settings by following the instructions in the Export as a GIF or PNG-Indexed File section on pages 251–252. (*Note:* The Indexed option creates a GIF file, not a PNG-Indexed file.)
   or
   If you chose **Truecolor**, choose a color Resolution (bit-depth) for the image (1–8). A Resolution of 8 will create an image with millions of possible colors; a Resolution of 1 will create a black-and-white image. Specify the opacity resolution by dragging the slider or entering a value between 0 and 8 in the text box. High values will raise the quality of colored areas in the image. Smaller values will result in a smaller file size, but may cause color banding and a loss of transparency. The Truecolor option generates a PNG file.

Shop and compare

With Preview checked, select an object that will export as a bitmap (the bitmap icon is visible on the composition/application window). Try JPEG, Indexed, or Truecolor to see which option produces the smallest export size with acceptable image quality. Repeat for other objects.

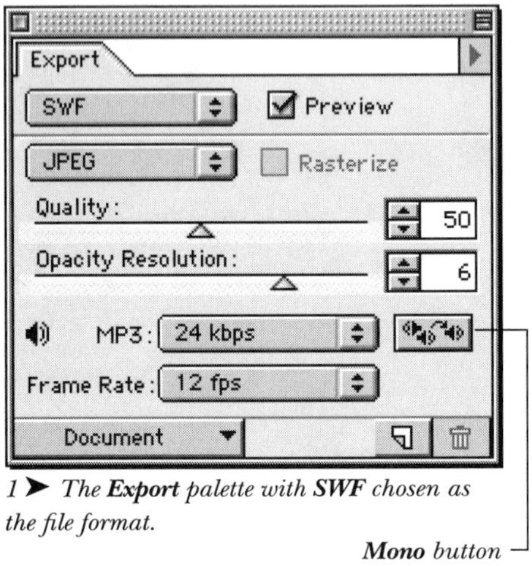

*1 ➤ The **Export** palette with **SWF** chosen as the file format.*

Background color problem

If you have a background color in your composition, it will also be exported. But if you export your composition as a SWF file, the bounding box around your image may display in a noticeably different color. This problem may be fixed in future releases of LiveMotion.

7. If your SWF file contains sound, choose the sound compression rate from the MP3 pop-up menu. Press the Mono button to decrease the file size.
8. Choose a frame rate from the Frame Rate pop-up menu.
9. *Optional:* To choose optimization settings for an object that differ from the document settings, select that object in the composition, click the Create Object Settings button at the bottom of the palette, then choose settings by following steps 5–6 on the previous page.
10. To choose optimization settings for other objects, select them one by one. Click the Create Object Settings button each time and choose settings as per the instructions above.

    Note: To change the composition settings at any time, choose Document from the drop-down menu. If you reselect an object, choose Object from the drop-down menu to view its settings.
11. To actually export the file, choose File menu > Export (Command-E/Ctrl-E).
    or
    If the file has already been exported and you don't want to write over the exported file, choose File menu > Export As.
12. Enter a file name, choose a location in which to save the exported file, then click Save (Return/Enter).

➤ When you choose object settings for a vector object, you can check the Rasterize box to export the object as a bitmap, but we don't really see the advantage to doing this.

LiveMotion also allows you to export specific objects or selections individually. This can be useful if you wish to use only specific elements of your composition on your Web page.

Note: Keep in mind that when you choose to export a selection, LiveMotion will export the smallest rectangle that encompasses the currently selected object. If other unselected objects overlap this rectangle, LiveMotion will also include the parts of those objects that overlap! The program will also export objects that are grouped with the selected object.

To export a selection:

1. Use the selection tool to select the objects or group of objects you want to export.
2. Show the Export palette, then choose file and compression settings (see pages 251–257).
3. Choose File menu > Export Selection.
4. Name your file, choose a location in which to save it, then click Save.

Web color palette

If you've ever created an image with millions of colors and then viewed your image on a monitor that can only display thousands or 256 colors, then you have some idea what Web-safe colors are all about.

No matter how few—or how many—colors a monitor can display, all monitors with at least eight bits of color can render 216 specific colors without dithering. This is because eight bits of color can be expressed as two to the eighth power, or 256. Subtract 40 for the colors that Mac and Windows systems reserve for other uses, and you're left with 216 colors that you can use with confidence in your Web graphics.

But keep in mind that not even these 216 colors will display in the same way on every machine. Windows and Mac systems use different color gamma values (colors appear brighter on the Mac than in Windows—see the tip on page 259), and each monitor may be calibrated somewhat differently.

Add a browser to the Preview In menu

If a browser you have installed is not showing up when you choose File menu > Preview In, you can add it easily. Create an alias (on a Mac) or a shortcut (in Windows) for your browser and place it in the Adobe LiveMotion > Helpers > Preview In folder. When you restart LiveMotion, the browser will appear as one of the choices.

The brower names are listed in alphabetical order on the Preview In submenu. The "default" browser is the first name listed, and it is assigned the keyboard shortcut. If you want to change the order in which a browser name appears on the Preview In submenu, rename its alias/shortcut (it's in the Preview In folder).

The best way to preview the optimization settings you have chosen for your LiveMotion composition is to view it in a browser.

To preview a composition in a Web browser:

1. Choose Edit menu > Composition Settings (Command-Shift-N/Ctrl-Shift-N).
2. If you have chosen Export: Entire Composition or Trimmed Composition, be sure to check the Make HTML option. An HTML header will then be included with the file, which will enable the browser to read the file.
3. Choose a browser from the File menu > Preview In submenu (Command-0/(zero)/Ctrl-0). The browser will launch automatically and display a preview of your composition.

➤ When a LiveMotion file is exported as a SWF, LiveMotion automatically generates an Export Report along with the LiveMotion file. Both Internet Explorer versions 4.5 and later and Netscape Navigator 4.6 and later can display such a report. Click Export Report to review download information on the file and the objects in the file.

➤ The same colors tend to look darker on a Windows system than on a Mac OS system. Mac OS users: To see how this will affect a particular composition, choose View menu > Preview Windows Gamma (Command-8) in LiveMotion. Windows users: Choose View menu > Preview Mac Gamma (Ctrl-8).

Using HTML

If you are using a lot of text in your composition, consider adding the text as HTML code rather than as a graphic. When you use LiveMotion's text tool, your text is saved as a graphic, which has a much larger export file size than HTML. HTML text is also searchable for words or phrases using Javascripts or search engines.

If you decide to use HTML instead of the text tool, LiveMotion can reserve an area in your composition for your HTML text. You can add the text within the LiveMotion program or you can export your file and add the text later in an HTML-editing program like Adobe GoLive.

But keep in mind that however you choose to add your HTML, you must export your composition using the AutoSlice or AutoLayout option in GIF or JPEG format. Only these options will export the HTML text. If you try to export your composition in SWF format, the HTML text won't display.

To make a space for your HTML text:

1. Choose the HTML text tool (Y).
2. Drag a rectangle within your composition to create a box in which you will put the HTML code (Fig. 1).
3. Use the Selection tool to double-click the box. The Edit HTML dialog box appears.
4. Type your text into the dialog box between the <P> and </P> tags (Figs. 2–3). You can also paste text from other sources into this box. Remember, you can double-click the HTML text box to change your text at any time.
5. Choose Export palette settings, then export the file (Fig. 4).

➤ Consider using the HTML text option as a place marker for HTML text that will be added in the Web page design program (e.g., GoLive or Dreamweaver). This way, the person who does the Web layout will know exactly where to place the HTML text.

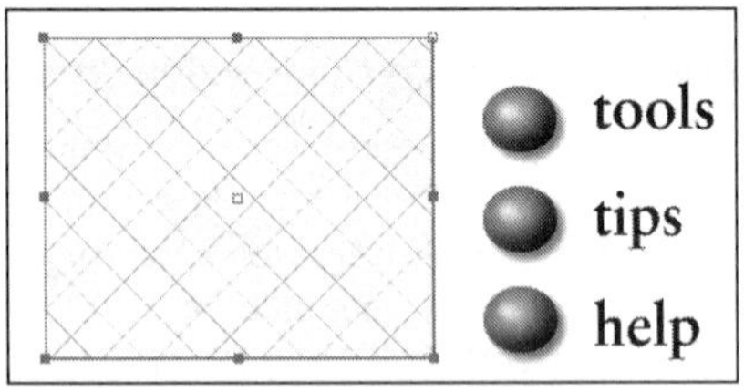

*1 ➤ A rectangle is created in a composition with the **HTML Text** tool.*

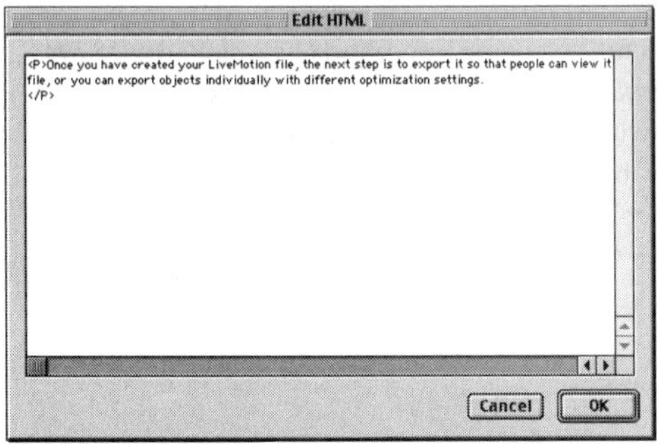

*2 ➤ Text is typed into the **Edit HTML** dialog box. Don't worry about line wraps—the <P> tags control where paragraph breaks will occur.*

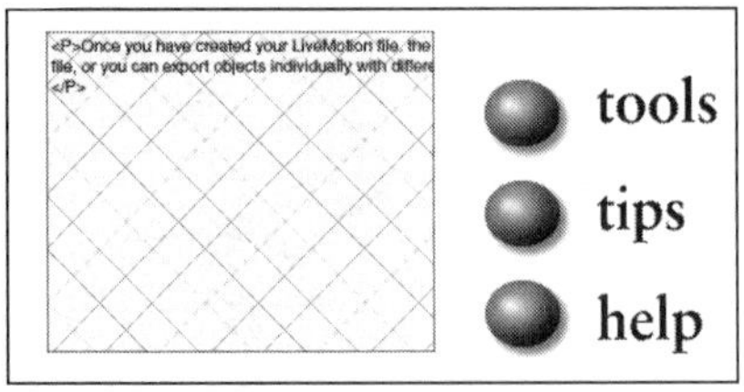

3 ➤ The HTML text box shows the text that was entered. The text runs off the right edge of the box here, but it will format properly to the width of the box in the browser.

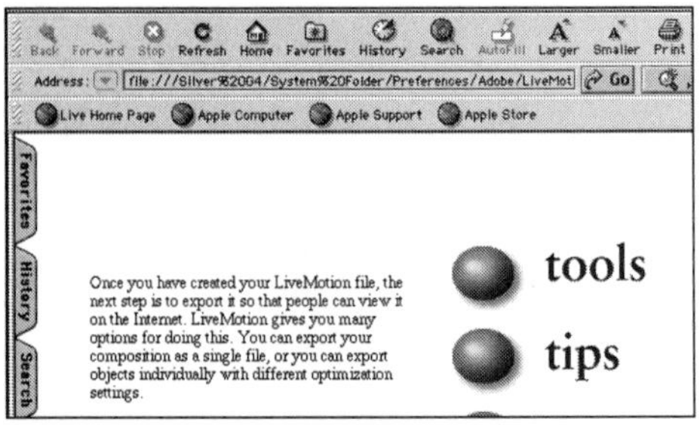

*4 ➤ The composition viewed in the **browser**.*

Browser alert!

HTML text that is created in Windows will appear smaller when viewed in a browser on the Mac due to the different OS screen resolutions. To alleviate this size discrepancy, viewers using Internet Explorer 5.0 on Mac OS can set the browser resolution to match the OS screen resolution.

Batch replacement

LiveMotion includes an innovative feature that allows you to automatically replace heading text in an HTML file with a graphic that includes the same text. To do this, you can create styled text within LiveMotion and use the style as a template.

Since LiveMotion is an object-oriented program, it can generate Web page text graphics by reading text tagged with a particular HTML headline style in an HTML file and then style that text to look like the objects in an existing LiveMotion file.

- First you'll create the text objects that will be used as a style in a LiveMotion document. This document is referred to as the template. The objects in the template are marked as replaceable.
- Next, you'll create an HTML file containing the replacement text with appropriate headline tags.
- Finally, you will use the Batch Replace HTML command in LiveMotion to generate the necessary Web graphics and HTML files for displaying the replacement text in a browser.

Batch replacement can be of assistance if you have to update a Web site that's composed of several linked HTML pages. By having a method to restyle replaceable text objects and then quickly replace text strings that use particular HTML headline tags, you can quickly update and restyle graphic text on the entire Web site.

To create a template file for a batch replacement:

1. Create a text object. The actual text you type in isn't important. We will use "Headline1" as the text. Decide whether you want the text to be aligned left, center, or right. This alignment choice will be carried over into the replacement text graphics for the Web page.
2. Style the text using the Properties palette and color the text using the Color palette.

3. With the text object selected, show the Web palette. From the Replace pop-up menu, choose H1 as the HTML headline tag that will contain the replacement text (Fig. 1). (It doesn't matter if other objects also get marked as Replace: H1, since only text objects will be replaced.)
4. *Optional:* Create an object to serve as a button shape behind the text object. Make the button object larger than the template text, and send it to the back. (Object menu > Arrange > Send to Back) (Fig. 2).
5. Select the text and button objects, then choose Object menu > Group. Objects that don't overlap should be grouped to make them export as one image. LiveMotion will export all overlapping or grouped objects as a single image for the replacement graphic.
6. If you have grouped the objects, you should choose Object menu > Maintain Alignment. With this option checked, the button object (the object behind) will automatically resize to fit the replacement text object. With this option unchecked, the button object will remain the same size, and may not correctly align behind a short or long replacement text string or phrase.
7. Save this document using the name "Template 1." Click the New Folder button in the Save dialog box, and create a new folder named "Batch" to hold this file and all the batch replacement files to be generated.

➤ You can include more than one text object in the template file, but only the text in the frontmost text object will be replaced with the text in the HTML file. Choose Object menu > Arrange> Bring to Front for the desired text object.

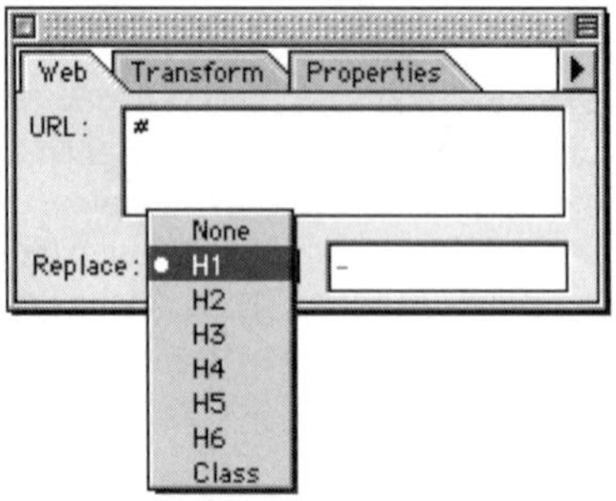

*1 ➤ The **H1 HTML** tag is chosen from the **Replace** pop-up menu on theWeb palette.*

2 ➤ The template 1 file contains a group consisting of a text object and a button object. Maintain Alignment has been turned on for the group.

*1 ➤ The replacement text as viewed in SimpleText on the Mac. The text is styled with the **H1** tag, the same tag that was chosen on the LiveMotion Web palette.*

To create the replacement text with the proper HTML tags:

1. Open your HTML editor of choice and enter some replacement text using the following format:

   ➤ What, you don't have an HTML editor?! Well, then just use SimpleText (Mac) or Notepad(Windows).

   <H1>Sales Team</H1>

   <H1>People</H1>

   <H1>Marketplace</H1>

   You can replace "Sales Team," "People," and "Marketplace" with your own text.

   The <H1> tag makes each string of text a replacement choice for any object assigned an H1 replace tag option in LiveMotion. The order of the HTML lines of text is the order in which they will appear from top to bottom in the browser.

2. Save this file under the name "replace.html" in the Batch folder you created earlier.

To choose the file format and optimization settings:

1. Back in the LiveMotion template file, Choose Edit menu > Composition Settings, choose Export: AutoLayout, then click OK.
2. Show the Export palette (Fig. 1).
3. Since the files will contain text, check the Preview box and choose the GIF file format.
4. Choose the Web Adaptive palette, and set the Colors slider to 32 or 64. Readjust the slider lower or higher to create the optimal setting for color quality versus file size (as indicated in the size readout area of the composition/application window (Fig. 2)).
5. *Optional:* Press the Include Transparency Info button if transparency was produced for your template objects using an alpha channel or an active matte that you want to include in the exported image.
6. Save the template file.

To perform the batch replacement:

1. With the template document open, choose File menu > Batch Replace HTML.
2. Locate and select the "replace.html" file, then click Open.

   LiveMotion will create an Images folder, in the same location as the replace.html file, to hold the GIF images that were created for each replacement text string. The program will also copy and then update the replace.html file to reference the newly generated GIF images. The original replace.html file will be left untouched and will be renamed "replace.old" (Fig. 3).

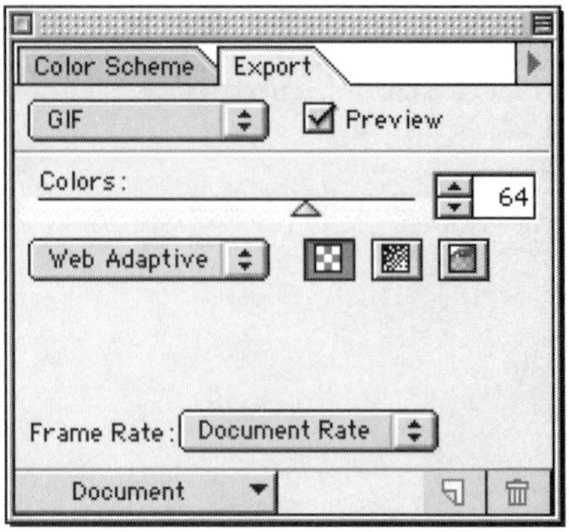

*1 ➤ The **Export** palette set to **GIF** format.*

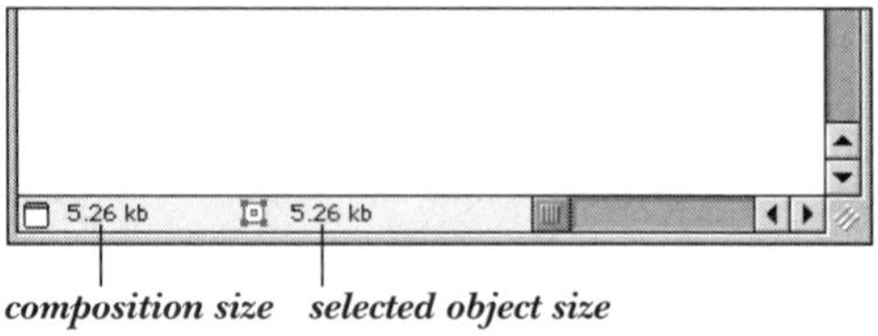

*2 ➤ The template object is currently selected, so both the **composition** size and **object** size readouts appear on the composition window.*

*3 ➤ These files appeared in the batch folder on the Desktop after we used the **Batch Replace** command. An image folder was created and the original replace.html file was renamed "replace.old."*

1 ➤ *The replaced text as viewed in the browser. Because Maintain Alignment was turned on, in each case the object matches the replacement text.*

To view the replacement text graphics in the browser:

1. Launch your browser.
2. Choose File menu > Open File.
3. Locate and open the Batch folder, then open the replace.html file (Fig. 1).

To edit the template and then update the batch replacement:

1. Edit the text object or any other objects in the template file. Use the Subgroup selection tool to select objects in a group.
2. Resave the file.
3. Verify that the Export palette has the proper export settings.
4. Open the Batch folder on the Desktop (Mac)/Explorer (Win).
5. Delete the replace.html file and the images folder.
6. Rename the replace.old file "replace.html."
7. Back in LiveMotion, choose File menu > Batch Replace HTML.
8. View the changes in the browser (see the first set of instructions on this page).

➤ Other objects and image objects can be grouped with the topmost text object to create a more complex unit that will be repeated for each line of replacement HTML text. These objects can include other text objects that will not be replaced (e.g., phrases that you want to remain constant along with replacement text). Don't assign the H1 tag to any text objects that you want to remain constant.

Printing

You might want to print a LiveMotion file if, for example, you'd like to show it to a client or to other members of your design team. To get an animation on paper as a storyboard, you can print your composition as it looks at one static point in time or make multiple prints for a series of static points in time. It's impossible to print a continuous animation because an animation is really a string of a gazillion individual frames.

To print a composition:

1. If you're working with an animated file, open your timeline window by choosing Timeline menu > Show Timeline Window. Use the selection arrow to scroll to the part of your animation you would like to print. What you see in your document window is what will print.
2. Choose File menu > Page Setup/Print Setup, then choose printing preferences for your printer. You may, for example, wish to print your composition in landscape mode if it is wider than it is long.
3. Choose File menu > Print to print the current state of the composition.

Slice 'n' dice

Slicing is the division of an image into sections. Each section fits into one cell of an HTML table. Each slice can be optimized independently and can contain its own links, animations, and rollover effects.

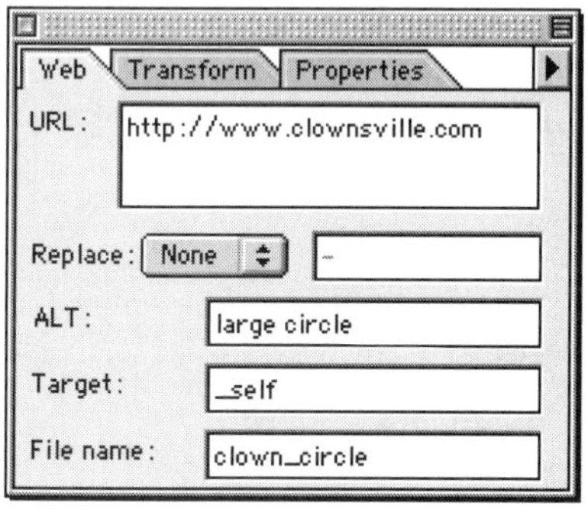

1 ➤ *The* ***Web*** *palette.*

Slicing

In LiveMotion, slicing is performed automatically on an object or group basis. Each object, set of overlapping objects, or group becomes a separate slice. If you choose **AutoLayout** as your composition setting, LiveMotion will create an HTML file for export that places your separate objects into an HTML table. This helps to preserve the appearance of your LiveMotion composition in its exported version.

If you choose **AutoSlice**, on the other hand, LiveMotion will put your image files in one HTML file, beginning with the top-left portion of your composition and ending with the bottom-right portion.

As you arrange your composition for automatic slicing, you can choose file names for your images (if you don't, LiveMotion will create file names for you). You can also specify alternate text that will appear in visitors' browsers if an image doesn't load, and you can choose a target window or frame for any links in your composition. For example, if you include an image that links to another page, you can have that page open up in a new browser window.

To enter slice information for a composition:

1. Select the object you want to export.
2. Show the Web palette (Window menu > Web).
3. Choose Detail View from the Web palette menu (upper-right corner of the palette) to display your choices for alternate text, target, and file name (Fig. 1).
4. In the ALT field, type the alternate text you would like to appear instead of your image.
5. If a URL was entered for your image, you can choose one of the following browser frames for the URL content to target (flow into):

   _blank loads the new page in a new browser window.

(Continued on the next page)

_parent loads the page into the page that contains the current page's frameset.

_self will load the page into the same frame that contains the page with your selected image.

_top loads your page into the top frame of your frameset.
or
Enter the name of the frame in the frameset into which you want to load the page.

6. Finally, you can specify the file name for your exported image by entering it in the file name box.

➤ If you use AutoLayout to export your files and nothing appears in one of your image slices, it may be because similarly named files have overwritten each other. To avoid this, use distinctly different file names (e.g., don't name files "button1," button2," etc.).

To export a sliced composition:

1. Choose Edit menu > Composition Settings, choose either AutoSlice or AutoLayout, then click OK.
2. Show the Export palette, and choose format and quality settings as described on pages 251–257.
3. Choose File menu > Export, choose a location in which to save the file, then click Save.

➤ You can preview how your composition will slice by choosing View menu > Preview AutoSlice Area. Green rectangle(s) will mark the slice areas. Overlapping objects will be sliced into the same area.

Extras

Working with properties

When you export files from LiveMotion, there are certain issues you should consider regarding properties that seem to produce similar results (e.g., Shape Resize vs. Scale, Object Opacity vs. Object Layer Opacity, and other property "pairs"). Object attributes and layer properties affect specific rollover states or specific layers. Transform properties, on the other hand, affect the entire object.

Shape Resize (an Object Attributes property) will resize an object, but it will produce a larger export size than Scale (a Transform property) because Scale is applied to the whole object. Object Layer Opacity (a Layer property) will produce more than one alpha channel when applied to an object, whereas Object Opacity will produce only one alpha channel for the whole object. (But obviously, if you only want to reduce the opacity of one layer in a multi-layered object, you need to use Object Layer Opacity.) Using a Transform property instead of an object attribute or layer property will yield a smaller export file size.

Whenever possible, export animations using Composition Settings: Entire Composition, and check the Make HTML box, then choose SWF from the Export palette. The SWF format can greatly reduce a file's size when LiveMotion property changes are compatible with drawing functions that are built into the SWF format, as most of the Transform properties are.

A larger export file will result when your animation incorporates property changes that the SWF format doesn't support. This is what the bitmap icon by the object size readout signifies. LiveMotion will then export a series of pixel images for downloading instead of the nice, compact SWF instructions.

Becoming Web-design savvy

- **Surf** and **study**. When you're going about your business on the Web, shopping, researching, killing time at the office, whatever—take notice. What is your all-time least favorite site? Why? Is it confusing to navigate through? Do the images take too long to download? Is it packed like a sardine can? You can learn as much from a lousy site as you can from a successful one. Surf with a purpose.

  Now study your favorite site (or two or three). What makes it successful? Is it easy to use? Do the images download quickly? Do you get enough information—but not too much? Is it fun, informative, eye-catching, elegant? Is it easy to find the links? Why do you think it stands out among the dozens, if not hundreds, of sites you've visited?
- Keep it **simple**. The site doesn't have to be poker-faced—it just has to be easy to use. Cartoony graphics and loud colors are great, as long as they convey the message and image you want the site to project and they don't interfere with the purpose of the site—whatever that purpose is.
- Always keep the **purpose** of the site in mind. The nature of the site should control the atmosphere you create. Are you trying to sell something? Recruit volunteers? Dispense information? Soft sell or reach out and grab?
- Keep your viewers' **strengths** and **limitations** in mind. If the site is trying to attract kids, for example, use bright colors and lots of rollovers.
- Challenge yourself. **Rollovers**, **animations**, and rollovers that trigger animations are the wave of the present, and they add an important dimension to Web pages. They help compensate for the fuzziness and imprecision of on-screen type and graphics. Animations help keep viewers entertained while they're waiting for the important stuff to download; well-placed rollovers make it easier for viewers to find links. Together or separately, they can add a delightful and refreshing element of surprise to Web pages. If you have a good sense of humor, this could be your time in the sun.
- Test it out. **Preview** it in the **browsers**. Put a little sign on your desk that says "Preview!" Or "This time, preview it!" Or "This time, preview it, dodobird!"
- **Read** books by the experts. Check out *The Non-Designer's Web Design Book* by Robin Williams and *Designing Web Graphics* by Lynda Weinman (one "n" at the end; no relation to Elaine Weinmann—at least as far as we know! Wouldn't that be amazing?).

Appendix A
Shortcuts

	Macintosh	Windows
Tools		
Selection	V	V
Subgroup-selection	A	A
Drag-selection	U	U
Layer-offset	O	O
Rectangle	M	M
Rounded-rectangle	R	R
Ellipse	L	L
Polygon	N	N
Pen	P	P
Pen-selection	S	S
Type	T	T
HTML Text	Y	Y
Crop	C	C
Transform	E	E
Paint Bucket	K	K
Eyedropper	I	I
Hand	H	H
Temporary Hand tool	Spacebar-drag	Spacebar-drag
Zoom	Z	Z
Create objects		
Show Properties palette	Double-click Ellipse, Rounded Rectangle, Rectangle, Polygon, or Type tool	Double-click Ellipse, Rounded Rectangle, Rectangle, Polygon, or Type tool
Constrain to square (Rectangle or Rounded-rectangle tool); circle (Ellipse tool); or proportional polygon (Polygon tool)	Shift-drag	Shift-drag

	Macintosh	Windows
Views		
Zoom in	Command-+	Ctrl-+
Zoom out	Command--	Ctrl--
Actual Size	Command-Option-0	Ctrl-Alt-0
100% view	Double-click Zoom tool	Double-click Zoom tool
Grids, rulers, and guides		
Show/Hide Grid	Command-'	Ctrl-'
Snap to Grid (Show Grid on)	Command-Shift-'	Ctrl-Shift-'
Show Rulers	Command-R	Ctrl-R
Show Guides	Command-;	Ctrl-;
Snap To Guides	Command-Shift-;	Ctrl-Shift-;
Lock Guides	Command-Option-;	Ctrl-Alt-;
General		
New	Command-N	Ctrl-N
Composition Settings	Command-Shift-N	Ctrl-Shift-N
Open	Command-O	Ctrl-O
Undo	Command-Z	Ctrl-Z
Redo	Command-Shift-Z	Ctrl-Shift-Z
Preferences	Command-K	Ctrl-K
Save	Command-S	Ctrl-S
Save As	Command-Shift-S	Ctrl-Shift-S
Close	Command-W	Ctrl-W
Quit/Exit	Command-Q	Ctrl-Q
Work with objects		
Select All	Command-A	Ctrl-A
Deselect All	Command-Shift-A	Ctrl-Shift-A
Move selection 1 pixel	Arrow	Arrow
Move selection 10 pixels	Shift-Arrow	Shift-Arrow
Make alias of object by dragging	Option-Shift-drag	Alt-Shift-drag
Make Alias	Command-M	Ctrl-M
Break Alias	Command-Option-M	Ctrl-Alt-M
Edit Original	Command-Shift-M	Ctrl-Shift-M

	Macintosh	Windows
Add or subtract object from selection (any selection tool)	Shift-click object	Shift-click object
Move clone of selection	Option-drag	Alt-drag
Move clone of selection (constrain to *x*/*y* axis)	Option-drag, then add Shift	Alt-drag, then add Shift
Duplicate (same *x*/*y* location)	Command-D	Ctrl-D
Copy and paste		
Cut	Command-X	Ctrl-X
Copy	Command-C	Ctrl-C
Paste	Command-V	Ctrl-V
Paste Style	Command-B	Ctrl-B
Béziers		
Convert last point or existing point from smooth to corner (Pen or Pen-selection tool)	Option-click	Alt-click
Add/delete point using Pen-selection tool	Command-click	Ctrl-click
Convert corner to smooth point (Pen or Pen-selection tool)	Option-drag from point	Alt-drag from point
Transform		
Show Transform palette	Double-click Crop tool	Double-click Crop tool
Resize object from corner	Option-drag opposite handle	Option-drag opposite handle
Rotate using selection tool	Command-drag corner handle	Ctrl-drag corner handle
Skew using selection tool	Command-drag side handle	Ctrl-drag side handle
Constrain rotation to 15° increments	Shift-drag upper right corner handle	Shift-drag upper right corner handle
Multiple objects		
Group	Command-G	Ctrl-G
Ungroup	Command-U	Ctrl-U
Bring object forward	Command-]	Ctrl-]
Send object backward	Command-[	Ctrl-[
Bring to Front	Command-Shift-]	Ctrl-Shift-]
Send to Back	Command-Shift-[	Ctrl-Shift-[

	Macintosh	Windows
Layers and styles		
New layer	Command-L	Ctrl-L
Select layer 1	Command-1	Ctrl-1
Select layer 2	Command-2	Ctrl-2
Select layer 3	Command-3	Ctrl-3
Select layer 4	Command-4	Ctrl-4
Select layer 5	Command-5	Ctrl-5
Sample and apply style to selected object	Shift-click object that has desired attributes using Eyedropper tool	Shift-click object that has desired attributes using Eyedropper tool
Acquire objects		
Place	Command-I	Ctrl-I
Place Sequence	Command-Option-Shift-I	Ctrl-Alt-Shift-I
Replace (Selection)	Command-Shift-I	Ctrl-Shift-I
Apply Last Filter (image objects)	Command-F	Ctrl-F
Animation		
Show Timeline window	Command-T	Ctrl-T
Make animation play or stop	Spacebar	Spacebar
Next keyframe	Option-K	Alt-K
Previous keyframe	Option-J	Alt-J
Make Time Independent Group	Command-Shift-G	Ctrl-Shift-G
Move time marker back 1 frame	Page Down	Page Down
Move time marker back 10 frames	Shift-Page Down	Shift-Page Down
Move time marker ahead 1 frame	Page Up	Page Up
Move time marker ahead 10 frames	Shift-Page Up	Shift-Page Up
Move to beginning of timeline	Home	Home
Move to end of timeline	End	End
Preview		
Preview mode/Edit mode	Q	Q
Preview in assigned browser	Command-0 (zero)	Ctrl-0 (zero)
With the composition window active:		
Active Export Preview toggle	Command-9	Ctrl-9
Preview Windows Gamma toggle	Command-8	

	Macintosh	Windows
Preview Mac Gamma toggle		Ctrl-8
Preview AutoSlice Area toggle	Command-7	Ctrl-7
Preview Motion Path toggle	Command-Shift-H	Ctrl-Shift-H
Show/Hide Object Edges	Command-H	Ctrl-H

Export

	Macintosh	Windows
Export Settings (on Export palette)	Command-Option-Shift-E	Ctrl-Alt-Shift-E
Export dialog box	Command-E	Ctrl-E
Export As	Command-Shift-E	Ctrl-Shift-E
Page Setup	Command-Shift-P	
Print Setup		Ctrl-Shift-P
Print	Command-P	Ctrl-P

Another well-designed site

Goodstein Communications, Stephen Beigner, Designer

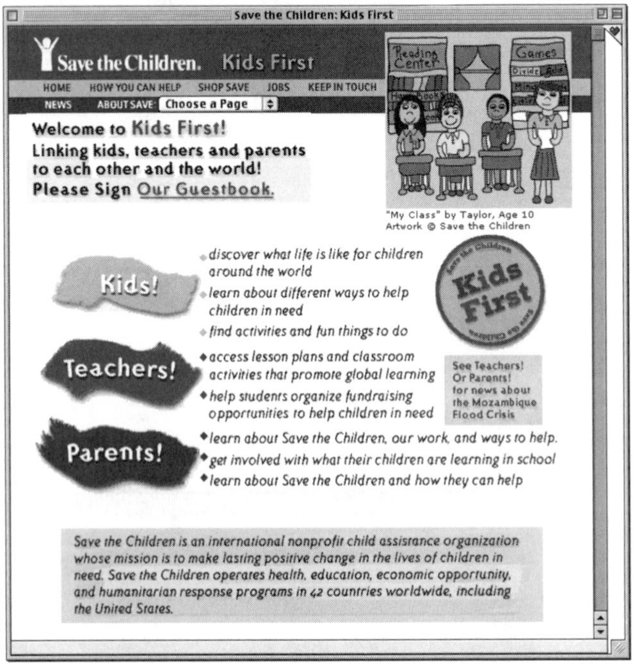

Goodstein Communications, Stephen Beigner, Designer

Index

B

M

U

V